Ideology and Rationality in the Soviet Model

First published in 1989, *Ideology and Rationality in the Soviet Model* assumes that since the October Revolution the development of the Soviet Union has essentially been a process of trial and error. Economic rationality has been sacrificed to political expedients, and the cultural sphere has been put to use as a legitimating and rationalizing device. This book analyses the internal logic of this process from the 1917 Bolshevik Revolution to Gorbachev's 'revolution from above', including coverage of the Stalin, Khrushchev and Brezhnev eras. The book focuses on the structural determinants of the Soviet Model, thus seeking to reveal the specific rationalities that characterizes 'Soviet man'. Its conclusion casts serious doubt on the likelihood of new policies defeating seven decades of Bolshevik rule and social indoctrination. It will be of interest to students of economics, political science and history.

T0382715

Ideology and Rationality in the Soviet Model

A legacy for Gorbachev

Kristian Gerner and Stefan Hedlund

Routledge
Taylor & Francis Group

First published in 1989
by Routledge

This edition first published in 2022 by Routledge
2 Park Square, Milton Park, Abingdon, Oxon, OX14 4RN

and by Routledge
605 Third Avenue, New York, NY 10017

Routledge is an imprint of the Taylor & Francis Group, an informa business

© 1989 Kristian Gerner and Stefan Hedlund, and Lena Jonson (Chapter 3)

Publisher's Note
The publisher has gone to great lengths to ensure the quality of this reprint but points out that some imperfections in the original copies may be apparent.

Disclaimer
The publisher has made every effort to trace copyright holders and welcomes correspondence from those they have been unable to contact.

A Library of Congress record exists under ISBN: 0415021421

ISBN: 978-1-032-21190-9 (hbk)
ISBN: 978-1-003-26720-1 (ebk)
ISBN: 978-1-032-21191-6 (pbk)

Book DOI 10.4324/9781003267201

Ideology and Rationality in the Soviet Model
A legacy for Gorbachev

Kristian Gerner

and

Stefan Hedlund

Routledge
London and New York

First published 1989
by Routledge
11 New Fetter Lane, London EC4 4EE
29 West 35th Street, New York, NY 10001

© 1989 Kristian Gerner and Stefan Hedlund, and Lena Jonson
(Chapter 3)

Typeset by NWL Editorial Services, Langport, Somerset.
Printed and bound in Great Britain by
MacKays of Chatham PLC, Chatham, Kent

British Library Cataloguing in Publication Data

Gerner, Kristian, 1942–
    Ideology and rationality in the Soviet model: a legacy for
    Gorbachev.
    1. Soviet Union. Society
    I. Title II. Hedlund, Stefan, 1953–
947.085'4

ISBN 0-415-02142-1

Library of Congress Cataloging-in-Publication Data

Gerner, Kristian, 1942–
    Ideology and rationality in the Soviet model: a legacy for
Gorbachev / Kristian Gerner and Stefan Hedlund.
        p.   cm.
    Bibliography: p.
    Includes index.
    ISBN   0-415-02142-1
    1. Communism–Soviet Union. 2. Soviet Union–Economic
policy–1986– 3. Soviet Union–Politics and government–1982–
4. Gorbachev, Mikhail Sergeevich, 1931- . I. Hedlund, Stefan,
1953– . II. Title.
HX313.5.G47   1989
335.43'0947–dc19   89-31075
                                        CIP

Dedication

This book is dedicated to those Soviet citizens, of great moral integrity, who are able to face Gorbachev's policy of glasnost without hesitation about their own past words and actions. They may be few and far between, but they are worthy of all our respect.

Contents

viii

Tables

Preface

This is not just another history of the USSR. Nor is it an attempt to provide an exposé over the economic, political and cultural development of the Soviet Union. Such works already exist, written by eminent scholars in their respective fields. Our endeavour is rather to attempt a synthesis of the main trends in these developments, seeking to explore the internal logic of the 'Soviet model'. With this ambition in mind, it is obviously necessary to incorporate into the presentation a good deal of material that is largely descriptive in nature. The contents of these sections have been chosen in order to give a factual background to the main points of our overriding argument. Consequently, they are not intended to be either exhaustive or all-embracing. In particular, they are not concerned with any specific policy issues. Two classic topics, foreign policy and the military, have been deliberately and entirely omitted. Both of these are certainly important in the sense that the Soviet leadership – as any government – can be safely assumed to take a keen interest in its own power and security *vis-à-vis* the rest of the world. Nevertheless, we shall maintain, first, that issues in relation to the interplay between the foreign and the domestic spheres form a largely separate problem area, and, second, that this is not where the *differentia specifica* of the Soviet model can be found.

Work on the book was begun in early 1984, when General Secretary Andropov was still alive. The original intention was to summarize and synthesize Soviet experience primarily against the background of the processes of fossilization and ritualization that increasingly had come to mark the Brezhnev era. There lay a challenge in finding out how stagnation came about and what it might lead to. With the entry of General Secretary Mikhail Gorbachev on the stage, these original plans and intentions have acquired a new significance. It is now probably safe to say that irrespective of the ultimate fate of *perestroika*, the Soviet Union will never again be the same. The ideological impact of events during the past 2–3 years has quite simply been too profound. In this sense, the present situation offers an excellent historical vantage point for retrospection. As Gorbachev himself likes to say, the very fate of socialism in the world is at stake. If *perestroika* fails, the implication is that socialism will be hopelessly discredited. If, on the other hand, it should succeed, that will also mean the end of (Soviet) socialism – as we know it. The time would thus seem ripe for a balance sheet to be drawn up.

The approach used is based on methodological individualism. The presentation concentrates on the behaviour of individuals, as actors in different situations and at different positions in Soviet society. Their actions are analysed within a loose game-theoretic framework which incorporates elements of Albert Hirschman's work on *Exit, Voice and Loyalty* and of the discussions of various interpretations of rationality that have been offered by Jon Elster and others. The approach is also structural, in the sense that Hirschman's concepts are used heuristically, in order to reveal the structural determinants of the Soviet model, those that condition and constrain the actions of individuals.

With the onset of *glasnost*, the new policy of openness, the situation of Western Sovietologists has been transformed more or less overnight. The present book bears a clear imprint of this change. It is no longer the case, as it was to some considerable extent under Brezhnev, that each and every scholar in the field of Soviet studies is familiar with the bulk of the hard evidence that appears in the Soviet mass media and in scholarly journals. The task has suddenly become the frustrating one of trying to keep up with the veritable flood of information, regarding most spheres of Soviet society, that is now continuously being published. On balance, this flow of information is, of course, for the better. Nevertheless, certain new problems do arise.

One immediate effect concerns the problem of evaluating the significance of various sources of information, in the entirely new environment of *glasnost*. It is no longer justified to accept everything that appears in Soviet media as expressions of a strictly monitored Party line. If *glasnost* is allowed to continue, one might even think that the very rationale for 'Sovietology' as a separate discipline should vanish. Not only will the sheer quantity of available information make it impossible to be a 'Sovietologist', 'specializing' in all aspects of Soviet affairs. The highly specific skills of the profession may also be rendered obsolete. With the new attitudes towards information and the freedom of expression that are associated with *glasnost*, Soviet sources can increasingly be accepted as colleagues putting forward arguments rather than as simple 'archaeological' evidence, as it were. It shall be a main point of the concluding chapter, however, to demonstrate that things may not work out to be that simple. If we assume that Soviet citizens in general are not able to shrug off at will the psychological imprints of decades of manipulated realities, it may then actually turn out to be even more difficult to sort out the significance of events that take place in the post-*glasnost* and post-*perestroika* environment.

Research for this book has been made possible by a generous grant from the Bank of Sweden Tercentenary Foundation. This is gratefully acknowledged. Apart from the undersigned, the original research team also included Lena Jonson. She has undertaken background research for Chapters 3, 7 and 11, and has also provided a draft for large parts of Chapter 3. Her assistance has been of great value and is hereby given due credit. All views expressed and conclusions drawn are, however, the joint responsibility solely of the authors. Finally, a word of thanks should be directed to Alan Harkess, whose skilful eye has purged the text of a multitude of linguistic infelicities.

Lund, August 1988,

Kristian Gerner
Stefan Hedlund

Part one

Introduction

Chapter one

Setting the stage

Economic stagnation and social decline were prominent features of Soviet development during the late Brezhnev era and during the period of interregnum under Andropov and Chernenko. Before the introduction of Gorbachev's policy of *glasnost*, or openness, this proposition would have been subject to some considerable controversy. Since then, however, the new General Secretary and his top economic advisors, together with leading representatives of the cultural intelligentsia, have presented us with a picture of past development which in many respects is even gloomier than most Western 'crisis-mongers' had suspected. At the June 1987 plenum of the Central Committee, for example, which launched a broad package of economic reform measures, Gorbachev presented his audience with a picture of emergency that was without parallel since the Civil War and since the Great Patriotic War against Germany. In order to understand the needs for *perestroika*, Gorbachev argued, one must realize that economic developments during the past decades had placed the country in a 'pre-crisis' situation (*predkrizisnoe sostoyanie*).[1] Less than a year later, at the February 1988 plenum of the Central Committee, he returned to explain the underlying causes of this development:

> During a period of 70 years, our people and our Party have been inspired by the ideas of socialism and socialist construction. But due to external as well as internal reasons, we have not been able to fully realize Lenin's principles of constructing a new society. Serious obstacles have been the cult of personality, the establishment in the 1930s of the command-administrative system of management and control, bureaucratic, dogmatic and voluntaristic distortions, arbitrariness, and at the end of the 1970s and the beginning of the 1980s – brake mechanisms and a lack of initiative which served to produce stagnation.[2]

Naturally, the present Soviet leadership, like any new political leadership, has a strong incentive to paint the past in dark colours, simply in order to denigrate its predecessors in office and to stress the need for substantial changes to be undertaken. In this context, it is important to note that some Soviet writers even go so far as to present a distinct impression of pending apocalypse.[3] In the April 1988 issue of *Novyi Mir*, for example, the well known reform economist Nikolai Shmelev speaks of the 'dead-end situation that we find ourselves in after the years of stagnation (*gody zastoya*)',[4] and in the same issue of that journal a certain Academician N.N. Moiseev goes even further. He starts by commenting on the fate of the world in general, saying that 'M.S. Gorbachev is certainly right in speaking of the need for a new global thinking. But we, the specialists, have an even deeper insight. We know that the previous stereotypes of thinking and behaviour inevitably must lead to disaster.' This, of course, has a certain familarity with opinions being voiced in Western media. The interesting point comes when he goes on to say the following:

> It is not only a matter of stagnation. The moral foundations of society have begun to wither away. People's norms and values are changing. Black turns into white and white into black. People are beginning to forget that there are other ways to live, that they are not there to serve the bureaucrats, that the bureaucracy is there to serve the workers. The motivation for good work disappears.[5]

Having read these and other similar statements, one is left with a distinct impression of *perestroika* actually being seen as the last chance of communism on earth.

The point of departure for this book is the rather peculiar fact that this so obviously dangerous process of deterioration has proceeded so quietly. From a Western perspective, we would most certainly expect to see political instability and perhaps even social upheaval follow in the steps of serious economic decline. The Polish case, moreover, serves as a reminder that the countries of 'real socialism' are not immune in this respect. Yet, in the 'good old days' of the late Brezhnev era, before Gorbachev's *glasnost* and *perestroika*, it was not only the case that all queries about mounting social and economic problems in the Soviet Union would be vehemently branded as 'anti-Soviet slander'. In addition, even initiated observers were struck by the rather remarkable stability of Soviet society at large.

In the social sphere, strikes, demonstrations and other such open manifestations of discontent were almost totally absent, and in the political sphere the surface was greyer and smoother than ever. To some extent, this apparent contradiction can of course be explained by the efficiency of the repressive organs. The achievements of the

KGB under the leadership of Yurii Andropov were no doubt quite impressive. At least, this is certainly the case in comparison with the record of some neighbouring countries. Such an explanation, however, is not sufficient. The ambition of this book is to investigate the nature of those economic, political and cultural forces that made this stability possible to achieve.

Having said this, we shall immediately backtrack somewhat, in order to recognize some important conceptual difficulties. *First* of all, the notion of a 'Soviet model' or a 'Soviet-type system', which is frequently encountered in the literature, raises important questions regarding the transferability of specifically Soviet – or indeed Russian – experience on to those other countries that are members of the family of 'real socialism'. To put it simply, the concept of a 'Soviet model' is of course no more than a convenient shorthand for a certain set of political ambitions, a certain structuring of the economic system, and a certain overall ideological framework. As such it will also be used below.

At the same time, we must also recognize that those highly specific – perhaps even unique – social and historical environments which characterize each of the countries in which this model has been introduced will necessarily, in a very broad sense, determine its degree of both acceptance and performance. Most important perhaps is the fact that in all cases but that of the Soviet Union proper regime legitimacy can be enhanced by referring to 'external restrictions', i.e. to the threat of Soviet intervention. Together with a number of other features, which will be referred to as we go along, this makes the Soviet Union a logical special case amongst the 'Soviet-type' systems. We shall certainly claim a general validity for those analytical tools that will be put to use below, but it should be made explicit right from the start that it is precisely this special case that is the focus of the present investigation. An application of the same tools to another 'Soviet-type' country might well present us with a highly different picture.[6] In short, rather than pretending to present a general theory of 'real socialism', ours is a specific study of the Soviet case which hopefully will also have some general implications for the other members of the 'family'.

Our *second* conceptual difficulty concerns the very notion of 'stability', which of course is a rather elusive one. Our sole comfort at this point is that we would seem to be in good company in noting its elusiveness. The following, for example, is the opening line of a recent book by Alexander Motyl, on the threat to the stability of the Soviet Union that is implicit in the national minorities question:

> The concept of stability, so central to contemporary political science, enjoys a dubious distinction. Most scholars use the term without specifying what they mean by it; those who attempt to do so have yet to agree on a common definition.... Confusion reigns, for although all political scientists appear to have a gut feeling about stability, few can describe that sentiment with any degree of precision.[7]

Motyl is of course entirely correct in his observation as far as a definition of the word is concerned, and his subsequent discussion of the difficulties involved illustrates that he knows what he is talking about. For the purpose of our own study, however, we shall seek refuge behind the simple fact that, pending the finding of a broadly accepted definition, issues that are related to the problem of stability will still have to be discussed. As far as a *definition* is concerned, our strategy in this volume is to rely on our 'gut feeling'. It is by focusing on the *functional* aspects of stability that we hope to make a contribution to the understanding of the Soviet system. The same will apply to our use of the equally elusive concepts of 'ideology' and 'rationality', both of which shall figure prominently throughout the book.

Our *third* conceptual point concerns the *nature* of the alleged contradiction between political and social stability, on the one hand, and economic decline, on the other. Here the problem largely concerns the point of reference. At first glance, our comparison with a Western perspective serves little purpose other than drawing attention to an important distinguishing feature between those two systems that are sometimes known as East and West. Since the Soviet-type societies in general lack most of the social and political mechanisms that serve in Western societies to cushion and perhaps absorb popular discontent, stability in the former will – if achieved – necessarily be of a highly different nature from that in the latter.

From a Soviet perspective, the essentially pluralistic Western market economies no doubt render a rather chaotic impression, seemingly lacking in all forms of order and control. The causes for their stubborn refusals to submit to the Marxist predictions of eventually inevitable apocalypse are perhaps not always well understood. (Indeed they may not always be all that well understood in the West either.) It is a main contention of this book that we have at this very point an important *differentia specifica* between the two systems. It will be our task below to penetrate those mechanisms that serve, in the face of economic decline, to provide the Soviet system with a basic political and social stability.

Our deeper understanding of the problems at hand can thus actually be seen as the very opposite of the contradiction that was referred to above, between decline and stability. Even a cursory reading of current Soviet writings on the problems of *perestroika* give a distinct impression of serious forces being at play under the apparently placid surface,[8] forces which harbour ominous threats to the stability of the Soviet system and which are most certainly taken seriously be the Soviet leadership. The following (1987) statement by Sergei Zalygin, editor of the prestigious journal *Novyi Mir*, is rather illustrative of the clearly apocalyptic atmosphere that marks the current Soviet debate:

> And it is quite clear that if we do not manage to bring about order and democratization, within fifteen years we shall be reduced to one of the ... poorest countries, we shall once and for all have squandered our outstanding natural resources – nature itself – and will then ourselves perish.[9]

It should be emphasized, in this context, that we are not interested solely in analysing the process of decline as such. We shall also argue that measures taken by the successive Soviet leaderships that preceded Gorbachev, in order to counter the threats of destabilizing influences, became increasingly subtle and in the process also more successful. Our reference to an apparent 'contradiction' has been made in order to underline this latter point.

The legacy left to Gorbachev by his predecessors evidently harbours this success in promoting stability, but it is a main conclusion of our presentation below that it does so in a perhaps unfortunate dual sense. Many of the mechanisms that have served so successfully to promote political and social stability in the past may now actually emerge as formidable obstacles in the way of Gorbachev's policy of economic reform, or *perestroika*. In this sense, the Soviet rulers can be seen as prisoners of their own past successes. If, on the one hand, the old style prevails, the current 'pre-crisis' situation will most certainly develop into a real crisis, the outcome of which may be dire indeed. If, on the other hand, *glasnost* and *perestroika* should succeed in bringing about the desired changes, that will put in jeopardy some of the most basic mechanisms of stability in Soviet society. As recently phrased by Daniel Franklin, writing for *The Economist*: 'The stakes in the Gorbachev gamble could hardly be higher.'[10]

Since our focus will be on the broader aspects of the system as such, it is perhaps only logical that our approach is an interdisciplinary one. We shall approach the problems at hand in four different historical phases and from three different disciplinary perspectives, the latter representing those of the economic, political and cultural dimensions. The objective function of the process of Soviet historical development will be sought in the political sphere, in terms of ambitions of the rulers to achieve power and security. This means that the economy will to some extent be seen as a dependent variable and the cultural dimension as a compensating device, designed to attenuate conflicts between political ambitions and economic possibilities. This, however, is the overriding approach. Needless to say, we are quite conscious of various feedback mechanisms, from the economic and cultural spheres, which serve to constrain political ambitions. To penetrate and understand this mutual dependency will be an important task of our study.

Our presentation will be strongly focused at the level of the individual, as an actor within the system, and it will consciously seek to challenge a number of those features of the Soviet system that to a Western eye may appear irrational. One example of the latter is the all too frequent picture of an irrational ideology that stands in the way of rational economic action. Here we shall attempt to find explanations that are based on the non-economic objectives of the Soviet leadership and that explicitly recognize an active and instrumental function of ideology.

Much of the discussion will consequently focus on malfunctions in the economic system and on things that apparently 'go wrong', in the sense once given to that concept by Alec Nove.[11] One observation to be made here is that various apparently obvious sub-optimalities may not always be seen as such by the Soviets themselves, since a proper point of reference may be lacking. If the malfunctions are endemic they may not be as easily perceived as if they were localized. Our approach will be to identify and explain such macro-level problems by attempting to establish (a) that malfunctions are logical consequences of rational individuals acting according to given incentives, and (b) that these micro-level incentives, while perhaps irrational from a narrow economic point of view, may from a broader political and ideological point of view assume a quite distinct rationality, albeit of a very different nature. To investigate the latter is another important task undertaken below.

The question of whether or not certain incentives or policies are rational obviously hinges on what we take their goals to be, since misspecified goals may put a false stamp of irrationality on measures that are actually highly rational. The real crux of this matter has been pinpointed by Alexander Yanov, in a book about the abortive 'link' reform in Soviet agriculture during the 1960s:

> Inevitably the answer to the question 'Does the system work?' depends on what one means by 'work'. If it refers to political control,

then the *kolkhoz* system works very well; if it refers to food production, then the system does not work, for it was not designed to.[12]

Given this perception of the problems at hand, our analysis will of necessity be heavily geared to studying the behaviour of individuals and the attempts by the political leadership to influence and control that behaviour. Consequently, we shall make extensive use below of an implicit game-theoretic framework which views social and political processes as the outcome of actions taken by single individuals – or groups of individuals – who are 'playing' against each other. Two key concepts that figure prominently in this undertaking are 'ideology' and 'rationality', both of which also figure in the title of our book.

Given the nature of the Soviet system, ideology naturally plays a prominent role in all spheres of society and its function will thus be an important topic of study as well as a tool of analysis in the following chapters. The other key concept underlies the whole ambition of the book. By focusing on the distinctions between individual and collective rationality, on the one hand, and economic and political rationality, on the other, we hope to have found a suitable format for a study of the problems stated above. As we have already indicated, both of these key concepts suffer from the same problems of definition as does 'stability'. Since, however, they will be operational in a sense that the stability concept will not, we shall discuss them in somewhat greater detail here, before proceeding with the study proper. Let us start with 'rationality'.

Rationality

Rationality is a concept about which much has been written and it is certainly not our ambition here to add anything essentially new to these writings. On the contrary, by extracting those aspects of the discussion that may be conducive to our purposes, we shall to a large extent draw on the fruits of the mental labour of others. In this endeavour, we will tread gently, avoiding as far as possible the pitfalls of attempting to *define* rationality and rational action. The following excerpt from one of Jon Elster's numerous books on the subject illustrates rather vividly that such an undertaking would constitute a research programme of its own:

> There is a bewildering multitude of entities that are said to be rational or irrational: beliefs, preferences, choices or decisions, actions, behavioural patterns, persons, even collectives and in-

9

stitutions. Also, the connotations of the term 'rational' range from the formal notions of efficiency and consistency to the substantive notions of autonomy or self-determination. And in the background of the notion lurks the formidable pair of 'Verstand' vs. 'Vernunft', be it in the Kantian or in the Hegelian senses.[13]

From Elster's above statement can be extracted the multitude of aspects of rationality that we shall *not* be concerned with here. One such set concerns the rationality of beliefs, ideas and ideological constructs. These certainly play an important role in our presentation below, but they do so primarily from the instrumental rather than the definitional end. We return to this issue in the following section of the present chapter, where our understanding of the concept of ideology at large will be discussed.

A somewhat more complicated issue is that of the rationality of the system as such. This, as we know, was the real centrepiece of the Socialist Controversy of the 1920s and the 1930s, the outcome of which was that Oskar Lange and Abba Lerner carried the day in theoretical terms while Ludwig von Mises and Friedrich von Hayek managed to cast some serious doubt on the practical feasibility of the proposed model of 'optimal' socialism.[14] To engage further in this discussion would carry us far into the more narrow realm of the rationality of the Soviet *economic* system, an endeavour which would be of a rather technical nature and of limited relevance to the broader scope of the problems outlined above. Yet, there is implicit in this context also an issue which is of considerable relevance to our presentation, namely that of economic versus political rationality.

Since it is a main premise of this book that there is an important conflict between these two concepts, the question may need some elaboration. Let us start by listening to a definition of rationality that has been suggested by Nove:

> All that is meant here by 'rationality' is the following rather simple proposition: that the economic purposes of society, whatever these may be *and* whoever decides them, are achieved with maximum economic efficiency – or alternatively, that maximum results are achieved at minimum real cost.[15]

Nove is quoted here from an article originally published in 1958 and the context is that of Khrushchev's de-Stalinization. After indicating a number of subsequently well established economic absurdities in the Soviet economic system, he proceeds to point at precisely that conflict between economic and political rationality which was just referred to. On the one hand, the 'leaders, and especially Khrushchev, like to be able to direct economic life, and do not take kindly to limitations on the power of arbitrary decision on any issue', while on the other a 'rational use of resources is essential if the aims of the Party's own policies are to be effectively realized. Thus the Party has, in this connection, a split personality.' Rather than being 'attracted by rationality *per se*', the leaders 'now feel that they *need* economic rationality *because of* (not despite) their power ambitions.'[16]

Our aim throughout this book is to investigate the nature and consequences of the 'split personality', and we shall do so by directing our attention to the rationality of actions, or – to be more specific – to the rationality of *individual* actions. The sum total of those individuals who together make up the Soviet Union, or the Communist Party, will thus be dealt with only in so far as they form a larger group or entity *within* which the single individuals act according to their own preferences, be they Party chieftains, economic planners, rank-and-file workers, common peasants, or members of the intelligentsia. It is here that we shall deploy the game theoretic framework that was referred to above.

Our approach thus comes close to the toolbox end of the discussion of rationality. By using the concept of rationality as an instrument – or a framework – for the discussion, it is our hope that we shall be able to approach and shed some new light on some important aspects of the Soviet system. The starting point for this endeavour will be *strategic behaviour*, which is held by Elster to be the truly distinguishing feature between *homo sapiens* and other animals.[17]

In a market system, interest in the workings of institutions and the behaviour of individuals is diffused and sometimes even lost in the hazy concept of the 'market mechanism'. No doubt, the growth of bureaucracies and 'Big Government' has increasingly prompted Western economics to focus also on the importance of institutional analysis. In a centrally controlled system, however, such interest is not simply a valuable addition. It is of paramount importance. When individual behaviour can no longer be assumed to be guided by some abstract profit or utility maximizing concept, we must attempt to isolate what the real determinants of that behaviour might be.

Under a perfect market regime, Adam Smith's invisible hand sees to it that what is good for the individual is also good for society. Of course, such a perfect regime has never been encountered in real life, but it serves to illustrate that there is a broad spectrum of situations where administrative control, and all the associated problems, becomes increasingly visible towards one end of that spectrum. In such cases, which include hierarchies of Western bureaucracies as well as of the centrally planned economies, the single individual will increasingly need to take into account what action others may take

11

when making his own plans. His behaviour will become *strategic*, to an extent and in a way that would not be warranted under a more anonymous market regime.

It is from this perspective that we shall address the problem of things that 'go wrong'. If we assume that all individuals behave rationally, according to some individually perceived utility function, may we then conclude that the global outcome will also be rational? Not necessarily, and here lies the very root of the dilemma of irrationality and things going wrong. Moreover, we also have here a very typical situation of a 'game' being played between the different actors, such as was referred to above.

Game situations can, however, arise in many different formulations, with different strategies and with different numbers of players. For the sake of illustration, we shall take a closer look at the Prisoner's Dilemma, the classic showpiece of game theory. In the original presentation by A.W. Tucker,[18] two individuals have been apprehended following a serious crime. Evidence against them, however, is insufficient for a conviction and so the District Attorney puts each in a separate cell – with no means of communication – and proposes to each the following deal: 'If you confess and your partner does not, you will go free while he will receive a maximum sentence. If both confess, you will both receive a moderate sentence, whereas if nobody confesses, you will both get a light sentence on some petty charge.'

The outcome of the game in this case is given. For each individual – or player – there is a *dominant* strategy. Irrespective of what the other person does, you should confess. If the other does not – you will go free, whereas if he does you will get a moderate sentence. The fact that both would be better off *as a group* by not confessing is the core of the dilemma, since this outcome is unattainable without co-operation – or solidarity.

This example holds all those ingredients that are vital to our following presentation. It highlights the importance of *strategic behaviour*, since each individual must carefully consider what the other might do, and it highlights the importance of *communication* and *co-operation*, since it is the lack thereof that produces the inferior outcome. Most importantly, however, it highlights the difference between *individual* and *collective* rationality. For each individual it is clearly rational to confess, whereas for the group as a whole it would have been rational not to do so. Thus, as each individual pursues his own rational strategy, the attainment of collective rationality is blocked. It is from this perspective we shall discuss our initial claim, that things apparently going wrong (collective irrationality) are the results of rational (individual) action based on erroneous incentives, only now we have to ask ourselves in which way incentives are 'erroneous'.

Let us use another example. During the Soviet reform attempts of the 1960s, Yanov wrote a series of articles in *Literaturnaya Gazeta*, on the needs and problems of reform in agriculture. In one of these,[19] he used an example that has later become classic. The theme of the article is an engineer at an agricultural machinery testing station who, having developed new equipment that showed very good results at the experimental fields, was puzzled by the total lack of success in the *kolkhoz* fields. When visiting one of the *kolkhozy*, however, he soon found the reason. The new equipment required precise handling and should not be driven at speeds over 2.5 km per hour. The tractor, however, was capable of doing 24 km. As soon as the supervisor had left, that was also the speed that it would do, as the tractor driver's work norm was set in *hectares*. The fact that high speed would cause great damage to the coming harvest was irrelevant to him, as that cost would be shared equally by all members, while the benefit from getting the work done quickly would accrue to him alone. Many other examples in a similar vein could be quoted. Nove, for example, cites as 'a common saying among tractormen' the caution to 'plough deeper: I see the director coming' (*zaglublyai, direktor edet*).[20] Shallow ploughing will of course render sowing impossible, but this is another thing that was irrelevant to the driver, whose only interest was to cover as many hectares as possible.

Yanov's example has been chosen partly because he has subsequently moved to the West, and written an admirable little book that elaborates on the theme,[21] and partly because it holds all those features that are crucial to the Prisoner's Dilemma. From *his* point of view, the tractor driver does behave rationally in ploughing shallow and driving fast. As Yanov points out, for simply meeting the norm he would be paid three rubles, for three times the norm – nine rubles, and for five times the norm – twenty rubles. Thus the higher speed.[22] Though it is obvious that the outcome of the labour of the entire collective of tractor drivers, combine operators, etc., is sub-optimal, are we right in drawing the conclusion that incentives are erroneous or irrational? The answer to that question will depend on what the incentive system is actually *supposed* to achieve, as was indicated above by Yanov.

That such incentives are erroneous in a perspective of aiming for macro-level economic efficiency is an obvious fact which is endemic to the entire process of Soviet economic planning. A classic textbook illustration is the nail factory which turns out minute size nails only when the plan is formulated in numbers but shifts into giant size nails when ordered to produce tons.[23] To a Western eye, this may appear to be a completely absurd situation and that is also the attitude taken in many Soviet books and articles condemning such practices (although of course they stop short of drawing conclusions as to the causes). Yet, in spite of decades of criticism, the problem has persisted and indeed become firmly entrenched in the practice of Soviet economic planning. Its root is the severe constraint on the amount of information that can be handled by the planners at the centre, a constraint which necessitates using aggregate targets. The latter in turn leaves plenty of scope for strategic behaviour by managers playing against the system, e.g. in deciding whether to produce large or small nails. The essence of this game has been analysed in the pioneering efforts of, among others, Joseph Berliner[24] and will not be discussed further here.

The situation depicted above is an obvious illustration of a Prisoner's Dilemma. All actors pursue their own individually rational strategies and the result is Berliner's play against the system and a sub-optimal final outcome. At the same time, there *is* a collectively rational strategy, which requires all players to give up their individually preferred strategies, in order to secure a better outcome for the group – and indeed for themselves too, as compared to the breakdown of the Prisoner's Dilemma. The problem is whether this collectively rational strategy can actually be implemented in practice, i.e. to make all tractor drivers plough deep and slow, thus increasing the harvest and making the total cake bigger.

From the discussion above it should be clear that there are only two ways to achieve this: by supervision or by co-operation. Let us put supervision on one side for a moment and concentrate on the prospects for successful co-operation. The problem of whether or not to co-operate (or, more properly perhaps, whether or not to be a free rider) is of course common to all forms of organization of work. As a *principle* it applies equally to East and West. Why is it then that problems of shirking and poor labour discipline appear to be more rampant in the Soviet bloc than in the Western countries? Moreover, why is it – as Anders Åslund has shown in his impressive study of private enterprise in Eastern Europe – that private entrepreneurs in Poland and in the GDR, respectively, exhibit such widely different patterns of behaviour?[25]

In a formal sense, the root of the problem derives from the link (or absence thereof) between effort expended and reward received by the single individual. If a single member of a group decides to increase his contribution, his rewards will depend on whether or not the other members follow suit. If they do not, the fruits of his extra labour will be shared equally by all members and his own reward will amount to no more than $1/N$, with N members in the group. Such being the case, the incentive for him to exert himself more than the minimum absolutely necessary will be small indeed. We have here the classic case against communes and co-operative enterprise.[26]

If, however, other members decide to follow his example, the strength of the incentive will grow and in the limiting case the reward to the single individual will simply be equal to the result of his extra effort (assuming identical individuals). What then would make the others follow suit?[27] One glaring example of success in this respect is the Israeli *Kibbutz*, which functions according to the principle of full communism, often even to the point of communal dining. The absence of a wage nexus means that the individual's share of the total cake is independent of his contribution to production. Under such circumstances, rational action would prescribe to minimize that contribution. It is precisely this that has been the Achilles heel of many attempts at co-operation, but not so in the *kibbutz*.[28]

The explanation is simple. If all members of the group have strong common interests, formal incentives to work will not be necessary. A personal moral code – or peer control in the form of community opprobrium – will simply rule out shirking. As the Israeli economist Haim Barkai has pointed out, an application of the classical case against communes to the *kibbutzim* is fallacious, precisely because the free rider problem will be an exception rather than the rule.[29] Although the explanation may be straightforward, the attainment in practice of this outcome is far from simple. In stark contrast to the *kolkhozy*, the *kibbutzim* have relied heavily on a voluntary and strongly selective recruitment of members with Zionist-socialist convictions and with strong preferences for the *kibbutz* way of life. This reduces the Israeli experience to a special case. The great emphasis that is placed by the *kibbutz* movement on matters of social tissue and group relations does, however, bring out quite clearly the crucial role that is played by such factors.

We have here a first step towards explaining the East-West dimension of shirking. Soviet beliefs in large rather than small scale, and in compulsion rather than choice, create a poor starting point for group solidarity and peer control to emerge. No doubt, the KGB informer system aggravates the problem, by its systematic fanning of distrust between people. Add to this a gradual degeneration of social tissue, caused by the sustained gap between promised and actual living standards, and we have a vicious downward spiral where the solidarity between individuals, and their interest in doing something for the group, become rapidly eroded. Hence, in this case, the situation of breakdown which is typical of the Prisoner's Dilemma will have particularly wide-reaching effects.

If a co-operative solution cannot thus be achieved, supervision and control will have to step in and this is indeed precisely what has happened in the Soviet-type economies. This will be dealt with at length in the following chapters of our study. First, however, let us look at the prospects for achieving the co-operative solution by introducing an explicit ideology, as a moral code to promote co-operation. As with rationality, our ambition will not be to contribute any original ideas to the already substantial discussion on the nature, role and function of ideology. Rather, we shall attempt to shape it into an instrument, for use in our analysis below.

Ideology

As in the case of 'stability', and perhaps even more so, most people would probably claim to have a 'gut feeling' type of understanding of the concept of 'ideology'. It may be hard to define an elephant but you would surely know one if you saw one. Such an intuitive definition is of course not to much avail for any practical purpose. Yet, in spite of the fact that the concept has a long tradition, it still remains controversial: 'Surely by now some specific meaning [of ideology] should have developed out of common usage. And yet it has not. The word remains both descriptive and pejorative, both analytical and normative,'once wrote Daniel Bell.[30]

In spite of this confusion, some form of a working definition is obviously needed and here Bell presents four different classes of interpretation. *First*, there is the one used by Marx in *Die deutsche Ideologie*, which views ideology as 'false consciousness' and derides the belief that ideas have the power to shape or determine reality. *Second*, there is the view that all ideas are socially determined, which has produced the sociology of knowledge. The *third* use is somewhat different, in that it sees ideologies as justifications which represent some specific set of interests. Here, the focus is not on the origin of ideas but on their consequences. *Last*, there is the use of ideology as a social formula, as a belief system to mobilize people into action. Revolutionary ideology would come under this heading.[31]

Other classifications would of course be possible, but that of Bell adequately serves our purpose. It illustrates the difference between looking at ideology for what it *is* and for what it *does*. The first two uses listed above deal with the origin and nature of ideas, while the latter two are concerned with their uses. Below we shall concentrate on the functions of ideology rather than on its origins or nature. For this purpose, Bell's definition will suffice: 'The function of an ideology, in its broadest context, is to concretize the values, the normative judgements of society.'[32] A similar understanding can be found with Motyl, who argues that one function of Soviet ideology is 'to mould perceptions'.[33] This is not to say, of course, that there is some easily identifiable centre from which the ideological prescriptions emerge. Our understanding is rather that of a self-generating system, the inner dynamics of which shall be an important topic for study below.

Values and value-systems in a society are of course of great importance to any discussion of ideology. By approaching the problem from this angle, we may find a suitable starting point for identifying those aspects of ideology that we shall need below. One problem that immediately arises in this context, and which we shall have to deal with right away, is that of the East-West dimension of ideology. The following is written by Sidney Verba, in conclusion of a volume of papers on 'political culture' in different political systems: 'In fact, explicit political ideologies arise when one wants to create a political system that is not supported by the implicit primitive beliefs of the population. If one has the beliefs, one does not need the ideology.'[34]

An immediate impression that might be gained from this statement is that ideology is something peculiar to revolutionary socialism. Verba is careful to guard against such an impression by using the word 'explicit', but the impression remains. Moreover, it is definitely the case that to a casual observer, it is the socialist systems that exhibit the most 'visible' ideology. Which American physicist, for example, would quote Abraham Lincoln in an article on quantum mechanics, in the way that Lenin's name is used by Soviet scientists across the board?

The problem at hand, however, is rather more complicated than one of simple visibility. As Motyl correctly points out, ideology in the democratic states differs from that of the authoritarian ones with respect to content, rather than function: 'American idealization of George Washington may not be so effusive as Soviet exaltation of Lenin, but it serves the same purpose – to provide a time-honoured, glorious reference point for the mass of citizens being socialized in the present.'[35] Having made this observation, we must also note that there does indeed remain two important distinguishing dimensions. *First*, we have the simple fact that the Soviet Union expends considerably more resources – human and others – on maintaining and propagating its ideology than do the Western democracies, a fact which Motyl ascribes 'not to some psychological quirk of Soviet leaders but to their appreciation of its indispensable role in the state's effective pursuit of survival'.[36] *Second*, we have the issue of visibility. Obviously, there are very special reasons for the strongly liturgical features that characterize Soviet ideology. These will be dealt with at length in our discussion below of problems of culture and legitimation. For the time being, however, we shall dwell on the function of ideology at a more general level.

The American economic historian Douglass North has offered an interesting approach to this complex issue by recognizing a built-in dilemma in the neo-classical economic model. On the one hand, he argues, all individuals are assumed to act so as to maximize their own personal welfare, while on the other they are simultaneously assumed to agree on a given set of rules for this behaviour, the latter being an obvious necessity for a viable political system. Rational action on the first count, however, implies irrationality on the second. As North points out, it is 'in the interests of the neo-classical actor to disobey those rules whenever an individualistic calculus of benefits and costs dictates such action.'[37]

At the root of this dilemma lies the classic free rider problem. We would probably all agree that littering, for example, leads to a reduction in total welfare. For the single individual, however, there is a cost involved – in terms of effort – in not littering, while the impact on the environment of *his* littering is negligible. Since his loss in welfare is most likely larger on the former than on the latter count, the rational action would be to litter. North's pointed question becomes: 'How much additional cost will I bear before I become a free rider and throw the beer cans out the car window?'[38]

In this narrow formulation, the answer is obvious and if all individuals act rationally we will end up in a Prisoner's Dilemma situation. If nobody would litter everybody would be better off, but given the rules of the game this outcome is blocked. The attraction to the individual of littering is simply too great. Enforcement would be one possible way out, but for most rules underlying a working society the cost of enforcement would be greater than the increased welfare that could be thus achieved. It is obvious that it pays to enforce rules against, say, murder, but what about jaywalking, or smoking in public? If all individuals were to act rationally, from their own points of view, we would expect very few of the rules that constrain their behaviour to be obeyed and thus society would break down. Yet, we observe that most people abide by most rules most of the time, although it is costly for them to do so. It is here that 'ideology' enters the picture.

The root of the evil in the free-rider problem is the attraction to the individual of increasing his own personal welfare at the expense of the others. To solve this problem, we must increase the costs he has to pay for doing so and, as we have noted above, legal and economic sanctions may not be a feasible way to achieve this. In such cases, we are left with imposing *moral* costs: 'Strong moral and ethical codes of a society is the cement of social stability which makes an economic system viable.'[39] Co-operation was also seen to be the solution to the Prisoner's Dilemma, as outlined above.

Only by explicitly recognizing this function of ideology can we explain the substantial investments that are made by societies in acquiring legitimacy. Above all, this explains much of the investment in the educational system that cannot be explained as investment in human capital in order to increase individual productivity. By instilling certain norms and values into people, certain decisions will be ruled out. Ideology thus helps simplify their decision-making processes. It also helps to socialize individuals within the given social system. If we take total and brutal repression to be the alternative, or the point of reference, ideology can thus actually be seen as a cost-saving device when attempting to build a society.[40]

Now we are approaching the East-West dimension of ideology. 'Its [ideology's] fundamental aim is to energize groups to behave contrary to a simple, hedonistic, individual calculus of costs and benefits', writes North, and proceeds to point out that the necessary investment will depend on how much the new system deviates from the old: 'The costs of maintaining the existing order are inversely related to the perceived legitimacy of the existing system.'[41]

If we assume that any given population holds a set of values and beliefs on what is, in some sense, 'fair', then every attempt to impose an order that differs from these beliefs will have to be followed by an effort to bring beliefs and reality into line with each other. As Rousseau observed in his *Contrat social*, the 'strongest is never strong enough always to be master unless he transforms strength into right and obedience into duty.'[42] Thus it follows that an attempt at making revolution and at maintaining the new order will be more dependent on an explicit and vigorous ideology than will a gradualist policy: 'To the extent that a society does not mobilize its people and becomes pluralistic and diverse, the ideology becomes more diffuse,' writes Bell.[43]

Proceeding to compare developments in East and West, we find that the political systems of the Western world have evolved gradually, over a relatively long period of time. Beliefs and reality have thus had plenty of time to blend together and ideology is rather muffled, to some maybe not even perceptible.[44] In the Soviet case, on the other hand, the existing political system is very young and, moreover, when introduced it was – in some important respects – radically different from the old order. It is thus natural to ask the question of what has happened to the process of 'ideological realignment' and perhaps to assume – as we shall do below – that it may still be far from complete.

This distinction between East and West may appear subtle but it is definitely not harmless. In a society such as the Soviet, where explicit ideological constructs serve important legitimating purposes, a diffusion of that ideology will have important implications for the political stability of the regime. We shall consequently have much to say below about this process of realignment. It is an interesting question, for example, to ask *what* is to be aligned? How are beliefs adjusted to the new structure? Is it perhaps possible to influence this process in such a way that continuity with the old structure of beliefs and reality come to dominate the revolutionary change? However this may be, it will remain of crucial importance whether a convergence between beliefs and reality will actually take place. Alfred Meyer once observed that 'convincing the Soviet citizens that theirs was the best of all possible worlds was difficult':

> Hence the ideology became implausible. The effect of this was not only increased rigidity, but the further intensification of the indoctrination effort.... The intensity of indoctrination and the rigidity of official dogma are inversely proportional to the credibility of the doctrine. Moreover, these elements mutually reinforce each other.[45]

We certainly do not agree with Meyer's sweeping generalization about *the* Soviet citizen. On the contrary, we shall have repeated call below to return to differences in perception between the Russian and the non-Russian elements of the Soviet population as one highly important aspect of the constant search for legitimacy. What Meyer does capture, however, is the dynamic interaction between popular beliefs and official policy, in the ideological sense. This is clearly an important aspect of the realignment process. As North points out, individuals 'alter their ideological perspectives when their experiences are inconsistent with their ideology. In effect, they attempt to develop a new set of rationalizations that are a better "fit" with their experiences.'[46] In the case of a *utopian* ideology, by which we mean one whose promises relate to the future, it is of crucial importance that reality should at least develop in the right direction.[47] If this does not happen, it will be necessary either to revise the ideology or to face the fact that individuals will alter their ideological beliefs, away from the desired course.

While thus agreeing with Meyer that the plausibility of ideology is an important – perhaps even crucial – aspect of legitimation, we shall challenge his view that in the Soviet case it had become implausible. At this point it may be useful to distinguish between the respective functions of *legitimation* and *socialization*.[48] In the former case, ideology is used to make the citizen accept the system as a whole, in the latter to accustom him with his place within it. Although both tunes will have to be played at the same time, the difference is of some considerable importance. In order to legitimate the system, a clearly perceivable but at the same time carefully screened link with the past will need to be maintained, in terms of doctrine as well as national values and rituals. To socialize the subjects, on the other hand, the promises of the revolution must be kept alive and somehow at the same time be aligned with observable reality.

Here we should note the importance of the gap between utopia and reality, which explains the very different challenges faced by Western and Soviet ideologies. Since there can hardly be a *Weltanschaung* that provides consistent answers to all possible questions, any ideology will by necessity contain a number of inconsistencies and contradictions. The consequences, however, will depend on the challenge that the ideology is called upon to face. In the Western world, democracy has evolved over centuries without ever being closely codified. A process of pragmatic give and take has been sufficient to solve problems that have appeared along the road.

In the Soviet bloc the reverse is true. Having never had the time to settle down, Marxism-Leninism has been presented from the very outset as a scientifically correct body of thought that provides the only (correct) answer to all questions. Although Western democracy has certainly been ascribed certain philosophical foundations, this has happened *ex post* and is a far cry from the *a priori* claims that are laid to the scientific and philosophical nature of Marxism-Leninism.[49] Against the background of such claims, it is obvious that any inconsistencies will be quite serious, threatening the general acceptance of the ideology. Much energy has consequently gone into writings attempting to reconcile the various parts with each other.

As David Comey once observed, this situation may produce a vicious circle.[50] Every attempt at more detailed codification will highlight further inconsistencies, which in turn demand yet more detailed codification, etc. These constant interpretations of doctrine that occupy so many Soviet officials and which give rise to imcomprehension on the part of so many Westerners are thus not to be taken lightly. Although many may realize that the search for logical coherence is a hopeless enterprise, it is not possible to abandon since that would mean admitting the existence of inconsistencies in the 'scientifically correct' theory.

The rigidity of Soviet ideology is also reflected in the demands placed upon Soviet citizens in general and on Party members and officials in particular. Marxist-Leninist thought must not only be accepted but also studied and digested extensively. This necessity of actually practiscing the ideology is reflected in the important principle of *partiinost* (Party-mindedness), which grants the Party a monopoly on interpreting the creed and which also guarantees that it is the truth that is spoken, much in the same way as for the Pope when speaking *ex cathedra*. As Meyer notes:

> The cohesiveness of the Party apparatus places a premium on the constant interpretation of the doctrine. When such demands are made in the name of 'rational, scientific' thought, the consistency of the doctrine becomes imperative, for to the extent that glaring inconsistencies are tolerated, the complete acceptance of the doctrine is endangered.[51]

Bell even takes *partiinost* to the point where 'it is not the creed but the insistence on the infallibility of the interpreters that becomes the necessary mechanism of social control.... Only in this way can the Party rationalize the abandonment of once-hallowed doctrines and adopt new doctrines that may have little justification in old dogma.'[52] He also goes on to pin-point the importance of the ideology in moulding together the officials selected to interpret it:

> An *official* ideology is both a principle of inclusion and a principle of exclusion. It defines the official creed and it identifies the enemy or heretic against whom sentiments must be mobilized. By its very formulation of a public creed it requires an overt statement of allegiance from those who occupy responsible positions in the society.[53]

So far we have dealt with the general aspects of the concept of ideology. In this brief introduction, there are three things that we wish to bring out. *First*, that ideology is not a particular feature of the Soviet system, or indeed of socialism, although there are reasons why these cases may exhibit the most visible manifestations of ideology. In the general sense, it is at work everywhere – East and West. *Second*, in the value-belief dimension, the process of ideological realignment can act as a brake as well as an energizing force on a regime's attempt to change societal order. The dynamic feedback effects are thus important here. *Third*, status as an official ideology creates rather special circumstances of inclusion/exclusion, heretics, etc. This is of particular importance for our purposes below, since it means that both explicit and covert elements of ideology may be used by the regime as a tool, in a way for which there is no parallel in the West.

This concludes our general remarks on ideology and rationality. Before we turn to our study proper, however, we shall look briefly at one more tool in our box. Since our investigation is an interdisciplinary one, aiming to blend strands of evidence as seen from three different disciplinary perspectives, it is obvious that we shall need a tool that spans over the three disciplines involved. Moreover, given the strong emphasis that has been placed above on strategic behaviour by individuals, our tool must also be geared into analysing the behaviour and reactions of individuals to changes in their environment. Precisely such a theoretical framework can be found in the concepts of *Exit, Voice and Loyalty* (EVL) that have been developed by Albert Hirschman.[54]

Exit, Voice and Loyalty

The main ambition of EVL can be illustrated by the sub-title of Hirschman's seminal work on the topic: 'Responses to Decline in Firms, Organizations and States.' Briefly put, we are dealing here with situations where an individual is faced with deterioration in the quality of goods he normally purchases, or in the performance of organizations to which he belongs, and it is assumed that he can choose either to protest (Voice) or to leave (Exit). The point made by EVL is that the choice made between these two options will be of crucial importance for the prospects of eventual recuperation.

A vital assumption in this context is that of 'repairable lapse',[55] i.e. that decline in the performance of a firm or an organization need not be intentional but may rather be the result of 'organizational slack'.[56] In such a case, the decline may well be reversible, if brought to the attention of management. To an economist, this assumption may be slightly surprising, as it is generally assumed that if one firm goes bankrupt (due to reasons other than falling demand) its place in the market will be taken over by another, and no difference will be seen. If we grant, however, that recovery is possible, then various feedback mechanisms become of interest, as signals to management that something is amiss. It is here that Exit and Voice differ in their respective functions.

Signals to management in the form of Exit are generally assumed to be weaker than those emitted in the form of Voice, as Exit will normally occur in the form of a slow seepage. Indeed, in the special case where customers simply move between different producers in the same market, Exit and Entry may actually cancel each other out.[57] If there are many producers on the market, such movements may serve to prevent management from absorbing any signals until the problem has assumed serious proportions. In contrast, even a few outspoken individuals may create quite a lot of noise by using the Voice option and thus perhaps also succeed in transmitting a powerful message.

The ideal situation would thus be to achieve a sufficient delay in Exit for the discontent of the individuals concerned to be channelled into Voice, which in turn sets in motion the desired process of recuperation. It is here that Loyalty – the third ingredient in the EVL triad – enters the picture. Hirschman assumes that individuals who are possessed with a certain Loyalty to the firm or organization in question will be prepared to put up with decline longer, in the hope that by resorting to Voice they may actually succeed in promoting recuperation, and thus incidentally also in justifying their delay in Exit.[58] This use of the concept of Loyalty is obviously somewhat different from the everyday understanding of that word, and harsh criticism has been directed at this part of Hirschman's theory. As we shall argue below, however, the special nature of our application succeeds in avoiding much of this critique.

An important advantage of EVL lies in the fact that it is an unusually successful example of an interdisciplinary approach, combining economics and political science.[59] The Exit option, with its clean dichotomy, comes naturally to the economist, who is accustomed to thinking in binary terms (purchase or no purchase), while the Voice option, with its drawn-out and often inconclusive perspective, comes equally naturally to the political scientist, who is used to thinking in terms of processes *per se* rather than focusing on the results of those processes. In his original book on the subject, however, Hirschman argues that EVL is equally applicable *in toto* to both disciplines. He also expresses a 'hope to demonstrate to political scientists the usefulness of economic concepts and to economists the usefulness of political concepts'.[60]

Our approach is to use EVL as a tool with which to analyse those mechanisms of stabilization that were referred to above. Methodologically, the approach is heuristic and the model will be used as a loose analytical framework, rather than as a Procrustean bed of rigid definitions. In the present context, it might be argued that the tool is ill chosen for the problems at hand. Political repression and censorship may be argued to inhibit the use of Voice. Closed borders and a general absence of competition can be seen to preclude the use of Exit. The diffuse nature of the concept of Loyalty makes it hard to operationalize and interpret, and the long-term nature of social processes invalidates the essentially short-run nature of Hirschman's framework. Yet, it is precisely by bringing up objections of this kind that we hope to demonstrate the usefulness of the EVL paradigm to the case at hand.

If we start with the problem of 'response to decline', it may actually be seen as a strength that we are *not* dealing with short-term adjustment processes. As we have indicated above, the concept of

Loyalty is that part of Hirschman's theory which has drawn perhaps the harshest criticism from reviewers. A.H. Birch, for example, has argued that Hirschman has the wrong correlation between Voice and Loyalty. To Birch's way of thinking, Loyalty ought to mean a 'disposition to accept rather than a disposition to criticize'.[61] In a further critique, Michael Laver sees the concept of Loyalty as 'probably the most self-contradictory part' of the whole theory.[62] Perhaps one of the most serious criticisms that has been directed at the EVL theory, however, has been voiced by Brian Barry, who has argued that Loyalty in Hirschman's use is no more than an '*ad hoc* equation filler', with no independent theoretical role to play.[63]

Barry's main objection is that Loyalty does not capture a 'real social phenomenon', and it is here that we shall present our application as largely escaping those criticisms that have been directed at EVL in its original formulation.[64] While the perspective used by Hirschman is essentially one of short-term utility maximizing adjustments, ours is that of a more long-term process of socialization of individuals within the sphere that is controlled by government policy. Their 're-sponse' should thus be seen not as short-term adjustments in behaviour, but rather as a more long-term formation of attitudes and a corresponding conditioning and adaptation of actions.

What we are dealing with here is something very similar to the 'real social phenomenon' that was originally found lacking by Barry. The long-term nature of this process illustrates the importance of the time dimension and highlights the role of the process of ideological 'alignment'. Most importantly, however, it emphasizes the sluggish nature of social change. Even if there were a favourable change in official policy, in order to arrest a perceived 'decline', it might be quite some time before a corresponding transformation occurs of those popular values and beliefs which make up our concept of Loyalty, and which determine how the change in policy will be received.

Although this illustrates the difficulties that may face a policy which relies on incentives and encouragement, there are of course also corresponding problems connected with a policy that relies on repression. In order to elaborate on the latter point, we shall need to make a distinction between *vertical* and *horizontal* Voice. Hirschman has been rightly criticized for failing to realize that Voice has charac-teristics of a public good, i.e. that if some people get together and organize a protest against some public problem – say poor educa-tional standards – this will benefit all, while the costs of Voice will be borne by the activists alone. Consequently, the single individual may be expected to hope that others will perform the service for him.[65] In essence, this amounts to the problem that is described in Mancur Olson's book on *The Logic of Collective Action*.[66]

This line of reasoning is clearly valid in relation to Voice in Hirschman's original formulation, i.e. protests or complaints raised by citizens – or their organizations – against authorities or enterprises. The formation of such Voice – which we shall refer to as vertical – will suffer from precisely those problems of collective action that have been outlined by Olson and will consequently be rather easy to suppress. The crux of the matter is that there is also another form of Voice, one which operates on the horizontal level. *Horizontal* Voice – as defined by the Argentinian economist Guillermo O'Donnell – represents the daily exchange of opinions – approval or disgruntlement – *between* people and as such it represents a phenomenon altogether different from its vertical counterpart.[67] In the West, sentiments of the latter kind are regularly surveyed, for example via opinion polls regarding political preferences, consumer satisfaction with various goods, etc. Such surveys are of course carried out in the Soviet bloc countries as well, but they are sparsely publicized and rather differently handled.

An illustration of how such polls can be used is provided in an article in the Soviet Party journal *Kommunist*, where the Polish Party chief Jaruzelski speaks about the need for polls in the following terms: 'We see in this a mechanism for early warning and a timely prevention of situations of potential conflict.'[68] In late 1982, Jaruzelski established a Centre for the Study of Public Opinion. According to the head of this institute, Colonel Stanislaw Kwiatkowski, its purpose was to 'aid the government in adopting correct decisions and in improving the style and method of using power.'[69] Significantly, however, expressing his views to a Soviet audience, Jaruzelski was careful to declare that 'socialist pluralism must serve to promote a creative and constructive emergence and application of a variety of ideas, opinions, values and suggestions, all on the foundations of socialist construction.' Furthermore, in 'order to move ahead, we must defend the reform process from subversive actions of the class enemies and limit or remove the influence of anti-socialist slogans and concepts'.[70] In other words, public opinion should be surveyed simply in order for the regime better to control and influence it.

An important difference of principle between opinion research in East and West lies in the fact that, in the former case, the single individual will never learn the full picture. Information gained in this way will thus, on the one hand, serve as a more powerful tool for *manipulation* in the hands of the Soviet leaders than it will in the hands of their Western collegues. On the other hand, however, it will be a more important source of *information* for the latter. Forgoing this information can be seen as a price paid for the use of opinion polls as a tool of manipulation.

The importance of the horizontal type of Voice must be underlined. Not only is it virtually immune to all forms of collective action problems, since there is little cost and probably quite substantial individual benefits *per se* involved in communicating with your fellow citizens. It is also a prerequisite for the formation of vertical Voice. The real challenge to a repressive regime is thus not so much to suppress the open manifestations of popular discontent, which is a relatively simple question of expenditure on censorship, police and the military. In order to be successful, repression must also be directed at suppressing horizontal Voice, which is where the real trouble starts. Before proceeding to examine how this crucial issue has been addressed, let us briefly outline how the remainder of our book is organized.

Plan of the Study

In the following section we deal with the foundations of the 'Soviet model', as they were laid down under Stalin. The initial step is to show that the development of economic policy had political rather than economic motivations. In particular, this will be seen to hold for mass collectivization and the introduction of five-year planning. Secondly, we will show how relative political pluralism and debate *within* the Party was gradually suppressed and replaced by the Stalinist dictatorship *over* the Party. Finally, attention will be directed to how the regime increasingly came to seek its legitimacy in selected traditional Russian values. The conclusion from this section will attempt to demonstrate the supremacy of politics over economics and the resultant need to seek legitimacy in non-economic terms.

The third section is devoted to an investigation of Khrushchev's attempts to change the basic Stalinist model. The main focus is first directed at the failure of changing growth strategy – i.e. the failure of intensification – and at the search for a new *format* for old policy rather than for a new policy. Then we investigate the political effects of de-Stalinization, and the attempts made at changing and revitalizing the Party state. Finally, we discuss the impact of Khrushchev's cultural policy on the rigid Soviet ideological universe of the late Stalin period. The conclusion from this section is that Khrushchev represents an 'aberration', a partial break with a number of ingrained structural continuities and restraints.

Section four deals with Brezhnev's increasingly stagnant leadership, the *period zastoya*. Particular emphasis is placed on the reforms that 'never were', and at the increasing fossilization of the economy, where each new attempt at 'reform' produced smaller and smaller effects. The political dimension exhibits a similar pattern of fossilization in the political leadership – with its associated consequences for the running of the economy, on the one hand, and for the emergence of competing interests and opinion groups, on the other. Finally, we show how a gradual return was made to the traditional values and how these came to be increasingly ritualized in the search for legitimacy. This section emphasizes the interrelation between economic and ideological development on the one hand, and demographic trends and nationality problems on the other.

In the concluding section of the book, we outline a 'Legacy for Gorbachev'. After a brief perusal of the interregnum under Andropov and Chernenko, we examine the contents of Gorbachev's attempted 'revolution from above'. The prospects for successful reforms are discussed against the background of current developments in the natural environment, and in the spheres of demographic change and tensions between nationalities. The real obstacle to reform will be sought in terms of the impact on the psychology of Soviet Man of seven decades of Bolshevik rule.

Part two

Foundations of the Soviet model

Chapter two

Searching for the economics of early Soviet planning

The title of this chapter has quite deliberately been chosen in a somewhat provocative manner, seeking to indicate our intention to penetrate the *rationale* behind, rather than the practice and system of, economic planning as it emerged during the early stages of Bolshevik rule. The assumption underlying this endeavour is that the emergence of the vast planning apparatus, and of the tasks placed before it, had an essentially political rather than economic rationale. Hopefully, the ensuing discussion will live up to the expectations that are implied by this introduction.

As a starting point, we shall invoke the support of two independent observers, both reflecting on the problem of the economics of the 'Soviet model'. Upon returning to Harvard from a visit to the Soviet Union, in 1960, Professor Vasily Leontief, one of the founding fathers of input-output techniques, is reported to have made the following remark: 'Western economists have often tried to discover the "principle" of the Soviet technique of planning. They have never succeeded since, up to now, there has been no such thing'.[1] This puzzlement, moreover, can be found not only in the West. During the campaign of the 'hundred flowers' in China in 1957, a Chinese economist trained by the Soviet Gosplan, summed up the same problem in the following, rather blunt manner: 'The theory of the political economy of socialism does not exist. This chapter is essentially empty.... We are moving blindly, fumbling and just imitating the Soviet pattern. Our economic planning represents a mixture of dogmatism and empiricism.'[2]

It is against this background that we shall discuss the concept of economic versus political rationality. When confronted with some of the apparent absurdities of the Soviet economic system, it may certainly be tempting for a Western observer to condemn it as 'irrational'. It is our hope here, however, that by introducing political and ideological objectives into the analysis of the more narrow 'economic' system, it will be possible to demonstrate that the logic of the system we are observing may indeed be quite rational, albeit according to criteria different from those of Western economics.

We shall start our inquiry by looking at the periods of War Communism, in 1918–21, and of the New Economic Policy (NEP), in 1921–28, as two lessons in 'feasible socialism'.[3] The main assumption here is that the Soviet model was built in an *ad hoc* fashion, with few premeditated plans or concepts. The cornerstones of the model came into being as responses to urgent political and/or economic problems. Only *ex post* did the Soviet leaders realize that certain policy measures carried highly palatable side effects. These were then adopted as logical parts of the model of 'scientific socialism'. Ideology served an important legitimating function in this process, by masking what was actually happening, and by presenting a series of *ad hoc* emergency measures as a logical sequence of premeditated steps.[4]

We will then move on to see how the foundations of the centrally planned model were laid, during the First Five Year Plan (FFYP) in 1928–32. By focusing on the suppression of economics, and the promotion of politically motivated policy measures, we will seek to show the limited value of searching for a narrowly defined economic rationality. This approach will also allow us to present the model of 'extensive' growth as the very antithesis to the much vaunted 'intensive' growth model, which has been heralded by the Soviets for decades. We will argue that the establishment of the former model required the suppression of the main ingredients necessary for the latter to work. This will cast serious doubts on the possibility of a gradual transition from one to the other.

In the concluding section we will pull together the threads of an argument that attempts to explain the apparent economic irrationality of the Soviet model by presenting it as politically rational and ideologically in conformity with the Russian intellectual tradition.

Two lessons in feasible socialism

First lesson: a taste of power

> We have knowledge of socialism, but as for knowledge of organization on a scale of millions, knowledge of the organization and distribution of commodities – that we have not. This the old Bolshevik leaders did not teach us.... Nothing has been written about this yet in Bolshevik text-books, and there is nothing in Menshevik text-books either.[5]

Thus wrote Lenin only months after the Bolshevik take-over. Not only had the revolution arrived in the wrong country, and at the wrong time. It had also arrived unexpectedly. Moreover, once it had arrived, nobody seemed to know what to do with it. It is a striking fact, for example, that both Kamenev and Zinoviev forcefully opposed that fateful Central Committee decision on insurrection which was to produce the Bolsheviks' successful October 1917 *coup d'état*. It was quite simply up to Lenin's superior oratory to secure the votes that would carry the day.[6] To say that the Bolsheviks started with an economic *tabula rasa* would thus hardly seem to be an over-statement. On the contrary, Napoleon's famous maxim *On s'engage, et puis on voit* would seem to be rather fitting.

Policy-making during the first few years of Soviet power was consequently to be characterized by an *ad hoc* attitude. As Maurice Dobb has put it: 'In those days of "touch and go" for the Soviet power, few of the Bolsheviks looked further into the future than a week or two at the time.'[7] It was not emergency alone, however, that characterized events. In his famous 'April Theses' of 1917, Lenin's aim had been 'not the "introduction" of socialism as an *immediate* task, but immediate transition merely to *control* by the Soviet of Workers' Deputies over the crucial production and distribution of products.'[8] Apart from the seizure and maintenance of power, there were few other plans for the future. In the light of that picture of a planned long-term strategic nature of Soviet development which was subsequently to gain currency in the West, among friends and foes alike of the Soviet system, this latter fact is of some considerable importance to note.

What the true ambitions were during the first 8 months leading up to the Civil War is impossible to say. Nove, for example, argues that the 'evidence, though mixed, is still consistent with the intention to maintain a mixed economy for a considerable period.'[9] For our purposes it will be sufficient to assume, in accordance with the 'April Theses', that it was a desire for power and control *per se* that was the overriding concern. Otherwise, the attitude was one of wait and see. This assumption, however, will not be made at the cost of totally ignoring such emergencies that were brought about by Civil War, and by foreign intervention and blockade. Rather, we shall take a dialectic approach, assuming that the desire for power and control conditioned *responses* to successive emergencies. Measures taken in this fashion would then *ex post* be rationalized as desired and intended policy. As Moshe Lewin says, in regard to this process of policy formation:

It evolved because of the interplay of action imposed by the contingencies of war and the combination of psychological needs of leaders and followers alike engaged in the battle for survival, which only the hope for 'utopia' can provide, with a set of vague notions about communism – which had never been thought out seriously and which Marx had deliberately left obscure because its establishment was too far in the future.[10]

The unfolding events certainly provided both the opportunity and the need for rather drastic policies. In the winter of 1917–18, food shortages were such that rations in Petrograd were down to 50 grams of bread per day – workers alike.[11] After the peace with Germany, in March 1918, followed the outbreak of Civil War in June, accompanied by foreign intervention and a naval blockade of Petrograd. Finally, there was the war with Poland in 1920.

All in all, there is good cause for labelling the 1918–21 policy 'War Communism', or to characterize it as the policy of a 'besieged fortress'.[12] Once we penetrate below the chaotic surface, however, a highly interesting problem emerges in the relation between action taken and some more basic principles of management. Let us look at this important feedback mechanism against the background of four important problem areas: agriculture, industry, labour and finances.[13]

Agriculture, or perhaps more properly put – food procurement, was the real centrepiece of the War Communism policy. In order to secure food for the cities and the Red Army, force and coercion were used. In the spring of 1918, a state monopoly on grain trade was declared and armed detachments were sent out from the cities to procure forcefully from peasants who refused to sell against payment in useless paper currency. The whole operation came to be known as *prodrazverstka*, and it was presented as a part of the class struggle in the villages, where the procurement agents were aided by committees of poor peasants (*kombedy*) who in reality acted as informers.[14] Initially, large quantities of grain were procured, but soon the peasants responded by drastic reductions in sowing, and by 1921 the country faced mass starvation.[15]

In *industry*, the dominant feature was nationalization. In contrast to land, however, which was nationalized wholesale on the very day after the October *coup d'état*, a general nationalization of industry was not decreed until June 1918. In the intervening period, nationalization would occur either for political reasons – to punish obstructing capitalists – or as a result of spontaneous takeovers by the workers. It is interesting to note that when a general nationalization was finally proclaimed, this was regarded as a remarkable surrender to the left wing of the Party.[16] It is of crucial importance to note that all spontaneous attempts at establishing worker control over enterprises were firmly discouraged and derided as syndicalism.[17] As in the case of agriculture, control from above was the prime objective.

In the field of *labour*, the outstanding feature was Trotsky's attempt to militarize the trade unions, seeking to introduce military organization and discipline, with heavy punishments for 'desertion'. In accordance with this policy, detachments of the Red Army were drafted into 'labour armies', for civilian purposes, and in April 1919 forced labour camps were set up for 'dissenters', their labour to be put at the disposal of Soviet institutions in the area.[18]

In the *financial* area, finally, action was swift. In the very week after the revolution, the State Bank was seized and soon after all private banks were expropriated and foreign debt repudiated.[19] Then a gradual deterioration in the value of the ruble followed, which resulted, in 1920, in a total collapse of the currency and in an attempt to introduce a money-free state budget.[20] A stable currency would not be restored until February 1924.

In short, the model of War Communism featured centralized control, harsh rationing, coercive mobilization of labour, coercive requisitioning of agricultural produce, elimination of markets – and terror. As Laszlo Szamuely has concluded, this system had its own logic: 'Its main features outline a model of the centralized directive system of planned economy in its purest historical form ever implemented. (Let us remember that since then not even the most rigidly centralized mechanisms have abolished monetary economy or – apart from war and other extraordinary circumstances – the free movement of labour.)'[21] Many of these traits were obviously wartime expedients, but there is also a more subtle dimension which has been indicated by Oskar Lange, in writing about the early stages of planning in a socialist state:

> I think that, essentially, it can be described as a *sui generis* war economy. Such methods of war economy are not peculiar to socialism because they are also used in capitalist countries in wartime.... The difficulty starts when the methods of war economy are identified with the essence of socialism and considered to be essential to socialism.[22]

This agrees well with our basic contention that *ad hoc* policy measures were presented – *ex post* – as logical steps in an allegedly premeditated strategy. One distinctive feature of the early period of Bolshevik rule was that there were hardly any traces of the comprehensive planning apparatus that has later been described as an integral part of 'scientific socialism'. On the contrary, when, already in May 1917, a group of Mensheviks urged the Petrograd Soviet to issue a call for planning, they were derided and charged with 'left wing childishness'.[23] Lenin blamed the Mensheviks in general for creating extremely complex, cumbersome and bureaucratic planning agencies, and condemned their planning projects as 'bourgeois hare-brained schemes'. In *State and Revolution*, written in July 1917, he himself held planning to be an exceedingly simple task:

> Accounting and control – these are the *main* requirements for a proper functioning of the *first phase* of communist society.... These have become greatly simplified under capitalism, being re-duced to operations that can be performed by any literate person: observation and note taking, knowledge of the four arithmetic operations, and the issue of receipts.[24]

The one really concrete and clearly defined part of the Bolshevik programme concerned the banks. On the eve of the Bolshevik take-over, Lenin was unconditionally in favour of the traditional socialist view of the big banks as being *the* state apparatus: 'Without the big banks, socialism would be unrealizable.'[25] To our minds, this extreme belief in the magic of taking over the banks merits a label of 'account-ancy socialism'. It also helps explain the rather lax attitude taken to the concrete problems of running the economy. Leon Smolinsky makes the following observation:

> This informal, if not impulsive, approach to the solution of intri-cate problems of economic planning and organization was to characterize Lenin on various important occasions.... Improvisa-tions that were to follow the October revolution were rooted in impatient oversimplifications abounding in Lenin's prerevol-utionary works.[26]

Lenin's own ideals were clear-cut. Inspiration was to come from Ger-many. German economic organization, together with the Soviet political revolution, would be the road to socialism.[27] One example of this was the famous GOELRO plan for the electrification of Rus-sia. This plan has been hailed by the Soviets as 'the first long-term development plan in human history',[28] and important it was, albeit in a somewhat different way.

The man put in charge was Krzhizhanovsky, an old Bolshevik and an engineer who had advocated electrification already before World War I. When actually faced with the task of carrying out his ideas, Krzhizhanovsky argued strongly that the GOELRO plan must be preceded by an *economic* plan to determine the interrelations be-tween different sectors of the economy,[29] but his plea was not heeded. The GOELRO turned out an exclusive engineering product, and we have here the first manifestation of a disease later to become deeply embedded in the practice of Soviet planning, namely the separation of *what* from *how*. The former is known in Russian as *planirovanie* (planning) and should be the task of economists, striving for the best possible allocation of scarce resources between competing uses. The latter is known as *proektirovanie* (projecting) and is the task of engineers, striving to reach a given target at least possible input cost. In economic terminology, the latter is a question of technical efficiency, whereas the former concerns economic efficiency. The difference between the two is crucial.

With politicians determining *what*, and engineers figuring out *how*, there is no mechanism to co-ordinate and balance total resource use in any manner remotely efficient. Technically, single projects may be efficient, but economically the choice of projects will be efficient only by pure chance. One example of the consequences of this separation can be found in the Volkhov river project, the first Soviet hydropower plant. Seeking political favours, local management decided in 1929 to increase the head of the dam by 20 percent. As a result, power output increased by some 100–150 million kwh per year, while about 250,000 acres of fertile floodplain, meadow and pasture land were flooded and rendered useless for agriculture, all at a time of agricultural crisis and impending starvation.[30] The increased power output may have been achieved in a *technically* efficient manner, but from an *economic* standpoint it was pure disaster. The system, however, had no mechanism to generate such information. The combination of politicians and engineers was a most powerful one.

Interestingly, under Gorbachev's *glasnost* Soviet scholars have also begun to recognize the real core of this dilemma. In an article entitled the 'conservative syndrome', L.G. Ionin delivers scathing criticism of 'social demagoguery', 'administrative wilfulness' and 'objective-optimistic' conceptions of the laws of economic development. His main thrust is to identify two mutually reinforcing principles which together make up the nature of the 'practical ideology' of economic management:

(1) A technocratic principle of arbitrariness, derived from the illusion of the simple nature and unlimited possibilities of social transformation, and (2) the sacral principle of 'organicness' (*organichnost*) which, by missionary 'objective superiority', makes it possible to justify any kind of activity, irrespective of its potential social consequences. This combination of technocratic arbitrari-

ness and its 'organic' foundations presents a *conservative syndrome*, the manifestations of which have been numerous.[31]

Ionin's account fits strikingly well into our overall perspective. If we look at the emergence of central planning from the perspective outlined above – i.e. the desire for power and control – we will find that several of the pieces in the puzzle fall neatly into place. The *prodrazverstka* makes sense as a way of breaking the political power of the food producers over the army and the cities. The militarization of labour makes sense as a way of breaking the power of Workers' Councils, and also offers considerable control over resource allocation. The absence of both planning and markets created a need for 'shock' methods (*udarnost*), and the destruction of the monetary system created a need for physical allocation of supply from the centre, all of which placed considerable power in the hands of the central government.

While this model may not have performed well in practice, it did have important demonstration effects. Forced requisitionings may certainly have been necessary under the initial circumstances, but soon they also presented an excellent way of controlling the peasants. The destruction of the currency can hardly have been intentional, but it did present an excellent way of controlling industry, etc. It is here that we find the interaction between wartime expediency and the masking function of ideology. As Lewin puts it, 'when Lenin suddenly found himself in a situation in which all the allegedly "capitalist" mechanisms began to disintegrate under the strain of the war, the Party leaders fell prey to the illusion that the dream was becoming real.'[32]

While the model of War Communism, as a vehicle of extraction and of political control and mobilization, may not have been originally visible, it 'grew' (so to speak) on the leadership, and soon became integrated into their ideology. The process was speeded up and each blow directed at some aspect of markets, and the price mechanism was hailed as a glorious victory. Thus we have arrived at precisely that which Lange warned about – the rationalization of war-time necessities as ingredient parts of socialism: 'Under the heading of "socialism" a centralized apparatus grew to massive proportions and enhanced the power of the state on an unprecedented scale.'[33]

The fact remained, however, that in practice the control model did not work. By the beginning of 1921, the country stood at the brink of total disaster, facing mass starvation and a total disintegration of the economy. The NEP was introduced.

Second Lesson: A Taste of Opposition

The decree that is normally taken as the introduction of NEP was rather simple, calling for a replacement of forced requisitionings of agricultural produce by a predetermined tax in kind.[34] Yet, 'this first move triggered the rest and led to a remarkable *volte-face* which astonished the world as well as the Bolsheviks.'[35] Each step taken to relax controls over the peasants was followed by further liberalization, in a virtual landslide: freedom to market commodities led to a booming private trade, increased purchasing power stimulated light industry, return to a free labour market abolished the 'labour armies', nationalization of small scale industry was revoked, large parts of major enterprises were leased to private entrepreneurs and concessions were offered to foreign capitalists. Finally, the enhanced role of the market created a need to stabilize the currency; this was achieved by 1923–4, thereby producing a balanced state budget.

Lenin tried to maintain that the 'commanding heights' of the economy (i.e. banking, foreign trade and large scale industry) remained firmly in the hands of the state, but this must have seemed a rather hollow claim. His public appearances also showed considerable embarassment and confusion in trying to explain the about-face to bewildered Party members.[36]

The effects of introducing the NEP were rapidly felt. As Carr notes, the 'New Economic Policy was, in its inception, a policy for agriculture, and, by implication, for internal trade, but not for industry.'[37] This fact was clearly borne out. Liberalizations and a restored faith in the regime stimulated the peasants to expand production as well as marketing, whereas industry continued to exhibit problems of inefficiency, rent-seeking trusts, and general disorganization. As a result, agricultural prices fell rapidly, in relation to industrial prices, and the country was approaching yet another crisis. This was the so-called scissors crisis, where the 'scissors' were the diverging indices of agricultural and industrial prices.[38]

This time, however, the crisis was nipped in the bud by swift action to force down industrial prices, which were still controlled by the state. The scissors were closed. There is a striking contrast between this action and those taken both earlier and later at similar stages. It is also characteristic of early NEP. The economy was recovering fast and several of the leading Bolsheviks took this as an indication that War Communism had been an erroneous policy. The greatest turncoat was Bukharin, who completely abandoned his earlier left-wing position and instead came out strongly pro-peasant and in favour of a cautious and gradual policy.[39] In 1925, NEP reached its peak.

As the economy was gradually healing its wounds, the need to formulate a long-term policy became pressing and the Great Debate over the future course of the industrialization of Russia was started.[40] Underlying this debate was a general consensus on the needs to catch up with the West economically and to prepare for a feared war with the hostile imperialist powers.[41] Both were seen to imply rapid industrialization and it was only when it came to the way in which to achieve this that opinions differed. Space unfortunately prohibits a closer scrutiny of the arguments presented in this highly interesting but inconclusive debate. It should be pointed out, however, that both left and right wings of the Party adhered closely to Lenin's principle of totally rejecting the use of force in relation to the peasantry.[42] This is important to bear in mind when we turn in a moment to the policy of mass collectivization.

While the debate was still in full swing, actual events overtook it. After 1925, opposition to NEP started to increase markedly within the Party. Peasants, who for a brief period even had the right to lease land and hire labour, were becoming better off. Private traders were becoming rich. In production as well as in trade, activities for personal gain totally dominated attempts at promoting co-operatives. The Party was forced to watch its grip over the all-important grain supply slipping. Considerable power was implicitly shifted into the hands of the peasants, at least in terms of obstructing government policy. Party supremacy was threatened, and with it the power and security of its leadership.

Ever louder voices called upon the Party to put an end to this spread of capitalism in the countryside, and to settle the score with the better-off peasants, who were branded as *kulak* oppressors. The actual truth behind allegations that the peasants were holding back supplies in order to starve the cities will probably never be found, but it has been established for a fact that Stalin presented deliberately falsified statistics in order to substantiate this claim and to pave the way for a harsher policy.[43]

As a result, liberalizations were revoked, step by step, and the terms of trade were once again turned against agriculture. Peasant reaction was the same as during War Communism, and during the scissors crisis. By the winter of 1927–8, the country faced yet another serious grain crisis. Government reaction, however, was back to 'normal'. Stalin answered by sending out armed detachments to procure grain, much in the same way as during the *prodrazverstka*.[44] For all practical purposes, NEP was dead.

The mass collectivization which followed has been characterized by Arthur Wright as a 'sudden desperate lunge to extricate the leadership from a deep economic and political crisis, a crisis which was largely of its own making.'[45] This point can hardly be overstated. The shortage of grain has been pictured as the result of a conscious and hostile act by the peasants, or alternatively as a result of an improvement in their own consumption. This picture is largely a false one. When the terms of trade were turned against agriculture, it was mainly grain prices that were falling. As a result of this change in *relative* agricultural prices, peasants shifted out of grains and into other lines of production, notably livestock. This not only brought about a direct reduction in the output of grains. Since animal production is biologically more demanding than vegetable production, it also brought a reduction in gross *calorie* production.[46] With very little realistic thinking, this grain crisis could have been predicted, and indeed some may have seen it coming. At the fifteenth Party Congress in 1928, which was admittedly to some extent after the event, Molotov referred to agricultural price policy as a series of 'colossal stupidities'.[47]

Again we find the same pattern as during War Communism. Mass collectivization was an *ad hoc* measure, brought about suddenly in order to forcibly extract from the peasants produce that was crucial for the survival, above all, of the cities and the Red Army. Once such measures were introduced, however, they proved to be a powerful tool in the struggle to control the peasantry. Similarly, official ideology was *ex post* twisted to show that agricultural co-operation was a logical part of socialism, which had been consciously promoted throughout. Against this, we can contrast not only Lenin's warnings against the use of force, but also his view on co-operation, as expressed in one of his last pamphlets (*On Co-operation*).[48] Lewin summarizes: 'Lenin primarily used co-operation to mean the grouping of peasants for the commercialization of their produce; common production, rather realistically, was not even mentioned in this article.'[49]

In sum, the perceived lessons of events during the first decade after the revolution can be put rather simply. If the Soviet Union was to catch up with its enemies, it must industrialize. For this purpose, accumulation must take place in agriculture. In order to transfer resources out of agriculture and into industry, the peasants must be compelled. All of this was seen to be inconsistent with market exchange.

The model that was introduced, however, was not the one of alleged central *planning*. It was simply one of centralized political *control* over the economy, which is a very different matter.[50] Centralizing political and administrative control offered unique possibilities for those at the centre to push the economy in a desirable direction, to break the economic power of potential and real political opponents, such as the peasantry, and to reward loyal vassals by granting lucrative fiefdoms in the rapidly expanding controlling bureaucracy. As Eugene Zaleski has noted on the War Communism experience, 'its most important role was the link it established in the minds of the planners between the idea of planning and that of centralization based on coercive measures'.[51] The cost, however, was that of losing *economic* control. As Charles Lindblom has put it, political levers have 'strong thumbs but weak fingers'.[52]

The Birth of the 'Soviet Model'

In 1931, and with a ghostly foresight, Stalin made the following remark: 'We have fallen behind the advanced countries by as much as fifty to one hundred years. We have to overcome this lag within ten years. Either we accomplish this, or we perish.'[53] As we know, the task was just barely accomplished in the stated time, but how was it accomplished and what was the price that had to be paid?

The Soviet Union in the 1920s was an underdeveloped and largely rural country, and agriculture was consequently destined to play an important role in any attempt at economic development. The demands that would be placed on agriculture in such a process are summarized by Bruce Johnston and Andrew Mellor under the following five headings: (a) to provide labour for an expanding industrial sector; (b) to provide food for a growing urban population; (c) to contribute towards capital formation in industry; (d) to provide exports for foreign exchange generation; and (e) to provide a market for industrial output.[54] The last point, as we know, was of negligible importance. Consequently, the basis for Soviet development strategy came to be the release of rural manpower for industrial expansion and the suppression of domestic consumption for the purpose of maximum accumulation. The way in which these two squeezes were achieved is of crucial importance in understanding the future development of the Soviet economy, and we shall now proceed to take a closer look at them, starting with the labour squeeze.

Forced Labour

At the end of the 1920s, the Soviet economy was subject to considerable agricultural overpopulation. The normal trend towards increased urbanization had been broken during War Communism, reducing the urban population from 29 million (20.4 per cent of total) in January 1917, to 21 million (15.7 per cent) by the end of

August 1920. The chief cause behind the shift was the severe problems of obtaining food in the cities. Although the food situation improved considerably during NEP, the cities still did not achieve a sufficient edge over the countryside in order to produce more than a slow transfer back. It would not be until 1930 that the pattern of 1917 was once again reached.[55]

Given the tremendous economic growth rates that were envisaged in the finally accepted, extreme version of the FFYP, this situation presented a serious obstacle. Labour must somehow be transfered out of agriculture, and here two expedient measures were found: the use of terror to scare free labour into the cities (and industry); and the use of arrests and deportations to create a pool of forced labour. As Stalin put it, 'new methods' were necessary in order to secure a sufficient supply of labour for the rapidly growing industrial sector.[56]

An important ingredient in the collectivization campaign was the process of *dekulakization,* aimed at eliminating the *kulaks* – the better off peasants – 'as a class'. There had been much debate about whether or not they should be allowed into the newly formed *kolkhozy*, but eventually Stalin settled the issue and a veritable witchhunt began.[57] There were obviously important political motives involved, such as to break once and for all the economic and political power of the peasantry, and thus to bring agricultural procurements under the firm control of the state. From top secret documents, however, that were subsequently captured by German troops, we can make out a picture that presents an additional and perhaps equally important motive.[58] The sheer numbers of people deported, the extreme vagueness of definitions of 'kulaks', and the existence of categories such as 'ideological kulaks',[59] all point in the direction of a wholesale terror which may well be interpreted as aimed at driving the peasants off to the relative safety of the towns – where their labour was desperately needed.

Intentional or not, dekulakization produced precisely that effect. According to estimates made by Frank Lorimer, on behalf of the League of Nations, net migration to Soviet towns and cities during the period 1927–38 amounted to 23 million people, while the total increase in the urban population was only about 28 million. In 1939, more than 40 per cent of the urban population consisted of people who had arrived from rural communities during the preceding 12 years. Moreover, 9.5 of the 23 million had arrived in the years 1930–2, when dekulakization was carried out.[60] This addition to the urban workforce, which came about without the government having to offer any benefits or incentives, was of obvious and decisive importance to the progress of the FFYP.

Parallel to this increase in the urban workforce, a pool of forced labour was built up, as another by-product of political repression and terror. Two important points can be made here. First, it had been an axiom of early Soviet justice that crime would wither away under socialism. Thus, the prevailing view was that prisons should be made to serve for correction, not for punishment, and that penal labour should serve a humanitarian ideal of correction and re-education. This attitude was reflected in the Criminal Code of 1924.[61] As we know, however, by the 1930s it had undergone a drastic transformation.[62] The second point concerns the concentration camp, another feature of early Soviet justice, which has been mentioned above. With penal labour and concentration camps we can thus observe, already during War Communism, two necessary prerequisites for turning forced labour into an economic institution. Yet, much in the same way that the ancient Egyptians were familiar with the steam-engine, but failed to put it to economic use, forced labour did not take on any economic importance during this time.

Again, however, the demonstration effect was important. In March 1928, a first decree was issued calling for 'a greater use of penal labour', and, in a step-by-step process, forced labour was integrated into the system. Planners were told to incorporate it into the FFYP, and prosecutors were ordered to reopen old cases against 'class-alien' elements who had received sentences of 3 years or less. Labour camp was made compulsory for all those sentenced to more than 3 years.[63] New demands were placed on the repressive apparatus. With plan targets being based upon the labour of prisoners, their numbers must also be determined in advance. All that was needed was an organizational framework, and as a finishing touch, the infamous GULAG (*glavnoe upravlenie lagerei*), the main administration of labour camps, was set up as a separate department within the secret police.

How many camps there were and what their total population was is a matter that is open to considerable dispute.[64] For our purposes, however, it will suffice to establish its structural importance rather than its magnitude, and here the evidence is clearer. The first large-scale application came in 1930, as a result of a desperate labour shortage in the northern lumber industry. After consultations with the secret police, the industry was virtually taken over by forced labour from the GULAG.[65] The experiment was successful and many similar examples followed, thus laying the foundations for what was to become a vast economic 'empire', so to speak, within the economy.

In this process, arrests acquired an important economic meaning. Any decline in the supply of fresh labour to the camps would not only risk production targets (with consequent repercussions for other enterprises dependent on GULAG output), but would also reduce NKVD profits and thus jeopardize its other operations. Consequently, the number of prisoners had to be determined in advance, and it is hardly surprising to find evidence that local NKVD officials were assigned quotas for the number of people that were to be arrested within their respective areas.[66] The latter also explains why so many of the people arrested in the 1930s were tried for things said or done 10–15 years back – any excuse would do in order to produce the required number of arrests. The economic importance of the oppressive apparatus had come to rival its political functions.

In sum, we can thus say that dekulakization and forced labour together served the important function of relieving the labour bottleneck. At the end of the 1920s, agricultural overpopulation was estimated at about 30 million people. As a result of various measures of 'organized recruitment', about the same number were removed from the villages during 1926–39. Of course, the natural increase in population to some extent offset this drain, but it is still significant that the farm labour force fell from 70.5 to 45.7 million over the period.[67] As we have said above, the exact extent of forced labour is unknown, but a conservative estimate points to around 10 per cent of the total labour force by 1939.[68] It constituted not a marginal addition, but a substantial part of the resources mobilized to carry out the process of industrialization.

Forced labour was also a logical part of the command model. It made possible the conquest of the vast natural resources of Siberia, without which Soviet industrialization would not have been possible, but which free labour would not go near. In this way the basis for 'extensive' growth was laid. At the same time, however, an effective obstacle was raised against the introduction of 'intensive' growth. The latter rests on productivity increases and improved factor allocation, and all thoughts of optimality or cost calculations were obviously alien to the NKVD. When the basic economic philosophy is to 'storm' and 'conquer', at any cost, the price of labour becomes immaterial. The system effectively suppressed *economic* rationality. This is above all reflected in the case of capital accumulation, to which we shall now turn.

Forced Accumulation

During NEP, an attempt was made to attract foreign capital, but this failed to produce any significant results, largely due to the refusal of the Bolsheviks to acknowledge Tsarist foreign debt. The Soviet state would thus have to rely largely upon its own resources for any development effort, and these were limited to labour and natural resources. Given the high growth rates envisaged, moreover, the gap between available resources and the implied demand was of quite substantial proportions. If industrialization was to succeed, this gap must somehow be bridged, and here policy was aimed both at increasing supply and at curbing all demand other than for directly productive purposes.

One of the main features on the former count was mass collectivization, which did produce a substantial short-run transfer of resources out of agriculture. Another was the use of 'shock' tactics in industry and the spread of the Stakhanov movement. It should be beyond doubt that these features had detrimental long-run effects, especially in the case of agriculture, and we shall not go further into these matters than to note that it was not increased productivity that was to be the key to rapid Soviet industrialization. The importance of this point can hardly be overestimated. The need to move from 'extensive' (more) to 'intensive' (better) growth has been at the centre of Soviet economic debates up until the present discussion of *perestroika*.

The real key to success, in terms of rapid economic growth, is instead to be found on the demand side, in a drastic reduction in all demand other than for directly productive purposes (i.e. heavy industry). Paul Baran gives an indication of how this was done:

> If great urgency is attached to the attainment of the developmental (and/or defence) goals, consumption standards can be fixed at 'rock bottom'. This 'rock bottom' is indicated by the need to preserve health and *productive efficiency* of the population and to maintain *political stability*. It goes without saying that the reduction of current consumption to such 'rock bottom' levels is highly undesirable.... Thus the First Five Year Plan although programming extremely high rates of expansion, was very far from scheduling a reduction of consumption to 'rock bottom' levels. In actual fact it anticipated an increase of consumption by as much as 40 percent over the quinqueannum.... This increase did not materialize in view of *unexpected* difficulties associated mainly with the peasants' resistance to collectivization.[69]

Baran's basic point is, of course, correct, but his appreciation of the actual course of events is either naive or grossly apologetic. It is, however, shared by other writers and thus merits some comment.[70] First, consumption standards were fixed *below* 'rock bottom', at least for the millions who perished by starvation. Second, the disruptions caused by collectivization and the crazy pace of industrialization can hardly be made to agree with any desire to preserve either productive efficiency or political stability. Third, it is rather hard to take seriously the claim that difficulties associated with collectivization could have been unexpected, particularly in the light of the many and repeated warnings issued by both the left and right wings of the Party. Instead, we shall argue below that the increases in consumption that were allegedly envisaged by the FFYP may never have been intended as anything but very cynical propaganda.

Our interpretation of the Soviet model is close to Preobrazhensky's theory of primitive socialist accumulation (i.e. the notion that agriculture must be 'over-charged' in order for rapid industrial growth to be achieved). His understanding, however, was that this should take place by ways of turning the terms of trade against agriculture, and he failed to indicate how the peasantry should be made to accept such 'unequal exchange'. Here we shall argue that Stalin found a solution in terror and coercion. Logically, the outstanding features of the collective farm system are precisely those needed to *extract* rather than to *produce* – forced membership in collectives that were made jointly responsible for imposed delivery obligations, a wage system that made payments to labour a residual factor, detailed Party control over the minutiae of farm operations, and, finally, in December 1932, the introduction of the passport system that would prevent peasants from leaving their farms.[71]

With this apparatus it was possible to control the consumption standards of the rural population and, as can be seen from Table 2.1, it was precisely the ability to depress consumption that made room for the necessary investment. While national income increased by some 60 per cent during the FFYP, consumption remained virtually unchanged.

Table 2.1 National income, 1928–32 (billion 1928 rubles)

	1928	*1929*	*1930*	*1931*	*1932*
National income	25.0	27.4	32.4	36.4	40.1
(a) consumption	21.3	22.6	23.2	22.7	22.4
(b) investment	3.7	4.8	9.2	13.7	17.7

Source: Ellman (1975), p. 845.

The squeeze that was applied to the rural population can be seen from Table 2.2.

Table 2.2 **Grain balance, 1928–32 (million long tons)**

	1928	1929	1930	1931	1932
Harvest	73.1	71.7	77.2	69.5	69.6
Marketed output	15.7	19.5	22.6	23.7	19.4
– of which export	0.1	0.3	4.8	5.1	1.7

Source: Ellman (1975), p. 847.

Not only did both marketings and exports rise continuously. They did so even during the extremely difficult year of 1931. This indicates rather clearly that the harvest retained on the farms (i.e. the livelihood of the peasants) was used as a residual to absorb fluctuations. It was only in 1932, in the face of mass starvation, that the pressure was eased somewhat, but even then exports were not discontinued altogether.

Agriculture, however, provided far from *all* the resources needed for industrialization; if nothing else this is borne out by the fact that total investment in the economy in 1932 was more than double the total value of agricultural production.[72] Moreover, the requirement of feeding the rapidly growing urban population was met not by increasing production but by a shift in the composition of production. The massive slaughtering of livestock that took place as a peasant response to forced collectivization, caused a substantial drop in feed requirements and thus made it possible to increase the production of such basic goods as bread, potatoes, and cabbage quite substantially.[73]

The real truth behind Soviet rapid industrialization may perhaps never be found. It is a fact that rapid accumulation took place. It is a fact that the prevailing intention was to achieve this by 'over-charging' the peasantry, and it is a fact that the Soviet leadership took steps in order to do so. There is, however, a serious danger at this point of falling into the trap of a *post hoc, ergo propter hoc* argument. The simple fact that rapid industrialization followed in the steps of a substantial squeeze on agriculture does not necessarily imply any causality, irrespective of the statements of intent made by those responsible for policy-making at the time. Most – if not all – students of the Soviet 1920s and 1930s would certainly agree that the long run consequences for Soviet agriculture of mass collectivization were something of a disaster. Yet, the conventional wisdom has long been that an 'agricultural surplus' was indeed extracted in the short run, which contributed to the industrialization effort. This view has been challenged by James Millar, and the ensuing debate illustrates the complicated nature of the issues at hand.[74]

If we take into consideration that the real extraction imposed by government policy took place only between the *state* and the peasantry, then with food shortages in the cities it may have been possible for the latter to shift the burden of extraction on to the urban population, via high black-market prices for whatever food supplies that were not discovered by the state procurement agents. Evidence can also be found of drastic increases in these prices.[75] The net position of the peasantry, and thus the net contribution by agriculture to industrialization, will then depend on which of these forces was stronger. The absence of reliable data, primarily regarding prices on the various resource flows, long made empirical work impossible. In the late 1960s, however, interesting new archival materials on developments during the FFYP were made available by the Soviet economic historian A.A. Barsov.[76]

Barsov's data has made it possible to argue: (a) that the terms of trade actually moved *in favour* of agriculture, (b) that deliveries of industrial goods to agriculture were quite substantial, and (c) that the agricultural surplus may have been quite small or even negative.[77] Barsov's own conclusion is rather striking: 'Nevertheless, the majority of accumulation, necessary for carrying out socialist industrialization, was obtained from the non-agricultural branches of the economy and was created by the working class.'[78] Millar takes an equally harsh stance: 'In any event, we may discover that the Soviet Union achieved growth and development not because the peasantry was exploited and agriculture neglected, but despite it.'[79] Needless to say, this leaves very little room for an apologetic attitude towards the horrors of mass collectivization, and it effectively rejects the argument that collectivization should have been carried out for reasons of improved agricultural efficiency.

The matter, however, unfortunately appears to be rather far from conclusively settled. Although theoretical agreement on the problems of proper sectoring of the economy, and on proper definitions of the concepts involved (viz. 'agricultural surplus'), may certainly be reached, we will still be left with substantial empirical difficulties. It is a fact, for example, that Barsov's new data cover only the period 1928–32, and judging from his own comments on the availability of data for the second five year plan, this appears to be all that we are going to learn. In addition, it is doubtful whether Barsov's data really warrant drawing the conclusion that the conventional wisdom regarding the extraction of an agricultural surplus has been wrong. David Morrison has submitted serious criticism both regarding the reliability of the basic materials used by Barsov, and concerning a failure to account properly for inflationary effects and for distortions in measuring labour productivity. Morrison concludes that 'the confidence placed by Western researchers in both his methods and results seems to have little foundation'.[80]

Fortunately, the main thrust of our argument does not require the precise truth to be found in this respect. All in all, it remains true that the foundations of Soviet industrialization implied a massive mobilization of manpower, a reduction of consumption standards to, and at times below, starvation level, and a tight system of control, repression and exhortation in order to *prevent* evasion rather than *stimulate* effort. The system was big stick and very little carrot, and in this way it was possible to squeeze out the massive resources needed. Whence the resources actually came is certainly an interesting issue, but it is not crucial to our argument. In important respects, the 'model' outlined above took its roots in the period of War Communism. Under Stalin, some of the missing links were perfected. Let us now proceed to see how the central planning system was erected, in a way that effectively covered up what was really happening in the economy.

Something Called Planning

Although the concepts of planning and central control over the economy fell into the background with the introduction of NEP, Gosplan continued to be concerned with both long-term prospects and with the effects of short-term policy. The first manifestation of the latter was a set of 'Control Figures', prepared for the fiscal year 1925–6, which in essence amounted to an annual economic plan. The ambition of this 'plan', however, was mainly to seek out bottlenecks. Consequently, its main function is best interpreted as an additional means for evaluating policy. This forecasting and evaluating function can be said to have applied equally to the 1926–7 Control Figures, and it was not surprising that the Council for Labour and Defence (*Sovet Truda i Oborony*, STO), which at the time still held considerable executive power, did not see fit to give mandatory status to either of these 'plans'. In May 1927, however, Gosplan was ordered to transform its Control Figures into an economic plan for 1927–8, a plan which was not only given compulsory status, but was also integrated with work then in progress on a national Five Year Plan. Although chiefly forecasting devices, these three annual 'plans' were important in gathering experience for the coming FFYP. Moreover, they showed a reasonably high degree of accuracy.[81]

If, on the other hand, we shift our attention to work on the FFYP, the first version of which was begun already in 1925, we get the opposite impression. As one draft succeeded another, targets for growth and investment were adjusted upwards at a rate that made the finally accepted version a wildly unrealistic document that stood virtually no chance of being fulfilled. This transition period is of crucial importance for understanding how 'central planning' came into being.[82]

The outstanding characteristic of the first drafts of the FFYP was that of flexibility. In May 1928, for example, M.G. Grinko, one of its main architects, reported that:

> It must be categorically emphasized that all the figures and qualitative indices contained in these directives [of the FFYP] are there merely to illustrate the envisaged pace of reconstruction; it is impossible to combine them in the form of balances or to harmonize developments in individual branches of the economy.[83]

This impression of flexibility is also compatible with the preparation of minimum and maximum variants of the plan, where the former had a cautious approach, warning of possible dangers, while the latter was to be a bold projection, based on the most favourable circumstances. When the final version was adopted, however, it was an augmented version of the already tight maximum one, leaving no room whatsoever for flexibility. In the annual plan for 1928–9 (the first year of the FFYP) industrial output was assumed to double in the coming five years. The maximum variant foresaw a hypothetical growth of 150 percent for the period. The final version called for 179 per cent. Similar developments can be noted for other sectors.[84] Jasny, for example, notes that the final version of the FFYP was based on perfect weather for agriculture throughout the period, something that is blatantly absurd, given the highly variable climatic conditions facing the country.[85]

The attitudes of those involved are important to note. Bazarov spoke of impending 'hunger and cold', Lyaschenko of 'targets suspended in the air', Shanin branded financing as 'inflationary', and, on the eve of adopting the plan, Kalinnikov voiced the general Gosplan opinion: 'Everyone believes it to be unrealizable!'[86] Even orthodox Party spokesmen seem to have been well aware of what was happening:

> In other words, in their view the First Five Year Plan was primarily a plan for massive works, and the most important thing was to get them done, not to solve 'secondary' problems as delays, costs or market equilibrium. But in taking this view against the other Soviet economists, they were in fact condemning Soviet economic thought of the 1920–8 period.[87]

What was really happening had little to do with economic *planning*. Rather, one would easily agree with Naum Jasny's conclusion that 'the FYP's are largely façade, not playing the role in the economy ascribed to them, but serving principally as propaganda.'[88] A similar opinion is held by Zaleski:

> The fact that socialization of agriculture was to be used as a *criterion of success* of the five-year plan meant that the five volumes of official text, although they were given the force of law, were not really taken seriously by the authorities, and that their real function was to lay a smoke-screen that would hide unpopular measures from the people.[89]

It is important to establish the imbalances and gross incoherences of the FFYP, particularly in the light of the delusion that was spread in the West. In 1948, for example, Dobb wrote the following: 'We have seen that the upward revision of targets which started at the end of 1929 was not ungrounded on the evidence of successful achievements to date.'[90] A delusion of perhaps even greater importance was that the suppression of personal income and consumption to 'rock bottom' should have been an *unforeseen* consequence of the turbulent conditions. A comparison between the Control Figures for 1928–9 and for 1929–30 gives precisely the opposite impression, with the target for average *nominal* wages being increased by less than 1 per cent in the face of considerable inflation, with *planned* agricultural output being cut by 6.8 per cent and with food rationing already introduced on class principles. As Jasny puts it, 'there was nothing in those tables either on real incomes of wage and salary earners or incomes, whether nominal or real, of the rest of the population.'[91]

The perhaps ugliest part of the introduction of planning was the fate that befell the planners. Already in 1927, prominent people like Kondratiev started losing their positions, and even orthodox Bolsheviks like Strumilin and Krzhizhanovsky were swept aside. Then, with the 'Menshevik Trial' of March 1931, the score was definitely settled. Virtually all of the architects of Soviet planning were purged and their work discredited. In Jasny's words, it

> was not a trial of men, but the triumphal burial of planning without force, of planning combined with freedom for the worker to take and leave his job, of planning which allowed for small-scale enterprise and, to some degree, for freedom of thought and expression, in short, the kind of planning which many Western enthusiasts visualize and want for their own country.[92]

The people that took over were all members of the 'Stalin Guard' and the principles of their recruitment had been already manifested in recruiting for the Gosplan, back in 1921. Here, showing a characteristic mistrust of 'professors' who were lacking in 'healthy pragmatism', Stalin had urged Lenin to appoint 'men of live politics, ready to act on the principle of report fulfilment'.[93] All talk of equilibrium was openly ridiculed as 'bourgeois deviationism'.[94] Planning became a plaything of the worst kind of demagogy, well worthy of the term 'Bacchanalian', that has been assigned to it by Jasny.[95]

The role of early planning was to mobilize, to create an atmosphere of urgency and of a need to exert maximum effort. Thus, plans did not need to be consistent nor could they be set at reasonably attainable levels. Economic reason would defy this purpose. The view of plans as a smoke-screen, that was advanced by Jasny, comes in a slightly different guise in the words of Zaleski:

> The economic policy expressed in the plans is very attractive and popular; it flatters national ambitions and promises a better life for every individual in the immediate future. Therefore, it helps mobilize the people (especially Party militants) to implement such promising plans. The plans are put on a pedestal and surrounded with mystery, while information on their revisions is very hard to come by. A distorted presentation of the costs of growth in the final result and a misleading and rather naive presentation of achievements in standard of living are then intended to hide the real economic policy – that of austerity – and the immense cost of this authoritarian and economically inefficient planning.[96]

Conclusion

Many of the problems of early Soviet 'planning' can be summed up in terms of the debate between the 'geneticists' and the 'teleologists'.[97] The former held that the limits to effective planning were determined by the spontaneous forces of growth and that plans should not be made to upset these forces. In the 1920s, agriculture was the dynamic force and thus the need for balance and equilibrium between agriculture and industry was at the forefront of the discussion, with the disruptions of War Communism being used as a discouraging example. The teleologists, on the other hand, took the opposite view, arguing that the Plan should be the guiding force, that the limits of planning were determined not by objective economic conditions, but rather by the dynamic forces created by the Revolution and the Party. The latter position is captured in a 1928 speech by Kuibyshev, who was then Chairman of the VSNKh: 'The market situation can be one current, but a communist and Bolshevik has always been able and is able to swim against the current.'[98]

The pivotal point of this debate was that of economic rationality, in the Western sense, and it is hardly surprising that nearly all of the prominent economists of the time were to be found on the 'genetic' side, while their opponents on the 'teleological' side were predominantly engineers and/or Party *apparatchiki*. Thus, when the genetic school was ousted, this meant the end not only of the economists but also of economics. As Lewin puts it: 'Economics was stifled, as were the planners. The political leadership seized complete control over the process and brushed aside [economic reasoning, which was] discontinued during the 1930s and abandoned until at least the mid-1950s.'[99]

Here we find the real root of much of the economic troubles that would later beset the Soviet economy. The economic model that emerged was a derivative of the political needs and desires of the leadership and many features that had been tried during War Communism were brought back, only this time with more consequence. Planning in physical units facilitated control over supply, the use of material balances facilitated the use of priorities in allocation, planning with deficits ruled out calculation at lower levels and promoted bargaining, the use of 'shock' methods facilitated the use of administrative/political rewards, etc. All of this was conducive to the emergence of a feudal hierarchy of political rewards and loyalties. From the political point of view, it was a rational model for a leadership interested in personal power and security. As a machinery for the mobilization of resources it was also excellent – this was the birth of the 'extensive growth' model.

The price, however, that had to be paid for the introduction of this model was the suppression of most effective economic feedback mechanisms. Planners preferred to 'stand' for higher tempos rather than 'sit' (in prison) for lower ones.[100] Analysis and questioning was considered equal to treason, economists and statisticians were removed, and the leading journals in these fields were closed. Physical units, deficit planning, and bargaining all precluded the generation of data to be used for analysis, and all decision makers were engineers/politicians:

> The use of arithmetic (but not geometric!) average and manipulation of percentages came to be regarded as the acme of statistical sophistication. Ignorance was thus elevated to dogma, mathematical economics having been proclaimed 'anti-marxian', and whole generations of newly graduating economists and planning specialists acquired a vested interest in the perpetuation of this state of affairs.[101]

It is precisely this absence of feedback and of reliable data for rational calculation that forms the main obstacle to the much coveted 'intensive growth'. Thus, the long run costs of Soviet rapid in-

54

dustrialization may be much larger than is commonly realized. It was indeed possible to mobilize vast resources and to put them to use at an unprecedented scale. Up to date, however, it has not been possible to adapt the economy in such a way as to ensure an efficient utilization of these resources. The secret behind Soviet economic growth has always been 'more', not 'better'. In the 1930s, it was possible to achieve 'the five-year plan in four years'. In the 1940s, it was possible to mobilize enough resources to defeat the Germans, and to reconstruct a ravaged economy. Throughout, however, monumental waste and misallocations have been perhaps the most outstanding feature of the Soviet economy, and it is important to understand the roots of the system that produces these effects. As Lewin points out, these roots go back to the very first years after the revolution: 'As propaganda and dogmatization were pushing out scholarship and theory, a planning system that had adopted practices largely prevalent under "War Communism" when planning was practically non-existent, could become sanctified as dogma.'[102]

The Soviet economic system was shaped in order to suit essentially political motives, and this required the suppression of not only the mechanisms of a pluralistic economic structure but also those people who might question the economic rationality of the new order. Any attempt at economic reform must thus not only recreate an 'economic' system, it must also retrain those people who are to operate within it. Our presentation in the following chapters will consequently be strongly geared to examining the role of individuals in the Soviet system and the ways in which the authorities have attempted to influence and control their behaviour. In the next chapter we will pursue this approach by looking at the disappearance of politics from Soviet political life.

Chapter three

Formation of the Stalinist political system

In the previous chapter, we presented a picture of the formation of the Soviet economic system that bore a firm imprint of the supremacy of politics over economics. In a sense, this supremacy also implied a shift in the burden of analysis from the economic to the political field, since much economic policy making consisted of *ad hoc* – and at times even desperate – emergency measures, conditioned by political contingencies. In the present chapter we shall continue that line of argument, by presenting the formation of the Soviet political system as conditioned by the same political ambitions of achieving power and security – broadly defined – for those at the top.

An important tool that will be used in analysing this process is the concept of 'political forces'. This term will be used here not so much in the sense of various organized groups with goal-oriented strategies, but rather to denote sections of the population, with implicit common interests, who react jointly in an *ad hoc* and unorganized fashion to policy measures imposed from above, often to avoid the consequences of certain actions perceived to be taken against them. This interpretation of 'anonymous' forces is well in line with the official Bolshevik ideology of the time, which spoke of using 'levers' (*rychagi*) and 'transmission belts' (*privodnye remeny*) in order to harness such forces for the regime's own advancement. Attention in this chapter will be devoted to investigating *how* this was done. Here we shall distinguish between *tactics*, used in specific situations of political struggle, and an overall *strategy*, aimed at a long run transformation of society, in a direction that would consolidate the position of the Party leadership.

In relation to the latter, we must recognize that an important prerequisite for achieving power and security for those at the top was that the articulation and expression of opinions in society must be brought under control. The efforts to do so proceeded along three different lines. First of all, the number of channels available for voicing discontent was restricted, thus limiting the scope for alternatives to be formed. Second, within this restricted structure the preconditions for a true political process to emerge were suppressed, and, third, repression and terror were used, in order to forcibly deter individuals from opposition against the new 'political' system. We start, in the first section of this chapter, by looking at these three elements of strategy. The next section then focuses on the specific tactics used to centralize power within the strategic framework, and, in conclusion, we shall present a picture of the Stalinist political system completed.

Restricting the Channels for Opposition

The process of restricting the scope for interest articulation and political manouevre was initiated shortly after the October *coup d'état*. Step by step, most of those rights and liberties that had only just been so proudly proclaimed were either constrained or altogether removed. The main impression of this process is that of a gradual concentration of power, first to the Party within society, and then to Stalin within the Party. By the time of Lenin's death, in January 1924, the main features of the new system were already discernible. Its main pillars were the Party political monopoly, the principle of the leading role of the Party, and the ban on factions within the Party. To these, all the leading Bolsheviks subscribed. The system also had a certain internal logic, which would soon become revealed. Once a would-be dictator had reached the pinnacle of power, all the tools necessary for *staying* in power, i.e. for maintaining control over the Party, and thus over society, would also be available to him. Turning now to look at the actual steps taken, in this process of concentration of power, it may be profitable to divide Soviet political life into four different arenas: the *political*, the *implementary*, the *societal*, and the *internal Party* arena.[1] Let us start by looking at the political one.

The Political Arena

One of the very first steps taken by the new Bolshevik regime was the establishment of a Party monopoly over Soviet political life. The course was set already when the Second All-Russian Congress of Soviets, convened in October 1917, decided on a new government – the Council of People's Commissars – and on a new Central Executive Committee. The former consisted of Bolsheviks only.[2] The latter featured both Mensheviks and Socialist Revolutionaries, but an absolute majority of seats went to the Bolsheviks.[3] The real intentions of the Bolsheviks can be reflected in the fate of the Constituent Assembly, the formation of which had been a demand of paramount political importance during the months following the February 1917 revolution. In the elections to the Assembly, the Bolsheviks found themselves winning only a minority of seats, and at the first session a Bolshevik proposal was defeated by 237 votes to 136. On the following day – 6 January 1918 – the Assembly was forcefully dissolved and the Bolshevik-controlled Congress of Soviets became the representative organ of the Soviet system.[4]

In 1921, the Bolshevik monopoly on political power was *de facto*, if not *de jure*, formalized. It is true that no formal decree was issued to prohibit the other two socialist parties, but the following statement by Lenin, made in May 1921, serves to illustrate the actual situation: 'We shall keep the Mensheviks and the SRs, whether open or disguised as "non-Party", in prison.'[5] The rationale behind this move can be found in a strikingly honest statement by Karl Radek, who told the tenth Party Congress in March that 'if the Mensheviks were left at liberty, now that the communists had adopted their policy, they would demand political power; while to concede freedom to the Socialist Revolutionaries when the "enormous mass" of the peasants was opposed to the communists would be suicide.'[6] To Radek at least, it was apparently obvious that the question of power must be a main priority of the Bolsheviks. This is also consistent with our previous focus on the importance of Lenin's 'April Theses'.

The Implementary Arena

The reason for making a distinction between a political and an implementary arena lies in the fact that while the Bolsheviks managed to dominate political life, by reserving for themselves all important top-level decision-making positions, in the executive sphere their representation was weak. Above all, this was true for various forms of technical expertise, which was in very short supply amongst the Party cadres. As a rule, the heads of the Commissariats and of the most important Buros were Party members, but they constituted a very small percentage of the total number of government employees. It is certainly a strange paradox, for example, that the most important stepping stones towards the establishment of central planning were laid by formerly Menshevik economists.[7]

The initially high percentage of non-Bolshevik specialists in the administrative sphere provided a certain independence for the implementary arena, from the political one, but this was soon to change. In March 1928, a group of engineers and technicians from the coalfields near Shakhty in the Donbass were tried on fictitious charges of conspiracy and sabotage. This change in policy towards the old intelligentsia was to have important implications for the relationship between the Party and state hierarchies.[8]

The central issue at hand concerned the division of power between the state and the Party hierarchies, the complication being that if the state officials were to be given a certain autonomy, this would pose a threat to the Party power monopoly. Some did not see this as a problem. Bukharin, for example, explicitly argued in favour of a 'restoration and preservation of the official division between state and Party functions.'[9] The prevailing view, however, was in favour of a Party monopoly and a vigorous attack was consequently launched against Rykov, who was then Prime Minister. This attack soon turned into a general onslaught against the state apparatus as a whole, and thus became part of the process of a total submission of the state bureaucracy to the controlling Party organs. At the lower levels, the Soviets rapidly lost out to the Party and the revolutionary slogan of 'All power to the Soviets' lost its content. With Party members entering the ranks of the state bureaucracy, the character of the latter changed and the implementary arena was gradually deprived of its autonomy.

The Societal Arena

Another step that was taken by the Bolsheviks shortly after their October *coup d'état*, was to sieze control over the press. Already by November 1917, they controlled all news media and had in their hands the power to prohibit any paper that might be critical of the new regime. In a matter of days, a number of Socialist, Liberal and Conservative papers were closed down. By August 1918, the Bolshevik monopoly over the Press was completed.[10]

The wartime atmosphere of War Communism naturally placed a firm imprint on the Party. In order to harness all efforts for the purpose of a military victory, all autonomous organizations in Soviet society were abolished as such. Organizational life was subjected to a process of 'statization', i.e. an extension of control by the Party-state over associations, organizations and institutions. The prime example of this latter process is the Trade Union controversy of 1920–1, which featured a struggle between three different platforms. At one extreme was the Workers' Opposition, with Kollontay and Shlyapnikov as its most prominent exponents. They claimed a dominant role in economic management for autonomous unions and argued that communists in the unions should be bound by directives of higher union bodies rather than by those of local Party organs. At the other extreme was Trotsky, who argued in favour of a militarization of the working class for the ends of production, and stressed the role of education and discipline in leading the workers. In the middle position was Lenin, who argued that a certain degree of autonomy should be allowed for the unions, but also held that they should be denied all forms of direct responsibility in economic management. In March 1921 the issue was settled – Lenin's way.[11]

The relaxation of control over economic activities that followed the introduction of NEP also brought in its wake a certain relaxation of the political climate. The high degree of private ownership and of private economic activity, made it simply impossible for the Party to maintain a total grip over society. As a consequence, some 'political forces' started to slip. The political role of the intelligentsia, in particular that of the writers, appeared to be on the rise. Private publishing houses were allowed to operate and the Bolsheviks even toyed with the idea of creating a Society of Writers which would be open to non-communists.[12]

The seemingly incipient liberalism that marked the cultural sphere was brought to an end by two interlocking processes. The first was the so called Cultural Revolution, of 1928–31, a process which was obviously supported by Stalin, who sought to discredit the Party's right wing as supporting traditional and bourgeois values. Once the position of the old intelligentsia in cultural life had been broken, however, the left wing would in its turn come under attack. In 1932, RAPP, the Russian Association of Proletarian Writers (*Rossiiskaya Assosiatsiya Proletarskikh Pisatelei*) was dissolved, and with the decree on historical education and the establishment of the Union of Writers, both in 1934, proletarian romanticism was brought to an end. From then on, the task of the historians was to invoke Russia's glorious past and to depict the Soviet Union as the culmination of the progressive development of Russia. Writers and artists should draw aestethical inspiration from the Great Russian realists, such as Tolstoy, Gorkii and Repin. Class-based historiography and culture was superceded by a policy that stressed the common Russian heritage and culture of the Soviet people.[13]

The Internal Party Arena

Once political control over society had been firmly concentrated in the hands of the Party, a logical next step was to achieve a similar concentration of power *within* the Party. This brings us over to our fourth, internal Party arena. At this point, it is natural that much of the discussion will focus on the tactics used by Stalin in his struggle for power. At the same time, however, it is also of some considerable importance to note that most of the tools used by him in this struggle were in existence already at the beginning of the 1920s. It is a tragic paradox, for example, that those who would later find themselves in opposition to Stalin had with their own hands helped forge the weapons with which they were to be crushed.

The most important of these were found in two resolutions on internal Party democracy, both of which were presented to the tenth Party congress, together with the introduction of NEP. The first condemned Party opposition on the issue of the trade unions, stressing the leading role of the Party, while the other, on 'Party unity', called for an immediate dissolution of all factions with separate political platforms within the Party. With these two resolutions, the Central Committee was given full disciplinary authority. The resolutions were supported by an overwhelming majority of delegates at the congress and little criticism was heard.[14]

The ban on factions and the call for unity were used on a number of occasions throughout the 1920s, in order to eliminate opposition against current Party policy. During that time, the door had still not been closed and sealed and the top Party leadership was far from being a homogeneous group. Stephen Cohen, for example, has characterized the Politburo as 'a conditional alliance of convenience between different "groupings" not a single group of wholly like-minded oligarchs.'[15] Debate *within* the Party was fierce and three big struggles were to erupt before the decisive final showdown, between Stalin and Bukharin in 1928–9. The ban on factions and the call for unity form important parts of the tactical weapons, useful in specific situations of political struggle, that we have referred to above. As for strategy, however, it was changes in the organizational structure of the Party that formed the real backbone.

Already at the eighth Party Congress, in 1919, three separate organs had been created, subordinated to the Central Committee – the Politburo, the Orgburo, and the Secretariat. As Party control over society was strengthened, the power of these organs grew, and, for anyone who was in a position to manipulate them, great possibilities opened up for the attainment of personal power. By 1922, Stalin was alone in being a member of all three, and since organizational skills and control over the central Party apparatus are normally considered to have been his main assets, the way in which he was to use this position is important to note. In addition to the formal picture, Niels Erik Rosenfeldt has presented us with a covert picture, which shows how Stalin was able to create secret organs that worked directly for him and which concentrated in their hands all classified information and all questions of personel: 'Stalin was now, not "merely" the Secretary General, but the whole Party's *Vozhd*.'[16]

The reorganizations of the Party that took place after 1921 were certainly not all initiated by Stalin himself but they very clearly worked in his favour. Quite deliberately, he managed to create within the Party a personal *apparat* which became his main weapon in the struggle for power. Hereby Stalin could control the expression of opinions within the Party. Via the purges, moreover, he was also able to virtually crush the Party, without undermining his own regime, a regime which allegedly rested on the authority of that very same Party.

Reshaping 'Politics'

By 1929, the legal possibilities available to criticize the Party and to articulate political opposition had been effectively curtailed. At the same time, the programmes for collectivization and industrialization were about to achieve an almost complete remoulding of the social structure of Soviet society. No social class remained that could resist the Party on a collectively organized basis.[17] The kulaks were portrayed as the arch-enemies of the regime and 'had neither the ability nor indeed the desire to organize themselves as a vast anti-Soviet ideological force.'[18] The main beneficiary of the social upheaval was the new working class, if not in terms of actual living conditions, then at least in terms of upward social mobility and entry into the Party ranks. The militant traditions of the old Russian proletariat were broken. The working class was in no position to voice any serious political opposition. With the help of the institutional changes of 1932–4, the cultural intelligentsia was effectively pacified.

As a distinct exception we find the new technical intelligentsia, created by a massive process of educating and promoting workers from the shop floor. This group was the new elite of Soviet society, representing one of the few real winners – if such there were – outside the ruling political elite.[19] In spite of their knowledge of the 'horrors of collectivization, famine and terror',[20] they could be relied upon to provide an active support for the regime.

The social revolution that was carried out under the auspicies of Stalin could, however, not in itself guarantee a widespread political acquiescence. In recent Western Sovietology, an attempt has been made to explain the relative calm and stability of the 1930s by invoking two additional arguments, both of which essentially aim to show that there simply were no grounds for social discontent and political opposition. The first of these holds that the communist leadership was frank about its policies and that it did not try to manipulate its subjects. Consequently, there was no reason to question its decisions. The second line of argument asserts that even if the processes as such were cruel and bloody, the numerical loss of life due to collectivization and the Great Purge was relatively low. In this case, there was not much to be worried about.

In 1985, the American historian J. Arch Getty published a book about the Soviet 1930s, which must be considered as the apogee of Western revisionist historiography on Stalinist Russia. Using both the Smolensk Archives and officially published Soviet documents, Getty arrives at the conclusion that 'the Bolshevik Party was not the monolithic and homogeneous machine both totalitarian theorists and Stalinists would have us believe.'[21] Getty based his conclusion about diversity on the conviction that in public statements the Soviet leaders were basically truthful about their political intentions:

> All politicians dissimulate about their roles and plans. Yet it is not naive to assume that the speeches and articles of Soviet politicians reflect real conflicts, struggles, and policies. After all, in the political culture of the thirties, Stalin's speeches were taken as revealed truth.... Stalin's word was law, and for this reason alone his pronouncements are worth studying as certain reflections on political reality.[22]

Getty interprets the existence of opposing public views as a reflection of diverging opinions held by the Bolshevik leadership. Allegedly, softliners Ordzhonikidze and Zhdanov were in opposition to hardliners Molotov, Malenkov, and Ezhov. Stalin is seen as the moderator and 'the personification of the bureaucracy'.[23] Nevertheless, 'the Stalinist radicals and moderates both supported the General line.'[24]

Getty's main ambition is to refute the understanding, allegedly supported by adherents of the totalitarian model, that the terror and purges of the 1930s constituted one long process, causing the death of more than ten million people, and that these atrocities – albeit perhaps not so serious as is held by the 'totalitarianists' – were willed by Stalin and executed by his loyal servants. The main question, however, is whether public statements, which form the basis of Getty's conclusions, can actually be regarded as reliable information concerning actual policies? The current Soviet debate on the 1930s, which gathered considerable momentum in 1987, has offered some interesting new insights in relation to that crucially important question.

In discussing the years 1927–34, i.e. the period from the fifteenth until the seventeenth Party Congress, Soviet economist O. Latsis has concluded that while Stalin's public statements could swing between 'moderation' and 'radicalism', behind the scene, in statements and letters meant exclusively for the Party cadres, the leader was consistently radical.[25] The examples discussed by Latsis concern collectivization and the first five-year plan. Directives concerning the pace of both industrialization and collectivization, which were adopted at the fifteenth Party Congress, in December 1927, were actually quite conservative. Indeed, immediately prior to that congress, Stalin had told a delegation of foreign labour leaders that collectivization would be brought about gradually and mainly by economic means. The Soviet Union, Stalin asserted, was far from embarking on a comprehensive collectivization. That would not materialize in the near future (*ne skoro*). The Party Congress confirmed this policy.

After his visit to Siberia in January 1928, however, Stalin accused local Party cadres of leniency towards the kulaks. Moreover, at a plenum with the Central Committee in July 1928, he said that state procurement prices for grain should be lowered to such a degree that the peasants would be forced to sell all their surplus. This statement was in direct contradiction to decisions taken at the Party Congress earlier in the year and it was kept secret until 1949. On the following day, Stalin said in public that all methods similar to the *prodrazverstka* were illegitimate. At the same time, *Pravda* published Bukharin's 'notes of an economist', where it was argued that it would be wrong to attempt to increase state revenue by forcing the peasants to sell grain. The latter had grown prosperous not by high prices on grain but by working for wages in industry and in construction. In early 1929, Stalin criticized Bukharin's views for being an attempt to 'correct' the line of the Central Committee, but this criticism was also to be kept secret until 1949. Latsis concludes: 'In this way, [Stalin] publicly endorsed the lofty principles that were rejected in his "closed" speeches.'[26]

The important point to note is that there was an apparent unanimity in the Party leadership and that actual Party politics followed the tacit Stalinist line, rather than the officially endorsed one. As we have described above, 1929–32 witnessed brutally enforced collectivization, and although he publicly distanced himself, in March and April 1930, from 'excesses' committed by overzealous local officials,[27] in May Stalin sent a letter to the leading Party cadres where the following was declared:

1) There is not and cannot be *any* analogy between, on the one hand, the Central Committee's statement last March against excesses in collectivization and, on the other, the Brest period or the introduction of the NEP. Then there was a turn [*povorot*] of pol-

icy. Here, in March 1930, there has been no turn of policy. We have corrected comrades who went too far, nothing more ....

2) There really has been a turn in the policy of collectivization [when the middle peasants joined the *kolkhozy*] but it occurred during the second half of 1929, not in March 1930.[28]

The rather obvious conclusion that is reached by Latsis is that despite 'moderate' statements in early 1930, no real change in policy can be observed. Instead, such policies were confirmed that had been embarked upon in 1929, and which had probably been designed by Stalin already in 1928. It is Latsis' contention that Stalin and the other top Bolshevik leaders were carried away by overenthusiastic young workers and that Stalin was personally responsible for not curbing their zeal.[29] The most important conclusion, however, is that Stalin's public statements did not reflect the policy he actually advocated and pursued. Latsis' juxtaposition of sources corroborates the hypothesis that there was indeed a consistent radical policy from 1928 onwards. This way of reading Stalin is also Robert Conquest's methodological premise, stated in his introduction to *The Harvest of Sorrow*. After discussing economic analyses of the Soviet 1930s, Conquest says:

The other theme of the period on which much has been written is the factional struggle within the Communist Party, and Stalin's rise to power. This too is covered here, but mainly to the degree that it is relevant to the vaster events in the countryside; and even then not, as has so often been done, taking the various arguments at their face value so much as in the context of the prospects actually facing the Party mind.[30]

Against the background provided by Latsis, the following judgement by Conquest must be seen to express an insight that cannot be neglected in a discussion of Party policies and popular acquiescence in the 1930s:

Stalin looms over the whole tragedy of 1930–3. Above all, what characterizes the period is the special brand of hypocrisy or evasion which he brought to it. [D]eception was the crux of every move. In his campaign against the Right he never admitted (until the last moment) that he was attacking them, and compromised, if only verbally, when they protested; in the dekulakization, he pretended that there really was a 'class' of rich peasants whom the poorer peasants spontaneously ejected from their homes; in the collectivization, his public line was that it was a voluntary movement, and that any use of force was a deplorable aberration; and when it came to the terror-famine of 1932–3, he simply denied that it existed.[31]

Using contemporaneous Soviet printed sources, such as newspaper items and census data, together with eye-witness accounts by foreigners as well as Soviet subjects, made in the countryside – in particular the Ukraine – Conquest estimates the number of dead, due to agricultural policy and the concomitant repression of 1930–7, as 14.4 million. He regards this as a 'conservative estimate' and attributes the lack of precision to the Soviet government's policy of denying access to archives: 'Which is to say that to this degree the regime remains the accomplice, as well as the heir, of those who fifty years ago sent these innocent millions to their deaths.'[32]

In reviewing Conquest's work, Peter Wiles has discussed the presented figures, contrasting the calculations against his own, and he arrives at the conclusion that Conquest's data are basically correct.[33] Getty, however, has challenged the figures in question, characterizing as 'controversial' Conquest's argument that the famine in the Ukraine was consciously organized by Stalin. He holds that the thesis is simply part of anti-Soviet black propaganda promoted by 'circles of exiled nationalities'. Getty refers to calculations by Stephen Wheatcroft, Barbara Anderson and Brian Silver, that make Conquest's estimates look 'much too high'. Moreover, Getty also argues that since 'he was not insane or irrational', Stalin could not have planned any genocide. Getty's own explanation of some excess deaths is the following: 'Rigid ideological preconceptions, weak administrative centralization, bad information and a surplus of enthusiasm combined with poor planning and irresponsible leadership to produce the disaster.'[34] Getty dismisses the accusation of deliberate genocide, and argues that the Ukrainian peasants simply were the victims of Stalin's 'policies and *raison d'état*'.[35]

Conquest has refuted Getty's criticism of the accuracy regarding the number of alleged famine victims by quoting the Soviet revisionist historian V.P. Danilov, who published his calculations on the number of victims already in 1968. Danilov's estimates were in the order of 15–16 million. In 1988, however, when asked to comment on the Western debate on this subject, he retracted his earlier estimates, claiming them to have been based on erroneous assumptions.[36] Conquest accuses Getty of complicity with the evil-doers by referring exclusively to evidence purveyed by the Soviet government of the 1930s, which is 'known to have produced falsifications on a gigantic scale.'[37]

It is evident that the great divergence between the conclusions of Getty and Conquest originates in their respective ways of evaluating available sources. Getty obviously prefers to believe that all victims of Stalin's repression were arrested in an orderly fashion, meticulously registered, and subsequently filed away in the carefully kept records of the Soviet Supreme Court Archives. This squares rather poorly with the author's own emphasis on bureaucratic disorder when he denies that the Soviet Union in the 1930s was a totalitarian state run by a monolithic Party.[38] Getty's position, moreover, also seems untenable in the light of claims made by Soviet historian Roy Medvedev in 1987, that under Khrushchev the Politburo ordered that the archives of the NKVD should be destroyed. According to Medvedev, all documents concerning the labour camps were burnt. All that was saved concerned prominent Party members that were under posthumous rehabilitation. Stalin's personal archive was also purged after the Dictator's death.[39]

Getty's revisionism, we may conclude, relies on three highly debatable notions: (a) that Stalin's official speeches can be taken at face value; (b) that contemporaneous narrative accounts on mass deaths, as well as calculations based on demographic data, must be dismissed as invalid and unreliable; and (c) that all relevant documents have been preserved in official Soviet archives. To our minds, the futility of such a stand has been conclusively demonstrated by the Soviet scholars Latsis and Medvedev, as well as by Western scholars such as Conquest and Wiles.

The Soviet Union in the 1930s was a country run by a determined and ruthless leader, and also one struck by massive famines and massive purges, resulting in the deaths of millions of people. Evidently, this must have affected both the physical and the mental abilities of the subjects to voice politically relevant opposition against the rule of Stalin and his Commmunist Party. Incidentally, much the same has been suggested by Soviet historian Oleg Khlebnyuk, in a study on the background to the eighteenth Party Conference, held in February 1941. According to him, the great transformation (*velikii perelom*) in 1929–30 had resulted in strict centralization (*zhestkii tsentralizm*) and a widespread use of 'administrative methods' (a euphemism for brute force) in the economy. All signs of initiative and innovation, moreover, had been effectively curbed during the 'difficult years' of 1937–8 (the height of the repression). Khlebnyuk noted that it 'was necessary to take into consideration the fact that the creative potential of society was reduced due to the massive repression. The previously created cadres were either physically liquidated or had lost their good qualities in the atmosphere of intolerance and suspicion.' He explained the decision to convene the Party conference as an acknowledgement of the fact that Soviet society had run into a serious economic crisis, simply because nobody dared to show any initiative, and concluded that there was a limit beyond which 'extra-economic force' became distinctly dysfunctional.[40]

It is Conquest's rather than Getty's description of what happened to the Soviet population in the 1930s that makes sense when it comes to explaining why society as such abstained from any organized and politically relevant opposition. It was not a simple effect of the social changes as such. A deliberately cheated, subdued, and terrified population, placed in the midst of widespread starvation and state-sponsored massive violence was in no position to protest openly. It abstained from opposition not because it endorsed the policies of the leaders, but because it was discouraged and actively deterred from doing so. As the latter aspect was of crucial importance, we shall proceed now to examine it in somewhat greater detail.

Deterring from Opposition

In January 1934, the seventeenth Party congress – the Victors' Congress – was held. Although Stalin's personal power was clearly not absolute, his achievements had certainly been substantial. Collectivization had been completed. Industrialization was under way, and a long row of his former adversaries paid him tribute, by publicly confessing their 'mistakes'. In spite of all this, the following years were to be marked by continued terror and a number of intensive purges which would eventually place Stalin in undisputed control. How can we explain this?

Both repression and purges, it may be noted, had been elements of Party policy from the very beginning. Already in a 1919 Central Committee circular, the pattern for purges was set, in order to weed out all those who in the eyes of the leadership failed 'to justify the lofty title of member of the Party.'[41] Below, we shall focus on those purges that struck the Party and we shall separate the purges as such from the resulting trials since, as Brzezinski notes, 'an element of distortion would be introduced into this analysis should the theme of the purge be made the centre of these trials. They were in effect the frosting on the cake.'[42]

In this context, we may also note that most Western analysts differ between the purges of the early and those of the late 1930s. Schapiro, for example, argues that while the purges of 1933–4 were mainly aimed at eliminating new recruits who had not stood up to the test of experience, those of 1936–8 aimed at a complete transformation of the Party, and especially of its top echelon, into an elite of Stalin's own making. The latter, moreover, are presented not as official purges decreed by the Central Committee, but rather as operations privately launched by Stalin and Ezhov, almost behind the back of the Central Committee.[43] The latter period represents the violent peak of purges and trials in the 1930s, the infamous Ezhovshchina, named after Nikolai Ezhov who had risen to Secretary of the Central Committee in February 1935 and had been appointed People's Commissar for Internal Affairs in September 1936. In December 1938 he was executed and succeeded by Beria.

The dividing line between the two phases was connected with the murder of Sergei Kirov, the Leningrad Party Secretary who died under mysterious circumstances shortly after the Victors' Congress. Following this event, the Central Committee issued a classified letter to all Party organizations, dated 18 January 1935, and entitled 'Lessons of the Events Bound up with the Evil Murder of Comrade Kirov'. The text of this letter has never been published, but references to it can be found in the Smolensk Archives.[44] We may also note that Stalin quoted from it in his speech to the March 1937 plenum of the Central Committee. Then, in connection with the 1936 trial of the 'Trotsky-Zinoviev bloc', a second classified letter was issued by the Central Committee, this one dated 29 June. It, too, was quoted by Stalin in his 1937 speech. Both letters called for vigilance, demanding that the ranks of the Party be purged of all 'alien elements', and placing particular stress on the immediate need to oust all former followers of Trotsky and Zinoviev.[45]

However, simply noting that the purges served the function of terrorising the Party cadres into silence and submission, and thus placing Stalin in supreme power, leaves us without an answer to the important question of *how* this was achieved. How do we explain the purges as a political phenomenon? To this question two highly different explanations have been suggested.

The first explanation of the role of the purges is based on the existence of a 'moderate bloc' of opposition within the Party, a bloc which allegedly challenged Stalin's policy and thus threatened his position. Some Western observers have pointed at the existence of such opposition at the 1934 'Victors' Congress', opposition which was to have taken the form of an illegal bloc of 'moderates', under the leadership of Kirov.[46] These 'moderates' differed from Stalin in their analysis of the political situation, and are said to have favoured a more restrained 'liberal' policy, based on compromises.[47] The evidence of the existence of such a bloc, however, is weak. Attempts to verify its existence have produced only one source, the 'Letter of an Old Bolshevik', which was originally published anonymously but later turned out to have originated in discussions held in Paris in 1936, between Bukharin and the former Menshevik Boris Nicolaevsky.[48] The fact that no other sources have been found, which would indicate any divergence of beliefs between Stalin and Kirov,[49] has even been taken by some observers as proof that the two may in fact even have been allies. Getty, for example, holds that 'it seems more likely that Stalin and Kirov were allies ... and that Kirov's death was not the occasion for any change in policy.'[50] Hough and Fainsod, however, comment in the following way: 'This view of Politburo relationships ... we scarcely should accept ... as proved – or, in some of its central features, as even probable.'[51]

In stark contrast to the conspiracy theory, G.T. Rittersporn seeks to explain the purges as consequences of social tension in Soviet society. Using the Smolénsk Archives, he argues that such broader discontent with Stalin's policy that was reflected in economic and social problems – labour turnover, absenteeism, etc. – was perceived by the regime as a growing political threat. Lacking effective means of control over the local apparatus, the central leadership also lacked effective means for controlling the population and thus failed to come to grips with the problems outlined above. According to Rittersporn, the struggles of 1936–8 were most likely unleashed by a popular discontent with the arbitrariness, corruption and inefficiency of the ruling strata.[52]

As we shall see in greater detail below, a case in point was that the central Party leadership expressed a growing concern over the attitudes of disregard towards the demands of the workers that were displayed by local Party officials. This can be understood as a tactical device in the context of opposing interests between cadres in the Party and state hierarchies, on the one hand, and the remainder of society, on the other.

In a similar way, Rittersporn seeks to explain why the purges were suddenly discontinued by pointing at social tensions and popular discontent. The Party had to close its ranks in order to maintain its position: '... the abandoning of radical efforts to discipline recalcitrant officials was necessitated by the increasingly open disobedience of the masses and the need to counter this by closing the ranks of the apparatus, which internal conflicts had severely disorganized.'[53] The draconian labour laws of the late 1930s provide an additional indication of the regime's perception of the seriousness of the threat facing it. Repression had turned out to be counter-productive in making the population comply with Stalin's policy. Terrified apathy resulted.

Rittersporn is, of course, far from alone in pointing at the necessity of halting further purges, but while the reason normally given by Western analysts is that the survival of the Party was threatened by the absence of new cadres to take over after constant purges of the old,[54] Rittersporn adds an interesting social dimension to the picture. In spite of monoparty rule and the prohibition against factions within the Party, one might thus argue that there did in fact exist a certain scope for political forces to move. One may also hypothesize that this peculiar nature of politics served as a means to consolidate Stalin's personal power, by continually removing from the scene all emergent opposition. In an attempt to provide an answer to the question of how Stalin was able to weed out the final straws of opposition, we shall proceed now to take a closer look at the Party election campaign that took place in the spring of 1937.

The 1937 Party Election Campaign

The Sources

Such primary sources on the 1937 campaign that are available to us consist of official Soviet accounts, published primarily in the Central Committee monthly journal *Bolshevik*. In view of the principle of *partiinost* and Lenin's classic dictum that the function of the press was to agitate and propagate in favour of the Party line, thereby serving to mobilize the masses, one must assume that materials published in *Bolshevik* did not primarily reflect what was actually happening in Soviet political life. It would be more correct instead to view such materials as expressing the view of the Party leadership – i.e. ultimately Stalin himself – on what *should* be happening. As the campaign for increased democracy was carried out at the height of purges and terror, it would seem reasonable to assume that it was also part and parcel of that same policy. The following general background of events is provided by Medvedev:

> Throughout 1937 and 1938 the flood of repression rose, carrying away the basic core of Party leadership. This well-planned, pitiless destruction of the people who had done the main work of the Revolution from the days of the underground struggle ... was the most frightful act in the tragedy of the thirties.... In 1937–8 there were days when up to a thousand people were shot in Moscow alone. These were not streams, these were rivers of blood.[55]

Our interpretation of the materials published in *Bolshevik* will be to view them as instrumental. In particular, this will hold for the keynote speeches delivered by Stalin and Zhdanov to the February 1937 Central Committee plenum. Such criticism of the middle level Party cadres that was voiced by the Party leaders, allegedly in the name of the Party rank-and-file and of the broad masses of the population, will be seen as part and parcel of a clearly populistic strategy. Stalin and Zhdanov used criticism 'from below' as a way of channelling popular discontent regarding the conditions of life, for which the Party bore sole responsibility, and of targeting it against 'disposable' individuals. Consequently, the turnover of Party cadres was substantial.

In his famous study of the Smolensk Archives, Merle Fainsod has shown that, during the years 1933–8, the Western *Oblast*, where Smolensk is situated, 'was subjected to an almost continuous purge', which reached its peak in 1937.[56] No *raion* in this *oblast* was too small to be struck: 'As this view of the events of 1937 indicates, even a Party organization in as remote a rural backwater as Belyi found itself tragically caught up in the convulsions of the Great Purge. In the course of one year there were three first secretaries ... and the ranks of the *raion* Party and governmental leadership was decimated.'[57]

In 1936, a new constitution was adopted, the so called Stalin Constitution, which was presented as 'the most democratic constitution in the world.' Amongst its architects were Bukharin and Radek, who were both to be purged in 1938. This circumstance is symbolic as a succint expression of the fact that false democracy and real terror were two sides of one and the same coin. The setting is important, in the sense that the Great Terror coincided in time with the alleged democratization of, first, the structure of the State, via the 1936 Constitution, and then of the Party, via the 1937 election campaign. The purpose of the process was clearly to pave the way for a post-revolutionary state.

Already in 1942, an early student of the events of 1936-8, the Swedish slavist Anton Karlgren, pointed out what has subsequently been rediscovered by Sheila Fitzpatrick and others, namely that by ways of destroying both the old Bolshevik core of the Party and its social milieu, Stalin managed to create for himself a completely new polity. In the new constitution, industrial workers and peasants were no longer privileged and the illusion of an international workers' state was dropped as well. The 1936 constitution made no provision for the rights of foreign workers to become Soviet citizens. Some 20 years after the October *coup d'état*, a *Russian* state had finally been restored:

> The structure of the Stalinist state was definitely completed. At the top the 'Father of the People' himself, with a power more despotic than that of the old Russian *samoderzhavtsy*. Around him a small circle, diminished over the years, of his own satellites ... . And then, at great distance, the rest of society, a typical class society with a service nobility, an intelligentsia, for the time being three ranks, and a workers' aristocracy, the *stakhanovity*, classes

73

that were enlisted by means of different priviliges to be the props and servants of the system. And beneath them the great masses, politically incapacitated, socially degraded and severely exploited, albeit not by private exploiters but by an exploiter far mightier, the so called one hundred per cent socialist state itself.[58]

Keeping these general reflections in mind, we shall proceed now to look somewhat more closely at the contents of *Bolshevik* during that fateful year of 1937, the aim being to study how Stalin and Zhdanov used publicity – i.e. *glasnost* – in order to unleash a popular outrage that could be harnessed to further their own endeavours to reshape the Soviet political landscape.

A Background to the Elections

As we have indicated above, in 1937 Stalin started a campaign for 'democratization' within the Party. The new constitution had introduced direct elections with secret ballots, presented as a 'turn' (*povorot*) in political life,[59] and a broad transformation of Party life was to follow. A resolution taken at the plenum of the Central Committee in February 1937 called for elections to be held – before May – to Party organs at local, regional and republican levels.[60] In a major speech at that plenum, Zhdanov delivered a forceful condemnation of conditions within the Party, pointing to the lack of internal democracy and calling Party leaders at the lower levels to account. A few days later Stalin joined in the attack by accusing these same lower-level Party leaders of enemy infiltration within the Party. These two speeches, together with Stalin's opening speech to that same plenum, will be of central importance in our presentation below.

At the plenum, a decision had been taken on a reform of Party elections, stipulating: (a) secret ballots at all levels up to the republican, not only for members of Party committees and delegates to Party conferences, but for Party secretaries as well; (b) rights to cross out names on the ballot and to add new ones; and (c) no lists of candidates to be prepared in advance by bodies other than the Party conference. Such lists, moreover, should be drawn up after individual consultations with the presumptive candidates. Names could be removed during such discussions.[61] Those reports on the election campaign that were subsequently published in *Bolshevik* may well give a better insight into Party work and Stalin's policy than any other available sources. Part of the explanation for this can be seen in terms of the interest Stalin had in pointing out anomalies that could legitimate his policy of purging large sections of the Party *apparat*.

Judging from *Bolshevik*, internal Party conditions formed the starting point for the campaign. The tune was set in Zhdanov's speech, which focused on the lack of democracy and the poor contact with the masses. This we shall refer to below as the *democratization* model. In addition to Zhdanov's, two other lines of argumentation can be discerned, which prescribe a somewhat different medication. The first stressed enemy infiltration in the Party, the state apparatus and other Soviet organizations, demanding an improved vigilance. This we shall call the *enemy* model. The second stressed deficient ideological and political studies within the Party, recommending a higher priority for propaganda. This will be referred to as the *propaganda* model.

The Democratization Model

In his speech, Zhdanov described the situation in the Party in great detail, characterizing it as 'bureaucratic distortions of democratic centralism.'[62] He pointed out that elections to the Party committees had not been held according to the Party statutes. In fact, the only elections that had been held since 1934 had been in newly organized *krai* and *oblast* committees (regional level) or in individual *raion* or city organizations (local level), where Party work was seen to have failed.[63] According to the statutes, elections should have been held once yearly or at least once every eighteen months.

In the absence of elections, 'co-optation' had become the normal way of adding new members to Party committees at lower levels, and in several cases those properly elected had even come to form a minority. Party secretaries were sometimes appointed without even being members of the committees they were to direct. Organizational rules were not followed, notably the rule on quorum. An illuminating example was given from a session with a Kharkov *raikom*, where ten of its members, together with non-members, had managed to expel the remaining twelve members from the committee.[64]

Party elections were characterized by Zhdanov as a 'pure formality', being organized in such a way as to 'avoid as quickly and as simply as possible all obtrusive criticism from the Party masses in relation to one candidate or the other.'[65] Candidates were nominated and presented in a way that made it impossible for the Party membership at large to have any influence on the outcome of elections. The formal decision-making Party organs at various levels had been pushed into the background, and in many cases the Party committee plenum had ceased to be a collective leading body. Sessions were rare and mostly focused on general or purely ceremonial issues. Party meetings with the rank-and-file were rarely held and seldom concerned with local Party work.[66]

The obvious targets of the democratization campaign were leading Party officials at the lower levels. They were held responsible for the poor conditions within the Party and for shortcomings in Party policy. The ambition to break up local cliques within the Party leadership was also presented as a matter of democracy. Appointments in such power groupings were seen to have been made out of loyalty to the group rather than to the Party. Single individuals followed their 'patron' in his career.[67]

The Enemy Model

Stalin's concluding speech to the Central Committee was entitled 'On shortcomings in Party work and measures to crush the Trotskyites and other doubledealers', the underlying perspective being that the 'enemy' had infiltrated not only the lower levels of the Party but also responsible positions on higher levels.[68] The situation in 1937 was compared to the almost 10 years' older Shakhty affair, and Stalin stressed the difference that lay in the fact that the enemy at that time had stood outside the Party ranks. Since he had now infiltrated to within the Party, he was also in a better position to deceive politically the Party members.[69]

The notion of enemy infiltration had the advantage of explaining failures not only in Party life, but also in the economy at large. It is evident from *Bolshevik* that the 'enemy' was blamed for all that had gone wrong in the economy, from explosions, accidents and fires, to 'wrecking' the process of planning and projecting. The underlying reason behind such influences was seen to lie in 'the political blindness of the commanding cadres of our industry'.[70] Hence, the Party could swear itself free of responsibility and thus of the growing popular discontent. Zhdanov warned of hostile agitation and hostile candidates, claiming to have noticed an intensified activity from anti-Soviet elements: 'The enemy will use and exaggerate our shortcomings in their propaganda against us', he said and went on to argue that the Party must take control over the elections and be 'armed to its teeth to meet every attempt from hostile elements to use the legal possibilities given by the new constitution.'[71]

As in the democratization model, the targets of criticism were Party leaders at the lower levels. While these were not seen as direct enemies, they were accused of behaving in a way that facilitated enemy infiltration and activity within the Party, and of having protected its enemies. In addition, they were also accused of underestimating the threat posed by the Trotskyites, of not recognizing them as wreckers and enemy agents, and of being naive and unsuspecting, in short – of being insufficiently vigilant. Consequently, the enemy model recommended improved vigilance, purges and executions as necessary measures. The solution was seen to lie in wiping out the enemy mercilessly.[72]

The slogan of 'vigilance' was not in itself a new concept. Already in the summer of 1936, the Central Committee had proclaimed, in a secret letter to the Party organizations, that an 'inalienable quality of every Bolshevik under the present conditions should be the ability to recognize an enemy of the Party, no matter how well he might be masked.'[73] As Fainsod indicates, this move was clearly designed to prepare the ground for the pending trial of the Trotsky-Zinoviev bloc.[74] What was new in the campaign of 1937, was that the atmosphere of distrust, suspicion, and insecurity had been further heightened. The qualities of this atmosphere transpire clearly when we see the enemy threat painted in bright colours even at times when things worked smoothly. The simple fact that economic plans were fulfilled, was not seen as a guarantee that the enemy was not lurking in the background.[75]

Who then was this enemy? According to Stalin, 'capitalist encirclement' should not be understood in any geographical sense. The enemy could be found anywhere within the country. 'Trotskyite' was the most commonly used invective, but the perception of the enemy was far from limited to persons connected with the previous Left Opposition. Apparently, there was even some hesitation in the Central Committee, over whom to consider as Trotskyites, as Stalin himself referred to questions raised by committee members on this issue.[76] As the supporters of Bukharin and the Right Opposition were lumped into the same bag, however, the meaning of the word changed rapidly, becoming instead a general term for wreckers, foreign agents, and suchlike.

The Propaganda Model

In their speeches, both Stalin and Zhdanov stressed that the importance of political propaganda in Party work had been seriously underestimated, the target of the message again being Party leaders at the lower levels. This critique was aimed at two points in particular. First, propaganda activities had become subordinated to the needs of the economy. Party cadres had become 'totally absorbed by economic work', while political and ideological work had been left behind. Leading Party cadres were also accused of interfering direct-ly in management, thus sidestepping the state bureaucracy.[77] In order to change this situation, political work would have to be given priority.

Second, the importance of political indoctrination had been underestimated. This neglect was seen to have resulted in enemy in-filtration, and measures recommended in order to remedy shortcomings on this point were studies of the 'big political ques-tions', such as the international position of the Soviet Union, the concept of capitalist encirclement, the internal political situation, and the struggle against the enemy. Among more specific measures recommended were courses for all Party secretaries at the local level, ranging from 4 to 8 months.[78]

These three 'models' of argumentation that can be discerned from the keynote speeches by Zhdanov and Stalin, and from the accounts of the election campaign that were subsequently published in *Bol-shevik*, will be used below as tools, in an attempt to shed some light on the tactics used by Stalin in order to strengthen his own political position. First, however, we shall look briefly at the *process* of elec-tions, as revealed by these same sources. This will provide an important framework for understanding the tactical aspects.

The Process of Party Elections

In this account, we shall make the hopefully reasonable assumption that different tactics were used at the local level: in the primary Party organizations where people took direct part in voting; and at higher levels, where the Party statutes prescribed indirect elections. The main impression gained from election conferences at the higher levels is that they appear to have been better organized and more firmly controlled than meetings at the primary level.[79] Almost without exception, they also appear to have been focused on fighting the enemy. Criticism along the lines of democratization can be found only in connection with calls for improved vigilance. According to the written accounts of these conferences, it was stressed that, ever since 1933, the Trotskyites and the Bukharinites had been infiltrat-ing the Party up to the regional level. It was thanks only to Ezhov, and the verification and exchange of Party cards, that they had been unmasked. The conferences are presented as having taken place in an atmosphere of excited hatred for the enemy.

Inefficiency in Party work and a lack of overview and control over current matters was also pointed out and criticized. Allegedly, no control was exercised over the implementation of decisions made; in actual practice, many decisions made by Party committees had never been implemented.[80] Party committees at the higher levels were criticized for shortcomings in directing work at the lower levels, of being inclined to grandiose declarations, stereotypes, abstract reasoning, and an ignorance of detail.[81]

Turning now to reports about Party meetings and conferences that were held at the local level, we get a distinct impression of a political atmosphere that was highly charged and even inflammatory. The attendance at meetings was reportedly much higher than usual.[82] Conferences might last 4 to 5 days, instead of the more normal 5 hours.[83] In some extreme cases, they might even last for weeks. A case in point is the village of Belyi, presented by Fainsod.[84] In contrast to previous practice, when Party members had not normally found it worthwhile to listen to discussions which had the character of ceremonial rituals, they now themselves took an active part.[85] In one example, from the Donbass, more than half of those present at meetings were reported to have taken part in discussions.[86] Meetings were characterized as tumultuous. According to some accounts in *Bolshevik*, murmur, noise, and shouting in many cases made it hard to catch the names of candidates being nominated.[87] Discussions of individual candidates could take a long time and at times also became heated. In some primary organizations they could go on for days.[88]

Criticism of Party leaders that was voiced at meetings in primary Party organizations seems to have focused largely along the lines of the democratization model: the principles of internal Party democracy and democratic centralism had been violated, co-option had replaced elections, the practice of criticism and self-criticism had been lost, Party leaders had forgotten both their responsibility to the masses and their duty to report their work to the Party organizations.[89] The behaviour of Party committees during the election campaign was also criticized. Reports did not contain enough self-criticism and the committees tried to control the discussions and push through their own, previously prepared, resolutions.[90] Criticism was also voiced against the way in which the purges had been carried out, against the fact that members had been excluded because of 'passivity' or some insignificant offences.[91] In several cases, the local press was criticized for having covered up rather than exposed shortcomings.[92]

While our account thus far indicates that criticism voiced in the primary Party organizations seems to have been in accordance with the official intentions of the campaign, we can also find evidence presented which indicates that many Party committees had experienced difficulties in maintaining control over the process. A number of Party committees at both primary and *raion* level were strongly criticized for having given up on directing the campaign, for not intervening against hostile criticism, for not proposing their own candidates, and for not opposing proposals which were out of line with the official stand. They were accused of not having understood the principle of the leading role of the Party. In several cases, representatives of higher Party levels had been denied, or voluntarily abstained from, the right of being present during balloting. In one case, the election result had even been declared invalid because a Party instructor from the district committee, the *raikom*, had been present during the ballot. This incident was severely criticized in *Bolshevik*.[93]

It is an interesting task to explain the fact that Party leaders refrained from being present at, and thus exerting control over, election meetings. One possibility of course, is that they took the Central Committee directives on democratic elections and secret ballots *ad notam*. Evidence of this can be found in *Bolshevik*, where Party leaders are quoted as having explained their behaviour by saying that they would otherwise have been guilty of 'undemocratic' behaviour and of 'suppressing self-criticism'.[94] Another possibility is that they simply chose to refrain from being present because of the charged atmosphere. This too can be substantiated by accusations against Party leaders of having a 'cringing attitude' (*khvostistskoe ponimanie*).[95]

In one report, Stalin's words about different types of criticism were cited:

> Criticism can be counter-revolutionary. That is the kind of criticism which is directed at exposing Soviet power in front of the masses, at undermining the confidence of the masses in the Party, and at shaking the Party organization, seeking thereby to weaken the Party's leading role in the country.[96]

Bolshevik also reports that there had been self-criticism of a non-Bolshevik kind in the campaign, and that there had been efforts to blame the Party apparatus for all shortcomings. These accounts are quite striking. They show a picture of a mobilization from below which had been initiated by Stalin and which in some cases had come to pose a threat to the Party. Attitudes to Party leaders are presented as having been at times quite hostile. In one case, a Party leader was accused of being a 'Goebbels' and a 'barbarian bureaucrat'.[97]

One illustration of this wave of discontent, allegedly unleashed from below, comes from a Party meeting at the Pavlov factory in Rybinsk, which was attended by about a thousand Party members. The meeting went on day after day for a full month. Hundreds of candidates were nominated and scrutinized, and questions with no relevance to the elections were discussed. According to *Bolshevik*, the Yaroslavsk *obkom* was not even aware of the meeting and Party leaders from the Rybinsk *gorkom* who were present 'did not have the courage' either to act at the meeting or to try and control it.[98]

Stalin's Tactics

When considering the tactics used by Stalin in the election campaign, it is important to note that the accusations that were allegedly levelled against the Party leaders were presented, so to speak, from below. Stalin clearly presented himself as the champion of the interests of the 'little man' (*malenkie lyudi*) and the 'common people of the broad masses' (*prostye lyudi iz nizov*). The chief blame for the poor internal state of the Party was sought in the fact that the Party leaders had lost contact with the masses, and had stopped listening to them. 'A new type of management' was seen to be needed, as well as responsibility to the masses. The experience of the Party leaders was insufficient for management.[99] The old Bolshevik historian Em. Yaroslavskii criticized the Party for being bureaucratic. Party leaders must complement their own experience with that of the masses, the Party masses, the working class, and the people.[100]

This perspective 'from below', the call for Party officials to listen to the masses, was in itself nothing new to Bolshevik propaganda. What is more interesting is the perception of a gap between the rulers and the ruled that transpires both from Stalin's speech and from other subsequent articles in *Bolshevik*. Stalin talks in terms of 'us on the top' and 'you below', saying that 'we, the leaders, look at things, events and people from one side only; I would like to say from above', in contrast to the masses with their perspective from below. Party leaders were called upon to lower themselves to the common people: 'Comrade Stalin pointed out in his speech ... that leaders must travel around to the factories more, stay there for some time to work, to get to know better the factory workers, and not only teach people but also learn from them.'[101]

In dealing with Party leaders on the lower and middle levels, Stalin mobilized the grass roots to a broad political campaign. 'Criticism and self-criticism' was the slogan, and the campaign for democratization provided a framework for the offensive. Party meetings and conferences became the forum for preparing the Party cadres for their coming tasks during the election process.[102] One contributor to *Bolshevik* quoted Stalin's declaration at the sixteenth Party Congress, where the latter had presented four ways of fighting bureaucratism within the Party: self-criticism, control over the implementation of decisions, purges, and recruiting devoted workers for the Party apparatus.[103] When measures for democratization are also recommended in fighting the enemy, the enemy model coexists with the democratization model. A lack of contact with the Party rank-and-file, and of criticism and self-criticism, were parts of the explanation why Party leaders have not paid sufficient attention to signs of enemy activity.[104] Local cliques of lower Party leaders are presented as having protected enemies in those cases where they have infiltrated these cliques.

As for the outcome of the elections, some official results do exist from elections in the primary organizations, but none for the higher levels. It is obvious, however, that Stalin did succeed, with the help of 'criticism' from below, in replacing a large part of the lower-level Party leaders. The following example is provided by Fainsod: 'By the end of the year 1937, a completely new team had taken over in Belyi, and they were all strangers to the *raion*.'[105]

Many primary Party organizations had found the work of Party committees unsatisfactory. Information from 54,000 primary organizations reveals that about half of them had this view and in some regions the share was quite high. In Kursk *oblast*, for example, this view was unanimously held.[106] In more than half the 54,000 primary organizations, the members of the Party committees were reappointed, and, in more than a third of cases, the Party secretaries as well.[107]

The campaign that preceded the 1937 Party elections demonstrates Stalin's skill in eliminating internal Party opposition by removing Party secretaries. By mobilizing the grass roots within the organization to criticize local and regional leaders, he won support for his policy of purging the Party apparatus. His goal, however, seems not only to have been to crush remnant support for the old Left and Right opposition, but also to find a remedy for inefficiency and shortcomings of the apparatus. The method chosen to achieve this was to replace individuals within a structure that remained unchanged:

It is a curious fact that even at the height of the purge, Stalin maintained the fiction of 'the leading role of the Party'. Still trumpeting this scheme, Stalin proceeded in 1937 to use the NKVD to decimate the ranks of the leading Party workers in the Western *Oblast*. This was the ultimate irony of Party control.[108]

The System Completed

While the purges certainly had far-reaching consequences for Soviet society as a whole, the crucial blow was directed against the Party. Although the initial attacks left the Party apparatus virtually intact, or affected local officials only, the Ezhovshchina purged the leading cadres and the intelligentsia as well. Of those elected to the 1934 Central Committee, only 20 per cent remained in 1939. For candidate members the figure was only 10 per cent.[109] A majority of those Central Committee members who survived the purges – physically *and* politically – had been part of Stalin's inner circle already in the 1920s or had been drawn into it in the years preceding the purges.[110] Of the 1,966 delegates to the seventeenth Party Congress, in 1934, 1,108 were to be purged.[111] Of the ten members elected to the Politburo in that year, only six were left in 1939. One of the other four was executed and three died under unclear circumstances.[112]

There are no reliable figures on the extent of purges at the lower levels. Since no archives have been opened to either Western or Soviet scholars, only indirect calculations can be made. According to such data, about 75 per cent of the leading cadres at the primary level may have been removed (including 'normal' transfers), and about 80 per cent at the *raion* and *oblast* levels. At the top level, even higher figures were found, due to the exposed position of such officials.[113] About 36 per cent of the Party membership at large were purged in the years 1936–8.[114] Hence, the bulk of the membership in 1939 consisted of new entrants. Less than a third had been members before Stalin's rise to power. The make-up of the Party had thus undergone a radical transformation. The 'new' Party that emerged was loyal to Stalin, and the eighteenth Party congress, held in 1939, was 'a cowed and servile assembly':

> There was no debate, no criticism, no discussion. Speaker after speaker obediently echoed the line laid down by the authors of the main reports ... . Orators vied with one another in ingenuity to devise some novel form of praising the greatness of Stalin – the stenogram bristles with little poems, culled by delegates from all corners of the Soviet Union in honour of the Leader.[115]

Although it had been transformed into a corps of loyal Stalinists, the Party was completely sidestepped in the process of political decision-making. According to the Party statutes, Party Congresses should have been held at five-year intervals. Yet, the nineteenth Party Congress was not to convene until 1952, thirteen years after the eighteenth. In his secret speech at the twentieth Party Congress, in 1956, Khrushchev said that the Central Committee plenum was 'hardly ever called', although the Party statute prescribed meetings every four months.[116] During the war, no meetings at all were held and during the years 1934–53 there were altogether three Party Congresses, one Party Conference and twenty-three meetings with the Central Committee. This can be compared to the period 1918–34, when there were ten congresses, ten conferences, and 122 Central Committee plena.[117] Even the Politburo, which is normally considered as the real decision-making body, was gradually set aside. During the last years of Stalin's rule, its sessions 'occurred only occasionally, from time to time.'[118] Stalin himself decided which Politburo members were to take part in discussions and 'many decisions were taken either by one person or in a roundabout way, without collective discussion.'[119]

It would thus be hardly correct to describe the Party as a ruling Party. It was reduced to an apparatus, no doubt the most important of the mass organizations, but nothing more.[120] The real decision-making organ was Stalin's secret chancellery. This was in stark contrast to the official presentation of the Stalinist political system. According to the 1936 constitution, the leading role of the Party was the cornerstone of the system. While the political structure that was described in the constitution was pure façade, it did present on paper a model for a socialist political system, and it was to this model the post-Stalin leaders would turn when denouncing the Stalinist practice.

Having said all this, can we describe Soviet society after 1939 as totally controlled by the Leader? Subsequent research on the period 1945–53 questions this belief, by pointing at diverging views amongst the top leadership on a number of issues.[121] Such divergencies can be traced to a rivalry between groupings around Malenkov and Zhdanov. These studies, however, fail to produce a consistent pattern of standpoints, in relation to both political content and alliances. A politician would be characterized as a 'hard-liner' on some issues, and as a 'dogmatist' on others. How, then, do we interpret the importance of these diverging opinions within the top leadership? Some observers have seen them as nothing but elements in a struggle for power:

> Generally, in the Soviet Union and in the communist movement, factions seem to coalesce and part ways kaleidoscopically, operating on the basis of personal struggles for power and influence, rather than on any particular, consistent ideological lines or specific issue-orientations. It appears that members of the Politburo focus their factional struggles on tactically advantageous issues, rather than the issues determining the factions.[122]

This description of Soviet high politics as being without political conflict, has been questioned: 'Nonetheless, that melancholy history of failed reform shows, that, even during the worst Stalin years, a reformist impulse existed among the highest Party and state officials.'[123] Cohen puts forward Nikolai Voznesensky, director of the Gosplan during the late 1940s, as one representative of such a reformist tendency. Voznesensky was purged in the Leningrad affair, as a follower of Zhdanov, and is believed to have been executed in 1950. This conflict, however, could also be interpreted as a manifestation of the old Moscow-Leningrad (St Petersburg) regional conflict.

There is some evidence, however, that there did exist some latent forces in favour of reform in the 'mature' Stalinist system, forces which could not come out into the open until after Stalin's death. Dunmore argues that the reform process that emerged after Stalin's death had in actual fact begun earlier:

> Great changes were wrought within five years of Stalin's death. It is often assumed that discussion of these reforms was banned before 1953. Although Stalin may have blocked some reforms (for example abolition of the MTSs) he appears to have allowed discussion of most of them before his death. The thaw of 1953–8 presided over by Khrushchev, and to some extent Malenkov, had already begun in Stalin's declining years.[124]

Even if it had been the intention, Stalinist control was thus not total. Political forces did to a certain extent prevail on the internal Party arena. It is characteristic, however, that these diverging opinions were marked by a distinct absence of any organized links with broader groups within the Party or in society at large. They were not like those top politicians in an authoritarian system, who are described by Wrong as engaging in 'backstairs plotting, court intrigues and veiled efforts to win advancement for their members or to promote policies', serving thereby 'to "mediate" covertly between the Party-state regime and larger social groups.'[125] In the Stalinist system there were no longer any bonds of that kind between the leadership and the population at large.

Conclusion

The conclusions to be drawn from this chapter relate quite distinctly to two different time periods. During the formative years of 1917–34, we have seen how various political forces in Soviet society were gradually subjected to Party control. This process started with the establishment of the Party monopoly over the media and over political life, and was then extended to cover also the full extent of what we have referred to as the implementary and the societal arenas. The two outstanding features in this process are that it was very clearly based on trial and error, rather than on a premeditated plan or a strategy, and that it was a process of concentration of power and control to the Party – broadly defined. The endpoint is the year 1934, when the Victors' Congress, the decree on history and the creation of the Union of Writers all signalled that the Party leadership was in firm control of all spheres of society.

The latter period, which represents the years of consolidation, in 1934-8, is marked by a conspicuous absence of any of those autonomous political forces that previously played such an important role. This fact explains our shift of focus, from the *strategic* aspects of concentrating power and control in the hands of the Party, to the *tactical* aspects of concentrating power and control within the Party in the hands of Stalin and his secret chancellery. This latter process is very clearly marked by populistic features, aimed at weeding out the last remnants of internal Party opposition to Stalin as the *vozhd*. By 1938, the last show trial was staged and all political enemies – real or imaginary – of the Communist Party and the Soviet state were eliminated. The process of political normalization that had been inaugurated by the adoption of the 1936 constitution and by the Party elections in 1937, had been completed.

Chapter four

The Bolshevik order and Russian tradition

In the previous two chapters, we have followed the Bolshevik regime's processes of trial and error in the economic and the political spheres. We have seen economic policy swing from War Communism to NEP, and then to the reborn command economy of five-year planning. We have witnessed how the demands of economic rationality were systematically sacrificed to political expediencies, deemed necessary in order to preserve the power and security of the regime. In the political sphere, we have traced the process leading from the Bolshevik *coup d'état* in October 1917, via the suppression of the remaining rival socialist political parties in 1918–20, and the ban on factions within the ruling Party in 1921, to the establishment of Stalin's personal dictatorship and the creation of a 'new' Party, in the 1930s. As a result of terror and purges, politics as such was seen to have ceased to exist. For obvious reasons, these developments in the economic and political spheres were matched by similar processes in the ideological sphere. The latent conflict between the respective demands of economic and political rationality simply called for the introduction of another tool, a tool which had to be sought in the sphere of cultural and ideological legitimation. In the present chapter, we shall proceed to outline how such measures were exploited and to look at what degree of success might have been achieved.

The Continuity Problem

In the immediate post-1917 period, the new rulers consciously portrayed themselves as ushering in a new era in Russian as well as in world history. Although some noted that traditional Russian traits still prevailed in many respects, many contemporary observers took the declarations at face value. With Stalin's ascendancy, however, the continuity problem came to the forefront: could some basic continuity with Marxism be identified, or was there perhaps a more profound continuity with Tsarist Russia? The question was not one of a total exclusion of either tradition. It was rather concerned with which was the dominant and ideologically most efficient one.

In the late 1980s, seven decades (or more than two generations) after the Russian revolution, in official Soviet texts, in Soviet intellectual debate, and in Western historiography, the Soviet Union is treated as one with historical Russia. The exceptions are few, Aleksandr Solzhenitsyn and Michel Heller being the perhaps best known exponents of the idea that Soviet communism is not Russian. By and large, the issue seems to be settled. The multitude of links uniting the Soviet Union with Tsarist Russia is generally recognized. The Soviet Union of today is regarded by friend and foe alike as the Russian state of the late twentieth century. Whether the ruler is known as General Secretary or as Tsar does not seem to be very important. The centrally planned economy is compared with Tsarist industrialization programmes, mono-party rule with Tsarist autocracy, and communist ideology with the Orthodox faith. This judgement, however, may only be the effect of a long time perspective and of a cognitive mechanism that simply 'makes Russian sense' out of contemporary Soviet realities.

If interpreted as saying that nothing has really changed, or, inversely, that the whole truth lies in the eye of the beholder, the perceptions of apparent similarities between the late nineteenth and the late twentieth century may be misleading. The structural similarity between the Tsarist 1910s and the Soviet 1980s may, for instance, be superficial simply because the quality of the 'similar' phenomena is different. The apparent similarity between today and yesterday may also obscure the existence of that pendulum-like movement of changes back and forth that has marked the entire period of Soviet development, from 1917 onwards.

In addition, the Russia of 70 years ago represented many different ideological and political strands and potentialities. Different traditions were available for inheritance. The Soviet Union might have turned out a different society, we might have found other 'precedents' in Tsarist society, and we might also have found striking similarities between then and now in the hypothetical case of a capitalist and parliamentary Russia today.[1] The question should thus be reformulated: in what ways – if any – was the past brought to bear on the present by the Bolsheviks, once they had secured power in Russia? Or, to put it somewhat differently: given certain undeniable similarities between old Russia and the new Soviet state, *which* of the various past Russias was it that the Bolsheviks recreated? What did they eventually do on purpose, in order to emulate existing ideological beliefs, and which elements of the emerging ideology were due to an overwhelming impact of the peasant and Christian orthodox ideological setting of the new regime?

In relation to the question of continuity versus change it is also important to note that Russia had experienced previous upheavals of magnitudes similar to that of 1917 and the Civil War, without anyone denying that she had remained Russia: the *oprichnina* of Ivan IV (The Terrible) in the 1560s, the Time of Troubles in the early seventeenth century and the reforms of Peter I (The Great) in the beginning of the eighteenth century are cases in point. In spite of turbulent changes, there remained a basic continuity.

It is obvious that the events in 1917 must be regarded not as an isolated occurrence but as part of a process of some length, in the same way as the *oprichnina* and Peter's reforms were processes. Although it is reasonable to regard the events of 1917 in general, and of the October *coup* in particular, as the point of departure for an analysis of the Soviet experience, it is more difficult to point at a precise moment when revolutionary processes were terminated. One encounters a range of views among researchers who have approached this problem. The Australian sovietologist Sheila Fitzpatrick, for example, holds that 'The institutional and social structure and cultural norms that were to last through the Stalin period had been established before the Great Purge, and did not change as a result of it. By the mid 1930s, Russia's new regime had already settled into its mould.'[2] In contrast, the French historian Alain Besançon comes to the following conclusion:

> The Party-state ... would not be completed until the whole of the Soviet population had been brought under its control, through collectivization; until the Party itself had been entirely renewed, which was the object of the purges of the 1930s; and until Stalin's succession had been settled, which would take ten years more, from 1953 until the fall of Khrushchev. So it was only in 1964 that one could say that the Bolshevik Revolution had been completed and that the process begun on 7 November 1917 had come to an end and established itself as stable and lasting.[3]

The apparent contradiction between the two views presented above is dissolved if one interprets Fitzpatrick as asserting that the early 1930s saw the consolidation of Bolshevik rule, not least in the ideological sphere, and Besançon as saying that the mid 1960s saw the eventual stabilization of the Soviet system as a whole. What remains to be shown, however, is how the consolidation and stabilization agreed upon were related to Russian history and anchored in Russian culture.

Although the October *coup d'état* was proclaimed by the Bolsheviks to have been a great revolution and the inauguration of a new, socialist era, and although it was hailed as a radical break with the past, the leading Bolsheviks evidently regarded themselves as the heirs not only to the socialist revolutionaries of the nineteenth century but also to the great Tsars of earlier times. Lenin is reported to have seen in Peter I 'the first revolutionary on the Russian throne' and to have opposed the idea of renaming Peter's capital – Peter, Lenin reportedly declared, was his (Lenin's) 'political forefather'.[4] It is also well known that Stalin in certain respects consciously sought to emulate both Ivan IV and Peter I.[5] However, to invoke and even emulate Ivan the Terrible and Peter the Great would hardly by itself have been sufficient to 'Russianize' Bolshevik rule. In order to be historically significant and ideologically effective, this Russification must also have met with response and been actively acknowledged by the Russian people at large.

The Russia of Lenin as well as that of Stalin's early rule was a predominantly peasant country. While it is true that the political take-over in October 1917 was organized by intellectuals, i.e. by the Bolshevik leaders, it was peasants in military garb who carried out the social revolution, much in the tradition of Russian peasant rebellions. A structurally similar event in another historical epoch was the Botvinnik rebellion at the Time of Troubles in the early seventeenth century, in the midst of the collapse of central political authority and foreign military interventions. It would certainly be fruitful to regard the hypothesized 'Russianization' of the 1917 revolution as an amalgamation of the Bolshevik conceptualization of Marxism with the historical peasant frames of reference and modes of behaviour.

In the short run, the revolutionary upheavals in 1917 can be said to have had two main protagonists on the winning side – revolutionary intellectuals and the peasantry. The landed aristocracy and the class of capitalists were completely routed in the course of the Civil War, and the Orthodox church also lost its position as an institution in society. But these were not the only losers. The industrial workers, having been few already at the time of the revolution, were cut down almost to a man when fighting for the new regime in the Civil War. As a matter of fact, the working class had actually to be recreated under the Bolshevik regime well after the allegedly socialist, workers' revolution.

It soon became evident that the majority of the Russians, i.e. the peasants, stuck to traditional Russian notions and beliefs. Although the early twentieth century had seen radical class-consciousness and democratic ideas emerge in some quarters, as was revealed in the revolution in 1905,[6] the notion of Autocracy, Orthodoxy, and Russian-ness as an inseparable ideological whole must have been alive among the majority. Ideas of representative democracy, freedom of organisation and speech, and independence of the courts, those basic traits of 'modern' political culture, were certainly not motivating forces behind the peasant uprisings of 1917.[7] They can hardly be said to have been the goals of the population at large in the wake of the successful upheaval against the Tsarist order.

Emergence of the Lenin Cult

While the Bolshevik leaders no doubt identified themselves with the great Tsars of old, they were also the heirs to ideological traditions that had been developed in Russia in the 19th century. As has been underlined in earlier research, and recently analysed at length by Andrzej Walicki and Alain Besançon, not only the westernisers but also the slavophiles, were influenced by common European ideological currents. In the former case, the principal influence was that of the Enlightenment, while in the latter, Romantic philosophy, with its stress on the cultural national heritage of the people, exerted a major influence.[8] In the course of the century, local variants of these intellectual currents became part of Russian culture. It turned out that the German Romantic tradition was compatible with certain popular Russian currents of thought.

The Bolsheviks belonged to that part of the imported and adapted 19th century current which Besançon refers to as gnosticism. There is certainly not any causal link between classical gnosticism and that which became Marxism-Leninism, but gnosticism may be profitably used as a paradigm whereby to judge Marxism-Leninism.[9] Central to classical gnosticism – and to Marxism-Leninism – is the notion that a chosen few have gained true knowledge and that the world is divided between the forces of good and the forces of evil. The latter world-view is known as Manicheism.[10] Common to the two is also a peculiar non-rationalistic notion of knowledge:

> The gnostic temptation draws strength from two powerful and constant tendencies in human nature. It promises knowledge to man who, as Aristotle declared, 'has a natural desire for knowledge'. It is a total explanation, resolving all problems, capable of integrating everything. Transcendent realities, physical phenomena and historical events all find within it a place and an explanation. Even the phases of the moon can be explained as a struggle between the two principles. All the same, as Solignac has put it so well: 'This is not a rational science, in the sense of each

assertion having been rigorously demonstrated, but rather a superior knowledge, an intelligence in which each element is comprehended through its cohesion to the whole.' Such a doctrine can only be absolute in dogmatism: it does away with all criticism, since one either 'understands' it, and there is an end to any difficulties, or else one does not 'understand' it, and the whole thing collapses.[11]

This description fits Marxism-Leninism well, as the doctrine is presented in Lenin's treatise on 'empirio-criticism'. It is also perfectly compatible with Lenin's view of the role of the Party, as put forward after the revolution and summarised by the American historian Robert Tucker:

> His heavy emphasis upon 'educational work' as a long-range process of persuasion in the setting of a Party-led movement of the entire people to socialism was in keeping with Bolshevism's master theme, enunciated over twenty years before. It was still a matter of 'consciousness' overcoming popular 'spontaneity' by a pedagogical process.[12]

It should be underlined that what is rendered here as 'spontaneity' is the Russian word *stikhiinost*, which has connotations of 'element', or 'elemental force.'

In classical gnosticism, the knowledge of the initiated few is contained in a certain set of holy scriptures. Similarly, it is well known how the Marxist-Leninist 'classics' have been treated as repositories of truth in the Soviet Union. It is not a matter of theoretical and practical knowledge, collected in practical handbooks. Far from it. The 'classics' are used in quotations as sources of divine wisdom and authority. This is not accidental or ephemeral. On the contrary. Lenin's deep-frozen corpse had not yet reached its embalmers when the Central Committee of the Communist Party (Bolsheviks) decided – on 9 February 1924 – to saturate the people with Leninism. This is an eloquent example of gnosticism in the understanding of 'scriptures'. As the American historian Nina Tumarkin, quoting contemporary sources, has expressed it in her comprehensive analysis of the different aspects of the Lenin cult:

> Straight away the Commissariat of Enlightenment declared that Leninism should provide the basis of all study: 'We must use Lenin's works extensively when studying every problem (independent of the "topic" concerned) in order to formulate our view.' ... 'In every endeavour the individual should remember that there is no sphere of work about which Ilich has not thought, about which he did not leave clear and comprehensible words and be-

hests.' It was up to Party members to communicate those words and behests to the population at large.[13]

This monistic and fideistic view of knowledge must have been perfectly compatible with the beliefs of a semi-literate population, brought up on the teachings of the far from pluralistically inclined Russian Orthodox faith, with its clearly Russian nationalist message.[14] Equally important for forging the link between the Bolshevik rulers and the majority of the Russians must have been the personalization of this 'superior knowledge' in the figure of Lenin. Bolshevik propaganda at the time of the revolution skilfully adapted the basic tenets of the ideology – the principle of superior knowledge and the manichaean world-view – to Orthodox as well as folkloristic Russian traditions. Lenin was presented as the incarnation of these tenets. Many propaganda posters from the Civil War took their form from icons and their message was that there was a struggle between absolute good and absolute evil. One might say that the *form* was patterned upon the Orthodox tradition, while the *content* alluded to the stereotypes of popular religious imaginery, such as demonology.[15]

According to Tumarkin's analysis, the attempt on Lenin's life, on 30 August 1918, was the first event consciously used by prominent Bolsheviks in order to promote the gradually emergent Lenin cult. Already on 6 September, Zinoviev depicted Lenin as 'a saint, an apostle and a prophet', and described Lenin's treatise *What Is to be Done?* as the gospel of the Iskraists. Lenin was inscribed in the Russian tradition of princes who were canonized because of their suffering and martyrdom (Boris and Gleb). The fact that Lenin happened to survive Fanny Kaplan's shot did not matter in the mythological process. Parallel to texts sanctifying Lenin, the Party leaders distributed a popularized biography which described him as a son of the people, of peasant stock, and a kind of twentieth century reincarnation of the peasant rebels Stenka Razin and Emilian Pugachev. These attempts at inaugurating a Lenin cult met with positive popular response, manifested not only in August–September 1918 but also in connection with the Kronstadt uprising in 1921.[16]

According to the Soviet scholar, N. Zaitsev, 'unknown poets and bards' from the depth of the people portrayed Lenin, already during the latter's life-time, as a hero (*bogatyr*), a protector of the people and a brave warrior (*voitel*), and as a wise man. The writer N. Klyuev even described Lenin as a follower of Avvakum and as the 'Red Lord of the Commune' (*Krasnyi gosudar kommuny*).[17] Some members of Christian sects amongst the peasants saw in Lenin the bearer of the righteous Holy Wrath, the fulfiller of the prophecies of Isaiah. Many also regarded Lenin as Anti-Christ.[18] The point is that even as Anti-Christ, Lenin was inscribed in Russian tradition. In his time, Lenin's predecessor Peter I was also regarded by some as Anti-Christ, without his belonging to Russian history being thereby diminished.[19] The perception of Lenin as Anti-Christ could not but underline that the revolution was a genuinely Russian drama. The traditional frames of perception were obviously intact.

In addition, the Communist Party's treatment of Lenin drew directly on Russian traditions. The lying-in-state of the deceased ruler had been introduced by the Romanovs with Peter I. And the 'Lenin corner' (*leninskii ugolok*), which was introduced at an exhibition in Moscow in August 1923, when Lenin was still alive, and subsequently established in public buildings all over the country, 'was directed toward the peasant and was undoubtedly derived from the *krasnyi ugolok*, the icon corner of the Russian home.'[20] In the film *Ego prizyv*, by Ya. Protazanov, which was produced in 1925 and, according to a Soviet scholar, was one of the first Soviet films to carry abroad 'the truth about revolutionary Russia and Lenin', the young worker Katya is shown putting the portraits of Lenin and his forerunner Marx alongside the icons in the room of her babushka – with the approval of the latter.[21]

The latter example does not prove anything about the peasants' perception at the time, but it does demonstrate the officially sanctioned view of what this perception should be. Structurally replacing representations of God and Jesus Christ, the portraits of Marx and Lenin are presented as worthy of devotion in exactly the same manner as the Christian icons. Empirical examples from a distant corner of the Soviet Union and from another religious tradition – the shamanism of the Buryatian Mongols to the east of Lake Baikal – have shown how the cult of Lenin may easily blend with local religious beliefs and practices.[22]

This, of course, does not positively prove anything about the manifest beliefs of Russian peasants, but the example nevertheless shows that syncretism of traditional religion and communist rites had become part of Soviet reality. Although the emergence of the Lenin cult can be viewed as a continuation of Russian and Mongol traditions, the cult was also the outcome of deliberate actions by Bolshevik leaders such as Lunacharskii, Zinoviev, Krasin, and Trotskii. They chose to make Lenin into a Russian saint and a *bogatyr*. Or, in the words of Tumarkin, referring to the introduction of the *leninskii ugolok* and to the embalmment of Lenin's corpse: 'This seems to have been a deliberate attempt to use a religious form to arouse political allegiance in the common people.... As a relic, he [Lenin in the mausoleum] was to continue to legitimize Soviet power and mobilize the population.'[23] As Tumarkin has shown, the lying-in-state and the ensuing exhibition of Lenin's embalmed corpse were successful means of legitimizing the Bolshevik regime in the eyes of the popular masses. The popular adoration of the mummy also convinced foreign observers that the Bolsheviks had struck an agreement with the Russian people.[24]

The creation and promotion of the Lenin cult must be regarded as a perfect example of how a mixture of spontaneous reactions and deliberate machinations helped anchor the new regime in Russian culture and actually made it seem to be one with that culture. The original Lenin cult was gradually overshadowed by that of Stalin. This process was definitely established by December 1929, when Stalin's fiftieth birthday was celebrated.[25] Although the connotations became somewhat different, this did not change the cult as such. Stalin was honoured as the great successor to Lenin and as the one who fulfilled Lenin's work.[26] Of lasting importance in the Lenin cult was that it made the cult of the leader (*vozhd*) seem appropriate and 'natural'. This really ought to have nothing to do with either socialism or Marxism. In this fashion, the Bolshevik leadership style was inscribed in Russian tradition. Instead of Western Marxism modernizing the political culture of Russia, Russia cast Marxism in her own particular form.

National Bolshevism

As was hinted above, the Bolshevik leaders were neither sovereign nor isolated moulders of the minds of the Russians. Events in the ideological sphere were not brought about solely by skilful Bolshevik propaganda and primitive peasant responses. Even non-communist intellectuals came to see in Lenin and the Bolsheviks the saviours of Russia (and of mankind). Some viewed the October 'revolution' as an apocalyptic event, announcing the coming of mankind's Messiah – Russia. The Bolsheviks could quite simply draw on the support of millions of temporary allies, in the form of people who saw the demise of the old order as a pious act in which they gladly took part.[27]

Using Church slavonic expressions, poets such as Esenin, Mariengof, Mayakovskii, and Belyi depicted the revolution as a 'new Easter'. The revolution was 'the thunderstorm of Christ', 'the poetic translation of the idea that the Russian people has the vocation of a supreme mission: they want the kingdom *hic et nunc*.'[28] Even a Soviet scholar who plays down the transcendental, religious message of

Blok's famous poem *The Twelve*, cannot avoid admitting its apocalyptic interpretation of the revolution. According to a Soviet source, the poet Blok compared his own time with the epoch of early Christianity, and the dissolution of the Roman imperial structure with the fall of Tsarist Russia, using the figure of Christ as a symbol for the new world, in the name of which the heroes of the poem seek their righteous revenge on the old world.[29]

A somewhat curious but also significant phenomenon in revolutionary Russia was that while the 'godless communists' of foreign (i.e. Jewish) extraction were regarded and treated as evil villains in peasant Russia, the 'righteous Bolsheviks' were reportedly perceived as true and good Russians. Even staunch conservatives found it natural to support the Bolshevik cause in the Civil War, since they regarded the Bolsheviks as legitimate defenders of Russia against a hostile surrounding world.[30] The Bolsheviks were not slow to capitalize on such moods. They began to portray their war as one defending the empire (although they avoided the term), especially when in 1920 the Civil War grew into the war against the Polish archenemy. The campaigns of the spring and summer of 1920 marked a definite shift in Bolshevik propaganda, from 'proletarian internationalism' to 'defence of the socialist Fatherland', i.e. of Soviet Russia and Soviet Ukraine. Some Soviet texts even used the old nationalistic derogative expression 'Lyakhy' about the Poles.[31]

A further indication of the identification of the Bolsheviks with the fate of Russia is the fact that intellectually influential people outside the Party, not least the *smenavekhovtsy*, supported Bolshevik rule. They saw in it a restoration of Russian might and state power. Leading Bolsheviks, such as Trotskii, Radek and even Lenin (in connection with the Genoa conference in 1922), greeted the *smena vekh* movement and other non-communist intellectuals and welcomed the support. It is significant that they did this in direct struggle against the narrowly proletarian, anti-traditional, and anti-national Proletkult and RAPP organizations.

The background to the emergence of what already at the time was being called National Bolshevism was the radical cultural policy promoted by Proletkult. This organization was founded on the eve of the October *coup d'état*, under the direction of Aleksandr Bogdanov, Lenin's old comrade in arms and subsequent philosophical adversary within the Bolshevik movement. Among its leaders were also the commissar for culture *in spe*, Anatolii Lunacharskii. Proletkult became the rallying point for a new, very radical cultural intelligentsia. At the outset, it was regarded by many as an almost natural counterpart to the political radicalization brought about by Bolshevik rule. However, Lenin's view of culture and of how to educate the workers and peasants into new Soviet Men differed sharply from the one promoted by Proletkult. Simply put, Lenin was a conservative in cultural matters.[32]

When he introduced NEP in economic life, in early 1921, Lenin also attacked Proletkult and its programme. The ideological significance of this move is that the demise of Proletkult was accompanied by an active endorsement of the non-communist Russian intelligentsia as the element best suited to cast the minds of the Soviet workers and peasants. Criticizing Proletkult and the similarly radical RAPP was not enough. The Soviet regime also authorized the establishment of independent, private publishers. As it turned out, however, the literature published by the latter was squarely anti-Soviet. A countermove was consequently deemed necessary, and in this situation one of the leaders of the Party *agitprop*, Ya. Yakovlev, presented the idea of selecting from the existing Soviet but non-communist literary groupings those that were close to the Bolsheviks and to create a Society of Writers. The Politburo authorized the establishment of a commission to prepare the ground, and in July 1922 this commission had reached the following conclusion:

> To organize a non-Party society with the use of the existing group around [the Bolshevik journal] *Krasnaya Nov*. To incorporate in this society: a) old writers, who approached us already at the beginning of the revolution (Bryusov, Gorodetskii, Gorkii and others); b) proletarian writers (The Assocciation of Proletarian Writers and the Moscow and Peterburg [!] Proletkults); c) the Futurists (Mayakovskii, Aseev, Bobrov and so on); d) the Imaginists (Mariengof, Yesenin, Shershenevich, Kusikov and so on); e) the Serapion Brothers (Vsevolod Ivanov, Shaginyan, Nikitin, Tikhonov, Polonskaya and so on); f) the group of ambivalent, politically unstable, talented youth (Boris Pilnyak, Zoshchenko); g) the *Smenavekhovtsy* (A. Tolstoi, Andrianov and others).[33]

The list of potential allies thus included not only known anti-communists but also those living abroad in voluntary emigration, such as Gorkii, and even Tolstoi, who at this time lived in Berlin and would return to Russia only in August 1923. The proposed Society of Writers did not materialize at the time, nor with the members envisaged. As is well known, the Union of Soviet Writers was not to be established until 1934, and under quite different circumstances. The point, however, is that the Bolshevik Party recognized the fact that non-communists were essential for cultural life and also recognized that such people might be willing to support the Party for the sake of Russia. This was something more than Lenin's traditional, conservative cultural taste. It meant an acknowledgment of the positive value of the work of 'talented' writers from different ideological quarters, the only provision being that they stood up for Russia and her present regime.[34]

In addition to gathering strength from this enlistment of non-Party intellectuals, the establishment of the new ideology of National Bolshevism was also furthered by the ethnic Russification of both the Party at large and of its central apparatus in 1924–7, a process which had begun with the 'Lenin campaign' (*leninskii prizyv*) immediately after Lenin's death in 1924.[35] Although the Society of Writers did not come about at the time, in the cultural realm the ideology of National Bolshevism succeeded in occupying a strategic position. An example of the importance in cultural life of the National Bolshevist conception of the early Soviet state was the foundation of the journal *Novaya Rossiya* (New Russia) in Petrograd in 1922. As has been pointed out by the Soviet scholar M. Chudakova, the noun 'Russia' was not used in the country at this time, except in standing formulations such as 'Soviet Russia'. The choice of name was thus significant, and the message was further underlined by ortography. 'Russia' was written in *Art Noveau*-style without any space between the letters. This was understood to imply 'the one and indivisible' (*edinaya i nedelimaya*) Russia.

Moreover, the journal *Novaya Rossiya* was related to the *Smena vekh* movement, which was a main pillar of the ideological construct of National Bolshevism. In July 1922, this movement opened a local Moscow office for its journal *Nakanune* (The Eve), which was published in Berlin. The *smenavekhovtsy* were praised already in early 1922 by Lunacharskii. He admitted that these new allies of the original Bolsheviks were yesterday's enemies. More important, however, was the fact that they were patriots with a keen interest in the well-being of both the Russian state and the Russian people. They came from the political right and were not contaminated by any democratic prejudices or any pseudo-socialist emotions, Lunacharskii observed. Although the local Party chief Zinoviev had the journal closed in Petrograd, it could continue its existence as a *tolstyi ezhemesyachnik* in Moscow. In issue number 7 in 1923, the editor of the journal, I. Lezhnev, made the following observation:

> Culture and life are built according to the law of continuity. After a revolutionary break of this line of continuity, there is either a rapid relapse towards the past, or an uninterrupted and stubborn forging of links, a cicatrization of the tissue, and the blood of the two epochs, the two cultures, is mixed. The idea of coalescence, synthesis of the two cultures is the most actual and topical idea,

and we have not ceased to speak about it from the first number of
the Petrograd *Novaya Rossiya*.[36]

Lezhnev's deliberations were spurred by his reading, in manuscript
form, of Mikhail Bulgakov's novel *The White Guard*. On 5 October
1926, Moscow's famous MKhAT theatre staged a play based on that
novel, now called *The Days of the Turbins*. The story is set in the time
of the Civil War. According to a contemporary observer, the play was
an extraordinary public success, one unprecedented since the revolution. What is of special interest is the alleged reason of the success:
'The audience was relieved by the demonstration of honest and not
Party-oriented self-sufficient emotions and the absence of deroga-
tion of the adversaries.'[37]

The Days of the Turbins was not perceived to be politically parti-
san. It was simply regarded as pro-Russian. The essence of the
message is clear when the White officer Myshlaevskii argues at the
end of the play that it is necessary to join the Bolsheviks. As Mikhail
Agursky has pointed out, Myshlaevskii's arguments are an expression of National Bolshevism. Agursky mentions that the wording was
a little too strong for some communist critics, who condemned the
play. It was, however, defended by Lunacharskii, the Commissar of
Enlightenment. During the period leading from September 1929 to
February 1932 the play was not performed, and in the official press
Bulgakov was mentioned together with such 'enemies of the Soviet
power' as Zamyatin and Pilnyak. After one of Stalin's mysterious
telephone calls, however, this one to Bulgakov in April 1930, the play
was finally restaged. In the conversation with Stalin, Bulgakov had
admitted that he did not believe that a Russian writer could live
abroad.

The latter was a confession of the basic Russian belief in the mystical unity of all Russians and the Russian state, i.e. a core element in
National Bolshevism as well as in what is known as Stalinism. Stalin
agreed with the writer on this point and promised to secure some
kind of backstage job for Bulgakov in Moscow. Although Bulgakov
did get such employment, he remained a non-person to his death in
1940 and was not allowed to publish further. *The Days of the Turbins*,
however, was shown from early 1932 until the outbreak of the war in
1941, for a total of 987 performances. Stalin demonstrated his approval of the message of the play by viewing it fifteen times.

Most likely, the ideology of National Bolshevism was contested in
the Party leadership during the turbulent years 1928–32. This would
explain why *The Days of the Turbins* was suppressed during these
years. The ideology became officially tolerated again only with the introduction of Stalin's and Zhdanov's cultural policy from 1932

onwards. According to Agursky, the ideological impact of Bulgakov's play with its blessing from above cannot be overestimated. The role of theatre in the Soviet Union of those days was so important that one single performance of *The Days of the Turbins* was more significant than all run-of-the-mill political literature of the time.[38]

The establishment of National Bolshevism should be viewed as a support for the Party, not as a complete substitute for Marxist influence on its ideology. Besançon has warned against believing that a complete merger took place between nationalism and Bolshevism:

> In fact, the Party remained the master of this alliance and knew how to maintain the subordinate relationship that Lenin had established: Party–class–nation. The revolutionary goal, which was utopian and ideological, was not abandoned for the sake of the nationalist goal: extension or maintenance of the empire. The problem for the Party was to keep the Party–class–nation hierarchy in the correct order.[39]

As we have noted in a previous chapter, the political sphere was put in order with the adoption of the 1936 constitution and with the Great Purge in 1937. Basically, the function of National Bolshevism was to rally new groups behind the Party line rather than to challenge the leading role of that Party.

The Stalinist Synthesis: The Great Leader of Russia

In 1928–31, Soviet ideological life was marked by the so-called cultural revolution, led by RAPP and directed against the 'rightist danger' in cultural life. RAPP succeeded in gaining control over the publication of literary journals and books and in squeezing out 'bourgeois' artists, such as Bulgakov, from cultural life. Once this was accomplished, the Party leadership – Stalin and his chief lieutenant Zhdanov – routed the 'proletarian' artists as well. What remained was thus a layer of largely non-political and non-ideological professional intelligentsia, representing something of the pre-revolutionary Russian mainstream, in combination with the recently trained new Soviet intelligentsia, the *vydvizhentsy*.[40] In April 1932, the Central Committee issued a decree on *perestroika* of the literary and art organizations. RAPP was dissolved, together with the remnants of Proletkult.[41] In 1934, the Union of Soviet Writers was created, together with similar organizations for the other fine arts, all at the Party's initiative. Cultural and ideological life was increasingly *gleichschalted*, homogenized.

Soviet cultural policy in the 1920s had also been marked by the so called *korennisatsiya* (rooting) with respect to the non-Russian languages and cultures. Cultural policy aimed at promoting native cadres in the national republics and autonomous regions. For example, the Slavic peoples of Belorussia and the Ukraine, who had been subjected to a severe process of Russification under the Tsars, could develop and spread the use of their native languages in different areas of societal life, write down their own separate histories and foster autonomous national Orthodox churches. The multinational character of Belorussia was symbolized in the republic's coat of arms, which carried the slogan 'Proletarians of the World, Unite!', in four different languages: Belorussian, Russian, Yiddish and Polish. Literacy campaigns were carried out among previously illiterate minorities in Russia and Central Asia. These, as well as the Turkish peoples, who had used Arabic script, adopted Latin script. The choice of Latin rather than Cyrillic symbolized a genuinely internationalist policy.[42]

Parallel with the elimination of first 'bourgeois' and then self-labelled 'proletarian' elements in the cultural life of the RSFSR in 1928–34, in the course of the 1930s, the different national Party leaders and cultural intelligentsias were eliminated as well, together with distinct national cultures and churches. Stalin's and Zhdanov's programmes for homogenization and Russification were crowned by a decree from the Central Committee on 13 March 1938, making Russian a compulsory language in all schools in the national republics and autonomous regions. Those peoples who a decade earlier had adopted the Latin script were now forced to switch to Cyrillic.[43] Another sign of the time was that the Yiddish and Polish texts disappeared from the Belorussian coat of arms.[44]

Stalin's own 'cultural revolution' of the 1930s can be viewed as a continuation and consolidation of the National Bolshevik tradition. We are concerned here primarily with the ideological aspect, but it is important to bear in mind that great social transformations also took place. Almost to a man, the generation of Old Bolsheviks, those Marxists who were internationalists 'without Fatherland', was crushed. What remained was, on the one hand, peasants and workers with their minds steeped in traditional Russian forms, and, on the other, a new generation of Party cadres and technicians, socialized with the help of a deliberate revitalization of the same Russian forms. The westernizing, anti-nationalist layer of intellectuals was destroyed, and in spite of the political and social rift separating the new class of administrators from the population at large,[45] both cadres and the people came to belong to the same community of ideological beliefs and of interpretations of the past.[46]

Stalin's rule meant *inter alia* a conscious and deliberate revival of the Russian autocratic tradition. Not only Aleksandr Nevskii and Dmitrii Donskoi, but in particular Ivan the Terrible and Peter the Great were invoked by Stalin as his forerunners. Not that any historical determinism was at work. It was rather a question of legitimizing extreme political measures by inscribing them in tradition, thus making them seem Russian: the Great Purge bore resemblance to the *Oprichnina* of Ivan, and it was deliberate policy rather than coincidence which made Soviet historians extol the terror and enserfment under Ivan as historically inevitable and 'progressive'.[47] In literature, especially that which praised the *stakhanovtsy*, Stalin was portrayed as the stern but benign father-tsar. The traditional hierarchical relationship between the ruler and the subjects was described as ideal.[48]

Once the regime had placed the mythological relation between the Soviet order and old Russia on the agenda, certain events lent themselves to mythological interpretation, although it is certainly debatable whether they were deliberately designed to be perceived in this way. A case in point is the murder of Sergei Kirov, Stalin's heir apparent, in 1934. Both Ivan the Terrible and Peter the Great had their own sons killed, their *tsarevich*, the heir apparent. This suffering of the son was interpreted in Russian Orthodox tradition as a repetition of the suffering of Christ, the son of God who was forced to die in order to save humanity. In this way, Tsarist power was inscribed in the Christian drama.[49] Kirov was certainly not Stalin's biological son, but in a structural sense he held the same position as once did the *tsarevich*. It is significant that although public homages to Stalin were commonplace at the time, it was Kirov who at the Party Congress earlier in 1934 had paid homage to Stalin on behalf of the Party and had praised him for being 'the greatest leader of all times and all nations.'[50] In a sense, a pattern repeated itself: the son paid homage to the father, the son was killed and subsequently hailed as a martyr for the people and posthumously celebrated as the one who was nearest and dearest to the Supreme Ruler.[51]

The *tsarevich*-Kirov parallel is structural and cannot be empirically proven to have been experienced consciously by the Russian people. The point, however, is that Kirov died under mystical circumstances and once dead was used by Stalin in a way that appealed to religious emotions and beliefs. The Soviet regime was inscribed in the mythological drama of Holy Russia.[52] The Russian past was being emulated not by the rationalization of history alone, but also with the help of myth. The main point in this context concerns not so much whether people actually believed in the central tenets of this ideology. This question obviously defies an answer.[53] The point is rather that people were forced to use – publicly at least – the associated terminology. This effectively precluded the emergence and formation – on the conceptual level – of alternatives. It is this, rather than terror as such, which we understand as the real essence of 'totalitarianism'.

Totalitarianism

Already in the 1930s, the Soviet system was labelled totalitarian by Marxists disappointed with developments in the Soviet Union under Stalin, as well as by the political and ideological adversaries of communism. This view was also rather common among researchers in the West in the 1950s, but in the 1960s and the 1970s the 'totalitarian model' went out of fashion as a tool of analysis in Western sovietology. Although the rejection more often than not was made upon false premises, i.e. based on the allegation that the 'model' was an invention of American Cold War warriors,[54] it became fashionable to treat Soviet society as just another version of modern industrial civilization, or perhaps as a slight perversion.

As developments in the Soviet Union in the late 1970s and early 1980s refused to adapt to the 'pluralist' antithesis to the 'totalitarian model', the latter was gradually reintroduced into the political and scholarly debate. Representative of this trend was a study by the French sociologist Edgar Morin.[55] Morin's central concern is the nature of political power in the Soviet Union. He takes internal as well as external aspects into consideration. Enumerating well known repressive traits in domestic Soviet politics, as well as imperialist actions in Soviet foreign policy, Morin argues that the Soviet Union can be labelled neither socialist nor communist. He instead holds that the label or concept of 'totalitarianism' is the most appropriate one for the mono-party, imperialist Soviet state. One need not postulate that the Party controls in minute detail every individual Soviet mind. The concept still covers the way in which the Party apparatus rules not only with the help of force, but also by using ideological devices, the latter being based upon the myth of a monolithically united people, directed by the Party.[56]

Another scholar who uses the concept of totalitarianism in the contemporary debate is the Polish philosopher and marxologist Leszek Kolakowski. It is noteworthy that his definition of the concept comes close to that of Morin. Thus Kolakowski in a discussion of the phenomenon of Stalinism:

I take the word 'totalitarian' in a commonly used sense, meaning a political system where all social ties have been entirely replaced by state-imposed organization and where, consequently, all groups and all individuals are supposed to act only for goals which both are the goals of the state and were defined as such by the state. ... not every despotic or terroristic system of ruling is necessarily totalitarian. Some, even the bloodiest, may have limited goals and do not need to absorb all forms of human activity within state goals; the worst forms of colonial rule in the worst periods usually were not totalitarian; the goal was to exploit subjugated countries economically, and, since many domains of life were indifferent from this point of view, they could be left more or less untouched. Conversely, a totalitarian system does not need to use permanently terroristic means of oppression.[57]

Both Morin and Kolakowski refer to empirical Soviet reality, stressing that complete totalitarianism is impossible and that 'no absolutely perfect totalitarian system has ever existed'.[58] Agreeing with these reservations one can argue that the three 'major defects' of the totalitarian model that have been indicated by the British political scientist Stephen White, are beside the point. According to White, the model must be dismissed because it assumes 'that the Soviet system was sustained almost entirely by coercion', because it is 'static' and 'resistent ... to comparative analysis', and because it fails 'to provide a satisfactory basis for the consideration of change over time in any political system thus categorized'.[59]

The question of whether 'change' can be allowed, without invalidating the concept of 'totalitarianism', is partly a matter of definition. Comparative analysis may be strictly conceptual and does not necessarily imply a search for empirical similarities between different political entities. Finally, 'coercion' is a concept that may be widened to include ideology – one merely has to recall the practice of brainwashing, which need not rely on physical violence to be efficient. Moreover, one may argue that all use of political power to a certain extent relies on coercion.

The logic of White's argument is that such a thing as totalitarianism simply cannot exist. After all, what we need is not a model, but a concept that is applicable in an analysis of the interplay between repression and ideology as instruments of political power in Soviet Russia. How and by which processes did that system develop which has inspired the definitions of a number of researchers up to contemporary scholars such as Morin and Kolakowski? It was obviously not any ideal type of totalitarianism that emerged but rather an empirical reality best understood as a situation where no politically effective opposition to the ruling apparatus could be articulated or aggregated into organized activity. The latter aspect is the really crucial one.

The basic traits of Soviet totalitarianism, as we understand it here, are a concentration of political power to the centre and an ambition by the regime to control society via force and indoctrination, without being bound by legal norms or rules. It is perfectly compatible with this understanding of totalitarianism to allow for infighting among the subordinated agencies – as long as these do not organize themselves and do not co-operate against the central state power. The totalitarianism in question, moreover, may well be tolerated by a majority of the population. As a matter of fact, tacit acquiesence by the majority, combined with the vociferous enthusiasm of a minority, were prominent features of ideological life in the Soviet Union in the 1920s and 1930s. What emerged was a kind of totalitarianism accepted by certain groups or layers in society.

Once it was evident, in 1917–20, that the Bolsheviks were determined to remain in power at any price, they gained the support of intellectuals who helped them legitimize their regime ideologically. In the mid-1930s, under the Great Purge, the pattern was repeated with new role-incumbents. The point is that although a sufficiently strong and ruthless state may induce a whole people to ideological lip-service, something else took place in the Soviet 1920s and 1930s. An active ideology emerged, supported by a substantial part of the population. The result has been well described by Fainsod in his classical study of Smolensk. Fainsod noted that by the end of the 1930s, there had emerged a formidable combination of vested interests in the survival of the regime, comprising Party and Komsomol *apparatchiki*, state officials, factory directors, engineers and the technical elite, the Stakhanovites, the collective farm chairmen, the new officer corps, the police and, in the cultural area, a well-kept elite of academicians, privileged writers, journalists, theatre and movie directors, actors, singers, musicians, and other 'engineers of the human soul'.[60] The phrase 'engineers of the human soul' was the Stalinist label on the cultural intelligentsia. This group was of crucial importance in producing a working ideology of the new Soviet state.

Although one may certainly agree with Cohen's assertion, that 'the important question of Stalin's popular support in Soviet society' is a problem which is 'largely ignored' in sovietological research, it is impossible to agree with his declaration that Stalin's popularity is 'inconsistent with the imagery of a "totalitarian" regime'. Cohen defines a totalitarian regime as one 'dominating a hapless, "atomized" population through power techniques alone.'[61] As a final point, we might add that if one does not consider Stalin's regime to be totalitarian, it will of course be impossible to consider the post-Stalin Soviet regimes as such.

Writing in 1987, however, assessing Mikhail Gorbachev's ways of exerting power in the Soviet Union of today, the seasoned 'revisionist' Jerry Hough admitted that the concept of 'totalitarianism' had perhaps been prematurely buried:

> Paradoxically, we have come to accept a basically Marxist view of the Soviet political system and to rely on Moscow rumours – often officially inspired by Moscow – about Kremlin politics. Had we continued to accept the interpretation of the literature on totalitarianism, our initial assessments of Gorbachev's prospects would have been far more accurate.[62]

The point in Hough's recantation is that although any single ruler may be toppled by his peers, the political system as such remains totalitarian. This belated observation by Hough makes clear that the error in Cohen's argument about the Stalin period lies in his phrase 'power techniques alone', and in his narrow interpretation of these as being exclusively of a terrorist kind. If one considers the structural properties of the political system to be important 'power techniques' and the ideological superstructure to be part and parcel of the system, then one may explain the basic political stability that has marked Soviet development from Stalin to Gorbachev without having to constantly refer to brute force as the sole 'technique'. It is exactly this aspect that has been under scrutiny in the present chapter.

Interestingly, after dismissing the concept of totalitarianism as misleading, White proposes as an alternative analytical tool the concept of 'political culture', this being better suited to the 'need for a more historically informed, developmentally-oriented approach to the analysis of communist political systems'.[63] We consider these two concepts to be supplementary, i.e. our historically oriented analysis of the culture of Russia should serve to deepen our understanding of how Soviet totalitarianism came about. This understanding of the concepts at hand underlines that it is the cultural dimension of totalitarianism, including the role and function of ideology, that is at the centre of our interest. As the concept of culture must have a time dimension, the concept of tradition is closely related to it. The aspect of tradition that interests us, however, is its actualization or revival in concrete circumstances, i.e. tradition as perceived, interpreted and used by the actors in society. As the past is supposed to be open to choice, this implies a non-deterministic stance. As the French philosopher Paul Ricoeur has expressed it: 'Preservation is as much a freely-chosen action as revolution and renewal.'[64]

Conclusion

In this chapter, we have seen how elements of Russian tradition were both consciously used by the Bolsheviks and spontaneously contributed to rally both peasants and intellectuals behind the new regime which, ironically, labelled itself a workers' government. Terror helped establish and confirm Bolshevik rule, but was hardly sufficient to secure popular support and political stability. These were instead won by the ideological appeal to the people at large and to the intellectuals, by the Russification of the ideological framework of the allegedly Marxist October 'revolution'. On an intellectual level, this development meant the triumph not only of Russian nationalism but also of the Manichaean world-view, which before the revolution had been a sub-culture among intellectuals. In the course of the Civil War, the black-and-white Manichaean view of both domestic politics and international relations became entrenched. According to Fitzpatrick, the 'war scare' of 1927 served to enhance this development, and by the late 1930s 'the "country in danger" mentality was ... firmly embedded in Soviet political culture.'[65] Already in 1927, however, Bukharin, who was then still an ideological spokesman for the Party, declared that the regime was not willing to allow the masses to become 'infected' by the enemy. Bourgeois influences from the decadent West should be fought by all possible means.[66]

The Soviet leaders showed that they mastered rather subtle power techniques, as they managed to use the Lenin cult as well as the ideology of National Bolshevism in their endeavour to suppress all political and ideological opposition. It stands to reason that Stalin and his collaborators succeeded in this way to forge the ideological environment of the ruthless economic policy to be carried out in the 1930s. While it took terror to eliminate physically any potential political opponent, the ideological struggle was already won. As indicated by our analysis, the totalitarian ideology was developed and ready to work when needed. During purges, collectivization and general suffering, substantial parts of the Russian population, including not a few intellectuals, acknowledged Stalin as the legitimate leader of Russia. As the result of a skilful adaption to vital currents in post-October Russia, the regime managed in the 1930s to gain support by tapping ideological beliefs which had grown out of Russian culture. That the totalitarian off-shoot was not the only one theoretically possible to emerge from this culture is quite another matter.

This analysis is an argument in support of the thesis that there is a basic ideological continuity between pre- and post-revolutionary

Russia. While a radical political break and a profound social upheaval undoubtedly did occur in 1917, culturally Russia remained very much the same. Modernism disappeared, but then again modernism had been a newcomer in Russia at the turn of the century. The re-emergence of the traditional popular and nationalist ideology was caused to a significant degree by the acts of the Bolsheviks, by their ability to appeal to different layers of the Russian people. This outcome was also aided by the fact that the socialization of the people, the shaping of a nation's collective identity, is a process of *longue durée*, a matter of generations.[67] Any basic change in the socialization pattern and in the ideological beliefs of a people will thus have to last long in order to have any crucial effects on the images of the past and on the understanding of the cultural meaning of the present.

The 'western' perspective that affected part of the Soviet intelligentsia in the first two decades of the twentieth century did not have time to establish itself in the minds of ordinary Russians during the 20-odd years it was offered. With the growing isolation of the Soviet Union from the West that took place under Stalin, and with the suppression of the non-Russian nationalities in the 1930s, Russia asserted itself. The Moscow Kremlin became not only the site but also the symbol of Soviet power. All this epitomized the ideological success of the new regime. Russia had remained Russia, retaining much of her empire and restoring political stability that had been seriously shaken first in 1905 and then in 1917. If it actually is possible to identify a specific ideological ahistorical content in Marxism, it was certainly not preserved in the state ideology of Stalin's Russia.

Chapter five

Summary: political forces

'Political forces' was a key concept used in our account of the emergence of the Stalinist political system. In this concluding summary over the first bloc of three chapters, which has comprised our presentation of the emergence of the Soviet system as a whole, we shall return to that concept, to use it as an instrument with which to integrate the three perspectives outlined in the respective chapters. Our approach shall in a sense be 'dialectic', i.e. we shall focus on the interplay between, on the one hand, such forces that were set in motion by certain actions taken by the Bolshevik leadership and, on the other, such policy measures that were in turn chosen by the leadership in order to deal with the former responses. In so doing, we shall recall the perspective of viewing policy as a series of *ad hoc* actions which only *ex post* would be rationalized as elements of a premeditated long term strategy.

Ideology will be seen in this context to have performed an important support function. The instrumental view of ideology that was outlined in the introductory chapter to this study will be used here in order to show how ideological statements were made initially as a smokescreen, to cover up unpopular and ideologically inadmissible policy measures, but then gradually came to acquire a legitimating and rationalizing purpose. In this sense, the emergence of Soviet ideology can also be given a dialectic interpretation, where the relative strength of various political forces conditioned the current profile and interpretation of ideology, and where certain of the more deeply embedded tenets of that ideology conditioned the character, or main direction, of the various *ad hoc* policy measures.

The conclusion that we shall seek to establish from the presentation so far will focus on the question of how successful the Bolsheviks were in managing to instil both sympathy for the cause and acceptance of the system among Party cadres and the population at large. In order to disentangle this thorny issue and arrive at certain conclusions, we shall use the instruments of Exit, Voice and Loyalty (EVL) that were previously presented, together with our interpretation of ideology. Our ambition will be to show the gradual emergence of a peculiar set of values and beliefs which in practice amounted to an operational 'ideology' that was well suited to further the political objectives of the Party leadership and which thus provided the system as a whole with a certain rationality of a rather subtle kind.

The fate and transformation of this ideology during the post-Stalin period will be dealt with in the summary sections following the two blocs of chapters on the Khrushchev and Brezhnev eras, and in the concluding chapter we shall seek to demonstrate how its main ingredients today have come to stand firmly in the way of the creation of the very conditions that are needed by Gorbachev for success with a policy of reform, or *perestroika*. Such essentially structural obstacles will be interpreted as a legacy left to Gorbachev by his predecessors. While in the three previous chapters we have used an essentially disciplinary perspective, we shall shift here to a chronological one. We start by looking at the period of War Communism, then move on to NEP and conclude with a discussion of the 'mature' model left by Stalin to his successors.

War Communism

When speaking of political forces, there is of course nothing that parallels those that fuelled – and were unleashed by – the revolutions of 1905 and 1917. As Lewin has put it, 1917 was a 'proletarian revolution, flanked by a peasant war'.[1] In all the three senses discussed above – economic, political and cultural – it is all too obvious how the Bolsheviks stood as if struck by lightning after their October *coup d'état*. There were no operational plans for the future and perhaps even little practical understanding of what needed to be done. As we have already shown, perceptions of the economic problems that lay ahead bordered on the naive.

Meanwhile, the economic manifestation of those political forces that were released amongst the peasantry was that of a spontaneous land reform, legalized *ex post* by the Bolsheviks. In terms of our EVL framework, we can describe these *unorganized* actions as a mass Exit by the peasantry from that sphere of society over which the Bolsheviks wanted to – indeed were forced to – extend their control. The seriousness of this Exit should be seen in terms of its implicit threat against the desire for control *per se* that has been amply documented above, from Lenin's 'April Theses' and onwards. The consequences of the Bolshevik reaction to this perceived threat would be dire.

As we have argued above, the 'siege' conditions of civil war and foreign intervention were certainly important factors behind the policy of forced requisitions, the *prodrazverstka*, which was the first step in the emergence of a Bolshevik agricultural policy. Under the circumstances, food simply had to be taken from the peasantry by force, if the cities and the Red Army were to survive. Few would probably quarrel with this.[2] The core of the matter, however, is something that will form the backbone of our 'dialectic' approach throughout the study, namely the *demonstration effect*. From Moscow's horizon, application of the *prodrazverstka* must undoubtedly have been considered a success. Against payment in virtually useless paper currency, twice as much grain was collected in 1919/20 as in 1918/19.[3] As Conquest puts it, 'the Party's success in confiscating the grain gave it the false, and shallow, idea that here was a simple method of solving the problem.'[4] The fact that the logical peasant response would be reduced sowings and an eventual crisis of production was – if at all understood – most likely overshadowed by the more immediate impression that the market had been crushed.

This experience forms an important first step towards the formation of early Bolshevik ideology, in its instrumental interpretation. The threatened Exit by the peasantry was blocked and their (thwarted) energies unwillingly harnessed for the cause. Gradually, that same 'model' was then extended to the other sectors of the economy. In the financial sphere, 1920 saw the experiment with a money-free budget and in industry a long neglected nationalization followed. The pieces were neatly falling into their places in the puzzle, as a new economic system was taking shape in front of the eyes of the bewildered Bolsheviks. *Ex post*, the main ingredients in this system would be rationalized as logical and necessary features of socialism.

A similar interpretation can be made of developments in the political sphere. As we have seen above, in October 1917 there was clearly no blueprint in the Bolshevik mind as to what the future Soviet political system would or should look like. Vacillations over the role of the Mensheviks and the Socialist Revolutionaries illustrate the differences of opinion that prevailed within the Party. Again the demonstration effect is paramount. In accordance with Lenin's April Theses, transition to power was still the overriding concern and the successful move of dissolving the Constituent Assembly illustrated what could be achieved in this direction.

The fact that three Socialist Revolutionaries had a brief tenure in the Council of Peoples' Commissars provides further illustration that the strategy was not a premeditated one, but rather a process of trial and error. If Lenin had lost the fateful October vote on insurrection, or if the other socialist parties had opposed the Bolsheviks more forcefully, those factions within the Party that favoured coalition might have prevailed. After all, Marx had spoken about a dictatorship of the proletariat, not of a power monopoly in the hands of the Party leadership. Once achieved, however, the political monopoly formed another neatly fitting piece in the emerging Bolshevik puzzle, making it possible to extend control over other 'arenas' in society as well. *Ex post*, these ambitions for power would be rationalized as a 'dictatorship of the proletariat'.

In order to consolidate the model that was thus slowly taking shape, the next requirement was to deal with any real or potential opposition, i.e. to achieve a containment of Voice. The original closure and censure of the Press was again most likely conditioned by wartime needs, as it would be in any so-called free society, but soon the benefits of an information monopoly must have emerged as yet another neatly fitting piece in the puzzle of the nascent Bolshevik state to be.

With the benefit of hindsight, these various steps can be pieced together into something that *looks* like a premeditated strategy, but such an interpretation – we shall argue – has little to do with reality. At the time, it was all 'touch and go', with the future of the revolution being at stake literally every minute of the day. It is in this perspective that our emphasis on demonstration effects and *ad hoc* policy-making should be seen. If the revolution had prevailed in Germany, all those emergency measures that were taken during War Communism could have been explained and excused as precisely that. This outcome, it may be noted, would not only have been 'theoretically' correct. It was also clearly the Bolsheviks' belief up until at least 1920. As it was, however, the emergency measures came to be rationalized as the foundations of socialism. We thus have here an illustration of precisely that danger of distorting socialism about which – as we may recall from Chapter 2 – Oskar Lange has issued serious warnings.

It might also be pointed out that even if there had been a master plan, the Bolsheviks simply would not have had the power to enforce such a new model by decree alone. Somehow they also had to create at least a minimal acceptance among as many as possible of those to whom Exit from the Bolshevik-controlled sphere was blocked and to whom Voice against its main characteristics was denied. If this could not be achieved, the model would simply blow up. It is here that ideology enters the stage, with the cult of Lenin as its mainstay. As we may recall, the Bolshevik leader was consciously portrayed on the one hand, as the true heir to old Russian heroes (*bogatyry*) and saints, the traditional protectors of the people against unjust rulers. This formed an appeal to Russian national and Orthodox religious values, seeking to portray the Party as the rightful ruler of Russia, above all

112

so in the eyes of the all-important peasantry. For internal Party purposes, on the other hand, promotion of the Lenin cult served even before 1924 to provide a charismatic aura for the Party leadership as a whole.

Although united in *function*, these two uses of Lenin were highly different in *nature*. To the people (chiefly the peasants), he was presented as a *Russian* popular leader while to the Party, he was a socialist revolutionary and a *Marxist* internationalist. In the former case, the aim was to instil faith in the re-establishment of a past – mythological – just order, while in the latter a future – utopian – just order was promised. Correspondingly, the two served to promote very different kinds of feelings.

Among the *peasants*, who were hardest hit by the blocked Exit, a pressure of discontent was rapidly building up which under peaceful conditions would perhaps have been released in forms reminiscent of today's actions by French farmers. As it were, however, it took a violent direction, with consequent repercussions for the Bolshevik struggle to survive in power. It would be a difficult exercise indeed to look for any attempt at ideological legitimation of Bolshevik rule in front of the peasants and it is rather symptomatic that it would only be after his death that Lenin succeeded in winning the peasantry. With the *urban* population, however, the situation was considerably different. They were undoubtedly severely affected by the food shortages, perhaps even worse than the peasantry, but in their case the prevailing exceptional conditions served partly to defuse Voice against the regime. The Party's ambition to gain legitimacy was also on considerably more firm ground here, with the policy of creating a working class and with conscious appeals being made to the need for sacrifices in the process of 'building socialism'.

These ideological differences between the case of the peasantry and that of the workers may merit some additional comment, as they were not just confined to the early period of the Soviet state. They would, for example, find an important symbolic representation in the 1937 statue by V.I. Mukhina – *Rabochii i kolkhoznitsa* (worker and *kolkhoz* woman) – which stands outside the permanent VDNKh exhibition in Moscow and which is also the official logo of Mosfilm. Mukhina's presentation of the peasantry as a woman has obvious connotations of Mother Russia and thus of presenting the peasants as a passive element in that process of progress which was led by the male industrial workers. *De facto* it can be taken to symbolize an effective exclusion of the peasant class as an active element in Soviet ideology. In this perspective, we may also recall our dual interpretation of the Lenin cult. To the workers he was the builder of socialism, while to the peasants he was merely an icon figure.

113

The really crucial and decisive factor in the Party's search for legitimacy, however, was the obvious need to win the cadres to the cause. Here the various tenets of the official ideology must have held a considerably greater appeal. Not only can we safely assume the Party workers to have been generally more receptive to *agitprop*. There must also have been strong feelings of all being together in the same boat, of having to keep a united front in order simply to hang on.

It may also be noted here that in comparison with the makers of the February revolution, Bolshevik activities in the sphere of legitimation give a distinct impression of skill and competence. Logically, they also met with remarkable success. A case in point, which has been advanced by Richard Stites, is the futile attempt by the provisional government to present a 'domesticated' twin eagle as a more peaceful symbol for the new state.[5] In the economic sphere, however, the Bolshevik success was somewhat less pronounced. In February 1921, a rebellion at the Kronstadt naval base provided the last straw needed for the model to collapse. As Trotsky was later to put it, 'the middle peasant talked with the Soviet Government through naval guns.'[6]

NEP

Those traumatic effects that resulted from the *volte face* that brought about the NEP have been amply illustrated in the three preceding chapters. What remains to be done here is to study the impact of the partly new set of political forces that was released by the apparently insignificant but in practice crucially important decision to substitute a tax-in-kind (*prodnalog*) for the hated and destructive policy of forced requisitions, the *prodrazverstka*. Once again, our initial concern is with the economic manifestations of such forces. As we have seen above, NEP was essentially a policy aimed at solving problems in agriculture and it is thus hardly surprising that this is where we find its most dramatic manifestations.

As in the months after the revolution, a mass Exit by the peasantry took place. Bolshevik control over the vital relations between town and country was reduced from direct administrative commands to an indirect and perhaps poorly understood market exchange. It must, moreover, also have become rapidly obvious that the 'infection' threatened to spread to other sectors of the economy as well, with the dreaded NEP-men taking over trade and with the large industrial trusts – which were still under central control – standing out as models of gross inefficiency.

The writing was on the wall but, in stark contrast to the period of War Communism, there were now no exceptional circumstances to defend and rationalize harsh measures. As their relative prosperity grew with increasing harvests, the peasants were gradually lulled into a belief that their dreams had finally come true, after the disappointments of 1861, 1905, and 1917. Such beliefs fed on the disarray of the Party's agricultural policy, which in 1925 allowed both the hiring of labour and the leasing of land. Once a decision was subsequently reached to launch another attack on the peasantry's relative independence, this would prove to have disastrous repercussions.

As we may recall from our introductory discussion of ideology, the process of alignment between utopia and perceived reality is of crucial importance. In this respect, a veritable gulf was opening up between the future as perceived by, respectively, the peasantry and the Party. The peasantry's Exit was accompanied by a radical transformation of their perceptions of both themselves and their future. As Moshe Lewin has phrased it, the 'NEP and its policies probably gave many peasants a sense of social promotion as millions of them became *khozyaeva*, i.e. independent, respected and self-respecting producers in their communities, even if many if not most of them were still very poor.'[7]

The peasantry had thus been effectively placed outside the reach of Party *agitprop* which rapidly lost both its relevance and credibility. The core of this process can be interpreted as the accumulation of a form of latent horizontal Voice against the Bolshevik model, Voice which could be unleashed by any attempt to curtail the Exit. Since the Exit was clearly neither organized nor controlled, this process can be taken as an important illustration of our understanding of 'political forces'. It was a spontaneous reaction, conditioned by previous events and triggered by the perceived retreat by the Party. Politically, Soviet society had been returned to a pre-modern state, with no separate or alternative organizations to which the peasants could turn. This was in stark contrast to the brief period of nascent pluralism, which came out into the open in 1905 and which had a last stand in the spring and summer of 1917.

The impact on the Party of these developments illustrates fairly clearly Lewin's claim that until 1929 the Bolshevik Party remained an 'alliance of factions'.[8] From this also stemmed the flexibility of its ideology, where Bukharin was the greatest turncoat. His call for the peasants to 'get rich' and his statement about reaching communism via trade and market exchange certainly combine to form a remarkable demonstration of the range of beliefs that could be – and were – held at the time.

In contrast to the landslide Exit that marked the economic sphere, the Party had in the politicial sphere not only managed to block Exit, by means of its sustained political monopoly, but also succeeded in controlling Voice, by means of the ban on factions within the Party and other similar actions aimed at both the 'implementary' and the 'societal' arenas. No other channels than those formally approved existed for the articulation and aggregation of Voice. The latter meant that the main tenets of what was currently approved as official ideology could be brought to bear on all open expressions of Voice, thus serving as a screening device with which to separate the 'heretics' from the reliable. Ideology had acquired one of its by far most important instrumental functions.

As we have previously emphasized, however, the controls on Voice that were thus imposed represented something very far from a total prohibition. What they meant was a restriction on channels, but within the approved sphere – above all on the 'internal Party' arena – a considerable amount of Voice was forthcoming throughout the 1920s, in the literary sphere as well as in the form of the Great Debate over the future course of Soviet economic development. The controls did, however, represent a certain 'softening' in the *nature* of approved Voice, as certain types of 'unreasonable' statements would certainly not be permitted (e.g. statements about the leading role of the Party).

On the surface, social relations during NEP can be seen to be marked by that same bifurcation of society into an industrial and an agrarian sphere, which was to be symbolized in the 1937 statue by Mukhina. In a deeper sense, however, the content of that symbol was being transformed. Among the *peasantry*, a 'false consciousness' of sorts emerged, as the utopia which was growing in their minds must have been something much more akin to the world of Chayanov than to that of the Bolshevik leadership. For the *urban* population, on the other hand, the situation was akin to the previous period of War Communism. They could still be reached by the message of *agitprop*, about the building of socialism, and they could view themselves as the elite of the new state to be. For the *Party cadres*, finally, the communist utopia was still alive and mixed with the mission of saving Russia it must have been a most potent and euphoric brew.

The sum conclusion of the NEP experience must be that the peasants were effectively disconnected from the official sphere of Soviet society and that the building of socialism consequently would have to rest on the shoulders of urban workers and Party activists alone. As NEP wore on, the implications of this message must have become increasingly obvious to the Bolshevik leadership and Stalin would

116

certainly not shy away from taking such measures that would be necessary in order to redress the situation.

Stalin

Stalin's rise to supreme power was a process of many dimensions. Most spectacular of course, was the curtailment of the peasantry's previous Exit and the consequent extension of effective Party control over agriculture. The terror and bloodshed that resulted illustrate forcibly the importance of the gulf between the two ideologies – or utopias – that was referred to above. The attempt to bridge the gulf, via mass collectivization and dekulakization, unleashed tremendous political forces, in terms of previously accumulated Voice. They produced the horror story told by Conquest, Lewin and others. As Stalin wrote to Sholokhov, it was 'a "quiet" war against Soviet power. A war of starvation, dear comrade Sholokhov.'[9]

Collectivization also provides a further important illustration of the demonstration effect. In the Soviet republic of Kazakhstan, almost 40 per cent of the population depended on livestock alone and a full two-thirds were semi-nomadic, migrating with their herds in summer. Given the social traditions connected with such an economy, it ought to have been unusually badly suited for collectivization. Yet, collectivized it was and the price paid was frightening. Possibly a quarter of the population perished, together with almost 80 per cent of the cattle and more than 90 per cent of the sheep. These horrible results may well have been partly unforeseen consequences but, as Conquest argues, 'the effectiveness of the unplanned Kazakh famine in destroying local resistance was a useful model for Stalin when it came to the Ukraine.'[10] The importance of this observation lies in the fact that it would be hard indeed to argue that the famine in the Ukraine could in any way have been an *unforeseen* consequence of the chosen policy.

Collectivization naturally looms large in any study of the onset of Stalinism and the peasantry undoubtedly suffered greatly from being perceived by Stalin as the main enemy. This time, however, it was not only they who were hit. In terms of our EVL framework, we can interpret Stalin's policy as a drastic and simultaneous curtailment of both Exit and Voice throughout Soviet society. If we assume, as does Hirschman, that there is a certain interdependence between the two options, such that if one is curtailed pressure on the other will mount, we can then conclude that this all-out repression had to produce a tremendous pressure of discontent within the system, a discontent which would simply have to find an outlet in some way.[11]

Such outlets, we shall argue, were of two kinds, both of which we shall refer to as 'soft options'. Let us start with the Exit.

Unproductive Soft Exit

With the 'hard' Exit being blocked, in its original Hirschman interpretation, various soft alternatives took its place, the most obvious of which was perhaps those private plots that were given to the *kolkhoz* peasantry, in a retreat from full collectivization. These not only filled the function of providing additional food, but must also have served as an important refuge from the 'new serfdom' on the collectivized fields.[12] For the urban population, activities in the second economy served a similar purpose. The psychological effects of such refuges can be seen as a combination of easing frustration, and of atomizing the individuals, thus precluding the aggregation of Voice. At the same time, however, it should be noted that the private plots and the second economy form a very special case of soft Exit, in the sense that the outcome of such activities is productive. Considerably more important, and widespread, forms of soft Exit were represented by drinking, slacking and general apathy, activities which were pursued throughout society and which far from being productive could actually be detrimental, in terms of a destruction of human capital. While different in *nature*, however, the various options were united in *function*, by providing a safety valve for the release of frustration and discontent, as an alternative to the prohibited 'hard' Exit.

Destructive Soft Voice

In the political sphere, the earlier controls on the *form* of Voice were supplemented by strict controls on its *content*. Whatever debate had previously been allowed within the approved channels was now replaced by a mechanical regurgitation of a blatant praise of the 'wise' leadership of Stalin. Voice thus underwent a definite transformation from hard to soft, with far-reaching repercussions for initiative and feedback. As in the case of Exit, however, we must distinguish between two different functions of Voice, one representing the *constructive* reporting of abuse and shortcomings, together with the making of proposals for improvements, while the other is the *destructive* practices of idle flattery and of denunciations and poison-pen letters.

With the constructive options being suppressed by terror, the destructive ones gained in prominence. Flattery may certainly be considered rather harmless here, but that was definitely not the case with the latter – particularly noxious – forms of soft destructive Voice. These were starting to spread like wildfire, and for good reasons. To the single individual, 'doing someone in' must have presented a golden opportunity for the release of fear and frustration, although for many people such actions would probably carry a bitter aftertaste once their consequences dawned upon the perpetrator. To those Party activists who were charged with the repeated purges, this type of Voice was an obvious help in the struggle to make sufficient arrests for their plan targets to be reached. To the Party leadership itself – i.e. ultimately to Stalin himself – it was instrumental in breaking up the preconditions for horizontal Voice. The latter, as we may recall, is in its turn the precondition for vertical Voice to be aggregated, and it was thus possible to nip in the very bud any whisper of opposition.

Passive Loyalty

For obvious reasons, however, simple terror was not enough in order to consolidate a position of absolute power. With a sufficient lack of conscience, it would no doubt have been possible to shoot and deport a sufficient number of the population for the remainder to be reduced to a state of terrified apathy, from which no political threat to the despot could come. Such a policy, however, has an important drawback in that apathy represents a soft Exit of the improductive kind, i.e. the costs in terms of output forgone might simply become so high as to be prohibitive. Moreover, what is there to guarantee that the punitive apparatus keeps its rifles pointed firmly *away* from the despot? It is symptomatic, for example, that the repressive organs themselves were subjected to extensive purges, and it is also relevant to recall Rosenfeldt's emphasis on Stalin's systematic ambition to create checks and balances in the system, in order to prevent the emergence of any rivals for power.[13]

No doubt, Stalin at times came very close to such a policy, in particular during the campaigns for collectivization and dekulakization, but at any given point in time a large enough section of the population simply had to be given some motivation to work – other than fear – for some production to occur. Here ideology provided the real challenge – and help – to Stalin. An appeal was made to national consciousness, which in practice meant a return to a set of selected Russian traditions and values. National Bolshevism confronted the Soviet population with carrying out Russia's holy mission, and the Stalin cult took over the function of the Lenin cult, changing its connotations from Russian *bogatyry* and saints, to the great Tsars Ivan the Terrible and Peter the Great. In this way, people were urged to work for the great Russian nation as well as for the empire. In striking contrast to Lenin, Stalin succeeded already during his lifetime in becoming a hero to all sections of the population.

To the *peasants*, Stalin was the *batyushka-tsar*, the distant Tsar who was unaware of and thus not to blame for abuse and excesses committed by his officials. To the *workers*, he was the great *vozhd* who was leading his Stakhanovite brigades in 'storms' and 'campaigns' to reach set targets, while to the *cadres*, finally, he was the benign *khozyain*,[14] offering an ordered bureaucratic hierarchy with simple rules for rising through the ranks. With this, Stalin had completed for his successors a social and economic legacy which would prove to be surprisingly and ominously resistant to all attempts at reform and restructuring.

Rationality and Loyalty

The issue of rationality in the Soviet model has two important and highly different dimensions. On the one hand, there is the question of *political* rationality, which we have interpreted in the broad terms of power and security for the leadership, and, on the other, there is that of *economic* rationality, which can be seen in terms of what degree of efficiency is achieved in the utilization of available resources. It should be rather obvious from what has been said so far that there is some form of – unspecified – contradiction between these two dimensions. The resolution of that contradiction has also been a persistent challenge to a number of successive Soviet leaderships. In the following chapters, we shall see how a process of learning by doing has served over time to produce a number of subtle mechanisms, which are of considerable help in this respect. As a starting point, let us outline the nature of the problem.

Simply put, economic efficiency requires initiative, while the political objectives require control. No easily identifiable policy measures seem to exist which will simultaneously affect both of these in a desired direction. On the one hand, too much emphasis on control and regulation will thwart productive effort and stifle productive feedback on performance. Using Hirschman's terminology, we could speak here of breaking through a 'floor' for Exit and Voice, a practical example of which would be the collapse of War Communism, in February 1921. On the other hand, as was illustrated by the NEP period, too great a play for the market forces will deprive the Party of the rationale for its existence, as alternative and perhaps more efficient structures arise and pluralism introduces competition. Again quoting Hirschman, we could speak of breaking through a 'ceiling' on Exit and Voice, with a resulting economic disintegration and/or political disruption.[15]

At first glance, it would seem possible to derive from this framework a challenge to the Party leadership which consists simply of manipulating the respective levels of Exit and Voice. From the presentation above, we could also draw the conclusion that such 'navigation' has been based on a long process of learning, a process which consists of a string of unconnected demonstration effects, illustrating likely responses to different policy measures. It should be emphasised, in this context, that although the outcome will be the same, this type of navigation process is something considerably different from adhering to a previously conceived economic and political strategy.

Reality is of course considerably more complicated than this first glance would lead us to believe, but as we proceed below to incorporate realism, this will be done within the outlined framework of 'navigation', and from the perspective of viewing policy as a process of trial and error. This latter process, moreover, will not be understood as a random walk, but rather as a systematic ambition to move in a certain given direction, as defined by the leadership's ambitions for power and security. Comparing Chinese and Soviet experience, Nove has argued that 'there are certain errors which communists repeatedly commit, possibly due to the suppression, in "anti-rightist" campaigns, of the voices of moderation and common sense.'[16] Our understanding is similar to that of Nove.

An important complication here lies in the simple fact that we are not dealing with a homogeneous population. Ethnic differences aside, we are concerned here with the three different groups of peasants, workers and Party cadres, each of which posed its own separate problems and thus required its own separate policy measures. We shall conclude this summary chapter by looking at the respective roles that were played by these three groups and we shall do so in terms of that Hirschman-type perspective where Loyalty serves to delay Exit, in order to promote constructive effort and feedback.

In this perspective, the case of the *peasantry* is the simplest one to assess. Throughout the whole of the period studied above, the peasants were effectively 'disconnected' from the official sphere of Soviet society and from its ideology. Although for a brief period during NEP they were brought out of their soft unproductive Exit, and incorporated into the economic sphere as efficient producers and providers, it is important to note that these activities were carried out on that fringe of the economy which was largely outside Bolshevik control.

121

Moreover, it is of paramount importance to note that those inducements which achieved this temporary incorporation were connected with factors that were *external* to both the Bolshevik societal concept and to its allegedly Marxist ideology.

Private initiative outside state control was the driving force and that had certainly never been part of any communist utopia. Even under Stalin, we can safely assume that those ideological devices which had served originally to adapt Bolshevism to the mind of the Russian peasant continued to be operational. The peasants continued to believe in the *batyushka* (Stalin) and in the saint (Lenin) and thus stood outside the mainstream of Bolshevik policy. To the extent that they were actually mobilized for the interests of the Soviet state, this was for reasons which had very little to do with either socialism or Marxism. It was more a case of Holy Russia having returned. Consequently, this *concordat* would eventually have to be curtailed. When that happened, it meant that the ideological distinction between worker and peasant was effectively made permanent.

The case of the *workers* is slightly more complicated. At first glance, it is of course rather obvious that they too suffered from the consequences of those repressive measures which aimed at restricting Exit and Voice. As we have indicated above, during some periods of desperate food shortages the situation in the cities may actually have been worse than in the countryside. There is, however, also a rather subtle difference which concerns the fact that, in contrast to the case of the peasantry, the measures which served to mobilize the newly urbanized workers for the Soviet cause were largely *internal* to both the Bolshevik societal concept and to its professed Marxist ideology.

To work as a Stakhanovite was certainly an activity of at least short-run benefit to the Soviet state. Shortages of consumer goods as well as harsh repressive measures could be accepted as being due to emergency, particularly in the light of that 'country-in-danger' atmosphere which was promoted by Party *agitprop*. In the eyes of the workers, the credibility of the Bolshevik programme was not beyond repair. They were mobilized for 'socialism' rather than for 'Russia'. We can thus speak of some first difficult steps being taken on the path of 'building socialism'.

The really crucial group, however, was the Party *cadres*, where we have seen how policy vacillated between commands issued to the middle levels and a broad policy of mobilization which was aimed at the base. Over time, there emerged here a pattern of obedience to neither the Party nor the state, but rather to the *Khozyain* at the peak of the power hierarchy. The essence of such obedience was reverence for neither Holy Russia nor the Socialist State, but only for the

Ruler. In history, such obedience has normally been associated with naked and ruthless authoritarianism.

Conclusion

The real strength of the economic model that emerged under Stalin was its capacity to mobilize both labour and other resources in order to achieve national goals that were perceived to be vital. There lie unquestionable achievements in rapid industrialization and in the formation of a vast military-industrial complex, ready to churn out sufficient numbers of tanks and aircraft to halt and defeat the German war machine. At the same time, however, a considerable long term price had to be paid for these achievements. The 'command-administrative' model, as it is known today, rested solely on vertical rather than horizontal relationships, and it achieved a near-total destruction of private enterprise and private initiative. As noted in our introductory chapter, these features are now being publicly recognized by Soviet sources.

The core of the inherent destructive forces of this model derives from the parallel suppression of both economic and political pluralism that marked War Communism and Stalinism. The contrast with NEP, which did feature considerable economic but very little political pluralism is illustrative of the interplay between the two spheres. If we start by recognizing that economic pluralism in a structural sense is a prerequisite for political pluralism, we may understand why control over the economy was seen as a precondition for the attainment of political power and security for those at the top. At the same time, we must also recognize that the suppression of political pluralism had seriously detrimental feedback effects on economic performance, as individuals resorted to various soft options for Exit and Voice. The crucial feature in this process, however, is more serious than simply paying a direct economic price for suppressing pluralism. It concerns rather the *de facto* segmentation of Soviet society that is associated with the practice of the soft options.

Already in his 1953 study, Fainsod observed how the Party consciously sought to 'utilize the mechanism of the Soviets to broaden its influence with the masses, to enlist sympathetic non-Party elements in the tasks of administration and government, and to reward outstanding achievement by designating the deserving for membership in the Soviets.'[17] In a subsequent work, Howard Swearer noted the same ambition, describing the Soviet government as 'a dynamic totalitarian government which sets as its ideal the total and active involvement of all citizens in the affairs of a rapidly changing and

123

ever more complex society.'[18] The rationale for this incorporation of large numbers of the population into the officially controlled sphere of society is of course close to the heart of the adherents of the totalitarian view of Soviet society. William Kornhauser, for example, has concluded that:

> If there were no controlled intermediate organizations in all spheres of society, people would be free to regroup along lines independent of the regime. That is why it is of the utmost importance to totalitarian regimes to keep the population active in these controlled groups. Totalitarian regimes search out all independent forms of organizations in order to transform them or destroy them.[19]

It is rather natural that Hough, being firmly against the concept of totalitarianism, disagrees with these and other similar views, arguing that political and popular participation in the Soviet case 'seem relatively little different on the surface from their counterparts in the West'.[20] Hough's examples are letters to editors and personal appeals to various committees and officials, as well as direct participation in commissions and councils, and it is of course true that 'on the surface' there may be little difference between East and West here. Yet we argue that the main importance lies not so much in what people *do* as in what they are *prevented* from doing. By incorporating the citizens into the controlled sphere, all Voice will have to be articulated and aggregated from within, where it can be effectively monitored and screened. This not only implies censorship and streamlining. Most importantly, it implies that there will be very little – if at all any – scope for the open formation of collective identities that represent values and ideas different from the officially approved ones.

If we recognize that no collective action will be possible without a collective identity, i.e. a feeling of common identification and a sense of a common cause, then we may understand the importance of precluding the formation of such identities. During War Communism, the overall situation was far too chaotic for this reasoning to be meaningfully applicable, but during NEP the inherent dangers were brought home with a vengeance. The *de facto* exclusion of the peasantry from the official sphere of Soviet society began the formation of a collective identity which was associated with goals and values considerably different from those of the Bolsheviks. The story of how Stalin managed to realign the ideological Soviet universe need not be repeated here.

Seen in the simple terms of political stabilization, the Stalinist model was successful because of its rather effective curb on Voice, on

124

the one hand, and the rather ephemeral nature of permitted Exit, on the other. A further contributing factor was that functional diversification of ideology which has been hinted at above. There were, however, also inherent in that model, latent challenges to stability. Once the economy had reached the limits of 'extensive' mobilization of new resources, once new interests had accumulated in a more developed society, and once the siege mentality could no longer be maintained, the problems of Exit, Voice, and Loyalty would acquire essentially new qualities. Accordingly, there would be new challenges in store for Stalin's successors. These challenges, and the policies chosen for their resolution, will be the topic of the following chapters of our study.

Part three

Attempts at Change

Chapter six

The failure of intensification

In his *Economic History of the USSR*, Nove summarizes Khrushchev's role in Soviet economic development in the following, rather fitting, one-line characteristic: 'But in the end he knew only the traditional methods.'[1] Much of our presentation in this chapter can be summarized in that very same sentence. It will be our ambition to examine and demonstrate how Khrushchev, although he certainly made a lot of noise about it, did not in any important way manage to alter the basic principles of running the Soviet economy. The question of whether he actually *intended* to do so, and in such a case to what extent, falls within the political realm and will thus not be dealt with here.

Our presentation in this chapter will focus mainly on policy-making in agriculture and industry, i.e. in the two central sectors of the economy. Policy in the former case will be analysed in order to show the continuation, and maybe even perpetuation, of that principle of extensive growth which was established under Stalin. There can be no more spectacular illustration of this than the Virgin Lands programme which, in less than a decade, succeeded in making the future of Soviet agriculture hostage to the vagaries of extremely unreliable weather conditions in the new areas.

Industrial policy will, on the other hand, be analysed with the intention of bringing out how a search for a basically administrative solution to pressing economic problems came to serve as a *de facto* substitute for serious economic reform. As in the case of agricultural policy, a series of administrative reshuffles were made, with the aim of finding an alternative *format* for a set of old *principles*. The many changes back and forth will be reviewed in an attempt to reveal what these principles may have been, in order to see whether they were conscious restrictions, or perhaps simply instinctive and *ad hoc* reaction patterns.

Against this background, agricultural and industrial policy will be seen to have an important common denominator in the fact that both in some sense served to ransom the future to current needs. Before we proceed to see how this was done, however, let us sketch briefly what it was that Stalin left for his successors.

Stalin's Legacy

The nearly two decades that passed between the Victors' Congress, in 1934, and the death of Stalin, in 1953, form a striking illustration of the claim that, in all important respects, the Soviet model – as we still know it – had already been established by the mid-1930s. The fact that the Second World War bisects the period adds a turbulent dimension to developments, but does not change the basic conclusion. The period leading up to the war was characterized by preparations, and the post-war period by restoration, but in neither case were there any substantial deviations from the basic model. As Lange has pointed out, the command model is a *sui generis* war economy. Changes brought about by the war were consequently a matter of degree, rather than of principle.

The similarities between the respective ways in which the economy was run in the 1930s and during the war might of course be explained by variations on the theme of 'encirclement', and by the need to be prepared for imperialist aggression. But what about the post-war period? In all nations but the Soviet Union, peace brought great changes to economic policy – a return to normalcy if you wish – as special wartime needs became obsolete. Why was the Soviet Union an exception? Was it simply that a state of war represented normalcy for the command economy?

It is also clearly reflected in official rhetoric that the Soviet approach to economic problems rests on a basic military logic. Reference is made to devising *campaigns*, in order to reach given *targets*, to organizing *shock* workers into *brigades*, which are *thrown* on to various *fronts* and to building labour relations on the basis of military discipline, where *traitors* and *spies* are accused of *wrecking* and *sabotaging* production.[2] This warlike philosophy constitutes an important trend of continuity in Soviet economic development. We have seen above how Bolshevik policy during the early stages of planning was marked by a strong belief in the ability to *storm* any kind of *fortress* and, as we shall see below, a similar, albeit perhaps less extreme, attitude has marked events up to the present date.

The real crux of the matter is that this type of approach to economic policy leaves very little room for any of those concepts of equilibrium, opportunity costs, and marginal analysis, that are such vital ingredients in non-Marxist economics. Not only was this true of statements from the top political leadership, which would have been serious enough, it even came to encompass the entire profession of economics and would thus have quite important long-term implications for the running of the Soviet economy. As we have seen in Chapter 2, by the mid-1930s, all prominent Soviet economists had been either shot or otherwise silenced. For the remainder of Stalin's rule, economics was reduced to a mechanical regurgitation of suitable quotations from the founding fathers and to the blatant ritual praise of the 'wise leadership' of the Great Leader, the *vozhd*.

In his 1952 textbook *Economic Problems of Socialism in the USSR*, Stalin himself added insult to injury by stating that 'burdening economics with questions of economic policy would mean destroying it as a science.'[3] Seen from the point of view of a destruction of human capital, this philosophy represented nothing short of a disaster, as a whole generation of Soviet economists was trained in the rejection of all those tools which really ought to have made up the very essence of their profession. Such was the price that was to be paid by future Soviet generations for Stalin's method of suppressing opposition to forced collectivization and to what Naum Jasny has referred to as 'Bacchanalian planning'.[4]

Of course, much has been done since that time, in an effort to remedy the consequences of this part of Stalin's legacy, but the results of that effort have not been overwhelming. It is symptomatic, for example, that under Gorbachev's current policy of *perestroika*, many Soviet economists appear to be almost childishly pleased that the top leadership is finally ready at least to listen to what they have to say. As we shall see in both this and in following chapters, the consequences of the suppression of economic thinking that accompanied the emergence of the Soviet model in the late 1920s and the early 1930s have remained so pervasive that even today they can be rightly considered as endemic to the Soviet system at large.

During the years immediately after Stalin's death, however, the atmosphere was different. As we shall argue at greater length in the following two chapters, opposition to Stalin's policies had been growing under the surface for quite some time before his death. Once the dictator was gone, such sentiments began to venture out into the open, albeit cautiously. At the twentieth Party Congress, in February 1956, both Suslov and Mikoyan came out strongly against Stalin's economic legacy, calling upon Soviet economists to undertake a revision.[5] According to Suslov, Soviet economists had 'lost the taste' for studying concrete problems, preferring instead to concentrate on the 'selection of quotations and on the art of their manipulation'. His portrayal of this 'science' was hardly a flattering one: 'Every little departure from quotations is considered a revision of its foundations. Such dogmatic activity is not only fruitless but even directly harmful.'

Although it is certainly difficult to tell if this stand was based on a genuine desire for economic reforms, or if it was chiefly part of the scramble to fill the power vacuum left by Stalin, it remains a fact that it did leave a number of observable traces. These will be subjected to closer scrutiny below.

For the moment, however, we shall leave the theoretical aspects of the problem, and return to those actual events that served to shape Stalin's legacy. Here we may profitably discern three separate stages. The *first* of these is the period of emergence of the Soviet model, which has been dealt with above. The *second* is the war with Germany, which is important here only in so far as it illustrates what minimal changes were needed in order for the Soviet economy to be adjusted to the needs of war. The *third*, which we shall be concerned with below, is the period of reconstruction, in 1945–53, which forms both an important transition period and an illustration to our claim of continuity. This stage has been characterized by Nove as an 'oddly shapeless period':

> Economic policy, organization, ideas, rapidly became frozen into their pre-war mould. Stalin spoke seldom, Party Congresses were not called, even Central Committee meetings were rare (and virtually unreported) occasions. An oppressive censorship made public discussion of serious matters impossible. Numerous, usually unexplained, reorganizations of the ministerial structure made little difference to the actual functioning of the system.[6]

In addition to the basic continuity in philosophy that was outlined above, regarding the role of economics and of economic principles, there are two further components of the Stalinist legacy which have their roots in the post-war period, and which may thus merit separate attention here. One is the remarkable economic recovery that was achieved in industry and the other the equally remarkable absence of any such recovery in agriculture. Let us start by looking at the former.

In 1945, industrial production in the previously German-occupied territories – i.e. in the bulk of the economically most developed European parts of the Soviet Union – was down to 30 per cent of its pre-war level.[7] The starting point for reconstruction was consequently not a favourable one. Although a large – albeit contested – amount of resources was transfered to the Soviet Union from the occupied territories in Eastern Europe, it would certainly be wrong to refute altogether the claim that reconstruction was chiefly the result of a remarkable effort by the Soviet population. The mobilization of labour was massive, and figures on capital investment reflect a similarly high tempo. The already ambitious 1946–50 investment plan was reported to have been overfulfilled by no less than 22 per cent.[8]

The population was thus subjected to hardship not only via long hours of hard work, but also via a substantial squeeze on consumption, in order to achieve the high rates of accumulation. By 1950, however, there was considerable reason for pride. The Soviet Union had rebuilt its industry to a point where its strength even surpassed that before the war. It may be pointed out that this reconstruction was above all a triumph of the traditional command model. There were a limited number of priorities, labour effort was elicited by means of exhortation, and central control was as strict as ever. The sense of triumph was thus to some extent built on false grounds, and the future would prove with a vengeance the growing inadequacies of the traditional model in meeting the challenges of an increasingly complex and interrelated economy.

In all fairness, however, it should be recognized that simple macro-economic indicators remain pointed towards an impressive industrial recovery. In this context, agriculture represents the reverse side of the coin. Here there was little reason indeed for pride.[9] Not only was there a noticeable lack of achievements in gross production terms, it should also be noted that agriculture by its very nature normally offers the best promises for a fast recovery. The poor showing of that sector is thus better ascribed to policy-related obstacles, than to a lack of support or potential for recovery.

During the war, state control over the farms had been somewhat reduced, and there had even been rumours among peasant soldiers that the *kolkhoz* system might be relaxed, or maybe even abolished, as a reward for military victory.[10] In 1946, however, all hopes along such lines fell flat, when a severe clamp-down was decreed on 'breaches of *kolkhoz* discipline'. Control was sharpened, taxation increased, and delivery obligations underlined. Large amounts of land that had been taken over by the private sector during the war were returned to the *kolkhozy*, which could often find no use for these scattered strips of marginal land. According to a Soviet economist, 'in the majority of *kolkhozy* such normally high-yielding lands became idle and overgrown with weeds.'[11] Then there was the Stalin Plan for the Transformation of Nature, and the Three Year Livestock Plan, both of which imposed additional burdens. Finally, there was Lysenko.

The only flow going into the villages was that of banners and medals to the 'heroes of socialist labour'.[12] Procurement prices were kept absurdly low and peasants survived only thanks to their – heavily taxed – private plots. Nove's conclusion on the absence of change in agricultural policy during Stalin's last years, and on those drastic changes which took place after the latter's death, is that there 'is no escaping the conclusion that he delayed long-necessary changes of policy by his obstinately hostile attitude to the peasantry.'[13]

All in all, we have little to add to this portrayal of Stalin's last years. The same old policies were continued, as if nothing had happened. Industrial reconstruction hinged on the mobilizing effects of tight planning, and on political control and exhortation – combined with hardships for the population, much in the same way as during the first years of 'Bacchanalian planning'. The old policy remained, moreover, even to the point of continuing to regard the peasantry as a hostile element to be exploited and controlled. Such was the legacy, and since problems were the greatest in agriculture, let us start our account there.

Agriculture on Centre Stage

To say that Stalin's agricultural policy had been one of mismanagement is hardly an overstatement. With the exception of hogs, livestock holdings in 1953 were still below their 1928 levels, as were crop yields for the period 1949–53. Farm income had fallen by 30 per cent in the period 1928–52, and peasants had in many instances survived thanks only to their private plots.[14] Soviet agriculture had thus, in the quarter of a century that followed collectivization, still not progressed beyond the level it had reached in 1928.[15] It was obvious that something needed to be done and the actions taken proceeded along three lines: administrative change, area expansion, and improved incentives. As we shall see below, there is a subtle logic that intertwines these three strands of policy.

In Search of an Administrative Solution

The majority of administrative measures taken during the Khrushchev period was aimed at strengthening Party control over agriculture. Having said this, there are two highly important facts that should be established. *First* of all, Khrushchev himself was exceptional, in the sense that he was of peasant origin and had made his career via the Party apparatus. Most of his rivals were of urban background, having their power base in the state hierarchy. *Second*, while the running of industry, due to its technical complexities, had been left to specialists ever since the Civil War, agriculture had throughout been strictly regarded as a 'Party affair'.[16] Both of these factors place a particular emphasis on the importance of agriculture in the struggle for power and consequently also in the formation of policy.

Khrushchev had started his bid for power already before Stalin's death, by launching a campaign for amalgamating the *kolkhozy* into larger units. In 1949–50 alone, their numbers were reduced from 250,000 to 124,000, and by 1958 they were down further, to 68,000.[17] That process has continued up to the present, albeit at a slower pace. The reduction in the number of farms to control had the obvious benefit of reducing the burden on the controlling Party apparatus. As the individual farms grew in size, so did the number of those that had a sufficient number of Party members in order to form a Primary Party Organization (PPO), which is the smallest organizational unit in the Party.[18] The importance of this extension of control to within the *kolkhoz* should be underlined. Once he had achieved the position of First Secretary of the Central Committee, in September 1953, Khrushchev took the logical next step on this path, by directing attention to the managerial level. Already in the 1930s, Stalin had sent some 20,000 people to the farms, to increase his grip over agriculture, and on this second occasion about 32,000 were sent, most of whom ended up as farm chairmen.[19]

With these two campaigns, the Party's grip inside the *kolkhoz* had been substantially strengthened. It now only remained to perfect the link between the centre and the local level. This, however, would not prove to be so easy. The struggle to find the right format for rural Party organization would last throughout the remainder of Khrushchev's rule.

The first step in this process was to introduce so called Instructor Groups (IGs) at the Machine Tractor Stations (MTSs).[20] The MTSs already had important powers over running matters on the farms, as the latter were not allowed to own major forms of machinery and equipment and were consequently fully dependent on the MTSs for most of their field work. The intention behind the IGs was that they would use that dependence in order to control and monitor *kolkhoz* operations. Political control rather than agronomic advice was thus on the agenda of the 'instructors'. A further important aspect of this change is that it took place at the expense of the Party district committee, the *raikom*, which had previously been in charge of rural affairs. The *raikom* agricultural department was abolished and its officials transferred. All this took place in an attempt to bring Party control 'closer to production'.[21] Simultaneously, an attack was made on the state agricultural bureaucracy, downgrading the All-Union Ministry and abolishing its local branches – once again to the benefit of the MTS system.

The new creation did not fare well though. The focus on political control over minute practical details caused disruptions in production. The recruitment task for the IGs proved overwhelming and the jurisdictional conflicts with the *raikom* added further strain. In 1955, the system came under heavy attack and was saved only after Khrushchev's personal intervention. In 1957, however, the IGs vanished quietly and the following year saw the end of the MTSs altogether.[22]

The second half of Khrushchev's reign was marked by a continued search for the Holy Grail of an optimal administrative set-up, but for our purposes nothing of consequence happened until 1961, when the Ministry of Agriculture was finally dissolved and the Minister – Matskevich – removed. In the following year, another radical change occurred, introducing a total of 960 Territiorial Production Administrations (TPAs), in lieu of the old agricultural bureaucracy. Each of these was responsible for a small number of farms and had a Party committee attached to it, much in the way of the previous MTSs. When the TPAs ran into the same – predictable – trouble as their predecessors, including jurisdictional conflict with the regular Party hierarchy, Khrushchev struck at the latter, abolishing the *raikom* altogether.[23]

Khrushchev never found what he was looking for and once he had been removed almost everything was restored to *status quo ante*, with the exception of the MTS network which had outlived itself for reasons stated above. While the importance of the administrative experience thus lies in what was *not* achieved, i.e. in the failure of finding an optimal administrative set-up, much of the importance of our next factor does lie in precisely those effects which *were* achieved.

Virgin Lands and Political Crops

In the midst of the turbulence that marked the immediate period after Stalin's death, there was one issue which stood out in front of all others, due simply to its strategic importance. This was the question of whether long term agricultural policy should be based on expansion or on 'intensification'. This issue was at the heart of the struggle between Khrushchev and Malenkov and it was particularly burning in view of the substantial shortfalls that marked agricultural production at the time. A growing urban population placed increasing pressure on food production, with an especially rapid increase in the demand for meat, and parallel to this there was a growing need for exports of agricultural produce, in order to earn foreign exchange.

A drive for intensification, which is essentially Soviet shorthand for improved productivity, had been initiated already during the final years of Stalin's rule. The Stalin Plan, which has been mentioned above, had aimed at planting tree shelter belts, in order to control erosion, and at digging canals for irrigation purposes. Then there was Lysenko and the Williams system for crop rotation. These schemes may certainly have left much to be desired, but they did represent an attempt at a new departure, chiefly by aiming at devoting more resources to rural development. It was made quite plain in Malenkov's speech at the memorial ceremony held in Red Square after Stalin's death that a continuation of such measures was on his agenda.[24]

Khrushchev, however, took the opposite stance, arguing on the one hand that there were no funds available for a programme of intensification, and on the other that needs were so pressing that there was simply no time available to rely on land improvement. The only way out was seen by him to lie in bringing more land under cultivation, in order to obtain a rapid increase in output. Whether Khrushchev was right in this judgement, or whether Malenkov's strategy would have been preferable, is a matter that has been subject to some debate.[25] Since, however, we are chiefly interested in what actually happened, and in the associated consequences, that debate need not concern us here.

At first glance there was nothing essentially new about going east to plough up virgin soil. Colonization of Siberia had, for example, been going on since the seventeenth century. What was new was the immense scale and the rapid escalation of the new programme. The first official figure was published in December 1953, calling for half a million hectares to be cultivated. By January it was 13 million, and by August it had been revised again, by over 100 per cent.[26] Actual development, moreover, outstripped even these ambitious goals.[27] By the end of 1954, more than 17 million hectares had been ploughed up and, by the following year, the total had reached almost 30 million. The peak was reached in 1960, when a total of 41.8 million hectares had been added.[28] By then, the limit of the agricultural area in the Soviet Union had been reached. The total sown area increased from 146 million hectares in 1950, to 203 million in 1960, the bulk of which was virgin land. Despite the massive investment in land reclamation that characterized the Brezhnev era, it stands today at no more than 228 million hectares.[29] Another Soviet resource had been exploited to its limit.

There can be little doubt that in terms of simple mobilization, this represented a major achievement. The area brought under cultivation – in but a few years – was equal in size to the entire cultivated area of Canada, or to that of France, West Germany, Belgium and

Scandinavia taken together. In production terms as well, it was an important achievement. The dominant crop in the new lands was grain, over half being spring wheat, and the contribution to total grain production was substantial. On average, Soviet annual grain production increased from 81 million tons in 1949–53, to 131 million in 1960–4. The new lands accounted for between one-third and one-half of that total.[30]

The problems encountered, however, were symptomatic. The great achievement lay in the mobilization of a large amount of resources, in a short period of time. But what happened with those resources once they reached their destination? Who was there to decide on crop selection, on the timing of operations, on the level of mechanization, and on the use of fertilizers and pesticides? Finally, what about investment in infrastructure? All these points illustrate the perhaps most basic of all weaknesses of the Soviet model, namely the inability to achieve efficiency in resource allocation, or precisely that which the Soviets refer to as *intensification*. Local decision making was unthinkable – even the Russian word for it (*samotek*) still has a bad ring – and the compilation of enough information for qualified central decision making was equally out. The programme needed simple rules of thumb, sloganizing if you wish. This is also clearly reflected in what materialized. Crop rotation was neglected and a widespread harmful monoculture was developed.

Not only was it a problem of a lack of information. Adherence to campaigns launched in Moscow became the litmus test of the political reliability of local Party officials charged with policy implementation. It is obviously impossible to pin-point from official sources how this process actually worked, but contemporary fiction gives a stunning account of what *could* happen. How about, for example, the *kolkhoz* chairman who was charged with 'political underestimation of silage', or the meteorological officer who was ordered to work out his weather forecasts in accordance with Party plans for coming agricultural operations – dry and sunny for making hay, etc?[31]

To put it mildly, the costs that resulted from this form of management were considerable. Yields fell rapidly, in some areas even to the point where seed was just barely reproduced. Fields were infested by wild oats and other weeds. The soil was exhausted. Even investment in infrastructure was almost totally neglected, although Kazakh Party officials had issued specific warnings about undertaking such a vast programme without sufficient roads, grain elevators, etc.[32] All opposition was swept away by the tremendous political momentum of the programme.

There were good reasons, however, why these had been Virgin Lands. Soils were poor, weather was highly volatile, infrastructure was seriously underdeveloped, etc. If intended only as a device for buying time, Khrushchev's programme might certainly have been a good idea,[33] but as we know the time thus bought was put to no better use than to postpone the problems. Today, Khrushchev's temporary solution has become a permanent problem. Soviet agriculture has ever since been heavily dependent on grains from these areas and yields have fluctuated greatly, under the influence of extremely variable weather conditions. Instability in agricultural production is one part of the price that is still being paid for time once bought and wasted.

Symptomatically, this 'campaign mode' of agricultural policy was not limited to the new lands. It was rapidly extended into other areas as well. For example, one of the basic ideas behind the massive expansion of grain production in the east was that land should be freed in the western parts of the country. These lands could then be used to grow feed crops, in order to expand livestock production. Of prime importance in this respect was corn, a crop which Khrushchev had dubbed the 'queen of the fields', after a visit to the famed US corn belt. Corn is normally an excellent feed grain and it was no doubt a wise move to expand the area under that crop. Predictably, however, this became yet another 'political' crop. In 1955, Khrushchev proposed to expand the area under corn from 4.2 million hectares to around 30 million by 1960 and, like the Virgin Lands programme, actual results were to outstrip plans. A peak of 36 million hectares was reached in 1962. For 'political' purposes, corn would be sown in areas where it would not have time to grow ears, and would thus be virtually useless for feed. Even Khrushchev himself admitted (at the February 1964 plenum of the Central Committee) that 'Some officials sometimes force *kolkhozy* to plant corn which they cannot profitably grow.'[34]

The very same story can be told for other campaigns as well, under Khrushchev's 'dynamic' leadership. An attack was made on the use of perennial grasses in crop rotation, which led local officials to force 'their' *kolkhozy* to plough up fields of growing clover, in order to score political points. Furthermore, a campaign against the use of fallow had serious consequences in the dry zone, where fallow was needed to preserve moisture.[35] The conclusion is the same. There were certainly sensible ideas behind the reduction of both grasses and fallow – in *some areas*. The system, however, proved incapable of fine tuning. Either all grasses go, or none. The 'campaign' mode of policy has only one gear – full speed ahead, across the board. The lessons drawn from such campaigning would rest as a heavy hand on policy-making after Khrushchev. Doing without major campaigns would certainly remove a number of costly side-effects, but it would also remove the primary effect of offering the centre a powerful policy instrument. The alternative would be a highly characteristic lethargy.

Incentives

While expansion of the cultivated area was seen as a temporary move, in order to bring about a rapid increase in available food supplies, it was no doubt realized that some more permanent changes would also have to be implemented. Once terror had been removed as the basis for agricultural policy, it was necessary to rely on incentives to make the peasants work. This was indeed a neglected area. As we have seen above, during some periods of early Soviet development, peasant survival had been critically dependent on food from the private plots. The task was thus to transform a basically feudal system, to turn serf-like labour in the collective fields into a lucrative and attractive alternative to working the plots.[36]

Changes made were drastic – and expensive. For both grains and livestock products, state procurement prices increased more than sixfold during the period 1952–6.[37] At the same time, a number of other measures, such as tax relief, bonus payments, etc., were undertaken, in order to improve the financial situation of the farms. The results of all these stimuli, however, were meagre. During the period 1950–65, agricultural production in the Soviet Union increased by 70 per cent, but more than *half* of this increase fell within the period 1956–60. On an annual basis, moreover, growth was highest in the first two years of the programme.[38] Average productivity grew by 25 per cent in the years 1950–65, but *all* this growth occured before 1959. The remainder of the growth in output was due to an increase in inputs by a third.[39] The Virgin Lands programme is of obvious importance here.

This incentive policy, however, was not only aimed at the farm level. Measures were also taken to improve the lot of the peasants, most importantly by abolishing the residual nature of *kolkhoz* pay, introducing instead a system of minimum payments based on *sovkhoz* wages. In addition, state delivery quotas for meat were abolished for all peasant households that did not have a cow, and for all others such quotas were reduced. By 1958, all deliveries from the plots were abolished.[40]

All of this meant the starting growth of an inflationary overhang which would later on come to assume dramatic proportions. Parallel with improving incomes, 1953 also saw reductions in consumer prices that in some cases could be substantial. The average reduction was 10 per cent, but in the case of some foodstuffs, prices were cut in half. During 1954, the average discrepancy between official and free market prices reached 34 per cent.[41] During the 1950s, this situation was still in flux, but after the general increase of food prices in 1955, and the rise in meat and dairy products in 1962, the consumer prices of most basic foodstuffs have remained unchanged.[42] Here we have yet another important legacy of the Khrushchev period.

What then is the picture that has transpired from our account so far? Let us bring together the three strands of argument that have been outlined above. The experience from those many administrative reshuffles that earned Khrushchev his epithet of having an 'organizational itch' is surprisingly that of continuity rather than change. Every time a new measure was tried, it was based on the same old principles, only appearing in a new guise – MTS political departments in the 1930s and during the war, MTS Instructor Groups in the 1950s, and TPA Party committees in the early 1960s. All of these were based on bringing control 'close to production'. Agronomic advice was seen as secondary to the need for administrative control.

It deserves to be pointed out, however, that the principle of closeness to production may well have embodied less of a desire for power *per se*, than of a deep distrust that agriculture would function tolerably if left to its own devices. The latter view, of course, departs from the assumption that the politically conditioned structure of Soviet collective agriculture is so contrary to the needs of efficient production, that constant interference by Party officials is simply unavoidable. This view is expressed by Yanov in the following way: 'The *kolkhoz* countryside, an invention of Stalin, the artificial fruit of dictatorship and the result of the destruction of the peasant elite, really cannot be left to its own devices. For it will cease to work (even as badly as it works now) as soon as the club is laid down.'[43]

The Virgin Lands programme illustrates, on the one hand, the preference for more over better, and, on the other the stark contrast between the great ability to *mobilize* and the equally great inability to *utilize*. The real crux of the matter is the apparently insoluble conflict between central control and local decision making. In a world of perfect information this conflict would not exist, but in the real world the problems outlined above are bound to arise, and to be aggravated by the rules governing the behaviour of local officials. None of the administrative reshuffles made by Khrushchev attempted to come to grips with these problems, and as long as they remain unsolved, there can be no real success along the lines of intensification.

The final, and perhaps most serious, problem was the attempt to replace the stick by carrots. In a certain sense, this represented a true policy failure. For incentives to work, there must be both rewards that are linked to effort, and penalties that are linked to inefficiency.

Neither of these materialized on a sufficient scale. With some experimental exceptions, in the form of the *beznaryadnye zvenya*, the 'unassigned links',[44] rewards continued to be awarded according to the traditional system, with all its familiar shortcomings in terms of 'ratchet effects' and suchlike.[45] All in all, the same old system was preserved. It only had an increasing amount of money poured on top of it, and the results were predictable. The carrots were eaten, but little else resulted.

The subtle logic that unites these three strands of policy was the search for an optimal format for some old principles of a policy which would not be questioned. The circle, however, would not square, and this is yet another fact that would rest as a heavy hand on the Brezhnev era. Let us now turn to industrial policy, the experience of which should be somewhat different, since industry has never been considered a 'Party affair' to the same extent as agriculture.[46] As we shall see below, however, the difference is again one of degree rather than of principle.

Industry: The End of Rapid Growth

We saw above that agricultural policy faced an important strategic decision in the choice of expansion versus intensification. When we move to the realm of industrial policy we can find a similarly important decision, only this time in the form of consumer versus producer goods production. Again, the two sides were championed by Khrushchev and Malenkov. The difference between the two cases lies in the rather surprising fact that while in agriculture, it had been Khrushchev's policy that prevailed, in industry the reverse was true. After having defeated Malenkov politically, Khrushchev simply abandoned his own previous stance and took up Malenkov's consumerist programme. Quoting a statement made by Khrushchev in 1964, on the eve of his being ousted, Yanov characterizes this about-face as follows:

> What eleven years previously had sounded in Malenkov's mouth like a manifesto of de-Stalinization, signaling the birth of a concordat with the consumer, and what nine years previously had sounded like the greatest political herecy, 'capitulationism', and even 'a slander on our Party', was now glorified as the newest wisdom of that same Party.[47]

This, however, was not the only major issue in industrial policy. There was also the question of relations between the respective Party and state bureaucracies, an issue which was seen above to have loomed large in agricultural policy as well. One tentative conclusion would thus again be that it was chiefly political rather than economic considerations that determined the actual content of policy making. As we shall see below, various interpretations can be made of the attempt to change course – Yanov in particular is elaborate on this point – but for the time being we shall dwell on policy as it actually unfolded.

One thing that stands out is the heavy concentration on producer goods production. In the period 1940–50, gross output of producer goods grew by a total of 105 per cent, while that of consumer goods increased by only 23 per cent.[48] It was this pattern that Malenkov set out to change. In the original plan for 1951–5, producer goods were to increase by 80 per cent and consumer goods by 65 per cent. After Stalin's death, however, new and considerably more ambitious targets were presented for consumer-goods' production in 1954 and 1955. Parallel with this shift in emphasis, there were also the reductions in retail prices that were mentioned above. For the year 1953, consumer-goods' production actually increased faster than that of producer goods (13 versus 12 per cent according to official figures), but by 1955 the attempt at change had been checked. Although the actual output of consumer goods in 1955 exceeded the original plan, it fell far short of those ambitious targets which had been championed by Malenkov.[49] Soviet economic history does not recognize this brief aberration in relative priorities.[50]

Another development that represents a continuity with the Stalin era, is that of rapid accumulation – the reverse coin of a low consumer goods output. Total investment in the period 1951–5 not only exceeded that of the previous Five Year Plan by 93 per cent. It even surpassed its own given plan target – albeit by a mere 3 per cent. Again the imprint of Malenkov is visible. As investment in 1953 increased by a mere 4 per cent, the achievement for the full 5 years stands out as all the more impressive.[51] This drive was to continue into the sixth plan, covering the period 1956–60, but here something went amiss. Within a year after its adoption, the plan was subjected to revision and would never more be seen.

The background to the changes in economic policy and structure that marked the latter half of the 1950s is of some considerable importance. The decision to revise the plan was taken at the December 1956 plenum of the Central Committee, and here we may yet again be justified in looking for chiefly political rather than economic motives.[52] The opposition attempted to circumscribe Khrushchev's rights to interfere in economic matters, and in February 1957 he struck back with a set of proposals that were adopted by the Supreme Soviet in May. The *sovnarkhoz* system was born.

Sovnarkhozy: A Conservative 'Reform'

The core of the 'reform' was the setting up of a number of regional economic councils – the *sovnarkhozy* – which initially numbered 105. Of these, 70 were in the RSFSR, while 11 of the republics made up single councils of their own. With the exception of those in charge of armaments, chemicals and electricity, representing the most vital sectors of the economy, the old industrial ministries were simultaneously abolished. Each *sovnarkhoz* now commanded all enterprises in its area and was directly responsible to the republican Council of Ministers, by which it was also appointed. The All-Union Gosplan was responsible for overall planning and co-ordination.[53]

The main reason given for this radical change in administrative structure was that of ministerial empire-building, which was accused of obstructing co-ordination and of leading to wasteful duplication of various functions. In particular, uncertainty over material supply forced each ministerial hierarchy to attempt as far as possible to cater to its own needs. The new regional structure – it was hoped – would be better suited to eliminate such waste. This hope, however, was poorly connected with reality. Soviet administrative history has been marked in this respect by a distinct pendulum-like movement. One extreme is *vedomstvennost*, which strictly denotes 'compartmentalization' but also has overtones of bureaucratic vested interests. The other is *mestnichestvo* which can be roughly translated as 'localism'. Khrushchev criticized the old structure for the former, and the latter was what he succeeded in replacing it with.

The problem, as Nove puts it, was that the 'cure was worse than the disease'.[54] True enough, the old system had been wasteful, but the 'reform' did not remove the *cause* of waste, it merely shifted it around. The new councils rapidly developed patterns of behaviour of their own, which produced *mestnichestvo*. Instead of a lack of co-ordination between a relatively small number of industrial ministries, a situation resulted where each of the new councils had little idea of – or care for – what the other 104 councils were up to. Moreover, while it had previously been possible, if need be, to fight out problems of specific enterprises at the ministerial level, under the new system the possibility of such 'protection' was removed. Consequently, local Party control over production strengthened.

This was most pronounced in the case of inputs. Under the ministerial system, the supply of inputs (*snab*) had been concentrated to within each ministry. Under the new system, it was spread between many hands and an enterprise producing several different goods could well end up having a number of different bosses. Most likely, the latter would frequently have conflicting interests. Although the

All-Union Gosplan was supposed to co-ordinate and ensure consistency between supply and production plans, it was precisely here that the weakest link of the new system was to be found. The *sovnarkhozy* were unable to take the place of the ministries, as effective bosses over production. Confusion was aggravated, and the risk of planning failures was correspondingly increased.[55]

Several questions arise in relation to the introduction of the *sovnarkhoz* system, but one looms larger than the others. Did it represent decentralization? The answer to this question was put very pointedly in a 1959 article by Oleg Hoeffding, who argued that the impression of decentralization was merely an optical illusion. Too much emphasis was placed on the abolition of central ministries, and too little on the strengthening of the Gosplan and on the severe limitations that were imposed on the *sovnarkhozy*. In his view, decentralization was 'an inaccurate and misleading summary description of these changes':

> Its administrative aspects apart, the 1957 reform impresses me not as a radical but as an eminently conservative measure, in the sense that it tries to correct various faults in the operation of industry and its structural and locational patterns, not by amending any of the basic institutions and operating principles of the Soviet economic system, as it applies to industry, but by organizational and procedural improvements.[56]

This view obviously agrees well with the underlying assumptions of our presentation, which are made with the benefit of hindsight. Hoeffding argues that the reform was radical only in the sense that it substituted the 'territorial' for the previous 'branch' principle of control over production, but he also holds that this brought tighter control, rather than an increased scope for managerial decision-making, as would have been implied by decentralization. The manager 'has been placed under, possibly, more immediate and intimate supervision by the regional economic councils than the more remote ministries and their *glavki* could provide.'[57] He also substantiates this view by quoting Khrushchev as having praised the 'shrewdness' of an anonymous American commentator who had suggested that the reform was not decentralization but 'transfer of centralism nearer to the immediate production process.'[58]

All in all, the *sovnarkhoz* 'reform' implied nothing new in terms of running the economy. All it did was to dress the same old problems in new guises, and to increase confusion in the process. Nove puts it accurately when he says that it was 'a step in the wrong direction, or at best a step sideways'.[59] That it would not be a lasting reform also seems to have been clear at the time. Nove, for example, wrote that the answer 'seems still to be sought in renewed centralization' and that 'logically a return to economic ministries is probably called for'.[60] Hoeffding wondered 'whether the next version of the organization chart of Soviet industry might not show some reappearance of branch-differentiated verticalism, at the expense of generalized territorialism.'[61] As we know, both these predictions would come true with a vengeance.

So far, our basic argument has been aimed chiefly at demonstrating the absence, during the Khrushchev era, of any such changes in economic policy that might merit the label of 'economic reform'. It is certainly true that many changes did occur, but these we have ascribed either to emergency measures, intended to buy time, or to basically political motives, which will be discussed further in our following chapter. This attitude, however, should definitely not be taken as saying that there was a total absence of any form of *desire* to implement serious reforms of the Stalinist model. On the contrary, under the official surface, a highly interesting awakening was taking place amongst the members of the economics profession. We shall devote the last section of this chapter to an investigation of the nature and fate of their proposals for change.

Prices, Costs, and the Law of Value

The Debate

The challenge for Soviet economists to revise Stalin's economic doctrines that was issued by Suslov and Mikoyan at the twentieth Party Congress focused very much on the Marxian law of value. In the 1920s, there had been a lively debate around the issue of whether that law could be applied to a socialist society, where the category of market exchange had been abolished.[62] As it were, however, Stalin would decide that issue, as he did so many others. Without much ado, he simply stated the law did indeed apply to goods sold for final consumption, but not to goods that were circulating within the state sector, i.e. to what we would call producer goods.[63]

At first glance, such definitional distinctions may perhaps appear somewhat esoteric. Nevertheless, their practical impact on Soviet economic policy has certainly been profound. The reason is very basic: if the law of value does not apply to producer goods, then prices of such goods need not reflect their values and will consequently not be able to provide decision makers with information on relative scarcities. The very essence of the task placed before Soviet economists was thus to undertake a price reform. Their response was swift and a vigorous general discussion ensued. The relation of the law of value to producer-price formation was the topic of three major conferences, held in December 1956, in May 1957, and in January 1958.[64]

One important line of criticism that was voiced in this debate concerned profits and turnover taxes, which theoretically represented the Marxian category of surplus value. Since prices on producer goods included a significantly lower element of taxes and profits than did prices on consumer goods, the former were priced below their value. Moreover, since surplus value was not properly distributed between the different spheres of goods, the relative prices of producer goods did not correspond to their relative values. In sum, both the level and the structure of producer-goods prices were thus seen to deviate from their Marxian values.

Given these distortions, producer-goods prices could obviously not be expected to supply correct information for planners and enterprise managers. Consequently, incorrect choices would be made, regarding inputs as well as outputs. In particular, this was seen to have serious consequences for the choice of labour versus capital. As wage rates would be adjusted to the level of prices on consumer goods, which was relatively too high, there would be an undue substitution of underpriced machinery and materials for overpriced labour.

In addition, it was also held that such distorted prices constituted a poor basis for control and evaluation of enterprise performance. Differences in profits and losses between enterprises were seen to be chiefly related to the rather arbitrary price structure, and not so much to variables that the enterprise could influence. To issue penalties and rewards on such grounds was considered unfair. Since control and evaluation is generally held to be the main function of the Soviet price system, this was a serious critique indeed. Finally, criticisms along similar lines were also voiced regarding the calculation of various macro-economic relationships, such as the relative contributions of different sectors of the economy to national income.

All in all, the general atmosphere was clearly one of openness and frankness about the shortcomings of the traditional system and there can be little doubt that many economists had a long felt need to come out with such criticisms. Morris Bornstein has grouped the resulting reform proposals into three different 'schools'.[65]

The 'traditionalist' school represented a conservative wing of economists who advocated modest and selective adjustments in the structure – but not in the level – of prices. According to them, the traditional system of price formation was basically sound and quite capable of achieving its assigned objectives. As for the relation between price and value, it was recognized that the use of prices as control instruments would at times require deviations between price and value, but neither scarcity nor demand were recognized as determining factors in this respect. According to Bornstein, this was 'not so much a theory of value and price as a set of rules for price-setting practice.'[66]

A somewhat more radical group of economists were those of the 'surplus mark-up' school, who advocated changes in both the level and the structure of producer prices. The core of this approach was to alter the distribution of surplus value, by reducing the level of consumer prices and increasing that of producer prices. In contrast to the 'traditionalists', whom they criticized heavily on this count, the advocates of this school really did seek a new *principle* for price formation, but when it came to the actual formulation of that principle, there was considerable disagreement. Some argued that a mark-up should be made on labour cost, some that it should be made on capital, and a third group argued for a compromise version. The 'mark-up' school did, moreover, share with the 'traditionalists' the view of the problem of value as being basically an *accounting* problem. If prices were to be assigned any allocative function, then deviations between price and value would have to be accepted.

The really radical reform proposals were instead made by the 'opportunity cost' school, the most notable exponents of which were Kantorovich and Novozhilov. Their approach was to use mathematical planning, such as input-output techniques, in order to formulate an optimal plan, from which prices could then be derived. This approach was clearly something very different and quite radical. Not only did it imply recognizing non-labour factors of production as capable of creating value. It was also based on such notoriously bourgeois concepts as scarcity and marginal calculation. It is significant that the proposals of this school were subjected to heavy ideological flak.

With the benefit of hindsight, we can certainly say that most of the efforts that were put into this debate would be in vain, at least as far as actual changes in the system of price formation were concerned. In our discussion below, of economic developments during the Brezhnev era, we shall see that those alleged reform measures which were introduced in 1965 would bear very little imprint of the preceding debate on price reform. At the time, however, the debate did produce two interesting practical manifestations which we shall proceed to review briefly.

Price Revisions

The first of these concerns prices, as they appear on price lists. At the July 1960 plenum of the Central Committee, a call was issued for a revision of industry wholesale prices, to be carried out in 1961–2. In the 1961 Party programme, moreover, it was stated that the 'price system should be continuously improved in conformity with the tasks of communist construction.'[67] The Party was thus clearly committed to some form of action, and a massive effort by economists and statisticians was initiated. The first manifestation of this effort was the 1963 industrial price revision, which Bornstein has termed a 'provisional resolution' of the debate that had been started in 1956.[68]

The crucial feature in this context, as Bornstein goes on to note, is that we are not dealing here with a *reform*, but merely with a *revision*, a *peresmotr tsen* as it was termed in Soviet parlance. As far as the basic principles of price formation went, it was the 'traditionalists' who prevailed. In essence, this stage of the price 'reform' amounted to no more than a recalculation of all prices, in order for them better to reflect the current structure of costs in the different branches of the economy. At the time, this outcome was probably seen by many as no more than a temporary setback. In a 1963 article, for example, Bornstein concluded that the reformers had 'lost this "round" in the controversy over the industrial price system.'[69]

As time wore on, however, such hopes rapidly lost out to reality, as it became evident that a revision was all that there was going to be. By June 1967, work on the revision was completed and, viewed simply in quantitative terms, the outcome was massive. 'Several million' prices had been recalculated and a total of 679 price handbooks were distributed.[70] The new prices took effect in light industry in October 1966 and in January 1967, while heavy industry made the switch in July 1967. The main effect of this gargantuan labour effort was that the major branches of industry became at least nominally profitable and that the spread in profitability rates between different enterprises was reduced.[71] It was a one-shot attempt at providing planners and managers with prices that could convey correct information about relative scarcities. It was, however, something very far removed from a serious reform.

Computopia

The second of our two practical manifestations of the reform discussion concerns the role of economics, in a broad sense. At the outset of this chapter, we indicated that the suppression of both economics and economists was an important ingredient of Stalin's legacy. We have seen how Stalin explicitly reserved for the Party all questions relating to economic policy. The search for a 'Political Economy of Socialism' (PES) that marked the residual development of economic theorizing during this time has been analysed by the Finnish economist Pekka Sutela, in an impressive study of Soviet economic thought.[72] Sutela is certainly not of the opinion that all Soviet economists of the time were reduced to dour commentary and dishonest nonsense, but the main thrust of his presentation of the quality of PES in general is hardly flattering. Sutela's argument can probably be best summed up by his quotation of a contemporary Soviet economist, commenting in 1964 on the role of Stalin: 'His mistaken doctrine condemned economic research into a general, closed and scholastic study of the socialist forms of ownership.'[73] The main importance of this observation concerns the fact that about two decades of training in economics was not merely lost. It was actually devoted to the teaching of techniques and practices that would later on constitute serious obstacles. When the call went out for economists to come to the rescue, there was consequently not much to build upon.

A saving grace could be found in the fact that during the 'difficult' years a number of former economists had gone into hibernation in the considerably less political field of mathematics. When the spring thaw arrived, they were consequently ready to come forward with a fresh alternative, dressed in the guise of mathematical economics. With the establishment, in 1963, of TsEMI, the Central Economic and Mathematical Institute in Moscow, this new school acquired an important institutional framework. Under the auspices of TsEMI, a major research effort was initiated, the purpose of which was to develop mathematical programming techniques that would be capable of acting as a substitute for market forces.[74] The very heading of the new programme – 'System for an Optimally Functioning Economy' (*Sistema Optimalnogo Funktionirovaniya Ekonomiki*), abbreviated SOFE – illustrates the ambitions behind the new programme. Sutela provides the following impression of its initial status:

> The official support given to mathematical economics was spurred by the generous promises economists were making. Balancing plans, drawing up plan variants, unifying the interests of the national economic hierarchy and putting an end to storming – all by mathematical methods – would raise social production by 30 to 50 per cent, according to Kantorovich and Novozhilov. Fedorenko and two other academicians, writing in *Izvestia*, promised that applying cybernetics in the national economy would at least double its rate of development.[75]

SOFE was part and parcel of the general euphoria of a promised 'computopia', a future where supercomputers held out the promise of eventually finding a solution to the problem of how best to introduce a 'visible hand'. As Sutela has shown, however, the outcome did not quite match the ambition:

> It is difficult not to judge SOFE as a failure. It has really not shown what an optimal socialist society might look like. It has certainly not provided for a strategy of transition to such a state, nor has it persuaded Soviet decision-makers of the need and possibility of such a transition. Furthermore, it has not provided us with an economic theory of really existing socialism.[76]

The reasons for the failure of SOFE should probably be sought in theoretical shortcomings as well as in political restrictions imposed from outside. However, as both of these are of a rather technical nature we shall not pursue this argument any further here. Although little can thus be said to have happened in practice, in the form of actual changes in the economy, it still remains a fact that the debate was both open and vigorous. In a 1963 article, commenting on the so-called Liberman proposals, which we shall have reason to return to at great length in Chapter 10 on economic development during the Brezhnev era, Marshall Goldman offered the following description of the general intellectual climate of the time:

> Absent is the use of doctrinal citation and flag waving. In contrast to the average Soviet economic discussion, almost no appeal is made to Marx, Lenin or even Khrushchev for ideological justification. Paeans to the superiority of the Soviet Union over the United States, a prerequisite in almost all past debates, have suddenly disappeared. In what appears to be an attempt to probe the essence of the problem, ideas are left to stand or fall on their own merit.[77]

There are obviously a number of interesting political aspects of this radical change in climate. These shall be the subject of discussion in the next chapter. Before proceeding, however, let us look briefly at the main events that characterized the final years of Khrushchev's reign, in order to see what it was that he left for his successors.

The Final Years

Economic development during the latter part of Khrushchev's reign was marked by the Seven-Year Plan (1959–65), which replaced the defunct sixth Five-Year Plan (1956–60).[78] In overall terms, there was substantial industrial progress during this period,[79] but there were also important shortcomings, which would contribute to the coming change in leadership. Of major importance here was the problem of declining economic growth rates. During 1963 and 1964, officially reported industrial growth fell to below 8 per cent. With the exception of 1933, that was the lowest peacetime figure seen thus far. Due chiefly to poor results in agriculture, national income in 1963 may have grown by no more than 4.2 per cent. The CIA even went on record with claims of no more than 2.5 per cent, which was well below the US growth figure of the time. A similar picture can be seen in terms of the falling rate of accumulation, as investment growth declined from 16 per cent in 1958, to 5 per cent in 1963.[80] Khrushchev's boasts of reaching the conditions of full communism and of catching up and overtaking the United States were becoming increasingly hollow.

In political terms, his greatest liability was the ever more chaotic manifestations of his 'organizational itch'.[81] Gradually, a large number of state committees were created, committees that came to resemble the former ministries but which lacked executive power. Gosplan, which had been split in 1955 and reunited in 1957, was split once again in 1960. In 1962, an All-Union *sovnarkhoz* was created and in 1963, a supreme co-ordinator was added – parallel to the Gosplan – which was given the memorable name of VSNKh. In that same year, a number of the 'regular' *sovnarkhozy* were merged, reducing their total to forty-seven. A number of planning regions were also set up, but in practice their achievements would prove to be rather insignificant. Finally, there was the famed bifurcation of the Party, into an industrial and an agricultural section. All in all, there is good reason to concur with Nove's conclusion, that 'By 1963 no one knew quite where they were, or who was responsible for what.'[82]

The ousting of Khrushchev, in October 1964, should consequently have come as no big surprise, but why did it happen? Where was it that he went wrong? These are certainly important questions, as they focus on the role and nature of opposition to change in the Soviet system, but they can be answered only when we agree on what the objectives may have been of all that activity which characterized the Khrushchev era. So what was it that he tried to achieve? In the eyes of Jerry Hough, Khrushchev's programme was a 'harebrained scheme', and Khrushchev himself a 'tinkering reformer – the man who ... is forever trying to make the existing machinery of government function perfectly in terms of some abstract ideal.'[83] To others he was the last utopian, who actually believed in the power of Marxism-Leninism, and whose boasts and promises should be taken to hold a certain element of sincerity.

A very different view is that of Yanov, who sees something far beyond political tactics: 'It was a formulation of a fundamentally new strategy. It was a philosophical-historical formula, diametrically opposed to the general line and the whole philosophy of Stalinism.'[84] To him, Khrushchev was the reformer, the man who was to take the Soviet Union out of the 'ascetic and isolationist philosophy of Stalinism'. The centrepiece of this reform was to have been the *beznaryadnye zvenya,* and the failure of the link movement is seen as a great tragedy by Yanov, who himself played an important role in it during the 1960s.

What can we make of this? Are the views really irreconcilable? If we subscribe to the view of Khrushchev as an economic reformer, then to what extent and in which sense we can speak of failure becomes an important question. On the one hand it is certainly true that the 1950s represented a new and difficult challenge to the Soviet model. Under Stalin, there had been plenty of resources to mobilize as fuel for the growth machine. Even major planning failures could thus be mitigated, to some extent, by the unplanned flow of labour from the villages. On the other hand, the realization was dawning in the 1950s that available resources were becoming scarcer and would thus have to be put to better use. This sparked the discussions about reform that have been reviewed above, and it also triggered various economic experiments, among them the 'links' in agriculture.

It is certainly a fact that Khrushchev did not manage in any important way to alter the basic functioning of the economic system, but had that really been on his agenda, as is suggested by Yanov? As we have seen above, there was no shortage of proposals for change, indeed in some cases the proposals were even quite radical. However, it was up to Brezhnev and Kosygin to implement these proposals. It may certainly be argued that those alleged reform measures which were to be introduced by Kosygin, in September 1965, were a legacy from Khrushchev and had a momentum of their own. Nevertheless, this tallies poorly with the fact that his successors managed, in all other respects, effectively to purge the system of his imprint. It seems hard to argue that controversy over the nature of economic reform was a major cause for the change in leadership.

However, if we subscribe to the view that much of his 'tinkering' was conditioned by political motives, then a whole different set of questions arises. In this perspective, it is certainly likely that his fall had more to do with simple power struggle than with the performance of the economy *per se.* These questions will be dealt with in the following chapter, on the political aspects of the Khrushchev era.

Conclusion

The many and occasionally drastic reshuffles of the state and Party bureaucracies undoubtedly constitute the most publicized feature of Khrushchev's rule. As we have just seen, some observers have taken all this activity as intended to bring about economic reform. To others, it had chiefly political motives. For the moment, these differences in interpretation will have to remain unresolved, nor will we concern ourselves here with what *might* have happened, if the 'reform' had succeeded. The fact is that it did not, and there were good reasons for this lack of success. Hough's description is fitting, in the sense that the search for an optimal format for policy was seriously constrained by the implicit objectives of the benefits of Party control *per se*. This also agrees well with Hoeffding's labelling of the *sovnarkhozy* as a 'conservative' reform. Whether or not Khrushchev was actually prepared to undertake serious reform, it remains a fact that all measures *actually* undertaken were based on the very same Stalinist principles of bringing control 'close to production'. One would have to search hard indeed in order to find an *economic* rationality behind that principle.

What then were the consequences of Khrushchev's programme? As we have seen above, no change was made in the basic principles of running the economy. Soon after the change in leadership, the old – pre-1957 – administrative structure was restored, even to the point of reinstating the former Minister of Agriculture, Matskevich. In one important sense, however, the programme did leave a firm imprint. In order to overcome current problems it ransomed the future in three particular ways, ranging from the purely political to the purely economic.

First, the previous record of incessant shake-ups forced the new leadership to issue an implicit promise of stability and continuity. In a sense, this promise to the cadres can be seen as the platform on which the new leaders were 'elected'. (The long-run effects of the administrative fossilization that resulted were to be amply documented during the long and increasingly lethargic Brezhnev tenure). *Second*, the Virgin Lands campaign not only extended the total cultivated area to its very limit, thus removing a possible future reserve, but also added a serious susceptibility to weather fluctuations. The consequences of this were also to be clearly felt. *Third*, the reversal of the flow of funds, which aimed to create incentives (especially in agriculture), served to initiate the growth of an inflationary overhang which would come to take on quite drastic proportions. One consequence of the latter is that monetary reform (i.e. a one-shot reduction in the value of the population's cash holdings) would be added to the list of critically necessary ingredients in a future reform package.

Khrushchev's legacy was thus very far from being a blessing. The fundamental structure of the economy had changed little from the days of Stalin, but the tasks placed before it had grown more complicated and the number of available policy options had been seriously reduced. Further organizational reshuffles were out, as was a further expansion of the area under cultivation. Most importantly, the bulk of the economics profession had been lured into a debate about economic reform, notably in the field of price formation, a debate which would produce no lasting imprint and which could thus *de facto* only serve to demoralize the corps of would-be reformers. This was indeed a serious part of the legacy, since, as we shall argue below, a major economic reform without a corresponding price reform is an impossibility. Let us now proceed to look at the Khrushchev era from a perspective of politics – Soviet style.

Chapter seven

The Khrushchev experience

In the previous chapter, we saw how Stalin's death brought to the surface a pressing need to reactivate the economy, which had fallen into serious decline. Activities connected with post-war reconstruction had served to some extent to obscure serious systemic problems, but, at the 1952 Party Congress, these problems could no longer be dismissed. Differences of opinion between the top leaders waiting to take over – notably Khrushchev and Malenkov – came out into the open. In the political sphere, the perceived need for an economic reorientation can be traced in the form of a realization that the Party would have to re-emerge in a leading role. In a sense, the core of Stalin's political legacy can thus be seen to have held the elements of a leadership crisis. As we may recall from our previous discussion, Stalin's consolidation of personal power had meant, essentially, a suppression of the Party as a decision-making apparatus. A realization of this latter fact can also be found in the pages of the Party press of the time.

Khrushchev's principal and possibly unwitting objective was to put the Party back on centre stage, where it could lead and direct activities in the economic sphere. The actual outcome of the latter ambition has been discussed in Chapter 6, where we saw that the economic legacy left by Khrushchev consisted more of a removal of previously available policy options, than of a record of actual changes made in the economic model left by Stalin. This understanding of economic policies during the Khrushchev era leaves us with one highly important question to address – namely, to what extent the failure to achieve seriously needed economic reforms can be traced back to malfunctions in the political sphere. Here we enter a strange land.

From the Kremlinologist's point of view, the Khrushchev years no doubt present serious and intriguing challenges concerning the actual mechanics of the power struggle at the very top. Several eminent Western scholars have also made their mark by investigating precisely this period.[1] We make no attempt here to add to these writings, since a concentration on personal struggles for power would pose questions that lie somewhat outside the main thrust of our argument. Instead, our approach will be structural, aimed at investigating the process by which the Party was brought back in from the cold. This latter ambition has three logical steps.

First we identify some internal forces, latent in the political legacy of Stalin, which served autonomously to produce 'de-Stalinization' and the subsequent resurrection of 'politics' – Soviet style. We shall then proceed to examine how the personal ambitions for power and security, that guided the actions of the players at the top, served to constrain the emergence of a potentially pluralist structure, and thereby blocked the cause of economic reform. Finally, we look at the outcome of these processes as an illustration of the limits to change in the Soviet model, as it emerged under Stalin. Let us start, however, by looking briefly at the political career of the leading actor in the cast.

Khrushchev's Political Career

Nikita Sergeevich Khrushchev was born in 1894. Having been admitted as a member of the Communist Party in 1918, he worked his way up in the Party hierarchy. In 1932-8, he was placed in Moscow, serving as First Secretary of the city and the *oblast* Party committees in 1935-8. After the Great Purge, he was appointed to lead the thoroughly purged Ukrainian Party organization. During the fateful years 1938-49, i.e. during the Second World War and during the post-war drive for Russification, he served as its First Secretary.[2] Having already been appointed to the Politburo in 1939, Khrushchev returned in 1949 to Moscow, which was the real centre of power. He was appointed Secretary to the Central Committee and First Secretary of the Moscow *oblast* committee.

In the struggle for succession that erupted after Stalin's death, Khrushchev's principal opponents were: Malenkov, whom he succeeded as First Secretary of the Party only a few days after Stalin's death; Beria, who was arrested in June and subsequently put to death at Christmas in 1953; and finally, Molotov and Kaganovich, who would both be expelled from the Party Presidium in 1957, together with Malenkov. The latter three would gain notoriety in Soviet parlance as the 'anti-Party group'. In October 1964, Khrushchev himself was in turn forced to retire, but his life was spared. In stark contrast to previous Stalinist practice, he was simply pensioned off.

The change in political climate that had taken place between the execution of Beria and the overthrow of Khrushchev has been strikingly well captured by the unofficial – or 'permittedly dissident' – historian Roy Medvedev, in his biography on Khrushchev. Medvedev does not acknowledge any source, which unfortunately makes the account somewhat apochryphal. However, even if it should only be a matter of Soviet folklore, *si non e vero, e bene trovato*:

> When he arrived home that evening he threw his briefcase in a corner and said, 'Well, that's it. I'm retired now. Perhaps the most important thing I did was just this – that they were able to get rid of me simply by voting, whereas Stalin would have had them all arrested.'[3]

The ups and downs of Khrushchev's tenure as leader have been thoroughly analysed in a number of works. Carl Linden, for example, has used a convincing conflictual approach in order to demonstrate that, in political terms, Khrushchev's reign was a period of transition from a personal to a more anonymous Party rule.[4] What has been documented in almost every analysis of Khrushchev's career is his great ability to change, his skill in adapting to new circumstances. No doubt, one may find strong elements of opportunism here, but the very way in which Khrushchev contributed to his own undoing as a top leader nevertheless betrays a certain goal orientation.

For once, it certainly appears that his de-Stalinization was seriously meant. A case in point is Khrushchev's treatment of the Ukraine. Although he himself had been instrumental, as First Secretary of the Ukrainian Party, in purging and streamlining – i.e. Russifying – the republican Party leadership in the 1930s, he was also responsible for a certain 'rehabilitation' of the Ukrainians both within the Party and in the Soviet Union at large in the immediate post-war years.

The latter process was already discernible in 1949, when the first post-war congress of the Ukrainian Party was held. Here Khrushchev called for a *perestroika* of the republic's industries and co-operatives.[5] It then continued and gathered momentum after Stalin's death. In 1954, on the occasion of the tercentenary celebration of the 1654 Pereiaslav Treaty (when Eastern Ukraine was 'reunited' with Moscow), the Ukrainians were officially hailed as the second 'Great Slav' people of the Soviet Union. Although chiefly intended as an ideological message, this also had an obvious political significance. Accordingly, the support of the Ukrainian leadership would prove to be decisive for Khrushchev's eventual victory over his rivals in the Politburo and in the Central Committee. According to Bohdan Krawchenko, the key to Khrushchev's success was that he, more than any other leader, 'recognized that the new national cadres in the republic had to be given a greater role in running their affairs.'[6]

As the events of 1954 turned out to be a confirmation of what had started already in 1949, the Ukrainian connection serves to underline an important continuity between the late-Stalin and the early-Khrushchev periods. This observation is basic to our understanding of political developments in the Soviet Union during the first two post-war decades, i.e. during the period from the end of the war until Khrushchev's fall from power.

From Stalin to Khrushchev

When speaking of a transition from Stalin to Khrushchev, it has unfortunately been rather common to focus on the death of Stalin as the precise time of transition. What we shall argue here, however, is first of all that we are dealing with a process of several years' duration, rather than with a sudden about-face. In addition, it will also be argued that the Soviet Union before and after the death of Stalin may not have been as *qualitatively* different as is often thought. In order to substantiate these claims, we shall subdivide the process in question into three stages.

In this section of the chapter, we look at the gradual erosion of Stalinist power during the last years of the Great Dictator's life, and at the resulting leadership crisis. This will cover the political legacy of Stalin. Then, in the following section, we will look at the symptoms of the crisis, as they were officially presented at and around the time of Stalin's death, and at the tactics that were used by Khrushchev in his subsequent bid for personal power. This will serve to illustrate the limited sense in which 'politics' came to be reintroduced. Finally, in the third stage, we will argue that the main reason behind the fall of Khrushchev should be sought not in any single 'mistake' *per se*, but rather in the fact that the Party apparatus had become strong enough to counter any attempt by a single leader to amass great personal power.

Erosion of Stalinist Power

The traditional view of the exercise of political power throughout the whole of the Stalinist period was that of a monolithic concentration of power in the hands of Stalin personally. This view, however, has been actively challenged by researchers such as Werner Hahn, William McCagg, and Nils-Erik Rosenfelt. What they have succeeded in demonstrating is that, during the latter years of Stalin's life, the monolithic surface was visibly cracking and a number of different – albeit cautiously expressed – factions emerged. We find it warranted to challenge the still rather widely held view that the Khrushchev regime meant a sudden and profound break with Stalinism. With his attacks on the 'personality cult', and the associated suggestions that a completely new era was dawning, Khrushchev himself must be said to have been instrumental in promoting this view. In this line of reasoning, the secret speech at the twentieth Party Congress, the removal of Stalin's corpse from the Lenin mausoleum, and the adoption of the clearly utopian 1961 Party programme, all form important landmarks. Although the end-product was obviously very different, in the sense that the rules of the game in 1964 had become considerably different from those prevailing under Stalin, the change was neither as sudden nor as profound as Khrushchev would have us believe.

A close scrutiny of Soviet sources has led some Western observers to question the alleged break in 1953. Once our interest is focused instead on the late-Stalin period, with knowledge of what would happen during the Khrushchev period providing necessary hindsight, it transpires that the process of de-Stalinization was rather gradual and, in fact, already took its origin in the late Stalin period. This judgement holds for foreign policy, which will not concern us here,[7] as well as for internal ideological developments.

Parallel with premonitions of renewed terror, such as the 'Leningrad affair' in 1948, and the 'Doctors' Plot' in 1952-3, both of which might seem to indicate that classical Stalinism still reigned supreme, there was also a certain diversity in the ideological sphere, suggesting the existence of a range of different policy options, not the least with respect to economic management. McCagg, for example, has shown how Stalin was forced after the war to deploy some classical 'Western' Marxist-Leninist revolutionary slogans, simply in order to re-establish central political control. During the war, a certain proliferation of power had taken place, e.g. to military and industrial elites, and to the security police. Consequenly, after the war there was once more a perceived need to anchor the regime's ideological legitimacy more firmly in Marxism-Leninism. The latter implied that there did indeed exist certain real differences of principle, which had to be smoothed over with the help of ideology.[8]

In his study on the 1946-53 period, Hahn has shown in meticulous detail what McCagg has demonstrated for the war period, namely that different actors or factions were at work during the last years of Stalin's rule. The following is the final note of Hahn's work:

> I believe that this book demonstrates that even during the dark days of Stalin's vicious and arbitrary personal rule, 'politics' existed in the Soviet Union and that the political struggles were

161

not solely over posts and power but also over ideas and policies. Moreover, I believe that such political struggles and policy differences can be detected and documented from a close study of the process itself. The struggles over ideas and policies documented in this study show that even under Stalin some people in the Soviet establishment were pressing for reform and [that] there has been a certain continuity in the struggle between 'liberals' and 'moderates' on the one hand, and 'conservatives' and 'dogmatists' on the other, through the decades.[9]

Stalin's personal power was not challenged, but the *vozhd* was evidently ailing. In the late 1940s, Grigorii Malenkov and Andrei Zhdanov quite obviously competed for influence over policy-making. After Zhdanov's sudden death in 1948, it was Khrushchev who came to stand against the Malenkov-Beria constellation. (As we may recall, Khrushchev himself had been brought to Moscow from the Ukraine in 1949.) The animosity that marked relations between these two camps became evident to all in their respective speeches to the nineteenth Party Congress, late in 1952. This was the first congress since 1939, and the mere fact that it was summoned could certainly be taken as an indication that politics were going to be made. The economy was in a shambles, and there does not appear to have been any clear programme for remedial action to be taken.

It is certainly likely that Stalin and Malenkov were, at the time, preparing a new Great Purge, of the kind unleashed after the Victors' Congress, back in 1934. With Stalin's death in March 1953, however, the stage was set instead for the ensuing struggle of 1953-5, when first Beria and then Malenkov were outmanoeuvred by Khrushchev.[10] All of this indicates that we may indeed speak of a continuous political struggle among the top leaders. Stalin's death probably turned the tables, as the supreme arbiter disappeared, but the political system as such did not change as abrubtly.

Although we would thus like to stress the existence of different competing factions, with somewhat different implicit platforms, it must also be emphasized that we are not dealing with political opposition in the Western understanding of that concept. For example, the very simple fact that Stalin never made his own personal views publicly known would seem to have effectively precluded the formation of any such opposition. Instead, what we are dealing with is something akin to the 'political forces' that have been repeatedly referred to above. There were certainly differences of opinion, but these could not be articulated and aggregated into explicit political platforms. Everybody, without exception, from the elegant suites of the Politburo (or the Presidium as that body was known after the nineteenth Party Congress) down to the simple peasant huts, knew that nobody was safe from arrest and incarceration, and that it might be fatal to have regular contacts with other people.

Was Khrushchev Really Necessary?

In sum, it may be said that, although there was movement under the ice, the different streams were not able to coalesce. This was the very core of Stalinist power – ruthless and seemingly arbitrary terror was sufficient to suppress all overt signs of political life but not to root out 'politics' as such. Totalitarian state power could be used to manipulate and kill anybody, but it could not make everybody the same. Had Stalin been granted eternal life, Soviet society would probably have died from entropy, leaving the Great Dictator alone in the Kremlin. Had Stalin not died, someone would have had to kill him, simply for Soviet society to survive. With a slight paraphrase of Alec Nove's classic piece *Was Stalin Really Necessary?*,[11] it may be warranted to ask here whether *Khrushchev* was really necessary.

This question concerning Khrushchev's potential 'necessity' is of course in some sense rhetorical. However, this also applies to Nove's original question concerning Stalin. If we interpret the question as to whether or not the actual *physical person* of N. S. Khrushchev was in some sense necessary, in order to deliver the Soviet people from the evils of Stalinism, then we are moving in the murky waters of the role of individuals in history, a topic which we have no desire to address at any length here.[12] Briefly put, if a Malenkov or a Beria had prevailed, the *direction* of change might have been somewhat different, but this does not detract from our basic contention that change as such was latent in Stalin's political legacy. The main point is rather that Khrushchev as a *phenomenon* was indeed necessary, from the simple perspective of survival of the Soviet system. As Hahn and McCagg have shown, there were forces at play under the surface which were no doubt fuelled by such a realization of the need for change. In this sense, Khrushchev was 'born' already some time before Stalin's death, and the process of de-Stalinization as such appears to have been predetermined.

A Changing of the Guard

Revitalizing the Party

The political implications of the death of the physical person Joseph Stalin should be seen against the background of what has just been said about the distinction betwen his personal political power and his personal potential to exercise arbitrary terror against real and perceived political opponents. As long as Stalin was well and alive, nobody would dare to put his head above the balcony, but as soon as this restriction was gone, those political forces which had accumulated under the surface would suddenly burst out into the open. The traditional perception of de-Stalinization as a sudden about-face in Soviet development is in this sense no more than an optical illusion.[13]

Immediately after Stalin's death, some rather important changes took place in the leading State and Party institutions. A Presidium was created above the Council of Ministers, and the Party Presidium (formerly the Politburo) had its membership cut by half. Those who were removed from the new Presidium were the newcomers of Stalin's latter years. The senior members thus reasserted their influence.[14] All of this also meant that the relative political weight of the Party Presidium was strengthened. A supreme leader and a number of 'puppets' were now replaced by a tightly knit political body that incarnated the notion of collective leadership. This reassertion of the central Party apparatus was matched by a campaign in the Party press which was obviously aimed at revitalizing the Party as such and at preparing the ground for its 'comeback' as an active political force in Soviet society.

If we start by looking at the internal state of the Party in 1953, as it was presented in the Party's own ideological organ *Kommunist*, it is rather striking to note a number of almost identical similarities with our previous account of the same presentation in its predecessor *Bolshevik* of 1937. On both occasions, attention was focused on local officials rather than on the top Party leadership. The essentials of the picture are disorder, apathy, and poor leadership, i.e. qualities that would call for purges of the incompetent, those who – according to a previously quoted 1937 Soviet source – did not merit 'the lofty title of Party member'.[15]

According to accounts in *Kommunist*, Party meetings at the lower levels were called irregularly.[16] Such meetings, moreover, would have to be both initiated and supervised by higher Party organs, since local officials could 'hardly take a step without a "direct order" from above.'[17] Agendas were set at the higher levels and included nothing but 'conclusions and decisions' from above, all of which made it impossible for the primary Party organizations to discuss local problems.[18] Lists of speakers were made up in advance, and speakers would deliver previously prepared speeches, in splendid isolation from each other. Such speeches, moreover, would mainly consist of self-assertion and glorification of 'successes'.

In a typically contradictory manner, strongly reminiscent of the 1937 Party election campaign, local Party officials were not only presented as passive and incompetent – as being deaf to the grass roots – but also as actively suppressing criticism and opinions of the Party rank-and-file. The same type of behaviour was ascribed to both primary and *raion* level Party organizations. The power structure was presented as strongly hierarchic, with Party secretaries being ordered from above to decide both which individual committee members would hold speeches and what those speakers would say.[19]

A prime target of critique in *Kommunist* was the *raikom* First Secretary, who was presented as a local despot, ruling a cowed and servile assembly:

> One can still find committee members who forget about their responsibilities to the Party ... who worry only about how to speak in line with the First Secretary. This is incorrect behaviour. Even if deep in their hearts, individual members consider the opinion of the First Secretary to be wrong, they will not say so.[20]

Briefly put, the description of the internal state of the Party that transpires from the pages of *Kommunist* may be summarized as bureaucratic distortions of centralism and as violations of the principles of collective leadership and of Party democracy. The dual aim of the critique found in *Kommunist* can thus be seen as being directed against the Party cadres, who were 'a group of submissive statists',[21] and against the Party secretaries, who were accused of being despotic and self-interested. Both categories consequently merited being purged.

Seen from a tactical point of view, we may also note that the concept of 'criticism from below' again figures prominently. The following understanding can be found in *Kommunist*:

> It is necessary to infuse the Party members with feelings of intolerance towards disorder, failures and neglect. A communist who notices shortcomings must do everything in his power to redress them. We must note that a true communist is activated if he sees shortcomings redressed which he has pointed out, or cadres corrected or removed whom he has criticized, or positive suggestions made by him not only decided upon but also implemented.[22]

A parallel which may be brought out here again concerns the 1937 Party elections, which have been discussed at length above. The tactical set-up is the same, and although the Khrushchev years would very definitely not be marked by purges and bloodshed of the Stalinist kind, this was due to different external circumstances and modes of behaviour rather than to qualitative differences in the 'political' process. As we shall now proceed to argue, the tactics used by Khrushchev in order to make his way to the top were in principle strikingly similar to those used by Stalin in his previous endeavour to purge the Party apparatus of every conceivable form of opposition.

Khrushchev's Way to the Top

The few points regarding Khrushchev's political career that were given above were concerned merely with the outwardly visible signs. On the basis of these observations, one would certainly be tempted to conclude that Khrushchev's way to the top was completed in 1957. In this perspective, three points in time stand out as being of particular importance. In June 1953, Lavrentii Beria was arrested. In 1955, Nikolai Bulganin, at the time a close Khrushchev ally, replaced Malenkov as Prime Minister, and in 1957 the three final remaining Presidium members most closely associated with Stalin, i.e. Malenkov together with Lazar Kaganovich and Vyatcheslav Molotov, were all expelled from that body, although they were not yet excluded from the Party, in spite of the sharp criticism of their respective contributions to Stalinist terror that was voiced at the twenty-second Party Congress in 1961. Molotov was reported to have been expelled from the Party in 1964, and was readmitted only in 1984, not long before his death. These developments in themselves illustrate that the alleged break with Stalinism was, in a certain sense, rather superficial.

The arrest and shooting of Beria no doubt served to trim the powers of the security police, which by then had acquired the subsequently infamous name of KGB, the Committee for State Security (*Komitet Gosudarstvennoi Bezopasnosti*).[23] With Stalin gone, and with its own leader defamed, the KGB could not emerge as an independent political actor, an outcome which certainly must have been feared by the other contenders for power. This meant that the struggle for power would be fought in the internal Party arena, rather than in the cellars of the Lyubyanka prison, the KGB Moscow headquarters. This was an important change in the rules of the game which has apparently been adhered to since that date.

The second point concerns Khrushchev's incomplete victory over Malenkov in 1955. Here the picture is somewhat more complicated. The outer manifestation was the removal of Malenkov from his post as Prime Minister, but at the same time we should note that he remained as both member of the Presidium and as a Deputy Premier of the Council of Ministers.[24] The significance of this event is thus rather that of an important stage in a process. Malenkov was replaced by Bulganin, who would subsequently become an important Khrushchev ally.

The really crucial point, however, concerns the final showdown, in the summer of 1957, between Khrushchev and the final remaining survivors of the Stalin Guard. Here, much in the way of Stalin's previous manoeuvres against the respective left and right wings of the Party, Bulganin and Zhukov were initially recruited as temporary allies in order to expel the anti-Party group. Then, while Bulganin was pensioned off, Zhukov was dismissed as Minister of War, expelled from the Party Presidium and sent on his way to 'another job'. What the latter might have been was not reported at the time.[25] It is also of some considerable importance to note that no blood was shed. Molotov and Malenkov met with their respective natural deaths in 1986 and 1988, and, at the time this is being written, Kaganovich is still alive.

It is, of course, of paramount importance that political struggles can be – and have been – fought without bloodshed. It is, however, also of some considerable importance to note that apart from this humanization of Soviet politics, the rules of the game have remained largely intact, from Stalin via Khrushchev and – as we shall see below – up to the present.

This brings us back to the setting of the stage, in 1953, and to the problem of 'criticism from below'. As in 1937, the problem has two rather contradictory dimensions. On the one hand, we can see from writings in *Kommunist* and *Partiinaya Zhizn*, both important Party journals, how lower-level Party officials were being accused of inactivity. This wave of criticism was once again presented as having such strength that local Party officials would be loath to intervene in debates, for fear of being accused by the rank-and-file of suppressing criticism.[26] On the other hand, however, we can also find simultaneous admonitions of the rank-and-file, who in their turn were told that 'one cannot be liberal with those who abuse Party democracy, and the right to discuss Party affairs in a positive way, for purposes of undermining discipline.'[27]

As in 1953, the years around the all-important twentieth Party Congress, in February-March 1956, were marked by a process of alleged 'democratization'. This time, however, the picture contained a rather novel ingredient, in that emphasis was placed on the rights of higher Party organs to intervene in local level elections.[28] The central feature of this process was that Khrushchev sought to strengthen his own personal power by means of debarring the remainder of the central Party leadership from influence, preferring instead to make the lower echelons his base of power. In order to understand how this could be brought about, it is necessary to remember that the Party's *raison d'être* as the vanguard of society lay in its role as director of the national economy. Khrushchev's policy was to reduce the role of the central state organs – controlled by high-level Party functionaries – in economic policy, and to increase instead the role of territorial Party organs. Carl Linden, who has made a detailed study of this process, has underlined that those who were in opposition to Khrushchev – i.e. the 'anti-Party group' – were opposed to precisely this policy. The opposition, however, was ill prepared. It lost out because Khrushchev could summon, in the Central Committee, 'the support of the middle-level functionaries of the territorial Party organizations'.[29]

A distinctly noticeable feature of the entire period from Stalin's death until the twenty-second Party Congress, in October 1961, was that of a characteristic pendulum movement between 'thaws' and 'frosts', in political as well as in cultural life. Immediately after the Dictator's death there was a brief thaw, which was followed in 1954 by a moderate frost, that lasted until the twentieth Party Congress in 1956. The thaw that was announced at that congress was in its turn interrupted by the Polish and Hungarian events, which caused a new frost. If we look simply at the cultural sphere, an additional mild thaw can be observed with Khrushchev's speech to the Writers' Congress in May 1959, but, if we look at the political sphere, no such thaw can be noticed until 1961.

We will argue here that an important feature of this pendulum movement was that it reflected changes in the relative positions in the power game at the very top. The thaw in 1953 resulted from the fact that none of the main contenders for power seem to have been attracted by the idea of unleashing a new wave of terror and purges, of the kind that may well have been envisaged by Stalin shortly before his death. Beria, the notorious chief of the terror machine, Malenkov, who had been a close collaborator of Stalin in the latter's personal chancellery, and Khrushchev, who had been brought to Moscow by Stalin in 1949, all pleaded for more tolerance (although not using that word) towards non-Russian nationalities, towards consumers, towards peasants and intellectuals. These different categories obviously tended to overlap rather than form distinct groups. The point, however, is that all top leaders acknowledged that there was such a thing as a *society* to care for. The spectre of entropy that had been raised by Stalin and Stalinism was removed. 'Politics' could be brought back in from the cold. This return of politics was a necessary, but as we shall argue in a moment, not a sufficient condition for economic and social reforms.

Once Khrushchev had won the first round, with his promotion to First Secretary of the Central Committee, in September 1953, and with the replacement of Malenkov by Bulganin, in February 1955, there was a pause, a 'frost' or a period of consolidation. The next phase was initiated by Khrushchev's ambition to undermine all his main opponents ideologically, by tainting them (but not himself) with compliance with Stalin's abuses of power. The first step was the secret speech at the twentieth Party Congress. Then a new cultural thaw followed, serving to distance Soviet society still further from Stalinism. The second step was the removal of the anti-Party group, in itself possible only as a result of the conscious cadre policies of Khrushchev. Interestingly, the challenges of the Polish October and the Hungarian uprising in 1956 appear not to have had any major repercussions in Soviet politics. If anything, they seem to have strengthened Khrushchev's hand. The net result of both upheavals was that the Stalinists were removed from power, not only in Poland but also in Hungary. The latter took place in spite of Imre Nagy's defeat and subsequent death, probably at the hands of the Soviets.

Khrushchev's victory in 1956-7 was, however, far from complete. Differences of opinion prevailed within the Presidium, regarding his programme of dismantling the MTS system in agriculture as well as the rate of development of the Soviet chemicals industry. The latter in particular was a major issue in economic policy. The strains were evident in March 1958, when Mikoyan, in support of Khrushchev, criticized some – anonymous – comrades and when Khrushchev removed Bulganin from the premiership, taking over the post for himself. As Linden has shown, Khrushchev did not succeed in scoring a final victory at the twenty-first Party Congress, in January 1959. It is an indication of the strength of the opposition that Vorozhilov – one of the old guard – retained his posts as member of the Presidium and as the formal Head of State (Chairman of the Supreme Soviet). In the following two years, Khrushchev's opponents in the Presidium managed to keep their positions and to block potential reforms. Notable among those openly critical of Khrushchev was Mikhail Suslov, the Party's chief ideologist.[30] The latter had become a full member of the Presidium in 1955 and would remain in the Politburo until his death as an octogenarian in early 1982.

While the victory over the 'anti-Party group' in 1957 must certainly be regarded as a crucial stepping-stone in Khrushchev's consolidation of power, the resistance that was offered to him at the 1959 Party Congress indicated that he had by no means the same sort of power as Stalin once had. Since Khrushchev had placed high stakes on a successful foreign policy as a weapon against internal opposition, the U-2 incident in May 1960 did not exactly strengthen his position. When we speak of 'Khrushchev in power' this means that there were no constitutional or formal restraints to his exercise of power in 1958-64, when he was both Party First Secretary and Premier. The political system worked very much in the same way as it had under Lenin and Stalin. The main, and crucial, differences were that Khrushchev was unable to rely on the unique charisma of Lenin – the Father of the Party – as this charisma could (and would) be bestowed on any Party chief. Moreover, he was unable to completely crush all oppositional political forces, since he chose to refrain from terror and political murder on a mass scale.

Khrushchev in Power

The distinguishing feature of the period that followed the defeat of the 'anti-Party group' and the retirement of Bulganin is that Khrushchev seemed to be in control at the top. This meant that he could afford to be less concerned with Party politics, and instead place more emphasis on the economy and the 'societal arena' at large. By means of a conscious policy of recruiting as Party members increased numbers of workers and peasants (who were said to have become strongly under-represented in the Party ranks), Khrushchev sought to make the Party a better reflection of Soviet society.[31] In 1957, 17.3 per cent of the Party members were registered as 'peasants', 32.0 per cent as 'blue-collar workers' and 50.7 per cent as 'white-collar workers', half of the latter being 'specialists'.[32] In 1964, at the end of the Khrushchev period, the peasants accounted for 16.5 per cent, the blue-collar workers for 37.3 per cent and the white-collar workers for 46.2 per cent of the Party membership.[33] These figures should be compared to census data for 1959, showing 31.4 per cent peasants and 68.3 per cent blue- and white-collar workers in the population as a whole.[34] Of the latter, 48.2 per cent were blue- and 20.1 per cent white-collar.[35]

We may thus conclude that in 1957, white-collar workers, accounting for no more than a fifth of the country's total population, made up half of the Party membership, and that the change in the period until 1964 was hardly significant, especially if one takes into account that total Party membership increased from 7.5 million in 1957, to 11.0 million in 1964.[36] These developments were paralleled by Khrushchev's attempt to have the Party eclipse the central state apparatus as manager of the economy, a process which reached its climax with the 'bifurcation' of the Party in 1962. The change in composition of Party membership was certainly not sufficient to draw any conclusion about 'democratization' of the Party, in the sense that the vanguard should have become less of an elite. Nor does it warrant concluding that it had been made more representative of the population's overall demographic pattern.

The reality that faced Khrushchev in the societal arena was very much linked to the question of expectations. As we have seen in the previous chapter, a major difference between the respective stances of Malenkov and Khrushchev in the economic sphere concerned the former's very strong emphasis on the need to increase consumer goods production. We have also seen, moreover, how after his victory Khrushchev would take over that programme. Thus, it ought not to be controversial to assume that considerable expectations for the future had been instilled amongst the population. No doubt, such expectations were fuelled by the boasts of catching up and overtaking the United States, which has also been presented in the preceding chapter. As reality unfolded, however, it became increasingly evident that these expectations would be put to shame. A potentially dangerous popular discontent was thus growing, a discontent with which Khrushchev would be forced to deal.

In 1959-62, there erupted a series of disturbances which are perhaps best referred to as 'food riots': in Voronezh in early 1959, in Temir-Tau, Kazakhstan, in 1960, and in Novocherkassk, in June 1962. The event in Voronezh was a strike in the Thaelmann mill, while the Temir-Tau disturbance consisted of strikes by Komsomol 'voluntary workers' in a copper smelting works. Dissatisfaction in the former case concerned poor food in the canteen, and, in the latter, preferential treatment offered to Bulgarian guest workers. Rioting in the latter case was effectively suppressed by the KGB, but – according to eye-witness accounts – only at the price of 'truck-loads of corpses'. In Novocherkassk, the situation was considerably more serious. Here workers took to the streets, in order to demonstrate against price rises on meat and dairy products. They were met by KGB troops in armoured cars. According to one eye-witness, casualties mounted to between 200 and 250. These events made Presidium members Mikoyan and Polyanskii go to Novocherkassk on 3 June, in order to speak to selected workers. In that same evening, Mikoyan spoke over the local radio station, blaming the local authorities for mismanagement of food distribution and political information.[37]

Although there had certainly been uprisings in the labour camps of the GULAG during Stalin's time, the 1959-62 disturbances were qualitatively different, in the sense that they were carried out by 'free' workers. The authorities were thus confronted with spontaneous 'interest articulation', i.e. with primitive political action from below. A worker who took part in the Novocherkassk demonstration, and who was allowed to leave the Soviet Union in the following year, has given the following eye-witness account:

It is difficult for me to evaluate the events in Novocherkassk. ...
However, one thing is evident. Although these events and those in
other towns in the Donetsk area had economic causes, they were
politically meaningful. They were the first organized protests
against the decisions of the powerholders, protests originating in
the masses and above all in the whole of the working class. For the
first time, KGB troops and workers joined battle. ... I believe that
the events in Novocherkassk were useful. They showed that the
Party and the government did not stop at anything, in order to defend their power. However, these events also showed that our
people are unorganized, disunited and lacking in experience on
how to deal with the powers.[38]

Although the Komsomol and worker demonstrations were certainly
not directly concerned with either the political struggle in the top
leadership, or with the thaws in cultural life, they pointed at a similar
phenomenon. Soviet society had returned to life politically. We are
approaching here one of the many pardoxes of Khrushchev, albeit
perhaps not the one most frequently commented upon. The net
result of Khrushchev's years in power was that the foundations of un-
restrained terrorist dictatorship were eroded, at both the top and the
bottom levels of society. After the execution of Beria, as far as we
know, executions have not been part of Soviet political life.

After having been defeated politically in 1957, Malenkov, Molotov, and Kaganovich were not even expelled from the Party.
Moreover, in spite of the harsh repression of the disturbances in Voronezh, Temir-Tau, and Novocherkassk, no mass terror seems even
to have been contemplated. Even if the visit to Novocherkassk by Mikoyan and Polyanskii did not entail any recognition from their side
that the Party leadership had been at fault, their very behaviour was
certainly a far cry from Stalin's method of dealing with his subjects.
As Khrushchev's Party reforms aimed at transforming the Party into
little more than an economic manager, the political implications of
the worker unrest were fairly obvious. With the Party in charge, politics was made possible again. Within limits, of course.

Did Khrushchev Really Matter?

It is an observable fact that Khrushchev did not succeed in implementing any serious measures of economic reform. A question
that remains to be answered, however, is *why* this was so. We have argued above that the process of de-Stalinization, which was unleashed
after Stalin's death, and which gathered considerable momentum
after 1956, was in a sense a necessary condition for reforms to be suc-

cessful. The role of Khrushchev in this process, as we have also argued above, was merely that of an exponent of forces which had accumulated during Stalin's latter years, and which were released at the time of the Dictator's death. It is certainly true that Khrushchev's speech at the twentieth Party Congress served both to deepen and broaden this process, but it was still not he who started it.

The sense in which we have understood the process of de-Stalinization to be *necessary* for economic reform, is that it created the preconditions for introducing both political and economic pluralism in Soviet society. As we have further argued above, however, it was not *sufficient* for reforms to be effective, and this is where the question of Khrushchev's role enters in a more meaningful way. It was characteristic of Khrushchev's leadership style that he used economic policy measures as instruments in the political power struggle (e.g. the many reorganizations of agriculture and the bifurcation of the Party). This certainly was detrimental to the cause of reform, but was it due to Khrushchev as a person; in other words, would another leader have been more successful?

This question obviously borders on that of the role of personality in history, which we have touched on but not discussed above. It does, however, not do so in the same sense. Given the nature of the rules of the game in the political sphere, economics was bound to be subordinated to politics, and thus the question of who is at the top becomes one of degree rather than principle. Khrushchev mattered in the sense that he added flamboyance, turbulence, and unpredictability, to an extent that other possible successors to Stalin perhaps would not have done. In the sense, however, that it was the rules of the game that determined the outcome, one cannot realistically speak here of a profound break with Stalinism.

A sufficient condition for reforms to be effective would have been the introduction of true pluralism, but this would have implied a direct challenge to the Party's leading role, and thus to the associated privileges of its cadres. It is symptomatic, for example, that all questions of rehabilitation and of past political abuse only concerned Party members, rather than the broad masses of workers and peasants. It is equally symptomatic, that in his keynote speech at the celebration of the seventieth anniversary of the alleged October revolution, Gorbachev spoke of 'thousands of Party members' having suffered under Stalin.[39] In this sense, the very structure of Soviet society, and the role of the Party within that structure, served as a formidable obstacle to reform. Pluralism was in this context both an anomaly and an anathema. In this sense, again, Khrushchev did not matter. What did matter was the Party and its cadres.

The Party Rehabilitated

Khrushchev Challenged and Defeated

The twenty-second Party Congress, held in October 1962, reflected quite clearly the resumption of Party politics at the very top, and a consequent redirection of emphasis, from the societal and back to the internal Party arena. From then on, Khrushchev was no longer concerned with mobilizing the population at large, but rather with purging the Party. As in 1937, 1953, and 1956, local-level Party leaders were placed under attack for the very same old faults. There was, however, no recourse to terror. The rules of the game had, in this sense, undergone a serious change. In a way, Khrushchev himself was to benefit from this mitigation, as he was simply forced to retire in 1964, without being put to death or having to commit suicide. But if terror was out of the question, the art of 'scapegoating' and hypocritical blame of selected culprits certainly was not. Consequently, the type of criticism that is brought out in *Kommunist* in early 1961 should by now be rather familiar to the reader. The target of criticism is once again the individual, the 'careerist' who is described in the following way:

> The psychology of the cadre-*cum*-bureaucrat, who has distanced himself from the masses and who considers himself superior, is the psychology of the bourgeoisie, of the careerist who pays no heed to the common interest but is interested simply in holding on, by all means and for as long as possible, to his own position.[40]

A similar outburst can be found in a subsequent issue of *Kommunist:*

> Many people have risen through the ranks who regard management as the only worthy occupation, and who have no desire to work as common cadres. The time has come to tell these seekers after portfolios that important posts are not for life, but for those with the knowledge, skills and capabilities necessary to secure a steady improvement of production, culture and the standards of living.[41]

A distinct novelty in this phase of the struggle against the Party by subsequent would-be dictators was Khrushchev's idea of a 'permanent purge'. In the new Party Statutes, a special clause was included which provided for a continual process of replacement of the cadres. In the fall of 1962, Khrushchev presented his Party reform which, in addition to the agrarian-industrial bifurcation according to the 'production principle', also contained the prescription that 'a certain re-evaluation of leaders should be carried out, a cer-

tain reshuffling, so long as it is possible for them to adapt themselves
to new conditions and to new tasks.' The latter words belonged to
Lenin, quoted from a document which had been conveniently rediscovered and decoded at the time.[42]

The purpose of regular reshuffling was claimed to be that of 'increasing the responsibility of Party leaders, of facilitating a more
attentive and sensitive relation to the workers, and of making them
listen to the voice of the people.'[43] A continuous regeneration of the
Party cadres was said to promote favourable conditions for 'criticism
and self-criticism, for eradicating nepotism and the tendency to cover
up failures and shortcomings, and for breaking up relations of personal dependency'.[44] A certain P. Rodionov, who was a first deputy
director at the Institute of Marxism-Leninism, reported in *Kommunist* that as a result of purges carried out in conjunction with the Party
elections just before and after the twenty-second Party Congress,
about 45 per cent of the members of Party committees at republican
and *oblast* level, and about 40 per cent of those at *raion* level, were replaced.[45]

One may discern in Khrushchev's policies of 1961-2 a clear attempt to weed out any and all potential opposition, to weaken the
Party as a coherent body and to make individual cadres dependent on
the Leader. However, as he failed to tame his rivals in the top leadership, notably Mikhail Suslov, the combined effects of his rather poor
record in foreign policy (e.g. the 1962 Cuban missile crisis and the
steadily deteriorating relations with China), the poor harvests in the
Virgin Lands, and the plans to cut conventional armaments could
not but force him to retreat and resign.

This being the conventional wisdom concerning Khrushchev's
fall, we would again like to distinguish between necessary and sufficient conditions. Each and every one of these mistakes and
shortcomings was certainly sufficient – as a pretext – in order to
topple Khrushchev, but no more than that. A necessary condition
was that a broad section of the Party cadres had turned against him,
and that would certainly not have come about as a result of Khrushchev's stand on various specific issues. Of great importance in this
context was that the Party First Secretary had increasingly come to be
seen as a threat to the security of the cadres.

A New Class?

Already, during Stalin's time, outside observers of the Soviet scene
wrote about a 'new class' that had emerged to rule over the socialist
state. From the inside, Leon Trotsky saw in the rapidly swelling

Soviet bureaucracy a new ruling stratum, which he would not refer to as a 'class' in the Marxist sense. Since there was no individual, inheritable ownership of the means of production, Marxist terminology was not applicable. According to Trotsky, the Stalin regime relied on the security police and on the officer corps, while courting the masses with populist slogans. Using the two French Napoleons as models, he chose instead to speak of a Soviet *bonapartism*.[46]

Since the year which saw the publication of Trotsky's 1937 treatise also witnessed a very thorough purge of the officer corps, it is obvious that this analysis was wide of the mark. There was certainly not any ruling military caste to be found. The shooting of Beria and the subsequently successful taming of both the military (Zhukov) and the KGB, should lead us instead, in our search for a new class, to shift our attention to the Party cadres, the only real remaining pillar of power. It is precisely this that has been done by Milovan Djilas, in his classic study of the role of the Party cadres. In his book *The New Class*, which was published in the West only in 1957, Djilas spoke of the emergence of a new ruling class in the Soviet Union and in other socialist countries.[47]

Like Trotsky, but with greater ingenuity, Djilas focused on the relation between power and property. Where Trotsky had rejected the concept of 'class', because of the absence of individual, inheritable ownership of the means of production, Djilas argued that the New Class 'instinctively feels that national goods are, in fact, its property, and that even the terms "socialist", "social", and "state" property denote a general legal fiction.'[48] The ingenuity of this approach lies in its recognition of the crucial role of power, in the context of the general illegality of the way in which property rights are vested in the collective body known as the New Class.

While power, which is seen by Djilas as the 'quintessence of communism', had originally been perceived as a means, with which to achieve the goal of a utopian transformation of society, power had, precisely by filling this function, gradually become an end in itself. As the building of socialism 'is being completed, it becomes apparent that in communism power has not only been a means but that it has also become the main, if not the sole, end.'[49] Given the connection between 'usurped' power and 'illegal' ownership, it is obvious that to the New Class, any criticism of its 'monopolistic administration of property generates the fear of a possible loss of power.' As a result, it follows that 'the words of the leading group do not correspond to its actions', all of which will have rather unfortunate social consequences: 'The discrepancy between legal and actual conditions continuously results in obscure and abnormal social and economic relationships.'[50]

The latter observation in particular is of great relevance to our perspective of looking at strategic behaviour by individuals, and of examining conflicts between individual and collective rationality. Under 'obscure and abnormal' circumstances it will obviously be rather more difficult to achieve such psychological solutions to the Prisoner's Dilemma that were discussed in the introductory chapter to our study. The questions of moral and social tissue that are involved here will be subject to closer scrutiny in the following chapters.

Ingenious as the approach might have been, however, the notion of a New Class has not succeeded in winning general acceptance as the label on a ruling class, or stratum, in the Soviet Union. Its place has instead been taken by the word *nomenklatura*, which has been used in the 1980s almost as a household term by anyone wishing to discuss Soviet affairs, professionally or not. Originally, this term was used with reference only to the Party's system of controlling appointments to all important positions in Soviet society, be they Party or state, military or civilian. Having been used in Western Sovietology for quite some time,[51] it was popularized by the Soviet expatriate Mikhail Voslensky in the early 1980s, when his book with the same title was published in the West, in Russian and in a number of other languages.[52] The book provides a good summary of much previous research on the political aspects of the Soviet system under Khrushchev and Brezhnev.

Voslensky shares with Trotsky the notion that the police and military leaders are *part of* the New Class. He differs, however, in stressing that the 'class' – the *nomenklatura* – excercises its power with the *help of* the security and military apparatuses. Voslensky notes that a strong repressive apparatus is a must in order for the *nomenklatura* to be able to exert its rule, and that military might is indispensable to safeguard it from any direct or indirect external threat. According to Voslensky's analysis, the *nomenklatura* is an exploiting class which reaps the fruits of the labour of the masses with the help of so-called extra-economic force. What is not needed in order to sustain the police and the military is used for luxury consumption: dachas, limousines, fine foods, and so forth. The ordinary subjects receive no more than necessary for work and survival: cheap but extremely poor quality housing, bread, cabbage, potatoes and, of course, vodka.[53]

According to Voslensky, the key to understanding the rule of the *nomenklatura* lies in a historical analysis of the Soviet system. By explaining the genesis of Soviet society one also explains its structure.

While we would add that the functional processes of and in a certain structure must also be taken into account, we agree with Voslensky's basic observation that Lenin's creation of a guard of dedicated Party revolutionaries, and Stalin's skilful purges and recruitment policies, were necessary preconditions for the emergence of the *nomenklatura*.[54]

As shown in both this chapter and in the previous one on Stalin's political actions, the rank-and-file of the Party had been subject to frequent purges. They can thus hardly be considered part of any ruling class. Instead, Voslensky argues, the real *nomenklatura* consists of about three-quarters of a million people, or, if family members are included, of roughly three million people.[55] It would thus constitute little more than 1 per cent of the Soviet population, which amounted to around 250 million at the end of Khrushchev's rule and to about 285 million in 1987. It was this Party apparatus that had emerged as a New Class, structurally stronger than its own leader, and in practice powerful enough to block all attempts at reforms which might threaten its 'monopolistic administration of property'. The New Class emerged under Stalin, as a Party bureaucracy where the situation of every individual member was precarious indeed. Under Khrushchev, it began to establish itself, and under Brezhnev a real consolidation of its power and privileges would take place. The latter period, however, was a mere confirmation of a trend of development which had started in the Khrushchev period.

Conclusion

'If Khrushchev had not emerged, it would have been necessary to invent him.' This statement may serve to illustrate the main gist of our above argument, concerning the transition from Stalin to Khrushchev. In the late Stalin period, there were clear symptoms of economic problems, social fatigue and cultural sterility in Soviet society. As Nettl has observed, developments 'could easily lead to a completely static society unable to meet the pace of industrialization.'[56] Soviet society tended towards political entropy, but the time was not yet ripe for this final stage. Differences of opinion could be observed in Stalin's closest environment, from the Second World War and until the death of the Dictator. Still, it is symptomatic that none of the contenders for power would lay claims to being Stalin's heir, in the sense that Stalin had done in relation to Lenin. The emergence of Khrushchev was not a sudden bolt out of the blue. It was the logical outcome of a gathering storm.

Khrushchev's right to dictatorial rule was contested throughout by his peers. The writers and artists refused to accept him as an arbiter in cultural matters, in spite of his obvious pretentions in this respect. On a few occasions, workers also dared to challenge the Party state. The de-Stalinization campaigns, which had been especially intense in conjunction with the Party Congresses in 1956 and in 1961, were not causes of political change. They were rather confirmations of the fact that the Soviet Union, at least for the coming quarter of a century, had left the archaic stage of the cult of the leader and was set on a course to a more subtle political system. It was Khrushchev's reign that made Western observers seriously question the totalitarian model as an adequate instrument for analysis of the Soviet political system. Khrushchev's ascendancy in 1953–7 essentially meant a victory for the Party as such.[57] Since he failed to change the whole of the Party apparatus, he never succeeded in acquiring dictatorial power.[58] In short, Khrushchev presided over the period when the Soviet Union became *politicized*. As we shall see in the following chapter, this process was closely connected with a certain *secularization* in the ideological sphere.

Chapter eight

Promoting patriotism: the era of mature Stalinism

In the previous chapter on culture and ideology, we saw how Stalin quite explicitly sought to legitimize his own personal rule by posing as the heir to a deified Lenin and to the old rulers of the Great Russian Empire. Traditions of authoritarian rule were thus imprinted upon the Soviet state, reinforced by notions of Russian supremacy in the multinational state and by a deliberate official comparison between Stalin and the great Tsars, Ivan the Terrible and Peter the Great. A distinctly Russian historical frame of reference gained prominence in Soviet society. In the present chapter, we shall be concerned with the process of transition from this time of vigorous high Stalinism to the subsequent period of Brezhnevian stagnation. It is certainly true that the Khrushchev regime accounts for the bulk of this phase, but since it is our understanding that the really fundamental ideological transition had already taken place before the outbreak of de-Stalinization, we shall be rather brief concerning Khrushchev's years in power. Our main interest shall be devoted to the years 1949–53, which we consider to be the crucial period of maturation of the official ideology. The Khrushchev years will be dealt with merely to examine the nature of the process of apparent 'secularization' of Soviet society. The latter will be done in order to examine what basic conclusions may be drawn, not only about continuities but also about irreversible changes in Soviet ideology during the transition from Stalinism to Brezhnevism.

At first glance, it may seem strange to categorize a period which covers both Stalin's last years and the Khrushchev era as 'the era of mature Stalinism'. It is our belief, however, that a closer examination of actual developments in the ideological sphere during this period does actually warrant such a label. While we have argued in the previous chapter that a certain de-Stalinization was in a sense predetermined for the political sphere, once Stalin was actually dead, and that a 'Khrushchev' – who might of course also have been named

Beria or Malenkov – was in this sense inevitable, we have also seen that there were definite limits to the practical consequences of de-Stalinization. We have witnessed above the re-emergence of the Party apparatus as a political actor, a process which had been in the making already during Stalin's last years, and which had its ultimate triumph with the demise of Khrushchev in 1964. Logically, this was accompanied by corresponding changes in ideology and in scientific and cultural life. The cult of the living leader reached its zenith with the celebrations of Stalin's seventieth anniversary, in December 1949, and in the closing years of Stalin's rule it was increasingly over-shadowed by homages to the Party. In the scholarly field, for example, the notion of Stalin as a single arbiter was paralleled by praise of real scholars, such as the historian A.A. Shakhmatov (who had died in 1920), the latter no doubt serving to allow for a well pre-pared 'thaw' in historiography, that began already in 1953–4.[1] Before proceeding to a more detailed investigation of this important period, however, we look at some of the main ingredients in the ideological legacy of the 1930s.

The Legacy of the 1930s

The famous Soviet scholar, the linguist and semioticist Vyacheslav V. Ivanov has used Mikhail Bulgakov's play *Ivan Vasilevich* to il-lustrate the nature of the Russian framework that was established under Stalin. The play in question was written in the 1930s and is set in Moscow in the 16th century as well as in the 1930s. The Soviet citizen Ivan Vasilevich changes places with Ivan the Terrible. Ivanov underlines that as one epoch is superimposed on the other, similarities as well as dissimilarities emerge. The description of Mos-cow life under Ivan thus sheds new light on life in Moscow under Stalin.[2] For Bulgakov in the 1930s, and for Ivanov in the 1970s, there is an explicit parallel between Ivan and Stalin. It is obvious that the writer – who died in 1940 – as well as the scholar took for granted that their Russian compatriots were equally well able to interpret what happened under Stalin as a kind of recurrent Russian phenomenon.

An implicit, but equally revealing reference to the same parallel can be found in a recent Soviet historical analysis of certain aspects of sixteenth-century Russian history. Soviet historians A.A. Zimin and A.L. Khoroshkevich offer the following description of the condi-tions of cultural life, historiography, literature, and art under Ivan the Terrible:

One can say that there was not a single field of culture, the development of which was not directly subordinated to the orders of the Tsar.'The earthly God' interfered in everything, in material as well as in spiritual matters. The writing of general Russian chronicles was turned into an exclusive matter for the state, to be carried out in the ruler's palace (*v gosudareve dvortse*) .... The Tsar himself participated actively, 'rewriting' history in connection with new political cataclysms.... On the eve of the introduction of the *oprichnina* in Russia, there was one publicist who held complete sway – the Tsar himself.... The actual disappearance of publicism (*publitsistika*) as a genre bears witness to the profound and tragic crisis of the public mind.... The place of brilliant and autonomous works of leading writers is taken by the *vita* of saints, appearing as though written by a single pen and multiplied by the clerks in order to add local actors to the list of all-Russian saints.... In order to 'avoid confusion among the people', due to different patterns of compositions in the icons, the Stoglav assembly (*Stoglavnyi sobor*) decided to introduce icon portrait 'originals' to serve as models.... Such instructions served to standardize the look of the saints and to eradicate the 'self-thinking' of the icon painter, the foundryman, and the carver.[3]

This account highlights precisely those aspects that are familiar from discussions on the characteristic traits of Stalinism. One basic feature is the peculiar symbiosis between the Tsar and the Church, on the one hand, and the General Secretary and the Party, on the other. In both cases, the ruler is in a position to administer harsh punishment of individual members of the respective institutions, but is not able to dismiss the institutions as such. The symbiosis fills the need of bestowing ideological legitimacy on the ruler and of depriving any potential opponent of the possibility to acquire such legitimacy. Our knowledge of Stalinism, of its regimentation of historiography and of its directives on socialist realism and the positive hero in literature, gives the above a familiar ring.

Russian sixteenth century artists may well have believed in divine inspiration, i.e. that they were not painters but transmitters of holyness, but they most probably did not experience any instrumental standardisation of their work. What makes Zimin and Khoroshkevich perceive the instrumental aspect, and interpret the sixteenth-century reality in this way, is doubtless their experience of Soviet reality. Since ideology as a mass phenomenon cannot be transformed overnight, the ideological framework exemplified by Bulgakov, and by Zimin and Khoroshkevich, quite evidently had persisted from the days of Stalin and well into the Brezhnev period.

While Bulgakov's use of the Ivan-Stalin parallel was mythological, however, in the sense of having the same reality appear again and again, the text of the two historians reveals a distinct secularization. Their treatment of Ivan the Terrible, and implicitly of Stalin, is historical rather than mythological. Taken together, these examples may therefore serve to focus our attention on some implicit changes in the ideology.

It has been correctly observed in previous research that one should not be too rash in treating the Stalin period as an ideologically homogeneous whole, from beginning to end. Contrasting early and late Stalinism, both Sheila Fitzpatrick and A. Kemp-Welch have warned against concluding from the rigid totalitarianism that marked the post-war period that regimentation was equally strict in the 1930s. Kemp-Welch summarises his study of the earlier period in the following way:

> Our account of the neglected phase, roughly 1932–6, discloses the institution of an 'order'. This should not be surprising: Stalinism was not simply terror, but became a huge, elaborated system, whose main pillars – those most visible in the thirties – were the ideas, institutions and individuals who constituted it. We identified: the Party organisers in various fields ... ideologists and trouble-shooters ... non-Party authorities in many spheres ... and specialists with professional opinions. There is plenty of evidence that actors in all four of these categories had wills of their own, and they would be miscast if simply seen as puppets manipulated by Stalin behind the scenes.[4]

Kemp-Welch makes two points that are of direct relevance to our presentation. The first is that what we have come to regard as Stalinism in the cultural and ideological sphere was in reality the result of a conscious policy, rather than something automatically inherited from the Russian past. The second maintains that far from being alone in this enterprise, Stalin had at his disposal a number of intellectuals in different spheres of society, willing to contribute to a cultural Russification of the Soviet Union. The process as a whole seems to have been not so much the result of Stalin's personal will and idiosyncrasies as the outcome of the actions of many, in consonance with Stalin's general intentions regarding the legitimation of his power. It was a matter of Russia reasserting itself, via its intelligentsia and with the help of a specific linguistic code. Stalin did not have to issue any specific directives, quite simply because the intellectuals already knew how to express themselves. The purges of the internationalists of the Old Bolshevik generation (the Westernisers) contributed to the development of ideological conformism by removing all independent thinking from the public domain.

The Khrushchev years meant a continuation of certain ideological trends from the late Stalin period, particularly so concerning the basic question of the ideological legitimacy of the regime. During Stalin's last years, the Soviet ideological 'discourse' became increasingly rigid and codified. In spite of the subsequent process of de-Stalinization, the official ideological constructs that were established at this time would remain in force under Khrushchev, as well as under Brezhnev. There did no doubt occur a superficial change after Stalin's death, in the sense that the worst aspects of Russian chauvinism and anti-Semitism were discontinued, but the really basic and profound trends of development, those of the secularization of the cult of the Leader and of the increasing importance of the Party in the ideological realm, had their roots in the late Stalin period.

Soviet Ideology as a 'Skaz'

It is evident that one may speak, during Stalin's last years, of a distinct process of moulding of Soviet ideology, a process which is of crucial importance in the sense that the basic forms and constructs of its final output were to remain largely unchanged up at least until the late 1980s. Official – or officially sanctioned – texts emerged in this process as expressions of an official ideology, designed to convey an official cultural framework, to be transmitted to the population at large and to be digested and acted upon by the Party rank-and-file. By examining the *ideological* output of this process in terms of an official collective identity, we may gain some new insights even when previously known and readily available texts are tapped anew. Our perspective is to regard Soviet texts of the time as expressions of mythology. This entails analysing the structure of the message, rather than the intentions of one or several actors. While recognizing our intellectual debt to previous research in this field, in particular of course to scholars like Barghoorn, Clark, Dunham, Fitzpatrick, and Joravsky, we shall argue that it is fruitful, when probing our special perspective, 'to start again, as far as possible, from the raw material'.[5]

We will interpret different Soviet sources as signs that transmit a certain code. A certain world-view is thus assumed to be inherent in the official language. When language is regarded as a code, the words used are deprived of their ordinary meaning in 'normal' language.[6] We will thus speak of the Soviet code as a 'discourse', i.e. as a language determined by certain particular conditions of production and

interpretation. The former may be represented in established ideological notions and the relative autonomy of the natural language,
neither of which can be entirely dismissed.[7] The latter are 'in the eye
of the beholder', i.e. dependent on the training or indoctrination of
the receiver/interpreter of the text.[8]

A basic conception in the Soviet ideological discourse, as it was
developed under Stalin, is the monolithic unity of the sender and the
receiver. The Party, as the holder of political power, is at one with society, with the people: ' "We" means "the power + the society".'[9]
This monolithic monologue, which includes the receiver in the sender, is directed against an absent Other, i.e. against the enemy who is
not allowed to speak in 'our territory' but against whom 'we' identify
'us'. Since there is no place left for any independent 'reality' to influence this kind of discourse, it in a sense *defines* reality.[10] This,
however, does not preclude a change of role incumbents both 'at
home' (Party leadership) and 'out there' (enemies to be countered).
As the French scholar Philippe Seriot has pointed out, the discourse
is not completely closed to the outside world. On the contrary, it is 'a
space invaded by its Other (*Autre*)', which constructs itself through
this opposition, answering implicitly the discourse of the adversary
without ever allowing this adversary to speak for himself.[11] Or, as
Seriot's colleague Alexandre Bourmeyster has formulated it, the
superficial solipsism of the Soviet discourse means that it exists
through itself and for itself. It does not necessarily convey any information about empirically observable Soviet reality.[12]

Bourmeyster analyses the Soviet discourse as an emanation of a
certain 'tale', or a *skaz*, the point being to indicate the uniting function of a predetermined ideological universe with fixed roles for
different actors and events. The *skaz* beneath the discourse 'becomes
a collective identification sheet for the USSR'. It denotes date of
birth, parenthood, the biography, the *curriculum vitae*, the projects of
the future for the new Soviet people produced by the advanced socialist society.[13] We will focus our attention on the actual message
derived from the fertile soil of the *skaz*, and although we speak of a
Soviet communist *skaz*, which during the years 1949–53 was also established in the vassal states, one must keep in mind that this *skaz* is
of Russian origin.

We shall base our analysis of the emergence of 'mature Stalinism'
on an examination of the contents of the central 'ideological and political journal' of the Communist Party, the journal *Bolshevik*, which
changed name to *Kommunist* in late 1952. It is of great significance
that the period chosen is marked by the transition of the Soviet
Union from being a regional great power to becoming a global superpower. Outwardly, the new identity of the 'socialist system' as a

Soviet-led world power was manifested in the consolidation of control over Eastern Europe, as well as in the worldwide political and military confrontation with the United States. The ideological discourse had to adapt to the post-war political changes, i.e. to the new global role of the Soviet Union and to the domestic reassertion of Party rule.

The ideological message contained in *Bolshevik/Kommunist* in 1949–53 was structured around certain core concepts and themes, such as the Leader, the Party, and Russia. Auxiliary concepts were those of patriotism, cosmopolitanism and imperialism. Central to the whole discourse was a pronounced paternalism, symbolized in a frequent use of the notion of 'up-bringing' (*vospitanie*). The various concepts are closely interrelated in the sources, but for obvious analytical reasons they shall be kept apart here. During the period 1949–53, there was an important change in the sense that the official ideology, whilst remaining metaphysical, was secularized. This was expressed in the fact that the cult of the divine Leader was replaced by reverence for a political organization, the Party. By counterposing these themes, we shall seek to demonstrate how the latter came to eclipse the former.

At the end of the chapter, we shall analyse the highly visible changes in the Soviet cultural landscape which took place during the 'thaws' of Nikita Khrushchev. Since the new signals at that time emanated from the creative intelligentsia, rather than from ideologists in the central Party organs, the focus of our attention will then be shifted to the leading literary journal *Novyi Mir*.

Mature Stalinism

The Divine Leader

In the official commemorative speech on the twenty-fifth anniversary of the death of Lenin, an interesting description of the great Lenin was offered by P.N. Pospelov, editor of *Pravda* in 1940–9 and Director of the Party's Marx-Engels-Lenin Institute in 1949–52. In his speech, Pospelov amalgamated the concepts of Leader, Party, and State in an overtly religious fashion, portraying Lenin as God and Stalin as Christ. He even stated explicitly that Lenin was immortal.

Stalin was hailed as Lenin's brother-in-arms, as the leader and teacher of the Party and the people, as the brilliant strategist of the proletariat, and as the greatest army commander of all times and all peoples.[14] The occasion of the twenty-fifth anniversary of Lenin's death was thus used to pay homage to Stalin. One may note in particular that Lenin and Stalin were described not as simple members of the Party but as its founder and teacher, respectively, and that Lenin was said to have created the Soviet state. One may also note the central role given to the mission of Russia, outside the confines of its own country and its own working class. Stalin was said to have taken an oath to expand both the Party and the state.[15]

On the following anniversary, in 1950, Pospelov said that 'the father of our Soviet revolution' was deceased. He also said that the father was immortal, though not actively interfering in Soviet life: 'if only Lenin had been able to see ...' is an invocation used by Pospelov when he describes paradise on earth, Stalin's Soviet Union. Lenin was said to have founded both the Party and the state, while Stalin was credited with having built the Party and the state together with Lenin, and with having sacredly fulfilled Lenin's last will. The celebration of Stalin's seventieth anniversary, on December 21, 1949, was also prominent in this speech. The concluding words were dedicated to Stalin, not to Lenin: 'Long live our beloved leader, father and teacher, the bright genius of humanity who leads the Soviet people towards the victory of communism, comrade Stalin! (Prolonged applause, changing to ovations. All stand up. In the hall greetings to the honour of I.V. Stalin are shouted.)'[16]

Lenin is now the predecessor who has died, and Stalin the heir who fulfils the mission. Stalin remains Christ, but Lenin is no longer God in Heaven. He is rather John the Baptist. This was the time when the personality cult reached its zenith. It had a distinctly religious character of a very emotional kind, clearly expressed in a description of the septuagenarian in *Bolshevik* by A.N. Poskrebyshev, Stalin's personal secretary from 1930 to at least 1952.[17] The following excerpt is notable not only for its symbolic content, but also for its verbosity, repetitiveness, and sterility, all of which were typical hallmarks of Soviet rhetoric as it developed under Stalin:

> It is of course impossible to record even an approximate number of those facts that bear witness to comrade Stalin's attentive and caring relation to people. The diversity of questions regarding which people turn to comrade Stalin for advice is, however, very telling. The authors of film scenarios ask comrade Stalin for his judgement of their work. Comrade Stalin pays great attention and makes his comments. His revolutionary comrades-in-arms in the Caucasus approach comrade Stalin. He gives them the necessary help. The author of a major work on military history sends it to comrade Stalin for a reaction. After careful scrutiny, comrade Stalin informs the author of his comments and delivers a rich criti-

cism of his mistakes. The personage of comrade Stalin, the wise leader of the peoples, the teacher, the friend of the toilers, is dear and close to the Soviet people and to humble people in the whole world. In songs and literature, in plays and movies, in sculpture and painting, the portrait of comrade Stalin is represented as the greatest man of our time, as the leader and guide of progressive mankind. The love and gratefulness to the great leader and teacher find expression also in the gifts to comrade Stalin from the Soviet people, and the peoples from many countries in the world. From all corners of the world gifts are sent to the Kremlin and comrade Stalin, gifts made with love and skill by the hands of the toilers. Comrade Stalin is a close relative (*blizkim i rodnym chelovekom*) to the toilers of all countries, to humble people in the whole world.... A number of cities in the people's democracies make comrade Stalin their honourary citizen. Comrade Stalin's name is given to streets and squares in the cities of foreign countries.[18]

The Soviet people and the world at large are presented here as children, taught and helped by the benevolent father. One should note that Stalin is described as *rodnoi*, which denotes relationship by blood, carnal bonds. This epithet was used also in slogans to Stalin, shouted at the end of Molotov's address and Malenkov's speech at the nineteenth Party Congress, in 1952.[19] It is both a paternalistic and an overtly religious personality cult, which intrudes into the most intimate sphere of every Soviet subject. Being both Christ (Saviour) and Father, Stalin is no longer anchored in historical tradition. He transcends time. Both Christ and Father are eternal phenomena in human life, since Christ exists forever, and because every child, regardless of all differences, must have a father. Going to this extreme, however, the cult was on the verge of being counter-productive. How could this authority be preserved, once Stalin was dead? What if Christ really should die without being resurrected? What if there was no father at all? Although the sources do not contain any expression of awareness of this potential risk, we can observe during the following years a distinct transformation of the cult of the Leader, a change in the direction of secularization.

Transition

On the 1951 Lenin anniversary, Pospelov labelled the ideas and teachings of Lenin as immortal. Interestingly, however, he also placed great emphasis on a distinctly empirical phenomenon which was of direct relevance for the day, namely Lenin's denunciation of

American imperialism. The lion's share of the speech was devoted to this theme, especially to the role of the United States in the Korean war. Stalin was praised only for his role in the Great Patriotic War. The speech ended with a stress on peace in the whole world and on Leninism as the banner of liberation for all of mankind. At the end of the session 'the Party hymn', *The International,* was sung.[20]

This was a distinctly more mundane and secularised commemoration of Lenin than those of 1949 and 1950. The role of Stalin was considerably less prominent than in the preceding years. The singing of *The International* had not been recorded in Pospelov's previous texts, and its inclusion at this time can certainly be interpreted as a stress on proletarian internationalism, giving the text a political rather than a mythical tinge. While playing down the theme of Russian exclusiveness, the reference to concrete political circumstances established the text in a more specific time and setting than had been the case in the previous years.

In 1952, Pospelov remarked that Lenin had 'left us'. But his immortal teachings remained. Lenin was declared to be 'the beloved leader, father and teacher of the toilers in all the world.' Quoting Stalin's speech on the first anniversary of Lenin's death, in 1925, Pospelov stressed the need to fight internal and external enemies. The struggles against opportunists in the socialist movement and against imperialists attacking and menacing the Soviet state, made up the main theme of the speech. The Party was hailed as the leader and organiser of these struggles and of all the victories. Stalin was declared to have saved mankind in the Great Patriotic War, by means of his political, organizational and strategic genius. The concluding phrases were dedicated to Leninism, to the Party of Lenin and Stalin, and to the invincible Soviet people. Lenin and Stalin were treated on almost equal footing, as master following master, but in the end it was Stalin who came to the forefront.[21]

In 1953, *Kommunist* did not contain any commemorative speech on the anniversary of Lenin's death. The leading article in the first issue was devoted instead to 'The conquering force of the ideas of Leninism'. It began by honouring the anniversary and went on to praise the Party, Marxism-Leninism, and Stalin, and especially the latter's recently published work *Economic Problems of Socialism in the USSR.* The concluding part of the article did not express any cult of either Leader or Party, stressing instead the doctrine of peaceful coexistence with the United States. Stalin was quoted as declaring that war with the United States was not inevitable. It was further stressed that the Soviet Union was prepared to engage in mutually advantageous peaceful economic relations with all countries in the world.[22]

We have here, already before the death of Stalin, a marked secularization of the anniversary of Lenin's death. As is well known, once Stalin was gone, the practice of celebrating Lenin's death would change into celebrations of his birthday. This transfer occurred in 1955,[23] but one may note the absence already in 1953 of a speech by Pospelov in *Kommunist*. At this time, the cult of the Leader as *svyatoi* (implied by choosing the day of Lenin's death as anniversary) and as Father (the living Stalin), was already being played down. Instead, the Party became the focus of adoration. In this way, the Soviet public was being ideologically prepared for the disappearance of Stalin and for the emergence of a faceless Party as leader. It is also noteworthy that the theme of the international policy of the Soviet Union was reiterated, having been prominent already in Pospelov's 1952 speech. The concrete international dimension drew attention to the role of the Soviet state in this world, to everyday concerns.

Denouncing the Cult of the Leader

The Party had never been absent from the Soviet discourse under Stalin. From the point of view of legitimacy of the regime, however, it is significant that, when Stalin died, the theme of Party supremacy was no longer tied exclusively to his person. The ground had been prepared for the explicit denunciation of the personality cult that was to be published in *Kommunist* in the spring of 1953, at the very time when Stalin was placed alongside Lenin in the mausoleum. It was then implied that, although the mummy of Stalin was worthy of adoration, just as that of Lenin, it was not appropriate to deify a living leader. The substitute cult of the Party was promoted already at the height of the Stalin cult. One may find here an incremental development towards a depersonalization of the Leader cult. The Party was increasingly presented as the diligent organizer, teacher, and leader of the people. One reason behind this development might, of course, have been the struggle for power that was associated with Stalin's growing weakness and eventual death. The contenders had a common interest in strengthening the authority of the Party. In this context, however, we are not concerned primarily with the input side of the Soviet discourse but rather with its presumed impression on the Party members and the population.

The leading role of the Party was stressed in *Bolshevik/Kommunist* throughout the investigated period. In one article in early 1949, Stalin's great role in inspiring the Party was mentioned, but it was the Party itself that was praised as the source and bulwark of all that was new, progressive, and communist. It was especially underlined that the Soviet Party was the leading force within the world communist movement and that it would keep its leading role because of its superior experience of political, economic, and ideological struggle to the benefit of the toiling masses.[24] In the same issue of *Bolshevik*, the leading article stressed the Party's role as caretaker of the patriotic traditions of both the Russians and the other peoples of the Soviet Union.[25]

Somewhat later on, Stalin was quoted to the effect that 'the working class regards the Party as the most sacred of all that is sacred (*svyataya svyatykh*)'.[26] Although not a person, the Party is holy. It is unlikely that the metaphor was perceived by the senders, but the receivers, used to age-old Christian traditions and to the recent deification of Lenin, may well have experienced a direct counterpart to the Christian Trinity, with Lenin as the Father in Heaven, Stalin as Christ, and the Party as the Holy Spirit. The point is that even if the parallel was not consciously perceived, there was a structural conceptual basis for the Party to find a legitimate position within the partly inherited and partly newly moulded ideological order of the Soviet state.

Much as God and Christ may inspire anthropomorphic representations in sacral art, Lenin and Stalin naturally did so in Soviet art (cf. the paintings by the two Gerasimovs and by Brodskii). In contrast, both the Holy Spirit and the Party can be said to be abstract and attainable mainly through symbols. The white dove (Picasso's well known picture) was used to represent the Communist Party in its campaigns for peace and the very same bird is the symbol of the Holy Spirit in the Christian tradition. The parallel between the two ideological universes in the late Stalin period is rather obvious.

In April 1950, still in the wake of Stalin's seventieth birthday, a leading article in Bolshevik extolled both the virtues of the Party and the people's trust in it: 'The Soviet people love their Party glowingly, have a limitless confidence in it and are proud of the fact that it is the basic guiding and directing force of the Soviet state. In the Party of the Bolsheviks, the Soviet people see the reason, honour and conscience of our epoch and regard its policy as its own policy, as the vital basis of the Soviet structure.'[27]

At the nineteenth Party Congress, in October 1952, Beria explicitly sought to promote the importance of the Party at the expense of Stalin. He described 'the Communist Party under the leadership of Stalin' as the architect of the victory in 1945, a victory which had previously been ascribed to the genius of Stalin alone.[28] Beria's unprecedented statement may of course be interpreted as an oblique criticism of Stalin.[29] Seen from an ideological rather than a political point of view, however, the importance of the declaration is rather that of preparing the ground for a shift of allegiance from the Leader to the Party.

In his speech at Stalin's bier, in March 1953, Malenkov naturally drew attention to the role of the Party. It had been created and steeled by Lenin and Stalin. It was a 'sacred duty' to strengthen further its monolithic unity in the face of internal and external enemies. This theme was also pursued in an editorial in the same issue of *Kommunist* where Malenkov's address was printed.[30] The role of the Party was further underlined in a subsequent editorial in that same journal. This time the late Stalin was quoted as having been vehemently opposed to the personality cult, and to the associated underestimation of the role of the people and the Party in history. It was underlined that Marx and Engels had led an incessant struggle against the personality cult. Overemphasis of the role of personality in history was seen to be non-materialistic, revealing a false, idealistic conception of history.[31]

In August 1953, *Kommunist* featured a lengthy, unsigned article, entitled 'The People, the Creator of History', which contained an elaborate refutation of the personality cult:

> In our propaganda in recent years there has been a deviation from Marxism-Leninism in the question about the role of the individual (*lichnost*) in history: instead of a correct explanation of the role of the Communist Party as the leading force, propaganda has often lapsed into personality cult, which has led to an underestimation of the role of the Party and its central leadership, and to a reduction in the creative activity of the Party masses and the broad masses of Soviet people.... The personality cult contradicts the principle of collective leadership and has nothing in common with a Marxist-Leninist understanding of the supreme importance of the leading organs and the leading officials.[32]

As noted above, this sharp criticism of the personality cult may be interpreted as an expression of a mutual understanding among those competing for power after Stalin's death that it was a vital common need to bolster the authority of the Party. On the other hand, it could be interpreted as saying that it was not the belief as such – in an actor sent by history – but only the *object* of adoration which had been wrong. In the following issue of *Kommunist*, the personality cult was vehemently attacked by the philosopher F. Konstantinov. An interesting aspect of Konstantinov's criticism is that he managed to combine it with some of the basic tenets of Stalinism, such as conspiracy theories ('capitalist encirclement'), xenophobia, and anti-Semitism. The personality cult was declared to belong to the same class of concepts as 'cosmopolitanism', 'bourgeois objectivism' and 'nationalist deviations', vices that were noticeable in non-Russian Soviet historiography and literature. The main thrust of Konstantinov's attack, however, was that the personality cult had defamed the role of the collective leadership and the role of the Central Committee of the Party.[33]

The message was Stalinism without Stalin, and a collective leadership as the incarnation of the Party. There was no direct criticism of Stalin, far from it. In the following issue of *Kommunist*, the late leader was again quoted as rejecting the personality cult.[34] The pattern of devotion was preserved, as it had been during the transition from Lenin to Stalin, but now the transition was to a faceless collective, to the Central Committee of the Party, rather than to another individual. Since their mummies remained in the mausoleum, neither Lenin nor Stalin was retrospectively secularized, but the contemporary source of authority certainly was. A social organisation, the Party, had become the *vozhd*, the leader.

A spell was broken, and any subsequent attempt to promote a new personality cult would be doomed to fail. Although they certainly made their attempts, neither Khrushchev nor Brezhnev would be successful in such endeavours, and although a smooth propaganda machinery has certainly succeeded in presenting Mikhail Gorbachev with a charismatic aura, the picture is hardly that of a *vozhd*. One is rather led to think of the diligent executive of USSR, Inc. The structure of the original Stalinist *skaz* had remained intact, but as the Party became the Leader, the main hero was depersonalized. Let us turn now from the role of the Party to the role of the state, i.e. to the mission of Russia.

Russia's Mission

Rather than being based on a class perspective, both the cult of the Leader and the subsequent cult of the Party were combined with the concepts of nationalism and *étatisme*. In this sense, the theme of National Bolshevism was continued. It was, however, not a question of non-communist intellectuals 'coming home', but rather of a strong Russian nationalism being actively promoted by the Party ideologists. This nationalism was directed not so much against external adversaries, as the case had been in the 1920s, but rather against internal enemies, against 'bourgeois nationalism' in the non-Russian republics and against 'cosmopolitanism' among the Soviet intelligentsia.

As the theme of 'Russia' and the associated concept of 'Soviet patriotism' were used in combination, with stress being placed on the need for 'upbringing', the ideological universe was one of both heated chauvinism and a pronounced infantilism. We are approaching here an important formative principle in the creation of Soviet Man. In order to demonstrate how this process developed, we shall take a closer look at the output of Party *agitprop* in *Bolshevik/Kommunist*. We will begin by examining how the cult of the divine Leader was combined with the cult of Russia, the Russians and the Russian language.

On the occasion of Stalin's seventieth birthday, Beria devoted part of his homage to the Russians, the leading people:

> In the fraternal family of equal peoples of the USSR, the Russian people is the most advanced (*vydayushchiesya*) nation. The Russian working class, led by the Party of Lenin and Stalin, took upon itself the basic burden of the struggle for the victory of the Great October socialist revolution. In the struggle for the victory of socialist construction, the Russian people formed the vanguard and the point of reference for all the other peoples in the industrialisation of the country, the collectivisation of agriculture, and the construction of socialist life. During the Great Patriotic War, the Russian people, with their clear mind, steadfast character, and sensible endurance, earned universal recognition as the leading force of the Soviet Union among all the peoples of our country. Comrade Stalin remarked in particular that 'the confidence of the Russian people for the Soviet government was the decisive force which guaranteed the historic victory over the enemy of mankind, over fascism.'[35]

One should note that Beria's stress on the Party, and not just on Stalin, was hardly accidental. Of greater relevance in our present context, however, is the fact that Stalin's thesis about the clarity of mind and other such alleged characteristics of the Russians, was also paramount in other ideological materials of the time. A definition of the words that Stalin had used took their origin in Old Russian:

> Take for example such a characteristic of the Russian people as *terpenie* (endurance). In Old Russian, *t'rpeti* (to endure) meant power, to be strong, to withstand; *t'rpenie* meant steadfastness, *t'rpelno* enduring bravely. And exactly courage, steadfastness and endurance constituted the firm, specific trait of the Old Russian people. It was developed under the influence of the conditions of their material, historical life.[36]

Although serfdom and capitalism had tried to instil slavishness in the Russians, the superior qualities of the people had emerged in their struggle against internal oppressors and foreign aggressors.

The Russian people had developed a broad and bold nature (*Shirota i udal russkoi natury*).[37] It should not come as a surprise, therefore, that the Russians must lead, because 'the Russian nation (*natsiya*) was the economically, politically and culturally most developed nation in [Tsarist] Russia.'[38]

The recurrent theme of Russian supremacy, so evident in Beria's 1949 speech in honour of Stalin, also appeared in the form of praise of the Russians from representatives of the smaller peoples. As Party leader of the Ukraine, Khrushchev underlined that Ukrainian culture had been enriched, not by any alleged Western influence, but by the great Russians.[39] In his praise of Stalin on the latter's seventieth birthday, Khrushchev mentioned Stalin's 'patriotic care' for the Belorussians, the Ukrainians, and the Moldavians as the main cause behind the 'reunification' of these peoples with the Soviet Union in 1939–40, but he also underlined that this mission could be fulfilled only thanks to 'the help from the great Russian people'. Paramount in Khrushchev's speech was the assertion that Stalin had made all the peoples of the Soviet Union love one another.[40]

Stalin was also hailed as the main cause for 'the renaissance and national existence' of the Azeri. According to M. Bagirov, Stalin had offered invaluable help in establishing the historical truth about the origins of the Azeri. *In nuce*, this truth was that all peoples except the Russians were historical enemies of the Azeri. In 1828, after the treaty between Russia and Persia, the people was split in two parts, and in 1950, the unhappy part still lived 'under the Persian yoke'. In contrast, the union with Russia had played an exclusively positive role for the Azerbaidzhanian people, because of the influence of the superior Russian culture and revolutionary philosophy. Moreover, the Russian people had given 'us' Lenin, and the Russian proletariat had taught Stalin what it meant to be the leader of the great Party of the working class. Bagirov also underlined that the Russians were the pioneering people in the world, the people who before all others had raised the banner of socialist revolution. Therefore, comrade Stalin brought up the Soviet people in a spirit of gratefulness and reverence for the great Russian people, which was the most advanced nation and the leading force of the USSR.[41]

In early 1949, N. Karotamm, the subsequently purged leader of the Estonian Party, stated that, although the Estonians' friendship with all the peoples in the Soviet Union was increasing, this was true in particular with respect to the great Russian people – even brotherhood with the great Russian people was on the rise. Without the help of the Russian Bolshevik Party, of Stalin, and of the great Russian people, the Estonians would not have been able to build socialism successfully.[42] There was even more to it than this. In 1953, a work on

196

the history of Soviet Estonia was praised in *Kommunist* because it showed the progressiveness of Estonia's incorporation (*prisoedinenie*) with Russia at the beginning of the eighteenth century. This was in the objective historical interest of the Estonian people, which had suffered under the yoke of German, Swedish and Danish occupants. Swedish colonial policy in the late 17th century was said to have been especially harmful to the Estonians, to have caused mass deaths and diminished the population by half, in some parts of the country even by two-thirds.[43] Russian benefaction, however, had started long before that. In the Middle Ages, the culturally superior Kievan Rus had blessed the Baltic peoples by its presence, helping them in their struggle against the Scandinavian occupants, who were heading south and east.[44]

The literature and art of the great Russian people had exerted a very strong influence on writers in the Baltic republics.[45] At the other periphery of the empire, the same was true for Uzbek literature and art, and for the struggle of emancipation among the Uzbeks. The toiling masses in Uzbekistan now studied Russian with love. They knew that this language was the means to cultural advancement and professional education.[46]

An eloquent summary of the theme of Russian supremacy and of the Russian historic mission was given in *Bolshevik*, in an article dedicated to the progressive role of the Soviet state in the building of socialism. This state was no abstract, non-ethnic entity. On the contrary:

> In the process of building communism, the peoples of the USSR are forged still harder around the great Russian people, the most advanced nation among all the nations of the USSR. The leading role of the Russian people guarantees the further growth of all socialist nations and the simultaneous growth of their mutual rapprochement (*sblizhenie*). This is the most important condition for the transition to communism.[47]

The argument about the progressive role of the Russians was carried to extreme in the distinction between 'Russian' and 'foreign' in the history of other peoples. The latter were declared incapable of taking care of themselves, thus having to be saved from foreign invaders by the Russians, who, by implicit definition, can never be either foreign or alien:

> Since ancient times, the peoples of the Ukraine, Belorussia, Moldavia, Pribaltika, Transcaucasia, Central Asia and the Eastern fringes of Russia have united their fate with the Russian people. Oppressed and hampered by foreign occupiers, they could be

saved from extinction and be delivered from perpetual hostile attacks only in union with the Russian people. Even when Tsarism sowed diversion, when they were oppressed and without rights in Tsarist Russia, they were drawn unchangeably to the Russian people.[48]

The argument that the Russians cannot be alien to any people drawn into their orbit could also be phrased in the following way: 'The Russian people united the peoples of our country in the struggle against the common external enemies and against Tsarism and imperialism.'[49]

In accordance with the historically leading role of the Russians, it was also stated that the great Russian nation, headed by the Party of Lenin and Stalin, played the leading role in the struggle for the victory of socialism. The Russian people had won 'the glowing sympathy and love of all the freedom-loving peoples of the world'. The peoples of the Soviet Union knew that they owed their free and happy life to the heroism of the great Russian people. In *Bolshevik*, the opening lines of the Soviet anthem were quoted as proof: 'The indivisible union of free republics was forged for ever by Russia the Great.'[50] It is evident from the statement by another contributor to the same issue of the journal that exactly this was the key note. He stated that the Soviet Union constituted 'a solid union of the peoples of our country lead by the great Russian people.'[51] At the end of the year, another article stated that 'the Soviet Union was created upon the strong basis of confidence for the great Russian people of the peoples formerly oppressed by Tsarism.' The help of the Russian proletariat was necessary to industrialize and develop the culture of the backward nations in Moscow's periphery.[52]

Referring to Stalin, another propagandist explained that many of the other peoples had been so severely suppressed by Tsarism that they would not have been able to develop economically and culturally without the help of the Soviet state and the Russian working class.[53] This argument implies that the Russians were alone in not needing any help, and it conforms to the assertion that Stalin learnt from the Russians what it meant to lead a revolutionary Party. On the other hand, the Russians were the helpers and teachers of the other peoples not only by their example but also because they educated the intelligentsia of all the other peoples of the Soviet Union, making it possible for them to move forward on the road to socialism. The successful spread of the knowledge of Russian was essential in this undertaking. To ignore the great positive role of the superb Russian culture was to be guilty of reactionary nationalism.[54]

The theme of Russian supremacy during the late Stalin period served to carry the ideology of National Bolshevism into the modern era. The theme is remarkable for the total absence of anything smacking of Marxism. Lenin and Stalin come to the foreground, not as Marxists but as Russians (Lenin), or as dignified leaders of the Russian people (Stalin). The core elements of early post-Stalin National Bolshevism were summarized in the last issue of *Kommunist* of 1953:

> The great Russian people is at the head of the Soviet peoples. The fraternal peoples know the invaluable contribution made by their elder brother, the Russian people, in their liberation and in the creation of a happy socialist life. The Russian people is fully entitled to the leading place as the most distinguished (*vydayushchayasya*) nation of all the nations of the Soviet Union. Devotion to the Russian people and a feeling of the most profound love and gratefulness, these bright, enliving emotions that are abundant in the hearts of all the fraternal peoples have deep historical roots. They were strengthened in the hearts of the peoples by ages of common struggle against 'their' oppressors and foreign occupiers. In this struggle, the peoples of Russia always had their true defenders and allies in the Russian people and their progressive politicians. The Russian working class proved to be the most revolutionary in the world. The glorious Communist Party stood out as the leading force in the people's struggle for happiness. The Russian people gave birth to the greatest genius of mankind, Lenin.[55]

The Soviet idea thus was the Russian idea. The theme of the Russians as *Kulturträger*[56] was paramount in official ideological treatises of the time. In practice, it was a handy rationalisation of what is normally known as imperialism and cultural colonialism. The alleged historical mission of the Russians to bring culture to the inferior peoples was particularly prominent when it came to literature and the fine arts. Soviet art was said to be the continuation and development of 'progressive, classical Russian art'.[57] Gorky was quoted as having declared that the classical Russian literature was the most humane and spiritual in the world.[58] Soviet writers were reportedly proud to be the pupils and inheritors of the coryphaei of Russian literature.[59]

The Russian language was also declared superior to all other languages. The year 1949 happened to be the 150th anniversary of Pushkin's birth, and in *Bolshevik* the poet was commemorated as the one who had demonstrated that Russian literature was of global significance, having the right to claim first rank. Since Pushkin had been witness to the Patriotic War of 1812, which brought Russia to the forefront in world history, his appearance in this role was certainly no coincidence. The course of history had made the Russian people the leader of the struggle for national liberation of all the peoples of Europe. Pushkin gave expression not only to the greatness of Russian literature and of the Russian people. In 1825, he had explained that the Russian vernacular language was superior to all other European languages. No wonder then that Pushkin was able to forecast the degeneration of Western European culture and to compare the declining West with 'the inexhaustive power of his motherland'. The commemorative article in *Bolshevik* identified Pushkin strongly with the current Party line, thus making him a champion of the regime:

> Pushkin loved his Russia and the Russian people with filial love, was proud of its heroic history and great historical role, believed in the great future of his country and his people and praised the richness of the Russian popular culture. He was proud of Lomonosov, Peter I, Kutuzov, Pugachev and Razin. He wrote: 'I solemnly swear that I will not for any price change fatherland (*otechestvo*) or have any history other than that of our forefathers'. ... Having learnt to know the cultures of contemporary Europe and America, Pushkin turned to Russia, to the Russian people, with still greater love. Pushkin loved the Russian language glowingly. In the enrichment and development of the Russian language he saw a socio-political task of utmost importance, which he solved successfully. More than that: the creation of a new literary language was regarded by Pushkin as a patriotic task equal to a political revolution.[60]

The Russian vernacular language (*narodnyi russkii yazyk*) was declared to have been developed and brought to perfection not only by Pushkin but also by subsequent Russian writers.[61] Russian literature was progressive and characterized by patriotism, humanism, populism and fidelity to the truth of life. The basic truthfulness of Russian literature had put it in the first place in the world. Gorkii had explained that Russian literature was the pride of the people, representing its major achievement as a people. In its turn, this literature had exerted influence on the Russian people and helped create their national character, which was 'active, energetic and creative, i.e. revolutionary.' Not only Pushkin and Gorkii, but also Tolstoi and Turgenev had praised the Russian language. Turgenev had even forecast the great historical role of a people capable of creating such a language. And Stalin himself had recently underlined that the Russian language had been victorious (*skreshchivalis*) in all confrontations with other languages. The traditions of Russian literature had helped the literature of the other peoples in the Soviet Union to perfection.[62]

The cream of Russian culture, however, was not Pushkin and the Russian writers following in his footsteps, but Leninism, 'the supreme achievement of Russian and world culture'.[63] The diligent Russians had not only produced the best culture in the world. They had also created new material values: 'The infinite spaces of Siberia, the north and the south of Russia have been called to life by the Russian people.'[64] So much for the achievements of the native population of the regions in question. What made the Soviet Union a just undertaking and a Great Power was its Russian identity and legacy. In order to underline this ideological message, an evil enemy had to be identified.

Infantilization

The respective cults of the Leader and of the Party, together with the elevation of Russia, all served as basic instruments of mobilization. Being based on emotional and religious or pseudo-religious beliefs, they were not subject to rational arguments. The irrational aspect was particularly pronounced when it came to the racist dimension of the ideological discourse. Here the blood relationship between the Slavic peoples was underlined, while the Jews were branded as traitors. The deliberate use of anti-Semitism was an obvious case of negative ideological mobilization. As August Bebel once observed, anti-Semitism is the socialism of the stupid.[65] Accordingly, one may characterize Soviet official anti-Semitism as an infantilization of the ideology. This infantilization was further promoted by the very structuring of ideological texts and by the prominent place given to the notion of 'up bringing'. Let us start by investigating Slavic blood mysticism and the situation of the Jews.

Russia and the Jews

An editorial in *Bolshevik* in March 1949 declared that the Party 'sacredly' preserved and developed the best patriotic traditions of the great Russian people and 'other' peoples. This thesis was supported by quoting Molotov from his speech at the 1939 celebration of the October revolution. This was a time when he, a Russian, had replaced the Jew Litvinov as foreign minister. It was also in the wake of the Soviet-Nazi pacts in August and September 1939, and of the ensuing partition of Poland. Here Molotov underlined that the Bolsheviks were not forgetting their blood relationship (*rodstvo*) with their (*svoim*) people. Stalin was also quoted as having urged the Soviet people during the war to defend the gains of the Russian people and the other peoples of the Soviet Union:

> At his performance at the audience in the Kremlin on 24 May 1945, comrade Stalin especially sharply and warmly underlined the decisive importance for the defeat of Hitlerite Germany of the patriotism of the great Russian people, the most exemplary (*vydayushcheisya*) people of all the peoples in the Soviet Union, the leading people among all the peoples of our country.[66]

Two circumstances are prominent in this text: first, that only the Russians are mentioned in their own right, the rest being referred to simply as 'other peoples', and, secondly, that there is a strong current of xenophobia and 'anticosmopolitanism'. Typically, the philosopher B. Kedrov was criticized for underestimating the importance of the great Russian culture by 'forwarding the cosmopolitan thesis that questions of [national] priority are not important in science.' Jewish contributors to *Voprosy Filosofii* (the journal was founded in 1947, on Kedrov's initiative)[67] were castigated for diminishing the importance of the revolutionary traditions of the Russian people for 'the historical development of Russia as the motherland (*rodina*) of Leninism'.

Jewish economists such as Blyumin and Shtein were criticized for playing down and denying outright the autonomy of Russian economic thinking. These and other conspiracies were said to aim at dividing the Soviet people and at destroying the love and confidence of the other peoples for 'their elder brother, the great Russian people'.[68] A special article in the same issue of that journal, which was devoted to a rebuttal of the 'cosmopolitan' economists, ended with the following statement of Russian supremacy:

> The most important task of Soviet economists is to reveal definitely the protrusion of cosmopolitanism into economic science and to demonstrate the genuine history of the development of Russian economic philosophy, which bears witness to the fact that Russian thinkers have been leading in the development of world science and that the Russian people have played an enormous role in the development of world civilisation.[69]

In a fully fledged attack on 'bourgeois cosmopolitanism', in the same issue of *Bolshevik*, the reader was reminded that comrade Stalin had demonstrated that the great Russian people was characterized by remarkable qualities, such as clarity of mind, steadfastness, deliberation, and sensible endurance (*terpenie*). Kedrov was attacked again, with the argument that 'the question of the priority of the leading (*peredovoi*) Russian science, Soviet science, was a vital question for the Soviet people and the socialist state.'[70] This line of reasoning was basic to the whole period under investigation. These were days when a Soviet physicist had to refer to Einstein as *Odnokamen* (one-stone).[71] In 1951, a historian noted that 'bourgeois-objectivist and cosmopolitan views' had become current among Soviet historians. This had found expression in homage to the foreign (*preklonenie pered inostranshchinoi*) and denial of the role of the Russian people.[72]

The blatant anti-Semitism that marked the Russian nationalistic campaign at the end of Stalin's rule is well known. It is of ideological importance to note that the campaign tapped vital, not to say virulent, emotions among the Russian people. De Jonge has given the following eloquent expression to what was happening:

> This was a time when persons of Jewish appearance found it prudent to avoid walking past beer halls, regular danger spots where they ran the risk of being beaten to death by patriotic drunks as the militia looked on in amused detachment. There were numerous cases of Jewish children, often of eminent parents, being beaten up at school.... The Russians' natural love of Jew baiting was given fuller rein in the last months of Stalin's life than at any time since the heady days of Nicholas II, when Jewish blood flowed freely in the gutters of small towns in southern Russia and the Ukraine.[73]

Intermittently, Soviet patriotism was contrasted with cosmopolitanism. An eloquent example of the combination of patriotism and anti-cosmopolitanism is a defence of Soviet patriotism in art and literature in early 1949. A certain F. Golovchenko castigated 'clanless' (*bezrodnye*) cosmopolitans in Soviet cultural life, listing a number of Jewish sounding names such as Yuzovskii and Altman. (Regarding a certain Kholodov, Golovchenko added in brackets 'Meyerovich', lest anyone should miss the message.) These people, according to Golovchenko, had slandered Russian culture, knelt to foreign, bourgeois culture and were notoriously lacking in feelings of Soviet national proudness and patriotism. He further declared that the time was ripe for 'annihilation (*razgromit*) of the anti-patriotic group of cosmopolitan critics'.[74]

As is well known, the theme of anti-cosmopolitanism reached its climax with the so-called Doctors' Plot, in early 1953. Here no bones were made about the Jewish nationality of the suspects, who were declared to be agents of 'the international Jewish bourgeois nationalist organisation "Joint" '.[75] Thus anti-Semitism can be said to have been at the core of Soviet patriotism. It should be stressed that both Soviet patriotism and anti-Semitism had their respective bases in a vehement xenophobia.[76]

Upbringing of the People

The chief aim of the means of mobilization that were mentioned above was to enhance 'Soviet patriotism', the latter being a recurrent theme in all major ideological texts in 1949–53. Soviet patriotism meant 'moral and political unity of Soviet society', being the 'powerful moving force' of that same society.[77] This patriotism was no doubt useful when references were made to the country's military capability. The concept was intimately united with 'proletarian internationalism', in the sense that the interests of Soviet patriots were common with those of all peoples that struggle for peace, democracy, and a bright future.[78] Soviet patriotism was not, however, something that was expected to grow naturally. Time and again editorials and writers in *Bolshevik/Kommunist* underlined the necessity of educating (*vospityvat*) the population. It was the task of the Party to educate the people in Soviet patriotism, in anti-nationalism (with respect to non-Russian nations) and in anti-cosmopolitanism. It must be underlined that education to hate was a central feature of this process. Devotion to the Socialist Motherland was understood to imply hatred towards the capitalist world and its culture.[79]

The recurrent theme of education can be seen as an expression of paternalism on behalf of the Party, and the implication was a profound infantilization of the Soviet people. Michel Heller argues that this was a necessary consequence of the Bolshevik ideology.[80] Leaving the question of necessity aside, one may at the very least conclude that his argument is empirically corroborated by materials in *Bolshevik/Kommunist* in the later Stalin years. It should be evident from quotations made in this chapter that the intellectual level of what was written in *Bolshevik/Kommunist*, and in other Soviet mass media at the time, was incredibly low. The ideology of mature Stalinism differs from the original National Bolshevism of the 1920s in the sense that it offered neither intellectual satisfaction nor visions of any kind. Although it is fairly certain that everyone who has been exposed to official Soviet texts of the time must have been struck by the massive idiocy of their contents, it has apparently not been *comme il faut* to give due attention to the fact in Western scholarship. Consequently, many people have been led to believe that Stalinist stupidities were confined to more well known fields, such as genetics and cybernetics. In order to stress the importance of this point, we shall refer to a recent Soviet evaluation of the phenomenon.

In early 1988, Boris Pasternak's novel *Doctor Zhivago* was finally published in the Soviet Union. Significantly, the publication occurred in *Novyi Mir*, and the event was widely discussed in the Soviet press. In an exchange of views in *Literaturnaya Gazeta*, the literary critic E. Starikova claimed that the novel had been prepared for publication already before the twentieth Party Congress, in 1956.[81] This implies that it must have been written during the period of what we have referred to above as mature Stalinism. It is highly interesting, in this context, to note a further contribution – where the literary critic G. Gachev comments on the novel's leading villain, the archetypal Bolshevik Strelnikov. According to Gachev, the emancipation of the serfs, in 1861, had given Russia a fresh start, but since then:

> As if envious of the reason of its inhabitants, the state rushed to play boss (*khozyainichat*) and to keep the sedate husband – the people – in eternal infancy (*v vechnykh nedoroslyakh*), pouring out slogans. Such a clever leader, who brandished the sword and the whip, was Strelnikov. He was an adolescent rising from the ranks of the workers; his mind quickly turned to death: he meddled in the living life, intending to transform it by force, according to theory, being himself emotionally underdeveloped (the hailed asceticism of the revolutionaries) and unable to see the richness of Being.[82]

The important point here is that Gachev praised Pasternak for his portrayal of the Bolshevik hero of the Civil War as infantilized and emotionally immature, the hero in question being a stereotype that was current in the early 1950s. Although Strelnikov of the novel committed suicide, it was the Strelnikovs in general who had won the Civil War, to become the new ruling caste under Stalin. Or, as a third contributor to the debate on *Doctor Zhivago*, the philosopher Arsenii Gulyga, observed: 'Stalin and the [fateful] year 1937 were but the consequences of more profound, earlier circumstances. The causes of our misfortunes are to be found in the Civil War. Exactly then began the great tragedy of our people, the self-annihilation.'[83]

It seems appropriate to end this comment on the infantile aspects of mature Stalinism by quoting de Jonge's verdict over the 'debate' on linguistics that was introduced in 1952 by a treatise of Stalin on the long since dead Soviet charlatan N. Ya. Marr:

> The fact that Stalin's idiotic ramblings were acclaimed by no fewer than eight professors of linguistics who published panegyrics in the same issue of *Pravda* is a miserable indication of the regime's reduction of every field of human endeavour to the crudest

thuggery. The Soviet Union was no place in which to profess anything but boundless admiration for the emperor's new clothes.[84]

De Jonge's conclusion is correct as far as the level of official ideology is concerned. Such 'pluralism' and sophistication that was displayed by some Soviet scholars in academic journals was rather esoteric and certainly quite incomprehensible for the Party rank-and-file, as well as for the masses under 'education'.[85]

The Soviet Union under Stalin has been compared to both barracks and labour camps,[86] and in some respects it certainly was a camp with barracks. In certain other respects, however, it was also the biggest nursery in the world. Outside the Party leadership, which acted as 'teachers', and the security police, which administered harsh punishments, there were practically no real adults in Soviet society of the time. In so far as the process of infantilization was successful, leaving a lasting imprint on the Soviet mind, we are approaching here a central cause of the Soviet 'crises' of the latter decades. There are obvious limits to the capabilities of infants to run a modern industrial economy, not to speak of a post-industrial society.

Secularization

In the late Stalin and the early post-Stalin periods, the Soviet *skaz* was structured so as to suggest a stable ideological universe with Moscow at its centre. By allowing the Party to eclipse the Leader as hero, the stage was set for Khrushchev's subsequent drive for 'secularization'. The themes of excessive Russian nationalism and of the need to fight particular, chosen enemies – Jews and Americans – soon turned out to be epiphenomena, as they would be softened substantially already in the period 1953–6. Not the least important for ideological developments was the revitalization of cultural life. Subdued and isolated notions that had been held by a few intellectuals under Stalin could now be openly published in journals of fairly wide circulation, addressing intellectuals in general rather than a few specialists in chosen, strictly segmented scientific areas.

The rather sudden and swift revival that marked cultural life can be taken as an indication that the ground had been well prepared in advance, during the late Stalin period. Again we thus meet with the fact that the change was not of Khrushchev's personal making. It might equally well have been accompanied by Beria or by Malenkov.[87] An obvious effect of the blossoming of Soviet cultural life under Khrushchev was to make the established *skaz* seem obsolete by suggesting polyphony also in the ideological sphere. We will highlight this aspect of ideological life in a broader sense in the Soviet Union under Khrushchev.

Whereas Stalin's activities during the 1930s, in the ideological sphere and in cultural life in general, had aimed at transforming the intellectuals into submissive instruments of the central Party propaganda apparatus, the initial lack of emphasis on the cult of the Leader and the associated neglect of ritualistic public behaviour in 1953, paved the way for a more polyphonic, in a way 'secularized', cultural life. As a result, there emerged in the Soviet Union a modern counterpart to the intelligentsia of old Russia. Although newspapers and journals remained subject to Party control and censorship, writers and other intellectuals could publish articles with highly different ideological implications. They were able to act in this role as the conscience of the nation and to criticize, if not the Party leadership, then at least certain shortcomings and dark sides in society. This meant that the mass media at times, albeit to a limited degree, became 'dissonant', thus adding a peculiar pluralism to the previously strictly regimented Soviet public ideological life.

A central role in the ideological secularization that took place during the respective 'thaws' of 1953–4 and of 1960–2 was played by the literary journal *Novyi Mir*. During both periods, the editor-in-chief was Aleksandr Tvardovskii, who had been appointed to the post already in 1950, under Stalin. The corpse of the late dictator had hardly cooled when Tvardovskii began publishing materials that challenged Stalinist orthodoxy. In the June 1953 issue, he printed a poem of his own, castigating Stalinist norms for Party-minded literature. Tvardovskii's criticism was not merely of an esthetic nature. He also analysed the fateful moral consequences of the so called *zhdanovshchina*, when writers had had to publish lies in order to survive. In the December issue of the same year, Tvardovskii published an essay by Vladimir Pomerants, about the necessity of straightforwardness in literature, and during the following spring, three further essays in the same vein were printed, by Mikhail Lifshits, Fedor Abramov, and Mark Shcheglov. All four of these writers stood up for such notions as honour, honesty, and integrity, rejecting the view that the Party should have a prerogative in deciding what should be considered true, right, and real.

The main ambition of this form of criticism was an attempt to restore private responsibility, and hence to promote polyphony in the cultural realm. Predictably, conservative forces in the Party leadership reacted strongly against these heresies. Khrushchev initially chose to side with the conservatives, apparently as a tactical retreat in face of the showdown with Kaganovich, Malenkov, and Molotov. Once the latter had been ousted, in mid-1957, cultural life was again liberalized. Tvardovskii, who had been forced to retreat from his post in 1954, was able to return in 1958. He did not stand alone, but his journal came to symbolize the cultural 'thaw', i.e. the liberalization of cultural life and the secularization of ideology. In *Novyi Mir* both established writers such as Ilya Ehrenburg and previously unknown ones such as Aleksandr Solzhenitsyn and Andrei Sinyavskii (subsequently to gain world renown as 'dissidents' under Brezhnev) could voice severe criticism of both past and present Soviet social phenomena.

The history of *Novyi Mir* under Khrushchev and during the early Brezhnev years, has been thoroughly analysed by Dina Spechler, in a book called *Permitted Dissent in the USSR. Novyi Mir and the Soviet Regime*.[88] The title is relevant in one sense but misleading in another. Dissent may be defined as illegal social criticism, in which case 'permitted dissent' is pure nonsense. If, however, 'dissenter' or 'dissident' is taken to refer to an *intelligent* of the Russian nineteenth century – a perspective which is missing in Spechler – *Novyi Mir* under Khrushchev may be regarded as one of the kind with Nekrasov's and Belinskii's *Sovremennik* and Herzen's *Kolokol*, both prominent literary journals in nineteenth-century Russia.[89] In this perspective, the function of *Novyi Mir* certainly takes on ideological significance as a trail-blazer on the road to 'secularization'.

In Spechler's analysis, five different kinds of 'dissent' can be found in *Novyi Mir*, and thus also in the ideological realm of Soviet society under Khrushchev. One was *social pragmatism*, as represented by literature criticizing some minor shortcomings in the building of socialism and proposing ways of improvement. Another was *cultural liberalism*, in a limited sense of the word, i.e. arguments for artistic freedom and demands for easing Party control over the written word. Third was *moral humanism*, criticizing the materialist and utilitarian official moral, and demanding rights to individual personal development without any restrictions from the authorities. These three kinds of unorthodoxy could be found in *Novyi Mir* already in 1953–4.

In the second period of real thaw, in 1960–2, they were complemented by *critical realism* and *historical revisionism*. The former current held that the communist regime had failed to improve the material and spiritual conditions of life in Russia and questioned obliquely the Party's right to rule, i.e. its legitimacy. The latter argued that the causes of the grave defaults were to be found in the Stalin era and in Stalinism. Those who were of this opinion openly demanded a total break with the entire heritage of the Stalin era: in the economy, in social life, and in culture. In a longer perspective, this was a plea for ideological pluralism or, as Spechler sees it, for a society of a Western, democratic kind.[90]

In general, the 'thaws' under Khrushchev entailed not only a certain polyphony in the cultural sphere but also secularization in the normal sense. Once Khrushchev had defeated the anti-Party group and ousted Bulganin from the post as Premier, the Party broke its truce with religion, a truce which had dated back to the Great Patriotic War. Anti-religious propaganda was intensified. After not having been published for 5 years, in 1959 the journal *Nauka i Religiya* (Science and Religion) resumed regular publication, and, at the same time, *Voprosy Filosofii*, the main philosophical journal, was ordered by the Central Committee to propagate 'scientific socialism'. Many churches, mosques, and synagogues were closed, and the Stalinist flirtation with the Russian Orthodox Church was discontinued. According to Soviet sources, the number of 'working' Orthodox churches declined from 22,000 in 1959, to 11,500 in 1962. The number of open synagogues was also significantly reduced.[91] Militant atheism once again became the order of the day. This downgrading of the Russian religious heritage was a departure from National Bolshevism. It aimed at anchoring the identity of the Russian nation and of the other Soviet peoples firmly in the present, rather than in myths of the past.

The other aspect of secularization concerned the Party itself. The personality cult was condemned and although the cult of Lenin was revived instead, no deification of a living leader took place. How little the person of the leader really mattered in Party liturgy became evident when Khrushchev was forced to resign. The Lenin cult provided the Party 'with legitimacy that was unassailable, not losing a beat when, in 1964, Nikita Khrushchev lost his job to Leonid Brezhnev.'[92] The new Party Programme of 1961 meant a revitalization of communist goals and implied concern with technological progress and welfare programmes. An enhanced role was envisaged for science and for economic rationality in a Western sense. During Khrushchev's later years in power, it seemed as if the Soviet Union was finally on the verge of becoming a modern, secularized, and urbanized industrial state, pragmatic rather than ideological.

Conclusion

Our examination of the contents of *Bolshevik/Kommunist* during the period 1949–53 has demonstrated how the cult of the Leader was subtly transformed into a cult of the Party, and how the theme of the greatness of Russia was further refined and brought to chauvinist extremes. The supreme form of this officially endorsed Russian nationalism was Soviet patriotism. The internationalist perspective that had marked the original Marxist ideology was absent. Instead anti-Semitism, known as anti-cosmopolitanism, and general xenophobia gained in prominence. The main difference between the previous period of National Bolshevism and the late Stalin and early post-Stalin periods lies in the pronounced imperialist and militant tone that marked the latter. This is evident not only from the many xenophobic statements made in connection with the campaign against cosmopolitanism, but also in the habit of describing the Russians as not being 'alien' to any of the other Soviet nationalities.

On the face of it, Russian nationalism of the late 1940s and the early 1950s was a mere continuation of National Bolshevism, but as all modern, secularized forms were banned from Soviet artistic and literary life, things must be said to have retrogressed to the 1920s, when National Bolshevism was born. The official ideological climate at the turn of the century had been recreated, when pogroms and the acts of the Black Hundreds ravaged Russia, and when intense Russification programmes were introduced in the non-Russian areas of the empire. As critical scrutiny of empirical reality was prohibited, the Soviet citizens were confined to a mythological world view. This was the frame of mind inherited by those who were to lead and inhabit post-Stalin Russia. At the end of Stalin's rule, however, there were indications that things had perhaps gone too far, reaching the point of self-defeating ideological exhaustion.

It was reported by non-Soviet contemporary sources (e.g. the British Embassy in Moscow), that Stalin was ailing long before his actual death.[93] This combination of a growing fatigue in the ideological tissue, and of a vacuum at the apex of political power, may explain why the cult of the Party could gradually outflank the cult of Stalin. The themes of Russian supremacy and Russian chauvinism could also be challenged at the time, in spite of the final outburst of virulent anti-Semitism in connection with the Doctors' Plot. At the Party Congress in 1952, Beria mentioned 'great-power chauvinism' as the main ideological danger in the area of national policies.[94] Already before the dictator's death, there were diverging ideological currents beneath the frosted surface. Khrushchev's famous 'thaws' were consequently long in the making.

Although politically impotent, the intellectuals must still be said to have benefited from Khrushchev's secularization of ideology. Not only literature but also the social sciences came to life in the 1950s and early 1960s. After the great 'Western' period in Russian and Soviet cultural and ideological life, lasting from the early 1900s until the end of NEP, Khrushchev's reign was the first period of a similar kind. The isolated Russian tradition once again was diluted, and it would take some years for the Brezhnev regime to reshape the basic traits of the previous Stalinist ideology.

After Khrushchev, however, Bolshevik ideology of the Stalinst kind could never be completely re-established. The counterpart to Christ (Stalin) had failed, and Khrushchev's voluntary withdrawal from the Porkkala base in Finland, as well as from the eastern part of Austria, in 1955, together with his visit to the United States, the structural arch-enemy of the Stalinist ideological discourse, caused serious damage to the idea that it was Russia's mission to 'liberate' other nations. The Stalinist spell was broken. Ideological polyphony under Khrushchev meant that the established Soviet *skaz* was dissolved. It did remain as a structuring principle for basic public ideological treatises, such as reports to the Party Congresses, but it no longer reigned supreme. Other modes of discussion became prominent in journals of different kinds, not only in *Novyi Mir* but also, for example, in *Voprosy Istorii*.[95] All this meant an irreversible 'secularization' of Soviet ideology. Although not a success in itself, the Khrushchev interlude thus served to change the rules of the game in the field of ideology.

Chapter nine

Summary: the role of ideology

We shall start this summary section by digressing briefly from the chronological perspective that has dominated the three previous chapters. The reason for this digression is directly connected with the issue of continuity versus change in Soviet development and is thus central to the main thrust of our presentation. In contrast to the rather commonly held belief, that the Khrushchev era represented a radical break with the previous Stalinist period, we have indicated at various points above that the manifestations of continuity between these two periods may be more important than those of change. In particular, we have shown good reasons to argue that the period of de-Stalinization in some important senses was begun already before the death of Stalin as a physical person.

It consequently becomes an important topic for investigation to find out if those outwardly substantial changes that are associated with Khrushchev's person, and which earned him the epithet of being a 'hare-brained schemer',[1] were largely ephemeral, or if he actually did manage to alter some fundamental operating principles of the Soviet system. The point of reference for this investigation is that model which we have claimed above to have been established already by the mid-1930s. We are thus dealing here with a time perspective which stretches over roughly two decades, rather than simply the first half of the 1950s.

The purpose of our digression is to create a model framework for investigating the issue of continuity versus change and we shall do so by recalling some of the basic points about the concept of ideology that were made in our introductory chapter above. By focusing on the role of ideology during this important period of transition, we shall bring together the various strands of evidence that have been outlined in the respective chapters on economic, political and cultural issues. The common traits that are thus produced will then be cast in the same framework of Exit, Voice and Loyalty that was used in the summary section that followed the first block of three chapters. While our focus at that time was aimed primarily at identifying various modfied options for soft Exit and Voice, we shall focus here on the concept of Loyalty, in order to produce the backbone of a Theory of Soviet Loyalty. With the help of the latter, which aims to capture the essentials of social and economic behaviour patterns, we shall then proceed to investigate in which respects Khrushchev actually managed to bring about change and, by way of conclusion, to outline the main ingredients in the legacy that was left for Brezhnev.

A Theory of Soviet Loyalty

Soviet Ideology

In the introduction to this study, three important points of principle were made regarding our use and understanding of the concept of ideology. The *first* of these was to establish that our understanding of Soviet ideology as a whole is basically an instrumental one, i.e. that we are concerned not so much with identifying its intellectual origins or internal consistency as with analysing its function in the emergence and development of the Soviet system. *Second*, even if we abstract from the actual content of an unspecified ideology, in order to focus on its instrumental aspects, it will nevertheless cover a rather wide spectrum, in this case of different functions. At the one end of that spectrum we can find it used in a sense which is perhaps best referred to as 'prescriptive'. Here, ideological principles serve to condition the behaviour of individuals, in the positive sense of inducing certain actions as well as in the negative one of blocking certain other actions. Revolutionary ideology would fall under this heading, as would those socialist-cum-zionist ideals that have produced the success story of the Israeli *kibbutzim*.

From what we have said above, about ideology being used as a smoke screen in order to cover up unpopular or inadmissible policy measures, and of its main tenets emerging as *ex post* rationalizations of largely *ad hoc* actions, conditioned by political necessities and emergencies, it would definitely not seem that our understanding of the function of Soviet ideology is a prescriptive one. The issue at hand, however, is considerably more complicated than this rather simple picture of black and white would have us believe. The complication stems from the fact that we must differ between official ideology and such beliefs regarding what is 'right and proper' that are held by wide sections of the population.

The third of our three points concerns precisely this distinction. The very notion of an 'official' ideology implies that there exists at each given point in time an officially sanctioned version of its currently correct interpretation, much in the way of the Pope speaking *ex ca-thedra*. The very high degree of 'visibility' that is so characteristic of official Soviet ideology and *agitprop* is an obvious derivative of this fact and, as we have noted above, the formation and interpretation of the ingredients in this ideology constitute an important part of Soviet political life.

However important this 'official' ideology may be, it is certainly doubtful to what extent its main principles agree with those of what we shall refer to below as a 'popular' ideology, in the sense of the widely held values and beliefs that were referred to above. In order to reflect this distinction, we shall separate our discussion of ideology into two parts, one concerning the population at large and the other relating to the specific case of the Party cadres. This separation is of a principally different nature from our previous distinction between peasants and workers. In that case, the separation was made on a horizontal plane, according to social status. Here we shall also recognize a vertical dimension, separating the Party cadres according to their status in the power hierarchy. This dimension is of a continuous nature, such that the higher up an individual is placed on the ladder, the greater will be the demands that are placed on him in terms of conformity and the ability to practice the ideology. It should be fairly obvious that Party membership means something altogether different to a rank and file worker than it does to a high level *apparatchik*.

In a broad sense, all three points just made regarding the use and understanding of ideology form crucial ingredients in the picture of an underlying political rationality in the Soviet model that we have presented above as the main objective of our investigation. The instrumental interpretation of ideology is, on the one hand, not directly connected with the object of investigation *per se*, but it is an important methodological point which reflects our view on tools available to the Soviet leadership. The view of ideology as an *ex post* rationalizing device is, on the other hand, intimately linked with our view of policy as a process of *ad hoc* measures, often of an emergency nature, which would *ex post* be rationalized as the essence of socialism. This is the real backbone of our argument on a political rationality.

The point about an official ideology is, finally, of perhaps equally crucial importance, as it derives from our separation of ideology into an 'official' and a 'popular' part and thus reintroduces to some extent a 'spectrum' interpretation of that concept. Elements of the official ideology may certainly be deployed in order to further some unspecified political objectives of the regime, but, in so doing, various elements of the popular ideology will of necessity be influenced and perhaps even altered in a counter-productive direction. The dynamics of the latter process will form the real mainstay of our discussion below. In particular, we shall have reason to address the problem of whence the ingredients in the official ideology come and how they are transformed over time.

In contrast to our simple two-dimensional understanding of an 'official' and a 'popular' ideology under Stalin, in the Khrushchev period, the cultural intelligentsia emerged as a peculiar 'intervening layer' (*sloi*), or a third element, which served as a bearer of a separate set of ideological beliefs and values. This became evident during Khrushchev's two 'thaws'. It was manifested in particular, albeit not exclusively, in the pages of *Novyi Mir*. This meant an end to the Party's monopoly in the production of ideologically relevant texts, signifying instead a certain polyphony in intellectual life. To an outside observer, however, the ideology of the 'popular masses' remained almost as obscure as before. Let us begin by considering the case of the workers and the peasants, the alleged 'builders of socialism'.

The Builders of Socialism

In our previous summary section, an important distinction was made between the respective places of the workers and the peasantry in Soviet ideology. It was argued that the latter had been placed largely outside the effective reach of Party *agitprop* and thus also outside that sphere of Soviet society over which Bolshevik control was effectively extended. By recalling some more detailed points from our introductory discussion of ideology, we shall now proceed to shroud that distinction in a somewhat more abstract model framework.

The real centrepiece of this presentation will be to assign an important role to the formation and function of what we have referred to above as a 'popular' ideology. As we may recall from our introductory discussion, both Elster and North placed strong emphasis on the importance of instilling in the population certain moral and ethical norms, regarding what should and should not be done. As was indicated by North, simple utility maximizing behaviour by all individuals would produce a Prisoner's Dilemma type situation. The sum of all individually rational actions would be a collectively irrational outcome where everybody is worse off.

The essence of introducing norms and values was consequently – and perhaps surprisingly – shown by Elster to lie in promoting a certain degree of individually irrational behaviour, simply in order to produce conditions necessary for the viable operation of a society. For obvious reasons, however, such norms and values cannot lead an existence of their own. Somehow they will either have to be brought into line with reality, or vice versa. The dynamic aspects of the problem at hand consequently become of paramount importance.

Any policy which sets out to achieve a radical transformation of society will of necessity create an initial gap between utopia and reality, a gap which may be of quite substantial proportions. The need to do so derives from the simple fact that individuals must be motivated to work for change, and will thus have to be presented with a utopia as a goal for their efforts. If, however, the regime should prove incapable of closing that gap, by lifting reality up to the level of the promised utopia, a potentially dangerous situation will arise. Either the utopia will have to be deflated, which implies political defeat and is thus hardly applicable to the Soviet case, or the regime will be forced to witness the emergence of a systematic discrepancy between official and popular ideology. The latter would very definitely seem to be the Soviet case.

The real root of this dilemma can be captured in what Elster has referred to as 'states that are essentially by-products'.[2] Classic examples used by him are faith, courage and humility, all of which represent states of mind that cannot be 'willed'. By direct action, it is true that one may succeed in producing religion, bravado, and meekness, but these are of course nothing but substitutes for the real thing. The difficulty, however, is that in their outward appearance, the two sets may be deceivingly similar. In some cases individuals may even successfully engage in what Elster refers to as 'faking'.

The importance of these observations lies in their relation to the effects and efficiency of political indoctrination. By means of *agitprop* and a corresponding system of penalties and rewards which promotes conformity, it will certainly be possible to instil in Soviet citizens an outward lip-service to the officially desirable set of values and ideals. As far as the rank-and-file are concerned, one may perhaps even plausibly argue that the Party's ambitions stretch no further than that. Simple faking will be sufficient in order to produce an acceptable façade of outward conformity with the Party line. The collective identity that is associated with the latter corresponds to the notion of Soviet Man.

The really crucial problem, however, concerns the question of what states of mind are produced as a by-product of the direct action. It is in this context that our discussion of Loyalty becomes relevant. Let us start by recognizing that we are dealing here with two essentially different kinds of action. On the one hand, we have normative *agitprop* statements about the desired utopia and on the other we have such concrete policy measures which actually affect the individuals in their daily life. As we may recall from above, an important point made by North was that individuals continuously alter their ideological beliefs in order to achieve a better 'fit' with observed reality. The interplay between the two different types of direct action will form the real driving force in our dynamic interpretation of the problem at hand.

If there is reasonable coherence between the message of *agitprop*, on the one hand, and perceived reality, on the other, a process of positive cumulative causation may be set in motion. As a by-product, economic and social policy measures will produce precisely such sentiments and states of mind that cannot be directly willed. If these correspond with the message of *agitprop*, the credibility of the latter will be enhanced. *Agitprop* will consequently be able to fulfil its purpose in the original – positive – sense of that concept, namely to mobilize and exhort individuals towards better deeds for the common good. The case of the Israeli *kibbutzim* serves to illustrate how a process of positive cumulative causation may be started in this respect.

If, however, there is a sustained gap between promised utopia and perceived reality, then we may expect a reversal of that process. Actual policy measures serve to produce sentiments and states of mind that are seriously out of tune with the message of *agitprop*. As the latter loses in relevance and credibility, its message will in turn serve to deepen the sense of alienation and to further stifle productive effort by individuals. A negative spiral will therefore become established, whereby individuals produce for themselves a set of ideological beliefs and rationalizations which may have very little to do with the officially accepted and propagated ones. Faking then enters the picture, in order to produce the smooth façade.

At this point, we may return to our previously made distinction between the respective places of workers and peasants in Soviet ideology and society. An important conclusion reached in our previous summary section was that both workers and peasants can be pictured in rather similar Prisoner's Dilemma type situations. Soft Exits into slacking, drinking and general apathy produce a collectively irrational outcome where everybody is worse off. The various soft options serve the purpose of delaying a 'hard' Exit, in the original Hirschman sense, but fail to achieve that of promoting Voice. This was referred to as a strategy of Stay-Silence, and the corresponding pattern of social and economic behaviour was referred to as a 'passive' Loyalty. In their outward appearance, the two cases can thus be seen to have a striking similarity. This, however, must not distract us from also noting the existence of an important difference.

The distinction between the two lies in the fact that the ingredients in the respective utopias are so very different. While those forces which served to exhort and mobilize the workers were largely *internal* to the Bolshevik concept of ideology and society, in the case of the peasantry, such forces were essentially of an *external* nature. The passive Loyalty of the workers was marked by a partial incorporation into the state-controlled sphere, while that of the peasantry was largely alien to the ideals and values of the Soviet state. This distinction has obvious implications for the respective prospects of eventually socializing the two groups in Soviet society. It also contributes to explaining why agriculture has performed so much worse than industry in Soviet economic development.[3] We are dealing here not only with a structure that is determined by the ambitions of the New Class for power and security, but also with an ideological heritage from Marx which was strongly anti-peasant.

So far we have dealt only with the *horizontal* dimension of Soviet society. In addition, however, we shall proceed now to argue that there is also a *vertical* dimension to the problem, a dimension which is of perhaps even greater importance.

The Party Cadres

We have chosen to treat the case of the Party cadres as distinct from those of workers and peasants because of the crucial political role that is played by this group. Of equal importance, however, is the fact that the instrumental role of ideology is so much more clearly observable in this case. In our introductory discussion of ideology, we emphasized the function of official ideology as a screening device, serving to separate the heretics from the reliable. We shall proceed now to elaborate that point and in so doing we shall make good use of Hirschman's original formulation of a Theory of Loyalty.[4]

In order to set the key for this discussion, we may begin by noticing that the very notion of 'Loyalty' gives an interesting indication of the general ideas involved. If we take, for example, cases such as family, tribe and church, which Hirschman refers to as 'primordial human groupings', it is rather obvious that interpersonal relations will normally be such that Voice is favoured over Exit, as a response to conflict. The word 'Loyalty' would thus be a rather adequate term to use. Similar conclusions can be seen to apply in a case like the Japanese, where the norms and values of society are such that response in the form of Exit is close to unthinkable. In cases such as these, people who do choose to Exit will often be branded as 'traitors', 'defectors', or 'deserters'.

If we were to apply these concepts to firms, organizations and states in a more general sense, it is of course no longer true that Exit is unthinkable. This has a profound impact on the interpretation of Loyalty. It is also here that the more controversial parts of Hirschman's theory enter the stage, with high costs of Entry and Exit being introduced as key determinants of Loyalty. On the one hand, it is assumed that individuals who have paid high fees to enter, or who have been subjected to some severe initiation rites, will be prepared to put up with decline longer than those to whom Entry was more freely available. One explanation of such behaviour is that of *self-deception*, a sub-conscious tendency to ignore any signs of deterioration. As the individual is in fact unaware of the decline, it will be accompanied by neither Exit nor Voice. We are dealing here with 'unconscious Loyalist behaviour', a situation which will have an obvious appeal to managers who desire an easy life, or indeed to the members of the Soviet *nomenklatura*. Another explanation of the effects of high costs to enter is that of *justification*. Those who have paid a high price – in some form – to join will be inclined to 'fight hard' in order to prove that their original decision, with all the associated costs, was a correct one. In both cases, Hirschman draws on evidence from experimental psychology.[5]

The reverse side of the coin is that of high costs of Exit, and here the situation has a perhaps even greater intuitive appeal. If Exit from an organization is associated with a heavy cost, such as excommunication, defamation or loss of livelihood, this will naturally act to deter from taking such a step. The most obvious examples are perhaps those 'primordial social groupings' which were referred to above, where the reluctance to Exit will serve to activate Voice.

If we proceed now to look more closely at the case of the Party cadres, it is quite obvious that the framework of high costs of Entry and Exit is directly applicable. Starting with the former, we may note that the Communist Party of the Soviet Union is and always has been a vanguard organization, where membership is open only to a minority of the population. To join the Party – or rather to be admitted into its ranks – is for most individuals the only way to acquire the better things of life, in terms of prestige, services and material goods. It is consequently understandable that many Soviet citizens are prepared to pay a high price in order to join, or – in some cases – in order to avoid the costs that are associated with non-membership.

An example of the former is that of proving one's political value and reliability. This can be done in many ways, for example by undertaking various forms of voluntary unpaid 'public service' (*obshchestvennaya rabota*), such as volunteer police (*druzhiniki*) or election canvassing. Empirically, it is fairly evident that anybody who wants to rise in the Soviet hierarchy will have to perform some such service. Intuitively, it should be equally clear that it will not be done with a light heart. Another type of Entry cost is that of learning to practice Marxist-Leninist ideology, a skill which might not be all that easily acquired.[6] If ideological concepts are to be assigned an instrumental role in Party *agitprop*, they must also be adaptable to the needs of specific situations. The rather striking flexibility which characterizes official Soviet ideology is, in this context, not only understandable but even absolutely necessary. Moreover, it also illustrates the demands that are placed on the ability of the cadres to follow various reorientations (which would seem, at times, to be rather subtle).

It is of some considerable importance, in this context, to note that research findings from experimental psychology, cited by Donald Barry and Carol Barner-Barry, have shown that people who expect distant rather than immediate rewards, as a result of active participation in the work of an organization, will be more susceptible to socialization to a given set of beliefs than those who are merely passive recipients of promises of milk and honey *hic et nunc*.[7] Based on such evidence, we may conclude that the Party cadres will be slow to react if something goes wrong, being more likely to 'adjust' their perceptions to what has been prescribed by the Party than to take some form of remedial action. Loyalty acquired through a vested interest in the existing social and political structure functions in this case as a filter to weed out 'inconvenient' information. In the sense that individuals will engage here in various psychological processes of justification and self-deception, the outcome is something akin to Hirschman's concept of 'unconscious Loyalty'.

If we turn now to the reverse side of the coin, once a person has been admitted as a member of the *nomenklatura* he simply does not choose to Exit. Not only would this mean the loss of a number of such priviliges that are available to the ruling elite, it would also mean incurring costs of the type that was indicated by Hirschman. A rather pointed illustration is the decision to apply for an Exit visa. Once an individual has taken the step to apply for permission to emigrate, he is effectively placed in a state of internal emigration and if he should eventually be granted the right to leave, he will then subsequently be treated as a non-person. Similarly, one simply does not take a public stand against the official Party line. This has also traditionally been associated with very high costs. It is quite significant to note, as does Hirschman, that in organizations of the 'primordial' kind, where Exit is either impossible or unthinkable, provisions for excommunication are generally made.[8] Expulsion from the Party serves this function in the Soviet context. It implies not only losing the status of Party member, but also a loss of all the associated material benefits.

While these observations indicate important limiting determinants of public behaviour by the Party cadres, they are certainly not meant to say that no opportunities whatsoever are open for either retreat or protest. As in the case of workers and peasants, a number of soft options enter in the place of their banned hard counterparts. Although open and organized opposition has been ruled out ever since the 1921 ban on factions within the Party, it is of course the case that there has remained some (variable) scope for 'political forces' to move under the surface. This process has important elements of what we have referred to above as 'horizontal Voice'. If nothing else, its existence is borne out by the long standing practice of Kremlinological speculations about pending changes in the top leadership.

We have again here an illustration of the importance of recognizing a vertical dimension, of making a distinction between the core of the Party apparatus, on the one hand, and the Party cadres in general, on the other. However, in order to fully understand the importance of these observations, we must recognize a further point of a rather subtle nature, a point which concerns the Soviet perception of the inner mysteries of the Party. This may call for some elaboration.

The Communist Party

Any but not All

With reference to the principle of methodological individualism, Elster has pointed out that there simply cannot exist such a thing as a collective desire or a collective belief: 'A family may, after some discussion, decide on a way of spending its income, but the decision is not based on "its" goals and "its" beliefs, since there are no such things.'[9] This argument is of obvious relevance to the formation of ideology in general, and in particular to the frequently made Soviet claims regarding 'the Party's will'. As an illustration of the latter, we may note a recent complaint by Grushin, that in spite of the changes in attitudes under Gorbachev, 'out of sheer inertia, we continue to use the established formulas: "the Soviet people thinks ...", "the inhabitants of our city all ...", "our collective is convinced ...", "for our consumers (viewers, listeners, etc.) this is not needed" '.[10]

Two aspects are immediately relevant here. First we have the 'sanctity of the Party',[11] i.e. its alleged infallibility, and, second, the claim that it also possesses some mystical power as an independent actor – independent of human beings that is. These observations call for a more detailed discussion of a highly peculiar trait of Soviet ideology, an aspect which has been approached by Western scholars but never, to our knowledge, been brought into discussions of Loyalty, or of the ideologically stabilizing function of peculiar Soviet metaphysics. At the core of this issue lies the notion that the Party is the repository of superior knowledge, possible to grasp only for a selected number of people, the initiated few. To become a Party member is thus something sacred and a voluntary Exit is theoretically impossible. Expulsion, on the other hand, implies that the person in question never really was a 'true' member of the Party. This, however, is not all.

During his lifetime, Stalin had been positively identified with the Party. Consequently, when Khrushchev initiated his de-Stalinization campaign it ought to have reflected upon the Party as well as on its former dictator. Furthermore, once Khrushchev himself had fallen and been defamed, the Party again should have stood to lose prestige – or so Western rationality would have it. Carl Linden's verdict on the situation after 'de-Stalinization' and 'de-Khrushchevization' is of interest in this context: 'The official refrain that the Party remained unsullied in spite of having been led by a succession of bad leaders is worse than no answer at all, and no amount of historical rewriting under the present leadership is likely to undo the damage.'[12]

Writing at the beginning of the Brezhnev era, Linden saw the loss of credibility of official ideology as a consequence of the 'devaluation' of the Party. The Party, however, remained firmly in power. Once Brezhnev had also been included in the ranks of bad leaders, it would paradoxically be hailed to an even greater extent by the new leader Gorbachev. Far from being tainted, after each revelation of wilfulness and mismanagement by its leadership, the Party seems to be elevated to a still more sublime level. Ernest Gellner's conclusion regarding developments in Czechoslovakia is relevant here, as a description not only of that special case but as a judgement about the Party and its role in the Soviet Model generally. Based on an analysis made by the Czech oppositional writer Milan Šimecka, Gellner starts with the rather obvious observation, that in order to function, the Soviet type system requires a Party which must rule alone. The crucial point in this context is that every single human being who contributes to make up this Party is expendable.

Against this, one might argue that such a view suffers from what Elster has referred to as a 'fallacy of composition'. It is of course true, on the one hand, that any single member is expendable, but on the other one must recognize that they are not all simultaneously expendable. Elster expresses the same by saying that 'although *any* worker may be seen as the marginal worker, not *all* workers can be at the margin.'[13] The Soviet case, however, defies this logic and it does so by virtue of a very specific feature, namely the existence of Lenin, a person who is eternally alive and beyond any reprehension.

Member Number One

It is a matter of historical fact that membership card number one in the Communist Party of the Soviet Union was once issued to Vladimir Ilich Lenin. It is perhaps less commonly known that every time Party cards have been changed, and membership revised, card number one has been reissued to that very same person. It should thus be fairly obvious that Lenin plays a role in Soviet politics and in Soviet ideology that transcends by far that of any other person – living or dead. Drawing on ideological tractates as well as on personal observations, made in Moscow during the late Brezhnev period, Barry and Barner-Barry have stressed that 'in a truly religious sense Lenin lives on.'[14] In a similar vein, Tumarkin has remarked that 'Lenin's immortality preceded his death.'[15]

When Stalin's body was removed from the mausoleum, one night during the twenty-second Party Congress, in 1961, a powerful argument in favour of that move was a testimony given to the congress by a certain comrade Lazurkina. She indicated that Lenin, who allegedly lived in her heart, had told her that 'it was unpleasant to lie beside Stalin, who had done so much harm to the Party'.[16] Stalin's corpse (which evidently did not tell anybody anything) was subsequently removed. The following illustrates the ideological reality that has been shaped by a consistent vilification of past Party leaders – with the notable exception of Lenin – and by the doctrine of the sanctity or infallibility of the Party:

> The Party rules, and rules alone. It selects its own membership, by unstated and obscure principles which in practice select for conformity and mediocrity. Šimecka quotes Brecht's joke that when things go wrong in a democracy one changes the government, and in a popular democracy one changes the people. In fact, the (slightly) enfranchised part of the people are the Party members, and they are literally replaced to suit requirements from above. The vanguard of the working class ensures that substantially progressive considerations prevail above mere formal considerations. But as there seems virtually no doctrinal substance left, *and the human content of the Party is itself variable*, we are left with substantialism without substance .... It is all a splendid new application of Leninism. The proletariat now not merely has a vanguard, but has a *disposable vanguard*, which can be replaced by a new one with perfect ease whenever necessary. This is perfectly

logical: you need a different vanguard according to where you want to go.[17]

It is essential to note that Lenin remains as the sole incarnation of the Party as such. This, however, is a complicated representation. Tumarkin makes the following observation: 'The collective ... is more than simply an ideal: it is Lenin. Lenin lives in the hearts of all worthy people, but every member of the Party *is* Lenin. This is a religious concept of communion, like being one with Christ.'[18] What this means, in essence, is that there can never be more than one member of the Party. Once a person has been accepted into the Party, he also becomes one with Lenin, and thus with the Party.

Although Stalin's Great Purge in the 1930s could be seen as a once and for all house-clearance, with some additional cleaning-up to be carried out in 1948–9, Khrushchev's defeat of the 'anti-Party group', in 1957, and his purges lower down the ladder, certainly could not. On the contrary, from now on it was evident for all that every single Party member and leader might turn out to be a culprit. The dismissal of Khrushchev and the ensuing criticism of his 'voluntarism' could not but reinforce this impression.

Dvoeverie and Pluralist Ignorance

A highly special problem with the Soviet model, as it matured under Stalin and Khrushchev, is the very marked difference that can be observed between views and attitudes shown in public and in private. There are two dimensions to this problem, which can be captured in the concepts *dvoeverie* ('dual belief') and 'pluralist ignorance'. The former is a concept that is normally applied to the medieval Russian state – the Kievskaya Rus – after its official conversion to Christianity. A recent Soviet book describes this situation in terms of an 'orthodox-pagan dual belief syncretism'. The dual belief, or dual culture, it is argued, made itself felt at all levels of medieval Russian social consciousness. It permeated all aspects of spiritual and ideological life. While the 'official' layer of social consciousness appeared to be Byzantine Christian, as far as ideology and value systems were concerned, the 'collective subconsciousness' of Rus was pagan.[19]

It should be noted that Dmitrii Likhachev, nestor of Soviet medievalists and Chairman of the Soviet Culture Foundation, has denied – on purely logical grounds – the very possibility of *dvoeverie*: 'it is not possible simultaneously to believe in pagan Gods and be a Christian'[20] and 'either one single faith, or none at all'.[21] Likhachev is distinguished by having come through the 'difficult' times without a record of 'faking' and can thus be assumed to reject the existence of a dual reality also on purely personal grounds. He does, however, appear to be rather alone in this belief. The existence of *dvoeverie* has been amply documented by the Soviet historian Igor Froyanov, in a recent empirical analysis of medieval sources. Froyanov concludes that there existed in medieval Rus two separate faiths, 'paganized Christendom, i.e. *dvoeverie*, and pure paganism'.[22]

There were two different aspects to the syncretism of Christianity and paganism, both of which can be derived from preserved medieval texts and archaeological findings. On the one hand, it meant that Christianity in Rus had acquired some special traits, inherited from the pagan Russian past. On the other hand, it also meant that while the official religion of the state was Christianity, and public behaviour 'Christian', in their daily life people remained pagan. They developed a mental tradition of living according to two sets of rules.[23] This may, of course, be said to be true for all newly christianized societies in medieval Europe, but Russian and Soviet scholars have long insisted that it is characteristic above all of the Russian case.

It is a striking fact, for example, that at the time of the Revolution, *dvoeverie*, or what Lewin has referred to as 'rural Christianity',[24] was still an observable phenomenon. When Marxism-Lenininism was superimposed on this reality it found fertile ground. Psychology was already structured to receive the inherent duality of the new ideology, as it has been described above. Contemporary Russians have thus been brought up in the belief of *dvoeverie* as something natural.

An important question that certainly begs an answer in this context is how the individual may hold the belief that other people are not true believers and that he himself is not alone in holding a set of beliefs and values that are out of tune with official ideology and public behaviour? This is where the concept of 'pluralist ignorance' enters the stage, representing what the American sociologist Robert Merton has defined as 'the pattern in which individual members of a group *assume* that they are virtually alone in holding the social attitudes and expectations they do, all unknowing that others privately share them.'[25] As Merton has further observed, there are two patterns of 'pluralist ignorance', one being 'the unfounded assumption that one's own attitudes and expectations are unshared', and the other 'the unfounded assumption that they are uniformly shared.'[26] The basic precondition for the situation is that 'mutual observability' between the individuals is low.[27]

This means that an outside observer – the investigator or the researcher – may register that the individuals all behave at odds with their value systems, while they themselves may not be able to do so. There are methodological problems involved here and we only want to call attention to the fact that there may exist widespread *dvoeverie* without the individuals knowing that it is widespread and common, *or*, conversely, believing that it is widespread when actually it is not. In any given social situation, there may be different levels of *dvoeverie*. In such a situation, the individual thinks that his innermost values and attitudes are those of a deviant small circle of friends and relatives, while the rest of society is supposed to believe in what they proclaim.[28]

What has happened after Stalin's death is that the gap between the official and the private spheres of Soviet society has in some sense been institutionalized. As Motyl has observed, control by the KGB has been restricted to the public sphere, i.e. to the sphere outside the homes of the citizens. Thus the opportunities for voicing 'dissident' views in private have increased. An interpretation of this is that the rulers, or 'the strategic elite', as Motyl calls them, have to an increasing extent been satisfied with conformism and faking. On the one hand, strict control has been excercised over the public sphere, but on the other, there has been a conscious ambition to 'expropriate' as much free time (hours after work) as possible for public purposes. The latter does not leave much space for 'deviant' activities.[29] This point recalls our previous argument on how the Party seeks to 'incorporate' the citizens into its controlled sphere, in order to prevent 'regrouping' and the formation of separate, autonoumous collective identities.

The observations regarding the existence of two separate sets of values, we may note, also find support in Soviet sources. In his June 1987 article in *Novyi Mir*, for example, Shmelev writes with respect to Gospriemka, the new system of state quality control, that if one is a 'pessimist', no more than about 7–8 per cent of the output of Soviet industry currently meets world standards, while to the 'patriot', a figure of 17–18 per cent would come to mind.[30] 'Pessimism', in this context, would correspond to the private sphere, while 'patriotism' would be its public manifestation.

The following excerpt from an article by Soviet sociologist B.V. Olshanṣkii, gets to the heart of the matter of two separate 'realities' in post-Stalin society:

A 'theory' has even emerged that makes a distinction between a normative approach to the way of life (the Soviet way of life [*sovetskii obraz zhizni*]) and a realistic one (the way of life of the Soviet people [*obraz zhizni sovetskikh lyudei*]). This distinction is based on a rift between word and action that is difficult to overcome .... The principal problem is revealed in the following: 'between culture as a system of spiritual values in society acquired from the experiences of the class, the nation and mankind, on the one hand, and individual and group cultural behaviour, on the other, there is a system which guarantees that every individual masters these values and that they enter the individual consciousness. This transfer [*translatsiya*] of culture and culture's transformation into individual cultural behaviour begin with the formation and elevation of spiritual ... needs, i.e. with what is, according to our view, the weakest point in the work of upbringing, its Achilles heel.[31]

Olshanskii's objective is to explain the causes of widespread alcoholism in the Soviet society of the 1980s and the passage quoted here was used in order to initiate a discussion about deviant behaviour. His own quotation, however, which is taken from a work published in 1986, reveals an important insight, namely a realization of the fact that Soviet 'upbringing' [*vospitanie*] has failed to socialize individual citizens into accepting official ideology. This is a legacy from the terror climate of Stalin's time which apparently has survived the Khrushchev and Brezhnev periods, most likely becoming increasingly subtle over time.

Continuity Versus Change

The experiences of Khrushchev's attempt at restructuring economic management, of his reshuffling of the Party apparatus, and of his tolerance of a strictly monitored polyphony in cultural life, illustrate quite conclusively the limited prospects for successful change in the basic operating principles of the Soviet system. In the economic sphere, the simplistic teachings of Marxism-Leninism prevailed, as did the principle of central control by the administrative bureaucracy. In the political sphere, an attempt was made to introduce organizational innovations based on functional criteria (e.g. the 'bifurcation' of the Party), but the fundamental principle of the leading role of that Party could not be questioned. In the cultural sphere, finally, the principles of Party control and censorship were not rejected. If anything, they became even more visible with the alternation between 'thaws' and 'frosts'.

Having said this, however, one should realize that not everything remained unchanged since the time of Stalin. Certain processes that had started during the latter years of the dictator's rule continued to develop. Most important in this respect was the definite innovation that mass terror ceased to be a pervasive trait in practically all walks of life. The scope for both Exit and Voice had increased somewhat.

The home had become the individual's 'castle', a place where he could temporarily escape control and give vent to certain misgivings. Different views could also be voiced in official media, up to the level of 'permitted dissent'.

The most striking feature of this development, however, is not the process of change but rather that of continuity. It is not so much the actual manifestations of a reaction to Stalinism that surprise, as the fact that so little was achieved. It is an empirical fact, for example, that collective and politically relevant violent behaviour has been a very rare phenomenon in Soviet society during the entire post-war era. Occasional riots in 1959–62 are notable exceptions to the rule.[32] The change of popular values and attitudes has obviously been a slow, discrete process. This means that any periodization of ideological development at the mass level becomes a hazardous and rather arbitrary exercise. For example, not even the de-Stalinization campaigns of 1956–7 and 1961–2 seemed to cause much turbulence among workers and peasants. In these quarters, there have simply not occurred any significant nationwide outbursts of Voice.

During the later Stalin years and during the Khrushchev era, however, certain things did happen in the ideological sphere that must have affected the perceptions of the 'masses'. The *first* was the change in the national composition of the Soviet Union, which we have referred to briefly above, in relation to our discussion of the new identity of the state. It was not only a matter of the enlargement of the Ukrainian and Belorussian republics, and of five additional Soviet republics being created. The acquisition of the East European empire, the 'socialist commonwealth' (*sotsialisticheskoe sodruzhestvo*) also played a part. These changes, i.e. the substantial geographical expansion of the Soviet empire, transformed pre-war Russian nationalism into an 'imperial nationalism'.[33]

Second, after the war, a renewed attack on the peasant way of life followed, with the creation of ever bigger *kolkhozy*. Under Khrushchev, the amalgamation of the *kolkhozy* was accompanied by two important ideological developments that also directly concerned the peasants. The first was the intensified atheist campaign, which, although directed against all creeds and social classes, struck at the very heart of the Russian peasant spiritual world. The second was the goal of total urbanization, i.e. the Party's intention, expressed at the twenty-second Party Congress, in 1961, to abolish rural life as such and to create instead agro-industrial complexes and erase the differences between town and countryside.[34] Although very slow in realization, in principle this programme implied the end of the peasantry. It should be underlined that Khrushchev's attempt in the final years of his regime, to launch the idea of 'the Party of the whole

229

people', presumed, on the basis of the industrial society, that all so-cial differences disappeared.[35] This was a further indication of the prospect of a Soviet Union without peasants.

What did all these material and ideological developments mean to the self-perception and self-esteem of the workers and the peasants? Although no opinion polls are available, a fairly safe educated guess would be that concepts such as 'atheism', 'urban', 'modern', 'indus-try', 'worker' and 'engineer' were perceived as positive, being connected with the Party and the future, while concepts such as 'reli-gion', 'rural', 'traditional', 'countryside' and 'peasant' were perceived as negative, being dismissed by those in power. In the ideological sphere, great prospects were accordingly promised for the workers, while for the peasants the promise was disappearance as a class. However, when 'modernization' failed to improve daily life notice-ably, when general welfare did not materialize, the working class must have felt cheated, not to say fooled. The peasant class, on the other hand, had already learned that its way of life was doomed in any case, and this experience was certainly not invalidated by any notable improvement in the material conditions of life in the countryside. Both the 'toiling' classes must consequently have experienced frus-tration. Such feelings, moreover, were not caused by the Brezhnev regime. Soviet sources in the late 1980s indicate that the social 'stag-nation' in the period 1964–82, was there from the beginning, i.e. as a legacy from the Khrushchev era.[36]

Under Khrushchev, neither the working class nor the peasantry had any alternative outlet for their feelings and misgivings than the soft Exit. The popular masses remained calm, but it was a sullen sub-mission, drenched in vodka. As we shall see below, the ideological movements from below that became visible in the Brezhnev era did not emanate from either of these two classes, but rather from the in-tellectuals, the separate 'layer'. It seems that at the end of the Khrushchev period, passivity among the masses served to dim and postpone the leaders' appreciation of the social crisis phenomena in Soviet society. There was less fear and more hope for rewards. That the Party apparatus and the Party cadres turned against Khrushchev as a person does not refute this conclusion. On the contrary, their support for the system in an abstract sense was evidently so strong that Khrushchev was toppled for trying to go too far in changing it. When Brezhnev took charge, the Soviet system had matured. After the trials of Stalinist terror and Khrushchevian 'voluntarism' and 'hare-brained schemes', the political leadership and the broad masses of workers and peasants looked forward to some peace and quiet. Al-most 50 years after the alleged socialist revolution, Soviet society was firmly set on its course towards economic and social fossilization.

Conclusion

In 1964, the Soviet Union had definitely emerged as one of the world's two superpowers. Stalin's empire had not only been preserved. It had become both consolidated and expanded. The uprisings in East Germany in 1953, and in Poland and Hungary in 1956, had been successfully suppressed. The establishment of the Warsaw Treaty Organization in 1955 may not have changed anything substantially, regarding Soviet control over Eastern Europe, but it certainly gave the empire a more consolidated appearance. In the Western hemisphere, the Soviet Union had acquired a foothold through the communist take-over in Cuba. In Asia, the prospects were not altogether bad. Although China had openly refused to follow Soviet orders, the country still seemed to be safe for socialism. French imperialism had been forced to leave Indo-China, and North Vietnam was added to the camp of socialist states. The emergence of the non-aligned movement, led by Egypt, India, and Yugoslavia, meant a further potential decline in the global political influence of the United States, the main adversary of the Soviet Union.

Internally, the Soviet economy seemed to be capable of steady growth, in spite of seriously distortive bureaucratic interference, and in spite of a waste of natural resources and manpower that lacks precedence in the industrialized world. Politically, all the main sectors were closely knit together, with the central Party apparatus, the leadership of the armed forces, and the KGB working hand-in-hand. Ideologically, the idea of a state-of-the-whole-people, envisioned already by the Stalin constitution of 1936, seemed to be an efficient precept for regulating the relations between social classes and different nations in the Soviet Union.

The system that had emerged and matured under Stalin had proven itself quite resistant to the impact of Khrushchev. It was a system marked by economic irrationality, political immobility and cultural sterility. Yet, the Party leadership saw only intoxicating growth figures, parading obedient masses, and a further spread of literacy and higher education. All seemed to be well, in all respects. The future was only a matter of refined management of an almost perfect machinery. To the world, this was announced in the new Party programme of 1961 and in Khrushchev's boasts about dancing on the grave of capitalism.

After Stalin's revolution from above, and in spite of Khrushchev's 'tinkering', in 1964 Soviet society was one of the most conservative and myopic imaginable. In theory, everything was splendid. In reality, much was fairly awful. *De facto*, the legacy for Brezhnev implied a choice between, on the one hand, belief in a fairy tale, or an image, and, on the other, recognition of the Leviathan that was devouring all social energy, a grim reality. The Brezhnev leadership chose to profess belief in the fairy tale. Against this background, it is hardly surprising that Gorbachev speaks today of 'years and decades' being lost.[37] It is, however, rather stunning when Shmelev says that 'the obstacles to change in our economic system were created over a period of six decades and are marked by an unbelievable force of inertia.'[38] Let us proceed now to take a closer look at what actually happened during the 'period of stagnation', the *period zastoya*.

Part four

The Precarious Victory of Stability

Chapter ten

Stagnation and the reforms that never were

The hallmark of the new leadership that took over after the ousting of Khrushchev was that of restoration. This was particularly the case in the realm of agriculture, where the disruptive effects of the previous years' policy had been the most pronounced. Restrictions on the private plots were eased, procurement prices were raised, the TPAs were abolished, and the *raikom* was reinstated. At the very top, the Ministry of Agriculture was restored to its former power, even to the point of reinstating the former Minister of Agriculture, Matskevich. The bifurcation of the Party was likewise abolished and the hierarchy of economic administration was restored to its former shape. The *sovnarkhoz* system was abolished and the old ministries brought back. The VSNKh went out and Gosplan came back in, under its old head Baibakov. A similar overhaul was made in the republics. The sum impression of these changes is that, with few exceptions, all traces of the Khrushchev years were removed.

Simply restoring the old order, however, could at best have been a halfway measure. It did undoubtedly remove much of the previous chaos and disruption, but at the same time, we must note that there had been good reasons – others than simple power struggle – for Khrushchev to seek change. Those reasons had certainly not been removed by his frequent administrative reshuffles. Simply put, the legacy of Khrushchev can thus be said to have consisted of two parts. On the one hand, restoration of the old order did not quite mean going back to square one. It meant going back to square one *minus* a number of the policy options that had been available to Khrushchev, but which were no longer either possible (the cultivation of new land), or feasible (further administrative reshuffles). In a sense, the situation in 1964–5 was thus worse than it had been in 1953–6.

The other part of the legacy consisted of a growing pressure for reform, in economic as well as in political terms. Far from being removed, this pressure had actually been exacerbated during Khrushchev's tenure, and we shall start our account here by looking at its main manifestations. In so doing, we shall consciously use the word 'reform', not because any measures were introduced during Brezhnev's time that would merit such description, but rather because the seriousness of economic stagnation and the inadequacies of the Stalinist control model *ought* to have called for such measures to be introduced.

Following this diagnosis of the nature of the problems that called for reforms, we shall proceed to examine what attempts were actually made in order to improve the functioning of the mechanisms of planning and control. This examination will give an impression of change and manipulation carried out *instead* of reform and when we move into the realm of agriculture, in the third section of the chapter, that impression will be strongly reinforced. The 1982 Food Programme, the *Prodovolstvennaya programma*, will be seen as a final splendid manifestation of the unwillingness – or inability – of the decaying Brezhnev leadership to face up to the real needs of the situation.

The Pressure for Reform

The pressure for reform came from many quarters and took on many guises. Particular emphasis should perhaps be placed on the increasingly open, cultural and ideological dissent that had emerged during Khrushchev's brief periods of thaw. This, however, falls largely within the political and the cultural realms, and will thus be left for discussion in the two following chapters. Below, we shall focus instead on three primarily economic reasons behind the growing needs to implement reform, all of which had a direct bearing on the traditional model and on the associated perception of economic planning and control.

First of all, the mid-1960s signalled the end of the 'easy growth' period. It should hardly be necessary to invoke a Rostowian take-off perspective in order to understand that an important ingredient in the early successes of Soviet economic growth had been the relative abundance of both labour and natural resources, in combination with an initially very low level of economic development. With the gradual exhaustion of both resources and high-yielding investment opportunities, growth rates were simply bound to fall, unless the 'economic mechanism' could, in some way, be adapted to changing circumstances. We thus have here a further sense in which the situation facing Brezhnev was relatively worse than that which once faced Stalin's successors.

236

Second, and in clear relation to the first point, with industrial development necessarily follows a growing complexity of the economy. Consequently, growing demands were placed on the system of planning and control. In the extractive branches of the economy, where output is homogeneous and there is a relatively narrow choice of production techniques, it may be sufficient to issue plan directives for, say, the production of X million tons of coal. As the secondary – manufacturing – sector of the economy grows, however, planners will be faced with rapidly growing problems of selecting optimal factor combinations for the production of a specified output. Early hopes that such problems could be overcome by high-speed computers and sophisticated mathematical planning techniques were dashed, partly due to the slow development of the Soviet computer industry. Instead of the hoped-for computopia, there was a steady growth in the number of plan indicators and material balances, which form the very backbone of the traditional planning mechanism. As the strain on the planning apparatus increased, the inadequacies of these methods became painfully obvious.

Third, as a result of peaceful coexistence with the West, and of the associated wager on materialism, the role of the consumer in the Soviet economy had undergone an important transformation during Khrushchev's reign. The implications of this transformation are rather subtle, as it was not merely a question of devoting more resources to the production of consumer goods. The simple fact that the consumer represents the end of the line, so to speak, means that changes in the plan for consumer goods will have no secondary effects on the planning process. This makes for an important difference between planning the respective outputs of consumer and producer goods. If the planner should decide to reduce the plan target for, say, the output of steel, this will affect the targets for all users of steel and for products made of steel, in an infinite process which, in practice, will be impossible to track down to its end. If, however, he should choose to cut back the output of some consumer good, then that will be the end of the chain. It is thus logical that planners are strongly inclined to use the consumer-goods sector as a buffer, serving to absorb unavoidable disruptions and bottlenecks. Increased priorities for the consumer would thus not only lay a higher claim on available resources, but would also place a serious additional stress on the actual mechanism of planning. This point is central to the under- standing of Soviet economic 'planning'.

The increasing inability of the traditional model to face up to the challenges of a modern industrial economy created a strong pressure for reform. A particularly worrying aspect must have been the implied long-run threat to vital military needs. No doubt there was a widespread awareness in Moscow that these pressures were mounting, and in the government resolution which introduced the 1965 reform, the urgent need for change was underlined. The planning system was accused of, *inter alia*, paying too much attention to administrative control, placing unreasonable constraint on managers, a lack of incentives for improvement, poor accountability of enterprises, frequent breaches of contracts, a poor use of various economic instruments, and essential shortcomings in pricing.[1]

On a first reading, this resolution may sound like a devastating condemnation of the Soviet economic system, as it emerged and developed under Stalin. It is also undoubtedly the case that, among Soviet economists at the time, there was a widespread optimism that there would indeed be change for the better. From a visit to the Soviet Union in 1967, for example, Nove reports having been told by a number of Soviet colleagues to 'Come back in two years and you will hardly recognize the system.'[2] In practice, however, such hopes were soon shown to have been misguided and a question that immediately comes to mind is *why* nothing of essence came out of all this. Why was there not a 'radical reform'? As we know, the Brezhnev era would be characterized by economic stagnation and a growing lethargy in both economic and political leadership. Indeed, the very same condemnation of the economic system that must have aroused great expectations in 1965, would subsequently be repeated so many times, and in much the same form, that it has taken on a ritual form of little practical implications.

It will be our main ambition in this chapter to investigate why this was so. Yet, before we release the full weight of reform pessimism, we shall pause briefly to look at what it was that the advocates of real reform were proposing, and we shall do so for one hopefully very good reason. Maybe their reform ideas were simply not workable? Let us take a closer look at the contents of the so called Liberman proposals, which are often presented as the theoretical antecedents to that package of would-be reform measures which was introduced in 1965.

The Liberman Proposals

Evsei Grigorevich Liberman was a Professor of Engineering Economics at Kharkov university, and hardly one of the most prominent Soviet economists of his time. The fame that he subsequently gained in the West[3] was clearly out of proportion to his importance in the Soviet economic debate. This is largely attributable to that very strong focus on the individual which characterizes Western media. No doubt it did arouse quite a debate both inside and outside the Soviet Union when his famous article 'Plan, Profit and Bonus' was published in *Pravda*, on 9 September 1962. It is also certainly true that he gained considerable publicity in the Soviet media. After that initial attention, however, his name quickly ceased to be mentioned, although his proposals continued to be discussed. Some Western observers even hold that he was consciously used as a figurehead for a liberal 'profit-group', which was advocating radical reform,[4] and it is certainly along such lines that his importance in the Soviet context should be seen. With the publication of his *Pravda* article, an official sanction was given for public debate. The paper's editors even issued an open invitation for economists to face that challenge.[5] The ensuing debate is particularly interesting in terms of the light it shed on the role of Liberman as a 'reformer'.[6]

Liberman's fame stems largely from his very strong emphasis on profit as a motivating force for enterprise managers, and perhaps also from his statement in *Pravda*, that 'What is profitable for society must be profitable for each enterprise.' It must be underlined, however, that he was very far from being a proponent of a 'radical reform' of the kind that was implied by the theories of economists like Kantorovich and Novozhilov, or indeed by Soviet reformists of today, like Zaslavskaya. The main thrust of the Liberman proposals was a reduction in what has long been known as the 'petty tutelage' of planners and Party officials over enterprise management. Liberman wanted profit to be the main determinant of enterprise behaviour and central plan directives to be limited to the quantity, assortment, and delivery of output. Given such directives, the enterprise should be free to make its own plans, for the simple reason that it 'alone knows and can discover its reserves best.'[7]

In order for the profit motive to make enterprises opt for maximum efficiency, an incentive scheme was outlined whereby a high bonus would be earned for reaching a set target, whereas a relatively low one would be paid for any additional output above that target. Enterprises that failed to meet their set targets would be deprived of all bonuses. There would thus be powerful formal incentives to strive for efficiency and to seek out cost economies. Liberman even provided a numerical example on how such incentive schemes could be arranged.[8]

As Alfred Zauberman pointed out in a 1963 article, it was precisely this incentive scheme, rather than the conceptual framework, that was really novel in Liberman's proposals.[9] Liberman himself was very specific in stressing that the overall framework of planning would remain intact. Central plans would continue to be drawn up, and directives issued, in much the same way as before, although the directives would now only reach the *sovnarkhoz* (which was still in existence at that time), and not the enterprise. Firms would indeed be allowed to devise their own plans, but only in negotiations with their customers, and subject to approval by the planning authorities. Once approved, moreover, the plan would be strictly binding. The profit motive was thus not intended to replace other control mechanisms. It was simply to be given a more prominent role among those other indicators.

Exactly how these negotiations were to be arranged, and what respective roles were to be played by planners and managers, was left unclear, and in the ensuing debate various interpretations were put forward. These institutional arrangements, however, were not the only weak point of the proposed model. Another, and considerably more important feature concerns the problem of stability. As we have noted above, decentralized enterprise decision making was to be based on a profit motive, and to be guided by centrally fixed norms, regarding resource use and production techniques. Here we have one of the most basic of all problems of Soviet planning. If centrally fixed norms are to have the desired influence on enterprise decisions regarding resource allocation, then they must remain stable over an extended period of time (Nemchinov suggested 10–15 years), but this requirement is clearly incompatible with the simultaneous desire that the norms in question should also reflect a current economic reality.[10]

Given this contradiction, it is hardly surprising to observe that views on how best to resolve this issue have tended to pendulate over time. Since central norms will in some way have to enter into evaluations of enterprise performance, and thus help determine enterprise penalties and rewards, it is rather understandable that frequent adjustments will produce bitter complaints from managers, about changes being made in the rules while the game is being played. Such complaints will in their turn produce promises from the centre, that norms will remain stable in the future, but as reality changes, the norms become obsolete and central interference becomes a necessity. A vicious circle is established, which is still waiting to be resolved.

The really crucial issue of the Liberman proposals is a direct consequence of the problem of stability versus adaptation. Since Liberman failed to come to terms with this issue, he never succeeded in formulating a proper theory for the role of prices in his system.[11] The latter were at the same time to be fixed by the centre, and subject to flexible adjustment in negotiations between enterprises,[12] hardly an arrangement which inspires much confidence in the theoretical underpinnings of his alleged 'reform' model. In the absence of a corresponding change in the *principles* of pricing, planners and enterprise managers would find themselves working in what Zauberman has referred to as different 'parametric frameworks', and the risk of conflicts between their respective choices is rather obvious:

> Presumably the planner would continue to rely largely on a physical-term calculation, and his hunches, allowing as he does sometimes now for profit achievable in feasible alternatives. How can he expect that he and the firm manager, the latter guided solely by the profit calculus, would opt for the same output and input structure?[13]

What, then, can we conclude about the Liberman proposals? Did they, for example, really imply decentralization? Liberman himself was very vague on this crucial issue, and it is, of course, not very productive – in this context – to engage in *ex post* speculation about what his own true ambitions might have been. We may note, however, that there was considerable scepticism amongst Western observers. Nove has concluded that the proposed model was simply not coherent,[14] and there was also considerable opposition amongst Soviet economists of the time. For example, the former Minister of Finance, A. Zverev, who was one of the main opponents to reform, suggested that 'the average profit rate of an enterprise cannot be substituted for the role and power of state planning.'[15]

We shall not venture any further into the theoretical coherence of Liberman's model. Nor shall we survey the various arguments that were put forward in the undoubtedly interesting Soviet debate on this matter.[16] Instead, we shall draw on the benefit of hindsight, in order to see what came out of that debate. By looking at those measures which actually were implemented, and at their respective degrees of success, we may perhaps draw some important conclusions regarding the viability of the proposed changes.

Swings of the Pendulum

The Reform that Never Was[17]

The contents of that package of reform measures which actually came to be introduced by Premier Alexei Kosygin, in September 1965, had two main thrusts, both of which were aimed at increasing the scope for autonomous enterprise decision making. The *first* of these concerned a reduction in the number of centrally fixed plan indicators, a step which was clearly in the spirit of Liberman. A case in point that was raised by Kosygin, in his speech to the Central Committee, was that of labour. Before the reform, enterprises had received four separate targets, controlling labour productivity, the number of workers, average wages, and the total wage fund. These were now to be amalgamated into one, controlling the wage fund alone, and Kosygin even hinted that, in the future, that indicator might also be abolished.[18] The only problem seen by him in this respect, was that until a substantial increase in production had been achieved, control had to be maintained over the total of wages paid out, simply in order to ensure a macro-economic balance between total demand and total supply in the economy.

Overall, the number of centrally assigned indicators was to be reduced from around twenty to thirty, depending on branch, to the following eight:

1. Total sales in rubles
2. Assortment of production
3. Total wage fund in rubles
4. Profits in rubles and in relation to capital
5. Transfers to and from the state budget
6. Investment and introduction of new capacity
7. Introduction of new technology
8. Material supply

The *second* thrust of the reform was expressed in a strong emphasis on financial levers, as a necessary complement to reducing the number of indicators. Perhaps the most prominent example here is the introduction of total sales as a target, to replace the old focus on gross output. Hereby a commendable attempt was made to curb some part of the classic practice of the *kult vala*, the 'output cult', the essence of which was (and still is) that the enterprise is rewarded primarily in relation to the total value of its output, rather than in relation to the efficiency with which that output is produced.

In a broad sense, the emphasis on financial levers was intended to mean much more than simply making accounts in rubles instead of in tons. In order to give a real content to the desire for an increased scope for local decision-making, resources would have to be put at the disposal of management. For this purpose, three separate enterprise funds were introduced, to be used by managers according to a set of fairly complicated rules. One of these was the *material incentive fund*, out of which premiums and bonuses of various kinds could be paid to workers, as well as to management. Another was the *production development fund*, which was to provide funds for decentralized investment, and finally there was the *socio-cultural fund*, which was to provide housing for the employees, as well as cater to various material, cultural, and educational needs.

Payments into these funds were to be made out of enterprise profits, as in the Liberman case, but according to a far more complicated system. The wage fund was to be used as a basis for calculating the magnitude of the payments, a measure which was clearly aimed at introducing an element of fairness between firms, such that capital-intensive firms with high profits would not be able to pay higher bonuses than those with labour-intensive techniques and many employees. The actual percentages of deductions and payments in various directions would then be determined by enterprise performance in relation to a number of different plan indicators. Here the rules were of such a nature that the resultant incentive schemes presented enterprise managers with an 'extremely intricate maximizing problem'.[19] According to Nove, the rules were 'barely comprehensible and often contradictory',[20] and Schroeder concludes that 'both the rules and the objectives are contradictory.'[21]

In addition to the complexity of the rules regarding payments and deductions, the funds also suffered from the problem of introducing different 'parametric frameworks' as was pointed out by Zauberman in relation to the Liberman proposals. Central plans would continue to be drawn up, and the appropriate authorities would be held responsible for their fulfilment, while the enterprises were simultaneously granted a wider scope for making their own decisions. One may perhaps realistically assume that the planners felt this asymmetry to be rather unfair, and the fate of the reform would be heavily marked by contradiction at this point.

According to the original decision, the reform was to be gradually implemented during the years 1966–70, and at first glance there would seem to have been considerable progress. By 1970, as many as 83 per cent of all industrial enterprises, accounting together for 92 per cent of total industrial production, had been transferred to the new system. These figures, however, reflect the official picture, and what may hide behind them is obviously difficult to tell. Schroeder, for example, argues that much of the initial increase in sales was due simply to a running down of unsold inventories, a move which had been triggered by the introduction of sales as a target, to replace the previous one for gross output only.[22] This could obviously provide no more than a once-and-for-all improvement. It might also be mentioned that the corresponding figure for progress in construction and material supply was only 10 per cent.[23] This indicates that the pace of the reform was at best uneven. Whatever the actual degree of original progress, however, the direction of change was soon to be reversed. There were good reasons for this reversal, reasons which we shall now proceed to look at in somewhat more detail.

The System Strikes Back

The original intention behind the reform had certainly been commendable. High profits would indirectly mean large bonus payments, more decentralized investment and more resources for purposes like housing and cultural activities. All of this would seem to provide powerful incentives for both labour and management to improve performance. In practice, however, evidence indicates that enterprises chose largely to ignore the proposed role of profit making, preferring instead to place a continued emphasis on gross output, or on gross sales. Furthermore, the promised freedom for enterprises to determine their own labour utilization, within the broad limits of the total wage fund, was circumscribed by continued interference from above, by the traditional enterprise desire to maintain reserves, and by strong resistence from the labour unions.[24]

Finally, even the attempts to promote a certain degree of decentralization in investment decision making, via the production development fund, were largely frustrated. The total volume of decentralized investment did increase, but mainly in enterprises with large profits, where the need to promote decentralization should have been the smallest. The introduction of a 6 per cent capital charge and the attempt to increase the role of bank credits met with similar disappointments. An important obstacle to success on these points was the anomaly that lay in decentralizing decisions over investment funds, whilst failing to make a corresponding change in the system of material supply. Consequently, the real scope for enterprise decision-making was affected to a very small degree.

As we have already mentioned, however, in spite of these problems and obstacles, a certain degree of progress was indeed recorded. Enterprise profits were increasing, bonus payments did go up, and so did the volume of decentralized investment. Maybe these modest advances were largely statistical, but the appearance of progress nevertheless seems to have been sufficient in order to start a process of counter-reform. The reasons behind the latter have been characterized by Schroeder in the following way: 'The experience of enterprises operating under the new procedures disclosed a number of inconsistencies and perversities in the rules and produced types of behaviour that the planners did not like.'[25] One part of what the planners did not 'like' was that increased payments of bonuses were made to white-collar workers, but there were a number of other criticisms as well, which, taken together, amounted to 'a tacit admission that the reforms were not really accomplishing their objectives.'[26]

At the beginning of the 1970s, strong feelings of discontent were generally assumed to be spreading within the planning hierarchy.

One may perhaps realistically assume that bureaucrats have an instinctive dislike for anything that smacks of reduced control and it is hardly surprising that strong demands for increased regulation started to emanate from this quarter. The result of such pressures took the form of a decree from the Central Committee, which aimed at changing the rules regarding the formation and utilization of incentive funds. The common denominator of these changes was to increase central control, and to combat the dreaded phenomenon of 'spontaneity'.

As a result, the pendulum started to swing back again. During the years 1971–3, six new central indicators were introduced, in addition to the previous eight. Among these, we may note that separate targets for labour productivity and for gross output were reintroduced. Detailed regulation was introduced for making payments both into and out of the bonus fund and a similar fate befell the production development fund. Briefly put, the enterprises had their newfound freedom effectively circumscribed and thus the entire reform attempt fell flat on the ground. As Schroeder has put it, the reform was 'bureaucratized into impotence'.[27] Her portrayal of the nature of the counter-reform is equally striking:

> In conclusion, the latest round of modifications in Soviet planning and incentives leaves the essentials of the system unchanged, but adds to the degree of centralization and to the complexity of administrative arrangements. The innovations also help to swell the administrative bureaucracy, which has increased nearly one-third since 1965.[28]

It is important to note this pattern of reaction, as there seems to be at this point an unavoidable dilemma. Reforms are originally introduced in order to improve economic efficiency in production, which essentially means granting the enterprises a larger degree of freedom in deciding over the use of resources. Soon, however, the planners discover that enterprise behaviour is not in line with the intentions in the plan, due chiefly to inconsistencies in the price system and in the system of material allocation. The only way out of this situation is then seen to lie in an increased detail of regulation, i.e. in introducing more plan indicators. Because the latter are, in their turn, the very antithesis to the original intentions behind the reform, a very characteristic pendulum movement is established.

Further Reform Decrees

The essence of this 'pendulum' is that of a constant probing for 'perfection', which in practice takes the form of a number of different experiments and alterations in the system of planning and control. The most well known of such experiments is perhaps that which was started at the Shchekino chemical combine as long ago as April 1967. The basic principle there was that the enterprise was granted the right to retain any savings in wages that could be made by shedding labour, provided that output was not reduced. Although much publicized, however, Shchekino was far from the only experiment, nor did it provide any panacea for the problems that have been outlined above.

Throughout the 1970s, a number of various experiments were carried out, but none of them really caught on and by the end of the decade, the time was obviously ripe for some pressure from the centre. In July 1979, the Central Committee issued a major decree which apparently was intended to inject some new life into the reform process. The content of that decree, however, was hardly designed to arouse much excitement. Morris Bornstein, for example, concluded that it 'indicates the Soviet regime's intention to try to modify and improve the traditional economic mechanism rather than to replace it; for example, with some kind of "marketizing" economic reform.'[29] A similarly pessimistic evaluation was offered by Philip Hanson: 'Almost nothing in the decree is new: it is a compendium of planning and incentive arrangements which have been tried out in various branches; what the decree does is to call for their general introduction, at least throughout the industrial sector.'[30]

Against this background, it would certainly seem out of context to speak of the 1979 decree as a reform. We may also note that the Soviets very carefully avoided using the Russian word *reforma*. Consequently, most Western observers were sceptical about any potentially beneficial effects, and it is interesting to note similarly pessimistic moods on the Soviet side. For example, Hanson quotes the subsequently influential economist Abel Aganbegyan[31] as first saying that it was 'a good, well founded, balanced plan for resource use', and then proceeding to add that 'in several respects we do not know how to make a good plan'. As Hanson points out, we have here the real 'nub of the matter': 'The new measures would work well if detailed planning from the centre were highly efficient. But if detailed planning from the centre had been highly efficient in the first place, there would be no scope for improvement, and no need for a "reform".'[32]

It is in precisely the latter respect that the 1979 decree is important, as it sheds further light on the prospects for achieving real improvements in the economy by means of simple manipulation of the system of plan indicators. The most important ingredients of the decree were as follows: for bonus purposes, attention was concentrated on three centrally fixed plan indicators; a completely new indicator was introduced, to replace gross output and sales; and profits replaced the wage fund as a basis for calculating bonuses. If we take a closer look at these points, we shall see our message about the limits to 'tinkering' being brought home rather forcefully.

The new indicator was called Normative Net Output (*normativnaya chistaya produktsiya*), and it was a concept which is reminiscent of but does not quite correspond to the Western concept of value added. We shall not go into technical distinctions here,[33] but it is important to note that this change represented yet another attempt to suppress the *kult vala*. Enterprises would no longer be rewarded in relation to the value of gross output, or sales, but in relation to the value of work performed. Norms would be calculated for the estimated volume of resources needed in order to produce a unit of a specified good, and the enterprise would then be rewarded according to its performance in relation to these norms.

In theory, this certainly represented an important step forward, since wasteful use of resources and preferences for expensive inputs would no longer be rewarded. In practice, however, it may just as well have been a step in reverse. As all other experiments were based on various norms, this also suffered from the lack of a reliable basis for calculation. Of course, norms regarding resource use must, in some way or other, depart from the price system, and the shortcomings of the latter should by now be rather familiar. Moreover, there is also the 'classic' problem of stability versus adaptation, which likewise has been discussed above. In essence, we have here one of the very many 'Catch-22' type situations that are so characteristic of the Soviet economy. Norms that agree poorly with reality produce bad plans, which create needs for revisions, which upset the stability of the norms, etc., etc.[34]

The introduction of a completely new concept also meant that the burden on the already overstrained planning apparatus was increased by another few million forms, to be read and evaluated (or perhaps simply ignored).[35] This could be expected to aggravate the already serious discrepancies between production targets and resource allocation for the individual enterprises. Hanson argues that there 'are, indeed, grounds for suspecting that the 1979 decree is making matters worse, not better, in so far as it increases the information overload.'[36] Finally, there also lay a serious inconsistency in the fact that sales continued to be planned in traditional gross terms, while production targets were now to be made in net terms. Enterprises were consequently burdened with two parallel sets of statistics. This can hardly have served to increase the efficiency of their decision making.

The *second* ingredient of interest in the 1979 decree concerns the three central plan indicators which were designated as 'fund forming'. The simplest of these to assess is total sales. According to Hanson, the 'most likely' interpretation is that it constituted a 'threshold' indicator, i.e. that all enterprises which fail to meet at least 98 per cent (in some cases 97 per cent) of their planned volume of sales would thereby automatically forfeit all bonuses.[37] No effects on payments into the bonus fund seem to have been intended here. This role is instead to be played by the respective indicators for labour productivity and for the share of high quality output.

The indicator for improved labour productivity is somewhat less straightforward than that concerning sales. Most likely, it represented nothing essentially new, but if it was intended to be measured in 'normative net' terms then the situation may be somewhat different. The really interesting point, however, concerns the ambition to link bonus payments with the quality of output produced. As an idea, this makes a lot of sense, but in practice there are considerable problems of definition and measurement. The main question concerns *who* is going to make the assessment, and according to which criteria. One is certainly tempted to suspect that products sold on the world market will be chosen as the standard and that in practice it will be up to the producing Soviet enterprise to identify its 'competitor'. After all, it is the enterprise, and not the planner, which has the relevant information. The situation will thus be characterized by the same type of 'game' which marks the process of plan bargaining at large. As Hanson puts it, 'who in his right mind is going to select "analogous" products for comparison which would make his own branch or enterprise product look inferior?'[38]

The *third* ingredient of a more important nature in the 1979 decree was that profits replaced the wage fund, as a basis for calculating bonuses. The importance of this step lay in the removal of the enterprise's previous incentive to maximize the volume of employment, in order to get a large wage fund and thus also large payments into the bonus fund. According to the new system, enterprise performance in relation to the indicators for labour productivity and the share of quality output would directly determine what share of profits should be paid into the various funds, without taking a detour via the wage fund.

To sum up, it was undoubtedly the case that the 1979 decree did contain features which were *both* novel *and* interesting. There was, however, also a number of drawbacks. Most serious, perhaps, was the heavy reliance that was placed on the practice of making 'counter-plans'. The basic idea behind this practice is that enterprises should be voluntarily induced to propose for themselves higher plan targets than those assigned by the planners. It should thus be possible to un-cover some 'hidden reserves'. It is certainly the case that Soviet enterprises are normally believed to hoard substantial reserves, which could be put to productive use, although it is unclear why they should volunteer to do so. Given the notorious uncertainty concern-ing future changes in plan obligations, and in particular with regard to material allocation, it is hardly surprising to find that, in 1981, less than 7 per cent of all industrial enterprises adopted counter-plans.[39] Hanson's conclusion is rather to the point:

> Counter-planning has therefore become a largely unrewarded act of voluntary uncertainty bearing. The only attraction is one that is not supposed to be on offer: the possibility of larger input alloca-tions to 'support' a counter-plan. That, presumably, helps to explain why any enterprises at all still offer counter-plans.[40]

The prospects for success with the 1979 decree were thus not overly promising. When faced with reality, it soon turned out that in prac-tice it would remain a dead letter. At a Central Committee plenum in November 1981, Brezhnev complained that it was only slowly and half-heartedly making its way through the bureaucracy.[41] Conse-quently, the time would soon be ripe for another attempt from the centre to push the reform process forward.

In June 1983, a number of further experiments were announced, to be introduced in January 1984. The main impression of this de-cree, however, is that it represented little more than an attempt to actually implement changes announced in 1965 and in 1979. As in the previous cases, the number of indicators was to be reduced, and the need for quality improvements and increased labour productivity was similarly emphasized. (There were certain technical distinctions, concerning *inter alia* the actual formulation of bonus functions and the stress that was placed on the need for technological progress, but these will not be dealt with further here.) It is of greater importance to note that on this occasion, as on others, no novelties of any prin-cipally important nature were announced. As a matter of fact, in the midst of Gorbachev's *perestroika* we can find Aganbegyan, one of the General Secretary's favourite economists, criticizing it for having been merely a repetition of the Kosygin reform, doomed to fail because it did not address the crucial issues of pricing and supply of inputs.[42]

When Brezhnev died, in November 1982, he left behind the experiences of close on two decades of a more or less continuous struggle to implement reform decrees which had changed very little in content, from the 1965 Kosygin 'reform' onwards. Andropov's attempt in 1983–4 was not much different in this respect. This process has been portrayed rather strikingly in Schroeder's metaphor of the Soviet economy being placed on a 'treadmill of reforms'.[43] Those vested interests which have served systematically to block any effective change are described in the following, rather conclusive manner: 'After 60 years of experience with a Socialist economy run by government agencies, however, nearly everyone seems to have found ways to turn its shortcomings to individual advantage.'[44]

Soviet post-war economic history is strongly marked by the swings of this peculiar reform pendulum. In particular, of course, this is true for the post-Khrushchev era. With the option of major administrative reshuffles being removed by Khrushchev's 'tinkering', and with the growth of vested interests against change in the basic principles of operation of the system of planning and control, the only remaining option was to work *within* the system. In Soviet terminology, such attempts at improvement are known as *sovershenstvovanie*, a term which can be roughly translated as 'perfecting'. This term has important ideological implications. In contrast to economic reform (which is known in Russian as *reforma*), *sovershenstvovanie* is based on the assumption that the existing system is basically sound, and thus in need only of some minor refinements, in order to find its 'perfect' and ultimate shape.

There are two reasons why it is important to make the distinction between these two concepts. *First* of all, we have the simple problem of misunderstanding. Since Western media have a tendency to publicize as 'economic reforms' such changes in the Soviet economy that would be more appropriately understood as experiments, or mere refinements, Soviet economic 'reformers' will to some extent be judged for not achieving goals that were perhaps never intended to be reached in the first place. As a rule, such attempts have generally been aimed at improving some partial aspect of the model, be it some specific industry, some specific ministry, some specific region, or some combination of them all. This brings us over to the second reason for making a distinction between the respective concepts of *reforma* and *sovershenstvovanie*.

The normal understanding of 'reform', we shall argue, is that of a comprehensive change in some general principles. Indeed, the very semantics of the word indicate that the subject to be reformed should acquire in the process an essentially new shape. We are thus dealing with something considerably different from a partial manipulation of some of its aspects. Experience, moreover, seems to suggest that real reform of the socialist economies cannot be a continuous process. The step from A to B has to be taken all at once, or not at all. Nove speaks about these dilemmas in terms of the 'inevitable failure of gradualness': 'Piecemeal reform does not work, and one is driven back to the old system. The point is that the system has an inner logic which resists *partial* change.'[45] In early 1988, Soviet Academician Vladimir Tikhonov comments on that very same problem in the following manner: 'Stage-by-stage reforms have never been realized in Russia [*sic*]. A resolute, once-and-for-all radical change is needed. It must include a reform of prices, of planning and the abolition of unnecessary personel.'[46]

The introduction of the New Economic Mechanism (NEM) in Hungary, in January 1968, is an obvious illustration.[47] Having fully realized the importance of the points regarding both comprehensiveness and gradualness, the Hungarians spent several years in preparation, and then took the full step overnight. The fact that NEM still did not succeed is today being ascribed to the fact that it was not comprehensive enough, i.e. that it left some parts of the economy (notably the institutional structure) outside the reform process. This certainly adds an important dimension to the prospects for success with Soviet *sovershenstvovanie*.

Before proceeding, we should note here two apparent Soviet exceptions, which may be advanced to the rules about comprehensiveness and gradualness. The *first* is the 1965 'reform', which we have discussed above and which was certainly viewed at the time – by Soviet economists at least – as a both comprehensive and radical step in a new direction. A. Birman, for example, called it the third great reform in Soviet history, after NEP and the introduction of five-year planning.[48] Against the background of what we have just said, however, it should be possible to conclude that it actually met neither of these criteria. As we have seen above, it was devoured by the bureaucracy, and perhaps even that is too generous a description. Already in 1968, Schroeder made the following prediction:

> Some Westerners have already suggested that the bureaucracy ultimately will sabotage the reform. It may well try, but there is little to sabotage in the reform as now constituted. It is a pale and sickly creature unworthy to stand in the same company with its robust and energetic predecessors – the NEP and the five-year plans – as one of the three great economic reforms in all Soviet history.[49]

The *second* seeming exception is Mikhail Gorbachev's *perestroika*, which is somewhat more problematic. In official statements, it is deliberately presented not merely as a 'reform'. At the twenty-sixth Party Congress, in February/March 1986, the General Secretary even went so far as to call for a 'radical' reform, a *radikalnaya reforma*.[50] In the concluding chapter of our study we will return to discuss whether this simply represents empty rhetoric, or whether Gorbachev is indeed serious, and in this case to what extent he will actually be able to realize his ambitions. Let us now shift the focus of our attention to the realm of agriculture, which represents the real Achilles heel of the Soviet system.[51]

The Enigma of Agriculture

When dicussing the Brezhnev era in Soviet development, it has long been common practice to talk in terms of stagnation, lethargy and a general inability to address increasingly serious problems. Our account above has certainly been no exception in this respect, and it is also rather interesting to note how the Gorbachev leadership has started to use a similar vocabulary when referring to that important period. As a matter of fact, one might even understand this as a reflection of a perhaps paradoxical but nevertheless important Soviet dependence on Western scholarship. Given the paranoid attitude towards information that marks their own society, Soviet social scientists have increasingly been forced to turn to Western research, simply in order to create a picture of their own, and it is thus hardly surprising if the respective analyses should coincide.[52] When moving into the realm of agriculture, however, we must recognize a rather subtle and also quite important nuance in this picture of stagnation. The nuance lies in the substantial shift of priorities in resource allocation that was actually implemented by Brezhnev, in favour of agriculture, and its importance in the very poor rewards that resulted from this change in policy.

A Black Hole in the Soviet Economy

In all fairness, we should perhaps start by recognizing that when viewed simply in terms of aggregate output figures, the performance of Soviet agriculture during the post-war period has been rather impressive. From Table 10.1 we can see, for example, that output of the all-important grain increased during 1956–85 by no less than 48.2 per cent. (If the highly unfavourable years 1981–5 are excluded, it increased by as much as 68.7 per cent.) With the exception of potatoes, other products show an even more impressive pattern. The vitally important output of vegetables was nearly doubled, while meat was more than doubled and eggs more than trebled, during the period in question.

Table 10.1 Soviet agricultural production, 1956–85 (in millions of tons; eggs per million pieces; annual averages)

	1956–60	*1961–65*	*1966–70*	*1971–75*	*1976–80*	*1981–85*
Grain	121.5	130.3	167.6	181.6	205.0	180.3
Vegetables	15.1	16.9	19.5	23.0	26.3	29.2
Potatoes	88.3	81.6	94.8	89.8	82.6	78.4
Meat	7.9	9.3	11.6	14.0	14.8	16.2
Milk	57.2	64.7	80.6	87.4	92.7	94.6
Eggs	23.6	28.7	35.8	51.4	63.1	74.4

Source: Narkhoz (1986), pp. 180–1.

As soon as we go beyond aggregate production figures, however, we encounter a picture which is rather less encouraging. First of all, a growing discrepancy between plan targets and actual production results indicates that performance has fallen far short of expectations. Let us again use grain as an illustration. For the period 1966–70, the plan was just about fulfilled. Subsequently, the gap between plan and reality has grown quite rapidly. In 1971–5, the total deficit between planned and actual output amounted to 67 million tons, for 1976–80 the total was 75 million, and for 1981–5 it reached as much as 300 million. In overall terms, the accumulated deficit for the period 1971–85 amounted to 442 million tons, or two and a half times the average annual harvest in 1981–5.[53] If we make the seemingly reasonable assumption that official plan targets reflect what is considered a desirable return to resources allocated, these figures certainly present a gloomy impression.

Furthermore, if we take into account that the Soviet population grew by 39.6 percent in 1956–85, or from 197.9 million to 276.3 million, it is evident that performance in per capita terms leaves even more to be desired.[54] Grain production thus defined increased from 0.58 tons in 1956–60, to 0.72 tons in 1971–5, and 0.78 tons in 1976–80.[55] These calculations present a clear impression of a rapid expansion at the beginning of Brezhnev's rule and of a subsequent stagnation. In 1981–5, moreover, an absolute decline to merely 0.66 tons per capita was registered.[56]

Disappointing as this may seem, however, it is only when we look at the input side, i.e. at the volume of resources that have been consumed in the process, that the real seriousness of economic mismanagement under Brezhnev is brought out. We have seen above how Khrushchev sought to postpone the need for agricultural reform by ploughing up the Virgin Lands, and how this policy not only led to an exhaustion of the remaining reserve of marginal lands, but also served to incorporate a rather serious sensitivity to weather fluctuations. In addition, there are now similarly gloomy accounts of agriculture's claims on labour and capital. Since, however, the period 1981–5 is marked by three changes in the top leadership, and by associated changes in policy, as far as statistics go we shall draw a line here at the end of the 1976–80 plan period, leaving the 1980s for discussion in the concluding chapter of our study. Let us start by looking at the Soviet agricultural labour force in an international perspective. Table 10.2 shows the Soviet case in comparison with the US and with Japan and Italy.

Table 10.2 Agriculture's share of total employment (in percentages, including forestry)

	1950	1970	1975	1980
Japan	51.6	17.4	12.7	10.4
Italy	43.9	18.2	15.2	13.2
United States	12.1	4.5	4.1	3.6
Soviet Union	53.9	32.2	28.8	26.4

Source: Goodman, Hughes and Schroeder (1987), p. 102.

The main impression given by this table no doubt concerns the remarkably high level of Soviet agricultural labour utilization. In particular, this is the case if comparison is made with the United States, which tends to be the favourite Soviet yardstick. The cases of Japan and Italy are certainly more illustrative, since they had a structure roughly similar to the Soviet Union at the beginning of the period in question, but even then the comparison indicates rather forcefully that something has gone seriously amiss in the Soviet case. Table 10.3 provides a more detailed picture.

Table 10.3   Soviet agricultural labour force, 1940–80

	1940	1960	1970	1975	1980
Rural population share[a]	67.5	50.1	43.1	39.3	36.6
Rural labour force share[b]	54.0	39.0	25.0	23.0	20.0
Agricultural labour force[c]	31.7	28.8	26.0	25.5	24.7
APK cadres[d]	n.a.	n.a.	n.a.	41.8	42.5

Notes: (a) per cent of total population (b) per cent, defined as the number of workers actually employed in agriculture plus forestry, including the private sector, in relation to total employment, (c) million man-year equivalents, defined as *sovkhoz* workers, *kolkhoz* peasants and workers in inter-farm agricultural enterprises, excluding the private sector, (d) million man-year equivalents, defined as the whole 'agro-industrial complex', which includes both socialized and private sectors of agriculture, plus all related activities, such as construction, processing, procurement, trade, repairs, etc.

Source: Narkhoz (1986), pp. 5, 303–4, 389–91.

If we start by looking at the first two rows of the table, we find that agriculture's claim on human resources has been reduced considerably over the period as a whole. The rural labour force share, for example, was more than halved in 1940–70. A closer inspection, however, reveals two disturbing facts: on the one hand, that the fall in agriculture's share of the total labour force slowed up considerably after 1970, and on the other, that the fall in the share of the rural population has been considerably less pronounced than that of the agricultural labour force. The latter reflects a rapidly growing demographic gap between rural and urban areas, due chiefly to a flight of the young for the cities. Although Central Asia certainly forms an exception here, what we are left with in overall terms is a definite impression of an ageing rural labour force.

If, moreover, we proceed to look at rows three and four, it is evident that the fall in agriculture's share of the total labour force has been due to an expansion in the urban workforce rather than a reduction in the rural one. In a narrow definition, the agricultural sector reduced its labour use by no more than five percentage points during the 1970s, and if we look at what the Soviets refer to as APK, i.e. the whole of the Agro-Industrial Complex (*Agropromyshlennyi kompleks*), agriculture has actually been *expanding* its claims, in absolute terms. The latter is true, in particular, for the controlling bureaucracy, which grew from 399,000 in 1975, to 480,000 in 1980.[57]

Substantial as these figures may seem, however, they still reflect only the officially recorded average annual workforce. In order to produce a more correct picture of agriculture's real claims on human resources, we must also include the additional labour that is tempo-

255

rarily put into agricultural work, during peak harvest time. Here the picture is rather hazy. Looking at official statistics on the number of workers on 'temporary attachment' to agriculture, we may find that this figure has been increasing steadily over time, from 0.6 million in 1970, to 1.0 million in 1975, and 1.3 million in 1980.[58] Seen in relation to the total agricultural labour force, this of course represents only a minor addition. If, however, we take into account that the figures are given as estimated man-years, a somewhat different picture will emerge.

What we then need to know is a conversion factor and here we are helped by a Soviet source from 1981, which claims that in 1978 a total of 15.6 million urban residents, about half of whom were industrial workers, were drafted into such activities for about a month each.[59] If we thus multiply our above figures by a factor 12, we find that the seasonal addition to the agricultural workforce, measured in terms of individuals, has increased from 7.2 million in 1970, to 15.6 million in 1980. This certainly gives a powerful impression of the outside help that is given to agriculture. These figures, however, still do not include students and others who are not officially employed and thus probably underestimate the true extent of the problem. This difference in coverage accounts for the difference between our two sources above, concerning the years 1978 and 1980, and indicates that the seasonal help may well be approaching 20 million people.

With the exhaustion of the reserve of marginal cultivable lands, and the already excessive agricultural labour force, it is rather natural that Brezhnev's wager would be placed on increased capital investment. Vigorous programmes for mechanization and land reclamation were launched, in an attempt to relieve the constraints on labour and land. The traces of the associated shift in priorities between agriculture and industry are clearly visible in the statistics. In the period 1965–80, annual investment in agriculture increased by almost 200 per cent – from 14.4 to 41.6 billion constant rubles – thus raising the share of agriculture in total investment in the Soviet economy from 22 to 28 per cent.[60] What we have here is essentially nothing but a *de facto* reversal of the process of industrialization, with the primary sector expanding its claims on available resources, rather than providing a surplus for the growth of the secondary (manufacturing) and tertiary (services) sectors of the economy.

The real seriousness of this process, however, lies not so much in the mere volume of resources that was devoted to agriculture, as in the fact that the rewards offered by the Black Hole, in return for the massive resource infusion, were meagre indeed. Before proceeding to examine the specific programmes, we may have a first impression

Table 10.4   **Capital-output relations in *kolkhozy*, 1965–80**
             (billion 1973 rubles)

	1965	1970	1975	1980
Capital stock	42.3	60.0	91.7	109.8
Output	35.5	42.3	42.0	41.5
Capital/Output	1.19	1.43	2.17	2.63

Source: Narkhoz (1981), p. 254.

of the overall picture by looking at the relation between capital and output in *kolkhozy* during the period in question.

From Table 10.4 we can see that in spite of an increase in capital stock by 160 per cent, *kolkhoz* output grew by a mere 17 per cent, and a similar picture can be presented for the *sovkhoz* sector.[61] One explanation might of course be that capital had been substituted for other factors, as would have been normal in any process of economic development. As we have seen above, however, this has not been the case. Both land and labour have been pushed to their respective limits. With this, let us proceed to take a closer look at the component parts of the picture, starting with mechanization.

Mechanization

In accordance with Lenin's classic statement, that if the peasants could only be provided with 100,000 tractors they would turn communists, Soviet agricultural policy has been aimed throughout at promoting large-scale and intensive mechanization. We have seen above how the process of amalgamations under Khrushchev served substantially to reduce the number of farms, thereby also increasing greatly the average farm size. With Brezhnev's entry on the stage, the process of mechanizing work on these giant farms was given a considerable boost. During the years 1965–80, the total number of tractors in Soviet agriculture increased by 58.8 per cent, the number of grain combines by 38.8 per cent, and that of trucks by 68.9 per cent.[62] At first glance, this picture would certainly not seem to inspire great worry. If, however, we compare inventories with the rate of deliveries, a dramatically different picture emerges.

During the same period, deliveries of tractors, combines and trucks were of such a magnitude that the actual annual increases in inventory amounted to no more than 10–15 per cent of deliveries.[63] The implied scrapping rates indicate that the service life of Soviet tractors and combine harvesters is no more than 7–8 years, and that of trucks 6–7 years. There were of course many reasons behind this development, not the least of which derive from poor care and maintenance on the farms. However, it must also be emphasized that some of them lay outside agriculture proper, in that system of 'material supply' which comprises agricultural machine building as well as the distribution and servicing of such equipment.

Information concerning the performance of agriculture's 'partners' have long been provided in both Soviet mass media and in scholarly journals. In 1982, for example, *Sotsialisticheskaya Industriya* reported that the combine harvesters Kolos and Niva, which are designed for an uninterrupted operation of around 300 hours during a season, had an average operating time – between breakdowns – of no more than 5.7 and 8.7 hours, respectively.[64] In this respect, the onset of *glasnost* under Gorbachev has not brought anything new. It has, however, added a sense of urgency to official comments. From a conference held in late 1986, at the Minselkhozmash, the ultimately responsible Ministry of Agricultural Machine Building, the following was reported: 'When machinery and equipment is put into operation, massive defects are revealed in welded joints, in assembly work, in adjustment and in painting.'[65] In 1987, moreover, Shmelev revealed that one out of every two tractors that are supplied to Soviet agriculture is destined to be stripped for spare parts, in order to keep existing machinery running.[66]

It was argued above that the most serious ingredient in the picture of Brezhnev's agricultural investment programme was not the volume of resources as such, but rather the poor results that had been generated. The picture of waste and misallocation that is provided by sources of the kind cited above certainly gives cause to suspect that, in spite of massive investment, the actually achieved level of mechanization may not be very high. Such suspicions are also well corroborated by official Soviet sources. At the beginning of the 1980s, no more than a quarter of all farm labour was classified as 'mechanized', which means that the bulk of the agricultural labour force was still engaged in heavy manual labour, aided by primitive and often makeshift tools and implements.[67]

If the programme for mechanization can thus be seen to conform fairly well with our previous metaphor of comparing Soviet agriculture to a Black Hole, this apparently is the case to an even greater extent with respect to the other major ingredient in the investment drive, that of the land reclamation schemes.

Land Reclamation

As the Soviets frequently point out, in comparison with the Western countries, Soviet agriculture is faced with highly adverse soil and climatic conditions. Although the country occupies about one sixth of the world's total land mass, large stretches of that land are too hot or too cold, too dry or too wet, or simply too broken for successful agriculture. Moreover, as we have indicated above, with the extension of cultivation into the Virgin Lands territories, the cultivable area was exploited to its outer limit. Any extra additions would consequently have to be 'purchased', by means of land reclamation. Such programmes are known in Russian as *melioratsiya* and their two main targets have been drainage in the non black-earth zone, and irrigation in Central Asia.

During the Brezhnev era, total investment allocated to such purposes increased considerably, from 16.2 billion rubles in 1966–70, to 40.0 billion in 1976–80.[68] Throughout the period, it has accounted for about 15–16 per cent of total agricultural investment,[69] and measured simply in hectares it appears to have been quite successful. Irrigated land increased from 9.9 to 17.5 million hectares, and land under drainage from 7.2 to 12.5 million.[70] Official statistics on the economic importance of the land reclamation programmes provide a similar picture of success. The area involved may not be so large, in relation to the total agricultural area, but the total value of output produced on irrigated or drained land nevertheless increased from 11.1 billion rubles in 1966–70, to 20.7 billion in 1976–80.[71]

What may unfortunately be less clear in this picture is the question of what costs have been incurred in the process. Here the case of irrigation assumes paramount importance. In 1980, no less than 29 per cent of all crop production, including *all* cotton and rice, was said to have originated on irrigated lands.[72] Given the fact that Soviet economic theory recognizes only labour as producing value, water has no price,[73] and it is consequently very hard – if at all possible – to tell what the real costs of producing this extra output have been. At this point, *glasnost* becomes of great importance. During 1987 and 1988, a number of writers and scholars have published information which indicates that the ultimately responsible Ministry of Water Management, the Minvodkhoz, is guilty of practices that border on the criminal.[74] For instance, accusations have been made that the Ministry deliberately manipulates statistics, in order to bolster its programmes. By choosing to report average rather than marginal yields, the actual contribution made by reclamation is lost. Moreover, as the fields chosen are most likely to be rather fertile to start out with, their eventual share in the total will be seriously biased.[75]

The Precarious Victory of Stability

What is lurking behind this, and other similar accusations,[76] is the simple fact that none of those concerned has any direct interest in keeping irrigation schemes in good repair and working order. The costs of waste will not be charged to any individual, and at the national level the Minvodkhoz has been excellently placed to cover up the true situation. The consequences, to put it mildly, are dire. At a 1984 Central Committee plenum on land reclamation, it was reported that the annual losses of water due to such causes amounted to no less than 43 km^3,[77] a figure which corresponds to almost half of the total volume of water that would be diverted from Siberia under the Davidov plan, the most grandiose of all the diversion schemes. If nothing is done – quickly and effectively – to reduce the waste or increase the supply of water in Central Asia, an ecological disaster of major proportions seems inevitable.

If the level of the once mighty Sea of Aral continues to fall at its present rate, by the year 2,000 it will be turned into a giant salt desert, with far-reaching ecological implications for the region as a whole. Humidity will fall, temperatures will become more extreme and the winds will carry salt over wide surrounding areas.[78] Unless new water can be brought in, or waste reduced, this would mean the end of Uzbek cotton production, and quite likely the end of permanent inhabitation in the area. Against this background, it is certainly hard to believe, as some Western observers apparently do, that the issue of river diversions should have been permanently crossed off the agenda. The problems of water shortage in Central Asia are simply too great, and the alternative solutions too unpalatable. Such is the legacy of Brezhnev's ambitions to 'conquer nature'.

Costs and Subsidies

If Soviet agriculture had been based on the rules of private enterprise, then the impact of all of those developments that have been outlined above could hardly have failed to produce a string of bankruptcies that would have wreaked serious havoc in the Soviet banking system. As it is, such effects are of course quite unthinkable. However, this does not remove the fact that both outputs and inputs have price tags and that farms are required by law to maintain financial accounts of their operations. Nor does it remove the fact that many farms will not be able to repay credits issued to them by the state bank. Consequently, the financial balance sheet of Soviet agriculture will by necessity have a rather interesting story to tell. Table 10.5 provides a first glimpse of this, by presenting the relation between investment and outstanding debt for the *kolkhozy*.

Table 10.5   *Kolkhoz* investment and outstanding debt, 1965–80
(billion current rubles)

	1965	1970	1975	1980
Investment	4.4	6.6	9.2	10.3
Short-term debt	0.3	2.4	10.1	25.7
Long-term debt	3.9	10.3	17.8	34.0

Source: Narkhoz (1981), pp. 341, 528, 531.

During the period 1965–80, *kolkhoz* investment more than doubled. From the simultaneous almost tenfold expansion of long-term debt we can deduce how the bulk of this was financed. During the 1970s, the relation of debt to own capital in *kolkhozy* rose from 21 per cent to 55 per cent.[79] In addition, the even more rapid escalation of outstanding short-term debt, clearly reflects the consequences of a decision taken in 1966, to make wages a priority payment. While total *kolkhoz* income (net of purchases of current material inputs) actually *decreased* during the 1970s, from 22.8 to 19.6 billion rubles, total wage payments *increased*, from 15.0 to 18.6 billion, thus increasing the proportion of wages to net income from 66 per cent to 96 per cent.[80] Those farms that have been unable to meet their wage bill out of their own revenue have apparently had liberal access to virtually free credit.

It should be fairly obvious that all of this must have serious implications for economic responsibility amongst farm management and the figures tell their story. If we look at changes in the costs of production in *kolkhozy* during the 1970s, measured in rubles per ton of output, we find increases ranging from about a third for vegetables, to 50 per cent for grains, and around 100 per cent for beef and potatoes.[81] The official reaction to these increases, however, has quite simply been to cover them up, by increasing procurement prices and by writing off debt. In 1979, following a round of price increases which was estimated at an annual cost to the government budget of 3.2 billion rubles, a Soviet economist stated frankly that 'We must realize that we cannot continually raise prices.'[82] Against this background, it is hardly surprising to find that Soviet food subsidies have risen to such a level that the question of their removal has become an issue of major political importance. Originally introduced in 1965, at about two billion rubles, they had grown by 1980 to no less than 37.2 billion.[83]

All of this highlights the importance of Soviet talk about the need to shift from 'administrative' to 'economic' methods of management. If the much vaunted principle of *khozraschet* (cost accounting) is ever going to have any real impact on farm-level decision making, then the lenient attitude towards matters of financial discipline must undergo a radical transformation. Currently, as Yanov has noted, there appears to be a long way to go: 'It turns out that money is being spent without results. Increasing the complexity of the operation leads to its decline. The *kolkhoz* seems to be a bottomless pit.'[84]

The 1982 Food Programme

Towards the end of the Brezhnev era, there seems to have been a growing consensus amongst the top leadership that something would simply have to be done about the agricultural problems. A bumper crop in 1978 was followed by two consecutive disappointments, in 1979 and 1980, and with the outright disaster of 1981 the situation was becoming untenable.[85] Substantial amounts of scarce foreign exchange holdings had to be spent on food imports and Soviet media were receiving a torrent of letters from readers and viewers, complaining about the food situation.[86] As a result, in May 1982 a 'Food Programme' was introduced, to cover the period leading up to 1990.[87]

The main impression given by that programme, however, is distinctly that of a programme to be implemented *instead* of reform, of a readiness to accept the costs of a further massive resource infusion simply in order to purchase yet another postponement of the inevitable serious reform. Virtually all of its ingredients can be captured under the heading 'more of the same'. State procurement prices were to increase for most agricultural products, at an estimated annual cost of 16 billion rubles. Outstanding debts amounting to a total of 9.7 billion were to be written off and a further 11 billion rescheduled. Available draft power was to increase by 60 per cent and deliveries of mineral fertilizer by 70 per cent. Areas under irrigation and drainage were to be expanded to 23–5 million hectares. Finally, state contributions towards investment in rural infrastructure, such as housing, schools and facilities for various cultural activities, were to increase at a further annual cost of 3.3 billion rubles.[88] Any mention of structurally important change was conspicuous by its sheer absence. This caps the legacy for Gorbachev in the realm of agriculture.

Conclusion

The conclusion from what has been said above, regarding the Brezhnev era, can in a sense also be said to form a sort of grand finale to the economic achievements of more than six decades of Bolshevik rule. The time span of our analysis here by and large ends with the death of Brezhnev, in November 1982. Due to the brief tenure and failing health of his two successors Andropov and Chernenko, the subsequent period of 28 months, leading up to Gorbachev's takeover, can essentially be seen as an interregnum. Consequently, we have arrived now at that point where the legacy for Gorbachev, in all its essential ingredients, was completed.

If we start by looking at the system of planning and control, we may note how, ever since its inception in the late 1920s, it has been marked by apparently insoluble conflicts between a desire for central control and a need to allow increased local decision-making, and – by implication – between a desire for stability and a need to allow flexibility. Under Stalin, the system of political control and repression was so tight that little feedback was forthcoming to indicate the existence of this conflict. Then, under Khrushchev, there was a sudden surge of such information, and pronouncements from the top political leadership which indicated a firm desire to implement change in some form. The experience, however, of the measures actually introduced was hardly encouraging. Computopia and SOFE, together with administrative reshuffles and debates on price reform, left few traces. Finally, under Brezhnev, with the range of policy options narrowed down to *sovershenstvovanie* within rather narrowly defined parameters, the search for solutions took on an increasingly Kafkaesque impression of changes that really were no changes at all, but which were nonetheless passed off as reforms. With *glasnost*, these 'steps on the treadmill' are now seen by the Soviets to have led the economy straight into a 'pre-crisis' situation, a *predkrizisnoe sostoyanie*, by way of a 'period of stagnation', the *period zastoya*.

If, on the other hand, we look at agriculture, we may recall that the origin of the Black Hole dates back to mass collectivization, in 1929–32, to the introduction of an economic structure whose main purpose was to excercise political control over the peasants. The systematic refusal during subsequent decades to implement any form of important change in the basic structure of this system is rather telling as to the true intentions of Soviet would-be reformers. Khrushchev's search for a new *format* for old principles that would not be questioned serves to illustrate this attitude, while Brezhnev's Food Programme represents a splendid last stand of the stubborn refusal to abandon control, in spite of the fact that the price for maintaining the old system was growing rapidly, as more and more resources had to be devoted to covering up its malfunctions.

In overall terms, it is a striking feature of the Brezhnev era that inefficiency and a lack of internal dynamic forces was compensated for by a steadily increasing reliance on external sources. Agricultural stagnation was offset by massive imports of grain, and the virtual absence of industrial innovation produced a well known dependence on Western technology. With the glaring exception of weaponry, these imports were paid for by exports of raw materials, such as oil, gas and gold. In the following two chapters, we shall turn to examine the political and ideological ingredients in the system that served to produce this rather peculiar outcome.

Chapter eleven

The politics of stagnation

In the previous chapter, we saw how the Brezhnev leadership began its rule by quite explicitly distancing itself from its predecessor in power. In the economic sphere, this entailed a thorough purging of the bureaucracy from almost every trace of Khrushchev's 'voluntarism'. The territorial organs were abolished and the central ministeries were brought back. Symbolically, the restoration of order even went so far as to reinstate, in their former positions, top-level officials who had been fired by Khrushchev. It is perhaps not surprising that a similar ambition marked events in the political sphere. Among the very first acts to be undertaken here was a re-separation of the posts of Party First Secretary – again known as General Secretary – and Chairman of the Council of Ministers. (After dismissing Bulganin, in 1958, Khrushchev had merged and occupied both of these posts.) Furthermore, the previous division of the Party and the Soviets into an industrial and an agrarian sector was abolished, with parallelism between Party and Soviets instead being stressed. Finally, and perhaps most importantly, in order to underline the intention to promote cadre stability within the Party, at the twenty-third Party Congress, held in 1966, Khrushchev's rule regarding a continuous rotation of the leading Party cadres was abolished.

These vigorous actions will be interpreted here as an implicit contract of sorts, issued by the new constellation of leaders in return for their being granted the right to rule. While this contract was clearly aimed at blocking further 'hare-brained schemes', and thus also at removing the associated threats to the security of the cadres, it should be noted that it did not entail a return to Stalinism in its original form. Although political 'dissenters', such as civil rights spokesmen and oppositional representatives of non-Russian nationalities, would no doubt be persecuted under Brezhnev, there would be no resort to mass terror. The new Party leadership had implicitly committed itself to enhance political stability, and to promote economic development, by relying on the joint mechanisms of popular participation in local government and expert administration at the central level. One may speak here of attempts at a certain authoritarian 'democratization', and at a peculiar 'scientification' of Soviet political life, but parliamentarism, as well as autonomous interest articulation and aggregation from below, were quite obviously out of the question.

At the end of the Brezhnev era, it was evident that this regime had in fact brought about 'a semi-covert re-Stalinization' of Soviet political life.[1] Although not completely eradicated, most of Khrushchev's reforms, concerning the operation of the Party as well as the state bureaucracies, had been largely undone. Nevertheless, in the mid-1960s the situation was different. There can be little doubt that to many people the implicit commitment to stability, in conjunction with the background of Stalinist terror and Khrushchevian 'voluntarism', must have held great promise for the Soviet future. Only – what exactly would that future bring? One is tempted, in this context, to quote Winston Churchill's classic statement to the House of Commons, made in the wake of the 1939 Ribbentrop-Molotov pact: 'I cannot forecast to you the action of Russia. It is a riddle wrapped in a mystery inside an enigma. But perhaps there is a key. That key is Russian national interest.'[2]

The problem this time was to find out what might have been in the 'national interest' of the Soviet Union. If the programme of the new leadership was based on a return to normalcy, then what was that 'normalcy' to be? If the Soviet Union was to embark on a new course, different from both Stalinism and Khrushchevism, then where would that course lead? What would be the new rules of the game? Before embarking on a more detailed study of these problems, let us look briefly at some contemporary Western perceptions of what was happening.

Whither the Soviet Union?

One of the features which distinguished the Brezhnev period was the proliferation of Western research on Soviet affairs. Political, sociological, and economic investigations undertaken in the West, drawing on first-hand experience as well as on studies of Soviet social science, kept pace with developments in Soviet society itself. Views on the 'essence' of that society may certainly have varied, depending on the value premises of the individual observer and on the more precise field of study chosen. Nevertheless, there emerged among Western scholars a fairly coherent and – with few exceptions – widely accepted view of Soviet society. Perhaps the most important ingredient in this process, as we have seen above, was an almost wholesale rejection of the previously predominant 'totalitarian model'. Already in Khrushchev's time, it had been possible to note competition amongst the top Soviet leadership. The circumstances surrounding his demise, moreover, also seemed to confirm the impression that there was a peculiar kind of pluralism within the Party. Consequently, many Western researchers found it both warranted and appropriate to adopt for the study of the Soviet political system certain theories and methods of Western political science.

Interest groups became a relevant topic for study. Investigations were carried out as to whether different bureaucracies tried to enhance their interest at the cost of others. Evidence was gathered which indicated that this was the case.[3] Different professional categories were analysed in order to demonstrate that there really were different interests at play, although these did not form the basis for co-ordinated actions among the various actors.[4] Regional processes were examined in order to establish that things were different in different parts of the Soviet Union and that regional bureaucracies would compete for allocation of resources.[5] At first glance, these studies would doubtless seem to indicate the existence of various interest groups – and thus of a nascent pluralism – in Soviet society.

One of those who grew increasingly critical of the interest-group approach to Soviet politics was, paradoxically, Hugh Gordon Skilling, himself the pioneer of this approach. As it seemed very difficult to establish unequivocally that institutionally defined groups or bureaucracies really were co-ordinating their endeavours, he suggested that the concept of 'opinion groups' might be more fruitful.[6] Skilling's conclusion also finds support in the findings of Donald Kelley and Thane Gustafson. In his study of the influence of different groups over the school and *sovnarkhoz* reforms in the Khrushchev period, Kelley found that only those actors who already possessed 'politically relevant resources' could exert influence, and then simply on the basis of *quid pro quo*, i.e. when other reasons made their support essential to the decision makers in question.[7] Covering a longer period of time, in his study on the respective land and water 'lobbies' Gustafson found that these could neither initiate nor oppose political decisions, but merely obstruct them.[8] Political power of this kind is normally referred to as 'negative', i.e. as the possession of a certain capacity to block or at least delay the implementation of decisions that are perceived to be detrimental to a certain agency.

Although these results may appear to have been rather meagre, they were still sufficient to challenge the notion of crude totalitarianism as the only model with explanatory potential. It was highly indicative of this change of view in the mainstream of Western sovietology that Jerry Hough chose to rename the new edition of Merle

Fainsod's classic handbook, from *How Russia is Ruled* (originally published in 1953, the year of Stalin's death)[9] to *How the Soviet Union is Governed*.[10] As Leonard Schapiro has observed, ' "governed" sounds rather less arbitrary and authoritarian'.[11]

In his review of Hough's revised edition of Fainsod, Schapiro noted a point which is of crucial importance to any understanding of Soviet politics in the Brezhnev period. It concerns the symbolic role of the Soviets. While Hough chose to discuss Lenin's political skills in terms of coalition building within the Left, Schapiro underlined, as Fainsod had originally done, that exploitation of popular support for the Soviets 'was possibly the most vital factor in Lenin's victory'.[12] The important point in this context concerns the manipulative *use* of the Soviets, rather than their own initiatives as such. By thus emphasizing the importance of the output side of the political process, Schapiro also brought out a basic difference between the 'totalitarians' and the 'pluralists':

> No one ... would ... dispute the fact that various interests, such as academics and their manifold institutes, and even individuals, make themselves felt before this policy is formulated. But the 'prototalitarians' would argue that not only is this input processed and channelled to the Politburo by the apparatus of the Central Committee. ... They would also argue that the Politburo, with no elections to fear, with no public opinion or independent courts of law to consider, and with ultimate control over all livelihoods, can ignore any pressures brought to bear on it with impunity. Again, no one would deny that all dictators have to take some account of the population's endurance and of opinion abroad. ... But this has nothing to do with pluralism, which means institutionalized opposition and opinion which the government is unable to ignore, even if it wishes.[13]

Schapiro's conclusion apparently was that changes in the Stalinist political system brought about under Khrushchev and Brezhnev were marginal and did not affect the essence of the system. As a matter of fact, in the late 1980s, this point of view would also be expressed by some Soviet social scientists, as Gorbachev's *glasnost* allowed them retrospectively to probe into the causes of 'stagnation'.[14] During the 1970s, however, in spite of rather heated debates in Soviet mass media, on economic as well as cultural matters, politics was beyond the scope of public discussion. It remained quite firmly the prerogative of underground debate among dissidents.

As we may recall from previous chapters, it was an important outcome of Stalin's ambitions to achieve supreme personal power that the Party was *de facto* crushed as a decision-making body. Given that it was replaced by a parallel, covert structure, which was loyal to and controlled by Stalin personally, it is rather logical that once the Great Dictator was gone a power vacuum of sorts would emerge. As we may further recall, none of the contenders for power managed to fill that vacuum single-handedly. Instead, the Party re-emerged, vaguely incarnated in a 'collective leadership'. In a series of decisive showdowns, this leadership was then, in turn, concentrated in the person of Nikita Khrushchev. Once he in his turn had been ousted, the by now familiar refrain of denunciations of the cult of personality was repeated, and his successors in their turn were again 'elected' on a programme of 'collective leadership'.

It is true that we have far from sufficient observations to speak here of a cyclical pattern. Nevertheless, it is still striking how history may repeat itself. In particular, this is the case with respect to statements about the Party and its role, which exhibit an almost liturgical similarity between the two different periods. Let us proceed now to see what would happen to the Party under Brezhnev's rule, to see if the previous pattern would be repeated once more?

The Leading Role of the Party

Soviet political life under Brezhnev became increasingly subject to a quite distinct process of routine. At least this was the case on the more readily observable output side. Although little appeared to change on the input side, in terms, for example, of an outside influence on Politburo decisions, Soviet society as a whole was explicitly invited to take an active part in the implementation of decisions made, either *ex officio*, as administrators, or as citizens, within the structure of the Soviets.[15] The attitudes and values of the population were also beginning to be taken more seriously by the Party leadership. While the Khrushchev period had been marked by both real and conceptual confusion in the political sphere, under Brezhnev there emerged a quite distinct pattern of a structural division of responsibilities. On the side of control was the ruling Party, representing the elite, the 'conscious vanguard'. On the executive side were the Soviets, administering local affairs and implementing the Party's decisions. In 'the state of the whole people' (a Khrushchevian concept which was retained under Brezhnev) the Soviets represented the 'people'.

Despite this apparent democratization, however, all major political decisions remained the firm prerogative of the Party and all forms of interest articulation continued to be channelled inside the Party.[16]

The Precarious Victory of Stability

In the sense indicated above by Schapiro, the Soviet Union could thus be said to have remained totalitarian. In order to investigate more closely what actually happened to the Party under Brezhnev, we shall now recall the perspective that was used in our chapter on political developments under Lenin and Stalin, namely that of looking at Soviet politics as taking place in different 'arenas'. Let us start with the *subjects* of Party control, i.e. the societal and implementary arenas.

The Party and Society

One important area that can be examined in order to trace distinctions between the respective Brezhnev and Khrushchev periods concerns the Party's status in Soviet society as a whole, i.e. to what extent it can actually be said to have been representative of the citizenry at large. In spite of a certain growth in its total membership, we shall argue that the elite nature of the Party was actually enhanced rather than diminished during the Brezhnev period. During 1957–65, the annual growth in Party membership had been around 5–6 per cent, but during 1965–71 it declined to no more than 2.0–3.5 per cent.[17] Hough's argument, that the Party was actually more representative of the masses than is commonly held in the West, is contradicted by his own figures, which rather seem to support the view that the Party was increasingly becoming a representative of the better-off in Soviet society. According to Hough, the total number of members and candidate members in 1973 amounted to 5 per cent of the Soviet population. If, however, youth under 18 years of age and women are subtracted from that total, the share of representation becomes considerably higher. Again according to Hough's estimates, about 22–3 per cent of all Soviet males in the 21–60 age bracket were Party members in 1973. Of males and females over 30, with at least high school education, 27 per cent were Party members.[18] Hough's conclusion was that these figures showed 'the mass character of the "elite" Party'.[19]

It is an important fact, however, that males in general and the well educated of both sexes in particular, were clearly overrepresented in the Party. We should perhaps be wary of considering all of the fifteen million members in 1973 as an elite, but it is nevertheless interesting to note that the figure of 6 per cent that was given for the share of Party members in the total population is actually less than the share of the nobility (*szlachta*) in pre-partition Poland. The latter had amounted to almost 7 per cent of the Polish population in the late sixteenth century, to 9 per cent in the late seventeenth century, and to more than 10 per cent in the eighteenth century. This 'democracy of nobles' is certainly regarded, in modern research, to have been the expression of rule by an elite, and not by the (peasant) masses.[20]

Another field which merits a search for potential differences under Brezhnev concerns the Party's role as an economic manager. During the early Brezhnev period, the central Party journals emphatically underlined that the Party's strategic role in guiding and controlling the masses must be strengthened. At the same time, it was also stressed that its involvement in routine administration, which had grown considerably in scope under Khrushchev, must be reduced. The dilemma that is hiding behind these statements was that the Party had quite simply become so bogged down in the everyday detail of the needs of production that it had lost sight of overriding political priorities.

In *Kommunist*, this was expressed in the observation that 'in recent years' it had been common practice to appoint local Party leaders from among the ranks of various specialists. A Party secretary in a rural *raikom*, for example, could be an agronomist or a zoo-technician. As a result of this policy, Party work and economic work had acquired equal importance and prominence, i.e. it was no longer necessary to rise through the ranks in order to obtain important Party posts.[21] The strengthening of the activity and militancy of the primary Party organizations was also seen 'in recent years' to have been hampered by frequent reorganizations and restructurings (*perestroiki*), and by 'confusing directives' regarding the role of the local Party organs in directing economic and cultural matters. The decisions of the Party plena in October and November 1964, however, had put an end to this 'abnormal situation' and helped activate all Party work.[22]

The main thrust of such criticism of the Khrushchev years that can be found in *Kommunist* was that the practice of appointing professional people, rather than experienced Party generalists or careerists, as local Party leaders, had served to erode the Party's control over the labouring masses. The new men, moreover, had been 'confused' by the orders to combine political and ideological work with control over economic and cultural life. This was apparently understood to have entailed less concern with the prerogatives of the central Party apparatus, and more interest in local, practical problems. As much was admitted in a roundabout way by two further contributors to *Kommunist*. They stated that recent local Party conferences had underlined that it was the task of the Party to organize and politically educate the workers, to set the key for socialist competition and to unite and organize the masses for successful execution of economic and political tasks. However, there had been many shortcomings in

271

the local Party activities, including a lack of Bolshevik élan (*strast-nost*), steadfastness (*nastoichivost*), and adherence to principle (*printsipialnost*).[23]

What is hiding behind the alleged lack of Bolshevik élan and other such qualities appears quite simply to have been an inability to implement and enforce directives received from above. The criticism was thus concerned with the Party's control function at the local level. Such a conclusion is borne out by the following judgement by another contributor to *Bolshevik*, writing about the situation in Zernograd:

> In the recent past, it occurred that the communists, the *aktiv*, at times felt themselves not to be masters in the regional Party organizations. This is hardly surprising. After all, in those conditions there essentially did not exist any single regional Party organization. Although living and working in the region, more than 200 communists were members of primary Party organizations attached to Party committees of other regions. ... The role and influence of the regional link had been eroded.[24]

However, with the re-establishment of the single Party organs at the regional level, and with the ensuing re-centralization of Party work, the Party apparatus was able to reassert its influence over the 'masses'. If Khrushchev can be said to have tried to create a comprehensible whole out of the previously distant worlds of Party decrees, on the one hand, and actual life, on the other, thereby losing some control but also reducing the sphere of non-public, illegal activities, the new rulers apparently deemed it essential to control all public life, even at the cost of losing control over the non-public sphere, over the increasing underground activities in the economic and cultural spheres, i.e. the second economy and the dissident movement.

The Party's overriding concern with outer appearances, i.e. with control over the public sphere, may be illustrated in its official comments on developments in Czechoslovakia in 1968. The so called Prague spring was important to Soviet development in the sense that from an official Soviet point of view, the Czechoslovak experience illustrated the dangers inherent in relaxing the Party's grip over the population, i.e. in reducing its ability to control potential political forces in society. The significance of the Soviet-led intervention in Czechoslovakia was that it demonstrated quite explicitly what the prospects were for serious reforms within the Soviet Union itself. In *Kommunist*, it was repeatedly stated that any weakening of the leading role of the Party might be used by the left and right opportunists in the Party in order to undermine socialist society. Left and right revisionism would thus merge with the subversive ideological activities of imperialism. As a safeguard against nationalist deviations, threatening to undermine the monolithic unity of the Party, its role must be strengthened, and the Party itself become even more disciplined and centralized.[25] This amounted both to an *ex post* legitimation of the intervention in Czechoslovakia, and to a firm commitment against any form of pluralism in the Soviet Union itself.

Symbolically, the leading role of the Party would also be more pronounced in the 1977 Brezhnev constitution than it had been in the 1936 Stalin counterpart.[26] The Party is mentioned here already in the first sentence of the preamble as the creator of the Soviet state. In Article 6, it is explicitly said that the Party guides social development, domestic as well as foreign policy, and the construction – on a scientific basis – of a communist society. At the same time, the Soviet state is described as 'the state of the whole people'. It may be worth noting that this state was no longer considered to be destined for a process of 'withering away', as it should have been according to the 'classics'. On the contrary, in a number of cases the constitution explicitly defines what people should and should not do. A case in point is Article 62, which tells the Soviet citizens to work for the strengthening of the power and reputation of the state. As the Swedish scholar Rolf Ejvegård has put it, the new constitution could be interpreted more as an instrument for establishing the permanency of socialist society in its given, Brezhnevian form, than as a pointer towards communism.[27]

The Internal Party Arena

Within the Party, as we have indicated above, Khrushchev's rather personal and arbitrary exertion of power was replaced by the collective leadership of the Politburo, the Party's top decision-making body which had been known under Khrushchev as the Presidium. The initial *troika* of top leaders consisted of Leonid Brezhnev, as General Secretary of the Party, Aleksei Kosygin, as Chairman of the Council of Ministers, and Nikolai Podgornyi, as Chairman of the Presidium of the Supreme Soviet. In a Western framework, these three could be said to represent Party chairman, Prime Minister, and Head of State. Given the past experience of a concentration of power in the hands of, first, Stalin, and then Khrushchev, as single individuals, it was unclear what the actual distribution of power would be under this new principle of collective leadership. Instead of a single leader, an oligarchy of more or less like-minded men had assumed power. During the following years, moreover, the rate of turnover amongst these oligarchs was so slow that the term 'gerontocracy' would eventually be used by Western observers.[28] During the interregnum between Brezhnev and Gorbachev, Michel Tatu would even coin the rather striking expression *le marxisme-sénilisme*. This development certainly served to obscure and perhaps even prevent any potentially effective and well defined pattern of leadership.

As time wore on, however, the previously familiar pattern of a cult of the Leader seemed to be repeating itself. Brezhnev was increasingly bestowed with symbols of prestige and power. In the Politburo, the General Secretary emerged in the early 1970s as the *primus inter pares*, known from 1976 onwards as the 'head' (*glava*) of that body of powerful men. In the same year, it was announced that Brezhnev, now a Marshal of the Soviet Union, was also Chairman of the State Defence Council, i.e. supreme commander of the Soviet armed forces.[29] In 1977, finally, he was elevated to the position of Head of State, i.e. to replace Podgornyi as Chairman of the Presidium of the Supreme Soviet. With the critically ill Kosygin having resigned from the Premiership in October 1980, to be replaced by Tikhonov, after this last move Brezhnev was the sole survivor of the original Brezhnev-Kosygin-Podgorny leadership *troika*.

At first glance, there would certainly seem to have been a new Leader cult in the making. Yet, this process stood in stark contrast to the previous ones. In spite of the many titles and orders that were bestowed on Brezhnev – among other things he was awarded the Lenin prize for his literary masterpiece *Malaya zemlya* (The Little Land) – he was by no means as powerful as Stalin – or even Khrushchev – had been. In practice, Brezhnev acted as a power broker of sorts, harmonizing various institutional interests. In the words of Archie Brown, his style of decision making was 'cautious and consensus-seeking'.[30] In retrospect, Seweryn Bialer would summarize the experience of the Brezhnev era as follows:

> The oligarchical Brezhnev leadership was formed from the heads of the major institutional interests and significant bureaucracies, such as the Party machine, the secret police, the military, the economic administration, the general administration, the foreign policy apparatus, and the leadership of the key republics and regions.[31]

For obvious reasons, this kind of rule could not be very dynamic. Since very few economic or political measures can be undertaken that benefit some without hurting others, the need to uphold the coalition by its own very nature served as a formidable obstacle in the way of effective leadership. Instead of leading and encouraging the development of Soviet economic and political life, the Party apparatus increasingly came to rest as a heavy hand over policy making, thwarting all initiative in the name of stability and unanimity. Subsequently, as we know, Soviet writers, scholars and even Party officials – led by Mikhail Gorbachev – would speak of this Party apparatus as a 'brake mechanism' (*mekhanizm tormozheniya*), and of the Brezhnev era *in toto* as a period of stagnation, the *period zastoya*.

Although it may not have been explicitly recognized at the time, there does seem to have been a dim awareness on behalf of the regime that something more than a consensus-ridden Party was necessary in order to lead the society of 'developed socialism'. The narrow focus on bureaucratic rules and relations, and the refusal to admit any form of true 'politics' – i.e. essentially pluralism – into the structure, produced a situation where the Soviet Union was increasingly led by a ruling but non-governing Party. The most serious ingredient in this picture concerns the simple fact that any economic and political system in the final analysis consists of *people*. In the absence of Stalinist terror to *compel* citizens to work and in the absence of a Khrushchevian utopia, to *induce* them to work, how was the Soviet population to be harnessed for the benefit of Soviet development? In this respect, we may find a highly characteristic distinguishing feature of the Brezhnev era.

In the absence of explicit sticks and carrots, the regime chose to engage in a systematic search for *substitutes* for politics, i.e. for some mechanisms that would make government more effective without resorting to pluralism. There were two sides to this endeavour, one seeking to 'incorporate' the citizens and the other looking for technical improvements in the methods of management. Let us start by looking at the former.

Incorporating the Citizens

If we return to our assumption from above, that the new leadership taking over after Khrushchev had been 'elected' by the Party cadres on an implicit commitment to stability and continuity, this immediately calls for a broader view to be taken of the problem of regime legitimacy. In previous chapters, we have discussed at great length the importance of historical and cultural traditions in providing a basic legitimacy for the regime, be it a Stalin or a conglomerate of oligarchs struggling for power. This focus on the non-material aspects of legitimation, however, implies a neglect of what is sometimes referred to as a 'social contract', between the rulers and the ruled. The main thrust of this latter argument is that in lieu of a broad range of political rights, such as free elections and freedom of speech, the regime provides its subjects with a package of basic material necessities, such as housing, food and public transport, at low or token cost. The exact nature and function of such contracts, which are sometimes also referred to as 'social compacts', is a matter of some controversy, the details of which we shall not pursue at any length here.

Given Khrushchev's explicit wager on materialism, and the associated neglect of Russian myths and traditions, it would, however, seem appropriate to also devote some general attention to the regime's search for a material basis for its legitimacy. Given, moreover, what we now know about the subsequent process of stagnation under Brezhnev, it is rather obvious that these aspects must also enter our discussion. As it became increasingly obvious that the Brezhnev regime was failing to meet its end of the bargain, a regime crisis would have seemed to be inevitable. Nevertheless, the system remained surprisingly stable. If we disregard for the moment the possibility that non-material factors of legitimation had either remained in place or reasserted themselves, an obvious conclusion regarding the apparent contradiction between decline and stability must be that there were some alternative stabilizing forces at play. In order to elaborate on this point, we shall draw on a general framework presented by Stephen White.[32]

Mechanisms of Adaptation

White's point of departure was to challenge the 'apocalyptic' views of Soviet economic development adopted by some Western observers towards the end of the Brezhnev era and during the ensuing interregnum.[33] His argument was that although many of the communist states were set in a serious process of economic decline, with associated social problems, it was not warranted to say that the communist systems were in the 'throes of a serious economic crisis',[34] or to argue that the 'ingredients for some kind of explosion are increasingly in place.'[35] In order to substantiate this claim, White suggested a framework of 'mechanisms of adaptation', which were seen to circumvent or defuse predictions of apocalypse based on the notion of a 'social contract' being violated. The main thrust of this argument is that there exists a number of ways in which the regimes concerned may 'absorb and process demands, expand the consultative capacities of their systems, give a stake in the system to various sections of their populations, and perhaps pre-empt demands for more far-reaching and anti-systemic change.'[36]

The first of four mechanisms listed here is *electoral linkage*, which refers to the growing practice of communist regimes to incorporate an element of genuine, or at least apparent, choice in general elections to various bodies. With Hungary leading the way, the trend on this count – from the mid-1960s onwards – has been for 'most communist countries' to move from the previously universal practice of single-slate elections to various models of choice in nominating and electing candidates. A second mechanism is *political incorporation*, which refers to the degree of involvement of the population in the actual political process, primarily of course via membership in the ruling Party. The general trend on this count was seen by White to point in the direction of both a proportionately increased membership and of an expanded share of members with a working-class background. The third mechanism is *associational incorporation*, which is indirectly related to the political one. Instead of direct involvement in the ruling Party, we are dealing here with activities in organizations that are controlled by but not directly affiliated with the Party, such as trade unions, people's control committees, and police auxiliaries. Again, the general trend was seen to point in the direction of an increased official emphasis and importance. Finally, there is the practice of *writing letters* to the media and of visiting the offices of Party and state organs.

White is careful to stress that neither of these mechanisms should be confused with their Western counterparts, i.e. with competitive free elections, pluralist politics, autonomous organizations, or a free Press, but he still maintains that they do serve to complicate considerably the simple picture that is provided by predictions based on the existence of a 'social contract' in some form. This latter claim being of obvious relevance to our presentation, we shall proceed now to examine its components.

The central issue here concerns the problem of citizen participation, as seen from the perspectives of both individuals and authorities. During the Stalin period, this was clearly not an issue of great relevance, and even during Khrushchev's years in power we would probably be hard put to establish any clear patterns. The Brezhnev era, however, with its explicit commitment to increased participation, would seem to offer fertile ground for study. Yet, little empirical work has actually been undertaken. In a study of political participation in Eastern Europe, Jan Triska has offered the following two explanations for the existence of an – understandable – bias among Western political scientists against studying the Soviet case: 'First, they found access to relevant information difficult, if not impossible; second, they considered political participation in the socialist countries largely ceremonial, government-sponsored and supportive, manipulative and mobilized, and thus not worthy of their attention.'[37]

While White's perspective is thus to some extent pioneering, he is not completely alone in observing that the issue of participation has taken on a greater importance in the post-Stalin period of Soviet development. Jan Adams, for example, has pointed at the 'remarkable revival and growth of public participation in community affairs that have occurred since the death of Stalin', and at the 'enormous pool of volunteers attached to the Soviets' that has come into existence.[38] Others have pointed to the increasing importance that is being placed on various forms of (unpaid) volunteer public service, such as volunteer police or election canvassing.[39]

Let us proceed now to investigate to what extent the mechanisms outlined by White can actually be identified in the Soviet Union under Brezhnev. We shall leave the mechanism of political incorporation aside, since we have argued above that Party membership did not develop in either of the directions indicated by White. The important aspects of associational incorporation, moreover, will be given separate treatment in a moment. Here we shall proceed to look at the process of political elections, i.e. at electoral linkage, and at the practice of writing letters to the media.

Soviet Elections

The real nature and purpose of Soviet elections, i.e. elections to the Soviets at various levels, from the local up to the Surpreme Soviet, has long been a subject of some puzzlement to outside observers. Some have regarded them as chiefly legitimating devices of the Soviet regime. Fainsod, for example, writes that elections 'offer a dramatic occasion for a campaign of agitation and propaganda',[40] while Schapiro sees them as 'a public demonstration of the legitimacy of the regime ... an invaluable educational and propaganda exercise'.[41] Others have adopted a more cynical view, referring to the routine reporting of over 99 per cent votes in favour of the offically approved single slate as proof that we are dealing here with no more than a façade, perhaps even of a rather farcical nature. While not subscribing to it himself, Everett Jacobs has expressed this view as 'mere propaganda exercises conducted by the regime to prove to itself and the world that the Soviet population is solidly behind it.'[42]

Such views have been challenged by Victor Zaslavsky and Robert Brym, who have argued, in a classic article, that there are indeed a number of important functions filled by Soviet elections, functions which are intended neither as mere window dressing nor to serve a narrow purpose of legitimation.[43] Although, according to them, it is certainly the case that legitimation was a prominent purpose of elections under Stalin, since then an important transformation has occurred: 'The typical Soviet citizen recognizes as well as the Western commentator that Soviet elections are not elections at all, a fact which hardly lends weight to our conventional assumptions about their legitimizing function.'[44]

An important background to their argument on the actual functions filled by Soviet elections is the recognition of the sheer numbers of people that are involved in the process as such. Once elections have been declared, normally 2-3 months in advance, it is up to an army of election canvassers, the so called *agitkollektivy*, to make sure that the Soviet citizens actually excercise their constitutional rights – first to register and then to vote. According to Zaslavsky and Brym, about 6 to 8 per cent of all electors can be assumed to take part in this process. In addition, there is a roughly equal number involved in district electoral commissions, which are responsible for voter registration and for actually counting the votes. All in all, a full 15 per cent of the electors may thus be assumed to take direct part in the elections on the organizational side.[45]

Two important questions arise in this context. First, why make this massive resource commitment, if there are not important ulterior motives involved? Second, why should so many people volunteer, if not because there are some important personal benefits involved? The *first* of these questions may find two answers in the article by Zaslavsky and Brym. Most importantly, the election process, by its very nature, offers an excellent opportunity to screen and reward potential entrants into the power hierarchy. Costly mistakes, in the form of promoting unsuitable canditates, may thus be avoided. A second important side-effect is that the elections serve as a test of the efficiency and reliability of the local Party organs, chiefly the *raikom*. Local officials are charged here with weeding out oppositional or deviant individuals who refuse to vote, and they are given a useful practice in the art of mobilizing the population for a campaign, a talent which as we know is of central importance.

Turning to our second question (i.e. to look at the election process from the point of view of the individuals), we may find additional reasons to take it seriously. For those who wish to rise in the power hierarchy, here is an obvious opportunity to prove one's salt, but there are attractions for others as well. On the one hand, as we have pointed out above, undertaking unpaid public service is a must for most, and election canvassing is probably a rather easy way to do so. On the other hand, those who do participate will be given priviliged information, in the form of special lectures and access to the foreign Press, and this may perhaps act as positive inducement for some.

While all these factors are no doubt important, it is the following, concluding statement from the article by Zaslavsky and Brym which really sums up the core of the ideological importance of Soviet elections:

> For elections encourage citizens to demonstrate that they have adjusted to the fiction of democracy in the Soviet Union. Elections buttress the regime – not by legitimizing it, but by prompting the population to show that the *illegitimacy* of its 'democratic' practice has been accepted and that no action to undermine it will be forthcoming.[46]

With this rather cynical statement, we shall leave the question of participation in elections and turn to the practice of writing letters to the authorities and to the Press.

Writing Letters

The practice of writing letters to Soviet media and to Soviet authorities, and indeed of paying personal visits to the offices of newspapers and of Party and state organs, is another area where the Brezhnev period stands in contrast to previous Soviet experience. Although both letter writing and personal appearances had certainly been common throughout previous Soviet history, under Brezhnev, the legal and administrative framework was made more explicit.[47] In 1967, the Central Committee issued a decree on how to handle letters from the citizens to Soviet authorities, and in the following year, a further decree introduced formal legislation, laying down standard procedures and obligations. The increased importance that was placed on such communications from below is also reflected in the 1977 Brezhnev constitution.

Here, Article 49 specifies the rights of all citizens to submit suggestions and criticisms to public bodies, which are then required to respond within given time limits. The same article also specifies that victimization of those who engage in criticism shall be prohibited and that those guilty of such persecution shall be held responsible. In Article 58, moreover, citizens are given additional rights to complain if they feel that improper action has been taken on previous complaints. Then, in 1980, the Supreme Soviet adopted revisions of the 1967 and 1968 decrees, further expanding the rights of the citizens. On paper, at least, it would thus seem that we are dealing here with a phenomenon of some importance.

The *contents* of the letters in question are obviously of a greatly varying nature, from idle flattery and malignant poison-pen letters, to constructive suggestions and the reporting of abuse and malpractice.[48] If we maintain the assumption that the regime does have an interest in allowing the citizens to indulge in such writings, two highly different motives may be identified. *First*, we have that of incorporation, which was indicated by White. If citizens experience that the media regularly publish letters that deal with issues of concern to them, or – even better – if letters are published that have been written by themselves or by someone they know, this will no doubt serve to promote a certain feeling of being part. White refers to this as the 'ombudsman' function of Soviet media, and it is hardly surprising to find Soviet surveys suggesting that the citizens 'in fact regard the press as perhaps the most effective means they have available of promoting their interests and resolving their particular problems.'[49] Letters to the authorities are seen in this respect to be less important, and the same can be said for the actual contents of the letters. 'Letting off steam' will be the prime objective.

The *second* of our two motives, however, concerns precisely the actual information that is contained in the various letters, and which is communicated at personal appearances. Here, the main question is to what extent the regime is actually prepared to listen. According to Soviet sources, a considerable amount of resources go into preparing digests and surveys of letters received, all for the benefit of the rulers. In 1978, for example, a separate Correspondence Department was set up within the Central Committee, and it is claimed that the letter departments of major newspapers like *Pravda* and *Izvestia* are the largest single departments of those papers, handling daily a mailbag which exceeds by far that received by major newspapers in the West.[50] Such claims might be dismissed as being mere façade, but there are good reasons for not doing so.

It is certainly true that the regime already has, in the vast KGB apparatus, an extensive network for gathering information about the working of Soviet society, but such information will be of a considerably different nature from that which the citizens themselves will supply, if given the chance to do so. Letters to the media and to the authorities are an excellent way of eliciting this information, without allowing autonomous articulation and aggregation of interests. We shall have reason below to return to other ways of solving the dilemma of feedback versus pluralism, but before doing so let us look in somewhat greater detail at the wager on the Soviets.

The Wager on the Soviets

In addition to the parallel endeavours of strengthening and disciplining the Party, and of 'incorporating' the citizens into the state-controlled sphere, the Brezhnev regime also sought to vitalize the Soviets, the local decision-making organs of the state apparatus. Ideologically, this was well in line with the ambition of presenting the Soviet Union as a modern, developed state, as the prime of 'real existing socialism'. There was much more to it, however, than simply putting up a nice façade. In his time, Stalin had seen, in the Soviets, an important means for obtaining information about attitudes among the population. He declared that 'the system of supreme organs must possess a number of barometers which will anticipate every change, register and forestall ... all possible storms and ill-fortunes.'[51] Stalin's point, which would also be preserved under Brezhnev, was that deputies elected to the Soviets should not be professional politicians, or citizens becoming full-time politicians, as in Western parliamentary democracies. Instead, they should remain amateurs, passive instruments serving to record the attitudes of their social environment, i.e. 'a human register, a human recording'.[52]

During the first years of the Brezhnev regime, it was a major theme in political speeches that an increased number of citizens should be drawn into active work in the local Soviets.[53] The latter were seen to serve not only as vehicles of socialization of the people, but also as 'barometers of public opinion', i.e. as a means for informing the Party authorities, which monitored the work of the Soviet organs, about popular sentiments and attitudes.[54] As we have seen above, this reflects a mixture of those parallel ambitions of incorporating Soviet citizens into the state-controlled sphere, and of obtaining information from below.

In addition to these two motives, moreover, we may discern also a third function of the expanded role of the Soviets, a function which may and may not have been intended. Since the local Soviets were organizationally subject to the Supreme Soviet, rather than to the republican leaderships, this development of 'Soviet democracy' in practice implied a decline of federalism. Given the important role that is played by this principle in the official presentation of the Soviet system, this was an important development. In spite of the apparent 'decentralization' and 'popularization' that was implied by allowing the Soviets to play a more prominent role in local government, the influence of the centre – and thus of the Russians – was further strengthened. Since the two chambers of the Supreme Soviet – Union and Nationalities – vote together, and the Russians were predominant, the tendency towards Russian supremacy was inherent in the very structure of the political system. It is also symptomatic that the Economic Commission of the Soviet of Nationalities was dissolved in 1967. This institution, which had been established in connection with Khrushchev's *sovnarkhoz* reform in 1957, was declared to be redundant when the branch principle was reintroduced in the economy.[55]

The main political importance of the attempted revitalization of the structure of the Soviets lay in its legitimizing function. When the regime could no longer resort to mass terror, and when the people could no longer be mobilized by promises of an immediate bright future, this function obviously had to become more important. Partly as an effect of their historical role in 1905 and 1917, and partly because they had roots in pre-revolutionary Russian history, in the *zemskii sobor* of the seventeenth century and in the *duma* of the 1905–17 period, the Soviets as an institution can be said to have possessed a certain 'residual legitimacy'.[56] By stating that the Soviets expressed the will of the masses, it was possible for the regime to draw on that legitimacy for its own purposes.

During the Brezhnev years, there was an increased overlap of membership in the Party and in the Supreme Soviet. The implications of this overlap were, at first glance, unclear, since it could be taken to mean either an increased degree of Party control over the implementary arena or an upgrading of the role of the Supreme Soviet, with an associated reversal of the flow of influence from the Supreme Soviet to the Party.[57] In practice, however, the outcome was a further entrenchment of the elite, at the expense of the people. Throughout the 1960s, the Supreme Soviet and its auxiliary bodies increasingly evolved into an instrument for legalizing and further centralizing the Party leadership's control over other major political institutions of the Soviet Union.[58]

Despite tight Party control, however, the Supreme Soviet was not completely devoid of political function under Brezhnev. The enhanced public visibility of this body provided the regime with a traditional legitimacy of sorts. As Peter Vanneman concludes, at the close of his study of the Supreme Soviet:

> The Supreme Soviet performs significant legitimizing, socializing, codifying, investigating, and monitoring functions. Also, an embryonic ombudsman function appears to be evolving. The continued evolution of these structures and functions could significantly facilitate the Soviet Union's gradual transition to a post-industrial society. ... The notion of direct popular initiative threads through the historical memory of the *Vieches*, *Sobors*, the

Paris Commune, and the Soviets to imbue the Supreme Soviet with a sometimes latent, but significant legitimating influence.[59]

Although Vanneman's conclusion contains imponderabilities and is rather speculative, the essence of what he is saying amounts to a recognition of the fact that the enhanced public role of the Supreme Soviet served to make the Soviet Union look orderly and 'normal', with its political system founded in both internal Russian traditions – the medieval *veche* and the seventeenth-century *sobor* – and in the traditions of the international workers' movement – the Paris Commune of 1871 and the Russian revolutions of 1905 and 1917. While continuing to be ruled by the Party, the state apparatus had acquired an institutional role that might eventually become the locus of political initiative, should one-Party rule be contested by new demands emerging from the development of Soviet society.

Borrowing a concept from the Finnish sociologist Erik Allardt, Theodore Friedgut has characterized the type of 'Soviet democracy' that emerged under Brezhnev as 'totalitarian populist'. This means that the broad mass of the people is well organized and active at the local level, while the centre still controls and commands the people, 'well insulated from any decisive pressures emanating from the mass.'[60] In this framework, Friedgut showed that, during the 1970s, the local Soviets acquired the function of enhancing the efficiency of administration, while at the same time educating the people to a better understanding of the political needs of society, and increasingly also to a view of this society as being 'theirs'.[61] Speaking in terms of Western concepts, the general idea was to merge civil and political society, or to ease out any attempt at individual withdrawal from public affairs. White's perspective of incorporation and adaptation is of obvious relevance here.

The main point in Friedgut's analysis of the local Soviets lies in his demonstration that 'political participation' was not intended to express conflicts or frictions between different societal interests, but rather to 'mobilize the Soviet citizen in support of state administrators'. The Soviets were to provide an institutional network necessary for implementing administrative decisions made by the Party.[62] Whereas regime legitimacy, according to Friedgut, might be thus enhanced, the central aspect was that All-Union administrative priorities could in this way be more easily placed before 'community self-determination'. Friedgut concluded that there had emerged under Brezhnev a combination of 'public self-government' and 'scientific administration'.[63]

In a judgement that closely resembles accusations levelled by radical critics at the Western parliamentary democracies, Friedgut labelled the Soviet outcome a 'democratic-manipulative system'.[64] He also remarked, however, that the system did have certain real political advantages, making it possible to rally the broad masses of the population against the intelligentsia in general, and against the non-conformists in particular.[65] The stress on local participation in administration through the Soviets can thus also be seen as an attempt to create checks and balances within the administrative apparatus.

The wager on the Soviets no doubt succeeded in incorporating large numbers of the Soviet population into the state-controlled sphere, in the sense that a part of their free time was expropriated for public service. In this sense, it was similar to the process of expanded associational incorporation, that has been exemplified above by various other forms of unpaid public service. Yet, it remains a fact that even in its expanded format, the activity of the Soviets was still confined to the implementary arena of Soviet society. Although it was apparently regarded as a main substitute for politics at the height of the Brezhnev regime, from a perspective of structure versus content, there still remained a large void where 'politics' should have been. Let us proceed now to look at some further attempts made at introducing substitutes for politics, starting with the question of 'scientific management of society'.[66]

Further Substitutes for Politics

'Scientific Management'

A central trait in the 'routinization' of policy that marked the Brezhnev era was the growth in size of the bureaucracy, and the enhanced role of its administrators and experts, in the implementation of political decisions. Both Soviet and Western scholars at the time applied systems theory to the Soviet system, the former in an attempt to render administration 'scientific', the latter in order to understand the system as a structure 'in which ideas and power ... flow up the administrative hierarchies as well as down'.[67] Writing in 1976, Paul Cocks, the author behind the quotation, could describe what seemed at the time to be a new direction, namely the use of systems theory 'aiming at strengthening the capabilities of central authorities to plan, co-ordinate and implement national policies and programme priorities.'[68]

According to Cocks, 'the systems movement' was part of 'a general drive to counter pluralist tendencies and particularist forces.'[69] The context was one of an increased significance of 'scientific management'. Government was viewed as a technical problem, a simple question of efficiency at the lower executive levels. We may regard this as the counterpart to the simultaneous promotion of 'Soviet democracy'. This approach, i.e. the desire to find a substitute for pluralism, was endorsed as the Party line at the twenty-fourth Party Congress in 1971, when Brezhnev introduced a programme designed to enhance and rely on the 'scientific-technical revolution'.[70]

The 'systems movement' was associated both with an import of Western management theories and with a return to ideas propagated in the Soviet 1920s, by heretics such as Bogdanov (Lenin's adversary) and Bukharin (one of Stalin's most prominent opponents and victims). Perhaps it was also these ideological implications which influenced the fate of the systems movement and of 'scientific management' in the late Brezhnev era. As the philosophers came dangerously close to the ideas of Bogdanov and Bukharin, the Party's legitimacy, being anchored in the heritage of Lenin and Stalin, was endangered. Writing in the early 1980s, Ilmari Susiluoto could paint another, darker picture than the one envisaged by Cocks a few years earlier. According to Susiluoto, it was an important sign of change when the yearbook 'Systems research' – *Systemnye Issledovaniya* – was suspended in the late 1970s. The ideological watchdogs in the Party leadership had caught the scent of Bogdanov: 'The seed of heresy had to be exposed and the escalation of systems thinking into a political movement prevented.'[71]

The crux of the matter was that a central part of regime legitimacy was – and still is – based on the notion that the Party is the main repository of scientific knowledge. A continuation of systems thinking implied a demonstration of the futility of the Party's Leninist 'science', indeed of its utter obsolescence, and would thus suggest the withering away of the leading role of the Party as an appropriate consequence. In a society where the independence of research was acknowledged and systems thinking freely applied, wherever suitable, demands would also increase for publicity, for better statistics and for social research, all in order to enable autonomous economic and social actors to adapt to a continuously changing environment. In a situation where equal access for all to available information is the basis for political decisions, there is no need for a vanguard Party of the Leninist type. If the ideas of autonomous social research and an open dissemination of social information were to become the order of the day, the Party would risk being seen as a reactionary force standing in the way of the growth and application of knowledge and hence also the progress of Soviet society.

It should be underlined that this interpretation is squarely at odds with Cocks' view that 'systems theory is consistent with the Leninist model of organization and a political culture that stresses the teleological nature of the system and the legitimization of the concentration of authority in a single command centre.'[72] Cocks' opinion is certainly an accurate description of what the Party leadership initially *hoped* to achieve with its endorsement of the 'systems movement'. According to Cocks, the spread of the 'systems movement' in the Soviet Union in the early 1970s reflected the persistence of the centralist command model in an increasingly differentiated and complex society.[73] This view, however, is hard to reconcile with the actual course of development in the following years.

In 1976, the Soviet philosopher G. Volkov could state that the problem of scientific management of society had still not been sufficiently investigated in the Soviet Union. Volkov proposed that a new concept, *homo dirigens*, should be added to the old notions *homo sapiens*, *homo agens* and *homo creans*. *Homo dirigens* would be the Soviet citizen, expressing the notion that society was governed directly by the toiling masses via their representatives. Volkov emphasized that management was complicated because it was a matter of both basis (economy) and superstructure (ideology), and of technological relations.[74] In a Soviet reader in sociology, published in the same year, Volkov's observation was further elaborated. It was stated that, as the role of the administrative apparatus increased, its links with the masses must be improved. The latter must develop a stronger sense of being the masters of society.[75]

Once it became clear that socio-economic reality was far too complex for a single centre to be in universal command, the presumed advantages of systems management were suddenly perceived as drawbacks – many sub-systems and second-level 'centres' would mean proliferation rather than concentration of power. When the dream of the giant central computer evaporated, the attractiveness of systems thinking, or rather 'scientific management', as a possible substitute for politics, was also significantly deflated. The implications were that yet another panacea solution to the dilemma of finding a substitute for 'politics', i.e. for pluralism, had fallen flat on the ground. The parallel with the previous beliefs in the blessings of SOFE and mathematical planning techniques is rather striking.

Social Science

Parallel to the Party leadership's interest in systems theory as a way of increasing management efficiency, there was also an attempt to enhance the role of social science in general. The social sciences, which had begun to develop under Khrushchev, were expected to provide the Party with 'social information' for the sake of improved social management and planning. In 1967, the Central Committee adopted the first resolution in Soviet history 'On measures for further development of the social sciences and strengthening their role in the construction of communism.'[76] The declaration was followed by a notable development of 'concrete sociological investigations' (the catchword for the Soviet equivalent of what was still regarded in the Soviet Union as 'bourgeois' sociology).[77]

The implications of an increased reliance on social research were discussed in *Voprosy Filosofii*, the leading philosophy journal. In an overview of recent Soviet research on the social and economic effects of the so called Scientific and Technological Revolution, the following points were made: planning and direction of production had ceased to be a matter for the enterprises only, becoming, instead, of interest to society as a whole; application of theoretical, scientific knowledge increasingly eased out 'direct empirical experience'; the knowledge of social science was put to systematic use in administration; modern technical devices – automation and cybernetic devices – were used; and the administrative system was 'democratized'.[78]

As always in Soviet texts of this kind, the borderline between empirical description and normative propositions is blurred. The main point, however, was the intention to understand 'social management' (*sotsialnoe upravlenie*) as encompassing direction of the economy and socio-political administration, as well as management of the cultural life of society and of the life of every citizen. This meant that social science would acquire a central role in gathering, processing and producing social information for the the benefit of the Party leaders. Science, the basis for management, should in its turn be directed by means of 'organization, co-ordination, motivation and control'.[79]

The phrase about direction of science indicated a growing realization that 'scientific management', the systems movement, and social science in general created a whole new set of problems, as seen from the perspective of the Party's desire for power and security. The challenge to the leading role of the Party that emanated from social science was eloquently formulated by the Soviet philosopher V. Zh. Kelle, who stated in 1978 that the autonomy of science – which he regarded as essential – implied that only professional scientists should deal with scientific problems. Under 'developed socialism', science could be said to influence social management in three different ways. The fundamental science was *Marxist-Leninist theory*, which revealed and determined the content, objectives, means, and forms of the struggle of the working class. Then came *science* (*nauka*), which stated the concrete goals, prognoses, plans, and indicators that were appropriate at any given historical moment, and, finally, there were *scientific methods*, used to design solutions to practical problems of management and implementation. As Kelle underlined that the 'contradictions' between technical and humanistic knowledge were superseded by a convergence (*sblizhenie*) of the natural, technical, and social sciences in socialist society, it is evident that his statement about the importance of professional, scientific knowledge also applied to social scientists.[80]

Arguments of the kind advanced by Kelle implied that while perhaps 'fundamental', the theories of Marxism-Leninism were not sufficient as a basis for the management of socialist society. The leaders must also rely on social science in order to acquire such social information that was apparently deemed crucial for the direction of society. The concept of 'social information' became a central feature in the Soviet discussion of 'social management'. In a book on social information and management, published in 1975, Viktor Afanasiev, social scientist and editor-in-chief of *Pravda*, stressed the importance of 'concrete sociological investigations' for the management of society. According to Afanasiev, sociological investigations reflected the multiform complexity of social processes and created a basis for evaluation of the efficiency of administration by providing the authorities with reliable information. Sociological investigations also helped the leaders understand how certain decisions influenced people, how different categories perceived them and how people's thoughts and behaviour were affected.

In order to improve the informative aspects of sociological investigations, it was necessary, Afanasiev said, to establish within the central statistical bureau 'a sociological service'. This institution would produce information about the effects of economic changes on social life and on people's thoughts. Other ways of obtaining information about public opinion were direct communication between rulers and ruled (*rukovoditelei i rukovodimykh*), mass media reports, and letters from workers. The letters were 'human documents' that revealed the feelings, goals, and wishes of people, as well as the socio-psychological climate on the shop floor and popular attitudes towards the commanding organs. Afanasiev mentioned that Pravda received 425,510 letters in 1973.[81] The daily Press was also increasingly used by experts from different sectors to call attention to burning economic, social, and environmental problems. The mass media became an unstructured arena for airing potentially politically relevant issues.[82]

The instrumental view of 'social information' that can be found in Afanasiev's argument, where sociology is put on an equal footing with oral and public printed communication, such as letters to the editor, indicates that social science and the special kind of problem-oriented Soviet journalism which is known as *publitsistika*, were regarded as substitutes for spontaneous articulation and aggregation of interests from below, i.e. for mass political initiatives, or 'politics' in the Western sense of the word. Not even the social scientists were given a loose rein. In 1972–3, the Institute of Concrete Sociological Investigations was reorganized, the Soviet Sociological Association purged, and the influence of the Party strengthened.[83] For the remainder of the Brezhnev regime, the social sciences would remain strongly circumscribed. Another endeavour to transform Soviet society had ended up in a *cul-de-sac*.

Public Opinion Research

When Soviet sociologists in the 1970s discussed the importance of undertaking public opinion surveys, this took place in a context considerably different from that of their Western colleagues. The Soviet context implied, quite simply, that public opinion should be surveyed for the benefit of the political leadership, not in the sense that economic and social policy-making should be better adjusted to the preferences of the population, but rather so that the regime's control over the 'masses' could be made more effective. The very recognition, however, of the existence of a phenomenon such as 'public opinion' (*obshchestvennoe mnenie*) could certainly be viewed as a first step on the road towards a real politicization of Soviet society. It may therefore be warranted to take a closer look at the rise and demise of research and theorizing concerning problems of public opinion in the Soviet Union under Brezhnev.

During the 1970s, opinion surveys were commissioned both by the Institute of Social Research, at the Academy of Sciences, and by Party Committees at various levels.[84] Ellen Propper Mickiewicz noted that Soviet public-opinion researchers had succeeded in demonstrating that, with respect to questions of local administration and industrial management, there was a difference between the public's view, on the one hand, and official assumptions, on the other. Public opinion, Mickiewicz held, had indeed been able to influence *the way* in which changes were made. Although this might certainly be regarded as a rather modest form of popular political influence, Mickiewicz nevertheless viewed the implications as 'wide-ranging' because to her they suggested 'a significantly increased and officially sanctioned role for public participation in decision-making.'[85]

By the time Mickiewicz had published her account, however, a main trend of Soviet public opinion research was subjected to severe criticism by A.A. Aleksandrov, then President of the Academy of Sciences, who argued that 'the mass of Soviet people was interested in improvements in daily life and not in participating in "mechanisms of functioning" (*mekhanizmy funktsionirovaniya*)'. According to Aleksandrov, precisely the latter was the rationale behind that branch of social research which was associated with the name and person of B.A. Grushin. Three years later, Aleksandrov's criticism was repeated in the sociological journal *Sotsiologicheskie Issledovaniya*, which only began publication in 1974.[86] The kind of public opinion research that was carried out by Grushin and his colleagues had apparently become politically sensitive. In order to gain a clear picture of the implied challenge, and of what would become 'de-politicized' when Grushin was subsequently declared a heretic (although he was able to continue with his research) it will be necessary to take a somewhat closer look at his 'school' of social science.

Grushin's central object of research was 'mass consciousness' (*massovoe soznanie*), which was considered to be a sub-system in society. It was seen to coalesce with the 'mass information relations', i.e. with the activities of the masses in producing, consuming, and using information. According to Grushin, there were two fundamental questions to be answered: (a) what is mass behaviour, as distinct from both individual and collective action, and (b) how is it expressed?

The spheres of mass behaviour that were chosen by Grushin for investigation were (a) mass migration of youth to construction sites, etc.; (b) movements of people both to certain professions and schools and to regions and towns; (c) people's amateur activities in leisure time; (d) the struggle of workers and officials to increase the profitability of production; (e) subscriptions to newspapers and certain other publications; (f) personal contacts in everyday life among neighbours, fellow travellers on public transport, etc.; (g) the population's reactions to certain acts, facts, and events; (h) mass purchases of certain goods; and (i) participation of the masses in social campaigns, etc.[87]

Moreover, at a colloquium with opinion researchers from different Soviet-bloc countries in Budapest in 1971, Grushin said that in 1970–1 All-Union opinion polls had been undertaken to find out popular views and attitudes concerning the following: the degree and spread of alcoholism and measures taken against the abuse of alcohol; sports, long-playing records, and the provision of quality consumer goods; and the role of money savings. In addition, a number of local polls had also been made, at the request of local Party organs.[88] As the results of the polls mentioned by Grushin in Budapest were not published, it is reasonable to assume that they were meant to inform the leaders, rather than the population at large. If ordinary people were to learn about each other's attitudes, they might well become aware both of the existence of different opinions and of the fact that a part, perhaps even a substantial part, of the population was in opposition to certain Party policies. Such 'popularization' of 'social information' was certainly not encouraged by the Brezhnev regime.

R.A. Safarov's work 'Public opinion and state management', which was published in 1975, was said by a reviewer to be the first Soviet monograph on the subject.[89] A central theme of the book was an attempt to answer the question whether Soviet public opinion was in accordance with the demands of developed socialism. Safarov showed that public opinion sometimes reached the leaders in a distorted form, and that information on public opinion was held up at the lower administrative levels, thus reducing the efficiency of management.[90] In order to educate public opinion, Safarov proposed, among other things, that one television channel should be allowed to specialize in systematically informing the population about the work of the Party, the Soviets and the economic organs.[91] Other Soviet sociologists implicitly supported such suggestions when they observed that the competence of public opinion increased with increasing information.[92] It was also asserted that it was especially important in studies of public opinion to analyse the efficiency of different media and propaganda organs.[93] Reporting on recent work within the Soviet Sociological Association, M.N. Rutkevich declared in 1977 that 'for historical materialism, public opinion is a certain aspect of social consciousness which reflects the conditions of social life and judges them through the prism of class interests.'[94]

One may note that while Grushin apparently considered public opinion to be a political force, and a potential source of influence, the main gist of both Aleksandrov's critique, and of the arguments presented by Safarov and Rutkevich, was not only that the leaders should be informed of public opinion, but also that the latter should be moulded and made to conform with the directives of the Party. Under conditions of preserved political stability but increasing social strains,[95] there was apparently among the Party leaders a recognition of the fact that the population at large must finally be heard. The 'solution', however, was not to allow different political opinions to be articulated freely and spontaneously and to be aggregated into autonomous organizations. The preferred method was rather to gather information in an orderly and controlled manner. In this way, the attitudes and hopefully also the behaviour of the people could be influenced.

This manipulative aspect of Soviet public opinion research transpired in a statement made at a joint meeting with the Institute of Sociological Investigations and the Soviet Sociological Association in 1976. Here it was deemed necessary to establish an 'information bank', fed by investigations of public opinion. It was also remarked that it was necessary to create a 'sociological information bank'.[96] At the same time, a Soviet reader on social management observed that a system of computerized information banks could rapidly furnish the controlling organs with essential information.[97]

Seen against the background of the subsequent stagnation of Soviet society, these declarations all bear witness to the fact that the regime's interest in opinion research was of the same nature as its interest in systems theory and in 'concrete sociological investigations', i.e. to improve the mechanisms of social management without allowing different interests to develop into distinct political currents or forces. We have seen above how both systems theory and sociology were deprived of serious content and purpose, once the signs of heresy were perceived by the Party leaders. At least this was the case with the published, observable results of these disciplines. In a parallel development, once Grushin's recommendations were understood to imply a greater influence from the public at large on questions of running the economy, i.e. the emergence of a true public opinion, the enquiries were brought to a halt.[98] These three examples illustrate rather clearly how deeply ingrained the Party's aversion actually was to allowing pluralism in any form.

Conclusion

The parallel attempts to activate the Soviets, to enhance the role of systems theory and sociological investigations, and to encourage public opinion studies, have all been seen here as ways of trying to create substitutes for politics in Soviet society. Once it had been recognized that different interests and attitudes existed, and that they perhaps ought to be heard and taken into consideration, the problem was how to accomplish this without allowing any organized, autonomous political forces to emerge, i.e. without threatening the leading role of the Party. What actually came about should not be seen exclusively as the result of manipulation from above. Given the experience of the thaws under Khrushchev, and the fact that Stalinist terror apparently was still not considered feasible, it is reasonable to assume that many people participated in the activities of the Soviets and of the social sciences out of a genuine personal desire to work for the improvement of Soviet society.

However, since all demands for political and economic pluralism, not to mention outright opposition, were simultaneously suppressed, these energies could not coalesce into a real reform. What was attempted was to encourage something that *resembled* politics, i.e. to allow a participation in policy implementation by the Soviets, and the gathering of 'social information' by social scientists, as substitutes for genuinely political inputs into the decision making process. It was a matter of allowing political processes without political actions. Writing about the Brezhnev period, Astrid Borcke and Gerhard Simon have characterized this tendency of ruling through a better informed autocracy as 'consultative authoritarianism'.[99]

Albeit implicitly, the different attempts to aggregate and articulate popular attitudes and values nevertheless allowed the emergence of a framework that resembled a political system. In a sense, the Brezhnev leadership staged the play without raising the curtain. The political arena remained opaque, but there was movement behind the screen. Groupings representing various opinions were beginning to form. Against this background, it is important to note that policies subsequently associated with the terms *glasnost* and *perestroika*, were outlined already in the late 1960s and in the 1970s, by officially recognized social scientists, by persecuted and harassed dissidents such as Andrei Sakharov, Valerii Turchin and Petr Grigorenko, and by the renowned 'official' or 'permitted' dissident Roy Medvedev.[100] From this perspective, the Brezhnev period can be seen as a period of hibernation for a set of political ideas and potential political forces that had been called to life under Khrushchev. When Gorbachev eventually raised the curtain, introducing *glasnost*, the backstage was transformed to the *avant-scne*. It is significant that the actors who then became visible to all turned out to be survivors from Khrushchev's days.

Chapter twelve

Return to Russia

Given the turbulence that had marked Khrushchev's years in power, and the implicit promise to restore order that was issued by his successors, it may perhaps seem somewhat surprising to argue that in the ideological and cultural spheres, the Brezhnev regime did not bring about any profound break with the preceding period. Gradually, however, certain differences in form did become visible. As the cultural 'polyphony' that had begun to flourish under Khrushchev was removed from the public scene, the rigid official ideology and culture of the 1949–53 period emerged largely intact. The heritage from the Khrushchev thaws had increasingly to be treated in the semi-secretive fashion of the Soviet underground 'second culture' which featured *samizdat* and 'dissidents'.

Having been strongly promoted under Khrushchev, atheist propaganda was continued under Brezhnev. The substitute Lenin cult was increasingly inflated, to the point even where it was becoming counterproductive,[1] and gradually, as we have seen in the previous chapter, it was supplemented by a Brezhnev cult. The latter was encouraged by the Party although it is doubtful whether it actually worked. Judging from the political anecdotes about Brezhnev's person that could be heard in the Soviet Union in the late 1970s and the early 1980s – he could mockingly be referred to as 'Ilich II' (Lenin being Ilich I) – this was hardly the case. The profound difference that could be observed between the vigorous Stalin cult, on the one hand, and the hardly plausible Brezhnev cult, on the other, was symptomatic of the general differences between the two regimes. It was certainly true that the Brezhnev era did not mean return to the wholesale terror of the 1930s and the immediate post-war period. It did, however, bring a lengthy period of rather deep 'frost', as a conventional police-state type of repression was introduced.

It was under Brezhnev that the concept of 'dissident' became an internationally well known term, denoting a Soviet intellectual who was persecuted and often imprisoned for being openly critical of the regime. The word was used even in Russian, in the official Soviet

Press, although of course in a derogative sense. Parallel with this 'creation' of a 'dissident movement', there also emerged an underground literature, under the internationally equally well known caption of *samizdat* (self-published). Much as had been the case in nineteenth-century Russia, Soviet culture was split into official and unofficial sectors. The *intelligent* of old had become the *dissident* of today.[2]

From the perspective of incorporation that was used in the previous chapter, this bifurcation of the cultural sphere can be seen to have quite serious implications. An important group of citizens had been deliberately placed outside Soviet society, with few opportunities to be enlisted to the cause of 'building socialism'. We shall return to the role and fate of the dissidents at the end of this chapter. First, however, we look at the ideological split of the cultural sphere. Here, the dimension of Russian versus non-Russian is of paramount importance.

Towards Recognition of the Phantom of Mamai

The Demographic Challenge to Russian Supremacy

As we have seen in the preceding two chapters, the Brezhnev era increasingly came to be marked by economic stagnation and political immobility. As a result, official cultural life and state ideology also became marked by 'stagnation' and 'immobility'. During this period of fossilization of the official surface, however, a demographic process with quite serious implications was beginning to change the ethnic balance, in a direction that was clearly unfavourable to the Russians, and thereby had serious implications for the stability of the state. Evidence from the 1979 Soviet census indicated that the relative weights of the different Soviet nationalities were changing. Fertility rates were falling among the Europeans, including the Russians, while they remained high for the Moslem Turks (and Tadzhiks) in Central Asia, Kazakhstan, and Transcaucasia. The implications for the future were rather drastic and evident to all.

Consequently, the nationality question acquired prominence as a major ideological issue in the multinational Soviet state. In absolute numbers, the Russians, together with the other Slavs – the Ukrainians and the Belorussians – continued to be predominant. However, the combined effects of Khrushchev's de-Stalinization, economic and social stagnation under Brezhnev, and the widespread perception of a 'yellowing' of the state, served to produce a certain ideological unease which resulted in a revival of nationalist feelings among the Russians. Partly as a result of these demographic changes, and partly as a form of defensive counter-reaction, a similar revival was taking place among the non-Russian nationalities.

We are dealing here with a process from below, originating amongst the intelligentsia, be it 'loyal' or 'dissident', rather than a repetition of Stalin's brutal programme for Russification from above, and the ensuing 'counter-nationalism'. The Russian revival was multi-faceted, ranging from literature, historiography, the arts and religion, to ecology and economic development programmes.[3] Especially vocal among the non-Russian peoples were the Ukrainians, the Balts, the Georgians, the Armenians, the Crimean Tatars, and the Jews.[4] These peoples are either linguistically different from the Russians, or belong to different religious categories. They are thus part of different cultural traditions. For the non-Orthodox, non-Slavic elements of the population this should be obvious. In the Ukrainian case, there were the intricate questions of the Autonomous Orthodox and Uniate Catholic Churches, both illegal and forced to operate underground, and of the long affiliation between Western Ukraine and Poland, and Catholic Europe in general.[5]

The Brezhnev regime's sensitivity to questions of demographic change was clearly revealed in its pronounced reluctance to publish data from the 1979 census. While data from both the 1959 and the 1970 censuses had been published within four years, the former in sixteen and the latter in seven volumes, only scattered information from the 1979 census appeared in journals and newspapers during an equivalent period of time.[6] Limited as the data were, they nevertheless confirmed the previous trend. The tendency towards secrecy, moreover, was not confined to the census. It was matched by a similar caution, or selectivity, in publishing research on the nationalities. Analysing published Soviet studies from these years, Zvi Gitelman even went so far as to declare that it was 'likely that empirical research on nationality questions is deliberately limited, that the results of studies are carefully screened before publication, and that even certain methods cannot be used by the researchers.'[7]

According to such census data that were published, total Soviet population growth in 1970–9 was about 0.9 per cent annually. The Russians, however, grew by merely 0.7 per cent, the Belorussians by 0.5 per cent and the Ukrainians by 0.4 per cent per annum, whereas the corresponding growth rates of the Moslems (Turks and Tadzhiks) was 2.5 per cent. Among children of up to 9 years, the discrepancy was quite significant. In the Slavic and the Baltic republics, this cohort amounted to 14–16 per cent of the population, while their share in the Central Asian republics was 29–30 per cent. Extrapolating this trend, Murray Feshbach concluded that by the year 2,000, the youngest cohorts of the six Moslem republics (Azerbaidzhan and Kazakhstan being added to the four Central Asian) would amount to 85 per cent of the corresponding numbers for the Russian republic.[8] This was well in line with a conclusion reached by Jeremy Azrael, on the basis of earlier data, that by the year 2,000 non-Europeans would constitute almost 40 per cent of the prime draft-age males in the Soviet Union.[9]

During the 1970s, purges of communist leaders accused of nationalistic deviations were carried out in the Ukraine, Georgia, and Latvia.[10] Demonstrations against perceived threats of Russification in school curricula and in the paragraphs on official state language in the proposed new constitutions, were reported from Georgia, Lithuania, and Estonia in 1978.[11] In the end, the primacy of the native languages was preserved only in Georgia and Armenia. Questions regarding the writing of history and the exploitation of natural resources and environmental protection also entered the picture of national/regional relations in the Soviet Union. The rigidity and narrowness that characterized the official understanding of these problems at the end of the Brezhnev era is evident from articles in *Kommunist*, and from statements by social scientists. A few examples will serve to illustrate.

In 1978, a certain N. Tarasenko elaborated on the theme of Russian supremacy. Because of their steadfast loyalty to the principles of solidarity and the ideals of communism, their generous soul and truly humanitarian actions, and their outstanding unifying mission, which they had fulfilled and were still fulfilling in the fraternal unity of peoples, the Great Russian people had deservingly become the object of love of all generations of Soviet citizens. The influence of the Russian people increased, and this helped the other nations develop their economy and culture.[12] The influence of national traditions meant that national peculiarities were still important, Tarasenko observed, and therefore it would be dangerous to accelerate artificially the pace of integration. The Party, however, still had to fight local nationalism and chauvinism, and overcome regional unwillingness to migrate. Because of the enhanced role of central economic planning, it was necessary to increase the role of the Russian language, Tarasenko concluded.[13] His statement was a combination of classical Marxist concepts and of Stalinist Russian nationalism.

Under Brezhnev, complete bilingualism for non-Russian Soviet citizens was an obvious goal. In 1978–9, conferences were held and decrees issued with the aim of improving Russian language training in the national republics.[14] At the same time, it was acknowledged that 'internationalization' under Russian auspices did meet with some difficulties. In 1980, Soviet academician P. Fedoseev (a one-time protégé of Andrei Zhdanov) noted some reaction against the process of merger (*sliyanie*) of Soviet peoples. According to him, the emergence of a unified Soviet culture was hampered by the fact that the Soviet peoples were insufficiently informed about each other, and about the Soviet Union at large. The classical Russian writers had been exemplary fighters against national prejudices. Pushkin had praised the Ukraine, Moldavia, and Georgia, and Lermontov the Caucasian region. The implication was, of course, that Russians should never be suspected of harbouring chauvinist emotions. Fedoseev underlined that the best way of fighting national prejudices was by means of a further spread of Russian, the international language of the Soviet Union. It was necessary to cease the unfortunate practice of printing scientific works in native languages only. They should be published in Russian as well.[15] The point here is that scientific communication should always take place *through* the Russian, and never directly from one minority language to another, say, from Estonian to Uzbek.

The very nature of the arguments put forward by Tarasenko and Fedoseev in *Kommunist* in 1978–80, together with articles in a similar vein by non-Russians, such as the Uzbek and Kazakh Party chiefs Rashidov and Kunaev,[16] indicated the existence of tensions between the Russian and the non-Russian elements of the Soviet population. Russian supremacy was apparently being contested, if not openly and in print, then at least in practice and in everyday life. The internationalism that had been proclaimed in the 1920s and in the 1950–60s, as well as the campaigns for Russification in the 1930s, 1940s, and 1970s, had evidently all misfired. At the end of the Brezhnev era, ethnic and regional differences were more prominent than ever in Soviet history. The early 1920s might be advanced as a parallel, but only in a very superficial way. Diversity at that time had been the *result* of Party policy, now proliferation occurred *in spite* of the Party's policy. The Soviet Union was approaching its sixtieth anniversary – in December 1982 – with its official ideology in disarray.

The process of ideological disintegration that marked the nationalities dimension was paralleled by obvious signs of social crisis with regard to housing, health, and social welfare in general. The latter process, which was implicitly of great ideological relevance, has been amply documented by Western scholars, and we shall not pursue it further here.[17] To our knowledge, it has not even been seriously denied by Soviet researchers. The only exception was that of a British sociologist, who based his conclusions on official Soviet statistics.[18]

Accepting the empirically well corroborated view that the life of ordinary Soviet citizens was somewhat less than prosperous under Brezhnev, Soviet sociological survey research, as reported by the prominent Soviet scholar B. Grushin,[19] takes on a particular interest.

The Precarious Victory of Stability

Although the topic of this chapter is neither the economy nor the society as such, we turn to Grushin because he succeeds in capturing the actually operative everyday ideology of Soviet society, as well as its immediate social background and surroundings. Our interest in Grushin's results originates with his description of the pattern of cultural life in the Soviet Union under Brezhnev. Although he does not indicate any direct causal link between culture consumption patterns and nationalist emotions, his picture nevertheless serves to illuminate some of the more profound reasons why the nationality question was gaining such prominence.

The Consumption of Culture

Grushin's approach to an examination of the patterns of culture consumption was to analyse various uses of free time. He observed that, for many years, the choice for most Soviet citizens on how to use free time had been largely academic, as there had quite simply not been any time to spare. Increasing welfare (of sorts) and the five-day working week, which was introduced in 1965–8,[20] should in this context have meant a final realization of Marx's visions of the creative human being. Instead, however, a major part of free time had become occupied by domestic work and child care. In Soviet cities at the beginning of the 1970s, men were reported to have 20 and women 12 hours of free time per week. Most of this time was spent rather passively, on activities that, according to Grushin, did not contribute to the development of a harmonious personality.

Soviet males, who had at their disposal an average of 14 hours a week for cultural consumption, chose to spend more than 13 of these watching TV, listening to the radio, and reading newspapers (judging from observations of Soviet citizens on public transport, the latter probably mainly about sport). The women, on their part, spent 5 of their 6 'cultural hours' a week in a similarly passive manner. Half of the total Soviet population never visited theatres and three-quarters never went to museums and exhibitions.

According to Grushin, the communist ideal was that man should develop a coherent ideological and aesthetic view of the world. This could only be attained by engaging in a diversity of cultural activities. Now research had shown, however, that Soviet citizens indulged in a one-sided, passive consumption of television programmes. This was seen to produce disturbed personalities, with a fragmentary and contradictory view of reality. In addition, there were gross social and regional differences in the patterns of cultural consumption. In 1980, 20 per cent of the Soviet population could not watch television (apparently not a big loss), or visit cinemas, bookshops, and public parks.

According to Grushin, the remedy would be either to evacuate all minor centres of population, which would certainly be in line with official policy, or to introduce an active cultural policy for the backward areas. To increase television broadcasts was not seen by him as a good solution, since this would diminish even further the scope for creative activities. Grushin also warned against the plans to increase the publication of books, from an annual 1.8 billion copies in 1978, to 5 billion in the year 2,000. Allegedly, this would entail a further withdrawal from public libraries and an increased privatization of cultural life. It was necessary to demand qualitative rather than quantitative goals for Soviet cultural policy.[21]

Grushin described a culturally apathetic mass society. He was not concerned in this study with the ethnic dimension of cultural policy, i.e. with the prospect that national traditions might assert themselves in the wake of the ideological and cultural vacuum. In the 1970s, it became evident that non-Russian nationalism was on the rise, a development which had obvious implications for Soviet cultural life.[22] Parallel to the much advertised increase in proficiency in Russian among the non-Russians, the latter were also gaining prominence in a number of other important respects, such as the rate of Party membership, tenure of administrative posts, spread of occupational skills, and access to higher education.[23] This certainly implied a potential challenge to the traditional supremacy of the Russians, a fact that was further underlined by the demographic developments in general, and the high fertility of the Moslems in particular.

There were no signs in the 1970s of an official ideological reassessment of the role of the forerunners of the Soviet Moslems, i.e. the Mongols of the Golden Horde who had converted to Islam in the fourteenth century and whose soldiers had increasingly been Turks. Nevertheless, the prospect of a future change of roles between the Russian (Slavic) and the Turkish (Moslem) elements of the population could be easily imagined. In a certain sense, the phantom of Mamai, the Mongol leader, was emerging on the Soviet scene in the late 1970s. This became evident in the intense celebration in 1980 of the 600th anniversary of the Kulikovo Battle, where according to the old Russian chronicles, Mamai had been defeated. Although this event was of paramount importance in official Soviet rituals of that year, it was hardly noticed by Western mass media. Since we consider it to be of great significance as a reflection of the ideological atmosphere in the Soviet Union at the end of Brezhnev's regime, it will be subjected to some considerable scrutiny below.

Interpretations of the Kulikovo Myth

The Background

The process of secularization that was associated with the Khrushchev era, as regards not only religious confessions but also Party ideology, had been accompanied by a social optimism and utopianism which was reflected *inter alia* in the new Party programme of 1961. As we may recall from above, however, the brave new world that was envisaged and promised by Khrushchev stubbornly refused to materialize. Faced with increasing economic stagnation and social fatigue, the Brezhnev regime gradually, albeit tacitly, began to dismantle the utopia. Ideology was turned around, to be anchored instead in the glorious Tsarist and Soviet Russian past. This process of reorientation was clearly manifested in a pronounced ritualization of Soviet public life.

After the ousting of Khrushchev, the Central Committee adopted certain principles for the introduction of new holidays and public rituals. Developments in this field have been thoroughly analysed by Christel Lane, who summarizes the original stipulations as follows:

(a) an organic connection of the new holidays and rituals with the whole system and way of life (*obraz zhizni*) of the Soviet people at the present stage of communist construction;

(b) the expression in every new custom of a definite progressive idea and of the principles of communist morality in combination with the specificities and forms of every custom;

(c) a synthesis of the logical and the emotional in every holiday and ritual. The utilization of varied means of aesthetic and emotional influence;

(d) an atheist direction, counterposing new to old religious rituals;

(e) the principle of the internationalism of the new rituals and holidays. Maximum utilization of everything progressive in national or popular traditions. Struggle against survivals of bourgeois nationalism;

(f) universality and systematic character of the new holidays and rituals, continuous and ubiquitous introduction of them into the daily life of the Soviet people.[24]

In the development of Soviet rituals under Brezhnev, Lane noticed as a striking feature 'the Russian chauvinist bias in the process of selecting a suitable cultural past.'[25] The existing Soviet order was treated in the new rituals as 'sacred'.[26] The three central Soviet holidays, the anniversary of the October revolution, on 7 November, international workers' day, on 1 May, and the anniversary of the victory over Nazi Germany, on 9 May, were all infused with military symbolism. According to Lane, this reflected 'the central position that the military-patriotic value complex has assumed in Soviet public consciousness.'[27] Worship of war heroes was recommended here as being important for 'patriotic upbringing', and Victory Day was said to be celebrated in reverence for the unsurpassed military heroism, courage and steadfastness of the Soviet people, the saviour of all of mankind from fascism.[28]

Central to any system of rites is its dependence on myths. Both rituals and myths belong to a cyclical perception of time, as distinct from a linear one. The myth is backward-looking, as both present and future realities are suggested to be merely instances of the mythical. Under Brezhnev, mythical events from the Russian past were combined with already ritualized Soviet 'counterparts' to create the image of an eternal Russian-Soviet cycle, all in accordance with the Russification of symbols and rituals that was noted by Lane. An outstanding example is the celebration in 1980 of the 600th anniversary of the Kulikovo Battle.

As we have noted above, in 1980 there were many signs that the Soviet Union was a society in decay. The economy was stagnating, alcoholism was rampant,[29] the creative intelligentsia was either leaving or being exiled in increasing numbers,[30] and the war in Afghanistan was rapidly turning into a failure. There was little for the Russians to be proud of. This was the social and emotional background to the Kulikovo celebration. By describing how Russia celebrated the Kulikovo Battle in 1980, we may draw certain conclusions regarding the meaning that was given to the concept 'Russia' in this fateful year, or, in the words of Mikhail Bakhtin, which 'fraternal bonds on a higher level' united the Russians of 1980 with their forefathers of 1380.[31]

It was an obvious subjective interpretation, serving to impute a certain meaning to the event, when the writer Valentin Rasputin labelled the celebration of the Kulikovo Battle, on 8 September, as 'the greatest event for Russian self-esteem since Victory Day'.[32] Bearing in mind Rasputin's statement, it is worth noting that he was not a member of the Communist Party but had become famous as a *derevyanchik*, a passionate defender of nature and old Russian culture against the assault of the industrial society. For more than a decade, the struggles to protect Lake Baikal and the Angara River, and to stop the vast river diversion schemes, had all been connected in large measure with the name and person of Valentin Rasputin.[33]

After briefly reviewing some basic facts about the Kulikovo Battle, we will proceed to analyse different levels in the official celebration of the Battle, as well as some observations by writers who are known to write in their own right. These interpretations will then be placed in the wider context of the Russian frame of reference that marked the late Brezhnev era.

The Official Interpretation

The Kulikovo – 'Sandpiper' – field is situated where the river Nepryadva enters the Don river. At this spot, on 8 September 1380, the Russians were led by Dmitrii, the Prince of Moscow, into battle against the Mongols under Mamai. This battle was subsequently commemorated in Russia as a great victory, and as the beginning of the end of the 'Mongol Yoke'. It was as a result of this feat, known in Russian as *podvig*, that Dmitrii earned his honourary epithet 'Donskoi'. As the American historian Charles Halperin has shown, the Kulikovo Battle was promptly exploited in contemporary Russian chronicles, such as the *Zadonshchina*, the *Troitskaya letopis*, and the *Skazanie o Mamaevo poboishche*, and also in Donskoi's *Zhitie* (*vita*). This was no doubt done in order to legitimize Moscow's rule over all Russian areas,[34] and it illustrates how the Kulikovo Battle was put to explicit ideological use right from the very beginning. It is this mythological/ideological interpretation which forms the basis of all recent Soviet elaborations on the theme.

An official interpretation of the significance of this event appeared in *Kommunist* on the eve of the anniversary, when the journal published a commemorative article, written in archaic prose by Sergei Narovchatov, who was then editor-in-chief of *Novyi Mir*. The style itself was a sign of 'Russianism', and the content stressed the importance of Russian unity and the historical mission of Russia. According to Narovchatov, *Rus* had been highly developed already at the time of the 'Rurik empire' (the phrase is borrowed from Karl Marx, without any indication that Marx was an adherent of the Russophobic Normannic theory). Narovchatov declared that neither Paris nor London was equal to Kiev, which was instead comparable with Constantinople, the seat of the emperor. Under the Mongol yoke, reminiscences of the old, flourishing Russian state were a source of power and unity for the Russians.

According to Narovchatov, it was a split between the Russian princes that had made possible the advancement of the Mongols and the establishment of the state of the Golden Horde on the Volga. The Mongol state was greedy and at least one historical epoch behind the Russians. At last, however, the Russians were united under Moscow, and in this process the Orthodox Church played 'a dynamic patriotic' role:

> The metropolite Aleksei and the authoritative church official Sergei of Radonezh were decided champions of the emancipation of the Russian soil from the heavy Yoke. They effectively helped the Great Prince of Moscow, Dmitrii Ivanovich, in his courageous deeds. Their moment was approaching.[35]

In 1378, Narovchatov observed, the Russians managed to score a minor victory over the Mongols at the Vozhe river. Mamai, the Mongol leader, sought revenge and in this endeavour he gained the support of Moscow's rivals, in particular the Lithuanian prince Jagiello. This was the background to the Kulikovo Battle, which the Russians waged under Dmitrii's slogan 'An honourable death is better than a life in shame'. The significance of the victory – as Narovchatov puts it – was the fact that 'with their bodies' the Russians had saved the Occident – Europe – and its culture from annihilation. Quoting Pushkin's famous letter to Petr Chaadaev, Narovchatov underlined that this mission had been adopted by the Russians already in 1240 – the year of the Mongol conquest. In his polemic against Chaadaev, who had argued that Russia had no cultural tradition and definitely not any European cultural heritage, Pushkin wrote that Russia not only belonged to Europe. It had even saved European culture, by absorbing the Mongol invasion.

A rather official, although perhaps somewhat more 'scholarly', treatment of the Kulikovo Battle and its lasting significance was given at the same time by the well-known historian V.T. Pashuto, in the journal *Istoriya SSSR*. Pashuto stressed that since it was a case of nomads attacking a more developed sedentary agrarian people, the Mongol assault should be seen as reactionary. The progress of history was delayed, without the labouring masses of Mongolia benefiting in any way from the conquest. When Russia was occupied by the Mongols, Sweden seized the opportunity to conquer Finland and a part of Carelia, while the Teutonic Order conquered Estonia and Latvia, which had been united with *Rus* since time immemorial.

After the victory in the Kulikovo field, however, a new era dawned. A centralized Russian state re-emerged. The Russians began to fight not only the Mongols in the south and the east, but also the Lithuanian state in the west. The Russians struggled to reconquer lands that had been usurped by foreigners. They protected and expanded both the Slavic and the non-Slavic core of the state, rejuvenating and strengthening the Old Russian nucleus. The key to success was centralized state power. As the Russians subsequently watched the decline of the Polish state, they learned to distrust parliamentarism.[36]

Another step further down the official ladder, we find a contribution in *Novyi Mir* written by Professor of History A. Klibanov. According to Klibanov, Dmitrii's *podvig* was the culmination of a long struggle against invaders, a struggle which had begun more than a hundred years previously when, at the time of the Mongol invasion, the Novgorod prince Aleksander Nevskii (from Neva, cf. 'Donskoi'), defeated Denmark, Sweden and the Teutonic Order, all coming from the West. The struggle continued in the form of popular uprisings against the Mongols in 1257, 1259, 1262, and 1289. In this contest, Russian Orthodoxy was the ideological lodestar of the popular resistance movement. The fight against the Golden Horde was waged under the slogan 'For the Russian soil and the Christian faith'. Like Narovchatov, Klibanov quoted Pushkin, arguing that since the Kulikovo Battle constituted a historical heritage that must be kept alive and be 'multiplied' (*umnozhenie istoricheskogo naslediya*), it had a direct relevance for today.

The Russians should be proud and delighted of the fact that their ancestors had defeated all their enemies and resurrected Russia as a mighty power. The victory had been preceded by the growth of a Russian nation (*narodnost*), characterized by patriotic self-esteem as well as ethnic, linguistic, cultural, and ideological unity. The new strength was confirmed by the Kulikovo victory, which Klibanov even claimed to have important implications for world history at large. It meant that a new East European great power emerged. Polemizing against earlier Soviet views, Klibanov held that religious, Christian motivations were important for the Russians in their struggle against the Mongols. Even today, the Russian people preserved the memory of the Kulikovo Battle as a historic symbol of emancipation and as an expression of national unity.[37]

Historians Pashuto and Klibanov must no doubt be considered to represent the official interpretation of Party-minded historiography. Their stress on the topicality and actuality of the Kulikovo Battle in 1380 for the Russians in 1980 was also reiterated in different ways in a number of monographs and anthologies especially published to commemorate the event. Historians analysed the battle from different perspectives in a special volume, *Kulikovskaya Bitva*,[38] which did not fail to stress that Russian patriotism was born in the Kulikovo field.[39] Apart from historical works, there was also fiction[40] and science fiction, in the latter case naturally oriented towards the past.[41] In one historical work it was said that 1380 had introduced a new transforming factor in Russian history, namely the factor of victory, based on the general insight that unity was necessary. The

306

experience of the Kulikovo Battle was successfully exploited by the
united Russian, Lithuanian, and Polish forces in the Battle of Grun-
wald in 1410. The influence, however, did not end there:

> In 1980, the Kulikovo Battle was 600 years old. This event is
> sacred for Russian history, as an unforgettable part of eternity.
> The Kulikovo epic recalls the great historical truth (*istina*), that in
> spite of suffering and terror a people that has risen in struggle for
> emancipation will not be defeated. It was no coincidence that in
> the days of supreme difficulty for our country, in the fall of 1941,
> Dmitrii Donskoi was counted among those great ancestors who by
> their courageous example had inspired the fighters in the Great
> Patriotic War.[42]

It is of great importance to note here how a line is drawn from the
day of the Kulikovo Battle straight down to the day of the victory over
Nazi Germany, the latter being one of the three great Soviet holidays.
This parallel formed an active endorsement of the theme of continuity which had been underlined already in 1941, when Dmitrii
Donskoi was hailed as a forerunner of the struggle against the German invaders, in line with Aleksandr Nevskii, Aleksandr Suvorov
and Mikhail Kutuzov.[43] This theme was elevated to a supreme level
in the finishing lines of a historical biography of Dmitrii Donskoi
which was also published in the year of the jubilee. Here it was stated
that, although 600 years separated 'us' from Dmitrii and the Battle,
they were both immortal:

> And the twentieth century with its terrible wars and invasions has
> sharpened and steeled our sense of history. The more bitter the
> sufferings bestowed in this century on our Fatherland (*Otchizna*),
> the brighter and the more inspiring have glittered in its sky the
> names of Russia's great sons.[44]

The official celebrations culminated on 8 September, the day of
the Kulikovo Battle. In *Literaturnaya Gazeta*, the prominent Moscow
writer Feliks Kuznetsov declared that not only the centralized Russian state, but also the Soviet state at large took its origins in Dmitrii
Donskoi's *podvig*. Quoting Pushkin, Kuznetsov added that not only
the Russia of old but also the Soviet Union of today was destined to
save Europe. Dmitrii's mission was continued with the victory over
fascism in the Great Patriotic War, and was also symbolized by the
Soviet Union's current struggle against nuclear war.[45] On 7 September, the eve of the anniversary, 30,000 people gathered in the
Kulikovo field to pay homage to the fallen heroes with a minute of
silence. On 8 September, a solemn celebration took place in the *Dom
Soyuzov* in Moscow, where Academician B.A. Rybakov, notorious

for his exaggerated view of the greatness of Old Russia,[46] gave a speech underlining the enduring impact of the spirit of Kulikovo and its significance for all Soviet citizens.[47]

The official interpretation of the Kulikovo Battle anniversary appealed to Russian nationalism, identifying it with Soviet patriotism. Prominent supporting themes were that of the centralized Russian state as a progressive factor in history, together with fulminations against the vices of parliamentarism, as manifested in the fate of the neighbouring Polish-Lithuanian state.[48] One may also note that one of Russia's great late poets, Aleksandr Blok, was reported to have been attracted by the Bolsheviks precisely because the latter were 'decidedly rejecting bourgeois parliamentarism'.[49] In a non-Russian frame of reference, the official celebrations may well be seen as an expression of aggressive Great Russian superpower chauvinism. It is also relevant, however, to see in the official celebrations a conscious attempt to give the Russian people a sense of community and meaning, in a time of economic stagnation, demographic crisis, and general ideological insecurity. If one sees the increasing ritualization of public life and the growing recognition of decay as mutually reinforcing processes, the celebrations of the Kulikovo Battle take on a deep ideological significance. As they met with a genuine response among the Russian intelligentsia, they also went beyond official rhetoric. Let us proceed now to take a closer look at this phenomenon of 'nationalism from within'.

Interpretations by Intellectuals

In 1980, the writer Fedor Nesterov published a philosophical/metaphysical account of Russian history where the Kulikovo Battle was placed in a grand perspective and given a profound significance. According to Nesterov, the Kulikovo victory was the first in a series of 'impossible feats', or 'exceptions', in Russian history. It was followed by the equally 'impossible' Russian victory over the Golden Horde, in the fifteenth century, and by Russia's conquest of the Eastern shore of the Baltic Sea, in the eighteenth century. What was the unknown factor, the hidden actor at work? The answer, according to Nesterov, was the state and the people. Centralization and discipline bestowed by Moscow on the Russian people were the necessary and most important preconditions for the triumph of Russia. These factors, however, would not have been efficient but for a 'third powerful factor' behind Russia's greatness, namely the power of national patriotism (*narodnyi patriotizm*).[50]

The relations of the old Russian intelligentsia and the modern Soviet writers to Kulikovo were highlighted in a special volume entitled 'Between the Nepryadva and Don Rivers' (*Mezh Nepryadvoi i Donom*).[51] Extracts from old Russian chronicles and from the works of Karamzin, Pushkin, Nikolai Rerikh, Lermontov and Tyutchev, of Akhmatova, Blok, Khlebnikov and Yesenin were printed here side by side with extracts from revered Soviet writers such as Vladimir Krupin, Petr Proskurin, and Valentin Rasputin. In his introduction to the anthology, Krupin placed particular stress on the 'educating significance' (*vospitatelnoe znachenie*) of the Kulikovo Battle. The purpose of the volume was to demonstrate the manifold nature of this significance, and to constitute 'our deep bow to the ground in honour of the ashes of the heroes of the Kulikovo Field'.[52]

In his contribution to the volume, Valentin Rasputin underlined how close he felt to the events of 600 years ago. He felt the appeal for his own generation to enter the Kulikovo Field and 'once again defend the Russian earth and the Russian blood'. Although *Rus* was not born in the Kulikovo Field, the battle had set the country on its exceptional course: 'In this moment its new history began, a history which would bring cruel and dark events but never slavery. In the Kulikovo Field a new era was begun for Russia.'[53] In the concluding chapter of the Kulikovo volume, the editor emphasized that the Russians had never experienced slavery, and that Russia was first among nations:

> Without any experience of slavery, albeit split up in principalities, long before the Kulikovo Battle *Rus* was the mightiest state of Europe. It was considered a great honour to be related to it. Voluntarily adopting Christianity, in which it believed more than all others, *Rus* created a people which was united by one language and one faith, a people that did not know the sound of gold, a people which placed spiritual purity above all.[54]

The views expressed by the writers quoted above are very much in line with those of the so-called New Russian Right.[55] In connection with the Kulikovo anniversary, however, Russian national traditions were perceived, or at least portrayed, in quite a different way by Yurii Trifonov and Yevgenii Yevtushenko, two prominent members of the liberal cultural intelligentsia. On the eve of the solemn celebration in the *Dom Soyuzov*, an article by Trifonov and a long poem by Yevtushenko were published in *Literaturnaya Gazeta*

Trifonov's commemorative article took, as its point of departure, the famous quotation from Pushkin that has been repeatedly referred to above. Choosing his own interpretation, however, he underlined that in 1380 the Russians had not fought in order to protect Europe but merely to defend themselves. In direct opposition to the rightist interpretation, moreover, Trifonov also held that the 240 years of Mongol supremacy (1240–1480) had allowed the lowest among the Russians to advance, while the best and the brightest had perished. Traitors and informers had thrived. The worst aspect of the Mongol yoke had quite simply been its long duration. The shrewd Ivan Kalita, however, managed to buy Russia a period of tranquility, and a generation of Russians could grow up without fear.

According to Trifonov, the significance of Dmitrii Donskoi's feat was not that he demolished the prison walls – which he did not – but that the 'walls of fear' were dissolved. As Russia's best sons fell in the Kulikovo Battle, however, the price paid was very high. And the memory of the Mongol yoke remained in the people: 'People grew up, grew old and died, their children grew old and died, whereas it all remained: *tamga, denga, yarlyk* and *arkan*.'[56] The words mentioned here by Trifonov symbolized Russian subservience under the Mongols. The first two, which denote certain fees, have been preserved in the Russian words for customs (*tamozhnaya*) and money (*dengi*), while the latter two were the written and physical signs of subjugation. By means of these words, the Russians were constantly reminded of their lack of freedom. It is interesting to note, however, that not even Trifonov spoke of slavery, and that the rightist nationalists stressed that the Russians were never slaves. This is well in accordance with the 'ideology of silence', i.e. the fact that the medieval Russian chroniclers and annalists never admitted that *Rus* was actually occupied by the Mongols.[57] This apart, however, the difference between Trifonov's interpretation and that of the others is obvious.

By declaring, in his poem, that in 1380 the Russians had defended Europe with their blood in exactly the same way as they would do again in the war against Hitler, when 20 million people of the Soviet population perished, Yevtushenko struck a more traditional note than Trifonov. He began the poem by stressing that the sufferings of the Russians were not in any way superior to those of other peoples. In addition, Yevtushenko took up his own anti-chauvinist line from the famous 1961 poem *Babii Yar*, where he came out strongly against Russian anti-Semitism. Now, in 1980, he stated that all peoples were equal and that the Mongols of today could not be held guilty for the atrocities of their ancestors. Yevtushenko then eloquently propagated the idea of peaceful coexistence, not only as an armed truce but as real co-operation. He also brought up the theme of conservation, of the protection of Russian nature, as he described the present-day Nepryadva as severely polluted by the spoils of modern industrial society.[58] Thereby he indicated that the struggles for tradition and for nature were one and the same.

The Wider Framework

As we have seen above, Pushkin's statement about Russia's defence of Europe was a central literary theme in the Kulikovo celebrations, both in the official use and in the works of individual writers. The latter were, of course, concerned with more than the Kulikovo Battle as such. The perspective outlined by Trifonov and Yevtushenko pointed to the wider cultural framework of the 1980 celebrations. We will examine the significance of the Kulikovo jubilee for Russian culture in the late Brezhnev era by analysing a few, selected political statements and cultural works that have no direct connection to the anniversary as such, but which are indirectly related to the theme.

Trifonov's remark that certain words denoted subjugation under foreign rule had an interesting parallel in a recent statement made at that time on the language question in the Soviet Union, by Sharaf Rashidov. Having been Party chief in Uzbekistan since 1959, Rashidov died in late 1983. Following serious accusations of corruption, he was posthumously deprived of his honourary orders and decorations. During his lifetime, however, he had been notorious as a most ardent promoter of the Russian language, and as a flatterer of both the Russian language and the Russian people.[59] In 1979, he argued that the great, progressive international role of the Russian language was revealed in the fact that the Soviet era had enriched the international vocabulary with new Russian words such as *leninizm, bolshevizm, kolkhoz, komsomol* and *pyatiletka*.[60] These words, of course, all denote the political and economic power of the Communist Party.

Trifonov's demonstration of the meaning of the Mongol words can also be seen to have a general relevance in a broader Soviet context, on this occasion with Rashidov symbolizing not the Mongols but rather communism, another 'foreign' power. There is of course nothing to say that Trifonov used the oblique parallel consciously, but it is quite evident that any Russian intellectual familiar with Party propaganda would have it close at hand. Although not original in itself, Trifonov's example thus turned the Kulikovo celebration into a critical commentary on contemporary communist rule over Russia.

As Yevtushenko was among the celebrators of the Kulikovo anniversary, and there were obvious similarities between his anti-Stalinist poem *Babii Yar* and the anti-chauvinist poem *Nepryadva*, the heritage from Stalin's rule was inevitably drawn into the picture. The juxtaposition of Trifonov and Rashidov suggests a further parallel between the present time and the Mongol Yoke. Now it is rather interesting to note that the tripartite structure of Mongol rule/ Stalinism/Brezhnevism squares very well with the famous director Andrei Tarkovskii's film triptych *Andrei Rublev*, *Zerkalo* (The Looking-glass), and *Solaris*. All three of these films concern the integrity of a Russian artist under harsh circumstances, i.e. the Mongol yoke, the Stalin era and – in the thin disguise of science fiction – the era of the 'scientific-technological revolution', the latter being the official catchword for Brezhnev's Soviet Union.

Zerkalo, the middle part of the triptych, which was first shown in 1976, fits strikingly well into Trifonov's way of celebrating the Kulikovo Battle. In this film, which is about individual and collective memory and responsibility, Pushkin's letter to Chaadaev is quoted. Tarkovskii, however, chooses to quote Pushkin's tragic verdict on Russia's fate without any pretext, and in a context that brings out the reverse side of the picture, i.e. the high price – in terms of despotism and suffering – which Russia had to pay for its alleged salvation of Europe. Because of this, Tarkovskii's triptych, and *Zerkalo* in particular, must have served as a peculiar sounding board for the official celebrations in 1980. In contrast to the 'pseudo-Marxist and pseudo-Slavophile messianism'[61] of the Brezhnev regime, which was so evident in the official celebrations of the Kulikovo anniversary, Trifonov's and Yevtushenko's nationalism, seen against the background of Tarkovskii's films, was certainly of a more inward-looking kind, an antidote to Russian expansionism both within the Soviet Union and beyond its borders.

In both Pushkin and Tarkovskii one encounters mystical-mythical themes. In Pushkin's letter, the country and the people are one as *Rus* absorbs the Mongol invasion. In Tarkovskii's *Andrei Rublev* and *Zerkalo*, the unity of the Russian people and nature is suggested as the camera eye 'caresses' the fields, the forests and the earth of Russia. This juxtaposition of the landscape and the people was also used by Dmitrii Likhachev, an individual who emerged already in the late Brezhnev era as the quintessential figurehead of non-chauvinistic Russian nationalism. Born in 1906, Likhachev, a literary historian specializing in the Russian Middle Ages, had a difficult past. In the early Stalin years, he was sent to the Solovetskii islands as a political prisoner – having opposed the reform of spelling. In the later Stalin years, however, he emerged as the leading specialist in medieval Russian literature, including the writings on Dmitrii Donskoi and the Kulikovo Battle. In Krupin's anthology he figured both as contributor in his own right and as translator of a fragment from Donskoi's *Zhitie*.[62]

In the wider perspective outlined here, however, another contribution by Likhachev is of special interest, namely his 'Remarks on the Russian' (*Zametki o russkom*), which was published in *Novyi Mir*. In this article, Likhachev did not mention Kulikovo, but, in the same vein as Tarkovskii, he underlined that history and nature merged into one in Russia and that Russian culture since time immemorial had regarded freedom (*volya*) and space (*prostor*) to be the essence of Russian nature, being both aesthetically and ethically good (*blago*). According to Likhachev, the country was the unity of people, nature, and culture. In the anti-chauvinist vein of Yevtushenko, Likhachev noted that Russian nature was not superior to that of other peoples, but that, like other peoples, the Russians, too, had a special relationship to their nature.

Among words that were seen to be especially 'Russian', i.e. anchored not only in culture but also in nature, in the landscape, Likhachev mentioned in particular the word *podvig*, used to describe Dmitrii Donskoi's feat. According to Likhachev, it was impossible to translate this word into any other language because it had a special Russian connotation of movement (*po-dvig*). Likewise, the monuments of Russian art and architecture were not static artefacts. They must be recreated by the perceiver, the co-creator, using his historical associations. The perceiving human being, Likhachev argued, must be regarded as a member of society in its living history. By history Likhachev meant not only the past as such but also the associated ideals. According to him, an abyss had emerged in Russian history, between the lofty ideals of culture and the base reality. In the old Russian ideals, there was a glaring lack of realization. The ideals never came true.

Likhachev was careful to stress that love of one's own people must not entail contempt for other peoples. Narrow nationalism was a sign of weakness, not of strength. It implied insecurity about the national traditions. A great people must help a smaller one to preserve its language and its culture. This assertion may certainly sound like a Russian counterpart to Kipling's 'white man's burden', but Likhachev seems more eager to stress that only a really Russian Russia could be a worthy member of the family of nations. It was therefore necessary to preserve the multitude, the dissimilarities, and the dynamic historical memory engraved in the great cities of Russia: Moscow, Leningrad, Kostroma, Gorkii, Yaroslavl, Kiev, Tobolsk, etc. Every place and every year of Russian history were present in today's reality, Likhachev argued.[63]

Likhachev's reflections on 'the Russian' were not political as such, but the implicit criticism against conformity and neglect of historical buildings and Russian countryside under Brezhnev was rather ob-

313

vious. This takes us back to Rasputin, the writer referred to in the introduction of the section on the Kulikovo anniversary (or motif). In 1976, the journal *Nash Sovremennik* published a novel by Rasputin entitled 'Farewell Matera' (*Proshchanie s Materoi*). The story is about an old Russian village being drowned by a hydropower dam built on the Angara River. It is impossible not to see in the village a symbol of Mother Russia and Russian culture. The hydroelectrical power plant, on the other hand, obviously signified the Soviet regime, which had used the necessity of producing energy intensive items for the armaments industry as a pretext for erecting the huge Bratsk power plant on the Angara. As Agursky has underlined, Rasputin managed to show how old Russian values were sacrificed in order to meet the demands of the Soviet imperialist military power.[64] In this perspective, it is evident that the Kulikovo Battle celebrated by Rasputin was that which entailed salvation of Russian nature and culture, not their destruction. Viewed in this way, Dmitrii Donskoi's *podvig* should be commemorated not as the first step in the building of an empire, but perhaps rather as the contrary.

It is fairly obvious that the Soviet intellectuals, Valentin Rasputin, Yurii Trifonov, and Andrei Tarkovskii, perceived the Kulikovo Battle from the same perspective as once Aleksandr Pushkin had done, that very Pushkin who stood in opposition to the Russian state power of his own time. In contrast, when official spokesmen such as Narovchatov, Klibanov, and Kuznetsov quoted Pushkin – all without specifying the context of Pushkin's statement – it amounted to a praise of the Russian/Soviet/state power, as symbolized by the Dmitrii Donskoi of the Russian chronicles, by Tsar Nicholas I of Pushkin's time, and by General Secretary Leonid I. Brezhnev of the Soviet Union.

We may conclude that by 1980, the Kulikovo Battle had become a myth. According to official spokesmen, the battle was a first instance on Russia's road to world supremacy as a defender of civilization. The non-official interpretation, however, placed the battle in quite another context, making it the first instance of defence of the Russian countryside, culture, and people. In 1380, this reading says, an *external* enemy incarnated the perpetual menace to Russia, but in 1980 Russia was threatened from *within* – or from above – by the imperial and militarist policies of the Communist Party.

We speak of a myth because there is no question here of any empirical analogy between the two dates 1380 and 1980. Reality did not repeat itself, but certain culturally significant Russians experienced a kind of repetition, or recurrence, of fateful events in Russian history. It is exactly this perception of an eternal predicament and fate, which makes the Kulikovo celebration mythical. It is a myth because the analogy was transcendental rather than empirical, according to Ricoeur's formula: 'My predecessors, my contemporaries and my successors were able, are able and will be able to designate themselves as I and to ascribe their experience to themselves.'[65]

There were even some signs that Russian nationalist fervour promoted by the Kulikovo celebrations actually went a bit too far to be really palatable to the Soviet authorities. In his speech to the twenty-sixth Party Congress, in February 1981, General Secretary Brezhnev warned against 'deviations from a clear class interpretation of certain historical events and figures'.[66] Subsequently, Brezhnev was echoed by G. Markov, then First Secretary of the Union of Writers, who underlined in his speech at the Union's seventh congress, in June 1981, that a class perspective was essential in historical novels.[67] It does not seem warranted to assert, however, as does Rutych, that the Politburo made an about-face and returned to the internationalist theme of 'the mossy swamp of Marxism-Leninism'.[68] In a neat summming up of both the Kulikovo celebrations in 1980 and of Brezhnev's subsequent admonition, in May 1981 *Kommunist* published an article devoted to the themes of nationalism and internationalism. Concerning the significance of the Kulikovo Battle, the following was said:

> This event occupies a special place in the history of our Fatherland. It would be narrow and one-sided to describe it only as the triumph of Russian weapons or as the defeat of a certain state. In reality it was a landmark which signified a fundamental moral and political change (*perelom*) in the 150-year-old struggle for national emancipation of the East and South Slav peoples, a mighty renaissance of the Russian consciousness of common national unity and a guarantee of total security for European and World civilization from barbaric annihilation. This date, as many other dates in our distant and recent past, owns exactly that 'globality' (*vsemirnost*) which makes it an international achievement.[69]

The quoted passage is an indisputable confirmation of the fact that the Party identified the cause of Dmitrii Donskoi with that of its own. In defending Russia, and in allowing Russian weapons to defeat the weapons of other peoples, both Dmitrii in the fourteenth and the Communist Party in the twentieth century stood as defenders of world civilization against barbary. Far from taking a stand against Russian nationalism, the Party, albeit with rhetorical reservations, gave the green light for Russian nationalism. Confronted with the rapidly vanishing appeal of Marxism-Leninism, the official ideology of the Communist Party and the Soviet state, this green light was apparently seen as a vital necessity.

Dissidence

Given the high hopes and expectations that must have been associated with Khrushchev's thaws, it is rather obvious that the process of what we have referred to above as cultural 'polyphony' would have ideological repercussions under Brezhnev. After Khrushchev's fall, some intellectuals actively sought to block what they saw as a road leading to a rehabilitation of Stalin and to a threatening re-Stalinization of Soviet society. On the eve of the twenty-third Party Congress, in 1966, they voiced their concern in an open letter to Brezhnev. The immediate cause of concern was the trial of Yulii Daniel and Andrei Sinyavskii, a trial which doubtless must have served as a reminder of Stalin's way of dealing with opposition and even mere dissent. Daniel and Sinyavskii were found guilty as charged and were promptly sentenced to 5 and 7 years, respectively, in prison camps. A stream of appeals, demands, new trials and new sentences, new appeals and new demands, followed.[70]

In a sense, this can be taken as a sign that an ideological discussion of sorts was taking place. Naturally, it was not held on equal terms for the discussants, nor with any immediate, tangible, positive results for the opposition. The 'dissident movement' was in this sense a political 'left-over' from the Khrushchev period. It had been awakened by the thaws associated with de-Stalinization, but it was only under Brezhnev that it would be branded as a separate 'movement'. Being a 'dissident' was not a self-appointed function. It was a structural phenomenon, reflecting the continued existence in Soviet society of a rigid and rather well-defined structure of communication, a remnant of the Stalinist *skaz*, within which only approved ideas and values could be expressed and given a wider distribution.

The emergence and proliferation in the 1970s of the underground *samizdat* literature is a symbolic manifestation of this structural divide. While the unofficial, semi-clandestine discussion certainly went further in its criticism than did the public discussion in Soviet mass media and scholarly journals, it is also interesting to note that there emerged a rather peculiar symbiosis between the two layers. A typically Soviet duality asserted itself, a system of double-think and double-talk which would subsequently be known as *dvulichie* (duplicity).[71] The existence of an overlap between the underground and the public discussions was notable, for example, in curious implicit overtures to dissidents such as Aleksandr Zinoviev, from public figures such as Viktor Afanasiev, the editor-in-chief of *Pravda*,[72] or vice versa, in expressions of sympathy from an exiled dissident such as Alexander Solzhenitsyn, to a Soviet writer such as Valentin Rasputin.[73]

As was underlined already at the time by Western observers, the main demand of the critical intellectuals was for an increased *glasnost*, i.e. for a free public exchange of different views and ideas. An obvious reason behind the demand for openness was that ideas about society and social change become politically significant only when they are freely distributed and – in principle – accessible to all. According to Gayle Durham Hannah, the new system of public communication that was suggested by the dissidents differed from the established one in suggesting pluralism instead of monopolist central control, equality instead of hierarchy, horizontal instead of vertical lines of communication, description and analysis instead of orders and prescriptions, and multiform variations instead of strict coordination of Soviet activities.[74] As regards the contents, or the substance of discussion which the dissidents attempted to make public, the central themes were political democracy, national and human rights, legalism, a rational strategy of societal development, religious freedom and quality of life.[75]

Two main points deserve to be underlined here: first, that 'dissidents' emerged not of their own volition but simply because the Party grew less tolerant of divergent views; and, second, that 'dissidence' covered a rather wide variety of values and attitudes, rather than a simple 'anti-Soviet' stance. Religious and nationalist dissidence, for example, usually concerned the collective rights of confessionally and ethnically well defined groups. Although the demands of such activists were, in principle, compatible with parallel demands for democratization, the latter ideal was not a main driving force in their dissidence. Civil and human rights dissidence, on the other hand, focused on the individual, calling for a Western-type democratic society where democracy was taken to mean not only mass participation in social activities but also a real possibility to exert political influence. Almost all dissident demands were, in theory, compatible with the Soviet constitution, both before and after 1977. However, in practice, the demands for certain collective rights were more in line with the Russian and Soviet ethos than was the struggle for individual rights. The latter must therefore be considered to have presented the more serious challenge.

All in all, however, despite internal differences, the overall programme proposed by the dissidents presented a radical challenge to many of the fundamental operating principles of the Soviet system. It is hardly surprising that repression by the KGB under Brezhnev was quite severe, but the interesting feature at this point is that it was carried out with an essentially new set of methods, which apparently met with some considerable success. Under the leadership of Yurii Andropov, who served as the head of that organization from 1967 until

317

his appointment as Central Committee Secretary, in May 1982, the KGB was transformed from a band of brutal thugs and hoods, relying on erratic terror, into an omnipresent and rather subtle machinery of refined repression.

It is symptomatic of the growing skills of the Soviet propaganda apparatus, that once he had been appointed General Secretary, in November 1982, 'well informed sources' (i.e. chiefly KGB disinformers) would spread rumours indicating Andropov's preferences for drinking whisky and listening to jazz records, tastes which had allegedly been acquired during personal acquaintance with the late British master spy Kim Philby. During his time as head of the KGB, however, the implied 'liberalism' and 'sportsmanship' was manifested *inter alia* in the imaginative use of 'political psychiatry', i.e. the practice of confining disturbing critics to mental hospitals where they would be subjected to treatment of such a type that they would very soon be in serious need of psychiatric help – in the normal Western sense of that concept.[76]

In spite of harsh repression, however, and in spite of the bitter fate of many dissidents, *samizdat* and the official discussion combined to produce a map of the Soviet ideological landscape which was squarely at odds with the myth of monolithic unity and conformity. Three main political currents could be identified in this picture, all cutting across the official-underground borderline. One of these was *Marxism-Leninism*, where the reformist ideas of a 'permitted dissident' such as Roy Medvedev were not far removed from those of the official spokesman, political scientist and journalist Fedor Burlatskii. Another was *liberalism*, where the ideas of the dissident academician, Andrei Sakharov, were matched by rather similar ideas, expressed in a number of books and articles by Viktor Afanasiev, and a third was *Russian nationalism*, where Solzhenitsyn was on common ground with a plethora of Soviet writers, such as Viktor Astafiev, Yurii Bondarev, Valentin Rasputin, and Vladimir Soloukhin. The categorization is certainly a very crude one. To mention but one aspect, 'nationalism' may be of very different kinds in different cases, ranging from socialist over liberal to conservative connotations. It does, however, serve to illustrate what we have referred to above as cultural 'polyphony'.

If they actually ever did harbour any notions of increased pluralism, international events such as the student demonstrations in Poland and the 'Prague Spring' in Czechoslovakia, both in 1968, can be safely assumed to have made the Soviet authorities still more suspicious of dissenting intellectuals in their own country. It is also an observable fact that known dissidents were increasingly arrested and sentenced for alleged crimes against the state, being sent to prisons, labour camps or mental hospitals. Solzhenitsyn was expelled from the Union of Writers in 1969,[77] and in 1974 he was finally deported to the West. As the publication of his novel *One Day in the Life of Ivan Denisovich*, in 1962, had been a landmark of de-Stalinization, this latter event was of great symbolic significance. Purges were carried out among the editors of cultural and scientific journals such as *Molodaya Gvardiya*, *Novyi Mir*, and *Voprosy Filosofii*. A number of social scientists and humanist researchers, such as Yurii Levada and Vyacheslav Ivanov, were fired from their 'proper' institutes and forced to work instead in obscurity in natural science departments. They were to re-emerge in broad daylight only in 1988.[78]

After the signing of the Helsinki agreement in 1975, the oppositionist intellectuals recovered some confidence in their cause. 'Monitoring' groups emerged in some of the Soviet republics, with the self-appointed task of scrutinizing the authorities' record on human, national and confessional rights.[79] As the 1980 Moscow Olympic Games drew near, however, the authorities obviously decided to clear the stage. Dissidents were yet again imprisoned or confined to mental hospitals, after being convicted of anti-Sovietism, and – on trumped-up charges – of espionage (Anatolii Shcharanskii). Some were exiled or allowed to emigrate to the West, in some cases in exchange for imprisoned Soviet (real) spies.

The dissident movement never succeeded in becoming a political force of significance, but the ideological influence of the Helsinki agreement would nevertheless prove to be of lasting importance. Recognition and support from well-known public figures, from leading politicians such as American President Jimmy Carter, and from humanitarian organizations such as Amnesty International, was obviously helpful both in softening the impact of repression in individual cases, and in making Soviet internal affairs a matter of increasing international concern. The cause of the Soviet dissidents was made increasingly international, and in this way Western ideas gradually and rather subtly began to make their imprint on Soviet life.

While Soviet leaders such as Mikhail Suslov, the Party's chief ideologist, and Semen Tsvigun, Andropov's deputy at the KGB, made violent attacks against 'capitalist subversion',[80] the lasting impact of Western interest in Soviet affairs, and of the associated attention paid to persecution of the political opposition, would prove itself once the old guard was forced to retire. Gorbachev's take-over provided further proof of the fact that economic stagnation and political immobility under Brezhnev was matched by a process of increasing dependence on the Western capitalist system.

We have argued in a previous chapter that the import of Western technology – and of grains – became substitutes for internal economic reforms. An important side-effect of this 'easy' solution was an increased Soviet exposure to Western political ideas and cultural values. While Khrushchev's attempted political and economic reforms were largely undone under Brezhnev, in a political return to Stalinism of sorts, a hardly noticeable but nevertheless profound Westernization of Soviet ideology was simultaneously under way. Since this ran parallel with the very strong Russian nationalist current, which we have examined above, the classical Russian dichotomy of 'Westernization' and 'Slavophilism' can in a sense be seen to have re-entered the stage, after an absence of almost a century.

The intellectual ferment was thus potentially relevant as a basis for the articulation of political demands. For the time being, however, repression effectively prevented the intellectual movement from becoming politicized outright. Although the ground was being prepared for political discussions once the grip slackened, the impact of the dissident movement, ranging from the nationalities question to demands for political pluralism, was primarily ideological.

Conclusion

Soviet ideological life under Brezhnev was an amalgamation of all previous Soviet experience. Here, the internationalism and secularization of the 1920s and of the Khrushchev years was merged with the Russification policies and Great Power chauvinism of the Stalin years. The Soviet Union finally established itself as a superpower with stakes all over the globe, from Vietnam and Afghanistan, via Ethiopia and Angola, to Nicaragua and Cuba. Having previously been confined to coastal waters, under admiral Gorshkov's leadership, the Soviet Navy took to the high seas. At the same time, however, Soviet demographic and cultural trends worked to the disadvantage of the Russians. Having all the reins of power in its hands, the Soviet regime was able to pursue a campaign for linguistic Russification, but it evidently did not meet with much success.[81] Instead, Russian historical memories were increasingly invoked by both official representatives of Moscow and by the more liberal cultural intelligentsia.

Ideologically, the perspective of Soviet internationalism was definitely superseded by Russian nationalism. It was not only, or even primarily, a matter of state policies, as under Stalin. In the first place, it was part of global developments in the 1970s, when national minorities reasserted themselves everywhere, not only in the Soviet

Union. In the second place, the Russian revival under Brezhnev signalled a final end to the utopian dreams that had been nurtured under Khrushchev. What was left for Brezhnev's successors was, on the one hand, a rather potent legacy of Russian Orthodoxy and nationalism, and, on the other, a greater prominence of local creeds and languages, in the Christian European and Trans-Caucasian republics as well as in the Moslem republics of Central Asia and Azerbaidzhan.

The development of cultural and ideological 'polyphony' that had been introduced under Khrushchev's thaws thus continued under Brezhnev, in spite of the repression of human-rights activists. In this respect, secularization continued. All in all, developments under Brezhnev had brought the Soviet Union ideologically and culturally into a pre-revolutionary situation which bore some resemblance to the Silver Age of decaying tsardom in the early twentieth century. On the surface, the Soviet Union at the time of Brezhnev's death, in November 1982, was a rigid society, marked by extreme ritualization of its political life and a sullen streamlined conformity of its official culture. Beneath the surface, however, there was a vigorous 'second culture', where the official rituals were undermined by the recreation of genuine myths, above all the myth of Kulikovo. Russia's intellectuals were ready for the arrival of a Prince Valiant, a modern counterpart to the mythical Dmitrii Donskoi of the old Russian chronicles.

Chapter thirteen

Summary: rationality and Soviet man

In our previous summary section, we began by making a brief digression, in order to recall some of the points about our understanding of ideology that were made in the introductory chapter to this study. This was done in order to create a framework for analysing the important issue of continuity versus change in Soviet development. With the help of our thus constructed model of 'Soviet Loyalty' we sought to establish two vital points. *First*, it was shown that a number of structural and behavioural patterns did indeed exhibit a remarkable continuity between the respective Stalin and Khrushchev periods, so much so in fact that we found it warranted to conclude that Khrushchev's 'tinkering' had not succeeded, in any fundamental respect, in altering the working principles of the basic Stalinist model. Our *second* point concerned those changes that actually were made. Here it was argued that the legacy left by Khrushchev contained the important feature of crossing off the agenda a number of previously available policy options. In a sense, Brezhnev could thus be seen to have found himself in a worse position than did Khrushchev at the time of his take-over.

With the addition of the three chapters on events during the Brezhnev era, we now find ourselves confronted with two important issues. The first is the repeated one of continuity versus change. Here we shall investigate whether Brezhnev actually succeeded in breaking old patterns or whether he was also frustrated in the pursuit of such ambitions. This task will be approached in a fashion similar to that of the Stalin-Khrushchev case. The second question, however, is somewhat more complicated and thus requires a somewhat different approach. Since we have arrived now, chronologically, at the end of the Brezhnev era, a point which in many respects can be seen as a crossroads for the Soviet system as a whole, it may be opportune at this time to backtrack somewhat, in order to consider the main lines of development that led up to that point.

In this summary section, therefore, we begin by making a brief digression, only this time we do so in order to recall some of the main points concerning the concept of rationality that were made in our introductory chapter. Our purpose in returning now to that discussion is to find some suitable tools for pin-pointing the real roots of the problems that are the focus of our investigation, and hopefully also to indicate why attempted solutions have not worked. The outcome of this discussion will be to present the essence of the legacy that was left for Gorbachev.

Soviet Rationality

In our introductory discussion of rationality, considerable attention was focused on the Prisoner's Dilemma, the classic show-piece of game theory. This was done in order to show that even if all single individuals pursue individually rational strategies, there is no guarantee that a collectively rational outcome will result. Or, to put it somewhat differently, even if all single individuals act so as to maximize their own utility, all individuals as a group may actually end up being worse off than if some other, individually less preferable, strategies had been chosen. As we have already indicated, the existence of such situations is in no way solely specific to the Soviet system. Applications of the Prisoner's Dilemma in economic analysis are by now so numerous and varied that even a brief survey would constitute a volume on its own. It is when we move into the domain of possible *solutions* to the dilemma that the Soviet case stands out. It is also mainly for the purpose of studying these aspects that we have chosen to use it here as a framework for analysis. Before proceeding to that discussion, however, we shall look somewhat more closely at the basic structure of the game.

The Prisoner's Dilemma

The Prisoner's Dilemma is an example of what is known in game theory as a two-person, variable-sum, non-cooperative game, i.e. we have two people playing against each other, in a game where they cannot co-operate but where the total pay-off to be shared will depend on the respective strategies that are chosen. These game characteristics are of some considerable importance and may thus merit a few brief comments. The fact that we are not dealing with simple two-person situations is of no major consequence. We may as well define the game as two groups playing against each other, or as a single individual playing against the remainder. The other two points, however, are somewhat more problematic.

The variable-sum nature of the Prisoner's Dilemma stands in contrast to zero-sum – or constant-sum – games, which are essentially games of pure conflict. It is fairly hard to find real-life situations where the total pay-off is not influenced by the players' choice of strategy. (One example is the tossing of a coin.) In our initial illustration, the dilemma concerned agricultural fieldwork; the respective strategies being 'to work' or 'to shirk'. The main reason for selecting that game was to identify the losses borne by everyone as a result of a universal defection strategy. It is obviously games of this kind that we are interested in here.

The aspect of non-cooperation is largely a question of interpretation. Since the Soviet system – in its official presentation – relies to a very large extent on various forms of co-operation, malfunctions in this respect will obviously have quite serious implications. The problem that arises out of this observation is to find out *why* co-operation tends to break down. In the literature, it is sometimes argued that it is the absence of communication that is the real *differentia specifica* of the Prisoner's Dilemma. Indeed, in the original formulation of the problem, as we may recall from our previous presentation, the very essence of the dilemma was that the two prisoners should be kept in separate cells, without the possibility of communication.

As with the zero-sum game, it may be difficult to find real-life situations where communication is totally impossible. As John Harsanyi has pointed out, however, it is not the absence of communication *per se* which is the main problem: 'The crucial issue is the possibility or impossibility of binding enforceable agreements. ... This will be true regardless of whether the players can talk to each other or not.'[1] As we shall argue below, it may actually be the case that a policy which is designed to facilitate communication, can, in practice, serve to deepen rather than resolve the dilemma. Before elaborating on this important point, however, we shall discuss briefly the different *theoretical* ways in which the dilemma can be resolved.

In a perceptive essay on prudence and morality in the Prisoner's Dilemma, Derek Parfit has structured available solutions into two different classes, according to the ways in which they approach the problem at hand.[2] The first of these represents *political* solutions, which aim either at making the undesirable activity *de facto* impossible, or at associating it with prohibitive costs. Illustrations of the former are the destruction of fishing nets, in order to prevent over-fishing, or the chaining of soldiers to their posts, to prevent desertion. Illustrations of the latter are rewards for those who abstain, or penalties for the culprits. If all deserters were to be shot, for example, the problem of desertion might thus be resolved. The other type consists of *psychological* solutions, and here Parfit presents four illustrative examples. One is for people to become *trustworthy*, i.e. to choose a co-operative strategy in the belief that others will do the same. Another is for them to become reluctant to be *free riders*. A third possibility is a *Kantian* influence, which can produce only that behaviour which one wants to see in others, and the final case is that of *altruistic* behaviour. While the political solutions seek to change the situation in which people find themselves, the psychological ones seek to change the individuals.

Given the highly different political and ideological implications that can be derived from these two classes of solutions, the distinction that is made between the two will play an important role in our discussion below. At the same time, however, it should be noted that one can obviously not exist in splendid isolation from the other. The distinguishing feature between various real-life illustrations will be where the main emphasis of a regime's policy is placed, on a spectrum of measures that runs from purely political to purely psychological. An outstanding illustration is the programme of 'African socialism' that is associated with former Tanzanian President Julius Nyerere. Having very strong moral and ethical overtones of equality and anti-colonialism, this programme placed heavy reliance on political exhortation and on achieving a radical change in popular values and beliefs. This, however, did not mean a total disregard for direct administrative and economic intervention. In both the economic and the political spheres, collectivist solutions were strongly encouraged and their private counterparts discouraged, or prohibited outright. The failure of the *ujamaa* programme for rural development, for example, is probably best understood as a failure in both the 'political' and the 'psychological' dimensions. Exhortation failed to produce the proper spirit, while direct intervention served to compound rather than diminish the problems that were associated with the gap between utopia and reality.[3]

The Soviet case lends itself admirably to interpretation in precisely these terms. Parfit's breakdown of the political solutions into two groups reflects the long-standing practice of speaking of a need to move from 'administrative' to 'economic' methods of management, i.e. from direct administrative commands and controls to a system of indirect economic penalties and rewards, and the distinction between 'political' and 'psychological' solutions reflects the multitude of situations where perfectly legal actions are condemned as morally unfair (e.g. high profits on the *kolkhoz* markets). As we shall see below, Soviet development exhibits an interesting interplay between these different solutions. Before proceeding to that discussion, however, we shall look briefly at some problems in relation to the introduction of the different solutions, or policy measures.

First of all, we have the simple problem of transaction costs, which was pointed out by North in our introductory chapter. In many cases, the costs of enforcing prohibitions, or of collecting taxes, may well turn out to be larger than the benefit that is derived from curbing the undesirable activity. This reduces the attraction of the political solutions. The psychological solutions, however, by their very nature, need not be enforced, and are thus in this sense costless. As North has indicated, the imposition of moral costs can, in this perspective, be seen as a simple cost-saving device, helping individuals to 'come to terms with their environment'.[4] We may perhaps best realize the importance of this dimension by visualizing what may happen if the regime fails in the latter respect, or – worse – if its policies actually serve to alienate the citizenry rather than help it to 'come to terms' with its environment.

Furthermore, we also have the inescapable dimension of *how* to introduce the desired solution. Here the political category stands out as the more readily available one. Direct prohibitions, or various combinations of taxes and subsidies, are much easier to introduce than subtle changes in the psychology of the subjects. In particular, this would seem to hold true in the Soviet case, where there are no drawn-out parliamentary proceedings, complicated by vociferous lobby groups, to accompany such actions. Reality, however, seems to belie this simple observation. While exhortation and political indoctrination have long been distinctive features of Soviet politics, it is only recently that such campaigns have gained wide currency in the West (e.g. environmental protection campaigns and anti-smoking drives).[5]

We shall return below to the important differences that exist between East and West in this respect. For the moment, however, it is sufficient to stress the fact that the ambition to find psychological solutions, in the form of exhortation and *agitprop*, has long been – indeed still is – a distinctive feature of the Soviet model. Our approach of focusing on the ideological dimension, rather than on the political process, would consequently seem to be rather appropriate.

If we move now from general reflections on the more abstract nature of the Prisoner's Dilemma, to the more specific details of the Soviet case, two points are in order. First, as far as the basic game is concerned, we shall concentrate on its *structure* rather than its actual formulation, and on its *solution* rather than on the dilemma as such. The former derives from the assumption that the players act strategically and that there is a dominant strategy for each player. This produces the contradiction between individual and collective rationality that was referred to above. The latter derives from our focus on ideology and serves to underline the important distinction between 'political' and 'psychological' solutions. This will also be seen to constitute an important difference between East and West.

Second, it is important to point out that, although situations akin to the Prisoner's Dilemma can certainly be identified in the political sphere, it is our basic ambition here to concentrate on the economic sphere. In good Marxist tradition, we believe that the productive forces are the basic determinants of development. Such ambitions and objectives that arise in the political sphere will consequently be seen as imposed on the economic one, in the form of restrictions. Indeed, it is precisely such restrictions (e.g. the collective-farm system or the absence of pricing for natural resources) that make the Prisoner's Dilemma endemic to the Soviet system. In this perspective, it becomes a task for the cultural and ideological sphere to impose norms that block undesirable behaviour, promoted by the failures of economic policy. Let us proceed now to examine what impact the imposition of such norms may have had on Soviet citizens.

Creating Soviet Man

It has been indicated on repeated occasions above that we view neither ideology nor Prisoner's Dilemma type situations as features specific to the Soviet system. In a similar vein, it should be pointed out now that the existence of social norms is not peculiar to Soviet society. As we have seen above, North points out that the imposition of such norms is a general phenomenon which we will expect to find in all societies: 'The educational system in a society is simply not explicable in narrow neoclassical terms, since much of it is obviously directed at inculcating a set of values rather than investing in human capital.'[6] As in the cases of ideology and the Prisoner's Dilemma, it will be argued here that the Soviet case stands out by virtue of degree rather than principle.

In a Western society, most people would probably say that they recognize the existence of (although perhaps not abide by) a large number of social norms which in various ways aim to constrain their behaviour. Equally probable, however, is that they would be at a loss when asked to explain the origin of most of these norms. In cases such as littering, the citizens of some countries would, perhaps, point to concerted national campaigns, but that would be exceptional. In most cases, the norms simply exist. People might agree that one should not spit, swear, or run naked in public, but would they be able to say from whom or for what reason such prohibitions are derived?

An immediate reference could certainly be made to family or school, but that would not be a satisfactory answer. It does indicate where in society the norms are stored, but it does not explain their actual origin. Another response might be that certain things should not be done simply because they are illegal. Then, however, we are no longer dealing with norms, but with formal acts of legislation. We shall return in a moment to the crucial interplay that must exist between these respective sets of rules for behaviour in society. First, however, let us look briefly at some distinguishing characteristics of the Soviet case.

The origins of a large number of the norms that constrain the daily activities of Soviet citizens are quite clear. There exists within the Party a huge apparatus the sole function of which is precisely that of propagating norms. It is this which we have referred to above as *agit-prop* and its main mission can loosely be said to be aimed at the creation of Soviet Man. This, of course, is not to say that the Party is in complete control of the entire spectrum of social and moral norms in Soviet society. Since many of the norms that are common to most civilized societies have existed much longer than the Soviet Union, that would be an obviously absurd claim.

Nevertheless, we shall argue that there are a sufficient number of norms that are controlled and propagated by the Party in order to warrant making the claim that there is, in this respect, an important qualitative distinction between East and West. The very nature of these norms, which we shall refer to below as 'political', makes them of a rather alien nature to a Western society. While social norms in a Western context chiefly serve to constrain public behaviour by individuals, political norms in the Soviet case also tend to invade the inner privacy of the individuals' perceptions of what is fair and just. By telling Soviet citizens that they are (or at least should be) Soviet men or women, the Party seeks to monopolize not only the function of control over public behaviour, but also the formation of moral and ethical values. The 'ambition' of Soviet political norms can thus in some sense be said to be higher than that of social norms in a Western context. Logically, the consequences of a failure, of an undesirable backlash effect, can also be expected to be more serious.

Another distinctive feature of political norms in the Soviet case is that they tend to be instrumental, to a degree that lacks parallel in the West. In order to elaborate on this point, we may profitably advance as parallels the biblical Ten Commandments, or various religious constraints on eating habits. Originally, these various restrictions were introduced in the form of decrees, by a priesthood that claimed to have received them from higher authority. Gradually, however, they began to assume the shape of widely accepted – and respected – social norms. Consequently, they were able in a natural way (i.e. without widespread policing) to fulfil their original intentions of curbing activities that were considered harmful to the members of society at large. In Parfit's terms, we would speak here of a 'psychological' solution having been achieved.

Over time, many of these early religious norms have been incorporated into the civil legislation of most civilized nations. The interplay at this point between norms and laws is important. Laws that do not reflect values that are shared by broad sections of the citizenry will be rather difficult to enforce. A case in point is the recent Swedish attempt to make jaywalking illegal. Since the bulk of the population appears not to have shared the conviction of the legislator that jaywalking should be punishable by law, no corresponding social norms emerged. Subsequently the law was repealed.

In the Soviet case, a large number of political norms are of a nature similar to that of the religious ones. As we have argued above, there are important similarities between institutionalized religion and the Communist Party's status as a repository of some sublime truth, outside the reach of ordinary humans. Although Soviet ideological tenets do not originate from a superior Divine authority, they are instead derived from the 'scientifically correct' body of thought that is known as Marxism-Leninism. The underlying authority and the instrumental function would thus seem to be rather similar.

The problem, however, is that among the Soviet population at large there seems to be a rather poor acceptance of the majority of the political norms that are thus derived. This failure of acceptance, moreover, has not been approached by adaptation of the creed but instead by high premiums for conformity and high penalties for overt non-conformity. In essence, this can be interpreted as an attempt to introduce political solutions (i.e. material penalties and rewards) in order to correct for the failures of psychological solutions (i.e. *agitprop* and exhortation), which in their turn were originally introduced to correct for problems of the Prisoner's Dilemma type that resulted from the change of economic system. This interpretation of the effects of various policy measures as a 'layered' structure has important implications for the psychology of Soviet Man.

To put it simply, the result of the intertwined processes of finding both political and psychological solutions has been to reinforce precisely that dual reality which we have described above in terms of the concept of *dvoeverie*. The response from the citizenry has, in turn, been what we have referred to above as 'faking', i.e. an effort to produce an outwardly acceptable façade. Inevitably, the outcome of these processes has been 'cognitive dissonance',[7] a psychological discrepancy between the two separate realities. Since such dissonance is unpleasant to live with, individuals will attempt to deal with it by resorting to the mechanisms of justification and self-deception that we

330

have discussed above.[8] To some extent, this process of artificial realignment will no doubt be successful, but only at the price of
introducing a certain element of latent self-contempt, for engaging in
that form of activity. We shall return to this mechanism in a moment.

Producing Ideology

Having thus outlined the impact on Soviet Man of the various
ideological pronouncements that are so characteristic of Soviet
society, we are left with the question of the origins of these pronouncements. As we have indicated above, it is our understanding that we
have here an important distinguishing feature between East and
West. In a formal sense, the question has an obvious answer. Within
the *apparat* of the Central Committee of the Communist Party of the
Soviet Union there exists a separate Department of Propaganda.
This department is responsible not only for *agitprop*, i.e. agitation
and propaganda, but also for the broader aspects of cultural and
sports activities in Soviet society. In essence, it attempts to cover and
influence both work and leisure activities of the citizenry. It is here
that speeches are written, texts are censored, and directives issued.
Soon after his elevation to the post as General Secretary, Gorbachev
appointed Aleksandr Yakovlev, former Soviet Ambassador to
Canada, to head this important department. Yakovlev, presumedly a
close associate of Gorbachev, is commonly believed to have been the
main architect behind *glasnost*, the new policy of 'openness'.

Once we proceed beyond the formal façade, however, it is obvious
that the process of deciding on what should be the currently correct
interpretation of official ideology is a fairly complicated process. In
particular, this will be the case if seen against the background of our
instrumental interpretation of ideology. If ideological pronouncements and the publication of ideologically relevant books and texts
have an important part to play in the line-up of forces in the power
game, then the actors in that game will naturally be rather keen on
exerting an influence over the production of ideology. This provides
fertile ground for various Kremlinological speculations.

There is, however, also a third dimension to this problem, a
dimension which for our purposes is of considerably greater importance than both the formal façade and the actual content of the power
game. It is not enough to identify a department of propaganda and a
number of politically correct officials who are able to determine what
should be currently produced. For obvious reasons, such pronouncements will also have to have an intellectual content. Someone will
have to write the speeches and the books, direct the movies and the

plays, compose the music and paint the pictures, that serve as the sugar coating on the pill. This is where the cultural intelligentsia enters the picture and the way in which their support is enlisted is rather intriguing.

With Gorbachev's revolution from above, words like *perestroika*, *uskorenie*, and *glasnost*, and concepts like *novoe politicheskoe myshlenie* and *period zastoya*, quickly start to appear. Suddenly, Soviet historian Danilov is interviewed by Western media, commenting on Conquest's book *The Harvest of Sorrow*, and on the film *Harvest of Despair*. Subsequently, moreover, the very same Danilov is allowed to publish, in *Voprosy Istorii*, a letter to the editor informing the Soviet readership about the Western slander contained in these works.[9] Why do such things happen? Why are the scholars, the writers, the composers and the other members of the creative intelligentsia so swift to emulate any new signals from the centre? Who, moreover, decides on what these new signals will be, and on which catch-words to use?

Some of these questions obviously defy scrutiny by outside observers, but the psychological implications of the process at hand can certainly be discussed. They are also of crucial importance to our presentation. With respect to political behaviour in a Western context, Elster has observed that 'in political debate one has to pay some lip-service to the common good.... One cannot indefinitely praise the common good "du bout des lvres", for ... one will end up having the preferences which initially one was faking.'[10]

There are two reasons why this observation is relevant in our context. First, it again shows that we are not dealing with exclusively Soviet problems. In both worlds, most people will no doubt at times find themselves in situations where some elements of faking will have to enter into their behaviour. There are certainly exceptions to this rule, in the form of people with great moral integrity, but they will be few and far between. The distinction between East and West, we shall argue, is again one of degree rather than principle. Faking in the Soviet context will not only be more pervasive but also associated with more extreme penalties and rewards (cf. our previous discussion on the role of Party membership).

The second point of relevance in Elster's observation is that it illustrates how prolonged faking will influence the psychology of those involved. Writers and other members of the creative intelligentsia probably perceive better than others the true nature of the system, and the associated problems of *dvoeverie*. Once they have been drawn into the process of producing ideology, they can thus be expected to suffer more acutely from the problem of cognitive dissonance. Being unable to influence reality, and being incapable of intellectually ac-

cepting the creed, they will then resort to those mechanisms of justification and self-deception that have been described above. As a
result, they will over time subconsciously come to believe – even in
private – in at least part of what they say in public.[11] In this way, the
production of ideology will become a self-generating system, where
the producers are highly sensitive to even minor variations in the tune
that is being played by the centre. At the heart of this process lies the
role of esoteric communication, the very keystone of Kremlinology.

An important consequence of this process, from an analytical
point of view, is that people inside the system will be slow to adapt if
the need to engage in faking should be suddenly removed, as to some
extent has been the case with the onset of *glasnost* under Gorbachev.
Rather than restoring a single homogeneous reality, *glasnost* will be
superimposed on the previous reality of *dvoeverie*, thus forming a
rather peculiar third layer. The response of individuals to the demands of this new situation will be to provide a false picture of
openness, tailored to the perceived new set of requirements. The
Russian term *pokazukha* captures precisely this phenomenon. The
root of the term is *pokazat*, which means to show, or to demonstrate,
and its meaning is mere window-dressing.[12]

Although the façade and the content of the message will change,
its bearing on reality may be rather limited. The same people as before will be doing the same things as before, only now they will be
saying different things. The satirical magazine *Krokodil* is an excellent source for understanding how such a new layer can be added.
During *glasnost*, a large number of cartoons have been presented,
showing, for example, enterprise managers smilingly presenting evidence of gross inefficiency and waste, and equally smiling workers
being portrayed on enterprise 'disgrace boards'.[13]

The point is that the *format* is exactly the same as in traditional
presentations of rising productivity and outstanding workers, only
now the picture has been inverted. There can be no better illustration
of this process than the *Krokodil* portrayal of a bureaucrat in the
shape of a weather vane. Facing left, under the heading 'yesterday', he
is smiling and utters phrases like 'Here everything is well! Wonder-
ful! Better than anywhere else!' Facing right, under the heading
'today', he has an angry look and says things like 'Here everything has
been bad! Terrible! Worse than anywhere else!'[14] Rather than
remove the old problems, this addition of a new reality may be assumed to introduce a further source of dissonance. The nature of the
latter process will be a central topic for discussion in the final, concluding, chapter of this study.

Lenin, Stalin and Khrushchev

If we return now to the problem of why the strategy of universal co-operation tends to break down in the Prisoner's Dilemma, we may recall Harsanyi's claim that the root of the evil was a failure to achieve binding enforceable agreements. When we look back at the experiences of Soviet development, as it has been described and discussed above, it is evident how different periods in time can be placed at different points on the spectrum between purely 'political' and purely 'psychological' solutions. During both Lenin's and Stalin's times, the Soviet regime consciously sought to block political solutions, hoping instead to promote psychological ones, via a massive investment in exhortation (viz, National Bolshevism and the Cult of the Leader). The obvious reason for this choice was the desire to suppress political opposition; without politics there can, of course, be no political solutions. To the extent that politics actually was suppressed, this also held true for the political solutions.

The outcome was the creation of what we have referred to above as passive Loyalty. Via a process of trial and error, an economic and political system emerged which to a myopic leadership was admirably well suited to further their perceived needs for power and security. It featured an economic system where inefficiencies and waste, derived from situations of the Prisoner's Dilemma type, had become endemic. Early attempts to promote collective incentives and to rely exclusively on exhortation (i.e. to seek psychological solutions) were already abandoned by the early 1930s, when Stalin branded all such ideas as 'petty-bourgeois *uravnilovka*'. Instead followed the Stakhanovite movement, which offered substantial material rewards to those few who were chosen as heroes and champions.[15]

This transition illustrates what we have referred to above as a 'layered' structure of solutions. The psychological solution represented by collective incentives was introduced in order to correct for the suppression of market forces that accompanied the end of the NEP. Then, when it became obvious that this engendered widespread free-riding, the political solution of Stakhanovism was introduced as a further corrective. For obvious reasons, however, the latter was far removed from the original situation under NEP. Given the way in which other workers had to be exploited in order to make the achievements of the Stakhanovites at all possible, the latter could in no way, other than for simple propaganda purposes, serve as role models. Economically, the system of 'shock work' had no advantage other than mobilization and a forced pace of production. All aspects concerning the quality of work and the efficiency of resource utilization were anathema. Morally, moreover, it had an inherent destructive potential of a rather obvious nature. Stalin, however, saw the situation differently. His prediction was that the 'Stakhanov movement will spread into all spheres, into all areas of our country, and will show us the wonders of new achievements.'[16] Already at this time, the need for economic reform was inherent in the Soviet Model.

The political part of the system that developed under Lenin and Stalin took a similar path towards inevitable needs for reform, moving from a restriction of available channels for Voice under Lenin, to outright terror under Stalin. In the short run, the benefits in terms of power and security were no doubt tangible. The model as a whole rested on a system of soft options for Exit and Voice that served effectively to decompress potentially explosive discontent among the population. At the same time, however, the resulting passive Loyalty was such that it also deprived the economy of vital initiative and feedback. If we recall Parfit's assertion, that to find binding enforceable agreements was the real solution to the Prisoner's Dilemma, it is obvious that no such solutions could be found under a reign of terror. In order to elaborate this important point, we shall bring out the following distinction, made by Hirschman, between vertical and horizontal Voice:

> It is the earmark of the more frightful authoritarian regimes that they suppress not only vertical Voice – any ordinary tyranny does that – but horizontal Voice as well. The suppression of horizontal Voice is generally the side-effect of the terrorist methods used freely and openly by such regimes in dealing with its real and imagined enemies. For once, this side-effect is not unintended: rather it is greatly welcomed by these regimes who hope to gain in power and stability by thus converting citizens into isolated, wholly private and narrowly self-centred individuals.[17]

It was certainly the case that Stalin not only succeed in curbing openly organized and aggregated Voice, but also in suppressing seemingly harmless horizontal Voice.[18] It is equally true that he did so by resorting 'freely and openly' to terrorist methods. No subtle analysis is needed to prove this point. Nor do we need to underline further the economic costs involved. There is, however, an important point involved in distinguishing between the vertical and the horizontal dimensions of Voice suppression. As we shall see below, subsequent leaders would find more effective ways of solving the dilemma of curbing Voice at a minimum cost.

The apparent discontinuity that marks the entry of Khrushchev on the stage forms an eminent illustration of the inherent limits to change that mark the Soviet model. As we have seen, Khrushchev consciously sought to revive economic thinking and to reintroduce politics into the Soviet system. In so doing, however, he shied away from the implied need to allow true pluralism in all spheres of society. As a result, the attempt to reform the economy was limited to 'tinkering', the attempt to revitalize politics produced little more than an increased level of sound within the same old channels, and the 'liberalization' of cultural life is better described as polyphony than as pluralism. In all important respects, continuity rather than change can thus be taken as the hallmark of the Khrushchev period.

De-Stalinization did, however, serve to dissipate some part of the previous pluralist ignorance. Not only were Soviet citizens being told some part of the story of atrocities committed under the late Dictator's rule. They were also becoming increasingly aware that they were not alone in being critical of this system. Intuitively, this limited openness should have served to promote collective action and the creation of an active Loyalty, in the original Hirschman sense of delaying Exit in order to promote Voice. In practice, however, it appears paradoxically to have served to deepen rather than resolve the dilemma. As people grew aware of the true nature of the reality that surrounded them, the problem of *dvoeverie* was sharpened. If true pluralism in economic and political life had been permitted, this might have been possible to overcome and 'binding enforceable agreements' could have been reached. As it was, however, the need to engage in faking remained and thus the problem of cognitive dissonance can be assumed to have grown more severe.

It is symptomatic, for example, that in 1988, speaking of the 'socio-economic and spiritual situation in the country', Shmelev would write that, in the 1950s, 'the price of spirits was considerably lower than it is today, and it was sold everywhere, yet the consumption *per capita* was 2.5–3 times less than it is today.'[19] It is difficult to say if the process of social degeneration started already during the Khrushchev era, or if it was part of the reaction to frustrated hopes that Khrushchev would really make a difference. It is certainly the case that its more visible manifestations belong to the 1970s in particular, but if we make the assumption that we are dealing with a social process that is slow in forming it would seem plausible to argue that it originally took its beginning in the early 1960s, or maybe in the late 1950s, as a reaction to the incomplete process of de-Stalinization rather than to Khrushchev's tinkering. This agrees well with our overall view of the Khrushchev period as a tumultuous parenthesis rather than as a break with the past. What, then, can we say about the issue of continuity versus change, and about ideology and rationality during the Brezhnev era?

The Brezhnev Era

The real hallmark of the Brezhnev era was that of economic stagnation, known in the current Soviet reform rhetoric as *zastoi*. Once the initial euphoria of the abortive Kosygin 'reforms' had worn off, and as the 1970s wore on, it became increasingly obvious to large numbers of Western observers that something was seriously amiss with the direction of Soviet economic development. Many books and articles were devoted to this theme and at the beginning of the 1980s the atmosphere was assuming quite alarming overtones. It was pointed out that the Soviet 'extensive' growth machinery was quite simply running out of steam. Natural resources were running low, technological change presented a sad picture and the demographic situation projected serious labour problems for the near future, in terms of shortages and spatial misallocation. All long-term indicators pointed firmly towards disaster.

Yet, to the Soviets all was apparently well. The official rhetoric continued to speak of 'perfecting' the system, a process which is captured in the strikingly characteristic Soviet expression *sovershenstvovanie*. Behind the façade there must obviously have been people who could see the writing on the wall, but one should not underestimate the impact of the massive distortions and falsifications that characterize Soviet statistics.[20] The *de facto* suppression of feed-back about actual economic performance that is represented by the practice of inflating production statistics, known in Russian as *pripiska*, together with the ostrich-like attitude of the regime, served in combination to produce a serious information black-out. In effect, the alarm bells had been disconnected. Happily babbling to itself, the Soviet colossus was slowly sinking into a morass of waste, inefficiency and indifference that almost defeats credulity. The grim details of that process are today being told with a vengeance by Gorbachev and his associates. If anything, this picture is even gloomier than that previously presented by Western observers.

From our perspective, however, the main cause for alarm in this process was not so much the economic decline *per se*, as its impact on the people that were living and working inside the system. The 'builders of socialism' resorted increasingly to various soft options of the unproductive kind. Drinking, slacking, and indifference were becoming endemic and the regime could only respond by further enhancing the mechanism of faking. As the production of ideology became increasingly ritualized and liturgical, the demands on its practitioners were gradually eroded. For increasing numbers of even senior Party cadres, simple regurgitation would often suffice.

One reflection of this erosion concerns the practice of issuing absentee ballots, known in Russian as *otkrepitelnye talony*, to citizens who for various reasons are unable to vote at their regular polling station on election day. In their study of the functions of Soviet elections, Zaslavsky and Brym have argued that, from the mid-1950s until the mid-1960s, it was necessary to show some proof from one's employer, certifying authorized absence, in order to receive such ballots. Since then, however, they have been issued fairly freely. Based on the assumption that virtually all of those who receive absentee ballots end up not using them, the authors conclude that maybe only three-quarters of the Soviet electorate actually participate in the 'fiction of democracy' that is represented by Soviet political elections.[21] This not only presents a dramatically different picture from the routinely reported electoral turnout of over 99 per cent. It also illustrates how the 'defences' of the official sphere of Soviet society were *de facto* pulled back rather significantly during the Brezhnev period, whilst maintaining an untroubled façade.

Another reflection of this process is the withdrawal of control by the KGB from the homes of the citizens. As Motyl has argued, an important characteristic of the Brezhnev era was that the authorities deemed it sufficient to control and monitor the public behaviour of the citizens, either by incorporating them into Party-controlled group activities or by deploying some more traditional means of surveillance over individual activities at work and in public places. An important consequence of this further pull-back has been that a distinct spatial dimension has been added to the previous psychological bifurcation of reality. The two sides of *dvoeverie* have thus acquired their own separate abodes, implying that *dvoeverie* has become institutionalized.

However, these various processes of pulling back must not be interpreted as a sign of relaxing political and ideolological control, as such, over the citizenry. On the contrary, it is another important hallmark of the Brezhnev era that the activities of the KGB met with remarkable success, from the leadership's point of view. Under the leadership of Andropov, the methods of the security police grew increasingly subtle and in the process also more efficient. At the horizontal level, Soviet citizens were subjected to a process of atomization and compartmentalization which rested on a characteristic 'satisficing' strategy. By allowing a wide latitude for various soft options for Exit and Voice, such as drinking, slacking, and grumbling, and by striking ruthlessly at any attempt at 'hardening' these options, such as the formation of alternative organizational structures or the organization of aggregated Voice, the regime succeeded effectively in curbing any potentially serious threats against its power and security, without wasting its energies on more insignificant phenomena, such as grumblings at the dinner table. What we have referred to above as pulling back the 'defences' should be seen in the light of this approach. It is also in this sense that we consider Soviet repression to have been more successful under Brezhnev than under Stalin.

If, however, we leave the horizontal dimension and proceed to look at the Brezhnev period from a vertical perspective, a considerably different impression will emerge. On the one hand, it was certainly true that the controls over individual behaviour, and the demands on their 'enthusiasm' in keeping up the façade, were eroded somewhat. At the same time, however, the deteriorating food standards, the persistent shoddiness of consumer goods production, and a growing ritualization of public life must have brought increasing numbers to a realization that something was seriously amiss. Assuming that the psychological imprint of the Stalinist *skaz* was deepened by ritualization, it follows that the gap between the separate realities actually widened. To those who were experiencing these developments, the psychological pressure of coping with *dvoeverie*, and with the inability of resorting to any form of remedial collective action, can be assumed to have grown intense.

At the lower levels of society, heavy drinking and a lapse into sullen apathy offered a way out, but higher up on the ladder such options would be less readily available. In order to deal with those who openly refused to play along with the rules of *dvoeverie*, and the implied demand for faking, the regime made increasing resort to the mechanism of ostracism. One way of doing so was quite simply to expel the undesirables from the country, treating them henceforth as 'non-persons'. Another way was the use of 'political psychiatry'. At the heart of these processes lay the introduction of a very explicit filter which served to separate the Soviet population into the categories of 'us' and 'them'. The test was the very simple question 'Are you a Soviet Man?'. If answered in the affirmative, the individual implied his acceptance of the rules of faking, if not he would be subjected to ostracism.

One consequence of this process was that the Soviet Union was purged, almost entirely, of the cream of its cultural intelligentsia. As Disa Håstad has shown, during the 1970s virtually all prominent writers, poets, painters, directors, and musicians emigrated – willingly or unwillingly – to the West.[22] Another consequence was the institution of a process of negative selection, whereby only those who were sufficiently cynical or incompetent would advance to the top, while the others would have to look for ways out.[23] The characteristically Soviet concept of 'dissident' symbolizes the very real existence of a filter, to separate out the heretics, while the spread of *samizdat*, the equally characteristic Soviet underground literature, forms a manifestation of the 'dissidents' ' search for alternative channels by means of which they could spread their ideas.

It is very difficult to tell what the actual costs of negative selection have been, but Gorbachev's repeated attacks on the bureaucracy gives some indication in this respect. We may also look to the Polish case, where the leaking of the Grabski report on how the events of 1980–1 could come about presents a rather shocking account of nepotism and incompetence. A considerably easier matter to assess, however, is the loss of the cultural intelligentsia. Although it is possible to rehabilitate and recall some of the previously expelled individuals, they will not be the same as when they left. The destruction of social tissue that was accomplished by the successes of political stabilization under Brezhnev is, in the near future at least, an irreversible process. Gorbachev's current attempt to undo that process will be the main topic of our concluding chapter.

Conclusion

Given our previous practice of building up stage-by-stage summaries in a telescopic fashion, to include all of what has been previously said, the conclusion to be drawn from this final summary will comprise a synthesis of the cumulative experiences of Soviet development from the fateful October 1917 *coup d'état* up until the beginning of the 1980s. As Gorbachev himself likes to point out, the legacy left by his predecessors consists of economic stagnation and of an overgrown bureaucracy which is solidly against *perestroika*.

If this was all, there would be little call for the outright apocalyptic perspective which is currently taken by people like Shmelev, Zalygin, and a host of other prominent intellectuals. To our minds, the core of the matter concerns not so much economic stagnation, political fossilization, and cultural sterility *per se*, as the impact on Soviet Man of the past decades of living and trying to cope with *dvoeverie*. Paradoxically, we shall argue, the main impression of seven decades of Soviet development is that of a remarkable success in creating a Soviet Man, a *Homo Sovieticus* who unfortunately bears very little resemblance to the New Man once promised and envisioned by Soviet ideologues.

The dynamics of this process have been described above and we shall only summarize very briefly here the main steps involved. The starting point is the suppression of economic and political pluralism, which we have previously referred to as curbing Exit and Voice. The economic manifestation of this suppression will be situations of the

Prisoner's Dilemma type, and an associated collective irrationality. In the political sphere, collective action is blocked by the absence of autonomous political processes. The regime attempts to compensate for these problems by making resort to psychological solutions, i.e. *agitprop*, but such measures will be superimposed on a reality that is marked by *dvoeverie*. Consequently, individuals will experience cognitive dissonance, which they will attempt to deal with by various processes of realignment, which we have referred to before as dissonance reduction. As these games are repeated, and people are forced into a prolonged process of faking, justification, and self-deception, a psychological deformation will occur, where parts of both realities are assimilated into a peculiar hybrid third reality.

The defensive mechanisms that people use in order to reduce dissonance can, in essence, be seen to produce a false consciousness of sorts. The processes of justification and self-deception go hand in hand with a preference for description over analysis, and the logical outcome is a poor perception of the true nature of accumulating problems. The status of the social sciences in Soviet society is an important manifestation of the costs that are associated with this type of reality. The well known sociologist Tatyana Zaslavskaya has delivered, in the Soviet sociological journal *Sotsiologicheskie Issledovaniya*, a scathing critique of the near-total absence in the Soviet Union of a separate discipline of Sociology, as it is understood in the West,[24] and the following is Zinoviev's satirical portrayal of the general role of the social sciences, which he refers to as the 'artificial sciences', in Soviet society, which he refers to as Ibansk:

> The artificial sciences occupy a special position in Ibansk. The ordinary Ibanskians neither know them nor understand them despite the fact that they study them throughout their lives and so call them, jokingly, social sciences. Nor do the specialists understand them, although they do recognize them. And since they have chosen to pursue them right to the tomb they seriously call them the social sciences.[25]

The seriousness of the situation that faces the reform proponents is thus not only a matter of the actual state of the economy, or of vested interests in the bureaucracy. More serious is the fact that people have learned over decades to block out unpleasant facts of life, and this will certainly take more than a couple of years to undo. The following is Shmelev's understanding:

> One is led to ask: what did we expect? Did we really expect some quick results? The population has been knit together over a period of sixty years. Is it really realistic to expect that a psychology

and a way of life that has been formed over that period can be changed in a mere two-three years?[26]

If Zalygin and the others are right, the situation looks bleak indeed. Against this background, let us proceed now to examine what Gorbachev is trying to do, and what the prospects may be for the future of the Soviet Union.

Part five

A legacy for Gorbachev

Chapter fourteen

Opening Pandora's box

In March 1985, Mikhail Sergeevich Gorbachev was elevated to the post of General Secretary of the Communist Party of the Soviet Union, and thus also to the leadership of one of the world's two superpowers. At the age of 54, he was then not only the youngest voting member of the Politburo, he was also the youngest to lead the Party since Stalin's take-over in the late 1920s. The impression of change and vitality that Gorbachev carried with him into the Kremlin stood in stark contrast to the combined images of his immediate predecessors and he certainly wasted no time impressing upon his audience that a new era had begun. In several major speeches during the following couple of months, he committed himself firmly to a programme of revitalization and reform.

At the April 1985 plenum of the Central Committee, for example, he struck a rather alarming note by declaring that 'the historical fate of the country and the position of socialism in the contemporary world' depended on whether the Soviet Union was capable of 'accelerating' its economic growth (*uskorenie tempov rosta*). He also underlined the need to 'reconstruct' (*perestroit*) management and planning, and stressed that it was essential to accelerate technological and scientific development (*kardinalnoe uskorenie nauchno-tekhnicheskogo progressa*). Most importantly, perhaps, he called on the mass media to create the necessary conditions for *perestroika* by 'organizing and educating the masses and by moulding public opinion'.[1]

Given this dramatic change in climate, it is hardly surprising that many people – both inside and outside the Soviet Union – were taken in by the new image. Hopes for the future, i.e. that the Soviet Union should finally manage to catch up with the West, were on the rise. Paradoxically, however, such expectations seem to have gained a much wider spread and credibility in the West than in the Soviet Union, or – significantly – in the neighbouring East European countries. After a meeting in London in 1984, for example, Margaret Thatcher went on record with the statement that Gorbachev was 'a man you can deal with',[2] and at the June 1988 summit in Moscow, President Reagan retracted his earlier statements about the Soviet Union as an 'evil empire', claiming these to have applied only to the time before Gorbachev. The new picture of Soviet openness and 'liberalism' that has come to dominate Western media in general awards high marks to the promotional skills of Politburo member and former Soviet Ambassador to Canada, Aleksandr Yakovlev, who is commonly believed to be the main architect behind the new charm offensive.

Although the game of *perestroika* is clearly not yet over, it is our aim in this final chapter to challenge any hopes that might exist for a quick and easy solution to be found, for some sort of short-cut out of the economic and social morass that Gorbachev has inherited from his predecessors. This argument will rest heavily on those conclusions regarding the nature of Soviet Man that have been reached in our previous summary sections. We shall argue that the problem of reforming the Soviet economy, and thus also Soviet society at large, is considerably more complicated than simply removing restrictions and 'unleashing' some unspecified market forces. Even if some people in the West might perhaps regard the latter as a 'return to normalcy', it is our firm conviction that this is not the case for the bulk of the Soviet population, or at least not for the bulk of the Russian population.

The systematic indoctrination of anti-capitalist values and sentiments, and the associated failure to introduce instead an operational collectivist and socialist ideology, forms an important background to this claim. Decades of explicit manipulation of *dvoeverie*, and frustration derived from the resultant patterns of cognitive dissonance, has become deeply ingrained in the psychology of Soviet Man. This mental pattern, we shall argue, presents by far the most important obstacle in the way of a successful *perestroika*. We shall start our account by looking briefly at the period of interregnum, between Brezhnev and Gorbachev, and will then proceed in considerably greater detail to examine the contents of Gorbachev's programme.

The Interregnum

Leonid Ilich Brezhnev, the foremost representative of the Soviet gerontocracy, died in November 1982, shortly after the Revolution celebration in Red Square and shortly before his 76th birthday. For years before his eventual death, however, Brezhnev's health had been deteriorating steadily, and it had consequently become increasingly obvious that a change in the top leadership of the Soviet Union was pending, the first since 1964. Yet, there was no heir apparent. The absence of formal rules and procedures for succession at the top created widespread confusion and speculation. The Kremlinologists were having a field day. In contrast to the respective successions after Stalin and Khrushchev, it was fairly widely held that there now existed some tacit rules saying that the successor must be firmly anchored in the Party hierarchy, that he must be both a (voting) member of the Politburo and a Central Committee Secretary. Against this background, it was an important occasion when Politburo member Andropov left his position as Chairman of the KGB, in May 1982, to assume instead the responsibilities of a Secretary at the Central Committee. The race for succession was on. The other main contender for power was Konstantin Chernenko, a close Brezhnev associate who had been a Central Committee Secretary since 1976 and a Politburo member since 1978.

As it turned out, both Andropov and Chernenko would make it to the top. Andropov prevailed in the first round, and when he in his turn passed away, in February 1984, Chernenko was next in line. Since both men belonged to the Brezhnev generation, Brezhnev being born in 1906, Andropov in 1914, and Chernenko in 1911, their short reigns may be seen in retrospect as a *de facto* twilight time of the Brezhnev era. Once Brezhnev was gone, however, a change of generations in the top leadership became an obvious prospect. New initiatives were more a question of *when* than *if*. In this sense, the Andropov-Chernenko period may also be seen as an immediate background, or perhaps a prelude, to the Gorbachev era.

In his first major speech as General Secretary, on 22 November 1982, Andropov spoke of the urgent need to make the economy more efficient and to raise the standards of living. Although such statements were certainly rather familiar from recent liturgical presentations by Brezhnev, one may note distinct nuances in the new General Secretary's speech. Among other things, he declared that Gosplan should be relieved of responsibilities for day-to-day decisions, which would be better handled by local organs. In stark contrast to Brezhnev, moreover, Andropov painted the state of the Soviet economy in fairly bleak colours. The latter might, of course, have been part of a typical Soviet 'post-election' campaign, i.e. a manifestation of the desires of a new leader to lodge the blame for the ills of society firmly with his predecessor in office. The substance of the complaints, however, was real.

According to Andropov, it was vital, for example, to economize on the use of energy resources. In order to achieve this goal, a *perestroika* of all branches of the economy was seen to be necessary. Another target of complaint was the poor performance of the respective Ministries of Transport, Construction, and the Iron and Steel Industries. As for the economy as a whole, new technology must be introduced and investment channelled to a few key projects, rather than being spread thin over the whole economy. Andropov declared that the major industries and trusts had to be allowed more autonomy, and that the experience of economic decentralization in other socialist countries (e.g. Hungary) should be emulated. He also underlined, however, that the Party would not tolerate any 'localism' (*mestni-chestvo*). All-Union interests must be placed above all others.[3]

Andropov's use of the term *perestroika* was neither emphasized by the Soviets nor recognized by Western media at the time, no doubt because this was a term which had been put to repeated previous use, from Lenin onwards.[4] Most symbolically perhaps, even Brezhnev himself, who is currently held up as the very anathema to *perestroika*, found it a useful expression in his time. Speaking to the twenty-sixth Party Congress, in 1981, about the need to utilize fully the 'enormous possibilities of our propaganda', the General Secretary had the following to say:

> Against this background, the Central Committee has formulated tasks for the improvement of ideological, political-educational work. They are spelled out in a decree from the Central Committee of 26 April 1979. That is a document of lasting importance. Essentially we are speaking here of a *perestroika* – yes precisely so, a *perestroika* – of many parts and areas of ideological work.[5]

The important point to note in this context is that the very slogan which would subsequently be used as perhaps the most important hallmark of the Gorbachev 'revolution',[6] actually has a long history of its own, a history which is distinctly lacking in bravado.

Turning to social science, which as we may recall had become increasingly circumscribed under Brezhnev,[7] Andropov further declared that there was a vital need for more and better research on the Soviet economy.[8] He also underlined that those who worked well should be paid well, and vice versa,[9] and that it was necessary to improve discipline in all walks of life. The latter implied, *inter alia*, measures aimed at an increased sobriety of the work force and a continued suppression of dissidents in combination with a heightened 'vigilance' against possible influences from the West.[10]

It is not our ambition here to show that a major economic reform was in the offing. We shall maintain, however, that Andropov apparently was serious, at least in his *intentions* of seeking to vitalize the Soviet economy. Compared to the Brezhnev period, the Soviet leadership had regained some initiative. There was a fairly large turnover of cadres within the Party apparatus, and in June 1983 a number of economic experiments were announced, to take effect in January 1984. In our previous discussion of economic developments under Brezhnev, we referred to these experiments as little more than a repetition of previous decrees. Nevertheless, the very swiftness of their introduction indicates a genuine desire to implement change. In terms of intentions, the Andropov period can be seen as a prelude to Gorbachev. This is perhaps most pronounced in the ideological sphere, where Andropov certainly appears to have been preparing a major new departure. According to rumours reported by Bialer, in the fall of 1983 he told his speech writers the following:

> You still do not understand the seriousness of the economic and social situations in which we find ourselves .... In the last decade, we adopted the formula that our country had entered the period of mature socialism, a stage next to full communism. But ... how can one reconcile this formulation ... with the relative backwardness of our economy, the lack of discipline and complacent dogmatism of our managers and our Party? ... We have to understand the needs for large-scale innovation and dramatic improvement of our social discipline. We have to forget the nonsense about mature socialism. Our Party has to be armed ideologically for this task.[11]

According to Bialer, all that Andropov said and did, including his reshuffling of the cadres, proved him to be 'a leader bent on preparing the ground for change'.[12] Be that as it may, before anything of lasting importance could be accomplished, in either the economic or the political sphere, on 9 February 1984, Andropov passed away, having been critically ill for at least half a year. He was succeeded by Chernenko, who was in critical health already at the time of his appointment. The interregnum was now obvious to all, and in practice very little – if at all anything – of consequence would happen during the coming 13 months.

Chernenko's brief time in office essentially amounted to a ghostlike rerun of the final years of the Brezhnev regime. A tragic farce of sorts was acted out in front of a bewildered world. The latter impression is perhaps best conveyed by a short glimpse of what occurred, not in the economy or in political life – where the lull was near-total – but in cultural life. Due to the ritualistic nature of Soviet cultural and ideological life, which revolved chiefly around various anniversaries, the simple passage of time would inevitably bring about further events in this sphere, even if pointless, emasculated, and perhaps even outright ridiculous.

For example, on 25 September 1984, the Union of Writers celebrated its fiftieth anniversary, an event of major cultural significance. To mark the occasion, the union was awarded the order 'Friendship of the Peoples'. The order was received directly from the hands of Chernenko, who himself, as a form of prelude, only 3 days previously had been awarded the Lenin Order and the 'Hammer and Sickle' in gold. These two ceremonies, and the extensive coverage awarded them in Soviet mass media, epitomized the rigid ritualization of Soviet life of the time. In his congratulatory speech to the Union of Writers, Chernenko revealed the official understanding of the word 'culture', by emphasizing militancy and incessant struggle against the imperialist West as a central task of Soviet writers.

The General Secretary also used the occasion to invoke the legacy of Stalin's time, by stressing the principles of *partiinost* and *narodnost* as the twin lode-stars for all artistic, creative activity in the country. It was the duty of Soviet artists to educate the Soviet people, and in particular the youth, in the spirit of class vigilance and a readiness to fight for the great Fatherland, Chernenko reminded his Soviet audience. Special attention should be paid to military-patriotic themes. Writers who slandered the Soviet order should not expect any favours of recognition, and those whose work sided with the ideological adversaries should never be forgiven.[13] Chernenko was promptly echoed by Georgii Markov, then First Secretary of the Union of Writers, who especially underlined the intimate relations between the writers and the military, and the militant spiritual unity of all true Soviet writers facing up to threats from the ideological adversaries.[14]

Chernenko's complacency was evident already in his first major speech as General Secretary, in March 1984. Here he painted a rather rosy picture of the economy, noting that order and discipline introduced in the preceding year had been fruitful. Now it was time to proceed with 'deep qualitative changes in the national economy', with a '*perestroika* of the economic mechanism', and with a 'serious *perestroika* of the system of management (*upravlenie*) of the economy'.[15] Although Chernenko repeatedly spoke of the need for *perestroika*, rather than implementing any radical new departures in the economy, he also continued to speak of a 'perfection of developed socialism and a gradual movement towards communism'.[16] In this sense, an important continuity with the Brezhnev period was evident.

In the midst of this self-glorification of the Soviet order, and of the associated fulminations against the decadent West, however, in his speech at the Union of Writers later in the year, Chernenko also made a curious reference to Andropov's previous dismissal of the view that the Soviet Union was approaching full communism:

Our experience has shown that before we can solve problems in direct connection with the building of communism, it is necessary to pass a historically long stage of developed socialism. Our country stands at the beginning of this stage.[17]

With the benefit of hindsight, we may conclude that there appears to have been during the late Brezhnev period, and during the brief Andropov and Chernenko tenures, a growing awareness that something was not quite in order with the Soviet economy. At the same time, key ideological pronouncements were marked by Russian chauvinism,[18] and constant appeals were made for cultural isolationism *vis-à-vis* the Western world, the latter, for example, in the above speeches by Chernenko and Markov. All of this resembled rather closely what happened during Stalin's last years. In this respect, a rather familar pattern of old was being repeated.

In our previous discussion of de-Stalinization, we argued that the ground for such a process had already been prepared during the last few years of the Great Dictator's life. Here we shall maintain that there were similar processes at work during the Andropov-Chernenko interregnum, processes which served to prepare the ground for Gorbachev's subsequent 'revolution from above'. More than 30 years had passed, however, between the ascendancy of Khrushchev and that of Gorbachev. From a reformist perspective, about 20 of these years had been 'lost' under Brezhnev, and this would, of course, mark Gorbachev's policies.

In his time, Khrushchev had been able to mobilize the population with promises of material welfare, allowing a relative cultural freedom to emerge almost as a by-product. Gorbachev faced a different reality. The economic situation was such that the option of promising material welfare had *de facto* been replaced by a need to call for sacrifices and hardship, and the inherent bureaucratic resistance to reform implied a need to whip up a fury amongst the Party rank-and-file against an obstructionist bureaucracy. Where Khrushchev's 'thaws' had followed in the steps of relaxed control, Gorbachev's *glasnost* would have to be instrumental, relying on clearly populist tactics. It is symptomatic that *glasnost* has produced very few new faces, and it is hardly a coincidence that literally the same intellectuals who had appeared out of the Stalinist night to act as supporters of Khrushchev's de-Stalinization, would re-emerge under Gorbachev to resume the previous process.

Perestroika and Uskorenie

Given what we know about the importance of campaigns in managing the Soviet system, it is rather logical that a new programme would have to be accompanied by an array of campaign slogans. In addition to *perestroika* (restructuring), we have become familiar with *uskorenie* (acceleration), *glasnost* (openness), and *novoe politicheskoe myshlenie* (new political thinking). Given, moreover, the highly-strung ambitions of that programme, it is perhaps equally logical that the new slogans would have to be introduced and propagated with considerable *gusto*. The cynic might certainly be tempted here to dismiss these concepts as no more than a peculiar Soviet form of Orwellian 'newspeak', but that would be misleading in two important respects.

First of all, we should recognize that in his classic novel *1984*, originally published in 1948, Orwell used 'newspeak' to describe the practice of introducing newly invented concepts in order to cover up the true nature of regime policies. An excellent example is the Ministry of Truth, which was charged with falsifying history. The parallel with the Soviet Commissariat of Enlightenment, which was charged with questions of education, culture and propaganda, is obviously not coincidental. Another illustrative example is Stalin's brutal terror against the peasants, a policy which was dressed in the guise of 'class struggle in the villages' and was accompanied by slogans claiming that life was 'becoming happier'. Gorbachev's programme, however, differs from both Stalin and Orwell in the dual sense that neither slogans nor policies represent anything essentially new.

The systematic use by previous regimes of the concept of *perestroika* has been documented above, and a similar case applies to the concept of *glasnost*. As we may recall from the previous chapter, *glasnost* has long been a demand of the dissident movement. Here we may add that is has an official history as well. In 1982, for example, it was used by A. Lyashko, the Premier of the Ukrainian SSR, to describe political life in his republic.[19] As in the case of *perestroika*, this also passed unnoticed, again undoubtedly because it represented nothing new at the time. A more serious task, however, than simply noting that the slogans are old, is to show that this lack of innovation in the sphere of propaganda corresponds closely to a lack of real content in the underlying policies. One way of doing this is to point to the simple fact that very little material improvement has actually been recorded since Gorbachev took over. In fact, some even hold that the contrary is true, that things are still getting worse rather than better. We shall listen in a moment to some Soviet voices on this count. Before doing so, however, let us review what has happened during Gorbachev's first years in office.

In its current official presentation, *perestroika* is said to consist of three separate stages. The first was devoted chiefly to preparatory ground work, stretching from March 1985 until the end of 1987. The second, which is currently under way, represents the actual introduction of a package of radical reform measures and an associated transformation of the economy to operate according to a completely new set of rules. This phase began in January 1988, when a new law on state enterprise went into effect, and is to be concluded by the end of 1990. The third phase, finally, will begin in 1991, with the introduction of the thirteenth five-year plan. It will represent a transformation of the Soviet Union into a modern industrial economy.

Our presentation, however, will not follow this agenda. We argue that the division into stages is merely a way of covering up the simple fact that it took 2 years before the Gorbachev regime managed to present a package of measures that even remotely resembles a coherent reform programme. Our periodization focuses instead on the political sphere. From this perspective, the period at hand is marked by three major occasions: the twenty-sixth Party Congress, in February/March 1986, the seventieth anniversary of the Revolution, in November 1987, and the nineteenth Party Conference, in June 1988. In addition, three Central Committee plena stand out as being of particular importance, namely those of April 1985, January 1987, and June 1987. We shall start by looking at the period from March 1985 until the end of 1986, a first stage which essentially represents time lost.

Time Lost

Given the structural importance of Soviet five-year plans, in determining both economic and political activities, it is perhaps fairly plausible to argue that the twenty-sixth Party Congress must have represented the first real hurdle on Gorbachev's marathon obstacle course. Since that congress would approve the twelfth five-year plan, covering the period 1986–90, the implications were that whatever reform measures could not be introduced in 1985 would have to wait until 1990. Once the new plan was approved, it would quite simply be too difficult to introduce any structurally important changes. Against this background, one might plausibly put faith in sources saying that Gorbachev swiftly dismissed the draft plan that had been worked out under Chernenko, demanding that its ambitions should be raised considerably. Against the same background, however, it was also rather worrying for the future cause of reform that very little actually seemed to be happening in the economy during 1985.

In the *political sphere*, it is certainly true that a considerable momentum was kept up. Under the impact of *glasnost*, Soviet newspapers, journals, and even official speeches suddenly started attracting considerable attention, if not overall then at least in some highly notable individual cases. A few previously 'impossible' movies were shown, and books published. Some of the more well-known political prisoners were released. The process of liberalization and of settling with the past may, in practice, have been considerably less important than is commonly imagined, but it is an undisputable fact that it did attract considerable attention, and – perhaps most importantly – that it provided the Gorbachev regime with a highly favourable Press in the West.[20]

If, moreover, we focus on the internal power game, a similar impression of vigorous change transpires. During the period from Gorbachev's take-over until the twenty-sixth Party Congress, no less than 38 per cent of the living, voting members of the Central Committe were either retired or seriously demoted, and a similar process marked the level of *oblast* First Secretaries. When the congress opened, 32 per cent of these important cadres were appointees of the Gorbachev regime, while a further 26 per cent had been appointed under Andropov-Chernenko.[21] The influence of the old Brezhnev guard was being rapidly reduced. Most importantly, perhaps, three out of ten voting members of the Politburo were removed in 1985.

At first glance, this rapid turnover would certainly seem to indicate that Gorbachev was in a position to wield considerable personal power, and it is hardly surprising that some Western observers have arrived at precisely this conclusion. Hough, for example, puts up the following argument:

> When Gorbachev added new members to the the Politburo, he was able to select men who had been much inferior to himself in status in November 1982 when Brezhnev died. ... And the fact that he did not promote a single member of the old Politburo strongly suggests that he did not have to cut any deals within the Politburo to get himself elected, that real power resided in the Central Committee, and that there he already had an extremely strong position.[22]

We shall not subscribe to this view. It is, of course, in no way possible to prove that Hough is wrong, but then again that holds equally well for his chances of proving that he is right. Our understanding shall be to look at the post-Chernenko Politburo as a constellation of oligarchs, men with different views and ambitions, who for simple

354

reasons of power struggle and due to the 1921 prohibition against factions within the Party, are forced into maintaining an outward appearance of consensus. We can obviously not prove that this is the case, but we shall maintain rather strongly that the latter interpretation of the political situation is the only one that squares reasonably well with the conspicuous absence of progress in the economic sphere.

Since well before Gorbachev's take-over, there appears to have been an established consensus among the bulk of Soviet experts that, given the sad state of Soviet agriculture, any seriously intended programme for social and economic reform would have to start there.[23] Given Gorbachev's personal experience, moreover, it would also appear that he should have been the right man for the job. He is said to have a double academic degree, in law and in agricultural economics, and his Party career has been intimately linked with agricultural affairs. In 1970–8, he served as First Secretary of the Stavropol *kraikom*, an important appointment in an important grain-growing area. In November 1978, he was promoted to the post of Central Committee Secretary, with responsibility for agriculture, and in October 1980 he was elevated to the Politburo. He is also believed to have been one of the main architects behind the 1982 Food Programme.

One might certainly argue that it would have been a wise policy for him to keep a low profile during the Andropov-Chernenko interregnum, but once he had become General Secretary that would no longer be tenable. *If* Gorbachev actually knew what needed to be done, and *if* he was as powerful as Hough and others seem to think, one would have expected to see the unfolding during 1985 of a vigorous programme of agricultural reform. Quick results in agriculture would not only have freed scarce resources for alternative use. Placing more and better food on the shelves of state food-stores would also have created a strong groundswell of popular support for the reform programme.

In spite of such potential gains, however, there was a conspicuous absence of any serious reform measures in agriculture during both 1985 and 1986. An apparent exception occurred in November 1985, when a reshuffling of the agricultural bureaucracy was announced, merging five ministries and one state committee into a new super-ministry, the Gosagroprom.[24] At first glance, this organizational reshuffle certainly presents more of a reminder of Khrushchev's 'organizational itch' than it does of economic reform. If, however, we consider that the merger is said to have been associated with a 47 per cent cut in central staff,[25] we may discern here a first sign of Gorbachev's subsequently very outspoken view of the bureaucracy as the main enemy of *perestroika*. Still, the actual outcome appears, at best, to have been a disappointment. In May 1986, Central Committee Secretary Viktor Nikonov, who was charged with supervision of agriculture, delivered sharp criticism of unclear boundaries and spheres of responsibility within the new hierarchy.[26]

Except for the draconian crack-down on alcohol, little else of consequence happened in 1985. From the summer onwards even Gorbachev's own speeches had a rather subdued character. Consequently, he went to the 1986 Party Congress with very little to show. Hough argues that this low profile represented a wise policy, designed not to upset the Central Committee constituency before the congress.[27] This interpretation can certainly be made to agree with the fact that in his speech to the congress, Gorbachev suddenly and vigorously spoke about the needs not only for reform, but even for a radical reform, a *radikalnaya reforma*.[28] It agrees rather poorly, however, with the fact that no measures were introduced – or even announced – at that congress which remotely corresponded to the proud pronouncements of 'radical reform'.

After the congress, moreover, there occurred a rather peculiar change of stage. Instead of economic reform, it was now democratization that was the order of the day. Suddenly, there was much talk about having more than one candidate at elections to the local Soviets, and of rights for the workers to elect factory managers, rather than having them appointed from above. Gorbachev had used his executive powers to change the agenda, a move which no doubt served to upset and realign the opposition. If we maintain our previous assumption on oligarchic rule, it is rather logical that a coalition of opposition formed on the issue of economic reform will not necessarily be viable on the issue of democratization. This change of stage provides an illustration of Gorbachev's tactical prowess, a skill which may well turn out to be his greatest single asset. It also illustrates, however, an explicit attempt to rely on the rank-and-file of the Party, rather than on the higher echelons. In this sense, a rather familiar pattern from Stalin's and Khrushchev's days is being repeated, where the policy of *glasnost* can be seen as a populistic campaign, designed to raise the fury of the grass-roots against obstructing bureaucrats.

Power politics aside, however, one economic area where some potentially important activity could be recorded during 1986 was, again, agriculture. In March 1986, i.e. only shortly after the Party Congress, a major decree was issued, the main thrust of which was to improve marketing and management functions.[29] The central part of this decree was a provision for farms to sell directly in the market up to 30 per cent of their planned deliveries of fruit and vegetables. Such sales, moreover, would count against their state delivery quotas. It caused quite a stir in the West when Gorbachev spoke of this change with reference to Lenin's *prodnalog*, the tax-in-kind which once brought an end to War Communism, triggering instead the New Economic Policy.[30] With respect to the actual outcome of the decree, however, Shmelev wrote the following, in April 1988:

> The rights that were granted, almost two years ago, for *kolkhozy* and *sovkhozy* to sell directly in the market not only above-plan production but also up to 30 per cent of their planned state deliveries, has in practice had no results whatsoever. Republican and *oblast* branches of the Gosagroprom have continued to plan in detail all agricultural production, down to the last cucumber, so that in practice nothing remains to be sold in the market.[31]

A similar absence of real change marks developments in the non-agricultural sector of the economy, where only three events deserve mention. The first was a May 1986 decree, calling for a struggle against 'unearned incomes' (*netrudovye dokhody*),[32] and the second a November 1986 law on 'individual labour activity' (*zakon ob individualnoi trudovoi deyatelnosti*),[33] permitting individual activities *in addition* to work in the socialized sector. Both of these were concerned with the fringe of the socialized sector of the economy, and can in this sense be seen to reflect a desire to legalize some part of the 'second economy'. In retrospect, one may also discern a certain logic here – first a harsh decree which satisfies the hard-liners that no NEP-type liberalization is pending, and then a cautious step forward. On paper, there was considerable progress, but it is obviously still too early to say whether this represents a true expansion of legitimate private enterprise, or if we are dealing simply with a formal façade for continued illegal activity. In comparison with similar arrangements in Hungary, moreover, one is struck by the narrow rights and considerable limitations that mark the Soviet case.[34]

The *third* event was a new system of independent state quality control – the Gospriem – which was introduced in the summer of 1985, and which was expanded during 1986 to cover a majority of Soviet manufacturing enterprises. Compared to the above two cases, this was of a principally different nature. It addressed a basic problem in the operation of the Soviet economy, and thus challenged important vested interests. During the first couple of months in 1987, it was vigorously enforced and drastic consequences resulted. Many enterprises failed to meet their targets and many workers experienced considerable reductions in pay. Wildcat strikes were reported,[35] and soon 'order' was restored. Publicity subsided and enterprises were again able to meet their targets. It is hard to understand this in any other way than as a retreat from the original ambitions of quality control. Gospriem represented the first real test of *perestroika* and it failed to achieve any lasting results.

With this we shall leave the preparatory stage, and turn to the phase of implementation. Although the economic aspects are certainly spectacular here, we shall maintain that the political sphere remains the more important one.

Full Speed Ahead

Already from the start of Gorbachev's 'revolution', Western observers pointed at the inherent contradiction in simultaneously wanting to have both *perestroika* and *uskorenie*. Any serious desire to 'reconstruct' the economy would inevitably result in a number of short-run disruptions that might actually reduce growth, whereas a desire to accelerate would in its turn imply a need to rely on the old methods. Interestingly, the very same observation was made by Shmelev in April 1988 that:

> The current situation in our economy illustrates that one cannot at the same time accelerate and reconstruct, that an increased rate of growth in all sectors, and a reconstruction of the economic mechanism in all its aspects, stand in contradiction to each other.[36]

Beginning in early 1987, however, one could find in every issue of *Kommunist* a separate section entitled precisely *Uskorenie i perestroika*. This would hardly seem to indicate any wider spread of the realization of a contradiction between the two.

One conclusion that may be reached from this latter observation is that Shmelev is intellectually above the run-of-the-mill *apparatchiki*, and, as far as the demands and prospects of *perestroika* are concerned, that is most probably the case. Another, more subtle, conclusion might be that the bureaucrats have quite simply become so used to the fact that slogans of various kinds live their own life, that they never really reflected on whether the new set was actually consistent or not. Finally, we might argue that during the initial phase there was in actual practice no signs of either *perestroika* or *uskorenie*. Accordingly, none of the inherent contradictions between the two could materialize. There is most likely an element of truth in all three of these explanations.

If we focus on the behaviour of the Soviet bureaucracy during what is now known as the preparatory stage of *perestroika*, one is struck by the rather obvious dominance of ritualistic passivity over active resistance. To the typical Soviet *apparatchik*, Gorbachev's calls for reforms must have sounded rather familiar, and experience certainly indicates that the best strategy in a situation like this is to drift along without making any commitments to either side. Such is the nature of demands on Soviet Man as we have outlined them above. The increasing frustration that marked Gorbachev's speeches and public appearances during this period reinforces the image of a man who is demanding rather unsuccessfully to be taken seriously.

With mass terror and old-style purges still apparently being considered unfeasible, the only way in which Gorbachev could drive home his message concerning the needs for reform was by increasing the power of his rhetoric, and by sanctioning the publication of facts concerning the state of the Soviet economy which would put the fear of God into any thinking official. This is most certainly an interpretation made with the benefit of hindsight, but even if it should be incorrect as far as Gorbachev's personal perceptions and intentions are concerned, it nevertheless fits the observable facts rather nicely. As we shall see in a moment, during 1987 and 1988 a number of articles were published in the Soviet media which actually surpass in gloom most of what previous Western prophets of doom had been suspecting.

It also fits the sudden change in the pace of Gorbachev's rhetoric, noticeable at the January 1987 Central Committee plenum, where he came across quite forcefully against surviving dogmas from the 1930s. This qualitative change in Gorbachev's appearances prompted Hough, for example, to take the new image as proof of the General Secretary's personal power: 'In my opinion, by the spring of 1987 Gorbachev was in as strong a political position as Stalin had been in 1927 or 1928.'[37] We do not agree with this interpretation of the political situation, but it is certainly a fact that in the run-up to the June 1987 plenum of the Central Committee, Gorbachev kept up a considerable momentum, which was crowned in his speech to that plenum, where he stated quite plainly that the Soviet economy had been placed in a 'pre-crisis' situation, a *predkrizisnoe sostoyanie*.[38]

This hard drive appears rather successfully to have prepared the ground for introducing in June 1987 a package of economic reform measures that most likely had been originally intended for introduction at the 1986 Party Congress. At first glance, it is certainly spectacular. The law on state enterprises, which had been subject to wide discussion during all of spring, was adopted, and in addition a veritable swarm of a near dozen major decrees was issued, calling for *perestroika* of virtually all aspects of Soviet economic life. Gosplan's direct control over the economy was to be considerably reduced, by means of a sharp trimming of the number of material balances under its jurisdiction. A shift to wholesale trade was to reduce the role of

Gossnab, and a decentralization of price fixing that of Goskomtsen, etc., etc.[39] One may certainly argue here that in comparison, for example, with the Hungarian reform process, the proposed Soviet measures are not very impressive. In particular, this holds for the total absence of a price reform. The main problem, however, is not so much the limited nature of the reform, as the fact that it is to be implemented at breakneck speed. The full package is to be completed by 1991, when the next five-year plan is introduced. This, moreover, is to be accomplished parallel with a slashing of the central bureaucracy in half. By thus implicitly *forcing* the bureaucracy into faking progress, *perestroika* is actually tearing itself apart from within.

The dubious economic rationality of Gorbachev's reform strategy may find its explanation in the political sphere, where sheer momentum appears to be 'do or die'. At the June 1987 plenum, three new voting members were appointed to the Politburo, while none of the previous candidate members was promoted. With Gromyko being moved to a purely ceremonial post in 1985, with Kunaev having been removed in 1986 and Aliev in 1987, six out of ten Politburo members had been neutralized since Chernenko's death. In addition to Gorbachev, only three survivors remained. By October 1987, eight new voting members had been appointed, and only two of the six candidate members were survivors. As Hough puts it, this 'was an unprecedented performance'.[40]

One should be wary, however, of taking this rejuvenation as a sign of Gorbachev's personal power. We have argued above that the Gorbachev Politburo is best seen as a set of oligarchs, and that impression was certainly reinforced during the 12 months leading from the June 1987 plenum to the June 1988 Party Conference. In his book on *perestroika*, which apparently was written during the summer of 1987, Gorbachev spoke of a 'brake mechanism in socio-economic development', as an explanation of economic stagnation,[41] and in his speech at Murmansk in October, he identified this 'mechanism' as an army of no less than 18 million bureaucrats, annually costing the Soviet economy 40 billion rubles.[42] The crucial feature in this context is that the *nature* of resistance from this 'brake mechanism' appears to have been changing. For example, the reformist writer Ivan Vasilev said that 'the colossal bureaucratic pyramid, which is beginning to feel a growing pressure from the active work of the masses, is shifting from a predominantly passive resistance to an open counterattack.'[43]

If we take this change as a reflection of conflicts at the very top, Lenin's famous maxim *kto kogo*, 'who beats whom?', would seem to be applicable. At the important November celebration of the seventieth anniversary of the revolution, Gorbachev delivered a speech that was so full of ambivalent and even outright contradictory statements that it could only have been the work of many conflicting wills.[44] *Glasnost* was now clearly being used as a weapon in the power game at the top, and during the spring of 1988, the political sphere was marked by an atmosphere of sharp struggle. Rumours of a pending *coup* were circulating,[45] and some even hinted that an attempt on Gorbachev's life might be made. The simple existence of such rumours is, of course, much more important than the question of whether or not they actually contained some elements of truth.

The so called Andreeva affair in March, i.e. the publication in *Sovetskaya Rossiya* of a blatantly Stalinist critique of *perestroika*,[46] was taken by some as the peak of this struggle. Gorbachev was in Yugoslavia at the time, Yakovlev was in Mongolia, and Yegor Ligachev, who was commonly held to be number two in the Politburo, is strongly suspected of having orchestrated the attack. After the return to Moscow of the former two, however, a long rebuttal was published in *Pravda*.[47] If indeed it was an attempted *coup*, it was certainly not a successful one. At the same time, however, nothing seems to have happened to the alleged conspirators. In stark contrast to Khrushchev's swift way of dealing with the 'anti-Party' group, in 1957, there has been a marked absence of visible change at the top. It is also interesting to note Gorbachev's very conciliatory tone at the June Party Conference, where he dismissed firmly and explicitly all demands for a purge, a *chistka*, to be carried out amongst the Party's 'ballast'.[48]

Given this interpretation of events in the political sphere, it is perhaps not surprising that very little happened in the economic sphere. In April, an All-Union *Kolkhoz* Congress was convened to ratify a new *kolkhoz* charter, the first since 1969.[49] At first glance, this should have been an important event, but as Karl-Eugen Wädekin has pointed out, a more lasting impression is that of an extension of the broader principles of *perestroika* to agriculture rather than an agricultural reform in its own right.[50] Another event was the adoption of a new law on co-operatives. Although one may say that this touches only on the fringe of the economy, it is still too early to judge its potential impact.[51] It is also striking that the June Party Conference announced no further novelties in the economic sphere. Apparently, the measures introduced in June 1987 will be the real core of *perestroika* in the economy.

It is undoubtedly the case that, seen in the simple terms of power struggle, Gorbachev has been quite successful. Yet, we must recognize also that a high price may have to be paid for these successes, in terms of potential backlash effects. First of all, there is a distinct risk that an overly apocalyptic perspective may actually serve to frighten and disillusion the population, rather than spur it on toward sacrifices that may bring about real improvements. One is certainly tempted here to take at face value Gorbachev's many recent claims that the actual state of the economy had turned out to be much worse than expected. A Pandora's Box of sorts has been opened, and the lid may well prove exceedingly difficult to replace. The second problem concerns the nationalities issue, where the policy of *glasnost* and the low profile of the repressive organs may produce an explosive situation. Let us start by looking at the former.

Apocalypse Now

Even a very cursory reading of the current Soviet debate on the need for *perestroika*, gives a quite firm impression that those who worry about the future tend to focus their worries along two distinct lines. One of these concerns a destruction of the natural environment of the Soviet system, while the other focuses on a degeneration of the human tissue inside that system. If we recall from our previous account that the two main sources of Soviet growth – indeed the only ones that were initially available – have been abundant natural and human resources, we may gain a first impression of the gravity of the present situation. It quite simply means the end of the road for the 'extensive growth' strategy.

It is of course nothing new that the Soviet Union faces serious problems in relation to pollution of the environment and a depletion of non-renewable natural resources. Pieces in that puzzle appeared regularly throughout the Brezhnev period, and the same holds for demographic problems, regarding inter-ethnic relations as well as fertility and mortality aspects.[52] The novelty that has been brought about by Gorbachev's *glasnost* lies in the fact that some Soviet intellectuals have now started linking these problems to the inner workings of the Soviet system as such, and the picture that emerges is not a pretty one. Evidence that has begun to appear in the Soviet media during 1987 and 1988 gives a distinct impression of pending apocalypse. We have argued above that there is an inherent conflict between economic and political rationality in the Soviet system. It would be hard to find a better illustration of that conflict than the one provided by the problems at hand here. Like a yeast bacterium that is hard at work producing alcohol which will eventually kill it, so the priorities of political and bureaucratic vested interests have been allowed over the years to erect a structure which *de facto* works toward a gradual destruction of those very resources – natural and human – that are supposed to feed it. Let us start by looking at the natural environment.

The Natural Environment

Environmental concerns have long been an object of vigorous debate in Soviet society. From time to time, that debate has even been marked by a surprising degree of openness, or *glasnost*. Many Soviet writers and intellectuals have developed a strong personal involvement in these issues, most importantly perhaps in the protracted struggle to save Lake Baikal. A prominent figure among these has long been the writer Sergei Zalygin, who prior to Gorbachev was perhaps best known for his 1964 novel *Na Irtyshe* (On the Irtysh), the theme of which is Stalin's mass collectivization. With his appointment to editor-in-chief of *Novyi Mir*, in the fall of 1986, Zalygin acquired a prestigious platform for his cause. He has used this platform quite deliberately to present himself as the main champion of the conservationists.

In the January 1987 issue of 'his' journal, Zalygin published an article of his own, with the ominous title *Povorot* (Turning point).[53] The article was important in two respects. On the one hand, it was a first major attempt to take *glasnost* seriously, by delivering scathing criticism of important malfunctions in Soviet society. It served as a path-breaker for Gorbachev's reform drive. On the other hand, since its main theme was the Siberian river diversion schemes, its very topic served in a natural way to merge the problems of demographic tensions and environmental protection. For both of these reasons, Zalygin's article merits closer scrutiny.

Having been subject to discussion and planning for decades,[54] the proposed river diversions have long been a major bone of contention between Russian and Central Asian intellectuals. The point of view of the latter has been that a diversion of fresh water from the north to the areas of the Caspian and the Aral Seas quite simply constitutes a precondition for economic development, and in some areas even survival, of the region. Here they have found vital support from the water lobby, the powerful group of technocrats and bureaucrats which has strong vested interests in the realization, or at least continued planning, of the diversion schemes. The Russian intellectuals, on their side, have pointed with equal fervour not only at the dubious economic rationality of the proposed schemes, but also at the wide ranging destruction of Russian cultural landmarks that would result from the creation of huge dams and reservoirs.

In August 1986, however, the issue was settled, at least temporarily so, with the issue of a Central Committee decree suspending implementation of the diversion schemes and calling for more research to be undertaken. It is hardly surprising that this decision was greeted with joy not only by Zalygin, but also by other prominent writers such as Valentin Rasputin and Vladimir Soloukhin. It was praised by Zalygin as a triumph of public opinion which, according to him, had now for the first time in Soviet history been enfranchized. He saw the river diversion schemes to be rooted in that 'autochtogenous bureaucratic conservatism' of Stalin's time which had caused the great ecological problems of the present day. In his article, Zalygin claimed that the projects, which had been under preparation for forty years, had in practice been 'owned' by the Ministry of Water Resources – the Minvodkhoz – and by the Institute for Water Management, at the Academy of Sciences. The sheer size of this empire is awe-inspiring. In 1987, 68,000 out of a total of two million employees in the Minvodkhoz worked on the projects, which up to date had cost between half a billion and one billion rubles.

Further details in this picture were provided by a certain geographer Khorev, who criticized plans presented in 1984 for the diversion of water from the Siberian rivers Ob and Irtysh. These projects, which were of the order of tens of billions of rubles, envisaged the irrigation and cultivation of several million hectares of land in Central Asia, without having anything to say about local infrastructure and labour supply, about possible effects on the environment, or about the costs of preventing such damage. Similar criticism was delivered against plans for diverting rivers to the west of the Ural mountains.[55]

In the July 1987 issue of *Novyi Mir*, a number of comments on Zalygin's article were published, critical as well as supportive, which all had in common the important feature of showing that the problems at hand are of such complexity that no simple solutions exist.[56] In a long keynote article, G.V. Voropaev, the Director of the Institute for Water Management, which is one of the main agencies involved in the diversion schemes, underlined the gravity of the water problem in the south and claimed that a solution would simply have to be found. In this he gained the support of an engineer of the Soyuzgiprovodkhoz, a certain O.A. Leontyev:

Everyone is aware of the importance ... of Western Siberia and of the industrial centre in the southern Urals, with cities like Tyumen, Sverdlovsk, Chelyabinsk, Magnitogorsk and Kurgan. A look at the water situation in this area shows that local water resources are on the verge of exhaustion.... The water situation in northern Kazakhstan is no less complicated. In order to appreciate the urgency of the problem there, one must consider that the population in the regional centre Turgai have fresh water only 2-3 hours per day, and the situation is similar in the province centre of Arkalyk ... A similar situation is at hand almost everywhere in the newly cultivated area. Water conservation is not an alternative, quite simply because there is no water left to conserve.[57]

Leontyev argued that the fate of Central Asia as a whole was at stake. With serious water shortage in the area already at the current level of population, an expected increase in population pressure by the year 2,000, from 35 to 50 million, would make the situation untenable. In addition, the people concerned were not prepared to leave the countryside, preferring instead to remain and to continue farming. From Leontyev's point of view, diverting water from the north was a precondition for Central Asia to be saved.

In a further contribution to the discussion in *Novy Mir* made by three colleagues of Leontyev's, V.S. Panfilov, A.A. Zhelobaev and V.V. Myasnikov, the Central Asian water shortage was presented as alarming. According to them, the surface level of the Aral Sea had already fallen by twelve metres and the lower reaches of the rivers Amur-Darya and Syr-Darya had been transformed into deserts. While more than 80 per cent of the country's population resided in the south, primarily in the basins of the Aral Sea, the Caspian Sea, and the Azov Sea, no more than 16 per cent of the country's total water resources could be found in these areas. Only two alternative courses of action were open. Either the population would have to be moved north and east, or water would have to be diverted to the south. Moving the population, however, would be far too costly and thus the only remaining alternative was river diversions.[58] Panfilov and his associates were joined by other scholars, who claimed that the people of Central Asia worry about the future of their children and their grandchildren. The water shortage was acute and the people were well aware that 'when the water runs out, the earth is finished'.[59]

The picture of doom that is presented by the protagonists of the river diversions is certainly to some extent purposely designed to inspire awe, but there would still appear to remain enough hard evidence to call for very serious measures to be undertaken. At the same time, however, we must recognize that the critics of the proposed schemes paint an equally gloomy picture. Minvodkhoz has been placed under particular attack here, its destructive potential being compared to that of the Mongol and the German invasions.[60] A Gosplan official argued that, on balance, this ministry had actually destroyed more land than it had improved. In parts of Southern Russia and the Ukraine, its activities had reduced rather than increased harvest yields. Senseless irrigation schemes had resulted in severe soil erosion.[61]

In 1988, further alarming information on the devastation of the natural environment was provided by Grigorii Baklanov, the editor-in-chief of *Znamya*, who claimed that, depending on which sources are cited, during the last decade between 25 and 40 per cent of the black earth had been lost. If we assume that the black earth accounts for about two-thirds of the cultivated area,[62] we are talking here of 35–60 million hectares of the very finest soils being lost. To Baklanov, this devastation was equal to 'tearing out a part of the motherland (*rodina*)'.[63] In addition, the economist G.K. Yuzufovich mentions that between 20 and 30 million hectares of agricultural land had been damaged by mining operations.[64] These are certainly stunning figures. Nevertheless, there are many others who convey similar impressions. In the July 1988 issue of *Novyi Mir*, Academician Andrei Monin claims that already in 1983 about 40 per cent of the irrigated land in the Turkmen republic was salinated. Today, the figure is greater. He also speaks of salinated ground water rising up to form veritable salt marshes, clearly visible on satellite photographs, and of dry salt plains, seemingly covered with snow, stretching from horizon to horizon. Most importantly, he quite bluntly states that the fate of the Aral Sea lies in store for the Caspian Sea as well.[65] The mind boggles at the consequences.

At long last, however, the authorities apparently have begun to realize that perhaps something will have to be done. In January 1988, the Central Committee issued a decree on *perestroika* of environmental protection, and a new state committee was created.[66] Commenting on this event, a Soviet zoologist, Academician Aleksei Yablokov underlined the importance of not repeating the 'mistake of the frog'. A frog swimming in a bowl of water that was slowly being heated would gradually adjust to the change in temperature and, failing to leave the bowl, would eventually perish, as the water came to a boil. According to Yablokov, this example had a striking similarity to Soviet environmental protection. In 1988, no more than 1 per cent of Soviet national income was earmarked for such measures. Merely to arrest a further deterioration, however, 3 per cent would be necessary, and to avoid irreversible processes – i.e. in the end to avoid sharing the fate of the frog – 5 per cent would be necessary.[67]

This picture is certainly alarming in its own right. However, it received further emphasis in May 1988, when some of the reasons behind Yablokov's apprehension were spelled out by none other than Valentin Koptyug, vice-president of the Academy of Sciences. Koptyug noted that with *glasnost* gradually revealing the effects of 'bureaucratic and egotistic activities', concern over the destruction of the natural environment was growing. He mentioned in particular 'the uninhibited felling of forests, the creation of hydropower dams without regard for forests and soil, the salination of soils due to senseless irrigation, the drying out of the Kara-Bogaz-Gol and the

Aral Sea, and the catastrophic pollution of the rivers and of the atmosphere in several industrial centres.' Of prime importance is Koptyug's straightforward dismissal of Siberia as a land of the future. Its nature was no longer virgin. The deterioration of the natural environment had already gone far and still continued to deteriorate. The upper and middle reaches of the Ob, and the whole of the Tom and Inya rivers, were severely polluted by emissions from the Kuzbass. High concentrations of dangerous substances were regularly recorded in the atmosphere above Kemerov, Novokuznetsk, Novosibirsk, Omsk, Prokopevsk, Barnaul, Tyumen, and other cities.[68] It is worth noting that both Yablokov and Koptyug stress that in 1988, the third year of *perestroika*, things are still deteriorating, rather than improving.

Seen from a long-run perspective, the facts reported here, and elsewhere, *de facto* amount to nothing less than a death-warrant of sorts over large areas of the Soviet Union. To put it bluntly, Central Asia is being transformed into a desert, Siberia is being suffocated by pollution and the previously fertile black earth is either being salinated by irrigation or swept away by the winds. Energy consumption is rising, in spite of efforts at conservation.[69] The once rich natural resources of Siberia are being depleted. The only extenuating circumstance in this picture is that the destruction of the human tissue appears – if at all possible – to present an even more worrisome picture.

The Human Environment

Gorbachev has repeatedly spoken of the 'human factor', the *chelovecheskii faktor*, as a centrepiece of *perestroika*. At the twenty-seventh Party Congress, for example, he said that 'the main driving force in the advancement of the agro-industrial complex, indeed its very soul, is, has been and will remain man.'[70] There is no doubt an element of empty rhetoric involved here, *pustozvonstvo* as Gorbachev would call it if uttered by someone else, but the underlying problems are nevertheless highly real and pressing. It has long been a well-known fact that the physical health of the Soviet population leaves a lot to be desired. If there had been any doubts about the low priority received by this sector, these were firmly dispelled by the former Soviet Minister of Health, Academician B. Petrovskii, in his (unpublished) speech to the June 1988 Party Conference. From our perspective, however, it is not so much the physical as the spiritual health of the population that ought to stand at the centre of attention. The basic question concerns whether the Soviet population will be able to face up to the demands of *perestroika*, after decades of psychological deformation, and the answer, as we shall see, is intimately connected with our previous arguments on *dvoeverie* and cognitive dissonance.

Intuitively, one would be tempted to focus here on the Party cadres in the administrative apparatus. Western observers have long pointed to the problem of vested interests as an important obstacle to reform, and during recent years Gorbachev has also quite consistently pointed his finger in this direction. At the June 1988 Party Conference, for example, he vehemently underlined his previous claim on the existence of 18 million bureaucrats, annually costing the Soviet economy 40 billion rubles. Adherents of Gorbachev's *perestroika* also seem to be in unanimous agreement that this 'layer' (the Russian word *sloi* is an established Soviet term for white-collar workers) has a vested interest in the established order, that it enriches itself at the expense of the people,[71] and that it is 'clearly incompatible' with *perestroika*.[72] Recently it has even been labelled a 'new class', in a belated tribute to Djilas.[73] As Soviet economist V. Chernyak puts it, moreover, any attempt to carry out *perestroika* with the help of this bureaucracy would be the equivalent of pulling oneself by the hair out of a swamp, a feat accomplishable only by a Baron Münchhausen.[74]

These critics are no doubt correct in the sense that this bureaucracy is in a position to obstruct, and perhaps even quash, *perestroika*. Soviet economist Vasilii Selyunin is rather explicit on this point:

> The established bureaucratic machine does not join *perestroika*. It may be crushed (in a revolution from above) or abolished (in a revolution from below), but it cannot be reconstructed (*perestroit*). ... Attempting to speed up scientific and technological progress, and to develop the economy under the deadly (*mertvyashchii*) control of the bureaucrats can only lead to economic stagnation and a demise (*upadok*) of the state.[75]

Interestingly, however, Selyunin sees the real danger to *perestroika* not so much in simple inertia and a deep-rooted conservatism of the administrative apparatus. 'Most important of all' is the impact on the mentality of the ordinary man, who has become used to obeying commands, to avoiding initiative, to demand from the state cheap food and housing, and to look down on his neighbour 'who decided to feed himself and who lives, the son of a bitch, better than me.'[76]

Rasputin argues in a similar vein, declaring that although the technocrats must assume great responsibility for environmental pollution, the Soviet people in general must also accept their share of the blame. The humanistic and spiritual, conservationist part of their brains had withered away to a dangerous degree, and that this disease was more dangerous than AIDS, because, in contrast, it had not been officially recognized and fought. Rasputin held that destruction of the natural environment is simply the outer manifestation of a widespread moral decadence. Individuals have been taught to avoid any commitment, any responsibility, and to praise the Party for everything, including the change of seasons.[77] Likhachev was equally critical, arguing that subservience and the habit of telling lies and half-truths had served to destroy the people's consciousness.[78] It is apparently not only the radicals among the intelligentsia that worry. The conservatives as well appear to be alarmed.

At the time of the June 1988 Party Conference, Yurii Bondarev, another well known Soviet writer, joined in the chorus, being more outspoken than Rasputin in blaming modernism in general, and the influence of Western mass media in particular, for the low moral standards of Soviet society. This influence, dressed in the veils of *glasnost*, had led to a negation of all traditionally cherished Russian values and to an obliteration of national traditions. Bondarev recalled the good old days before the revolution when life, although dirty and full of injustice, still had preserved a fresh *naiveté*. The world had not been at the edge of a moral and physical abyss. (One should note that Bondarev is referring here to the last years before the Great War!) In order to prevent the Soviet youth from finally degenerating into a bunch of 'flabby and clumsy scepticists' (*vyalykh i nepraktichnykh skeptikov*), at least the memory of the Great Patriotic War must be held in great esteem:

> Wilfulness in the evaluation of historical events, in the characterization of individual writers and military commanders, of the revolution itself and of *perestroika*, and the active fashion of banality in dress, sexual life, boulevard language and imitation of all kinds, [this wilfulness] has acquired influential positions in different publishing houses. In the end, this will cause irreparable damage to ideology and culture.

According to Bondarev, optimism might actually be more dangerous to society than pessimism. He referred to the 'administrative, official optimism' as a synonym of lies, and as a hallmark of the 'deadly season of stagnation'. The real problem was inertia, an indifference to social welfare and to fellow human beings, caused by the fact that Soviet Man had lost his faith.[79] Again referring to the serious problem of environmental pollution, Bondarev dismissed the hope for a better future with the following stern admonition: 'There will not be any tomorrow (*potom ne budet*).'

Time Running Out

As we may recall from above, in the July 1987 discussion in *Novyi Mir*, Zalygin said that if there were no tangible results of *perestroika* within a period of 15 years, the country would perish. The Russian word used was *pogibnem*, which has connotations of soldiers falling in battle, and the perspective was thus rather ominous. Yet, in May 1988, at a meeting between Gorbachev and a group of leading editors, Zalygin had shortened his time perspective considerably, saying that unless there are tangible results within 5–6 years, 'we may speak of *perestroika*, or of anything we please, but our resources will have been irrevocably destroyed'.[80]

Zalygin referred chiefly to the natural environment, but a similar perspective applies to the human counterpart. Already in June 1987, for example, Shmelev wrote that if 'people's expectations are once again (for the umpteenth time) put to shame, apathy may well become irreversible,'[81] and less than a year later, in April 1988, he returned to speculate over 'the notion of our people as some form of idle serfs, whom only the whip can force to move. One is led to ask if this really can be the case? Have we really (and our countryside in particular) grown up in such a way that any attempt to return people to normal, honest labour is doomed to fail?'[82]

To Selyunin, finally, 'time lost means everything lost. [Just] look at the years lost in discussion, and no changes can be seen. History will not forgive us if we yet again pass by an opportunity. An abyss may be passed in one leap, in two it cannot be done.'[83] Against the background provided thus far, one is certainly led to wonder if Gorbachev will be able to mobilize enough productive effort from the Soviet population in order to arrest these processes. Proceeding now to examine the impact on 'Soviet Man' of the policies of *glasnost* and *perestroika*, we shall find little grounds for optimism on this count.

Dismantling Soviet Man

The mainstay of our argument above has been to illustrate how a number of successive Soviet leaderships, by systematically placing priority on their own power and security, have promoted over time the emergence of a political and socio-economic structure which may certainly in some sense be stable enough but which is also devoid of internal dynamics. The previous section of this chapter underlined that Soviet perceptions of the current situation fully appreciate the disastrous impact on both the natural and the human environment that this 'command-administrative' system has had. Although such perceptions may perhaps not be universally recognized, in a descriptive sense they are no doubt quite penetrating and disquieting. What is missing, however, is an analytical perspective, aimed at assessing more seriously the combined response of the Soviet population to the demands of *perestroika* and the revelations of *glasnost*.

We began this study by stating that our focus should be directed firmly at the individual level, to seek explanations of the performance of the Soviet Model in terms of conflicts between individual and collective rationality, on the one hand, and economic and political rationality, on the other. By now, it should be fairly obvious that such conflicts are not only endemic to the system as such, but perhaps even instrumental in maintaining it. In Western literature, Soviet citizens are frequently described as atomized and narrowly self-centred. The socio-economic aspects of this approach have been captured above in our mechanisms of soft Exit, productive as well as unproductive. Taken to extreme, however, this approach would imply that no collective action of any kind would be possible in Soviet society. This is an obviously absurd proposition. In practice, of course, we do observe substantial collective action, in the economic as well as in the political and cultural spheres.

If, however, we recognize that collective action will not be possible without the existence of a collective identity, and assume further that, ever since the October 1917 *coup d'état*, the activities of the repressive apparatus have been geared into suppressing the formation of any kind of alternative structure that might serve as a basis for such identity formation, we are left with an apparent dilemma. In order to resolve this dilemma, we shall maintain that the aim of Party policy throughout has been to promote a substitute collective identity, known as Soviet Man. The mechanisms that keep the psychology of this political *homunculus* together have been captured above in terms of passive Loyalty. It may well be that no single living Soviet citizen actually holds the values and ideals that are associated with the official image of Soviet Man, but by means of mechanisms that reward conformity, penalize individuality, and promote pluralist ignorance, faking and self-deception have been introduced into the picture to make up for the lack of positive identification. The question that remains to be answered here is what will happen when these demands are removed.

Autonomous Groups

A process of great importance that marked Gorbachev's first years in power was the proliferation of 'informal', i.e. officially not recognized, groups. The phenomenon as such, which lacks precedence in Soviet history, appears to have been noted already in 1984, when *Literaturnaya Gazeta* opened a special telephone connection for young readers, with the explicit aim of 'finding out what exactly the informal youth groups are.'[84] In late 1986, *Komsomolskaya Pravda* observed that the 'informal' groups were 'growing as fast as mushrooms in the rain',[85] and it soon became evident that they represented a youth movement of significant dimensions. In 1987, a Moscow police officer by the name of I.Yu. Sundiev reported that, according to investigations carried out by the police, one-third of all Moscow high school students were members of 'informal' groups. (Moscow has an estimated ten million inhabitants.) The groups in question covered a wide variety of different interests, among which Sundiev mentioned in particular the following:

fanaty – sports fans, whose active rioting had to be restrained by strict police surveillance;

rokery – fans of rock music, subdivided into *bitlomany* (Beatles fans), *khardrokery* (hard-rockers), *metallisty* (heavy-metal, according to Sundiev representing the trash of society, constituting a 'cultural ghetto' of their own), and *panky* (punk-rockers);

breikery – break-dancers;

khippi – hippies, subdivided into *staraya generatsiya* (the old generation), *sistema* (the system) and *patsifisty* (pacifists);

karate, *konfu* and *ushu* – practitioners of oriental martial arts;

poppery – Soviet yuppies, elegantly dressed youngsters considering themselves to be the elite of society; and

optimisty – youth with an interest in social questions, turning against the use of alcohol and drugs.[86]

In addition, there were also a number of groups without flashy Western names, taking an interest in the protection of nature and historical monuments. The latter are apparently considered to be genuine Soviet phenomena, parallelling but not being patterned after similar movements in the West. Sundiev actually took great care in stressing that *all* informal groups are first and foremost a product of Soviet society, rather than of Western models. Much to the point, he observed that the lack of meaning in Soviet public life and the dullness of Komsomol activities were the main reasons behind the emergence of the informal groups:

For many young people, participation in Komsomol activities has become a ritual.... As is usually the case with rites, most of the participants never question the activity, but simply join in the voting and the shouting. Such a duplicity of behaviour and values in situations of strict social control (family, school, university) breeds duplicity also in norms and values.[87]

The Moscow police officer concluded his report by finding it 'symptomatic' that the informal groups focused on the sore points in Soviet life, on that which had been neglected for so long: cultural heritage, ecological problems, creative individual self-realization, aesthetic education, physical education,[88] and respect for the law. It was added that this interest 'not seldom took on abhorrent forms (*urodlivye formy*)'.[89]

In a discussion of the problems reviewed by Sundiev, a historian held that the youth worried not so much about things that concerned the older generation but rather with trying to come to grips conceptually with the country's past.[90] In this endeavour, the school system had failed to help. Young people were still educated in the spirit of duplicity (*dvoedushie*), in accordance with the rule of doublefacedness (*dvulichie*), which was the acknowledged format of Soviet education.[91] A Moscow school principal reported how the authorities had attempted to reach dissenting youth by admitting informal groups on to the school premises in the evenings and during holidays. The *panky* and the *rokery*, however, had not shown up, being 'allergic to all forms of organization'.[92]

The reaction of Soviet media to the 'mushrooming' of informal groups is best described as bewilderment. Although the emergence and spread of such groups is certainly understood as an indication that the Komsomol is becoming obsolete,[93] and although the groups that take an interest in culture, history and protection of the environment are welcomed, the authorities seem to be at a loss concerning what should be done with those who turn their backs on Soviet society. The informal youth groups represent an antithesis to the Soviet understanding of how society should be organized, and hence to Soviet ideology. In more abstract terms, they represent a break with the previous patterns of incorporation of large sections of the citizenry into the officially controlled sphere of Soviet society. As this incorporation breaks down, and autonomouos organizations are formed to pursue the separate interests of separate groups, a number of competing collective identities are formed. In a pluralistic setting, this would of course be a great asset, since in most cases it represents an articulation and aggregation of constructive ideas. In the Soviet case, however, it represents a threat not only to the Party's power monopoly but also to the stability of society at large.

We are obviously not dealing here simply with youth. There are many other autonomous organizations that should be mentioned as well; for example various literary groups, vigilante squads, and the ultra-conservative Pamyat[94]. Youth are, however, by far the most important, since a loss of a substantial part of the youth implies a failure of incorporating new generations into the Soviet project. But this is still only one dimension. A considerably more menacing phenomenon is represented by developments in the national and ethnic dimension, where a completely different panorama unfolds.

The Russians and the Others

Western observers have long pointed at the nationalities issue as perhaps *the* major problem to be addressed by Soviet policy makers. An underlying assumption has been that, if and when central control is relaxed, a number of explosive situations might emerge, posing a serious threat to the regime.[95] Recent events would certainly seem to confirm such suspicions. One need only think of the unrest in Alma-Ata, the capital of the Soviet republic of Kazakhstan, in December 1986, and of the bloody confrontations between Azeris and Armenians, in the Azeri town of Sumgait in February 1988. The situation is no doubt potentially dangerous to Moscow, but we must also recognize that the nationalities issue is considerably more complicated than simply posing a threat of destabilization. Essentially, there are three dimensions involved: ethnic conflicts, demographic change, and potential responses to the new demands of *perestroika*.

The demographic dimension is perhaps the easiest to assess. In their study of Soviet population policy, Jones and Grupp have concluded that, in contrast to 'the image sometimes presented in the Western press' the Soviet regime is not really worried about the 'imminent prospect of a USSR swamped by non-Russians'.[96] The demographic dilemma is concerned not so much with ethnic relations *per se*, as with regional labour-force projections. In a recent study, a group of Soviet demographers have stressed the fact that those eight Soviet republics where fertility rates are too low to allow a reproduction of the population, i.e. Moldavia, Georgia, and the Baltic and the Slavic republics, together account for 80 per cent of the country's total population. Consequently, the burden on the high-fertility republics becomes impossibly high: 'This is a threat to the mere net reproduction of generations ... which can be overcome only by higher fertility in the younger categories (under 30 years of age) in the republics with low fertility rates.'[97]

The latter point is of great importance, indicating the slight prospect of nationalities with a high fertility being able to compensate for the fall in population growth in the Soviet heartlands. Since the latter problem is intimately linked with overall socio-economic policies, the demographic dilemma may be taken as a reflection of quite serious problems. The picture is rendered even gloomier if we consider further that fertility rates in the high-fertility regions are expected to converge on the all-Union average,[98] and that the Central Asians and the Transcaucasians are unwilling to move, not only *from* their own republics but even from rural to urban areas *within* those republics. With an outmigration of Slavs, who tend to be city-dwellers, these 'labour-abundant regions' (*trudoizbytochnye regiony*) will in relative terms become increasingly rural.[99] The sum conclusion must thus be that the solution to the Soviet demographic dilemma lies neither in moving the Central Asians and Transcaucasians north and west, nor in moving the industrial base south and east. It too must be sought in economic and social reforms.

Turning to the ethnic dimension, one is given a quite distinct impression of a retreat *en masse* from everything 'Soviet'. Non-Russian writers and other intellectuals object to Russian influence in the Soviet state, and Russian intellectuals are blaming other nationalities, in particular the Jews, for having forced the Soviet order on them. All stress their own national identities. Ukrainians and Belorussians, who have long been regarded as especially intimate brothers of the Russians, are demanding that instruction in their own mother tongues should be made compulsory, from pre-schools to universities. Lithuanians, Armenians, and others demand that history books should be rewritten in such a way that their own respective pasts are placed on an equal footing with Russian and Turkish history. While the Russians relish the benevolent attitude shown towards the Russian Orthodox Church in 1988, the year of its millenium, the Ukrainians resent that their national Orthodox and Catholic (Uniate) Churches are still illegal, and the Moslems are expanding the number of unofficial mosques. The current religious revival thus serves to underline ethnic differences within the Soviet state. In order to illustrate the complexity of feelings underlying these differences, let us take a closer look at three cases of particular importance.

The background to the unrest in Alma-Ata in 1986 was that the republic's First Party Secretary, Dinmukhammed Kunaev, had been replaced by Gennadii Kolbin, an ethnic Russian. The reason for the replacement was apparently linked with the campaign against corruption, as Kunaev had been heavily involved in racketeering. What made the Kazakh youth take to the streets in violent anti-Russian rioting and demonstrations, however, was national pride. As a result of previous developments, the Russians had come to completely dominate economic, political, and cultural life in Alma-Ata, and, with Kolbin being placed as republican Party chief, growing ethnic tensions exploded in open conflict. The protest was not aimed against the Soviet Union as such, but rather at Russian dominance in local affairs.

A completely different situation can be found in the case of Nagorno-Karabach. A systematic neglect of the economic and cultural needs and demands of the Armenian population in this autonomous *oblast* in the republic of Azerbaidzhan, had led to growing demands for an incorporation of the *oblast* with the neighbouring Armenian republic. Once *glasnost* allowed the conflict between the Azeri and the Armenians to become articulated, it erupted in violence. A veritable pogrom was carried out in Sumgait. According to official Soviet sources, thirty-two Armenians were massacred. According to unconfirmed information, the death toll was much higher. By July 1988, the conflict had become a stalemate. At the Party Conference, Gorbachev took a firm stand against demands for border changes, and the immediate reaction of the Supreme Soviet of Nagorno-Karabakh was a unilateral declaration of affiliation with the Soviet republic of Armenia. The Azeri authorities promptly and correctly condemned this action as illegal and as a gross violation of the Soviet Constitution, but the Armenian Supreme Soviet gave its full support. Again, the conflict was not directed against the Soviet Union as such. Nor was it primarily an expression of anti-Russian sentiments. It was an expression of an old conflict between Turks and Armenians, illustrating the rather tenuous nature of the Soviet 'Union' and the dubious legitimacy of its internal boundaries.

The third illustration concerns Estonia, where the situation again is completely different. Here we are dealing not with open violence and rioting, but rather with a calm but nevertheless firm resistance against Soviet economic development plans. Plans for a further industrialization of the Estonian republic call for a massive immigration of Russian workers. According to Estonian intellectuals, this would exacerbate national tensions. The Russians are already a majority in the republican capital of Tallinn. They receive priority in housing, and they largely refuse to learn Estonian.[100] Of even greater importance, however, is the plan to open a huge phosphorite mine in the northern part of the republic. According to Estonian scientists, the open cast mining would lead to wide-ranging environmental damage, transforming as much as a third of the republic's territory into an industrial wasteland. Confronted with these threats to its people and its environment, the Estonian Communist Party has come out in open support of demands from Estonian economists for complete economic autonomy. The Estonian case is not primarily one of ethnic conflict, but rather one of simply asking to be left alone. There are no indications that remaining Russians would be maltreated if the Estonians were granted autonomy in some form.

These illustrations provide essentially static impressions of the nationality-related problems. In order to appreciate the full gravity of the situation, however, we must look at it also from a dynamic perspective, i.e. to examine how the various nationalities may be expected to respond to new demands of *perestroika* and to the new image of reality that is provided by *glasnost*. Here we may draw on the findings of Soviet ethno-sociological research.[101] In general terms, one may speak of a certain spectrum of attitudes and values, stretching from the Baltic republics, via the Russians, to the Central Asians. The main features of this spectrum can be summarized as follows.

The Balts, and especially the Estonians, show a much greater interest in social problems than do either the Russians or, especially, the Central Asians. While Estonia has the highest material standard in the Soviet Union, the Estonians are nevertheless the most dissatisfied with their situation. In comparison with, for example, Uzbeks, Georgians, and Moldavians, they are markedly more interested in 'developing democracy' and in 'showing economic initiative', and equally markedly disinterested in campaigns for improved discipline. The Baltic and Slavic peoples greatly appreciate 'interesting work' and 'conditions for creative activity', while the Central Asians are more inclined towards a 'quiet and peaceful life'. The Balts, furthermore, are the most extrovert and achievement-oriented, while the Moslem Central Asians are portrayed as introvert and rather complacent regarding current affairs. The Russians are placed somewhere in between these extremes.[102]

One should not interpret these survey findings as proof that the Central Asians and the Transcaucasians are in any way 'lazy' or antisocial. The point is rather that their focus of interest tends to go in a direction different from that of the Slavs and the Balts. The repeated Soviet campaigns against corruption and local 'mafias' in Central Asia and Transcaucasia reflect such differences. What is regarded as illegal in Moscow may be part of national traditions in Uzbekistan and Armenia.[103]

The main importance of these observations lies in what they can tell us about the potential responses of the various nationalities. To the Estonians, a successful *perestroika* would mean autonomy from Moscow, increased efficiency in the socialized sector, and probably also increased economic relations with the West. To Uzbeks and

Georgians, an ideal development would be an expansion of the second economy and a removal of central restrictions and interference. To the Russians, an unsuccessful *perestroika* would probably be the – myopically – preferred outcome, permitting a continued slacking and reliance on the state as a provider of goods and services, albeit at a low level. These are certainly crude stereotypes, but they still reflect the complicated patterns of ethnic composition. If the Soviet 'Union' were to be broken up in its constituent parts, the Estonians might do very well in the first economy, the Georgians and the Uzbeks in the second economy, while the Central Asians would have the population growth. Very little would be left for the Russians.

Conclusion

At first glance, one might certainly think that Gorbachev's programme for radical reforms should serve to restore normalcy to the Soviet Union, by eliminating the 'command-administrative' philosophy and all its manifestations. *Perestroika* in the economy, with the associated decrees on decentralization and on promoting individual and co-operative activities, should serve to improve the overall allocation of resources. *Glasnost* in the cultural sphere, with the associated curb on censorship, and with political rehabilitations and a more honest approach to the country's own history, should bring about a moral cleansing. Political reforms and democratization ought to improve the citizenry's feelings of participation and thus elicit more productive effort from the toiling masses. Legal reforms, finally, should put an end to political persecution and to wilfulness in the judicial system, thus in the end producing a long overdue transformation of the Soviet Union into a *Rechtsstaat*, a *pravovoe gosudarstvo*.[104] The question, however, is whether all of this is possible to reconcile with the parallel destruction of the collective 'Soviet' identity.

There are no doubt many who believe that all of the above is actually on offer, and there are certainly even more who hope and wish that this should be the case. Our ambition here is definitely not to reduce such hopes and beliefs to mere wishful thinking. All that has been said in the above, however, has been intended to demonstrate that the dilemma of Soviet reforms is not simply finding technical solutions to well-defined problems in the economic and political systems. It is rather a matter of social change, of a transformation of the mentality of the Soviet population, the *chelovecheskii faktor* as it were. The latter is of course not impossible, but it is going to be a slow and vulnerable process. In an interview with *Moscow News*, early in 1988, Academician Vladimir Tikhonov said that it would take two generations of Soviet leaders, or about 25 years, before any visible results could be registered.[105] Against this background, the apocalyptic visions that have been presented above certainly take on a new urgency. Even if the full reform package should meet with success, a number of irreversible processes are already at work. While not impossible in principle, Gorbachev's reforms will thus not be able to restore what was, but merely to salvage what remains. In which sense, then, can we understand the reforms to 'work'?

In essence, Gorbachev's programme boils down to what O'Donnell has referred to as a 'resurrection of civil society',[106] and it might be illustrative, in this context, to draw a parallel with the latter's account of the resurrection of civil society in the Argentine, after the Falklands débâcle in 1982. A crucial role in this account is played by the concept of horizontal Voice, which O'Donnell argues that 'not even the most efficiently terroristic regime could ever completely suppress'. After the 1976 coup, however, the military regime certainly did what it could to prevent a repoliticization of Argentine society. During the period of military rule, Argentinian citizens could use vertical Voice, by 'respectfully petitioning' the authorities on various less sensitive matters, but any attempt to keep alive former collective identities, by resorting to horizontal Voice, was regarded as 'subversive contamination', and thus tantamount to 'almost certain death'. As a result, people shifted their involvements out of the public and into the thoroughly depoliticized private sphere of society.

The most interesting feature in O'Donnell's account is that he shows how former collective identities managed to survive under the surface, in spite of brutal repression. The key here was 'oblique Voice'. Unconventional ways of dress, excessive hand clapping at public functions, visits to certain cultural events, and other such activities, served as signals that could be understood by 'others like me' but hopefully not by the repressive organs. Although certainly not devoid of risk, this form of signalling had great emotional and cognitive impact, serving to confirm the surviving identities. Once the military was gone, there were consequently alternative structures ready, in terms of values as well as loose forms of organization. As open vertical Voice once again became the normal format of political life, the oblique horizontal counterpart was rendered superfluous. 'Resurrection' represented a return to normalcy.

In a superficial sense, there are important similarities between the Argentine and the Soviet cases. Regimes bent on total power deal with opposition by resorting to terror. The populations are relegated to the private sphere of society, and soft Voice replaces political pluralism. In a deeper sense, however, the importance of the parallel rather lies in illustrating some profound differences. The key to the latter lies in the active Soviet policy of incorporation, and the consequent need to engage in faking. While the Argentine military regime was simply authoritarian, Soviet Party rule has been totalitarian. Where the Argentine military was content with brutal suppression of open manifestations of discontent, Soviet repression has increasingly sought to invade the inner privacy of the citizens. In the Argentine, repression rested on fear. In the Soviet Union, fear has increasingly been replaced by a perverse form of socialization, described above as passive Loyalty. From the perspective of resurrection, there are three concepts of crucial importance to be addressed here, namely 'normalcy', 'resurrection' and 'surviving identity'.

In the Argentinian case, repression lasted less than a decade, and under the surface there remained a civil society to resurrect. In the Soviet case, the time-span is measured in generations and the picture is rather complicated. The forces that were set in motion by de-Stalinization may certainly be taken as an indication that ideals, values, and identities had survived from before the imposition of totalitarian repression. In Khrushchev's time, a relaxation might thus have been enough to resurrect civil society, had it been allowed to run its full course. Under Gorbachev, however, this is definitely not so. It is not simply the case that many people, notably of course the 18 million bureaucrats, have strong vested interests in the established order. While undoubtedly true, that observation has a limited explanatory value. It is of much greater importance to realize that the bulk of these people have laboured mentally over the years to eliminate cognitive dissonance between, on the one hand, that actual Soviet reality which is currently being so brutally exposed, and, on the other, that picture of Soviet society as it should be, which has been propagated by the official ideology. To the extent that people have been successful in harmonizing these two sides of the *dvoeverie*, it is very difficult to say what represents 'normalcy'.

The reality that is promised by the utopia of the official ideology does not yet exist. The observable reality that confronts the Soviet citizen in everyday life is not allowed to exist, and the hybrid reality that is the outcome of dissonance-reducing psychological processes is, of course, merely that – a psychological construct. The keystone in this construct, indeed the very force that has kept it all together, has been the official ideology, with the associated principle of *partiinost* and the need to behave as Soviet Man, all reinforced by pluralist ignorance and harsh repression against those who step out of line, against those who point out that the Emperor in fact has no clothes.

The concept of 'resurrection' is difficult to interpret in this setting. *Glasnost* and the new approach to history essentially means an end to pluralist ignorance, allowing individuals to learn that they are not alone in holding certain negative views about the regime, and the relaxation of repression allows them to say so. Superficially, this ought to mean the end of the need to engage in faking. Moreover, as previous lies and dishonesties are being exposed, the official ideology is simultaneously being seriously discredited. Is it possible, under these circumstances, to identify a new collective identity, which may serve to promote remedial collective action? Here we must distinguish between creation and resurrection.

On the one hand, it has been shown above how a broad range of 'informal' groups have suddenly started to emerge. This no doubt represents a proliferation of collective identities, but in the great majority of these cases we are dealing with identities that are being created, that have no roots in the Soviet past. In fact, we have seen above that many of the new groups explicitly turn their backs on Soviet society. On the other hand, we have also seen how various nationalities are beginning to assert themselves. Here we are very definitely dealing with a resurrection of 'surviving identities'. In the case of the Estonians, for example, we may even observe important outer symbols being displayed, such as the old Estonian flag and national anthem. A common denominator, however, is that neither of these identities is compatible with the Soviet project. In the case of youth, we may speak of a vertical disintegration, as future generations are being disconnected, and in the case of nationalities, we may speak of a horizontal disconnection, as the periphery is being spun off.

Given these centrifugal forces, one might be tempted to conclude that Gorbachev's programme actually threatens to tear the Soviet Union apart at its seams, vertically as well as horizontally. Such a conclusion, however, would neglect the very specific nature of the Soviet milieu. Although there may undoubtedly be a few individuals of great moral integrity, who have come through the 'dark decades' untarnished, it is very difficult to believe that the bulk of the Soviet population would be able, at will, to shrug off completely the previous imprints of faking, self-deception, and pluralist ignorance. Recognizing that the new demands of *perestroika* relate to a 'normalcy', or a reality, that conceptually does not exist, we may assume that they will serve only to introduce yet another 'reality', and thus a further source of cognitive dissonance. Hence we shall argue that a plausible outcome will be the addition of a new layer of faking. Rather than returning to 'normalcy', in order to deal with self-contempt for having actively engaged in the previous practice of faking, which is now being vehemently denounced, people will again resort to self-deception. In this perspective, the violent fulminations against obstructing and conservative bureaucrats and managers assume a rather simplistic appearance.

We shall not conclude this book by predicting that the Soviet Union is going to perish in the near future. We would, however, like to maintain that the Soviet Union as we have known it up to date in certain important respects is already dead, and maybe Secretary Gorbachev would agree with us here. The question then becomes what will appear in its place. By perverting the new collective identities, the new layer of faking, which is contrary to the demands of *perestroika*, will serve to counter the centrifugal tendencies, thus preventing a total break-down. Simultaneously, however, such faking also stands firmly in the way of replacing the old discredited structure with something new and more efficient. The wide range of new collective identities that are emerging 'like mushrooms in the rain' are simply too badly co-ordinated for them to be conducive to the building of a viable state. Paradoxically, the main failure of the Party's systematic endeavour over the decades to create a Soviet Man appears to be that it has been rather successful.

Notes and references

Notes

Chapter 1 – Setting the stage

1. Gorbachev (1987a), p. 27.
2. Gorbachev (1988a), p. 9.
3. A visual representation of this atmosphere can be found in a *Krokodil* cartoon which shows a man sailing down a stream on a raft. The man is fixing the horizon through binoculars. The raft is headed for a waterfall, being only feet away from going over the edge, into the abyss (*Krokodil*, no. 12, 1988).
4. Shmelev (1988), p. 160.
5. Moiseev (1988), pp. 182, 186.
6. In Gerner and Hedlund (1988) we deal briefly with the Polish case.
7. Motyl (1987), pp. 1–2.
8. Cf. e.g. Nastavshev (1988).
9. Kak sovershaetsya (1987), p. 234.
10. *The Economist*, 9 April 1988, p. 3.
11. Nove (1977), p. 9.
12. Yanov (1984), p. 22.
13. Elster (1985b), p. 1.
14. For a brief overview of the main arguments and participants in this highly interesting debate, see Gregory and Stuart (1974), ch. 9.
15. Nove (1964), p. 51.
16. Ibid., pp. 55, 61–2. (Emphasis in the original.)
17. Elster (1984), pp. 18–28.
18. The matrix formulation behind the example formulated by Tucker was presented earlier. For a general discussion of the Prisoner's Dilemma, see Rapoport (1982).
19. Yanov (1968). See also Yanov (1984), pp. 19–22.
20. Nove (1977), p. 143.
21. Yanov (1984).
22. Ibid., p. 20.
23. The original source is a cartoon in *Krokodil*, cited in Nove (1977), p. 94.
24. Berliner (1957).
25. Åslund (1985), ch. 4, *passim*.
26. There are many sources for this, but perhaps the most clearly put indictment of communal incentives is found in Israelsen (1980).

27. The various dimensions of incentives in co-operation are discussed in Hedlund (1985).
28. The *magnum opus* on problems in the *kibbutz* economy is Barkai (1977). See also Barkai (1987).
29. Barkai (1987), pp. 250–3.
30. Bell (1965), p. 591.
31. Ibid., pp. 592–3.
32. Ibid., p. 595.
33. Motyl (1987), p. 72.
34. Verba (1965), p. 546.
35. Motyl (1987), p. 71.
36. Ibid.
37. North (1981), p. 45.
38. Ibid., p. 47.
39. Ibid. Elster comes even closer to the mark, in a more subtle sense, when he says that 'irrationality rather than duty may be the cement of society, a socially beneficial illusion, like Voltaire's God. It may not be a good thing if social scientists spend too much of their time discussing such connections among rationality, morality and collective action' (Elster, 1985a, p. 145). In both North's and Elster's formulations, the importance of staving off the threat of the Prisoner's Dilemma is highlighted.
40. See further North (1981), pp. 48–54.
41. Ibid., p. 53.
42. Quoted by Bell (1965), p. 594.
43. Ibid., p. 601.
44. A parallel with economics is rather striking here. Under 'perfect competition', no outward signs are visible to indicate that firms are actually competing against each other, whereas under various forms of imperfect competition, such as oligopolies or monopolistic competition, the manifestations of competition are very obvious. The absence of public regurgitation of ideological dogma should not be taken as the absence of ideology, but maybe instead as an indication that it is working rather well.
45. Meyer (1966), pp. 279–80.
46. North (1981), p. 49.
47. A case in point here is Khrushchev's promise, made in 1961, that the Soviet Union would not only catch up with but even overtake (*dognat i peregnat*) the US by 1970, a prophecy close enough in the future to be relevant, but still distant enough at the time to pose a small risk of falsification to the prophet.
48. See further Meyer (1966), p. 280.
49. As an illustration that this practice persists in the midst of Gorbachev's *glasnost*, we may quote the following, from the introduction to a 1987 Soviet book on a subject as remote as the Christianization of Rus, a millennium ago. Speaking of different views among the scholars, the editor of the book underlines that in the final analysis they 'all stay within the framework of a true Marxist approach to the problem, this being

the only guarantee of genuine objectivity and historical truth.'
(Sukhov, 1987, p. 5.)
50. Comey (1962), pp. 308–10.
51. Meyer (1966), p. 309.
52. Bell (1965), p. 602.
53. Ibid., p. 595.
54. Hirschman (1970).
55. Ibid., p. 1.
56. See further Williamson (1976).
57. Hirschman (1970), p. 26.
58. See further ibid., ch. 7.
59. Other examples of such use of economic models in political science are Downs (1957) and Olson (1965).
60. Hirschman (1970), p. 19. On the applications of EVL, see Hirschman (1986).
61. Birch (1975), pp. 74–5.
62. Laver (1976), p. 477.
63. Barry (1974), p. 95.
64. The defence of the original version is handled in Hirschman (1986).
65. Barry (1974), pp. 88–95.
66. Olson (1965).
67. O'Donnell (1986), pp. 251–2.
68. Jaruzelski (1987), p. 69.
69. Hahn (1987), p. 334.
70. Jaruzelski (1987), pp. 66, 69.

Chapter two – Searching for the economics of early Soviet planning

1. Quoted by Smolinsky (1967), p. 124.
2. Ibid.
3. Expression borrowed from Nove (1983).
4. See further Comey (1962).
5. Lenin quoted by Carr (1952), p. 365.
6. Hough and Fainsod (1979), p. 63.
7. Dobb (1929), p. 41.
8. Quoted by Carr (1952), p. 270. (Emphasis in the original.)
9. Nove (1969), p. 54.
10. Lewin (1974a), p. 77.
11. Nove (1969), p. 55.
12. According to Dobb (1929), p. 61, War Communism was 'the product not of theories, but of war-time improvisation.' Nove's characteristic is also rather striking: 'A siege economy with a communist ideology. A partly organized chaos. Sleepless leatherjacketed commissars working round the clock in a vain effort to replace the free market' (Nove, 1969, p. 74).
13. On the general course of events during this period, see Carr (1952), ch. 17, Dobb (1929), ch. 4, and Nove (1969), ch. 3.
14. Cf. Selyunin (1988), p. 175, who makes precisely this latter point.

Notes and references

15. For developments in agricultural policy, see also Hedlund (1984), ch. 2.
16. On nationalization policy, see Carr (1952), pp. 82–100, and Dobb (1929) ch. 2, *passim*, in particular pp. 59–60, where it is argued that the decree on general nationalization was prompted by German speculation in Russian shares, aiming to establish foreign holdings and thus control over Soviet industry.
17. Carr (1952), p. 72, and in particular note D, pp. 394–7, on the attempt by the railway workers to take over and run the railways.
18. Ibid., pp. 210–17.
19. Nove (1969), p. 50.
20. Dobb (1929), p. 90, presents the astonishingly rapid increase in currency circulation during 1917–20.
21. Szamuely (1974), p. 22. (This was written before the Khmer Rouge period in Kampuchea.)
22. Lange (1965), pp. 200–1.
23. Smolinsky (1967), p. 108.
24. Lenin (1928), p. 440. (Emphasis in the original.)
25. Quoted by Carr (1952), p. 133, who traces this belief back to Saint-Simon and Hilferding.
26. Smolinsky (1967), p. 111.
27. Carr (1952), pp. 93, 361. See also Smolinsky (1967), on GOELRO and German inspiration.
28. Nove (1969), p. 70. See also Zaleski (1962), pp. 35–40.
29. Smolinsky (1967), p. 117.
30. Gustafson (1981), p. 103.
31. Ionin (1987), p. 23.
32. Lewin (1974a), p. 81.
33. Ibid., p. 83. In the spring of 1921, with industrial output at a mere fraction of the prewar figure, the number of administrative personnel in the VSNKh agencies above enterprise level was up to 230,000, or 96 times as great as those employed in the pre-war ministries of trade and industry (Smolinsky, 1967, p. 115).
34. For general events, see Carr (1952), ch. 17–18, Carr (1958), part II, and Dobb (1929), *passim*. Agricultural policy is dealt with in Hedlund (1984), ch. 2.
35. Lewin (1974a), p. 84.
36. See Roberts (1970) and Szamuely (1974), ch. 3–4, for the confusing statements issued at the time. Against this background, it is hard to understand writers who argue that NEP was 'a well prepared return to normalcy' (Dobb, 1928, p. 128) or 'the creation of transitional conditions that would permit the socialist government to retain political power until the triumph of socialism in the West' (Baran, 1970, p. 5). See also Brutzkus (1935), p. 103.
37. Carr (1952), p. 297.
38. See e.g. Nove (1969), pp. 93–6.
39. In complete contradiction to his earlier stand, he would say: 'We thought that we could, at a blow and swiftly, abolish market relations. Yet it turns out that we shall reach socialism through market relations'

(Nove, 1969, p. 188). The advance towards socialism should be at 'the speed of a tortoise' (Nove, 1964, p. 22) and his view that strong peasants were an asset to the country produced the famous call for them to 'Get rich!' (*obogoschaites*) (Nove, 1969, p. 123). Bukharin's gradual realization of the need to adopt a different approach to the economic problems is described in Cohen (1980), pp. 139–49.

40. There are many sources to this debate, the *magnum opus* being Erlich (1960). See also Gregory and Stuart (1974), part 1, ch. 3, and Nove (1969), ch. 5.

41. Erlich (1960), ch. 4, *passim*. Recognizing that this belief existed does not, of course, imply accepting it as a justification for the events that followed. Ibid., p. 168, for example, characterizes the rationale of implementing the FFYP as a way of preparing for war as a 'suicide prompted by the fear of death'. Had the German attack come in 1928–32, the Soviet economy would have been in dire straits indeed.

42. Wright (1979), p. 7.

43. One example is a table presented in 1928 that showed grain marketings to be down to half of their 1913 level. The table long went undisputed, but eventually a debate followed over its reliability. Jerzy Karcz, for example, has argued that the calculation 'is completely misleading and provides an exceedingly distorted picture of the relation between 1913 and 1926/7 grain marketings' (Karcz, 1967, p. 402). See also Davies (1970) and Karcz (1979). The disputed table can be found, *inter alia*, in Karcz (1967), p. 402.

44. The operation was mainly directed against areas in the Urals and in Siberia, where the harvest had been comparatively good. Hence, it later came to be known as the 'Ural-Siberian Method'. See Davies (1980), ch. 2, Lewin (1974b) and Taniuchi (1981).

45. Wright (1979), p. 6.

46. On events immediately preceding mass collectivization, see Lewin (1965).

47. Ibid., p. 165.

48. Published in *Pravda* on 26 and 27 May 1923.

49. Lewin (1974a), p. 95.

50. Zaleski quotes the head of the Polish Gosplan in the late 1940s as having made the following remark: 'Centralization is a substitute for a plan, and a bad one. When one is incapable of foreseeing, he reserves for himself the right to intervene at any moment, on any pretext' (Zaleski, 1962, p. 34).

51. Ibid., p. 31.

52. Lindblom (1977), p. 65.

53. *Pravda*, February 5, 1931. Quoted by Smolinsky (1966), p. 88.

54. Johnston and Mellor (1961), p. 571.

55. Swianiewicz (1965), pp. 66–7. As we have noted above, the NEP was primarily an agricultural policy, and given the improvement of rural life that followed, combined with the traditional Russian attachment to the soil, it was difficult to induce the peasants to leave for the cities, where food was hard to get and housing conditions in particular were appalling. Towards the end of the decade, moreover, the renewed grain crisis

caused a further deterioration in the food situation. Black market prices for grain more than trebled between April 1928 and April 1929 (ibid., p. 73).

56. Ibid., p. 112.
57. Stalin put an end to the debate in December 1929, and his attitude to the problem is characteristic: 'When the head is off one does not mourn for the hair' (Nove, 1969, p. 166, and ch. 7, *passim*, on the campaign).
58. These are the so called Smolensk Archives, which were captured by the Germans at Smolensk, and later fell into American hands. Selected documents have been edited, translated and published in Fainsod (1958).
59. Carr (1958), p. 99, says that 'it was no longer true that the class analysis determined policy. Policy determined what form of class analysis was appropriate to the given situation.' See also Hedlund (1983).
60. Lorimer (1946), pp. 147, 150.
61. Dallin and Nicolaevsky (1947), p. 152, and ch. 7 *passim* on early policy. Penal labour was started already in January 1918: 'Work details are to be formed from among the prisoners able to work, for the carrying out of tasks necessary for the state, *tasks no more strenuous than those of unskilled workers*' (emphasis added) (ibid., p. 157). See also Swianiewicz (1965), pp. 17–19 on the policy of re-education by work.
62. In 1937, the journal *Sovetskaya yustitsiya* (Soviet Justice) wrote that 'A prison is a prison, why so much shyness? ... We must overcome the sugary liberalism, the compassionate attitude towards the offender' (Dallin and Nicolaevsky, 1947, p. 156).
63. Ibid., pp. 206–8.
64. A look at a historical atlas of the Soviet Union shows that well over half of the total area of Siberia was designated as territories of various camp administrations, and that even European Russia was liberally dotted with such areas (Gilbert, 1979, pp. 29–31).
65. Dallin and Nicolaevsky (1947), pp. 197–201. Swianiewicz (1965), pp. 113–1⟨
66. Dallin and Nicolaevsky (1947), p. 259, quote evidence for this: 'At least once, in 1937.' Swianiewicz (1965), p. 14, also seems convinced of the economic importance of arrests: 'A demand for a compulsory labour force seems to have become a contributory factor in the number of arrests and deportations carried out by the security police.' Ibid., p. 49, also cites the importance for these arrests of the 'Special Conference' (*osoboe soveschanie*, or OSSO) that existed within the security police, and which had the right to sentence people for alleged crimes, or even without alleged offences, 'simply as a preventive measure'. See also Fainsod (1953), pp. 384–7, on the growth of the NKVD economic empire.
67. Swianiewicz (1965), pp. 125–6.
68. Ibid., pp. 39–40.
69. Baran (1970), p. 8 and note 14. (Emphasis added.)
70. Maurice Dobb, for example, has the following to say: 'Certainly the Plan did not envisage any lowering of consumption as the *conditio sine qua non* of the high rate of investment for which it budgeted. ... It is

often supposed that this high rate of investment was designed at the expense of an absolute fall in consumption. But this is a misconception so far as the original design was concerned. Nothing of the kind, at least, was contemplated when the Plan was originally made. ... So far as consumption at least was concerned, things did not work out according to these preliminary estimates. This was largely because of the occurrence of certain unfavourable factors which could scarcely have been foreseen. ... Such factors could not be regarded as necessary concomitants of industrialization and are at any rate without much relevance to an estimate of the consequences of industrialization elsewhere' (Dobb, 1948, pp. 26, 235, 237).

71. This argument is pursued in Hedlund (1984), ch. 2, *passim*.
72. Ellman (1975), p. 847.
73. Ibid., p. 845.
74. Millar (1970, 1971a), Nove (1971a, 1971b).
75. According to one Soviet source, inflation caused urban real wages to fall by as much as 49 per cent during 1928–32. An important contributory factor here was a fall by over 40 per cent in the volume of available grain per worker during 1930–2 (Ellman, 1975, pp. 847, 850; Carr and Davies, 1969, p. 703). Note also that 1928 was the starting year for both food rationing and for the system of 'closed shops' for the privileged that has later become an integral part of the Soviet system.
76. Barsov (1968, 1969).
77. See Millar (1974) and Ellman (1975).
78. Quoted by Ellman (1975), p. 844.
79. Millar (1970), p. 93.
80. Morrison (1982), p. 581.
81. For details, see Zaleski (1962), pp. 47–8.
82. See further ibid., pp. 74–5.
83. Quoted by ibid., p. 52.
84. Ibid., pp. 74–5.
85. Jasny (1961), p. 61, See also ibid., pp. 56–7, for target increases.
86. Quoted by Zaleski (1962), p. 70.
87. Jasny (1961), p. 12.
88. Ibid.
89. Zaleski (1962), p. 72.
90. Dobb (1948), p. 245.
91. Jasny (1961), p. 66. Ibid., p. 28 also notes that inflation during the Stalin era would bring consumer prices to a peak of 36 times their 1928 level, while producer prices would rise only six times.
92. Jasny (1954), p. 57. See also Jasny (1961), p. 69, Davies (1960) and Zaleski (1962), pp. 107–9.
93. Lewin (1974a), p. 101.
94. Zaleski (1962), p. 72.
95. Jasny (1961), p. 73.
96. Zaleski (1980), p. 504.
97. See Swianiewicz (1965), pp. 139–47, and Carr (1958), ch. 10.

98. Quoted by Davies (1960), p. 28. Many similar quotations could be listed on the alleged Bolshevik ability of 'storming' various 'fortresses'.
99. Lewin (1974a), p. 100. Ibid., pp. 99, 105 also notes the 'astonishingly inadequate development of theory' during industrialization, and the bizarre fact that 'in this "planned economy", the very idea of planning was sacrificed'.
100. Statement by Strumilin, quoted by Lewin (1974a), p. 105.
101. Smolinsky (1967), p. 123.
102. Lewin (1974a), p. 109.

Chapter three – Formation of the Stalinist political system

1. The concept of 'political arena' is discussed in Lasswell (1964).
2. During December 1917 – March 1918, three seats were temporarily held by the Socialist Revolutionaries.
3. Hough and Fainsod (1979), pp. 74–80.
4. Ibid., pp. 79–81.
5. Quoted by ibid., p. 87.
6. Schapiro (1970), p. 215.
7. Susiluoto (1982), pp. 114–19.
8. Hough and Fainsod (1979), p. 149.
9. Cohen (1980), p. 231.
10. Kenez (1985), pp. 36–44.
11. Hough and Fainsod (1979), pp. 98–100.
12. Baranov (1987), p. 2.
13. See Enteen (1978), pp. 166–7, and Clark (1978), pp. 204–6, on this transition from 'radicalism' to 'Russianism'. The topic will be pursued at greater length in Chapter 4 below.
14. See further Hough & Fainsod (1979), pp. 101–3.
15. Cohen (1980), p. 214.
16. Rosenfeldt (1978), pp. 99–116.
17. Cf. Lewin (1985), p. 222.
18. Lewin (1968), p. 472.
19. Fitzpatrick (1978), pp. 181–8, 240, Fitzpatrick (1979), p. 386.
20. Bailes (1978), p. 259.
21. Getty (1987a), p. 198.
22. Ibid., pp. 203–4.
23. Ibid., p. 205. The quote is from Trotsky.
24. Ibid., p. 14.
25. Latsis (1987), pp. 88–9. Cf. also Getty (1987a), p. 204, who notes the former of these two aspects, but neglects the latter.
26. Latsis (1987), p. 88.
27. See 'Dizzy with Success' (*Golovokruzhenie ot uspekhov*), in *Pravda*, 2 March 1930, and 'Answer to our *Kolkhoz* Comrades' (*Otvet tovari-shcham kolkhoznikam*), in *Pravda*, 3 April 1930. These articles are reprinted in Stalin (1953).
28. Latsis (1987), p. 89.

29. Ibid., pp. 89–90. The attribution of the 'excesses' to overzealous young workers can also be found in Getty (1987b), p. 7.
30. Conquest (1986), p. 6.
31. Ibid., p. 7.
32. Ibid., pp. 306–7.
33. Wiles (1987), pp. 44–5.
34. Getty (1987b), p. 8.
35. Ibid.
36. Danilov (1988), p. 120.
37. Conquest (1987), p. 4.
38. Getty (1987a), p. 198, Getty (1987b), p. 7.
39. Novachitch (1987), pp. 46–7.
40. Khlebnyuk (1988), pp. 29–30.
41. Fainsod (1958), pp. 210–11.
42. Brzezinski (1960), p. 72.
43. Schapiro (1970), pp. 440–1.
44. Getty (1987a), p. 114.
45. Stalin (1937a), pp. 2–3.
46. Hough and Fainsod (1979), pp 159–61.
47. Cohen (1980), p. 342.
48. Ibid., pp. 365–8.
49. Schapiro (1970), p. 400.
50. Getty (1987a), p. 82.
51. Hough and Fainsod (1979), p. 159.
52. Rittersporn (1979a), pp. 41, 87, Rittersporn (1979b).
53. Rittersporn (1982), p. 109.
54. Schapiro (1970), p. 431.
55. Medvedev (1971), pp. 192, 239.
56. Fainsod (1958), p. 55.
57. Ibid., p. 137.
58. Karlgren (1942), p. 550.
59. Zhdanov (1937), p. 2.
60. Informatsionnoe (1937), p. 1.
61. Postanovlenie (1937), pp. 28–31.
62. Zhdanov (1937), p. 11. On Zhdanov's speech, cf. also Getty (1987a), pp. 141–3.
63. Zhdanov (1937), p. 11.
64. Ibid., p. 13.
65. Ibid., p. 14.
66. Ibid., pp. 15–16.
67. Stalin (1937b), p. 20. On Stalin's speeches, cf. also Getty (1987a), pp. 145–9.
68. Stalin (1937a), p. 1.
69. Ibid., p. 8.
70. Povysit (1937), p. 33.
71. Zhdanov (1937), pp. 8–9.
72. Stalin (1937a), p. 11, Nekotorye uroki (1937), p. 77.
73. Stalin (1937a), p. 3.

74. Fainsod (1958), p. 233.
75. Povysit (1937), p. 37.
76. Stalin (1937b), p. 19.
77. Ibid.
78. Molotov (1937), p. 15. On Molotov's speech, cf. also Getty (1987a), pp. 134–5.
79. Nekotorye uroki (1937), p. 79.
80. Ibid., pp. 80, 82.
81. Ibid., p. 79.
82. Pervye (1937), p. 75.
83. Pospelov (1937), p. 61.
84. Fainsod (1958), pp. 132–3.
85. Pospelov (1937), p. 61.
86. Pervye (1937), p. 75.
87. Ibid., p. 78.
88. Ibid., pp. 75, 77.
89. Pospelov (1937), p. 62.
90. Pervye (1937), p. 76.
91. Pospelov (1937), p. 67.
92. Ibid., p. 62.
93. Nekotorye itogy (1937), p. 11.
94. Ibid., p. 12.
95. Ibid.
96. Pervye (1937), p. 84.
97. Ibid.
98. Nekotorye itogi (1937), p. 10.
99. Stalin (1937b), pp. 21, 23–4.
100. Yaroslavskii (1937), pp. 31, 43. On Yaroslavskii's article, see also Getty (1987a), pp. 154–5.
101. Yaroslavskii (1937), p. 42.
102. Peredovaya (1937), p. 31.
103. Yaroslavskii (1937), p. 44.
104. Pospelov (1937), p. 59.
105. Fainsod (1958), p. 137.
106. Nekotorye itogi (1937), pp. 6–7.
107. Ibid., p. 16.
108. Fainsod (1958), p. 172.
109. Rigby (1983), p. 5.
110. Ibid., p. 7.
111. Khrushchev (1956), p. 23.
112. Schapiro (1970), p. 444.
113. Brzezinski (1960), pp. 100–1.
114. Ibid., p. 101.
115. Schapiro (1970), p. 437.
116. Khrushchev (1956), p. 21.
117. Cohen (1985), pp. 180–2.
118. Khrushchev (1956), p. 82.
119. Ibid., p. 83.

120. Tucker (1972), p. 179.
121. McCagg (1978), Dunmore (1980, 1984), Hahn (1982), Raanan (1983).
122. Raanan (1983), pp. 8–9.
123. Cohen (1985), p. 142.
124. Dunmore (1984), p. 156.
125. Wrong (1979), p. 161.

Chapter four – The Bolshevik order and Russian tradition

1. Cf. Moore (1978), p. 363, who argues that there were in 1905–7 prospects for a 'reformist integration', prospects that were quashed by Tsarist repression during 1907–12.
2. Fitzpatrick (1982), p. 3.
3. Besançon (1981), pp. 274–5.
4. Fulöp-Miller (1928), p. 54. Lenin obviously was prey to the popular notion that the city had been named after Tsar Peter, but this was not the case. The new capital was actually named after Saint Peter, in order to substantiate Tsar Peter's claim to have founded the New Rome – the original city being that of the apostle, i.e. Saint Peter (Lotman and Uspenskii, 1982, pp. 239–40).
5. Yanov (1981), p. 213, Tucker (1977), pp. 95, 98–101. Cf. also Selyunin (1988), pp. 180–2.
6. White (1979), pp. 34–5, Shanin (1982).
7. Cf. White (1979), pp. 30–1.
8. Walicki (1980), pp. 8–34, 106–11, Besançon (1981), pp. 37–45.
9. Besançon (1981), p. 9.
10. Ibid., pp. 9–10.
11. Ibid., quoting Solignac (1962), p. 125.
12. Tucker (1985), p. 36. Cf. also Susiluoto (1982), pp. 120–2.
13. Tumarkin (1983), p. 214. Tumarkin quotes two articles in the Soviet journal *Kommunisticheskie prosveshchenie*, No. 1, 1924.
14. Cf. Bodin (1987), pp. 38–40.
15. Tumarkin (1983), pp. 69–70, 86.
16. Ibid., pp. 89, 108. We may note here that the notion of presenting the Communist Party leader as a prophet is not exclusive to the Lenin cult. In April 1988, the Patriarch Pimen of Moscow addresses General Secretary Gorbachev as *provozvestnik*, which is the Russian literary form for prophet (*Pravda*, 30 April 1988).
17. Zaitsev (1980), pp. 6, 25.
18. Fulöp-Miller (1928), p. 38.
19. Uspenskii (1977), p. 113.
20. Tumarkin (1983), p. 127.
21. Zaitsev (1980), pp. 32–3.
22. Humphries (1983), p. 408.
23. Tumarkin (1983), pp. 127, 179.
24. Ibid., pp. 179, 196–7.
25. See Maslov (1988), p. 97.

26. Ibid.
27. Agurskii (1980b), pp. 16–21, 24–7, 34–49, 97.
28. Nivat (1982), pp. 62–79.
29. Zaitsev (1980), pp. 193–4, quoting Orlov (1964).
30. Agurskii (1980b), pp. 103–4, 135.
31. See Gerner (1972) and Agurskii (1980b), pp. 154–5, 251.
32. See Kleberg (1980), pp. 18–34.
33. Quoted from Baranov (1987), p. 2.
34. Ibid., p. 2, stresses precisely this point. Although he may certainly be suspected of ulterior motives, in trying to promote a similar view of the dissidents and emigrants in Gorbachev's Russia, this does not detract from his evaluation of the original process.
35. Agurskii (1980a), pp. 158–61, 185, 194, 260.
36. Chudakova (1987), p. 183.
37. Fulöp-Miller (1928), p. 469.
38. Agurskii (1980a), p. 218, Chudakova (1987), pp. 187–201.
39. Besançon (1986), p. 4.
40. Fitzpatrick (1978), pp. 28–40.
41. Literaturnyi (1987), pp. 41, 307.
42. Simon (1986), pp. 34–40.
43. Ibid., pp. 153–79.
44. Kozlowski (1988), p. 6.
45. Rittersporn (1979a), p. 861.
46. Fitzpatrick (1979), p. 399.
47. Lewin (1977), p. 130, Yanov (1981), pp. 254, 280.
48. Clark (1977), pp. 180, 187, 192–3.
49. Sironneau (1982), p. 227.
50. Ibid., p. 443.
51. Sinyavskii/A. Tertz (1983), pp. 251–6.
52. See Cherniavsky (1961), pp. 101–27.
53. Cf. Jancar (1984).
54. Jensen (1981), pp. 4–11.
55. Morin (1983).
56. Ibid., pp. 13–14, 127–31, 154–5, 163.
57. Kolakowski (1977), pp. 285–6.
58. Morin (1983), p. 165, Kolakowski (1977), p. 284.
59. White (1979), pp. 4–5.
60. Fainsod (1958), p. 454.
61. Cohen (1977), p. 27.
62. Hough (1987), p. 21.
63. White (1979), p. 5.
64. Ricoeur (1983), p. 73.
65. Fitzpatrick (1982), p. 112.
66. Fulöp-Miller (1928), pp. 477–8.
67. Braudel (1969), pp. 41–56.

Chapter five – Summary: political forces

1. Lewin (1968), p. 132.
2. A notable exception is Selyunin (1988), p. 166, who argues that the famine was actually created by government policy rather than *vice versa*. According to him, a crucial role was played by the 10 November 1917, decree against 'speculation'.
3. Carr (1952), p. 151.
4. Conquest (1986), p. 90.
5. Stites (1987), p. 28.
6. Quoted by Conquest (1986), p. 53.
7. Lewin (1985), p. 268.
8. Ibid., p. 191.
9. Conquest (1986), p. 232.
10. Ibid., pp. 190, 196, and chapter 9, *passim*, on the Kazakh tragedy.
11. In an interesting parallel, Hirschman notes that Castro, when deciding to reduce the scope for Voice in Cuban society, first allowed a considerable amount of Exit (to Miami) simply in order to defuse some of the pressure of discontent that would unavoidably follow (Hirschman, 1981, p. 227).
12. Conquest (1986), p. 152, makes the observation that the peasantry increasingly came to interpret the letters VKP as *Vtoroe Krepostnoe Pravo* (second serfdom), rather than in their correct meaning of *Vsesoyuznaya Kommunisticheskaya Partiya* (All-Union Communist Party).
13. Rosenfeldt (1978).
14. In a recent issue of *Sotsiologicheskie Issledovaniya* a rather striking personal account of precisely this perception of Stalin was published, authored by a certain A. T. Rybin (Rybin, 1988). Cf. also a penetrating discussion of Rybin's account, which was published in the same issue of that journal (Bestuzhev-Lada, 1988). Incidentally, the view of Stalin as a *Khozyain* also forms the mainstay of Alexander Zinoviev's presentation in *The Yawning Heights* (Zinoviev, 1981).
15. Hirschman (1981), p. 224.
16. Nove (1964), p. 29.
17. Fainsod (1953), p. 324–5.
18. Swearer (1960), p. 42.
19. Kornhauser (1960), p. 82.
20. Hough (1976a), p. 14–15.

Chapter six – The failure of intensification

1. Nove (1969), p. 368.
2. See further Gerner (1985), p. 181.
3. Stalin (1952), p. 73.
4. Jasny (1961), p. 73.
5. *Pravda*, 17 and 18 February 1956.
6. Nove (1969), p. 287.
7. Ibid., p. 290.

8. Ibid., p. 293.
9. The account of developments in agriculture during this period relies heavily on Hedlund (1984), ch. 3, *passim.*
10. Nove (1969), p. 296.
11. Shmelev (1964), p. 136.
12. Nove (1969), p. 299.
13. Ibid., p. 303.
14. Karcz (1979), p. 122. The livestock comparison holds true for Soviet territory within its present as well as its pre-war boundaries.
15. Cf. also Selyunin (1988), p. 177.
16. Yanov (1984), p. 40. See also Kaplan (1987), *passim,* on the nature of Party involvement in agriculture.
17. Hough (1971), p. 109.
18. In 1954, 76,000 out of a total of 87,000 *kolkhozy* had PPOs. By 1956, there were only about 7,000 which lacked them (Swearer, 1963, p. 19).
19. Hough (1971), pp. 108–16. Like the amalgamation campaign, this process had started already during Stalin's final years, but it did not gather momentum until after his death.
20. The *magnum opus* on the MTS system is Miller (1970).
21. Ibid., ch. 12.
22. See ibid., p.312, on the demise of the MTS system. The dominant explanation is that the growth in size of the farms had removed both economic and political reasons for having the MTSs. The political struggle over agricultural affairs is studied in Ploss (1965).
23. On this new agricultural bureaucracy, see Fainsod (1963), p. 226, Miller (1971), pp. 94–7, and Swearer (1963), pp. 28–39. Yanov's interpretation is that for a period of about 6 months an open struggle was allowed to develop between the Party professionals and the managerial elite in the countryside. When the latter came out on top, the former were crushed (Yanov, 1984, pp. 87–8).
24. Malenkov (1953).
25. McCauley (1976), ch. 7, discusses possible alternatives.
26. See Mills (1970) on the prelude to this gigantic programme.
27. See McCauley (1976), p. 83, Table 4.2.
28. For various reasons, much of this land was quickly lost again. According to ibid., p. 82, the 'true' total comes to no more than 32.7 million hectares. This of course remains a quite impressive figure.
29. Narkhoz (1987), p. 222.
30. Ibid., pp. 86, 88.
31. These two examples are from Abramov (1963), p. 109, and Yanov (1984), p. 50. A number of similar accounts can be found in Nove (1964, ch. 8, 1967). Hedlund (1984), ch. 5, *passim,* relies heavily on this type of source, in order to document the daily running of agricultural affairs.
32. In the Tselinnyi Krai, which was at the heart of the new lands, grain yields fell from 9.0 quintals per hectare in 1958, to 6.4 in 1961 and 3.1 in 1963 (Zoerb, 1965, p. 34). The record in terms of weed infestation goes to a farm in the Kochetav oblast, where 3,700 shoots of wild oats were

counted on one square meter of cropland. The roots went down 20 centimetres. Overall, the amount of grain containing more than 5 per cent weeds rose from 6.1 per cent in 1954–7, to 50.5 per cent in 1958–61 (McCauley, 1976, p. 181). On warnings issued by the Kazakh officials, see Mills (1970), pp. 60–1.

33. Indeed, in retirement, Khrushchev claimed that Soviet economists had estimated that yields amounting to only half of the official target of 10 centners per hectare would be needed to make the programme profitable (Talbott, 1974, p. 124). This may have been valid in the short run. However, one wonders if, on balance, there have not been more resources (labour, machinery, fertilizer, etc.) going into the new lands than produce coming out, taking the entire period together.

34. Volin (1970), pp. 497–8, 502.

35. Hedlund (1984), pp. 77–8.

36. Cf. Selyunin (1988), p. 186, who argues that War Communism reversed the process of agricultural reforms that had been initiated by Stolypin, after the abortive 1905 revolution, and brought back agricultural practices that had been prevalent in 'Old Russia'. As collectivization was in many ways a structural continuation of feudalism, Soviet agriculture is thus structurally more backward than Russian agriculture under the last Tsar.

37. Volin (1970), p. 384.

38. Diamond (1966), p. 346.

39. Ibid., p. 343.

40. Nove (1969), pp. 329, 337.

41. Ibid., p. 324.

42. On agricultural subsidies, see Treml (1982).

43. Yanov (1984), p. 56.

44. See Pospielovsky (1970) for the history of this experiment, and Hedlund and Lundahl (1982) for a more formal analysis of its possible effects.

45. Cf. Berliner (1957), pp. 78–9.

46. The reasons for this are dealt with at great length in Kaplan (1987).

47. Yanov (1984), p. 77.

48. SYP (1960), pp. 16–17.

49. Nove (1969), tables on pp. 325, 340.

50. Ibid., p. 326.

51. Ibid., pp. 326, 340.

52. These aspects will be left for our following discussion of the political dimension of the Khrushchev era, but it may be noted here that Nove reports having been told by a Soviet economist that the original 1956–60 plan was fundamentally feasible, and that the objections were chiefly political (ibid., p. 343).

53. See further ibid., p. 344.

54. Ibid., p. 343.

55. See further Nove (1962), *passim.*

56. Hoeffding (1959), pp. 65–6.

57. Ibid., p. 67.

58. Ibid., p. 70.

59. Nove (1969), p. 358.
60. Nove (1962), p. 14. See also Nove (1957).
61. Hoeffding (1959), p. 76.
62. See Meek (1956) on the early debate, and Zauberman (1960) on its flare-up in the 1950s.
63. E.g. Stalin (1952), pp. 19–25, 51–4.
64. Our following discussion of the debate on producer price formation relies heavily on Bornstein (1964). For some more general aspects of Soviet price theory, see also Bornstein (1962).
65. Bornstein (1964), pp. 23–45.
66. Ibid., p. 27.
67. Bornstein (1963), p. 44.
68. Ibid., p. 43.
69. Ibid., p. 52.
70. Schroeder (1969), p. 466.
71. Ibid., p. 470.
72. Sutela (1984), part I, ch. 3.
73. Ibid., pp. 76–7.
74. See further ibid., part II.
75. Ibid., p. 89.
76. Ibid., p. 203.
77. Goldman (1963), p. 498.
78. SYP (1960) presents and evaluates its proposed targets and objectives.
79. See Nove (1969), pp. 352–4.
80. Ibid., p. 361.
81. See further ibid., pp. 359–62.
82. Ibid., p. 360. In addition to the sources cited above, Kaser (1959) should also be mentioned in relation to the post-1957 period.
83. Hough (1965), p. 26.
84. Yanov (1984), p. 77.

Chapter seven – The Khrushchev experience

1. Viz., Conquest (1967), Linden (1966), Ploss (1965, 1971), Rush (1958), and Tatu (1969). A pioneering work in the genre, which deals with the Stalin period, is Nicolaevsky (1966).
2. Krawchenko (1985), pp. 149–50, 242–3.
3. Medvedev (1982), p. 245.
4. Linden (1966), *passim*. This was a process of development which was to be reversed, perhaps, only with the rule of Mikhail Gorbachev (cf. Hough, 1987, p. 21).
5. Khrushchev (1949a), p. 14.
6. Krawchenko (1985), p. 245.
7. Cf. Shulman (1963).
8. McCagg (1978).
9. Hahn (1982), pp. 184–5.
10. Cf. de Jonge (1986), pp. 488–99.
11. Nove (1964).

12. Cf. Carr (1961), p. 98, and ch. 4, *passim.*
13. Cf. Nettl (1967), p. 197, who says that 'without doubt all the developments since 1953 were built on Stalin's foundation.'
14. Conquest (1967), p. 200.
15. Quoted by Fainsod (1958), pp. 210–11.
16. Yakovlev (1953), p. 31, Shimarev (1953), p. 64.
17. Razvitie (1954), p. 10.
18. Ibid., p. 5.
19. Ibid., pp. 6, 11, Yakovlev (1953), p. 33.
20. Yakovlev (1953), p. 35.
21. Ibid., p. 36.
22. Razvitie (1954), p. 7.
23. Exactly when this change occurred is not known. The new name was first mentioned on 27 April 1954, but it had apparently been in existence for some time before that (Conquest, 1967, p. 222).
24. Ibid., p. 256.
25. Ibid., pp. 338–45.
26. See, for example, O demagogii (1957), p. 61.
27. Partiinaya (1956), p. 4.
28. Kakova (1955), p. 61, Partiinaya (1956), p. 7.
29. Linden (1966), p. 33.
30. Linden (1966), pp. 72–89.
31. Churaev (1957), p. 38.
32. Kerblay (1983), p. 249.
33. Lane (1976), p. 99.
34. Pisarev (1962), p. 77.
35. Lane (1971), p. 121.
36. Lane (1976), p. 99.
37. Schwenke (1980), pp. 9–10, 91–104.
38. Ibid., pp. 103–4.
39. Gorbachev (1987e), p. 14.
40. Kritika (1961), p. 80.
41. Podbirat (1961), p. 22.
42. Linden (1966), pp. 149–51.
43. Rodionov (1962), p. 73.
44. Ibid., p. 74.
45. Ibid., pp. 72–3.
46. Trotsky (1937).
47. Djilas (1957).
48. Ibid., p. 65.
49. Ibid., p. 169.
50. Ibid., p. 65.
51. Cf. Nove (1975).
52. Voslenskii (1984) is the first Russian edition.
53. Ibid., pp. 197–217.
54. Ibid., 119–42.
55. Ibid., pp. 177–81.
56. Nettl (1967), p. 206.

57. Cf. ibid., p. 218.
58. Cf. Conquest (1967), p. 283.

Chapter eight – Promoting patriotism: The era of mature Stalinism

1. Mazour (1971), pp. 32, 282, 284, 306, 314–17.
2. Ivanov (1973).
3. Zimin and Khoroshkevich (1982), pp. 160–6.
4. Kemp-Welch (1983), p. 132. See also Fitzpatrick (1976).
5. Conquest (1967), p. 15.
6. Cf. Heller (1985), p. 274.
7. Seriot (1985), pp. 51–3.
8. Cf. Heller (1985), p. 274.
9. Sambor (1985), p. 369.
10. Cf. Seriot (1985), pp. 49–53.
11. Ibid., pp. 339–41.
12. Bourmeyster (1983), p. 35.
13. Bourmeyster (1985), p. 5.
14. Pospelov (1949), p. 12.
15. Ibid., p. 9.
16. Pospelov (1950), pp. 12–16, 24. (Quotation on p. 24.)
17. See Rosenfeldt (1978), pp. 129–30.
18. Poskrebyshev (1950), p. 23.
19. Molotov (1952), p. 4, Malenkov (1952), p. 63.
20. Pospelov (1951), pp. 9–16.
21. Pospelov (1952), pp. 9–18.
22. Vsepobedayushchaya (1953), pp. 3–13.
23. Tumarkin (1983), pp. 257–9.
24. Stepanyan (1949a), pp. 14–16.
25. Peredovaya (1949a), p. 2.
26. Peredovaya (1949b), p. 4.
27. Peredovaya (1950), p. 4.
28. de Jonge (1986), p. 494, quoting *Pravda*, 9 October 1952.
29. Cf. de Jonge (1986), pp. 494–5.
30. Malenkov (1953), p. 13, Peredovaya (1953c), pp. 23–32.
31. Peredovaya (1953c), p. 15.
32. Narod (1953), pp. 46–7.
33. Konstantinov (1953), pp. 60–1.
34. Khrustov (1953), p. 81.
35. Beria (1949), p. 30.
36. Blagoi (1951), p. 36.
37. Ibid., p. 37.
38. Yakubovskaya (1953), p. 29.
39. Khrushchev (1949a), p. 29.
40. Khrushchev (1949b), p. 83.
41. Bagirov (1950), pp. 46, 51.
42. Karotamm (1949), pp. 29–30.
43. Zytis and Krastyn (1953), p. 115.

44. Latsis (1953), p. 24.
45. Ibid., p. 29.
46. Niyazov (1953), pp. 30–7.
47. Stepanyan (1949b), p. 20.
48. Fedoseev (1953), p. 13.
49. Yakubovskaya (1953), p. 29.
50. Kammari (1949), p. 39.
51. Zhudin (1949), p. 29.
52. Gorkin (1949), pp. 53–6.
53. Azizyan (1950), p. 29.
54. Kammari (1953), pp. 15, 23, 25.
55. Bazhan (1953), p. 82.
56. Cf. Karklins (1986), p. 207.
57. Trofimov (1950), p. 37.
58. Myasnikov (1951), p. 39.
59. Peredovaya (1951), p. 7.
60. Maslin (1949), pp. 31–43. (Quotation on pp. 42–3.)
61. Blagoi (1951), p. 43.
62. Ryurikov (1952), p. 43–7.
63. Berestnev (1951), p. 27.
64. Ivanov (1951), p. 73.
65. Cf. Silberner (1983), p. 291.
66. Peredovaya (1949a), p. 3.
67. Cf. Hahn (1982), p. 164.
68. Peredovaya (1949a), pp. 5–11.
69. Khromov (1949), p. 76.
70. Chernov (1949), p. 32. The repetition of 'Russian science, Soviet science' is a direct translation.
71. See de Jonge (1986), p. 502.
72. Burdzhalov (1951), p. 20.
73. de Jonge (1986), p. 501.
74. Golovchenko (1949), pp. 39–48.
75. Peredovaya (1953b), p. 13.
76. See Khrushchev (1949a), p. 29.
77. Pospelov (1949), p. 12.
78. Peredovaya (1953c), p. 21.
79. Berestnev (1951), p. 32.
80. Heller (1985), pp. 41–52.
81. Doktor (1988), p. 3.
82. Ibid.
83. Ibïd.
84. de Jonge (1986), p. 489.
85. Cf. Hahn (1982) and Rosenfeldt (1971).
86. Cf. Selyunin (1988), p. 178.
87. Cf. Conquest (1967), pp. 195–227.
88. Spechler (1982).

89. *Kolokol* was published in London, but it 'poured into Russia in numerous copies', to become in 1857–61 'the principal political force in Russia' (Mirsky, 1958, p. 220).
90. Spechler (1982), pp. 240–2.
91. Luchterhand (1976), pp. 123–34, Rothenberg (1978), p. 185.
92. Tumarkin (1983), pp. 260–1.
93. See de Jonge (1986), pp. 490–5.
94. Ibid., p. 495.
95. See Heer (1971).

Chapter nine – Summary: the role of ideology

1. *Pravda*, 17 October 1964. Quoted by Rakowska-Harmstone (1976), p. 70.
2. See further Elster (1985b), ch. II.
3. Hedlund (1989) analyses the case of the peasantry in a perspective similar to the one used here.
4. Hirschman (1970), ch. 7.
5. Ibid., pp. 94–5, in particular notes 10–11. In an appendix, a tentative design is set up for actual testing of the effects of severity of initiation on activism (ibid., appendix A).
6. It may be noted that the collected works of Marx and Engels run into forty-one volumes while those of Lenin occupy no less than fifty-five.
7. Barry and Barner-Barry (1978), p. 45.
8. Hirschman (1970), p. 76.
9. Elster (1986), p. 3.
10. Grushin (1988), p. 29. We must, of course, recognize that this is not an exclusively Soviet problem. We might also refer, for example, to frequent American phrases such as 'Congress thinks' or 'Congress has decided', which analytically make no more sense than the phrase 'The Party has decided.' In the Soviet case, however, it is not simply a question of a certain manner of speech, but rather of a deep symbolic meaning.
11. Barry and Barner-Barry (1978), p. 32.
12. Linden (1966), p. 229.
13. See further Elster (1986), p. 19.
14. Barry and Barner-Barry (1978), p. 8.
15. Tumarkin (1983), p. 130.
16. Barry and Barner-Barry (1978), p. 3.
17. Gellner (1987), pp. 127–8. (Emphasis added.)
18. Tumarkin (1983), p. 148.
19. Milkov and Pilyogina (1987), p. 266.
20. Likhachev (1988a), p. 10.
21. Likhachev (1988b), p. 253.
22. Froyanov (1988), p. 328.
23. Ibid., pp. 288–329.
24. Lewin (1985), p. 70.
25. Merton (1968), p. 431.

26. Ibid.
27. Ibid.
28. One consequence of this phenomenon is that one must be wary of the results of Soviet sociological survey research. Frankness to strangers or – worse – to local Party officials will in this context be a rare flower indeed. Cf. Karklins (1986), pp. 108–9.
29. Motyl (1987), pp. 107–10.
30. Shmelev (1987), p. 154.
31. Olshanskii (1987), pp. 16–17.
32. Guerilla fighting in Lithuania and Estonia in the late 1940s should be seen more as an immediate consequence of the Soviet occupation, than as an endogenous feature of the Soviet system as such.
33. Bialer (1986), p. 266.
34. Pisarev (1962), pp. 109–10.
35. Linden (1966), p. 209.
36. Ulyanov (1987), pp. 52–3.
37. Gorbachev (1987a), p. 13.
38. Shmelev (1988), p. 174.

Chapter ten – Stagnation and the reforms that never were

1. See further Kushnirsky (1982), p. 12.
2. Nove (1972), p. 360.
3. In 1965, he even made the cover of *Time* magazine (12 February 1965).
4. Gregory and Stuart (1986), p. 397.
5. It may be of interest to note here, that many of the same ideas and criticisms had been expressed by the very same Liberman as early as 1955, in the economics monthly *Voprosy Ekonomiki*, and in 1956, in the official Party journal *Kommunist*. This certainly supports the idea of him being used, in 1962, as a mere figurehead, for the expression of opinions that had been sanctioned by the general change in atmosphere that characterized the 1961 Party Programme. His *Pravda* article is reprinted (in English) in Liberman (1972).
6. On Liberman's career, see Stuart (1967). On his proposals and their general background, see Goldman (1963), Nove (1963) and Kaser (1968).
7. Liberman (1972), p. 313.
8. Ibid., pp. 310–11.
9. Zauberman (1963), pp. 736–7.
10. See further ibid., pp. 742–3. Nemchinov is quoted from *Pravda*, 21 September 1962. An English translation of that article can be found in Bornstein and Fusfeld (1970).
11. This too is a problem that is still waiting to be resolved at this present time.
12. Liberman (1972), p. 315.
13. Zauberman (1963), p. 740.
14. Nove (1977), p. 309.

15. Zverev (1962), p. 97. An English translation of that article can be found in Bornstein and Fusfeld (1970).
16. See, further, Sharpe (1965), Felker (1966), pp. 58–67, and Goldman (1970). A number of contributions to both the debate around Liberman's original proposals, and around those reform measures which were subsequently introduced, have been collected – in English translation – in Sharpe (1966).
17. Expression borrowed from Nove (1972), p. 354. See also Gregory and Stuart (1986), pp. 399–408, and Schroeder (1973).
18. Kosygin (1972), p. 321.
19. Schroeder (1968), p. 14. Ibid., pp. 13–14, also provides an illustrative example of what this could look like.
20. Nove (1972), p. 356.
21. Schroeder (1968), p. 16.
22. Ibid., p. 7.
23. Gregory and Stuart (1986), p. 402.
24. Although considerably different in nature from their counterparts in the West, the power of Soviet trade unions should not be underestimated. The following account by a Swedish diplomat is rather striking: 'During one visit to an industrial enterprise, we thought that we had spotted the *politruk*, an abrasive, loud man who interrupted the director without hesitation or apologies. It turned out to be the senior trade-union representative in the enterprise' (Åslund, 1987a, p. 78).
25. Schroeder (1973), p. 30.
26. Ibid., p. 31.
27. Ibid., p. 22.
28. Ibid., p. 38.
29. Bornstein (1985), p. 25.
30. Hanson (1983), p. 11, footnote 2.
31. On Gorbachev's economic advisers, see, further, Åslund (1987b).
32. Hanson (1983), p. 9.
33. See further ibid, pp. 2–5, and Bornstein (1985), pp. 9–11.
34. See further Bornstein (1985), pp. 3–5.
35. According to Selyunin (1988), p. 188, the Soviet bureaucracy 'every year prepares one hundred billion pages of documents, i.e. about one page per day *per capita* of the population. Of these, at least 90 per cent are pointless – they will simply not be read by anyone.'
36. Hanson (1983), p. 9.
37. Ibid., p. 6.
38. Ibid., p. 5
39. Bornstein (1985), p. 6.
40. Hanson (1983), p. 8.
41. *Pravda*, 17 November 1981.
42. *Nedelya*, 8 January 1987.
43. Schroeder (1979).
44. Ibid., p. 340.
45. Nove (1977), p. 313.
46. *Moscow News*, supplement, no. 4, 1988.

47. Kornai (1986), provides an excellent overview of the problems and prospects of the Hungarian reform process. For further references, see the sources cited therein.
48. Quoted by Schroeder (1968), p. 1.
49. Ibid., p. 21.
50. Gorbachev (1986), p. 29.
51. With the benefit of hindsight, one is easily impressed by the main thrust of Naum Jasny's classic 1951 article '*Kolkhozy*, the Achilles' heel of the Soviet regime' (Jasny, 1951). Achilles, we might add, died from his wound.
52. Cf. Bialer (1986), p. 78, who reports astonishment when being informed by a Soviet scholar of the latter's dependence on materials concerning Soviet development that are regularly published by the US Congress' Joint Economic Committee.
53. Hedlund (1984), p. 88, and Narkhoz (1986), p. 180.
54. Narkhoz (1963), p. 6, Narkhoz (1987), p. 5.
55. Table 10.1, and population data from Narkhoz (1972), p. 7, and Narkhoz (1981), p. 7.
56. Table 10.1, and population data from Narkhoz (1987), p. 373.
57. Narkhoz (1986), p. 303.
58. Ibid., p. 304.
59. Manevich (1981), p. 60.
60. Narkhoz (1987), p. 275. The definition used here is *po vsemu kompleksu rabot* (the whole complex of works), which includes farm construction, agricultural research, material supply and services (the former Selkhoz-tekhnika), food processing, and irrigation and drainage (the Minvodkhoz). A narrower definition, which includes only the actual farm sector, gives a figure of about 20 per cent, while a broader definition, which includes the entire APK, as defined in Table 10.3, produces a figure of around one third of total Soviet investment.
61. Narkhoz (1987), p. 292.
62. Narkhoz (1981), p. 218. Tractors increased from 1,613,000 to 2,562,000, combines from 520,000 to 722,000, and trucks from 945,000 to 1,596,000. One is certainly tempted, in this context, to recall an expression once used by Daniel Yergin in a review of Joseph Berliner's book *The Innovation Decision in Soviet Industry*: 'The Russians are keeping score in the wrong game.' (*Guardian Weekly*, 5 September 1976, p. 18).
63. Narkhoz (1981), p. 251.
64. *Sotsialisticheskaya Industriya*, 1 October 1982.
65. *Izvestia*, 6 December 1986.
66. Shmelev (1987), p. 158.
67. Goodman, Hughes and Schroeder (1987), pp. 108–9.
68. Narkhoz (1987), p. 278.
69. Ibid., p. 277.
70. Narkhoz (1966), p. 366, Narkhoz (1981), p. 239.
71. Narkhoz (1987), p. 252. (Annual averages, 1983 prices.)
72. Ibid., p. 242.

73. Fees for the use of ground water were introduced in 1984, but many users, including the farms, still get it for free – and use it accordingly (Yuzufovich, 1988, p. 71).
74. See in particular Shmelev (1988), p. 172.
75. Kak sovershaetsya (1987), p. 218.
76. See, further, ibid., *passim.*
77. *Izvestia*, 24 October 1984.
78. According to a recent Soviet source, the total salt deposit already amounts to no less than 75 million tons annually. A freight train carrying this load would be 12,000 km long (Kaipbergenov, 1987, p. 6).
79. Khachaturov (1982), p. 27.
80. Suslov (1982), p. 27.
81. Hedlund (1984), p. 132.
82. Gumerov (1979), p. 86.
83. Treml (1982), p. 179.
84. Yanov (1984), p. 9.
85. It is symptomatic that the immediate Soviet reaction to the 1981 harvest failure was the classic one of trying to cover up what was happening. Figures on the grain harvest for that year were withheld, and when the same practice was repeated in the following four years, many Western observers were beginning to accept the permanent loss of yet another official Soviet statistic. In 1986, however, under the auspices of Gorbachev's *glasnost*, the publication of grain harvest figures was resumed, and the figures then released were strikingly similar to those estimates which had been circulating in the West (Narkhoz, 1986, p. 180).
86. White (1986), p. 481, argues that this pressure may actually have been a determining factor in the decision to launch that programme.
87. *Pravda*, 25 May 1982. See also Prodovolvstvennaya (1982).
88. Prodovolvstvennaya (1982), pp. 18–19.

Chapter eleven – The politics of stagnation

1. Barghoorn and Remington (1986), p. 277.
2. Quoted by Schuman (1967), pp. 6–7.
3. See Skilling and Griffiths (1971), Skilling (1983), Gustafson (1981).
4. See e.g. the various contributions to Skilling and Griffiths (1971).
5. Dienes (1983).
6. Skilling (1983).
7. Kelley (1971), p. 321.
8. Gustafson (1981), p. 158.
9. Fainsod (1953).
10. Hough and Fainsod (1979).
11. Schapiro (1979), p. 8.
12. Ibid.
13. Ibid. See also Barghoorn and Remington (1986), pp. 303–4, on the prerogative of the Politburo.

14. Cf. Shmelev (1987, 1988), Medvedev (1988), Popov (1988), and Selyunin (1988). We return to these at great length in our final chapter.
15. See Barghoorn and Remington (1986), p. 211.
16. See Rakowska-Harmstone (1976), p. 76.
17. Ibid., p. 61. See also Leninskie (1965), p. 89.
18. Hough (1976b), pp. 118–23.
19. Ibid., p. 132.
20. Cf. Davies (1982), pp. 214–15.
21. Edinstvo (1965), pp. 41–2.
22. Ibid., pp. 46–7.
23. Karpov and Melkov (1965), p. 46.
24. Kulikov (1965), p. 61.
25. Slepov and Yudin (1969), p. 50, Stepin (1969), pp. 37–8, Tsvigun (1969), pp. 103–4.
26. Sharlet (1984), p. 251.
27. Ejvegård (1981), p. 75.
28. As an illustration, we may note that while half of the members of the Central Committee were replaced between 1956 and 1961, the corresponding rate of replacement between 1966 and 1971, and between 1971 and 1976 (the points of reference are given by the years when Party Congresses were held), was only about a quarter (Kerblay, 1983, p. 263).
29. Carrre d'Encausse (1982), p. 100.
30. Brown (1975), p. 147.
31. Bialer (1986), p. 154.
32. White (1986), p. 470.
33. Some representative targets for the attack were Drewnowski (1982), Goldman (1983), Burks (1984), Hedlund (1984), and Pipes (1984).
34. Burks (1984), p. 71.
35. Pipes (1984), p. 50.
36. White (1986), p. 470.
37. Triska (1977), p. 149.
38. Adams (1983), p. 179.
39. Zaslavsky and Brym (1978), p. 368, argue that, among other records, 'documentation attesting to public service work is required for changing jobs, travelling abroad, obtaining better housing, and so forth.'
40. Fainsod (1953), p. 323.
41. Schapiro (1965), p. 117.
42. Jacobs (1970), p. 61.
43. Zaslavsky and Brym (1978).
44. Ibid., p. 363.
45. Ibid., pp. 364–5.
46. Ibid., p. 371 (Italics in the original.)
47. This section relies heavily on White (1983), *passim*. On the role of letters under Stalin, see also Inkeles and Geiger (1968).
48. On this topic, see further Adams (1981).
49. White (1983), p. 57.
50. Ibid., pp. 47–9, 54.

51. Quoted in Vanneman (1977), p. 157.
52. Ibid.
53. See Thompson (1985), p. 185.
54. Vanneman (1977), pp. 25–6.
55. Ibid., pp. 50–2, 126.
56. Ibid., pp. 19, 153.
57. Ibid., p. 222.
58. Ibid., p. 231.
59. Ibid., pp. 232–3.
60. Friedgut (1979), pp. 22–3.
61. Ibid., pp. 17, 44, 314.
62. Ibid., pp. 289, 301.
63. Ibid., pp. 299, 302.
64. Ibid., p. 319.
65. Ibid., p. 323.
66. Cf. the title of Afanasiev (1975).
67. Cocks (1976), p. 163.
68. Ibid.
69. Ibid., p. 170.
70. Brezhnev (1971), pp. 44–6.
71. Susiluoto (1982), p. 187.
72. Cocks (1976), p. 176.
73. Ibid.
74. Volkov (1976), pp. 116–18.
75. Osipov *et al* (1976), p. 15.
76. O merakh (1967).
77. See Weinberg (1974).
78. Sotsialno (1976), pp. 47–50.
79. Ibid.
80. Kelle (1978), pp. 38–41.
81. Afanasiev (1975), pp. 78, 88, 99–102.
82. Cf. Gerner and Lundgren (1985), pp. 412–14; Laird and Hoffmann (1984), pp. 829–30, Kerblay (1983), p. 260.
83. Barghoorn and Remington (1986), p. 190. For relevant policy declarations, see also Elyutin (1972), Fedoseev (1972) and Suslov (1972).
84. Smolyanskii (1987), pp. 41, 184.
85. Mickiewicz (1972), pp. 574–80.
86. Aleksandrov (1972), *passim* and, especially, pp. 64–5; Povyshat (1975), p. 6.
87. Grushin (1970), pp. 46–8.
88. Grushin (1972), p. 206.
89. Sherkovich (1976), pp. 211–13.
90. Safarov (1975), pp. 120–1, 173–4.
91. Ibid., pp. 237–8.
92. Osipov *et al* (1976), p. 106.
93. Problemy (1976), p. 188.
94. Rutkevich (1977), p. 15.

95. Cf. Warshofsky Lapidus (1984), pp. 703–11.
96. Problemy (1976), pp. 188–9.
97. Zapasewicz (1977), pp. 329–30.
98. According to Rutkevich, in 1987, work undertaken by the Centre for Study of Public Opinion at the Central Committee of the Communist Party of the Georgian republic 'remained a single beacon in the night' (Intervyu, 1987, p. 32.)
99. Borcke and Simon (1980), p. 147.
100. See e.g. Saunders (1974).

Chapter twelve – Return to Russia

1. Tumarkin (1983), pp. 262–8.
2. See Etkind (1978), Lourie (1975), Maltsev (1976), Shatz (1980), and Feldbrugge (1975).
3. See further Allworth (1980).
4. See Alexeyeva (1985), ch. 1–3.
5. See Krawchenko (1985), pp. 186–202, 250–4, on general aspects, and Kolarz (1961), pp. 227–44, on the Church.
6. See further Feshbach (1982).
7. Gitelman (1983), p. 39.
8. Feshbach (1982), p. 33.
9. Azrael (1978), p. 365.
10. See Carrre d'Encausse (1978).
11. Solchanyk (1982), p. 33–9.
12. Tarasenko (1978), pp. 66–76.
13. Ibid., pp. 68, 73, 75.
14. See Simon (1986), pp. 369–95.
15. Fedoseev (1980), pp. 62, 66–9.
16. Rashidov (1979), Kunaev (1980).
17. See e.g. Connor (1979).
18. McAuley (1979), p. 317, writes that 'after a quarter of a century of barbarity under Stalin, the USSR bids fair to become more civilized than the rest of Europe.'
19. Grushin (1980).
20. McAuley (1979), p. 206.
21. Grushin (1980), pp. 72–82.
22. See Carrre d'Encausse (1978), Simon (1986).
23. Jones and Grupp (1982).
24. Lane (1981), pp. 46–7.
25. Ibid., p. 238.
26. Lane (1984), p. 213.
27. Ibid., p. 215.
28. Sinitsyn (1977), pp. 8, 26, 110–12.
29. Petrovskii (1980).
30. Cf. Håstad (1983).
31. Bakhtin (1979), p. 369.

32. Personal communication to the authors from Malcolm Dixelius, former Moscow correspondent of the Swedish Broadcasting Company, after an interview with Rasputin.
33. Cf. Håstad (1979), pp. 53–5, 85, Agursky (1980a).
34. Halperin (1976), pp. 76–82.
35. Narovchatov (1980), p. 74.
36. Pashuto (1980).
37. Klibanov (1980).
38. Kulikovskaya (1980).
39. Beskrovnyi (1980), p. 245.
40. See e.g. Borodin (1980).
41. Alekseev (1981).
42. Kirpichnikov (1980), pp. 110, 115, 119–20 (quotation).
43. Kargalov (1980), p. 59.
44. Loshchits (1980), p. 363.
45. Kuznetsov (1980).
46. Cf. Kruglyi (1988), *passim.*
47. Nemerknyshchaya (1980), Zhivaya (1980).
48. Pashuto (1980), p. 90.
49. Kozmin (1980), p. 18.
50. Nesterov (1987), pp. 33, 60.
51. Krupin (1980a).
52. Ibid., p. 4.
53. Rasputin (1980), p. 16.
54. Krupin (1980b), pp. 262–3.
55. See Yanov (1978), pp. 130–1, and *passim,* Szporluk (1980), Dunlop (1983).
56. Trifonov (1980).
57. Halperin (1985), pp. 5, 61–74.
58. Yevtushenko (1980).
59. Simon (1986), pp. 289, 381, 391. For eloquent examples, see Rashidov (1976, 1979).
60. Rashidov (1979), p. 15.
61. Barghoorn (1980), p. 64.
62. Likhachev (1980a, 1980b).
63. Likhachev (1980c).
64. Agursky (1980a).
65. Ricoeur (1978), p. 9.
66. Brezhnev (1981), p. 50.
67. Markov (1981), p. 2. Cf. also Rutych (1981), pp. 27–9.
68. Rutych (1981), p. 27.
69. Vsegda (1981), p. 44.
70. Lourie (1975), pp. 46–7, Kerblay (1983), p. 297.
71. Ideologicheskie (1988), p. 18.
72. Afanasiev (1978).
73. A cryptical dialogue between the latter two took place by means of Rasputin's 'answering' a sympathetic statement by Solzhenitsyn over the

BBC in February 1979, with an equally sympathetic declaration in *So-vetskaya Rossiya* in May of that same year (Agursky, 1980a).
74. Durham Hannah (1976).
75. Tökes (1974).
76. See, further, Bloch and Reddaway (1977), Bukowskij (1971), Medvedev and Medvedev (1971), Pliouchtch (1977).
77. See Labedz (1972), pp. 187–233.
78. Cf. O lektsiyakh (1970), Ivanov (1988), and Zwykle sprawy (1988).
79. Alexeyeva (1985).
80. Suslov (1977, 1980), Tsvigun (1981).
81. Cf. Bromlei (1983), p. 63.

Chapter thirteen – Summary: rationality and Soviet man

1. Harsanyi (1986), p. 92.
2. Parfit (1986), pp. 37–8.
3. It is a tragic historical irony that Nyerere would unknowingly repeat a number of mistakes previously committed by Stalin, during the process of Soviet collectivization. It is also symptomatic of the difference in personality between the two that, when peasant opposition grew strong, Nyerere chose to back down rather than proceed to crush all opposition.
4. North (1981), p. 49.
5. It might be argued here that commercial sales promotion has long functioned in this way in the West, and there are undoubtedly important psychological similarities between the ways in which the respective 'products' are sold. This analogy, however, is seriously misleading in the sense that Western commercials are not instrumental in the hands of the regime in the same way as are the pronouncements of ideology in the hands of the Soviet leadership.
6. North (1981), p. 54.
7. Cf. Elster (1985b), p. 110.
8. Ibid., Part III uses La Fontaine's fable of the 'Sour Grapes' as an illustration of such a process of dissonance reduction.
9. Danilov (1988).
10. Elster (1985b), p. 36.
11. Zinoviev (1981), *in toto*, forms an illustration of the absurdities involved in this process.
12. A Soviet dictionary offers the following more precise definition: 'actions intended to produce an outwardly favourable impression' (Slovar, 1984, p. 244).
13. See, in particular, the cover illustration of *Krokodil*, no. 9, 1987.
14. *Krokodil*, no. 35, 1987.
15. Sutela (1987) presents the interesting Soviet debate on the role of economic incentives that took place during the decisive years 1929 and 1930.
16. Stalin (1953), p. 543.
17. Hirschman (1986), p. 82.

18. One illustration of the dangers inherent in simple social life is the case of Isaak Babel, who was arrested in late 1940, charged with having had connections with Ezhov, the former head of the security police. The latter having been shot as an 'enemy of the people', Babel's crime was that he had known Ezhov's wife. He, too, was subsequently shot. The story is reported in Vaksberg (1988), p. 12.
19. Shmelev (1988), p. 168.
20. Cf. Selyunin and Khanin (1987).
21. Zaslavsky and Brym (1978), pp. 365–6, 370.
22. Håstad (1983).
23. In an interview on Danish Television, on 24 March 1988, the eminent Soviet writer Fazil Iskander, who is a valiant champion of *perestroika*, underlined the importance of realizing the consequences of 20 years of negative selection. Commenting on the same in *Literaturnaya Gazeta*, Yevgenii Yevtushenko simply says that 'the best people were mowed down' (Yevtushenko, 1988, p. 13).
24. Zaslavskaya (1987).
25. Zinoviev (1981), p. 526.
26. Shmelev (1988), p. 163.

Chapter fourteen – Opening Pandora's box

1. Gorbachev (1985), pp. 6–7, 15.
2. Tatu (1987), p. 109.
3. Andropov (1982), pp. 14–22.
4. According to Listov (1988), p. 12, the expressions *perestroika, glasnost*, and *uskorenie* were all ubiquitous in Party statements and documents in 1920–1. There is also a wealth of illustrations to their subsequent use. To give but three examples, we may recall that the 1932 decree which sealed the fate of RAPP and Proletkult was entitled '*O perestroike literaturno-khudozhestvennykh organisatsii*' (On *perestroika* of literary-cultural organizations), and that speaking to the sixteenth Congress of the Communist Party of the Ukraine, Khrushchev underlined the necessity of energetically 'initiating a *perestroika*' of the republic's industries and co-operatives. Moreover, in the article on Kuibyshev in the second edition of the Great Soviet Encyclopedia, it is said that, while serving as chairman of the Gosplan in the early 1930s, Kuibyshev had laboured hard to carry out a *perestroika* of its organization (Bolshaya, 1953, pp. 620–1).
5. Brezhnev (1981), p. 61.
6. Cf. the title of Gorbachev (1987b).
7. Cf. the testimony of Soviet sociologist Shkaratan in a 1988 interview with the Polish weekly *Polityka* (Zwykle sprawy, 1988, p. 10).
8. Andropov (1983).
9. Andropov (1982), p. 15.
10. Andropov (1983).
11. Bialer (1986), p. 95.
12. Ibid.

13. Chernenko (1984c), pp. 1–2.
14. Markov (1984), p. 3.
15. Chernenko (1984a), pp. 5–7.
16. Chernenko (1984b), p. 35.
17. Chernenko (1984c), p. 2.
18. Cf. e.g. Effendiev (1982), p. 61.
19. Lyashko (1982), p. 39.
20. One would certainly be less sceptical of the true Soviet intentions if, for example, it had not been the case that news of the release of political prisoners is routinely communicated by the press secretary of the MID, the Ministry of Foreign Affairs.
21. Hough (1988), pp. 29, 31.
22. Ibid., pp. 34–5.
23. See, for example, Tatyana Zaslavskaya's 1983 'Novosibirsk report' (Zaslavskaya, 1984).
24. *Pravda*, 23 November 1985.
25. Doolittle and Hughes (1987), p. 36.
26. Ibid.
27. Hough (1988), p. 39.
28. Gorbachev (1986), p. 29.
29. *Pravda*, 29 March 1986.
30. Gorbachev (1986), p. 8.
31. Shmelev (1988), p. 162.
32. *Pravda*, 28 May 1986.
33. *Pravda*, 21 November 1986.
34. It is also interesting to note here that, according to Maslov (1988), p. 100, the very concept of a *Rechtsstaat*, which is now known in Russian as *pravovoe gosudarstvo*, has been absent from the Soviet debate since the 1920s. Although a *perestroika* of the legal system was indeed announced at the June 1988 Party Conference, there is obviously a long way to go from discussion to practice.
35. Cf. Radio Liberty (1986, 1987).
36. Shmelev (1988), p. 166.
37. Hough (1988), p. 37.
38. Gorbachev (1987a), p. 27.
39. See further Schroeder (1987).
40. Hough (1988), p. 34.
41. Gorbachev (1987b), p. 13.
42. Gorbachev (1987c), p. 3.
43. *Sovetskaya Rossiya*, 4 October 1987.
44. Gorbachev (1987d).
45. Cf. Shatrov (1988), p. 5. In August 1988, the *Ogonek* journalist Anatolii Golovkov speaks of this period as 'the three weeks of counter-revolution' (Golowkow, 1988, p. 12).
46. *Sovetskaya Rossiya*, 13 March 1987. The article was promptly reprinted in *Neues Deutschland*.
47. *Pravda*, 5 April 1988.
48. Gorbachev (1988c), p. 38.

49. A draft text of this charter was published in January 1987 (*Ekonomiches-kaya Gazeta*, No. 3, 1987). Gorbachev's speech at the congress can be found in Gorbachev (1988b).
50. Wädekin (1988).
51. Cf. Hanson (1988).
52. For recent accounts of the former problems, see Gerner and Lundgren (1985), and Ziegler (1987); for accounts of the latter, see Jones and Grupp (1987), Arutyunyan and Bromlei (1986), and Vishnevskii *et al.* (1988).
53. Zalygin (1987).
54. See Gerner and Lundgren (1978).
55. Khorev (1986), p. 10.
56. Kak sovershaetsya (1987).
57. Ibid., p. 193.
58. Ibid., pp. 198–203.
59. Ibid., p. 206.
60. Ibid., p. 208.
61. Ibid., pp. 218–19.
62. Ådahl and Perlowski (1978), p. 62.
63. Cherez (1988), p. 2.
64. Yuzufovich (1988), p. 34.
65. Monin (1988), pp. 164–5.
66. *Pravda*, 17 January 1988.
67. Yablokov (1988), p. 11.
68. Koptyug (1988), p. 25.
69. According to Koptyug, the Soviet Union has failed in its attempts at conserving energy. The plan in 1987 was to decrease energy consumption by 1.8 per cent, but in reality it increased by 0.9 per cent (ibid., p. 26).
70. Gorbachev (1986), p. 28.
71. Andreev (1988), p. 11.
72. Ideologicheskie (1988), p. 10.
73. Andreev (1988), p. 11.
74. Chernyak (1988), p. 10.
75. Selyunin (1988), p. 188.
76. Ibid., p. 189.
77. Rasputin (1988), p. 10.
78. Likhachev (1987), p. 11.
79. Bondarev (1988), p. 11.
80. Cherez (1988), p. 1.
81. Shmelev (1987), p. 146.
82. Shmelev (1988), p. 164.
83. Selyunin (1988), p. 189.
84. Shchekochikhin (1987), p. 1.
85. See further Tolz (1987), p. 1.
86. Sundiev (1987), pp. 58–61.
87. Ibid., p. 58.
88. On this rather striking point, cf. also van den Heuvel (1987), pp. 70–1.
89. Sundiev (1987), p. 61.

90. Cf. the suicide of the Party Chief's (Beriya's) grandson in Abuladze's famous film *Pokayanie*.
91. Ideologicheskie (1988), p. 18.
92. Ibid., p. 20.
93. According to Smolyanskii (1988), p. 134, the result has been an 'avalanche of informal groups, counting millions of members'. Many have left the Komsomol simply by not paying their membership dues.
94. Cf. Popov (1988).
95. Cf. Carrre d'Encausse (1978) and Motyl (1987).
96. Jones and Grupp (1987), p. 268.
97. Vishnevskii *et al.* (1988), p. 58.
98. Ibid.
99. Makarova, Morozova and Tarasova (1986), pp. 75–81.
100. Cf. Kirch, Järve and Haav (1988), pp. 33–4.
101. Cf. Arutyunyan and Drobizheva (1987).
102. As an official reflection of these survey findings, we may note criticism for corruption and a lack of social dynamism, levelled against the Uzbeks at the 1986 Party Congress .
103. In a recent interview with a Polish newspaper, Soviet sociologist Shkaratan spoke of 'feudalist conditions' in Uzbekistan and of 'capitalist mafias' in Armenia (Zwykle sprawy, 1988, p. 10).
104. See Gorbachev (1988c), p. 41. Cf. the statement by G.A. Borovik, President of the Soviet Peace Committee, to the 1988 Party Conference (*Pravda*, 2 July 1988).
105. *Moscow News*, supplement, no. 4, 1988.
106. O'Donnell (1986), p. 263 and *passim*.

References

Abramov, Fedor (1963), 'Vokrug do okolo', *Neva 9* (1).

Ådahl, Andreas and Perlowski, Adam (1978), *Sovjetunionens näringsliv*, Lund: Liber.

Adams, Jan S. (1981), 'Critical letters to the Soviet press: an increasingly important public forum', in: Donald E. Schultz, and Jan S. Adams (eds) *Political Participation in Communist Systems*, New York: Pergamon.

— (1983), 'Citizen participation in community decisions in the USSR', in: Peter J. Potichnyj, and Jane Schapiro Zacek (eds) *Politics and Participation under Communist Rule*, New York: Praeger.

Afanasiev, Viktor G. (1975), *Sotsialnaya informatsiya i upravlenie obshchestvom*, Moscow: Politizdat.

— (1978), 'V.I. Lenin o mirnykh i nemirnykh putyakh sotsialisticheskoi revolyutsii', *Voprosy Filosofii*, no. 6.

Agursky, M. (1980a), 'The new Russian literature', *Research Paper* no. 40, Hebrew University of Jerusalem, Soviet and East European Research Centre.

— (1980b), *Ideologiya natsional-bolshevizma*, Paris: YMCA.

Aleksandrov, A.D. (1972), 'V zashchitu sotsiologii', *Vestnik AN SSSR*, no. 7.

Alekseev, Oleg (1981), 'Rassvet na Nepryadve', in: A. Kuznetsov, and V. Shkiratov (eds) *Fantastika-80*, Moscow: Molodaya Gvardiya.

Alexeyeva, Ludmilla (1985), *Soviet Dissent. Contemporary Movements for National, Religious, and Human Rights*, Middletown, Ct: Wesleyan University Press.

Allworth, Edward (ed.)(1980), *Ethnic Russia in the USSR. The Dilemma of Dominance*, New York: Pergamon.

Andreev, S. (1988), 'Obrok s gosudarstvennoi nivy', *Literaturnaya Gazeta*, 18 May.

Andropov, Yurii (1982), 'Rech Generalnogo sekretarya TsK KPSS Yu.V. Andropova na plenume TsK KPSS 22 noyabrya 1982 goda', *Kommunist*, no. 17.

— (1983), 'Uchenie Karla Marksa i nekotorye voprosy sotsialisticheskogo stroitelstva v SSSR', *Kommunist*, no. 3.

Arutyunyan, Yu.V. and Bromlei, Yu.V. (eds)(1986), *Sotsialno-kulturnyi oblik sovetskogo obshchestva. Po resultatam etnosotsiologicheskogo issledovaniya*, Moscow: Nauka.

Arutyunyan, Yu.V. and Drobizheva, L.M. (1987), 'Natsionalnye osobennosti kultury i nekotorye aspekty sotsialnoi zhizni sovetskogo obshchestva', *Voprosy Istorii*, no. 7.

Åslund, Anders (1985), *Private Enterprise in Eastern Europe: The Non-Agricultural Private Sector in Poland and the GDR, 1945–83*, London and Basingstoke: Macmillan.

— (1987a), 'Berliner revisited', *Nordic Journal of Soviet and East European Studies 4* (4).

— (1987b), 'Gorbachev's economic advisors', *Soviet Economy, 3* (3).

Azizyan, A. (1950), 'Razvitie tovarishchem Stalinym marksistko-leninskoi teorii po natsionalnomu voprosu', *Bolshevik*, no. 3.

Azrael, Jeremy R. (1978), 'Emergent nationality problems in the USSR', in: J.R. Azrael (ed.) *Soviet Nationality Policies and Practices*, New York: Praeger.

Bagirov, M. (1950), 'Velikii vozhd narodov', *Bolshevik*, no. 1.

Bailes, Kendall E. (1978), *Technology and Society under Lenin and Stalin: Origins of the Soviet Technical Intelligentsia 1917–1941*, Princeton, NJ: Princeton University Press.

Bakhtin, Mikhail M. (1979), *Estetika slovesnogo tvorchestva*, Moscow: Iskusstvo.

Bandera, V.N. (1984), 'Capital accumulation and growth in a socialist economy: the case of Soviet NEP', *Journal of European Economic History, 13* (1).

Baran, Paul A. (1970), 'National economic planning: the Soviet experience', in: Bornstein and Fusfeld (eds) *The Soviet Economy: A Book of Readings,* 3rd edn.

Baranov, Vadim (1987), 'Pouchitelnye uroki', *Literaturnaya Gazeta*, 30 September.

Barghoorn, Frederick C. (1980), 'Four faces of Soviet Russian ethnocentrism', in: Edward Allworth (ed.) *Ethnic Russia in the USSR. The Dilemma of Dominance*, New York: Pergamon.

— and Remington, Thomas F. (1986), *Politics in the USSR*, 3rd edn, Boston, Mass. and Toronto: Little, Brown & Co.

Barkai, Haim (1977), *Growth Patterns in the Kibbutz Economy*, Amsterdam: North-Holland.

— (1987), 'Kibbutz efficiency and the incentive conundrum', in: S. Hedlund (ed.) *Incentives and Economic Systems: Proceedings of the Eighth Arne Ryde Symposium, Frostvallen, 26-7 August, 1985.*

Barry, Brian (1974), 'Exit, Voice and Loyalty', (review article), *British Journal of Political Science, 4* (1).

Barry, Donald D. and Barner-Barry, Carol (1978), *Contemporary Soviet Politics: An Introduction*, Englewood Cliffs, NJ: Prentice Hall.

Barsov, A.A. (1968), 'Selskoe khozyaistvo i istochniki nakopleniya v gody pervoi pyatiletki (1928–32)', *Istoriya SSSR*, no. 3.

— (1969), *Balans stoimostnykh obmenov mezhdu gorodom i derevnei*, Moscow: Nauka.

Bazhan, M. (1953), 'Druzhba narodov, druzhba literatur', *Kommunist*, no. 18.

Notes and references

Bell, Daniel (1965), 'Ideology and Soviet Politics', *Slavic Review*, 24 (4).
Berestnev, V. (1951), 'O sotsialisticheskoi kulture i kulturnoi revolyutsii v SSSR', *Bolshevik*, no. 10.
Beria, Lavrentii P. (1949), 'Velikii vdokhnovitel i organisator pobed kommunizma', *Bolshevik*, no. 24.
Berliner, Joseph (1957), *Factory and Manager in the USSR*, Cambridge, Ma.: Harvard University Press.
Besançon, Alain (1981), *The Rise of the Gulag: Intellectual Origins of Leninism*, New York: Continuum.
— (1986), 'Nationalism and Bolshevism in the USSR', in: Robert Conquest (ed.) *The Last Empire: Nationality and the Soviet Future*, Stanford: Hoover Institution Press.
Beskrovnyi, L.G. (1980), 'Kulikovskaya bitva', in: *Kulikovskaya Bitva. Sbornik statei*, Moscow: Nauka.
Bestuzhev-Lada, I.V. (1988), 'Nado li voroshit proshloe?', *Sotsiologicheskie Issledovaniya*, no. 3.
Bialer, Seweryn (1986), *The Soviet Paradox. External Expansion. Internal Decline*, New York: Alfred Knopf.
Birch, A.H. (1975), 'Economic models in political science: the case of "Exit, Voice and Loyalty" ', *British Journal of Political Science*, 5 (2).
Blagoi, D. (1951), 'Natsionalnye osobennosti russkoi literatury', *Bolshevik*, no. 18.
Bloch, Sidney and Reddaway, Peter (1977), *Russia's Political Hospitals: The Abuse of Psychiatry in the Soviet Union*, London: Victor Gollancz.
Bodin, Per-Arne (1987), *Världen som ikon*, Skellefteå: Artos.
Bolshaya (1953), *Bolshaya sovetskaya entsiklopediya*, vol. 23, Moscow: Sovetskaya Entsiklopediya.
Bondarev, Yurii (1988), 'Bol i nadezhda', *Literaturnaya Gazeta*, 22 June.
Borcke, Astrid and Simon, Gerhard (1980), *Neue Wege der Sowjetunion-Forschung. Beiträge zur Methoden und Theoriediskussion*, Baden-Baden: Nomos Verlagsgesellschaft.
Bornstein, Morris (1962), 'The Soviet price system', *American Economic Review 52* (1).
— (1963), 'The 1963 Soviet industrial price revision', *Soviet Studies 15* (1).
— (1964), 'The Soviet price reform discussion' *Quarterly Journal of Economics 78* (1).
— (1985), 'Improving the Soviet economic mechanism', *Soviet Studies 37* (1).
Bornstein, Morris and Fusfeld, Daniel R. (eds.)(1970), *The Soviet Economy: A Book of Readings*, 3rd edn, Homewood, Il.: Irwin.
Borodin, Sergei (1980), *Dmitrii Donskoi*, Moscow: Sovremennik.
Bourmeyster, Alexandre (1983), 'Utopie, ideologie et skaz', *Essais sur le discours sovietique*, vol. 3, Grenoble: Université de Grenoble III.
— (1985), 'Le discours politique sovietique, le programme narratif et le theorie du skaz', *Essais sur le discours sovietique*, vol. 5.
Braudel, F. (1969), *Ecrits sur l'histoire*, Paris: Flammarion.
Brezhnev, Leonid I. (1971), 'Otchetnyi doklad Tsentralnogo Komiteta KPSS XXIV sezdu Kommunisticheskoi Partii Sovetskogo Soyuza. Doklad

Generalnogo Sekretarya TsK tovarishcha L.I. Brezhneva, 30 marta 1971 goda', *Kommunist*, no. 5.
— (1981), 'Otchetnyi doklad L.I. Brezhneva Tsentralnogo Komiteta KPSS XXVI sezdu Kommunisticheskoi Partii Sovetskogo Soyuza i ocherednye zadachi partii v oblasti vnutrennei i vneshnei politiki, 23 fevralya 1981 goda', *Kommunist*, no. 4.
Bromlei, Yulii (1983), 'Etnicheskie protsessy v SSSR', *Kommunist*, no.5.
Brown, Archie (1975), 'Political developments: some conclusions and an interpretation', in: Archie Brown and Michael Kaser (eds) *The Soviet Union Since the Fall of Khrushchev*, London and Basingstoke: Macmillan.
Brutzkus, Boris (1935), *Economic Planning in Soviet Russia*, London: Routledge and Kegan Paul.
Brzezinski, Zbigniew (1960), *The Soviet Bloc: Unity and Conflict*, Cambridge, Mass.: Harvard University Press.
Bukowskij, Wladimir (1971), *Opposition: Eine neue Geisteskrankheit in der Sowjetunion?*, München: Carl Hanser Verlag.
Burdzhalov, E. (1951), 'Stalinskii "Kratkii kurs istorii VKP(b)" i istoricheskaya nauka', *Bolshevik*, no. 18.
Burks, R.V. (1984), 'The coming crisis in the Soviet Union', *East European Quarterly 18 (1)*.
Carr, Edward H. (1952), *The Bolshevik Revolution*, vol. II, London: Macmillan.
— (1958), *Socialism in One Country*, vol. I, London: Macmillan.
— (1961), *What is History?*, Harmondsworth: Penguin.
Carr, Edward H. and Davies, R.W. (1969), *Foundations of a Planned Economy*, vol. I, London: Macmillan.
Carrre d'Encausse, Helen (1978), *L'empire eclaté*, Paris: Flammarion.
— (1982), *Confiscated Power: How Soviet Russia Really Works*, New York: Harper & Row.
Cherez (1988), 'Cherez demokratizatsiyu – k novumu obliku sotsializma', *Literaturnaya Gazeta*, 11 May.
Chernenko, Konstantin U. (1984a), 'Rech tovarishcha K.U. Chernenko na vstreche s izbiratelyami', *Kommunist*, no. 4.
— (1984b), 'Rech tovarishcha K.U. Chernenko na Plenume TsK KPSS', *Kommunist*, no. 6.
— (1984c), 'Utverzhdat pravdu zhizni, vysokie idealy sotsializma', *Literaturnaya Gazeta*, 26 September.
Cherniavsky, M. (1961), *Tsar and People: A Historical Study of Russian National and Social Myths*, New Haven: Yale University Press.
Chernov, F. (1949), 'Burzhuaznyi kosmopolitizm i ego reaktsionnaya rol', *Bolshevik*, no. 5.
Chernyak, V. (1988), 'Polumery ne pomogayut', *Literaturnaya Gazeta*, 11 May.
Chudakova, M. (1987), 'Neokonchennoe sochinenie Mikhaila Bulgakova', *Novyi Mir*, no. 8.
Churaev, V. (1957), 'Edinstvo partii i vnutripartiinaya demokratiya', *Kommunist*, no. 17.

Notes and references

Clark, Katerina (1977), 'Utopian anthropology as a context for Stalinist literature', in: R. Tucker (ed.) *Stalinism: Essays in Historical Interpretation.*

— (1978), 'Little heroes and big deeds: literature responds to the first five year plan', in: S. Fitzpatrick (ed.) *Cultural Revolution in Russia, 1928-1931.*

Cocks, Paul (1976), 'The policy process and bureaucratic politics', in: Cocks, Daniels and Heer (eds) *The Dynamics of Soviet Politics.*

Cocks, Paul, Daniels, Robert and Heer, Nancy Whittier (eds)(1976), *The Dynamics of Soviet Politics*, Cambridge, Mass.: Harvard University Press.

Cohen, Stephen F. (1977), 'Bolshevism and Stalinism', in: Tucker (ed.) *Stalinism: Essays in Historical Interpretation.*

— (1980), *Bukharin and the Bolshevik Revolution: A Political Biography, 1888–1938*, Oxford: Oxford University Press.

— (1985), *Rethinking the Soviet Experience: Politics and History Since 1917*, New York and Oxford: Oxford University Press.

Comey, David Dinsmore (1962), 'Marxist-Leninist ideology and Soviet policy', *Studies in Soviet Thought 2* (4).

Connor, Walter D. (1979), *Socialism, Politics, and Equality. Hierarchy and Change in Eastern Europe and the USSR*, New York: Columbia University Press.

Conquest, Robert (1967), *Power and Policy in the U.S.S.R.*, New York: Harper Torchbooks.

— (1986), *The Harvest of Sorrow. Soviet Collectivization and the Terror Famine*, New York and Oxford: Oxford University Press.

— (1987), 'Starving the Ukraine', *The London Review of Books 9* (9).

Dallin, David J. and Nicolaevsky, Boris (1947), *Forced Labour in Soviet Russia*, New Haven: Yale University Press.

Danilov, V.P. (1988), 'Diskussiya v zapadnoi presse o golode 1932–1933 gg. i "demograficheskoi katastrofe" 30–40-kh godov v SSSR', *Voprosy Istorii*, no. 3.

Davies, Norman (1982), *God's Playground: A History of Poland* vol. 1, Oxford: Clarendon Press.

Davies, R.W. (1960), 'Some Soviet economic controllers', *Soviet Studies 12* (1).

— (1970), 'A note on grain statistics', *Soviet Studies, 21 (3).*

— (1980), *The Industrialization of Soviet Russia*, London: Macmillan.

de Jonge, Alex (1986), *Stalin and the Shaping of the Soviet Union*, London: Collins.

Diamond, Douglas (1966), 'Trends in output, inputs and factor productivity', in: US Congress, Subcommittee on Foreign Economic Policy, *New Directions in the Soviet Economy*, Washington, DC: Government Printing Office.

Dienes, Leslie (1983), 'Regional economic development', in: Abram Bergson, and Herbert Levine (eds) *The Soviet Economy Toward the Year 2000*, London: Allen & Unwin.

Djilas, Milovan (1957), *The New Class: An Analysis of the Communist System*, New York: Praeger.

Dobb, Maurice (1929), *Russian Economic Development Since the Revolution*, London: Routledge & Kegan Paul.
— (1948), *Soviet Economic Development Since 1917*, London: Routledge & Kegan Paul
Doktor (1988), ' "Doktor Zhivago" vchera i segodnya', *Literaturnaya Gazeta*, 15 June.
Doolittle, Penelope and Hughes, Margaret (1987), 'Gorbachev's agricultural policy: building on the Brezhnev food program', in: US Congress Joint Economic Committee, *Gorbachev's Economic Plans*, vol. 2.
Downs, Anthony (1957), *An Economic Theory of Democracy*, New York: Harper & Row.
Drewnowski, Jan (ed.)(1982), *Crisis in the East European Economy*, London: Croom Helm.
Dunlop, John B. (1983), *The Faces of Contemporary Russian Nationalism*, Princeton, NJ: Princeton University Press.
Dunmore, Timothy (1980), *The Stalinist Command Economy: The Soviet State Apparatus and Economic Policy 1945–53*, New York: St Martin's.
— (1984), *Soviet Politics 1945–1953*, London and Basingstoke: Macmillan.
Durham Hannah, Gayle (1976), 'Soviet political communications in the post-Stalin period', in: Jane P. Shapiro and Peter J.Potitchnyi (eds) *Change and Adaptation in Soviet and East European Politics*, New York: Praeger.
Edinstvo (1965), 'Edinstvo obyazannostei i prav kommunista', *Kommunist*, no. 13.
Effendiev, M. (1982), 'Luchi odnoi zari', *Kommunist*, no. 17.
Ejvegård, Rolf (1981), *Sovjetunionens konstitution: En analys*, Stockholm: Esselte studium.
Ellman, Michael (1975), 'Did the agricultural surplus provide the resources for the increase in investment in the USSR during the first five year plan?', *Economic Journal 85*.
Elster, Jon (1984), *Ulysses and the Sirens: Studies in Rationality and Irrationality*, Cambridge: Cambridge University Press.
— (1985a), 'Rationality, morality and collective action', *Ethics 96* (1).
— (1985b), *Sour Grapes: Studies in the Subversion of Rationality*, Cambridge: Cambridge University Press.
— (ed.)(1986), *Rational Choice*, Oxford: Blackwell.
Elyutin, V. (1972), 'Zadachi kafedr obshchestvennykh nauk vysshikh uchebnykh zavedenii na sovremennom etape', *Kommunist*, no. 1.
Enteen, George M. (1978), 'Marxist historians and the cultural revolution: a case-study of professional in-fighting', in: Fitzpatrick (ed.) *Cultural Revolution in Russia, 1928-1931*.
Erlich, Alexander (1960), *The Soviet Industrialization Debate*, Cambridge, Mass: Harvard University Press.
Etkind, Efim (1978), *Notes of a Non-Conspirator*, Oxford: Oxford University Press.
Fainsod, Merle (1953), *How Russia is Ruled*, Cambridge, Mass.: Harvard University Press.

Notes and references

— (1958), *Smolensk under Soviet Rule*, Cambridge, Mass.: Harvard University Press.

— (1963), *How Russia is Ruled*, revised edition, Cambridge, Mass.: Harvard University Press.

Fedoseev, P.N. (1953), 'Sotsializm i patriotizm', *Kommunist*, no. 9.

— (1972), 'XXIV sezd KPSS i osnovnye napravleniya issledovanii v oblasti obshchestvennykh nauk', *Kommunist*, no. 1.

— (1980), 'Teoreticheskie problemy razvitiya i sblizheniya natsii', *Kommunist*, no.1.

Feldbrugge, F.J.M. (1975), *Samizdat and Political Dissent in the Soviet Union*, Leyden: A.W. Sijthoff.

Felker, Jere L. (1966), *Soviet Economic Controversies*, Cambridge, Mass.: MIT Press.

Feshbach, Murray (1982), 'Between the lines of the 1979 Soviet census', *Problems of Communism 31* (1).

Fitzpatrick, Sheila (1976), 'Culture and politics under Stalin: a reappraisal', *Slavic Review 35* (2).

— (ed.)(1978), *Cultural Revolution in Russia, 1928–1931*, Bloomington, Ind.: Indiana University Press.

— (1979), 'Stalin and the making of a new Soviet elite', *Slavic Review 38* (3).

— (1982), *The Russian Revolution*, Oxford and New York: Oxford University Press.

Friedgut, Theodore H. (1979), *Political Participation in the USSR*, Princeton, NJ: Princeton University Press.

Froyanov, Igor Ya. (1988), 'Nachalo khristianstva na Rusi', in: Georgii L. Kurbatov, Eduard D. Frolov, and Igor Ya. Froyanov (eds) *Khristianstvo: Antichnost Vizantiya, Drevnyaya Rus*, Leningrad: Lenizdat.

Fülöp-Miller, R. (1928), *Geist und Gesicht des Bolschevismus*, Zürich, Leipzig and Berlin: Amalthea Verlag.

Gellner, Ernest (1987), *Culture, Identity and Politics*, Cambridge: Cambridge University Press.

Gerner, Kristian (1972), 'Polen i sovjetrysk utrikespolitik 1920', in: Christer Jönsson (ed.) *Sovjets utrikespolitik*, Lund: Studentlitteratur.

— (1985), *The Soviet Union and Central Europe in the Post-war Era*, Aldershot: Gower; New York: St. Martin's.

Gerner, Kristian and Hedlund, Stefan (1988), 'Die polnische Dauerkrise', *Osteuropa 38* (5).

Gerner, Kristian and Lundgren, Lars (1978), *Planhushållning och miljöproblem: Sovjetisk debatt om natur och samhälle 1960–1976*, Stockholm: Liber.

— (1985), 'Nature's revenge: the Soviet debate over nature and society, 1960-79', in: Kendall E. Bailes (ed.) *Environmental History: Critical Issues in Comparative Perspective*, Lanham: University Press of America.

Getty, J. Arch (1987a), *Origins of the Great Purges. The Soviet Communist Party Reconsidered, 1933–1938*, Cambridge: Cambridge University Press.

— (1987b), 'Starving the Ukraine', *London Review of Books 9* (2).

Gilbert, Martin (1979), *Soviet History Atlas*, London: Routledge & Kegan Paul.

Gitelman, Zvi (1983), 'Are nations merging in the USSR?', *Problems of Communism 32* (5).

Goldman, Marshall I. (1963), 'Economic controversy in the Soviet Union', *Foreign Affairs 41* (3).

— (1970), 'Economic growth and institutional change in the Soviet Union', in: M. Bornstein and D.R.Fusfeld (eds) *The Soviet Economy: A Book of Readings*, 3rd edn.

— (1983), *USSR in Crisis: The Failure of an Economic System*, New York and London: Norton.

Golovchenko, F. (1949), 'Vysoko derzhat znamya sovetskogo patriotizma v iskusstve i literature', *Bolshevik*, no. 3.

Golowkow, Anatolij (1988), 'My dzieci Arbatu', *Polityka*, August 13.

Goodman, Ann, Hughes, Margaret and Schroeder, Gertrude (1987), 'Raising the efficiency of Soviet farm labor: problems and prospects', in: US Congress Joint Economic Committee, *Gorbachev's Economic Plans*.

Gorbachev, Mikhail S. (1985), 'O sozyve ocherednogo XXVII sezda KPSS i zadachakh, svyazannykh s ego podgotovkoi i provedeniem. Doklad Generalnogo sekretarya TsK KPSS M.S. Gorbacheva na plenume TsK KPSS 23 aprelya 1985 goda', *Kommunist*, no. 7.

— (1986), 'Politicheskii doklad tsentralnogo komiteta KPSS XXVII sezdy Kommunisticheskoi Partii Sovetskogo Soyuza. Doklad Generalnogo sekretarya TsK KPSS tovarishcha Gorbacheva M.S. 25 fevralya 1986 goda', *Kommunist*, no. 4.

— (1987a), 'O zadachakh partii po korennoi perestroike upravleniya ekonomikoi. Doklad Generalnogo sekretarya TsK KPSS M.S. Gorbacheva 25 iyunya 1987 goda', *Kommunist*, no. 10.

— (1987b), *Perestroika i novoe myshlenie dlya nashei strany a dlya vsego mira*, Moscow: Politizdat.

— (1987c), 'Perestroika – pryamoe prodolzhenie oktyabrya. Torzhestvennoe sobranie, posvyashchennoe vrucheniyu gorodu Murmansku ordena Lenina i medali "Zolotaya Zvezda". Rech tovarishcha Gorbacheva M. S.', *Ekonomicheskaya Gazeta*, no. 41.

— (1987d), 'Oktyabr i perestroika: revolyutsiya prodolzhaetsya. Doklad Generalnogo sekretarya TsK KPSS M.S. Gorbacheva na sovmestnom torzhestvennom zasedanii Tsentralnogo Komiteta KPSS, Verkhovnogo Soveta SSSR i Verkhovnogo Soveta RSFSR, posvyashchennom 70-letiyu Velikoi Oktyabrskoi sotsialisticheskoi revolyutsii, v Kremlevskom Dvortse sezdov 2 noyabrya 1987 goda', *Kommunist*, no. 17.

— (1988a), 'Revolyutsionnoi perestroike – ideologiyu obnovleniya. Rech Generalnogo sekretarya TsK KPSS M.S. Gorbacheva na Plenume TsK KPSS 18 fevralya 1988 goda', *Kommunist*, no. 4.

— (1988b), 'Potentsial kooperatsii – delu perestroiki. Vystuplenie Generalnogo sekretarya TsK KPSS M.S. Gorbacheva na IV Vsesoyuznom sezde kolkhoznikov 23 marta 1988 goda', *Ekonomicheskaya Gazeta*, no. 13.

Notes and references

— (1988c), 'O khode realizatsii reshenii XXVII sezda KPSS i zadachakh po uglubleniyu perestroiki. Doklad Generalnogo sekretarya TsK KPSS M.S. Gorbacheva na XIX Vsesoyuznoi konferentsii KPSS 28 iyunya 1988 goda', *Kommunist*, no. 10.

Gorkin, A. (1949), 'Stalin – sozdatel i rukovoditel mnogonatsionalnogo sovetskogo gosudarstva', *Bolshevik*, no. 23.

Gregory, Paul R. and Stuart, Robert C. (1974), *Soviet Economic Structure and Performance*, New York: Harper & Row.

— (1986), *Soviet Economic Structure and Performance*, 3rd edn, New York: Harper & Row.

Grushin, B.A. (1970), 'Logicheskie printsipy issledovaniya massovogo soznaniya', *Voprosy Filosofii*, no. 7.

— (1972), 'Vystuplenie i doklad', in: *Obshchestvennoe mnenie i massovaya kommunikatsiya*, Budapest: Hungarian Broadcasting Corporation.

— (1980), 'Tvorcheskii potentsial svobodnogo vremeni', *Kommunist*, no. 2.

— (1988), 'Obshchestvennoe mnenie v sisteme upravleniya', *Sotsiologicheskie Issledovaniya*, no. 3.

Gumerov, R. (1979), 'Zakupochnye tseny i stimulirovanie selskokhozyaistvennogo proizvodstva', *Planovoe Khozyaistvo*, no. 3.

Gustafson, Thane (1981), *Reform in Soviet Politics. Lessons of Recent Policies on Land and Water*, Cambridge: Cambridge University Press.

Hahn, Werner G. (1982), *Postwar Soviet Politics. The Fall of Zhdanov and the Defeat of Moderation, 1946–53*, Ithaca, NY: Cornell University Press.

— (1987), *Democracy in a Communist Party: Poland's Experience Since 1980*, New York: Columbia University Press.

Halperin, Charles (1976), 'The Russian Land and the Russian Tsar: the emergence of Muscovite ideology', in: *Forschungen zur Osteuropäischen Geschichte*, Band 23, Berlin: Osteuropainstitut.

— (1985), *Russia and the Golden Horde. The Mongol Impact on Medieval Russian History*, Bloomington, Ind.: Indiana University Press.

Hanson, Philip (1983), 'Success indicators revisited: the July 1979 Soviet decree on planning and management', *Soviet Studies 35* (1).

— (1988), 'The draft law on cooperatives', *Radio Liberty Research Bulletin*, RL 111/88, 15 March.

Harsanyi, John C. (1986), 'Advances in understanding rational behaviour', in: Elster (ed.) *Rational Choice*.

Håstad, Disa (1979), *Samtal med sovjetiska författare*, Stockholm: Askild & Kärnekull.

— (1983), *En elit far västerut. Den nya emigrationen från Sovjetunionen*, Stockholm: Norstedts.

Hedlund, Stefan (1983), 'Stalin and the peasantry: a study in red', *Scandia 49* (2).

— (1984), *Crisis in Soviet Agriculture*, London and Sydney: Croom Helm; New York: St. Martin's.

— (1985), 'On the socialization of labour in rural cooperation', in M. Lundahl (ed.) *The Primary Sector in Economic Development. Proceedings of the Seventh Arne Ryde Symposium. Frostavallen, August 29–30, 1983*, London and Sydney: Croom Helm.

— (ed.)(1987), *Incentives and Economic Systems: Proceedings of the Eighth Arne Ryde Symposium, Frostavallen, 26–27 August 1985*, London and Sydney: Croom Helm.

— (1989), *Private Agriculture in the Soviet Union*, London: Routledge.

Hedlund, Stefan and Lundahl, Mats (1982), 'Linking efforts and rewards: the Zveno system of collective farming', *Economics of Planning 18* (2).

Heer, Nancy Whittier (1971), *Politics and History in the Soviet Union*, Cambridge, Mass.: Harvard University Press.

Heller, Michel (1985), *La machine et les rouages*, Paris: Calmann-Levy.

Hirschman, Albert O. (1970), *Exit, Voice and Loyalty: Responses to Decline in Firms, Organizations and States*, Cambridge, Mass. and London: Harvard University Press.

— (1981), *Essays in Trespassing: Economics to Politics and Beyond*, Cambridge: Cambridge University Press.

— (1986), *Rival Views of Market Society and Other Recent Essays*, New York: Viking.

Hoeffding, Oleg (1959), 'The Soviet industrial reorganization of 1957', *American Economic Review 49* (2).

Hough, Jerry F. (1965), 'A harebrained scheme in retrospect', *Problems of Communism 14* (4).

— (1971), 'The changing nature of the *kolkhoz* chairman', in: J. Millar (ed.) *The Soviet Rural Community*.

— (1976a), 'Political participation in the Soviet Union', *Soviet Studies, 28* (1).

— (1976b), 'Party "saturation" in the Soviet Union', in: Cocks, Daniels and Heer (eds) *The Dynamics of Soviet Politics*.

— (1987), 'Gorbachev consolidating power', *Problems of Communism 36* (4).

— (1988), *Opening Up the Soviet Economy*, Washington, DC: The Brookings Institution.

Hough, Jerry F. and Fainsod, Merle (1979), *How the Soviet Union is Governed*, Cambridge, Mass.: Harvard University Press.

Humphries, Caroline (1983), *Karl Marx Collective: Economy, Society and Religion in a Siberian Farm*, Cambridge: Cambridge University Press.

Ideologicheskie (1988), 'Ideologicheskie problemy perestroiki. Kruglyi stol zhurnala "Kommunist" ', *Kommunist*, no. 7.

Informatsionnoe (1937), 'Informatsionnoe soobshchenie ob ocherednom plenume TsK VKP(b)', *Bolshevik*, no. 5–6.

Inkeles, Alex and Geiger, Kent (1968), 'Critical letters to the Soviet Press', in: Alex Inkeles (ed.) *Social Change in Soviet Russia*, Cambridge, Mass.: Harvard University Press.

Intervyu (1987), 'Intervyu s chlenom korrespondentom AN SSSR M.N. Rutkevichem', *Sotsiologicheskie Issledovaniya*, no. 5.

Ionin, L.G. (1987), 'Konservativnyi sindrom', *Sotsiologicheskie Issledovaniya*, no. 5.

Notes and references

Israelsen, Dwight (1980), 'Collectives, communes and incentives', *Journal of Comparative Economics 6* (4).
Ivanov, L. (1951), 'Ob uchebnike istorii SSSR', *Bolshevik*, no. 14.
Ivanov, Vyacheslav V. (1973), 'The category of time in twentieth-century art and culture', *Semiotica 8* (1).
— (1988), '... i dyshat pochva i sudba', *Literaturnaya Gazeta*, 1 June.
Jacobs, Everett M. (1970), 'Soviet local elections: what they are and what they are not', *Soviet Studies 22* (1).
Jancar, Barbara (1984), 'Political culture and political change', *Studies in Comparative Communism 27* (1).
Jaruzelski, Wojciech, (1987), 'K novym gorizontam', *Kommunist*, no. 11.
Jasny, Naum (1951), '*Kolkhozy*, the Achilles' heel of the Soviet regime', *Soviet Studies 3* (2).
— (1954), 'A Soviet planner – V.G. Groman', *Russian Review 13* (1).
— (1961), *Soviet Industrialization 1928–52*, Chicago: University of Chicago Press.
Jensen, Bent (1981), 'Forsvar for et foraeldet begrep', *Bidrag till Öststatsforskningen 9* (4).
Johnston, Bruce and Mellor, Andrew (1961), 'The role of agriculture in economic development', *American Economic Review, 51* (4).
Jones, Ellen and Grupp, Fred W. (1982), 'Measuring nationality trends in the Soviet Union: a research note', *Slavic Review, 41* (1).
— (1987), *Modernization, Value Change and Fertility in the Soviet Union*, Cambridge: Cambridge University Press.
Kaipbergenov, Tulenbergen (1987), 'Vystuplenie', *Literaturnaya Gazeta*, 6 May.
Kak sovershaetsya (1987), 'Kak sovershaetsya povorot', *Novyi Mir*, no. 7.
Kakova (1955), 'Kakova rol raikoma v podbore sekretarei pervichnykh partorganizatsii?', *Partiinaya Zhizn*, no. 15.
Kammari, M. (1949), 'Tovarishch Stalin o natsiakh burzhuaznykh i sotsialisticheskikh', *Bolshevik*, no. 16.
— (1953), 'Sotsialisticheskie natsii SSSR v usloviyakh perekhoda ot sotsializma k kommunizmu', *Kommunist*, no. 5.
Kaplan, Cynthia (1987), *The Party and Agricultural Crisis Management in the USSR*, Ithaca and London: Cornell University Press.
Karcz, Jerzy (1967), 'Thoughts on the grain problem', *Soviet Studies 18* (4).
— (1979), 'Agriculture and the economics of Soviet Development', in: A. Wright (ed.) *Jerzy F. Karcz. The Economics of Communist Agriculture.*
Kargalov, V.V. (1980), *Konets ordynskogo iga*, Moscow: Nauka.
Karklins, Rasma (1986), *Ethnic Relations in the USSR: The Perspective from Below*, Boston: Allen & Unwin.
Karlgren, Anton (1942), *Stalin*, Stockholm: Norstedts.
Karotamm, N. (1949), 'Borba bolshevikov Estonii za podem khozyaistva i kultury respubliki', *Bolshevik*, no. 6.
Karpov, M. and Melkov, Yu. (1965), 'Pervichnaya partiinaya organizatsiya i aktivnost kommunistov', *Kommunist*, no. 5.
Kaser, Michael (1959), 'Changes in planning methods during the preparation of the Soviet seven-year plan', *Soviet Studies 10* (4).

— (1968), 'Kosygin, Liberman and the pace of Soviet industrial reform', in: G.R. Feiwel (ed.) *New Currents in Soviet-type Economies. A Reader*, Scranton, Pa.: International Textbook.

Kelle, V. Zh. (1978), 'Nauka kak komponent sotsialnoi sistemy', *Sotsiologicheskie Issledovaniya*, no. 3.

Kelley, Donald R. (1971), *Interest Groups and Policy Formation in the USSR*, PhD Dissertation, Indiana University.

Kemp-Welch, A. (1983), 'Stalinism and intellectual order', in: T.H. Rigby, Archie Brown, and Peter Reddaway (eds) *Authority, Power and Policy in the USSR*, London: Macmillan.

Kenez, Peter (1985), *The Birth of the Propaganda State: Soviet Methods of Mass Mobilization 1917–1929*, Cambridge: Cambridge University Press.

Kerblay, Basile (1983), *Modern Soviet Society*, New York: Pantheon Books.

Khachaturov, Tigran S. (1982), 'Puti realizatsii prodovolstvennoi programmi', *Voprosy Ekonomiki*, no. 11.

Khlebnyuk, Oleg (1988), 'XVIII partkonferentsiya. Vremya, problemy, resheniya', *Kommunist*, no. 1.

Khorev, B. (1986), 'Volga vpadaet v Kaspicheskoe more', *Literaturnaya Gazeta*, 3 September.

Khromov, P. (1949), 'Protiv kosmopoliticheskikh izvrashchenii istorii russkoi ekonomicheskoi mysli', *Bolshevik*, no. 5.

Khrushchev, Nikita S. (1949a), 'Bolsheviki Ukrainy v borbe za vosstanovlenie i razvitie khozyaistva i kultury USSR', *Bolshevik*, no. 3.

— (1949b), 'Stalinskaya druzhba narodov – zalog nepobedimosti nashei Rodiny', *Bolshevik*, no. 24.

— (1956), 'Secret Speech 24–25.02.1956', US Department of State, Washington, DC: 4 June 1956.

Khrustov, F. (1953), 'Istoriya kommunisticheskoi partii sovetskogo soyuza – marksizm-leninizm v deistvii', *Kommunist*, no. 14.

Kirch, A. V., Järve, P.E. and Haav, K.R. (1988), 'Etnosotsialnaya differentsiatsiya gorodskogo naseleniya Estonii', *Sotsiologicheskie Issledovaniya*, no. 3.

Kirpichnikov, A.N. (1980), *Kulikovskaya Bitva*, Moscow: Nauka.

Kleberg, Lars (1980), *Teatern som handling: Sovjetisk avantgardeestetik 1917–1927*, Stockholm: Norstedts.

Klibanov, A. (1980), 'O svetlo svetlaya i krashno ukrashennaya zemlya Russkaya', *Novyi Mir*, no. 9.

Kolakowski, Leszek (1977), 'Marxist roots of Stalinism', in: R. Tucker (ed.) *Stalinism: Essays in Historical Interpretation*.

Kolarz, Walter (1961), *Religion in the Soviet Union*, London: Macmillan.

Konstantinov, F. (1953), 'Rol sotsialisticheskoi ideologii v razvitii sotsialisticheskogo obshchestva', *Kommunist*, no. 13.

Koptyug, Valentin (1988), 'Ekologiya – ot obespokoennosti k deistviyu', *Kommunist*, no. 7.

Kornai, János (1986), 'The Hungarian reform process: visions, hopes, and reality', *Journal of Economic Literature 24* (4).

Kornhauser, William (1960), *The Politics of Mass Society*, London: Routledge & Kegan Paul.

Kosygin, Alexei N. (1972), 'On improving industrial management', in: A. Nove and M.D.Nuti (eds) *Socialist Economics.*

Kozlowski, Jozef (1988), 'Polacy na dalsszych kresach', *Polityka*, 23 April.

Kozmin, M. (1980), 'Velikii poet Rossii', *Voprosy Literatury*, no. 10.

Krawchenko, Bohdan (1985), *Social Change and National Consciousness in Twentieth-Century Ukraine*, Houndmills and Basingstoke: Macmillan.

Kritika (1961), 'Kritika i samokritika – nashe ispitannoe oruzhie', *Kommunist*, no. 1.

Kruglyi (1988), 'Kruglyi stol', *Voprosy Istorii*, no. 3.

Krupin, Vladimir (1980a), 'Ot sostavitelya', in: V. Krupin (ed.) *Mezh Nepryadvoi i Donom. K 600-letiyu kulikovskoi bitvy*, Moscow: Sovremennik.

— (1980b), 'Svyatoe Pole', in: V. Krupin (ed.) *Mezh Nepryadvoi i Donom.*

Kulikov, V. (1965), 'Selskii raikom partii segodnya', *Kommunist*, no. 11.

Kulikovskaya (1980), *Kulikovskaya Bitva. Sbornik statei*, Moscow: Nauka.

Kunaev, Dinmukhammed (1980), 'V blagotvornoi atmosfere leninskoi druzhby narodov', *Kommunist*, no. 12.

Kushnirsky, Fyodor I. (1982), *Soviet Economic Planning 1965–1980*, Boulder, Co.: Westview Press.

Kuznetsov, Feliks (1980), 'Pole russkoi slavy', *Literaturnaya Gazeta*, 10 September.

Labedz, Leopold (ed.)(1972), *Solzhenitsyn. A Documentary Record*, Harmondsworth: Penguin.

Laird, Robbin F. and Hoffmann, Erik P. (1984), 'The competition between Soviet conservatives and modernizers: domestic and international aspects', in: Laird and Hoffmann (eds) *The Soviet Polity in the Modern Era*, New York: Aldine Publishing Co.

Lane, Christel (1981), *The Rites of Rulers. Ritual in Industrial Society – the Soviet Case*, Cambridge: Cambridge University Press.

— (1984), 'Legitimacy and power in the Soviet Union through socialist ritual', *British Journal of Political Science 14* (2).

Lane, David (1971), *The End of Inequality. Stratification Under State Socialism*, Harmondsworth: Penguin.

— (1976), *The Industrial Socialist State. Towards a Political Economy of State Socialism*, London: Allen & Unwin.

Lange, Oskar (1965), 'The role of planning in a socialist economy', in: M. Bornstein (ed.) *Comparative Economic Systems: Models and Cases*, Homewood, Il.: Irwin.

Lasswell, Harold D. (1963), *The Future of Political Science*, New York: Atherton.

Latsis, O. (1987), 'Problema tempov v sotsialisticheskom obshchestve. K 60-letiyu XV sezda partii', *Kommunist*, no. 18.

Latsis, V. (1953), 'Velikaya sila druzhby narodov', *Kommunist*, no. 16.

Laver, Michael (1976), ' "Exit, Voice and Loyalty" revisited: the strategic production and consumption of public and private goods', *British Journal of Political Science 6* (4).

Lenin, Vladimir I. (1928), *Sochineniya*, Tom XXI, Moscow and Leningrad: Gosizdat.

Leninskie (1965), 'Leninskie normy partiinoi zhizni', *Kommunist*, no. 14.

Lewin, Moshe (1965), 'The immediate background of Soviet collectivization', *Soviet Studies 17* (2).
— (1968), *Russian Peasants and Soviet Power: A Study of Collectivization*, London: Allen & Unwin.
— (1974a), *Political Undercurrents in Soviet Economic Debates: From Bukharin to the Modern Reformers*, Princeton, N J: Princeton University Press.
— (1974b), 'Taking grain', in: C. Abramsky, and B. Williams (eds) *Essays in Honour of E.H. Carr*, London and Basingstoke: Macmillan.
— (1977), 'The Social Background to Stalinism', in: R. Tucker (ed.) Stalinism: *Essays in Historical Interpretation.*
— (1985), *The Making of the Soviet System: Essays in the Social History of Interwar Russia*, New York: Pantheon.
Liberman, Evsei (1972), 'The plan, profits and bonuses', in: A. Nove & M.D.Nuti (eds) *Soviet Economics.*
Likhachev, D.S. (1980a), 'Ozarennaya slovom', in: V. Krupin (ed.) *Mezh Nepryadvoi i Donom.*
— (1980b), 'Slovo o zhitii i o prestavlenii velikogo knyazya Dmitriya Ivanovicha, tsarya russkogo', (translation) in: V. Krupin (ed.) *Mezh Nepryadvoi i Donom.*
— (1980c), 'Zametki o russkom', *Novyi Mir*, no. 3.
— (1987), 'Trevoga sovesti', *Literaturnaya Gazeta*, 7 January.
— (1988a), 'Predvaritelnye itogi tysyacheletnego opyta', *Ogonek*, no. 10.
— (1988b), 'Kreshchenie Rusi i gosudarstvo Rus', *Novy Mir*, no. 6.
Lindblom, Charles (1977), *Politics and Markets*, New York: Basic Books.
Linden, Carl (1966), *Khrushchev and the Soviet Leadership: 1957–1964*, Baltimore, Md: Johns Hopkins Press.
Listov, Viktor (1988), 'Revolyutsiya molodaya', *Literaturnaya Gazeta*, 13 July.
Literaturnyi (1987), *Literaturnyi entsiklopedicheskii slovar*, Moscow: Sovetskaya Entsiklopediya.
Lorimer, Frank (1946), *The Population of the Soviet Union: History and Prospects*, Geneva: League of Nations.
Loshchits, Yu. (1980), *Dmitrii Donskoi*, Moscow: Molodaya Gvardiya (republished in 1983).
Lotman, J. and Uspenskii, B. (1982), 'Otzvuki kontseptsii "Moskva – Tretii Rim" v ideologii Petra Pervogo' in: V.A. Karpushin (ed.) *Khudostvennyi yazyk srednevekovya*, Moscow: Nauka.
Lourie, Richard (1975), *Letters to the Future. An Approach to Sinyavsky-Tertz*, Ithaca: Cornell University Press.
Luchterhand, Otto (1976), *Der Sowjetstaat und die Russisch-Orthodoxe Kirche. Eine rechtshistorische und rechtssystematische Untersuchung*, Köln: Wissenschaft und Politik.
Lyashko, A. (1982), 'V seme volnoi, novoi', *Kommunist*, no. 17.
MacAuley, Alastair (1979), *Economic Welfare in the Soviet Union. Poverty, Living Standards, and Inequality*, Madison, Wis.: University of Wisconsin Press.

Notes and references

McCagg, William O. (1978), *Stalin Embattled, 1943–1948*, Detroit: Wayne State University Press.

McCauley, Martin (1976), *Khrushchev and the Development of Soviet Agriculture: The Virgin Lands Programme, 1953–64*, London: Macmillan.

Makarova, L. V., Morozova, G.F. and Tarasova, N.V. (1986), *Regionalnye osobennosti migratsionnykh protsessov v SSSR*, Moscow: Nauka.

Malenkov, Grigorii (1952), 'Otchetnyi doklad XIX sezdu partii o rabote Tsentralnogo komiteta VKP(b)', *Kommunist*, no. 19.

— (1953), 'Traurnyi miting na Krasnoi ploshchadi vo vremya pokhoronya Iosifa Vissarionovicha Stalina. Rech tovarishcha G.M. Malenkova', *Kommunist*, no. 4.

Maltsev, Yurii (1976), *Volnaya russkaya literatura 1955–1975*, Frankfurt/M.: Posev.

Manevich, E. (1981), 'Ratsionalnoe ispolzovanie rabochei sily', *Voprosy Ekonomiki*, no. 9.

Markov, G.M. (1981), 'Sovetskaya literatura v borbe za kommunizm i ee zadachi v svete reshenii XXVI sezda KPSS', *Literaturnaya Gazeta*, 1 July.

— (1984), '50 let sluzheniya partii i narodu', *Literaturnaya Gazeta*, 26 September.

Maslin, N. (1949), 'Genialnyi russkii poet', *Bolshevik*, no. 9.

Maslov, V.P. (1988), 'Vne morale, vne zakona', *Sotsiologicheskie Issledovaniya*, no. 3.

Mazour, Anatole J. (1971), *The Writing of History in the Soviet Union*, Stanford, Ca.: Hoover Institution Press.

Medvedev, Roy (1971), *Let History Judge: The Origins and Consequences of Stalinism*, London: MacMillan.

— (1982), *Khrushchev*, Oxford: Blackwell.

— (1988), 'Kto byl przeciw?', *Polityka*, 28 May.

Medvedev, Roy and Medvedev, Zhores (1971), *A Question of Madness*, London: Macmillan.

Meek, Ronald L. (1956), *Studies in the Labour Theory of Value*, London: Lawrence & Wishart.

Merton, Robert K. (1968), *Social Theory and Social Structure* (enlarged edition), New York: The Free Press.

Meyer, Alfred (1966), 'The functions of ideology in the Soviet political system: a speculative essay designed to provoke discussion', *Soviet Studies 17* (3).

Mickiewicz, Ellen Propper (1972), 'Policy applications of public opinion research in the Soviet Union', *Public Opinion Quarterly*, no. 36.

Milkov, V.V. and Pilyogina, B.N. (1987), 'Khristianstvo i yazychestvo: problema dvoeverie', in: A.D. Sukhov (ed.) *Vvedenie Khristianstva na Rusi.*

Millar, James R. (1970), 'Soviet rapid development and the agricultural surplus hypothesis', *Soviet Studies 22* (1).

— (1971a), 'The agricultural surplus hypothesis: a reply to Alec Nove', *Soviet Studies 23* (2).

— (ed.)(1971b), *The Soviet Rural Community*, Urbana, Ill.: University of Illinois Press.

432

— (1974), 'Mass collectivization and the contribution of Soviet agriculture to the first five-year plan: a review article', *Slavic Review 33* (4).

Miller, Robert F. (1970), *One Hundred Thousand Tractors: The MTS and the Development of Controls in Soviet Agriculture*, Cambridge, Ma.: Harvard University Press.

— (1971), 'Continuity and change in the administration of Soviet agriculture since Stalin', in: Millar (ed.) *The Soviet Rural Community.*

Mills, Richard (1970), 'The formation of the virgin lands program', *Slavic Review 21* (1).

Mirsky, D.S. (1958), *A History of Russian Literature. From its Beginnings to 1900*, New York: Vintage Books.

Moiseev, N.N. (1988), 'Oblik rukovoditelya', *Novyi Mir*, no. 4.

Molotov, Vyatcheslav (1937), 'Uroki vreditelstva, diversii i shpionazha Yaponu-nemetsku-trotskistskikh agentov', *Bolshevik*, no. 12.

— (1952), 'Vstupitelnaya rech', *Kommunist*, no. 19.

Monin, Andrei (1988), 'Zastoinye zony', *Novyi Mir*, no. 7.

Moore, Barrington Jr. (1978), *The Social Bases of Obedience and Revolt*, White Plains, N.Y.: M.E. Sharpe.

Morin, Edgar (1983), *De la nature de l'URSS*, Paris: Fayard.

Morrison, David (1982), 'A critical examination of A.A. Barsov's empirical work on the balance of value exchanges between the town and the country', *Soviet Studies 34* (4).

Motyl, Alexander J. (1987), *Will the Non-Russians Rebel? State, Ethnicity and Stability in the USSR*, Ithaca, NY: Cornell University Press.

Myasnikov, A. (1951), 'A.M. Gorkii i sovetskaya kultura', *Bolshevik*, no. 11.

Narkhoz (1963), *Narodnoe khozyaistvo SSSR v 1962 g.*, Moscow: Finansy i statistika.

— (1966), *Narodnoe khozyaistvo SSSR v 1965g.*, Moscow: Finansy i statistika

— (1972), *Narodnoe khozyaistvo SSSR 1922–1972*, Moscow: Finansy i statistika.

— (1981), *Narodnoe khozyaistvo SSSR v 1980 g.*, Moscow: Finansy i statistika.

— (1986), *Narodnoe khozyaistvo SSSR v 1985 g.*, Moscow: Finansy i statistika.

— (1987), *Narodnoe khozyaistvo SSSR 1917–1987*, Moscow: Finansy i statistika.

Narod (1953), 'Narod – tvorets istorii', *Kommunist*, no. 8.

Narovchatov, Sergei (1980), 'I byst secha velika ...', *Kommunist*, no. 12.

Nastavshev, I. (1988), 'Prikosnis k istochniku', *Kommunist*, no. 6.

Nekotorye itogi (1937), 'Nekotorye itogi vyborov partiinykh organov', *Bolshevik*, no. 10.

Nekotorye uroki (1937), 'Nekotorye uroki partiinykh konferentsii', *Bolshevik*, no. 13.

Nemerknyshchaya (1980), 'Nemerknyshchaya stranitsa istorii', *Literaturnaya Gazeta*, 10 September.

Nesterov, F. (1987), *Svyaz vremen. Opyt istoricheskoi publitsistiki*, Moscow: Molodaya Gvardiya. (Originally published in 1980.).

Notes and references

Nettl, J.P. (1967), *The Soviet Achievement*, London: Thames & Hudson.
Nicolaevsky, Boris I. (1966), *Power and the Soviet Elite: 'The Letter of an Old Bolshevik' and Other Essays*, New York: Praeger.
Nivat, G.M. (1982), 'La révolution russe et le mythe de la "tempête christique" ', *Cadmos 5* (17/18).
Niyazov, A. (1953), 'V bratskoi seme narodov Sovetskogo Soyuza', *Kommunist*, no. 8.
North, Douglass C. (1981), *Structure and Change in Economic History*, New York and London: Norton.
Novachitch, Aleksandar (1987), 'Roj Medvedev govori za NIN. O novom mishleniyu i starim bolestima', *NIN 36* (1921), 25 October.
Nove, Alec (1957), 'Problems of economic destalinization', *Problems of Communism 6* (2).
— (1962), 'The industrial planning system: reforms in prospect', *Soviet Studies 14* (1).
— (1963), 'The Liberman proposals', *Survey*, no. 47.
— (1964), *Was Stalin Really Necessary?*, London: Allen & Unwin.
— (1967), 'Peasants and officials', in: Jerzy Karcz (ed.) *Soviet and East European Agriculture*, Berkeley, Ca.: University of California Press.
— (1969), *An Economic History of the USSR*, London: Allen & Unwin.
— (1971a), 'The agricultural surplus hypothesis: a comment on James R. Millar's article', *Soviet Studies 22* (3).
— (1971b), 'A reply to the reply', *Soviet Studies 23* (2).
— (1972), 'Economic reforms in the USSR and Hungary, a study in contrasts', in: A. Nove and M.D.Nuti (eds) *Socialist Economics*.
— (1975), 'Y a-t-il une classe dirigeante en U.R.S.S.?', *Revue des études comparatives Est-Ouest 6* (4).
— (1977), *The Soviet Economic System*, London: Allen & Unwin.
— (1983), *The Economics of Feasible Socialism*, London: Allen & Unwin.
Nove, Alec and Nuti, Mario D. (eds.)(1972), *Socialist Economics*, Harmondsworth: Penguin.
O demagogii (1957), 'O demagogii i demagogakh', *Partiinaya Zhizn*, no.1.
O lektsiyakh (1970), 'O "Lektsiyakh po sotsiologii" Yu. A. Levady', *Vestnik Moskovskogo Universiteta. Seriya Filosofiya*, no. 3.
O merakh (1967), 'O merakh po dalneishemu razvitiyu obshchestvennykh nauk i povysheniyu ikh roli v kommunisticheskom stroitelstve', *Voprosy Filosofii*, no. 9.
O'Donnell, Guillermo (1986), 'On the fruitful convergences of Hirschman's "Exit, Voice, and Loyalty" and "Shifting Involvements": reflections from the recent Argentine experience', in: Alejandro Foxley, Michael S.McPherson, and Guillermo O'Donnell (eds) *Development, Democracy and the Art of Trespassing: Essays in Honor of Albert O. Hirschman*, Notre Dame, Ind.: University of Notre Dame Press.
Olshanskii, B.V. (1987), 'Nachalo polozheno. Chto dalshe?', *Sotsiologicheskie Issledovania*, no. 1.
Olson, Mancur (1965), *The Logic of Collective Action: Public Goods and the Theory of Groups*, Cambridge, Mass. and London: Harvard University Press.

Orlov, D. (1964), 'Schastye videt', *Sovetskaya kultura*, 4 May.

Osipov, G.V., Gvishiani, D.M., Kolbanovskii, V.V. Rutkevich, M.N., Filippov, F.R., and Andreenkov, V.G. (eds)(1976), *Rabochaya kniga sotsiologa*, Moscow: Nauka.

Parfit, Derek (1986), 'Prudence, morality and the Prisoner's Dilemma', in: J. Elster (ed.) *Rational Choice.*

Partiinaya (1956), 'Partiinaya demokratiya i rukovodstvo', *Partiinaya Zhizn*, no. 19.

Pashuto, V.T. (1980), 'I v'skie zemlya russkaya', *Istoriya SSSR*, no. 4.

Peredovaya (1937), 'Peredovaya', *Bolshevik*, no. 5–6.

— (1949a), 'Peredovaya', *Bolshevik*, no. 5.

— (1949b), 'Peredovaya', *Bolshevik*, no. 13.

— (1950), 'Peredovaya', *Bolshevik*, no. 7.

— (1951), 'Peredovaya', *Bolshevik*, no. 14.

— (1953a), 'Peredovaya', *Kommunist*, no. 2.

— (1953b), 'Peredovaya', *Kommunist*, no. 4.

— (1953c), 'Peredovaya', *Kommunist*, no. 8.

Pervye (1937), 'Pervye uroki vyborov partiinykh organov', *Bolshevik*, no. 9.

Petrovskii, B. (1980), 'Preodolenie opasnogo neduga', *Literaturnaya Gazeta*, 3 September.

Pipes, Richard (1984), 'Can the Soviet Union reform?', *Foreign Affairs 63* (1).

Pisarev, I. Yu. (1962), *Narodonaselenie SSSR. Sotsialno-ekonomicheskii ocherk*, Moscow: Sotsialno-ekonomicheskaya Literatura.

Pliouchtch, Léonide (1977), *Dans le carnaval de l'histoire. Mémoires*, Paris: Seuil.

Ploss, Sidney I. (1965), *Conflict and Decision Making in Soviet Russia: A Case Study of Agricultural Policy*, Princeton, NJ: Princeton University Press.

— (1971), *The Soviet Political Process*, Waltham: Ginn and Co.

Podbirat (1961), 'Podbirat i vospityvat kadry v dukhe leninskikh printsipov', *Kommunist*, no. 5.

Popov, Gavril (1988), 'Pamyat i "Pamyat". O problemakh istoricheskoi pamyati i sovremennykh otnoshenii beseduyut dr. ek. nauk G. Kh. Popov i Nikolai Adzhubei', *Znamya*, no. 1.

Poskrebyshev, A.N. (1950), 'I.V. Stalin – velikii uchitel i drug trudyashchikhsya', *Bolshevik*, no. 1.

Pospelov, P.N. (1937), 'Bolshevistskaya samokritika – osnova partiinogo deistviya', *Bolshevik*, no. 8.

— (1949), 'Pod velikim znamenem Lenina- Stalina k pobede kommunizma', *Bolshevik*, no. 2.

— (1950), 'Pod velikim i nepobedimym znamenem Lenina-Stalina – k torzhestvu kommunizma', *Bolshevik*, no. 2.

— (1951), 'O XXVII godovshchina so dnya smerti V.I. Lenina', *Bolshevik*, no. 2.

— (1952), 'O XXVIII godovshchina so dnya smerti V.I. Lenina', *Bolshevik*, no. 2.

Notes and references

Pospielovsky, Dimitry (1970), 'The "Link" System in Soviet Agriculture', *Soviet Studies 21* (4).
Postanovlenie (1937), 'Postanovlenie TsK VKP(b) "Ob organisatsii vyborov partorganov" ', *Bolshevik*, no. 7.
Povyshat (1975), 'Povyshat rol sotsiologii v nauchnym issledovanii ideologicheskikh protsessov', *Sotsiologicheskie Issledovaniya*, no. 1.
Povysit (1937), 'Povysit bditelnost i ovladet bolshevizmom', *Bolshevik*, no. 5–6.
Problemy (1976), 'Problemy koordinatsii sotsiologicheskikh issledovanii v svete reshenii XXV sezda KPSS', *Voprosy Filosofii*, no. 4.
Prodovolstvennaya (1982), *Prodovolstvennaya programma SSSR na period do 1990 goda i mery po ee realizatsii. Materialy maiskogo plenuma TsK KPSS*, Moscow: Politizdat.
Raanan, Gavriel D. (1983), *International Policy Formation in the USSR: Factional 'Debates' During the Zhdanovshchina*, Hamden, Ct.: Archon Books.
Radio Liberty (1986), ' "Stormy Protests" at Soviet truck plant', *Radio Liberty Research Bulletin*, RL 461/86, 4 December.
— (1987), 'State acceptance commissions', *Radio Liberty Research Bulletin*, RL 114/87, 24 March.
Rakowska-Harmstone, Theresa (1976), 'Toward a theory of Soviet leadership maintenance', in: Cocks, Daniels and Heer (eds) *The Dynamics of Soviet Politics*.
Rapoport, Anatol (1982), 'Prisoner's Dilemma – recollections and observations', in: Brian Barry, and Russell Hardin (eds) *Rational Man and Irrational Society*, Beverly Hills, London and New Delhi.
Rashidov, Sharaf (1976), 'Yazyk bratstva i druzby narodov', *Kommunist*, no. 3.
— (1979), 'Moguchee sredstvo edineniya sovetskikh narodov', *Kommunist*, no. 13.
Rasputin, Valentin (1980), 'Vechnoe Pole', in: V. Krupin (ed.) *Mezh Neprydvoi i Donom.*
— (1988), 'Esli po sovesti', *Literaturnaya Gazeta*, 1 January.
Razvitie (1954), 'Razvitie vnutripartiinoi demokratii – vazhneishee uslovie podema aktivnosti kommunistov', *Kommunist*, no. 12.
Ricoeur, Paul (1978), 'History and hermeneutics', in: Yirmiahu Yovel (ed.) *Philosophy of History and Action*, Dordrecht: Reidel.
— (1983), *Hermeneutics and the Human Sciences: Essays on Language, Action and Interpretation*, Cambridge: Cambridge University Press.
Rigby, T.H. (1983), *Stalin: The Disloyal Patron?*, Kennan Institute for Advanced Russian Studies, Occasional Paper no. 166.
Rittersporn, G.T. (1979a), 'Societé et appareil d'état en Union Sovietique (1936–1938): contradictions et interférences', *Annales 34* (4).
— (1979b), 'The state against itself: socialist tensions and political conflicts in the USSR 1936–1938', *Telos*, no. 41.
— (1982), 'The 1930s in the *Longue Durée* of Soviet History', *Telos*, no. 53.
Roberts, Paul Craig (1970), 'War Communism: a re-examination', *Slavic Review 29* (2).

Rodionov, P. (1962), 'Vazhneishii printsip partiinoi zhizni', *Kommunist*, no. 15.

Rosenfeldt, Niels-Erik (1971), *Kapitalismens genesis: Et periodiseringsproblem i sovjetisk historieskrivning*, Copenhagen: Gad.

— (1978), *Knowledge and Power: The Role of Stalin's Secret Chancellery in the Soviet System of Government*, Copenhagen: Rosenkilde & Bagger.

Rothenberg, Joshua (1978), 'Jewish religion in the Soviet Union', in: L. Kochan (ed.) *The Jews in Soviet Russia Since 1917*, Oxford: Oxford University Press.

Rush, Myron (1958), *The Rise of Khrushchev*, Washington, DC: Public Affairs Press.

Rutkevich, M.N. (1977), 'Itogi pyatiletnei deyatelnosti SSA. Otchetnyi doklad pravleniya SSA', *Sotsiologicheskie Issledovaniya*, no. 3.

Rutych, N. (1981), 'Rossiya i ee problemy', *Posev*, no. 1.

Rybin, A.T. (1988), 'Ryadom s I.V. Stalinom', *Sotsiologicheskie Issledovaniya*, no. 3.

Ryurikov, B. (1952), 'Nasledie klassikov i sovetskaya literatura', *Bolshevik*, no. 12.

Safarov, R.A. (1975), *Obshchestvennoe mnenie i gosudarstvennoe upravlenie*, Moscow: Yuridicheskaya Literatura.

Sambor, Jadwiga (1985), 'Nowomowa – jezyk naszych czasow', *Poradnik Jezykowy*, no. 6 .

Saunders, George (ed.)(1974), *Samizdat. Voices of the Soviet Opposition*, New York: Pathfinder Press.

Schapiro, Leonard (1965), *The Government and Politics of the Soviet Union*, London: Hutchinson.

— (1970), *The Communist Party of the Soviet Union*, 2nd revised edition, New York: Random House.

— (1979), 'Rewriting the Russian rules', *The New York Review of Books 26* (12).

Schroeder, Gertrude E. (1968), 'Soviet economic "reforms": a study in contradictions', *Soviet Studies 20* (1).

— (1969), 'The 1966–67 Soviet industrial price reform: a study in complications', *Soviet Studies 20* (4).

— (1973), 'Recent developments in Soviet planning and incentives', in: US Congress, Joint Economic Committee, *Soviet Economic Prospects for the Seventies*, Washington, DC: Government Printing Office.

— (1979), 'The Soviet economy on a treadmill of "reforms" ', in: US Congress, Joint Economic Committee *Soviet Economy in a Time of Change*, Washington, DC: Government Printing Office.

— (1987), 'Anatomy of Gorbachev's economic reform', *Soviet Economy 3* (3).

Schuman, F.L. (1967), *The Cold War: Retrospect and Prospect*, Baton Rouge: Louisiana State University Press.

Schwenke Arnold (ed.)(1980), *Arbeiteropposition in der Sowjetunion. Die Anfänge autonomer Werkschaften. Dokumente und Analysen*, Hamburg: Rowohlt.

Selyunin, Vasilii (1988), 'Istoki', *Novyi Mir*, no. 5.

Notes and references

Selyunin, Vasilii and Khanin, G. (1987), 'Lukavaya tsifra', *Novyi Mir*, no. 2.
Seriot, Patrick (1985), *Analyse du discours politique soviétique*, Paris: L'institute d'études slaves.
Shanin, T. (1982), 'The peasant dream: Russia 1905–7', in: R. Samuel, and G.S. Jones (eds) *Culture, Ideology and Politics*, London: Routledge & Kegan Paul.
Sharlet, Robert (1984), 'The new Soviet constitution of 1977', in: E.P. Hoffmann and R.F. Laird (eds) *The Soviet Polity in the Modern Era.*
Sharpe, Myron E. (ed.)(1965), *The Liberman Discussion: A New Phase in Soviet Economic Thought*, White Plains, NY: International Arts and Sciences Press.
— (ed.)(1966), *Planning, Profits and Incentives in the USSR*, vols I–II, White Plains, NY: International Arts And Sciences Press.
Shatrov, Mikhail (1988), 'Vystuplenie', *Literaturnaya Gazeta*, 18 May.
Shatz, Marshall Z. (1980), *Soviet Dissent in Historical Perspective*, Cambridge: Cambridge University Press.
Shchekochikhin, Yurii (1987), 'O "Lyuberakh" i ne tolko o nikh', *Literaturnaya Gazeta*, 4 March.
Sherkovich, Yu.A. (1976), (Review of Safarov), *Sotsiologicheskie Issledovaniya*, no. 1.
Shimarev, G. (1953), 'Demokraticheskii tsentralizm i rukovodyashchaya deyatelnost partiinykh organov', *Kommunist*, no. 18.
Shmelev, Gelii I. (1964), *Raspredelenie i ispolzovanie truda v kolkhozakh*, Moscow: Mysl.
Shmelev, Nikolai (1987), 'Avansy i dolgi', *Novyi Mir*, no. 6.
— (1988), 'Novye trevogi', *Novyi Mir*, no. 4.
Shulman, Marshall D. (1963), *Stalin's Foreign Policy Reappraised*, Cambridge, Mass: Harvard University Press.
Silberner, Edmund (1983), *Kommunisten zur Judenfrage. Zur Geschichte von Theorie und Praxis des Kommunismus*, Opladen: Westdeutscher Verlag.
Simon, Gerhard (1986), *Nationalismus und Nationalitätenpolitik in der Sowjetunion. Von der totalitären Diktatur zur nachstalinschen Gesellschaft*, Baden-Baden: Nomos.
Sinitsyn, V.G. (ed.)(1977), *Nashi prazdniki*, Moscow: Politizdat.
Sinyavskii, A./Tertz, A. (1983), *Godnatt och sov gott*, Malmö: Brombergs.
Sironneau, J.P. (1982), *Sécularisation et religions politiques*, The Hague: Mouton.
Skilling, Hugh Gordon (1983), 'Interest groups and communist politics', *World Politics 36* (1).
Skilling, Hugh Gordon and Griffiths, F. (1971), *Interest Groups in Soviet Politics*, Princeton, NJ: Princeton University Press.
Slepov, L. and Yudin, I. (1969), 'Partiya v politicheskoi sisteme obshchestva', *Kommunist*, no. 14.
Slovar (1984), *Slovar russkogo yazyka*, Tom III, Moscow: Russkii Yazyk.
Smolinsky, Leon (1966), 'The Soviet economy', *Survey*, no. 59.
— (1967), 'Planning without theory', *Survey*, no. 64.

Smolyanskii, V.G. (ed.)(1987), *Ideologicheskaya borba i sotsiologicheskie issledovaniya*, Moscow: Nauka.

Solchanyk, Roman (1982), 'Russian language and Soviet politics', *Soviet Studies 34* (1).

Solignac, A. (1962), 'Preface', in: Solignac (ed.) *Augustine, Confessions*, Bruges: Desclée de Brouwer.

Sotsialno (1976), 'Sotsialno-filosoficheskie problemy nauchno-tekhnicheskoi revolyutsii (issledovaniya 1971–1975 gg.)', *Voprosy Filosofii*, no. 2.

Spechler, Dina R. (1982), *Permitted Dissent in the USSR: Novyi Mir and the Soviet Regime*, New York: Praeger.

Stalin, Iosif V. (1937a), 'O nedostatkakh partiinoi raboty i merakh likvidatsii trotskistskikh i inykh dvurushnikov (Doklad na Plenume TsK VKP(b) 3 marta 1937 g.)', *Bolshevik*, no. 7.

— (1937b), 'Zaklyuchitelnoe slovo tovarishcha STALINA na Plenume TsK VKP(b) 5 marta 1937 g.', *Bolshevik*, no. 7.

— (1952), *Ekonomicheskie problemy sotsializma v SSSR*, Moscow: Gospolitizdat.

— (1953), *Voprosy Leninizma*, Moscow: Gospolitizdat.

Stepanyan, Ts. (1949a), 'Postupatelnoe dvizhenie sovetskogo obshchestva k kommunizmu', *Bolshevik*, no. 5.

— (1949b), 'Sovetskoe gosudarstvo – glavnoe orudie postroeniya kommunizma v SSSR', *Bolshevik*, no. 14.

Stepin, A. (1969), 'Rukovodyashchii printsip zhizni i deyatelnosti leninskoi partii', *Kommunist*, no. 6.

Stites, Richard (1987), 'The origins of Soviet ritual style: symbol and festival in the Russian revolution', in: Claes Arvidsson, and Lars-Erik Blomqvist (eds) *Symbols of Power: The Esthetics of Political Legitimation in the Soviet Union and Eastern Europe*, Stockholm: Almqvist & Wiksell International.

Stuart, Robert C. (1967), 'Evsei Grigorevich Liberman', in: George W. Simmonds (ed.) *Soviet Leaders*, New York: Crowell.

Sukhov, A.D. (1987), 'Sotsialnye predposylki i posledstviya kreshcheniya Rusi', in: A.D. Sukhov (ed.) *Vvedenie khristianstva na Rusi*, Moscow: Mysl.

Sundiev, I. Yu. (1987), 'Neformalnye molodezhnye obedineniya: opyt ekspozitsii', *Sotsiologicheskie Issledovaniya*, no. 5.

Susiluoto, Ilmari (1982), *The Origins and Development of Systems Thinking in the Soviet Union*: Helsinki: Suomalainen Tiedeakatemia.

Suslov, I. (1982), 'Kolkhozy v sisteme narodnogo khozyaistva', *Voprosy Ekonomiki*, no. 12.

Suslov, Mikhail (1972), 'Obshchestvennye nauki – boevoe oruzhe partii v stroitelstve kommunizma', *Kommunist*, no. 1.

— (1977), 'Marksizm-Leninizm i revolyutsionnoe obnovlenie mira', *Kommunist*, no. 14.

— (1980), 'Istoricheskaya pravota idei Lenina', *Kommunist*, no. 4.

Sutela, Pekka (1984), *Socialism, Planning and Optimality. A Study in Soviet Economic Thought*, Helsinki: Suomalainen Tiedeakatemia.

Notes and references

— (1987), 'Economic incentives in Soviet pre-war economic thought', in: S. Hedlund (ed.) *Incentives and Economic Systems*.

Swearer, Howard (1960), 'Popular participation: myths and realities', *Problems of Communism 9* (5).

— (1963), 'Agricultural administration under Khrushchev', in: Roy D. Laird (ed.) *Soviet Agricultural and Peasant Affairs*, Lawrence, Ka.: University of Kansas Press.

Swianiewicz, Stanislaw (1965), *Forced Labour and Economic Development: An Inquiry into the Experience of Soviet Industrialization*, London and New York: Oxford University Press.

SYP (1960), *The Soviet Seven-Year Plan: A Study of Economic Progress and Potential in the U.S.S.R.*, London: Phoenix House.

Szamuely, Laszlo (1974), *First Models of the Socialist Economic System*, Budapest: Akademiai Kiado.

Szporluk, Roman (1980), 'History and Russian ethnocentrism', in: E. Allworth (ed.) *Ethnic Russia in the USSR. The Dilemma of Dominance*.

Talbott, Strobe (ed.)(1974), *Khrushchev, Nikita S.: Khrushchev Remembers*, vol. II, Boston and Toronto: Little, Brown & Co.

Taniuchi, Yuzuru (1981), 'A Note on the Ural-Siberian method', *Soviet Studies 33* (4).

Tarasenko, N. (1978), 'Sblizhenie natsii – zakonomernost kommunisticheskogo stroitelstva', *Kommunist*, no. 13.

Tatu, Michel (1969), *Power in the Kremlin*, London: Collins.

— (1987), *Gorbatschev: L'U.R.S.S – va-t- elle changer?*, Paris: Le Centurion.

Thompson, Terry (1985), *Developed Socialism: Soviet Ideology and Politics under Brezhnev 1964–1977*, PhD Dissertation, Georgetown University.

Tökes, R.L. (1974), 'Dissent: the politics for change in the USSR', in: H.W. Morton, and R.L. Tökes (eds) *Soviet Politics and Society in the 1970s*, New York: Columbia University Press.

Tolz, Vera (1987), ' "Informal groups" in the USSR', *Radio Liberty Research*, RL 220/87, 11 June.

Treml, Vladimir G. (1982), 'Subsidies in Soviet agriculture: record and prospects', in: US Congress, Joint Economic Committee, *Soviet Economy in the 1980s: Problems and Prospects*, Washington, DC: Government Printing Office.

Trifonov, Yurii (1980), 'Slavim cherez shest vekov', *Literaturnaya Gazeta*, 3 September.

Triska, Jan F. (1977), 'Citizen participation in community decisions in Yugoslavia, Romania, Hungary and Poland', in: Jan F. Triska, and Paul M. Cocks (eds) *Political Development in Eastern Europe*, New York: Praeger.

Trofimov, P. (1950), 'Edinstvo eticheskikh i esteticheskikh printsipov v sovetskom iskusstve', *Bolshevik*, no. 18.

Trotsky, Leon (1937), *Revolution Betrayed; What is the Soviet Union and Where is it Going?*, Toronto: Doubleday.

Tsvigun, Semen (1969), 'Borotsya s ideologicheskimi diversiyami vragov sotsializma', *Kommunist*, no. 11.

— (1981), 'O proiskakh imperialisticheskikh razvedok', *Kommunist*, no. 18.

Tucker, Robert C. (1972), *The Soviet Political Mind: Stalinism and Post-Stalin Change*, London: Allen & Unwin.

— (1977), 'Stalinism as revolution from above', in: R. Tucker (ed.) *Stalinism: Essays in Historical Interpretation*, New York: Norton.

— (1985), 'Lenin's Bolshevism as a culture in the making', in: A. Gleason, P. Kenez, and Richard Stites (eds) *Bolshevik Culture: Experiment and Order in the Russian Revolution*, Bloomington, Ind.: Indiana University Press.

Tumarkin, Nina (1983), *Lenin Lives! The Lenin Cult in Soviet Russia*, Cambridge, Mass.: Harvard University Press.

Ulyanov, M. (1987), 'Podem v gory po nekhozhenym tropam', *Kommunist*, no. 5.

US Congress (1987), Joint Economic Committee, *Gorbachev's Economic Plans*, vol. 2, Washington, DC: Government Printing Office.

Uspenskii, Boris A. (1977), 'Historia sub specie semioticae', in: Daniel P. Lucid (ed.) *Soviet Semiotics*, Baltimore, Md.: Johns Hopkins University Press.

Vaksberg, Arkadii (1988), 'Protsessy', *Literaturnaya Gazeta*, 4 May.

van den Heuvel, Martin (1987), 'Ten theses on sport and physical culture in the Soviet Union', *Nordic Journal of Soviet and East European Studies 4* (4).

Vanneman, Peter (1977), *The Supreme Soviet: Politics and the Legislative Process in the Soviet Political System*, Durham, NC: Duke University Press.

Verba, Sidney (1965), 'Conclusion: comparative political culture', in: Lucian W. Pye, and Sidney Verba (eds) *Political Culture and Political Development*, Princeton, NJ: Princeton University .Press..

Vishnevskii, A. G., Shchebrov, S. Ya., Anichkin, A. B., Grechukov, B.A., and Donets, N.V. (1988), 'Noveishie tendentsii rozhdaemosti v SSSR', *Sotsiologicheskie Issledovanya*, no. 3.

Volin, Lazar (1970), *A Century of Russian Agriculture: From Alexander II to Khrushchev*, Cambridge, Mass.: Harvard University Press.

Volkov, G. (1976), 'Obshchestvo, chelovek, upravlenie', *Kommunist*, no. 14.

Voslenskii, Mikhail (1984), *Nomenklatura. Gospodstvuyushchii klass sovetskogo soyuza*, London: Overseas Publications Exchange.

Vsegda (1981), 'Vsegda aktualnaya tema', *Kommunist*, no. 8.

Vsepobedayushchaya (1953), 'Vsepobedayushchaya sila idei', *Kommunist*, no. 1.

Wädekin, Karl-Eugen (1988), 'The new *kolkhoz* statute: a codification of restructuring on the farm', *Radio Liberty Research Bulletin*, RL 33/88, 3 February.

Walicki, Andrzej (1980), *A History of Russian Thought from the Enlightenment to Marxism*, Oxford: Clarendon Press.

Warshofsky Lapidus, Gail (1984), 'Society under Strain', in: E.P. Hoffman and R.F. Laird (eds) *The Soviet Polity in the Modern Era*.

Weinberg, Elisabeth Ann (1974), *The Development of Sociology in the Soviet Union*, London: Routledge and Kegan Paul.

Notes and references

White, Stephen (1979), *Political Culture and Soviet Politics*, London: Macmillan.
— (1983), 'Political communications in the USSR: letters to party, state and press', *Political Studies 31* (1).
— (1986), 'Economic performance and communist legitimacy', *World Politics 38* (3).
Wiles, Peter (1987), 'Stalin's two famines', *The New York Review of Books 34* (5).
Williamson, Oliver (1976), 'Some uses of the Exit-Voice approach – discussion', *American Economic Review 66 (2)*.
Wright, Arthur (ed.)(1979), *Jerzy F. Karcz. The Economics of Communist Agriculture*, Bloomington, Ind.: International Development Institute.
Wrong, Dennis H. (1979), *Power: Its Forms, Bases and Uses*, New York: Harper.
Yablokov, A. (1988), 'Ekologiya – eto vygodno', *Literaturnaya Gazeta*, 27 January.
Yakovlev, F. (1953), 'Kollektivnost rukovodstva – vyshii printsip partiinogo rukovodstva', *Kommunist*, no. 11.
Yakubovskaya, S. (1953), 'Obrazovanie i rassvet sotsialisticheskikh natsii v SSSR', *Kommunist*, no. 9.
Yanov, Aleksandr (1968), 'Spor s predsedatelem', *Literaturnaya Gazeta*, 7 August.
— (1978), *The Russian New Right. Right-Wing Ideologies in the Contemporary USSR*, Berkeley, Ca.: Institute of International Relations, University of California, Berkeley.
— (1981), *The Origins of Autocracy: Ivan the Terrible in Russian History*, Berkeley and Los Angeles: University of California Press.
— (1984), *The Drama of the Soviet 1960s. A Lost Reform*, Berkeley, Ca.: Institute of International Studies, Research Series no. 56.
Yaroslavskii, Em. (1937), 'Ob otvetstvennosti rukovoditelei pered massami', *Bolshevik*, no. 7.
Yevtushenko, Yevgenii (1980), 'Nepryadva', *Literaturnaya Gazeta*, 3 September.
— (1988), 'Priterpelost', *Literaturnaya Gazeta*, 11 May.
Yuzufovich, G.K. (ed.)(1988), *Sotsialno-ekonomicheskie problemy vzaimo-otnosheniya cheloveka s prirodnoi sredoi*, Leningrad: Leningradskii Universitet.
Zaitsev, N. (1980), *Pravda i poeziya leninskogo obraza*, Leningrad: Iskusstvo.
Zaleski, Eugene (1962), *Planning for Economic Growth, 1918–32*, Chapel Hill, NC: University of North Carolina Press.
— (1980), *Stalinist Planning for Economic Growth, 1933–1952*, Chapel Hill, NC: University of North Carolina Press.
Zalygin, Sergei (1987), 'Povorot', *Novyi Mir*, no. 1.
Zapasevich B. (1977), 'Organizatsionno-pravovye problemy mekhanizatsii i avtomatizatsii upravlenskogo truda', *Apparat upravleniya sotsialisticheskogo obshchestva*, Tom II, Moscow: Nauka.
Zaslavskaya, Tatyana (1984), 'The Novosibirsk Report', *Survey 28* (1).

442

— (1987), 'Rol sotsiologii v uskorenii razvitiya sovetskogo obshchestva', *Sotsiologicheskie Issledovaniya*, no. 2.

Zaslavsky, Victor and Brym, Robert J. (1978), 'The functions of elections in the USSR', *Soviet Studies 30* (3).

Zauberman, Alfred (1960), 'The Soviet debate on the law of value and price formation', in: Gregory Grossman (ed.) *Value and Plan: Economic Calculation and Organization in Eastern Europe*, Berkeley and Los Angeles: University of California Press.

— (1963), 'Liberman's rules of the game for Soviet industry', *Slavic Review 22* (1).

Zhdanov, Andrei (1937), 'Doklad na Plenume TsK VKP(b) 26 fevralya 1937 goda', *Bolshevik*, no. 5–6.

Zhivaya (1980), 'Zhivaya pamyat pokolenii', *Literaturnaya Gazeta*, 10 September.

Zhudin, S. (1949), 'Politika bolshevistskoi partii – zhiznennaya osnova sovetskogo stroya', *Bolshevik*, no. 20.

Ziegler, Charles E. (1987), *Environmental Policy in the USSR*, Amherst: University of Massachussetts Press.

Zimin, A.A. and Khoroshkevich, A.L. (1982), *Rossiya vremeni Ivana Groznogo*, Moscow: Nauka.

Zinoviev, Alexander (1981), *The Yawning Heights*, Harmondsworth: Penguin.

Zoerb, Carl (1965), 'The Virgin Lands territory: plans, performance, prospects', in: Roy D. Laird, and Edward Crowley (eds.) *Soviet Agriculture: The Permanent Crisis*, New York: Praeger.

Zverev, A. (1962), 'Protiv skhematizma v reshenii slozhnykh voprosov', *Voprosy Ekonomiki*, no. 11.

Zwykle Sprawy (1988), 'Zwykle Sprawy. Z radzieckimi prof. Jurijem Lewada i prof. Ofsiejem Szkarantanem rozmawia Andrzej Goszczynski', *Polityka*, 4 June.

Zytis, Ya. and Krastyn, Ya. (1953), 'Tsennyi trud po istorii estonskogo naroda', *Kommunist*, no. 9.

Index